CORPVS CHRISTIANORVM

Continuatio Mediaeualis

167

CORPVS CHRISTIANORVM

Continuatio Mediaeualis

167

IOHANNIS SCOTTI
seu
ERIVGENAE

Opera fere omnia

TURNHOUT
BREPOLS ❧ PUBLISHERS
2020

IOHANNIS SCOTTI ERIVGENAE
CARMINA

edidit

Michael W. Herren

adiuuante

Andrew Dunning

DE IMAGINE

cura et studio

Giovanni Mandolino

introductionem criticam praemisit

Chiara O. Tommasi

TURNHOUT
BREPOLS ❦ PUBLISHERS
2020

CORPVS CHRISTIANORVM

Continuatio Mediaeualis

in ABBATIA SANCTI PETRI STEENBRVGENSI
a reuerendissimo Domino Eligio DEKKERS
fundata
nunc sub auspiciis Vniuersitatum
UNIVERSITEIT ANTWERPEN
VRIJE UNIVERSITEIT BRUSSEL UNIVERSITEIT GENT
KATHOLIEKE UNIVERSITEIT LEUVEN
UNIVERSITÉ CATHOLIQUE DE LOUVAIN
edita

editionibus curandis praesunt
Rita BEYERS   Alexander ANDRÉE   Emanuela COLOMBI
Georges DECLERCQ   Jeroen DEPLOIGE   Paul-Augustin DEPROOST
Greti DINKOVA-BRUUN   Anthony DUPONT   Jacques ELFASSI
Guy GULDENTOPS   Hugh HOUGHTON   Mathijs LAMBERIGTS
Johan LEEMANS   Paul MATTEI   Gert PARTOENS
Marco PETOLETTI   Dominique POIREL   Kees SCHEPERS
Paul TOMBEUR   Marc VAN UYTFANGHE   Wim VERBAAL

uoluminibus parandis operam dant
Luc JOCQUÉ   Tim DENECKER
Bart JANSSENS   Christine VANDE VEIRE

D/2020/0095/15
ISBN 978-2-503-55174-6
Printed in the EU on acid-free paper

© 2020, Brepols Publishers n.v., Turnhout, Belgium

All rights reserved. No part of this publication may be reproduced,
stored in a retrieval system, or transmitted, in any form or by any means,
electronic, mechanical, photocopying, recording, or otherwise,
without the prior permission of the publisher.

PREFACE

The works of Iohannes Scottus Eriugena, the Irish master who served in the court of Charles the Bald in the second half of the ninth century, are already well represented among the volumes of the *Corpus Christianorum*. Beginning with the *Expositiones in Hierarchiam caelestem,* a commentary on the *Celestial Hierarchy* of Pseudo-Dionysius, which appeared in 1975 (*CC CM*, 54, ed. J. Barbet), and continuing with the polemical *De diuina praedestinatione* in 1978 (*CC CM*, 50, ed. G. Madec), the Latin translations of Maximus the Confessor, both the *Ambigua ad Iohannem* in 1988 (*CC SG*, 18, ed. É. Jeauneau) and the *Quaestiones ad Thalassium I et II* in 1980 and 1990 (*CC SG*, 7 and 22, ed. C. Laga and C. Steel), as well as the most recent volume, the *Homelia super "In principio erat uerbum" et Commentarius in Euangelium Iohannis* in 2008 (*CC CM*, 166, ed. É. Jeauneau), *Corpus Christianorum*'s Eriugenian corpus culminated in the towering five-volume edition of the Irish master's *Periphyseon*, edited by Édouard Jeauneau between 1996 and 2003 (*CC CM*, 161–165).

The present volume, the latest and perhaps last installment of the intermittent *Opera fere omnia Iohannis Scotti seu Eriugenae*, brings together two works that inhabit very different spheres of Eriugenian thought: the Latin translation of Gregory of Nyssa's fourth-century Greek treatise on theological anthropology, the Περὶ κατασκευῆς ἀνθρώπου or *De opificio hominis* (*On the Creation of Man*), entitled *De imagine* in Eriugena's translation, and his poetic corpus, composed almost exclusively for Charles the Bald and his royal court, celebrating both high occasions, such as Easter or political triumph, and the less elevated pleasures of his friends and drinking brothers. In the *De imagine* we see Eriugena the translator "at work" forging an influential theological and philosophical Latin vocabulary and engaging with an author whose work was cited in the *Periphyseon* more often than any other Greek patristic writer.[1] In the *Carmina* we see Eriugena the poet "at play" composing occasional verses that both repaid his debts to his patron

---

[1] Édouard Jeauneau, "Érigène et Grégoire de Nysse," in *"Tendenda vela": Excursion littéraires et digressions philosophiques à travers le Moyen Âge* (Turnhout, 2007), 204.

and provided him the opportunity "to speak publicly to the powers that ran his world."[2]

In both we see what could be called the hallmarks of Eriugena's intellectual and literary style: the creative, sometimes strained, but always dazzling synthesis of the linguistic and conceptual realms of Greek and Latin; and the encounter between ancient (and late-ancient) philosophical traditions of a perennial Platonism and the Christian theological debates and political complexities of the Carolingian court.

No modern editor has shaped our understanding of all facets of Eriugena's thought – including his translation strategies (and occasional errors), his compositional process, and even the ductus of his pen – more than Édouard Jeauneau. We had intended to dedicate this volume to Édouard as a gift, but we now publish it in honor of his memory. Fr. Édouard Jeauneau died in Chartres on the 10th of December, 2019. *Ad ueritatis contemplationem ... frequenti literarum diuinarum laboriosoque studio ducente et adiuuante et cooperante, et ad hoc mouente diuina gratia, redeundo perueniat, perueniendo diligat, diligendo permaneat, permanendo quiescat.*

Paris, France
15 December 2019
Andrew Hicks

---

[2] Paul Edward Dutton, "Eriugena and Virgil," in W. Otten and M. I. Allen (eds), *Eriugena and creation: proceedings of the eleventh international conference on Eriugenian studies, held in honor of Edouard Jeauneau, Chicago, 9–12 November 2011* (Turnhout, 2014), 9.

IOHANNIS SCOTTI ERIVGENAE

CARMINA

Michael W. Herren

with the assistance of
Andrew Dunning

INTRODUCTION

I. Biographical

A. Life

Very little is known of the life of the man who is widely regarded as the brightest light of the early Middle Ages and is sometimes viewed as the founder of medieval scholasticism. In 1933, Dom Maïeul Cappuyns devoted an extensive monograph to the topic of the life and work of Johannes Scottus Eriugena,[1] otherwise referred to as John Scottus or John the Scot. In the nearly eighty-five years subsequent to the appearance of this monograph, Eriugena has become the subject of intense scholarly activity.[2] Apart from numerous studies of his thought, there has been extensive research into his literary production, his influence as a teacher and scholar, and his intellectual milieu, much of this published in conference proceedings.[3] Since the appearance of the Dublin edition of the

---

[1] M. Cappuyns, *Jean Scot Erigène, sa vie, son œuvre, sa pensée,* Louvain – Paris, 1933.

[2] There are two indispensable bibliographical aids for Eriugenian scholarship, both prepared by M. Brennan: (1) 'A Bibliography of Publications in the Field of Eriugenian Studies', *Studi Medievali,* 3rd ser., 17 (1977), 401–447; (2) *Guide des Études Érigéniennes: Bibliographie commentée des publications 1930–1987 / A Guide to Eriugenian Studies: A Survey of Publications 1930–1987* (*Vestigia,* 5), Fribourg – Paris, 1989. For an assessment of the canon of John's writings, see M. Lapidge – R. Sharpe, *A Bibliography of Celtic-Latin Literature 400–1200* (*Royal Irish Academy Dictionary of Medieval Latin from Celtic Sources Ancillary Publications,* 1), Dublin, 1985, p. 83–92. See now the bibliography of Eriugena compiled by D. Ó Corráin, *Clauis litterarum Hibernensium: Medieval Irish Books & Texts (c. 400–c. 1600)* (*CC Claves,* 2), Turnhout, 2017, p. 550–606.

[3] The bibliographical data for the proceedings are as follows: (1) *The Mind of Eriugena: Papers of a Colloquium in Dublin 14–18 July 1970* – ed. J. J. O'Meara, L. Bieler, Dublin, 1973; (2) *Jean Scot Erigène et l'histoire de la philosophie* – ed. R. Roques (*Colloques internationaux du Centre national de la recherche scientifique,* 561, Paris, 1977; (3) *Eriugena: Studien zu seinen Quellen* – ed. W. Beierwaltes, Heidelberg, 1980; (4) *Jean Scot écrivain: Actes du IVe colloque international, Montréal 28 août – 2 septembre 1983* – ed. G.-H. Allard (Montreal – Paris, 1986); (5) *Giovanni Scoto nel suo tempo: l'organizzazione del sapere in età carolingia* – ed. C. Leonardi, E. Menestò, Spoleto, 1989. In addition to these conferences there were two colloquia held in Bad Homburg under the auspices of the Werner-Reimers-Stiftung; the *acta* of these conferences are as follows: *Eriugena Redivivus: zur Wirkungsgeschichte seines Denkens im Mittelalter und im Übergang zur*

poems in 1993, four additional volumes of proceedings have been published.[4] Claims have also been made for new works: translations, brief poems, and sets of scholia.[5] Yet few concrete details about John's life have emerged that were not already known to Cappuyns.[6] Some gains have been made, however. Recent research has led to a clearer understanding of the range of John's activities, his methods of teaching and learning, his scholarly milieu and his connection to his patron Charles the Bald, as well as his influence on his own generation and that immediately following.

Johannes Scottus, 'John the Irishman', was the name by which John was known to his contemporaries. Eriugena, 'born in Ireland', was the name he gave himself.[7] John was born in Ireland very probably in the first quarter of the ninth century. There is no information as to when he migrated to the continent, although it now seems certain that this event occurred at least by 847.[8] Eriugena emerged to prominence with the publication of his treatise on predestination, written very likely in the year 851 at the request of Charles the Bald and Hincmar, archbishop of Reims, in order to refute the theory of 'double predestination' held by Gottschalk

---

Neuzeit – ed. W. Beierwaltes, Heidelberg, 1987; *Begriff und Metapher: Sprachform des Denkens bei Eriugena* – ed. W. Beierwaltes (*Abhandlungen der Heidelberger Akademie der Wissenschaften, Philologisch-historische Klasse, Jahrgang 30, 3 Abhandlung*), Heidelberg, 1990.

[4] *Eriugena: East and West: Papers of the Eighth International Colloquium of the Society for the Promotion of Eriugenian Studies* – ed. B. McGinn, W. Otten, 1991), Notre Dame, IN, 1994; *Iohannes Scottus Eriugena: The Bible and Hermeneutics: Proceedings of the Ninth International Colloquium of the Society for the Promotion of Eriugenian Studies, held at Leuven and Louvain-la-neuve* – ed. G. Van Riel, C. Steel, J. J. McEvoy, Leuven, 1996; *History and Eschatology in John Scottus Eriugena and his Time: Proceedings of the Tenth International Conference of the Society for the Promotion of Eriugenian Studies* – ed. J. J. McEvoy, M. Dunne, Leuven, 2002; *Eriugena and Creation: Proceedings of the Eleventh International Conference on Eriugenian Studies, held in honor of Édouard Jeauneau, Chicago, 9–12 November 2011* – ed. M. I. Allen, W. Otten, Turnhout, 2014.

[5] These will be dealt with below, p. XV–XXII.

[6] See the very useful collection of *testimonia* to John's life assembled by M. BRENNAN, 'Materials for the Biography of Johannes Scottus Eriugena', *Studi Medievali*, 3rd ser., 27 (1986), 413–460.

[7] For evidence relating to John's name and its variants, see I. P. SHELDON-WILLIAMS, *Iohannis Scotti Eriugenae Periphyseon (De diuisione naturae), Liber primus* (*Scriptores Latini Hiberniae*, 7), Dublin, 1968, p. 1.

[8] For the evidence supporting this assumption, see *ibid.*, p. 2.

of Orbais.⁹ It seems clear that Eriugena's views on this theological topic went too far in the direction of human free will, and the author fell into strong disfavour with Hincmar and his supporters.¹⁰ Attacks on Eriugena by members of Hincmar's party refer to him as a *scholasticus et eruditus*¹¹ and describe him as *nullis ecclesiasticis gradibus insignitus*.¹² These descriptions render it likely that John was a lay teacher; in any case, he was attached to the court of Charles the Bald at the period of the controversy.¹³ In spite of his association with the king, John's treatise on predestination was twice condemned: first at the Council of Valence in January 855 and subsequently at Langres in May 859.¹⁴

It is not clear what, if any, punishment John suffered for his views. He continued to write and publish freely, beginning about 858 and throughout the 860s, the decade in which his most important works were produced. Moreover, it is clear that his relation to Charles the Bald continued on favourable terms, as Charles himself commissioned John's translations of the Greek works of pseudo-Dionysius and Maximus the Confessor. From 859 to 870 John enjoyed the role of 'royal poet', although he com-

---

⁹ For a detailed account of the controversy, see D. GANZ, 'The Debate on Predestination', in *Charles the Bald: Court and Kingdom* – ed. M. Gibson, J. Nelson (*British Archaeological Reports, International Series,* 101), Oxford, 1981, p. 353–373.

¹⁰ M. W. HERREN, 'Eriugena and Irish Christianity', in *Eriugena and Creation,* p. 70–83; J. C. THOMPSON, 'God's Own Dwelling Place: Oppositions in the Ninth-Century Predestination Debate', in *Eriugena and Creation,* p. 85–104. For a new edition of the *De praedestinatione* with an excellent introduction see *Giovanni Scoto Eriugena De praedestinatione liber: Dialettica e teologia all'apogeo della rinascenza carolingia* – ed. S. N. Mainoldi, Florence, 2003.

¹¹ FLORUS OF LYON, *Adversus Joannis Scotti Erigenae erroneas definitiones liber (PL,* 119), col. 101B–103A; see BRENNAN, 'Materials', no. 7.

¹² PRUDENTIUS OF TROYES, *De praedestinatione (PL,* 115), col. 1043A; see BRENNAN, 'Materials', no. 5.

¹³ This supposition is based on the words of Florus: 'regni illius ubi ... laudi et honori maximo habetur' (*ibid.,* col. 126B). See CAPPUYNS, p. 59–65. That John was attached to the court in some capacity is shown by the testimony of PARDULUS OF LAON, *De tribus epistolis liber (PL,* 121), col. 1051D–1052A: 'Sed quia haec inter se ualde dissentiebant, Scotum illum qui est in palatio regis, Joannem nomine scribere coegimus'; see BRENNAN, 'Materials', no. 6. In my view, it is not improbable that John was employed as a tutor to the royal children, just as Walahfrid Strabo had been employed by Louis the Pious as a tutor for Charles the Bald. It is also possible that John 'doubled' as court physician; see the evidence collected by J. J. CONTRENI, 'The Study and Practice of Medicine in Northern France during the Reign of Charles the Bald', in *Studies in Medieval Culture,* vi–vii (1974), 43–54; BRENNAN, 'Materials', nos. 1–4.

¹⁴ See CAPPUYNS, p. 120–125.

plained of his patron's parsimony in the subscriptions to several poems.[15]

It is very probable that Eriugena spent the second half of the 850s (after the Council of Valence in 855?) and all of the 860s at Saint-Médard de Soissons under royal protection.[16] In any case, it is well known that Eriugena shared close intellectual interests with Wulfad, abbot of Saint-Médard, 858–860, and later archbishop of Bourges (c. 866–876).[17] John dedicated his magnum opus, the *Periphyseon*, to Wulfad, and a list of books belonging to Wulfad survives that shows the strong influence of Eriugena's learning.[18] There is also palaeographical evidence to connect some of the manuscripts of John's work to Saint-Médard.[19] John may have travelled back and forth to Laon to visit the Irish colony there and to teach: it appears that he was a friend of the teacher and scribe Martin of Laon (Martin Hiberniensis), who, at some time between 870 and 875 made extracts of John's Greek poems and a collection of glosses to the Greek words in them.[20] We may also imagine that John travelled to the court and to the monastery of Saint-Denis. In any case, it appears that John's late career was largely confined to the region in northeastern France that formed the centre of Charles the Bald's political and spiritual world: Compiègne, Saint-Denis, Soissons, Laon, possibly Reims.

---

[15] P. E. DUTTON, 'Eriugena the Royal Poet', in *Jean Scot écrivain: Actes du IVe colloque international, Montréal, 28 août–2 septembre 1983* – ed. G.-H. Allard, Montreal – Paris, 1986, p. 51–80. For the complaints see poems 1, 80–81; 2, 69–72; 6, 37–48.

[16] A detailed case for situating John at Saint-Médard in Soissons for the latter period of his career has been made – convincingly – by G. SCHRIMPF, 'Johannes Scottus Eriugena', in *Theologische Realenzyklopädie*, XVII, Berlin – New York, 1988, p. 160.

[17] On the relation of John to Wulfad, see especially J. MARENBON, *From the Circle of Alcuin to the School of Auxerre*, Cambridge, 1981, p. 111–114. For Wulfad as intermediary between John Scottus and Heiric of Auxerre see J. J. CONTRENI, *The Cathedral School of Laon from 850 to 930: Its Manuscripts and Masters* (Münchener Beiträge zur Mediävistik und Renaissance-Forschung, 29), München, 1978, p. 145–146.

[18] The list occurs on the final page of Paris, Bibliothèque Mazarine, MS 561; cfr M. CAPPUYNS, 'Les "Bibli Vulfadi" et Jean Scot Érigène', *Recherches de théologie ancienne et médiévale*, 33 (1966), 137–139.

[19] B. BISCHOFF, 'Irische Schreiber im Karolingerreich', in his *Mittelalterliche Studien: Ausgewählte Aufsätze zur Schriftkunde und Literaturgeschichte*, 3 vols. (Stuttgart, 1966–1981), III, 52.

[20] For John's relation to the Irish at Laon, see J. J. CONTRENI, 'The Irish "Colony" at Laon during the Time of John Scottus', in *John Scot Erigène*, p. 59–67; on a treatise attributed to Martin of Laon reflecting Eriugena's teaching, see CONTRENI, 'John Scottus, Martin Hiberniensis, the Liberal Arts, and Teaching', in *Insular Latin Studies: Papers on Latin Texts and Manuscripts of the British Isles: 550–1066* – ed. M. W. Herren (*Pontifical Institute of Mediaeval Studies Papers in Mediaeval Studies*, 1), Toronto, 1981, p. 23–44.

The date of John's death, like the date of his birth, is unknown. Eriugena's last securely datable work, the poem *Aulae sidereae,* was written in the year 870.[21] According to a tradition beginning as early as the late ninth century, John migrated to England at the bidding of Alfred the Great and spent his last years in that country.[22] The tradition is attractive, but almost certainly false. At any rate, there is no unambiguous evidence for further literary activity after 870.[23]

B. Literary milieu

If we know little about the details of John's life, we know somewhat more about his contacts and the intellectual circles in which he moved. As already noted, he enjoyed the patronage of Charles the Bald throughout his life. Not only did Charles commission Eriugena to undertake translations from the Greek, it seems that he also commissioned poems. As we shall see, John's poems commemorate several important events in Charles's career. Close associations to scholars in Soissons and Laon have already been mentioned. In addition to Martin of Laon, John may have formed an association with Bishop Hincmar of Laon, who possibly acquired his reputed taste for Greek from John himself.[24] It was doubtless at Soissons where John met his pupil Heiric of Auxerre,

---

[21] M. W. HERREN, 'Eriugena's "Aulae Sidereae", the "Codex Aureus", and the Palatine Church of St Mary at Compiègne', *Studi Medievali,* 3rd ser., 28 (1987), 593–608. This article contains a review of the problems surrounding the date of the poem and the identification of the church.

[22] BRENNAN, 'Materials', nos. 14–16 and 23. The tradition is based on a conflation of a certain John mentioned by Asser (doubtless John the Old Saxon) with John the Scot by Ingulph in his Chronicle of the Abbey of Crowland, *Rerum Anglicarum Scriptores,* Frankfurt, 1601, p. 870 (Brennan, 'Materials', no. 15). The tradition was much embroidered by William of Malmesbury (see Brennan, 'Materials', no. 23). See S. KEYNES – M. LAPIDGE (trs.), *Alfred the Great: Asser's Life of King Alfred and Other Contemporary Sources,* Harmondsworth, 1983, p. 27.

[23] It is frequently asserted that Eriugena lived at least to 875, as there is a letter of the same year by Anastasius Bibliothecarius that is critical of the literal method employed by John in translating the pseudo-Dionysian corpus. But as Cappuyns rightly argues, p. 237–238, the letter proves only that John's translation had reached the attention of the papal librarian at that time. For a handy text and translation of the letter, see Brennan, 'Materials', no. 11. See below, *Addendum,* p. LXXVII-LXXVIII.

[24] For allegations that Hincmar of Laon employed not only Greek in his writings, but also Irish, see HINCMAR OF REIMS, *Opuscula (PL,* 126), col. 448B. However, caution regarding direct contact between John and Hincmar of Laon is needed; see CONTRENI, *Cathedral School,* p. 87.

who was instrumental in disseminating Eriugena's thought as well as his enthusiasm for Greek.[25] Wicbald (or Wibald), bishop of Auxerre, was another student,[26] and Hucbald of Saint-Amand came under Eriugena's influence.[27] A personal connection to Sedulius Scottus – after John certainly the most versatile and influential of the Irish scholars on the continent in the ninth century – has not yet been firmly established. Yet Sedulius's and John's notes on the liberal arts are found next to each other in one very important manuscript,[28] and the title for Sedulius's lost treatise on the logical works of Porphyry survives, comically corrupt, in one of the main manuscripts of John's poems.[29] The two may have had contact through the enigmatic Fergus, a much-admired friend of Sedulius who may also have assisted John as a scribe – and possibly glossator – of Greek texts.[30]

One other figure who deserves to be mentioned in connection with John is Hilduin of Saint-Denis. This influential ecclesiastic, who acquired several abbacies, is said to have been abbot of Saint-Médard at Soissons in 827, but, at all events, acquired the relics of St Sebastian for that monastery.[31] He was also abbot of Saint-Denis and is credited with acquiring the *Corpus Dionysiacum*, brought to the Frankish kingdom by an embassy from Constan-

---

[25] R. QUADRI, *I Collectanea di Eirico di Auxerre,* Fribourg, 1966, p. 18–21; É. A. JEAUNEAU, 'Les écoles de Laon et d'Auxerre au IXe siècle', in *La scuola nell'occidente latino dell'alto medioevo* (*Settimane di studio del Centro italiano di studi sull' alto medioevo,* 19), Spoleto, 1972, p. 495–522, 555–560 (reprinted in *Études érigéniennes* – ed. É. A. Jeauneau, Paris, 1987, p. 57–84).

[26] JEAUNEAU, 'Les écoles', p. 510.

[27] A. VAN DE VYVER, 'Hucbald de Saint-Amand, écolâtre, et l'invention du nombre d'or', *Mélanges Auguste Pelzer* (*Université de Louvain: Recueil de travaux d'histoire et de philosophie,* 3rd ser., 263), Louvain, 1947, p. 62–79.

[28] J. J. CONTRENI, 'The Irish in the Western Carolingian Empire (According to James F. Kenney and Bern, Burgerbibliothek 363)', in *Die Iren und Europa im früheren Mittelalter* – ed. H. LÖWE, 2 vols., Stuttgart, 1982, II, 769.

[29] Vatican City, Biblioteca Vaticana Apostolica, MS Reg. lat. 1587, f. 64v: 'Sedulius Donatus super imperium armenie et super Porfilium' (*sic*). The hand is of the thirteenth century. MARENBON, *Circle of Alcuin,* p. 105, n. 64 was unaware of this manuscript when he argued that evidence for the survival of a commentary by Sedulius on Porphyry had been misinterpreted.

[30] On this interesting but obscure figure, see J. J. CONTRENI, *Cathedral School,* p. 89–92.

[31] See the detailed discussion in *Hilduin of Saint-Denis: The* Passio S. Dionysii *in Prose and Verse* – ed. M. Lapidge (*Mittellateinische Studien und Texte,* 51), Leiden, 2017, p. 25, with n. 99.

tinople in 827.³² Hilduin lived to at least 855, and had certainly died before 862,³³ before which time he had been reinstated as abbot of Saint-Denis and, likely, Saint-Médard, which he had lost at his dismissal from the arch-chaplaincy by Louis the Pious in 832.³⁴ Given Hilduin's connection to these two monasteries, particularly Saint-Médard, it is not improbable that John and Hilduin crossed paths. Given Hilduin's earlier work on the *Corpus Dionisiacum* and John's close involvement with the works in that corpus, the hypothesis gains in plausibility. Finally, John's close knowledge of the actions and achievements attributed to St Denis may be owed to his reading of Hilduin's *opus geminatum*, as will be discussed later.

At all events, Eriugena was not the isolated figure he was often made out to be by earlier scholarship, which was wont to portray him as a lonely man ahead of his times.³⁵ His poems, surely our best contemporary source for his life, show him to be *au courant* with the activities of the king and by no means removed from the world of political controversy, although it is not always possible to identify particular events.³⁶

C. Writings

Eriugena's writings can be divided into four main categories: (1) learning aids, (2) translations, (3) commentaries and scholia, (4) original compositions. There is a close nexus among all these types. John's knowledge of the Greek language,³⁷ unrivalled in the transalpine West in his time and for more than three centuries afterwards, may have been acquired largely through the private study of glossed manuscripts, aided by Greek-Latin glossaries and whatever grammars were available.³⁸ However, given the plausi-

---

³² *Hilduin of Saint-Denis* – ed. Lapidge, p. 34.
³³ *Hilduin of Saint-Denis* – ed. Lapidge, p. 60.
³⁴ *Hilduin of Saint-Denis* – ed. Lapidge, p. 35–38.
³⁵ This point is nicely developed by DUTTON, 'Royal Poet', p. 52–53.
³⁶ DUTTON, 'Eriugena the Royal Poet', p. 79–80.
³⁷ The fundamental study of this topic is that by É. A. JEAUNEAU, 'Jean Scot Erigène et le grec', *Archivum Latinitatis Medii Aevi*, 41 (1979), 5–50.
³⁸ See the important study by A. C. DIONISOTTI, 'Greek Grammars and Dictionaries in Carolingian Europe', in *The Sacred Nectar of the Greeks: The Study of Greek in the West in the Early Middle Ages* – ed. M. W. Herren (*King's College London Medieval Studies*, 2), London, 1988, p. 26 (for the implication that John learned his Greek through private study). That a reading knowledge of Greek could be acquired through diligent home

bility of John's contact to Hilduin of Saint-Denis, it may be necessary to modify, or even abandon, that hypothesis. We do not know Hilduin's precise role in the translation of the *Corpus Dionisiacum*. We know, however, that he was aided by *interpretes* who were thought to be Greek-speaking.[39] Hilduin's translation was begun in 827, and completed in 834.[40] Accordingly, it is impossible to know if the native speakers of Greek involved in the Hilduin translation were still resident in Francia when John began his own translation, likely at some time in the 850s. All that is certain is that John had the translation by Hilduin and his team at his disposal when he began work on the corpus.[41] It strikes me as at least possible, however, that John met Hilduin at Saint-Médard in the mid-850s, and that Hilduin, who had contacts to Constantinople, could have arranged tutoring in Greek for a scholar who had already shown aptitude for that language.[42]

Since John later taught Greek in addition to using it for his study and writing, it comes as no surprise that he himself contributed to the preparation and dissemination of learning aids. It now seems certain that Eriugena was the editor of one branch of excerpts of Macrobius's treatise *De differentiis et societatibus graeci latinique uerbi*, which he used for teaching the rules of the Greek verb.[43] Moreover, a set of paradigms and a 'grammatical' word-list are transmitted above the name ΙΩΑΝΗΣ in London, British Li-

---

study is argued in the case of Bede by DIONISOTTI, 'On Bede, Grammars and Greek', *Revue Bénédictine*, 92 (1982), 111–141.

[39] LAPIDGE, *Hilduin of Saint-Denis*, p. 71.

[40] LAPIDGE, *Hilduin of Saint-Denis*, p. 61–62.

[41] If Hilduin did directly help John in this capacity, this probably would have happened after the death of Lothar in 855, as John, still a protégé of Charles the Bald, would have been outside of Lothar's fiercely loyal group of poets and intellectuals; see LAPIDGE, *Hilduin of Saint-Denis*, p. 52–56.

[42] For John's early Greek studies, see M. W. HERREN, 'The Study of Greek in Ireland in the Early Middle Ages', in *L'Irlanda e gli irlandesi nell'alto medioevo. Spoleto, 16–21 aprile 2009*, Spoleto, 2010, p. 515–518.

[43] See the review of this question in M. W. HERREN, 'Classical and Secular Learning among the Irish before the Carolingian Renaissance', *Florilegium*, 3 (1981), 135 (reprinted in HERREN, *Latin Letters in Early Christian Ireland*, Aldershot, Hampshire, 1996, no. 1, p. 31–32). For a positive opinion on John's authorship, see DIONISOTTI, 'Greek Grammars and Dictionaries', p. 19, 21, 39–40, n. 50. For the edition see *Macrobii Theodosii de uerborum Graeci et Latini differentiis uel societatibus excerpta* – ed. P. de Paolis, Urbino, 1990, p. xl–xlix. The crucial evidence for John's activity as compiler occurs in the explicit to the text found in Paris lat. 7186 (f. 42–56): 'expliciut defloratio de libro ambrosii macrobii theodosii quam iohannes carpserat ad discendas grecorum uerborum regulas'. For a useful summary of the three recensions of this work with bibliography see J. E. ZETZEL,

brary, Harley MS 2688.[44] It is also highly probable that John contributed materially to the preparation of Laon, Bibliothèque municipale, MS 444, copied by Martin of Laon. This codex is the most important repository of Greek paradigms, word-lists, and textual excerpts that survives from the Carolingian age.[45] We have no way of judging what his contribution may have been to numerous other surviving grammatical and lexical aids, the latter often containing the terminology of philosophical and theological treatises.

Eriugena translated at least four separate authors; some of his translations are of multiple works by the same author. His most famous and influential translation, commissioned by Charles the Bald, was a new rendering of the pseudo-Dionysian corpus,[46] a task carried out earlier less satisfactorily, by Hilduin of Saint-Denis.[47] The corpus comprises the *De caelesti hierarchia,* the *De ecclesiastica hierarchia,* the *De diuinis nominibus,* and the *De mystica theologia,* and ten *epistulae.* The work is thought to have been completed around 860. After this came another royal commission: a translation of the *Ambigua* of Maximus the Confessor,[48]

Critics, Compilers, and Commentaries: An Introduction to Roman Philology, 200 BCE–800 CE, Oxford, 2018, p. 300–301.

[44] See the discussion below, p. XXXVII.

[45] The literature on this important manuscript is quite considerable. See B. BISCHOFF, 'Das griechische Element in der abendländischen Bildung des Mittelalters', in *Mittelalterliche Studien,* II, 266–267; CONTRENI, *Cathedral School* (see the index, p. 204, for numerous references). DIONISOTTI, 'Greek Grammars and Dictionaries', p. 48–54, gives a full description of the contents of this manuscript. A partial publication of the contents of the manuscript is to be found in E. MILLER, 'Glossaire grec-latin de la bibliothèque de Laon', *Notices et extraits,* 29, 2 (1880), 1–230.

[46] See LAPIDGE – SHARPE, no. 696; additional references in BRENNAN, *Guide*. More recent bibliography: Ó CORRÁIN, *Clauis litterarum hibernensium,* I, 553–555 (no. 439).

[47] G. THÉRY, 'Scot Erigène traducteur de Denys', *Archivum Latinitatis Medii Aevi,* 6 (1931), 185–278; A. SIEGMUND, *Die Überlieferung der griechischen christlichen Literatur in der lateinischen Kirche bis zum 12. Jahrhundert,* Pasing, 1949, p. 182–187; R. ROQUES, 'Traduction ou interprétation? Brèves remarques sur Jean Scot traducteur de Denis', in *The Mind of Eriugena,* p. 59–76; J. PÉPIN, 'Jean Scot, traducteur de Denys: L'exemple de la Lettre IX', in *Jean Scot écrivain,* p. 129–142. Despite these titles which mention only John's name, Hilduin figures prominently and is subjected to a close comparison with John as a translator of Greek. Further to Hilduin's knowledge of Greek, see M. LAPIDGE, 'The Lost "Passio Metrica S. Dionysii" by Hilduin of Saint-Denis', *Mittellateinisches Jahrbuch,* 22 (1987), 56–79, especially 62–65, and most recently, *Hilduin of Saint-Denis* – ed. Lapidge, p. 64–80. For a negative assessment of Hilduin's work see LAPIDGE, *Hilduin of Saint-Denis,* p. 80.

[48] This work is now available in a critical edition by É. A. JEAUNEAU, *Maximi Confessoris Ambigua ad Ioannem iuxta Ioannis Scotti Eriugenae latinam interpretationem*

whose main interest to the Carolingians seems to have lain in his exegesis of pseudo-Dionysius. Eriugena also translated Maximus's work *Quaestiones ad Thalassium*.⁴⁹ Beyond these he completed a rendering of Gregory of Nyssa's *De opificio hominis* (*De imagine*), and the interesting *Solutiones ad Chosroem* by Priscianus Lydus, which transmitted excerpts of works by Aristotle.⁵⁰ To this I should add the interlinear translation of the four gospels found in St Gallen, Stiftsbibliothek, MS 48, which I believe to be a copy of a translation made by John.⁵¹

John's commentaries cover a broad array of secular, biblical and patristic works. He wrote a notable commentary on the *De nuptiis Philologiae et Mercurii* of Martianus Capella, which, arguably, survives in two or more recensions.⁵² John's interest in Martianus

---

(*CC SG*, 18), Turnhout, 1988. See also É. A. JEAUNEAU, 'Jean Scot, traducteur de Maxime le Confesseur', in *Sacred Nectar*, p. 257–276.

⁴⁹ *Maximi Confessoris Quaestiones ad Thalassium*, I, *Quaestiones I–LV, una cum latina interpretatione Ioannis Scotti Eriugenae iuxta posita* – ed. C. Laga, C. Steel (*CC SG*, 7), Turnhout, 1980; II, *Quaestiones LVI–LXV* (*CC SG*, 22), Turnhout, 1990. See P. MEY-VAERT, 'The Exegetical Treatises of Peter the Deacon and Eriugena's Latin Rendering of the *Ad Thalassium* of Maximus the Confessor', *Sacris Erudiri*, 14 (1963), 130–148; MEY-VAERT, 'Eriugena's Translation of the *Ad Thalassium* of Maximus: Preliminaries to an Edition of this Work', in *The Mind of Eriugena*, p. 78–88.

⁵⁰ See the edition by I. BYWATER, *Prisciani Lydi quae extant* (*Supplementum Aristotelicum* 1, 2), Berlin, 1886, p. 39–104. The best treatment of this work and the problem of its authenticity is that by M.-T. D'ALVERNY, 'Les *Solutiones ad Chosroem* de Priscianus Lydus et Jean Scot', in *Jean Scot Érigène*, p. 145–160. There is a new translation by P. HUBY et al., *Answers to King Khosroes of Persia/Priscian*, London – New York, 2016. See further Ó CORRÁIN, *Clauis litterarum Hibernensium*, I, 559 (no. 443).

⁵¹ M. W. HERREN, 'St Gall 48: A Copy of Eriugena's Glossed Greek Gospels', in *Tradition und Wertung: Festschrift für Franz Brunhölzl zum 65. Geburtstag* – ed. G. Bernt – F. Rädle – G. Silagi, Sigmaringen, 1989, p. 97–105. Additional arguments for the hypothesis were put forth in M. W. HERREN, 'John Scottus and the Biblical Manuscripts Attributed to the Circle of Sedulius', in *Iohannes Scottus Eriugena: The Bible and Hermeneutics* – ed. Van Riel – Steel – McEvoy, p. 303–320. See the discussion below, p. XXXV–XXXVI, p. XLV–L.

⁵² The version in Paris, Bibliothèque nationale de France, MS lat. 12960 (from Corbie) is edited by C. E. LUTZ, *Iohannis Scotti Annotationes in Marcianum* (Cambridge, MA, 1939). There is a partial edition of the second version, that in Oxford, Bodleian Library, MS Auct. T. 2. 19 (from Metz?), by É. A. JEAUNEAU, in *Quatre thèmes érigéniens* – ed. É. A. Jeauneau (*Conférence Albert-le-Grand*, 1974), Montreal – Paris, 1978, p. 92–184. For a review of the problem of the relation between the versions and their authenticity, see M. W. HERREN, 'The Commentary on Martianus Attributed to John Scottus: its Hiberno-Latin Background', in *Jean Scot écrivain*, p. 265–286, at 265–271. The authenticity of the Oxford version was challenged by B. PABST, *Prosimetrum: Tradition und Wandel einer Literaturform zwischen Spätantike und Spätmittelalter*, Cologne – Weimar – Vienna, 1994, p. 235–243. The whole question is confused by the fact that there are also ninth-tenth century Martianus commentaries that overlap in part with the Paris version

goes back at least to his time as a *scholasticus* in the court, as shown by the use of book 4 of *De nuptiis* in the *De praedestionatione*,[53] but that he had already composed the 'Paris' version has been convincingly challenged.[54] It is now no longer in doubt that Eriugena wrote glosses to the *graeca* in Priscian's *Institutiones grammaticae* and also corrected the Greek quotations in the copy of this work contained in Leiden, Universiteitsbibliotheek, BPL 67,[55] which appears to have been at Soissons in Wulfad's time.[56] Many of the notes are written in the hand known as i^1.[57] At the very least it can

---

(see e.g. the notes in Leiden, Universiteitsbibliotheek BPL 88, written in the hand of i^1), in part with the Oxford, and are also mixed with the commentary known as Ps.-Dunchad. A valuable census of Martianus manuscripts and Martianus commentaries was made by C. LEONARDI, 'I codici di Marziano Capella', *Aevum* 33 (1959), 443–489; 34 (1960), 1–99, 41–524; see further his 'Martianus Capella et Jean Scot: nouvelle présentation d'un vieux problème', in *Jean Scot écrivain*, p. 187–207. Building on Leonardi's work, Mariken Teeuwen and Sinéad O'Sullivan have made highly valuable contributions to sorting out the tradition and publishing the texts; see the bibliography in Ó CORRÁIN, *Clauis litterarum Hibernensium*, I, 573–576 (no. 448).

[53] Cfr Mainoldi's edition, p. 90, 92, 98, and passim.

[54] See the evidence for a dating to 859–860 based on computistical clues in the Paris version: C. C. COULTER, 'The Date of John the Scot's *Annotationes in Marcianum*', *Speculum*, 16 (1941), 487–488.

[55] For John's attempts to translate several Homer quotations in the Leiden Priscian see M. W. HERREN, 'The Humanism of John Scottus', in *Gli umanesimi medievali: Atti del II Congresso dell' "Internationales Mittellateinerkomitee"*, Firenze, Certosa del Galluzzo, 11–15 settembre 1993 – ed. C. Leonardi, Florence, 1998, p. 191–199. See P. E. DUTTON, 'Evidence that Dubthach's Priscian Codex Once Belonged to Eriugena', in *From Athens to Chartres: Neoplatonism and Medieval Thought. Studies in Honour of Édouard Jeauneau* – ed. H. J. Westra, Leiden, 1992, p. 15–45. Edition of the glosses by A. LUHTALA, 'In Priscianum', *Cahiers d'Institut du moyen âge grec et latin*, 71 (2000), 115–188.

[56] This manuscript is one of four ninth-century Irish copies of Priscian, some of which contain Old Irish glosses. See KENNEY, *Sources*, p. 556–557, 674–677. (It is important to note that in his discussion of the Leiden Priscian (no. 364) Kenney confused the shelfmark of this manuscript (BPL 67) with that of Sedulius Scottus's commentary on Priscian (Leiden Voss. lat. F. 67); this has been the source of some confusion in the secondary literature.) The evidence that the Leiden Priscian, written by Dubthach and dated precisely to 11 April 838 (subscription to text of the *Periegesis*) was for a time at Saint-Médard de Soissons is provided by a set of poems in the margins of f. 1r–2v: *Poetae Latini aevi Carolini* – ed. L. Traube (*MGH, Poetae*, 3), Berlin, 1896, p. 687–688, 690. In one of these, there is a reference to Wulfad and Carloman, the son of Charles the Bald, tonsured in 854 and abbot from 858–860. See KENNEY, *Sources*, p. 562 (no. 366). There is a strong likelihood that John wrote them; see below, p. LI.

[57] The presence of i^1 in this manuscript was, to my knowledge, first mentioned by Bernhard Bischoff in *Jean Scot Erigène*, p. 94. See P. E. DUTTON, 'Evidence that Dubthach's Priscian Codex Once Belonged to Eriugena', in *From Athens to Chartres: Studies in Honour of Édouard Jeauneau* – ed. H. J. Westra, Leiden, 1992, p. 15–45. On the problem of whether the hand known as i^1 is the autograph of John, a positive consensus was reached at the Laon Conference (see the papers by Bischoff, Bishop, and Contreni).

be claimed that the glossed recension of Priscian was carried out under John's supervision. Other scholia claim our attention as well. Although most scholars now think that John did *not* write a commentary to Boethius's *Consolatio,* there is at least a possibility that he wrote extensive notes to the metrical sections of Book IX of this work.[58] Another commentary possibly of Eriugenian authorship is that on the *opuscula sacra* of Boethius.[59] It now seems very likely that some notes on the *Aeneid*, particularly on the philosophical portions of Book VI, may be attributed to him.[60] A commentary on Prudentius has also been assigned to John.[61]

Eriugena's surviving scriptural studies comprise a commentary on the Gospel of John[62] and glosses to all the books of the Old Testament, including the apocrypha.[63] The Old Irish glosses to the Old Testament works show that John continued to use his na-

---

(However, see the review of the entire question by MARENBON, *Circle of Alcuin*, p. 88–96, and the reservations of J. VEZIN, 'A propos des manuscrits de Jean Scot' in *John Scot Érigène*, p. 95–100). The question now appears to be settled in favour of i¹; see É. A. JEAUNEAU – P. E. DUTTON, *The Autograph of Eriugena*, Turnhout, 1996.

[58] See the edition and study by H. SILVESTRE, 'Le commentaire inédit de Jean Scot Érigène au mètre IX du livre III du "De consolatione philosophiae" de Boèce', *Revue d'histoire ecclésiastique*, 47 (1952), 44–122.

[59] The edition is by E. K. RAND, *Johannes Scottus* I. *Der Kommentar des Johannes Scottus zu den Opuscula sacra des Boethius;* II. *Der Kommentar des Remigius von Auxerre zu den Opuscula sacra des Boethius* (*Quellen und Untersuchungen zur lateinischen Philologie des Mittelalters,* 1), Munich, 1906. The attribution was challenged by M. CAPPUYNS, 'Le plus ancien commentaire des Opuscula sacra et son origine', *Recherches de théologie ancienne et médiévale,* 3 (1931), 237–272. There is a valuable review of the whole question by G. D'ONOFRIO, 'Giovanni Scoto et Remigio di Auxerre: a proposito di alcuni commenti altomedievali a Boezio', *Studi Medievali,* 3rd ser., 22 (1981), 587–693.

[60] See J. J. SAVAGE, 'The Scholia in the Virgil of Tours, Bernensis 165', *Harvard Studies in Classical Philology,* 36 (1925), 91–164; CONTRENI, 'The Irish in the Western Carolingian Empire', p. 768–798.

[61] H. SILVESTRE, 'Jean Scot Érigène, commentateur de Prudence', *Scriptorium,* 10 (1956), 90–92; for a sceptical view, see M. CAPPUYNS, 'Jean Scot Érigène, commentateur de Prudence', *Bulletin de théologie ancienne et médiévale,* 7 (1954–1957), 657. The glosses are printed by J. M. BURNAM, *Glossemata de Prudentio edited from the Paris and Vatican Manuscripts* (*University Studies of the University of Cincinnati,* 1, 4), Cincinnati, 1905. If John did write a commentary to the poems of Prudentius, it is curious that there appear to be no echoes of Prudentius's poems in John's poetic oeuvre.

[62] *Iohannis Scotti seu Eriugenae Homilia et commentarius in euangelium Iohannis* – ed. É. A. Jeauneau (*CC CM*, 166), Turnhout, 2008.

[63] The glosses in Paris, Bibliothèque Mazarine, MS 561 (Soissons), have been edited by É. A. JEAUNEAU, 'Quisquiliae e Mazarinaeo codice 561 depromptae', *Recherches de théologie ancienne et médiévale,* 45 (1978), 103–104. There are four additional sets known as the IOH glosses. They occur in Vatican City, Biblioteca Apostolica, MS Reg. lat. 215; Bern, Burgerbibliothek, MS 258; Paris, BnF, MS lat. 3088; MS lat. 4883A. See J. J. CONTRENI, 'The Biblical Glosses of Haimo d'Auxerre and John Scottus Eriugena', *Speculum,*

tive language in teaching his compatriots.⁶⁴ The commentary on the gospel, which survives only in fragments, is usually thought to be a late work. In addition to the commentary there is also a homily on the prologue to the same gospel entitled *Vox spiritualis*.⁶⁵ There is good evidence that Eriugena used a Greek text of John's gospel for his commentary.⁶⁶ Perhaps John's most important achievement as a commentator was his study of three of the four works of the pseudo-Dionysian corpus (curiously not a unified commentary, as far as the text tradition goes).⁶⁷ In it John made use of his ever-growing knowledge of Greek to arrive at more accurate meanings of the text which he had translated some years previously.

In contrast to this extensive output of learning aids, translations and commentaries, the extent of John's original compositions looks small: the *De praedestinatione,* the *Periphyseon,* and a relatively small corpus of poems. However, one must note that the *Periphyseon* is a substantial work of five books;⁶⁸ it is a veritable 'summa of Eriugenism' – a systematic treatise in dialogue form dealing with every aspect of John's theological and philosophical

---

51 (1976), 411–434; P.-Y. LAMBERT, 'Les gloses bibliques de Jean Scot: l'élément vieil-irlandais', *Études celtiques,* 22 (1985), 205–224.

⁶⁴ See P. P. Ó NÉILL, 'The Old-Irish Words in Eriugena's Biblical Glosses', in *Jean Scot écrivain,* p. 287–297. Edition: *Glossae divinae historiae: The Biblical Glosses of John Scottus Eriugena* – ed. J. J. Contreni, P. P. Ó Néill, Florence, 1997. Confirmation of the authenticity of the glosses is provided by P. LENDINARA, using evidence of *nominatim* citation in Vatican City, Biblioteca Apostolica Vaticana, Barberini Lat. 477: 'On John Scottus' authorship of the biblical glosses', *Studi medievali,* 3rd ser., 33 (1992), p. 571–579 (reprinted in LENDINARA, *Anglo-Saxon Glosses and Glossaries,* Aldershot, Hampshire, 1999, p. 139–148).

⁶⁵ IOH. SCOT., *Homil. Ioh.*

⁶⁶ *Jean Scot, Commentaire sur l'évangile de Jean: Introduction, texte critique, traduction, notes et index* – ed. É. A. Jeauneau (*SC,* 180), Paris, 1972, p. 16; see L. BIELER, 'Observations on Eriugena's Commentary on the Gospel of John: A Second Harvest', in *Jean Scot Erigène,* p. 235–241.

⁶⁷ The only extant modern critical edition is limited to the *De caelesti hierarchia* (IOH. SCOT., *Ier. Dion.*); Timothy Budde is preparing a new edition. See now BUDDE, *The* Versio Dionysii *of John Scottus Eriugena. A Study of the Manuscript Tradition and Influence of Eriugena's Translation of the* Corpus Areopagiticum *from the 9th through the 12th Century,* Ph.D. diss., University of Toronto, 2011. For the entire corpus readers must rely on Floss's edition (*PL,* 122). Bibliography: Ó CORRÁIN, *Clauis litterarum Hibernensium,* I, 567–568 (no. 445). See the thoughtful study of this work, P. ROREM, *Eriugena's Commentary on the Dionysian Celestial Hierarchy,* Toronto, 2005.

⁶⁸ For a helpful summary of the contents of the *Periphyseon,* see J. J. O'MEARA, *Eriugena,* Oxford, 1988, p. 80–154.

thought.[69] Characteristically, the author revised and annotated his own work.

Eriugena's influence on his own and succeeding generations was considerable.[70] He was the main impetus behind the revival of Greek in the Carolingian age, and his ability to work directly with Greek sources brought the western world – in a limited way and for a short time – back into contact with some of the riches of Greek theology and philosophy. His interest in dialectic and in problems of the application of language were remarkable; these contributed to the development of a unique theology blending aspects of neo-Platonism with Aristotelian logic. Significant traces of this theology can be found in his poems, to which we now turn.

II. LITERARY

A. The poems: editions and scholarship

The poems of Johannes Scottus Eriugena have not enjoyed a favourable reception. They have largely been ignored by the majority of students of the Carolingian period, including Eriugenian specialists. They are rarely cited as evidence for Eriugena's thought and only occasionally used for information about the reign and times of Charles the Bald. Whereas the poems provide some material relating to these matters, they tell us a great deal more about the poet himself – his attitude towards his patron, his pride in his accomplishments, even his feelings about Jews. Most importantly, they reveal a new dimension of the complex intellect that dominated cultural life in the period of Charles the Bald, namely that of literary artist. The writing of Latin poetry can no longer be viewed as a 'leisure-time activity' in the life of a busy philosopher/theologian and teacher. Rather, poetry was for John a central occupation in which he was engaged for most of his known career. He was well read in the classical and Christian poets and was interested in the poetic works of his age; he was a keen (if somewhat imperfect) student of metrics; he possessed his own

---

[69] For a useful work on John's thought, see D. MORAN, *The Philosophy of John Scottus Eriugena: A Study of Idealism in the Middle Ages,* Cambridge, 1989.
[70] See, generally, *Eriugena redivivus* – ed. Beierwaltes.

image of the role of the poet in a Christian world – an image that he reshaped in late career to embrace the notion of the philosophical poet.

Those scholars not indifferent to John's poems have been at pains to disparage them. One critic speaks of their 'baneful influence'; another asserts that they are of 'no literary merit'.[71] It would appear that they are the sort of poems that only an editor can love. Angelo Mai lauded them, while Traube showed his esteem by the meticulous care with which he treated them. In more recent times, Paul Dutton demonstrated the historical importance of the poems in an appreciative and careful study.[72] I should like to add my own voice to those of this tiny chorus of admirers, and I shall presently attempt to show that Eriugena's modest corpus of poetic writings should be valued as much for its artistic achievement as for the information it yields.

If we ask the question of why Eriugena's poetry has fared so badly, two possible reasons emerge. First, John was a late Carolingian poet, and Carolingian poetry in general has been poorly appreciated, often disliked.[73] Not all dislike is without foundation. There are good grounds for it on occasion, and I can imagine what some of them may be in the case of Carolingian poetry: some poems are mechanical, repetitive, verbose, overly reliant on the quotation and paraphrase of better poems, and often constructed without much, if any, attention to artistic effect. It also seems obvious that many of them were hastily composed, written more to demonstrate a facility than to give pleasure or instruct. The result is that all Carolingian poets have been painted with the same brush. Even the best of them – Theodulf, Walahfrid Strabo, and Sedulius Scottus – have gained recognition only in the small field of Carolingian scholarship, and not in the larger world of Latin poetic criticism. To date, Eriugena has not been accepted even into this class.

---

[71] F. J. E. RABY, *A History of Secular Latin Poetry in the Middle Ages,* Oxford, 1957², I, 238; I. P. Sheldon-Williams in *Iohannis Scotti Eriugenae Periphyseon (De divisione naturae), Liber Primus (Scriptores Latini Hiberniae,* 7), Dublin, 1968, p. 4.

[72] P. E. DUTTON, 'Eriugena, the Royal Poet', in *Jean Scot écrivain: Actes du IVe Colloque international, Montréal, 28 août – 2 septembre 1983* – ed. G.-H. Allard (Montreal and Paris, 1986), p. 51–80.

[73] See the remarks by P. GODMAN, *Poetry of the Carolingian Renaissance,* London, 1985, p. xi. For a positive assessment of John's poetry see GODMAN, p. 58-60.

A second reason for the ill fortune of the poems may be that John's poems are difficult and intentionally so. John used a fair amount of Greek: individual words, short phrases, whole lines, consecutive lines, even whole poems. John loved Greek and believed that the Greek language had greater authority than Latin;[74] but he also wanted to impress. Perhaps, as well, he believed that the depth of his ideas should find expression in a 'deep' language. John's use of Greek was therefore a stumbling block for his contemporaries as much as it is for many medievalists today. Yet the Greek element is only one of the difficult aspects of the poems. What makes Eriugena's poetry hard is simply the arrangement of his ideas and his use of allusion. The challenge of grasping Eriugena's poetry often lies more in the thought itself than in its expression.

Nonetheless, Eriugena's poems have not been wholly ignored. The pioneering edition was made by James Ussher.[75] The first modern edition was produced by Angelo Mai.[76] It contains many able corrections to the text of the Vatican manuscripts known to the editor. The second, by H. J. Floss, introduced several good corrections (*PL,* 122, col. 1221–1234, 1237–1240). The third (and by far the best to that point) was given by Ludwig Traube.[77] A separate edition of the poem *Aulae sidereae* appeared in 1971 together with a French translation and notes.[78] There was no translation of the entire corpus before the Dublin edition of 1993, although Peter Godman in his anthology and study of Carolingian poetry provided some selections, and John O'Meara rendered two poems into English: *Aulae sidereae* (here edited as no. 25) and *Postquam*

---

[74] See, above all, the exemplary study by É. A. JEAUNEAU, 'Jean Scot Erigène et le grec', *Archivum Latinitatis Medii Aevi,* 41 (1979), 5–50, especially p. 6–9. For John's study of Greek, see also W. BERSCHIN, *Griechisch-lateinisches Mittelalter: von Hieronymus zu Nikolaus von Kues,* Bern – Munich, 1980, especially p. 145–157. See the English translation of the revised edition by J. C. FRAKES, *Greek Letters and the Latin Middle Ages: from Jerome to Nicholas of Cusa,* Washington, DC, 1988. Most recently: M. W. HERREN, 'The Study of Greek in Ireland in the Early Middle Ages', in *L'Irlanda e gli irlandesi nell'alto medioevo. Spoleto, 16–21 aprile 2009* (*Settimane di studio della fondazione Centro italiano di studi sull'alto medioevo,* 57), Spoleto, 2010, p. 511–528.

[75] *Veterum epistolarum Hibernicarum sylloge,* Dublin, 1632.

[76] 'Iohannis Sapientissimi Versus ad Karolum Calvum Ludovici Pii Filii cuius avus fuit Karolus Magnus', in *Classici auctores e codicibus Vaticanis editi* – ed. A. Mai, 5 vols. (Rome, 1833–1838), V, 426–450.

[77] TRAUBE (*MGH, Poetae,* 3), p. 518–556.

[78] M. FOUSSARD, '*Aulae sidereae:* Vers de Jean Scot au Roi Charles', *Cahiers archéologiques,* 21 (1971), 79–88.

nostra salus (here no. 9).[79] A Spanish translation of *Aulae sidereae* by Francisco Socas and J. A. Anton was published in 1986.[80] In 1993, I published an edition, English translation, and commentary of an expanded corpus for the Dublin Institute for Advanced Studies.[81] Francesco Stella reprinted Traube's edition of *Si uis OYPANIAC* (here no. 8), *Postquam nostra salus* (here no. 9), and a part of *Aulae sidereae* (here no. 25) with Italian translations.[82] Filippo Colnago followed these with a complete edition and Italian translation of the poems that follows the Dublin edition with only a few divergences.[83] The present edition is a revision of the Dublin edition; it contains a much expanded apparatus fontium and apparatus biblicus, and a few changes to the text that are indicated in the apparatus criticus. Some small omissions in the presentation of the fragments have been remedied. The indices have been expanded and corrected.

General treatments of the poems are given in the standard handbooks by Kenney, Manitius, Raby, Szövérffy, and Brunhölzl. There is a fine treatment of the epigrammatic aspects of John's work by Günter Bernt.[84] Small, but important, contributions to the corpus of John's poems were made in articles by Paul Lehmann,[85] Claudio Leonardi,[86] John Contreni,[87] and Paul Dutton with Édouard Jeauneau.[88] Dom Cappuyns dealt with the problem of the authenticity of some of the poems and made use of evidence

---

[79] GODMAN, *Poetry*, p. 300–307; J. J. O'MEARA, *Eriugena*, Oxford, 1988, p. 182–194 (with intervening discussion).

[80] *Rivista de filosofia*, 2 (1986), 129–134.

[81] *Iohannis Scotti Eriugena Carmina* – ed. M. W. Herren (*Scriptores latini Hiberniae*, 12), Dublin, 1993.

[82] *La poesia carolingia: testo latino a fronte* – ed. F. Stella, Florence, 1997, p. 246–263.

[83] *Giovanni Scoto Eriugena Carmi: un capolavoro nell'epoca carolingia* – ed. F. Colnago, Milan, 2014.

[84] G. BERNT, *Das lateinische Epigramm im Übergang von der Spätantike zum frühen Mittelalter*, Munich, 1968, p. 279–286.

[85] P. LEHMANN, 'Mitteilungen aus Handschriften II', *Sitzungsberichte der Bayerischen Akademie der Wissenschaften, philologisch-historische Abteilung*, Jahrgang 1930, Heft 2, p. 18–20.

[86] C. LEONARDI, 'Nuove voci poetiche tra secolo IX et XI', *Studi Medievali*, 3rd ser., 2 (1961), 139–168.

[87] J. J. CONTRENI, 'A propos de quelques manuscrits de l'école de Laon au IXe siècle', *Le Moyen Age*, lxxviii (1972), 5–39, especially p. 9–14. The poem was re-edited by É. A. JEAUNEAU, 'Les écoles de Laon et d'Auxerre au IXe siècle', p. 505. (Reprinted in JEAUNEAU, *Études érigéniennes*, Paris, 1987, p. 57–84.)

[88] P. E. DUTTON – É. A. JEAUNEAU, 'The Verses of the "Codex Aureus" of Saint-Emmeram', *Studi Medievali*, 3rd ser., 24 (1983), 75–120.

from the genuine poems for dating events in John's life.[89] Michael Lapidge provided an important study of John's stylistic influence on later poets with special reference to the use of Greek.[90] In the same volume Peter Dronke penned a sensitive article comparing the roles of poetry and theology in leading the mind to contemplation of the divine.[91] Paul Dutton contributed an excellent study of Eriugena's poems in their historical setting,[92] and Peter Godman commented on some of the political aspects of John's poems.[93] Gustav Piemonte made a significant contribution to our knowledge of the sources.[94] Four papers of my own on various matters relating to the poems have appeared: the first deals with the date and occasion of *Aulae sidereae* (here edited as no. 25);[95] the second with John's authorship of the poem ΓΡΑΜΜΑΤΑ ΓΡΑΙΥΓΕΝΩΝ (here edited as App. 2);[96] the third with the sources of John's anti-Jewish attitudes.[97] In the fourth I essayed a brief study of Eriugena's abilities as a poet in a festschrift for John O'Meara.[98] In the same year as the Dublin edition appeared, Francesco Stella published an excellent monograph on Carolin-

---

[89] CAPPUYNS, p. 76–78, 233–237.

[90] M. LAPIDGE, 'L'influence stylistique de la poésie de Jean Scot', in *Jean Scot Erigène*, p. 441–452.

[91] P. DRONKE, '*Theologia veluti quaedam poetria*: quelques observations sur la fonction des images poétique chez Jean Scot', in *Jean Scot Erigène*, p. 243–252.

[92] DUTTON, 'Royal Poet'.

[93] P. GODMAN, *Poets and Emperors: Frankish Politics and Carolingian Poetry*, Oxford, 1987, p. 169–173.

[94] 'Acotaciones sobre algunos poemas de Eriugena', *Patristica et Mediaevalia*, 10 (1989), 21–48; 11 (1990), 27–67. (The two parts of this article are subsequently referred to as 'Acotaciones 1' and 'Acotaciones 2'.)

[95] HERREN, 'Eriugena's *Aulae sidereae*'.

[96] HERREN, 'St Gall 48'.

[97] M. W. HERREN, 'Gli ebrei nella cultura letteraria al tempo di Carlo il Calvo', in *Giovanni Scoto nel suo tempo: l'organizzazione del sapere in età carolingia* – ed. C. Leonardi – E. Menestò, Spoleto, 1989, p. 537–552. Modifications in HERREN, 'John Scottus Eriugena and the Bilingual Bibles Attributed to the Circle of Sedulius', in *The Bible and Hermeneutics.*
Proceedings of the Ninth International Colloquium of the Society for Eriugenian Studies, 1995 – ed. G. Van Riel & al., Leuwen,p. 303–320.

[98] M. W. HERREN, 'Johannes Scottus Poeta', in *Studies in Neo-Platonism: Essays in Honor of John O'Meara* – ed. F. X. Martin – J. Richmond, Washington, DC, 1991, p. 92–106.

gian poetry, in which the biblical and theological themes in John's poetry play a central role.[99]

The wish that I expressed in the Dublin edition for a more thorough treatment of Eriugena's poems has been fulfilled, in large part, by Filippo Colnago.[100] The first part of this monograph is devoted to a careful presentation of John's theological doctrines as derived from the sources; the second consists of the application of the doctrines to a line-by-line analysis of the poems. Contemporary liturgical practices are also discussed in relation to the poems. It is to be hoped that Colnago's work will inspire future research on John's *carmina*, which remain understudied and underutilized, even by Eriugenian specialists.

B. The manuscripts and the transmission of the text

The poems of Eriugena, like those of most other Carolingian poets, have been preserved in a small number of manuscripts. There is no unified tradition for all the poems. There was, however, one collection that embraced the major poems directed to Charles the Bald and some shorter pieces written mostly in Greek. Outside this main collection, which I describe below, there are various other manuscript sources for John's poems. The poems that serve as metrical prefaces to his translations of Greek works (notably the pseudo-Dionysian corpus and the *Ambigua* of Maximus the Confessor) are preserved in the manuscripts that contain these works. The poem *Aulae sidereae*, a 'major work' addressed to Charles the Bald, belongs logically to the main collection. However, it was transmitted separately probably because it was written too late for inclusion there. All these are printed below as the genuine poems of John because they bear the attribution of the manuscripts. Other poems attributed to John on various grounds survive in disparate manuscripts. These are printed below in the Appendix. The problems surrounding their authenticity will be discussed in the next section.

---

[99] F. STELLA, *La poesia carolingia latina a tema biblico* (*Biblioteca di Medioevo Latino,* 9), Spoleto, 1993, p. 271-299 and passim.

[100] F. COLNAGO, *Poesia e teologia in Giovanni Scoto l'Eriugena,* Rome, 2009.

1. The main collection of John's poetic works (nos. 1–19)

The chief collection of John's poetic works was made in the author's own lifetime, probably towards the end of 869, which I believe to be the year of the last securely datable poem (no. 17), or else early in 870.[101] (See, however, the *Addendum*, p. LXXVII-LXXVIII). It is possible that the collection was made by John himself, since the *errores communes* by which the archetype can be established are few. I label this collection Ω. The *graeca* in this collection were extensively glossed, likely by John himself. The anthology was substantially fuller than our extant corpus, although, as already noted, it did not contain the whole of John's poetic oeuvre. It did, however, contain at least three additional poems, which we know only from groupings of Greek words with their Latin glosses (given below as Frs. 1–3). Moreover, one of the poems transmitted to us (no. 10) is incomplete, while no. 12a required restoration. It is a fair assumption that these poems were complete in Ω.

Ω can be reconstructed from the following manuscripts:

R   Vatican City, Biblioteca Apostolica Vaticana, Reg. lat. 1587 (Fleury?, s. IX), f. 57r–64v [poems 1–8][102] + Vat. Reg. lat. 1709 (France, s. IX), f. 16v–18r [poems 9–10][103]

L   Laon, Bibliothèque municipale, 444 (Laon, 870×875, written by Martinus Hiberniensis), f. 294v–298r [poems 11–17; fragments 1–3][104]

V   Vat. Reg. lat. 1625 (s. $IX^{ex.}$), f. 65r–66v + Paris, Bibliothèque nationale de France, lat. 10307, f. 246v [poems 18–19 + inscriptions by Martin attested in L])[105]

R is the most complete manuscript of the poems that we possess. It is generally thought to have been written at Fleury, but certainty

---

[101] Traube was the first to advance the hypothesis of a unified collection made at this time: see his edition (cited above, p. XXIV, n. 77), p. 523–525.

[102] M. MOSTERT, *The Library of Fleury: A Provisional List,* Hilversum, 1989, p. 284, BF 1513. B. BISCHOFF, *Katalog der festländischen Handschriften des neunten Jahrhunderts (mit Ausnahme der witigotischen),* Wiesbaden, 2014, III, p. 440, no. 6788, assigns this manuscript to 'Tours (?)' and dates to s. $IX^{med.}$ However, poem 10 transmitted in R can be dated to 867 (HERREN, Dublin edition, p. 148–149). Given that R is not an autograph, a dating of s. $IX^{3/4}$ strikes me as likelier.

[103] MOSTERT, *The Library of Fleury,* p. 287, BF 1526; BISCHOFF, *ibid.*

[104] BISCHOFF, *Katalog,* II, Wiesbaden, 2004, p. 35, no. 2120, assigns the manuscript to Laon, and dates it to s. $IX^{3/4}$.

[105] BISCHOFF, *Katalog,* III, 160, no. 4627: 'schon s. IX in Laon'.

on this point has not been attained.[106] The close similarity of the hands copying John's poems in the two Vatican manuscripts indicates that leaves from a single book were later divided. However, it is also clear that Reg. lat. 1709 did not pick up the text of the poems where Reg. lat. 1587 left off. This is shown by the presence of extraneous material that precedes the text of the poem *Postquam nostra salus* (here given as no. 9) on f. 16v of Reg. lat. 1709. This observation does not impugn the original unity of the two manuscript portions, for one can point to numerous cases in medieval manuscripts of the interruption of a continuous text or collection by extraneous material.

The scribe of *R* excerpted the 'long poems' addressed to Charles the Bald in a collection entitled: VERSVS IOHANNIS SAPIENTISSIMI AD KAROLVM CALVVM FILIVM LUDOVICI PII CVIVS AVVS FVIT KAROLVS MAGNVS. It is by no means clear whether these poems were already grouped in Ω under this title, or whether they were made into a separate collection by the scribe of *R*. As far as we can tell, *R* gives complete texts of nearly all the poems he transcribes (a probable exception being no. 10, *Graculus Iudaeus*). Where there are whole Greek lines in the text, *R* copies these in Greek characters. Individual Greek words are usually given in Greek characters, but not always. Greek words are regularly glossed. The Latin text provided by *R* is generally sound. Given its date and the general accuracy of its text, *R* is probably a direct descendant of Ω.

L consists of two parts which Traube termed L^I and L^{II}; I preserve this nomenclature. L^I (f. 294v–296r) consists of the list entitled 'Graeca ad Versus Iohannis Scotti'. This list gives Greek lemmata and Latin definitions of words drawn from John's poems in much the same order as they are presented in *R*. They also give *graeca* from poems not in *R*, but which are preserved wholly or partially in L^{II}. A coronis is used on occasion to separate the *graeca* of one poem from those of another.

L^{II} (f. 297r–298r; see **Plates I–III**) consists of two parts. The first part covers most of f. 297r down to the verses beginning ΖΕΣ ΝΥΝ ΖΗΣ (no. 11). This first part of L^{II} is a collection of Greek

---

[106] TRAUBE (*MGH, Poetae*, 3), p. 522 wrote of the two manuscripts 'uterque Floriacensis'. However, it has long been recognized that the two codices are composite volumes, with parts of varying provenances and dates. For a detailed study of manuscripts of Fleury provenance, see MOSTERT, *The Library of Fleury*), p. 284, no. BF1513 and p. 287, no. BF1526.

verses drawn from the long Graeco-Latin poems in Ω, which correspond – with few exceptions – to whole Greek verses as they are given in *R*. These verses are regularly labelled with the word ΣΤΙΧΟΙ.

The second part of L^{II}, which extends from near the bottom of f. 297r to a point near the end of 298r, contains Greek verses that do *not* belong to the collection in *R*. This material is disparate and not well organized. The scribe Martin does not make it clear which groups of verses are meant as excerpts, which as whole poems. Moreover, the intrusion of his own name as author of one of the poems in the second part (no. 16) raises problems of authenticity throughout the latter part of the collection. (See the detailed discussion below, p. LXII–LXV.) However, the collection ends with what appears to be a complete poem in Greek (no. 17) with an unambiguous attribution to John.

Two parts of Martin's 'edition' – L^I and L^{II}, part 1 – agree closely with each other except in some minor details of spelling, and in the fact that L^I preserves some *graeca* representing three poems (Frs. 1–3) that are not preserved or excerpted in either part of L^{II}. This inconsistency is to be explained by the hypothesis that the lost poems contained only individual Greek words rather than complete στίχοι. Moreover, the Greek poems or partial poems, nos. 14–17, are not represented in L^I. But these may have been omitted from the list of glossed *graeca* because nos. 14 and 15 are provided with metrical Latin interlinear translations, probably written by John himself. That Martin was the scribe of *L* (L^I and L^{II}) is proved conclusively from the subscription at the end of L^I on f. 296v:

ΕΛΛΗΝΙΣ ΓΡΑΨΕΝ ΜΑΡΤΙΝΟΣ ΓΡΑΜΜΑΤΑ ΑΥΤΑ.

The handwriting of L^{II} is identical.

V consists of two leaves of a portion of a quire now in Vat. Reg. lat. 1625 plus one leaf inserted at the end of Paris, BnF, lat. 10307.[107] All the Greek items on f. 66r clearly were copied

---

[107] CONTRENI, *Cathedral School*, p. 139–140. I am not as certain as Contreni that the final folio of Paris, BnF, lat. 10307 (246v) with its Greek glossary and poems, which clearly belongs with f. 65r–66v of Reg. lat. 1625, has any connection to the main part of Paris, BnF, lat. 10307. More likely, *La* is a part of a quire from a now lost manuscript. The quire may have been written in Fleury; see MOSTERT, *Library of Fleury*, p. 285, no. BF1518.

directly from *L,* as they include Martin's subscription cited immediately above and the attribution of one of the poems in L^{II}:

ΣΤΙΧΟΣ ΠΡΕΠΟΣ ΔΙΔΑΣΚΑΛΟΥ ΜΑΡΤΙΝΟΥ

V also contains the Greek distich ΙΔΕ ΒΑΘΟΥ (no. 13), which must have been copied from *L.* A Greek prayer, unattributed and arranged to resemble verses, was copied from the folio in *L* that follows the collection of John's verses (f. 298v, **Plate IV**):

ΠΡΟΣΤΑΞΙΣ ΚΥΡΡΙΕ ΕΥΛΟΓΕΙΝ ΕΥΛΟΓΕΤΟ ΣΟΙ Ο ΘΕΟΣ
ΣΥ ΔΕ ΚΥΡΡΙΕ ΕΔΕΗΣΟΝ ΕΜΩΝ

The scribe has wrongly separated Ο ΘΕΟΣ (producing the form ΣΟΙΟ) and has made the common mistake of confusing Λ and Δ in ΕΔΕΗΣΟΝ. These unmetrical *Scheinverse* follow immediately after the two 'Martin-inscriptions' in *V.* There is a faint possibility that these lines are Martin's own 'verses' that had been expunged at some time from *L,* where they were written under the inscription ... ΔΙΔΑΣΚΑΛΟΥ ΜΑΡΤΙΝΟΥ (see the discussion below, p. LXII–LXV). The other items in *V* are the two epigrams first published by Leonardi,[108] here edited as nos. 18 and 19. These are headed by the inscriptions *Versus Iohannis* and *item Iohannis,* and thus are included among the genuine poems.

What is the source of *V*'s material that is not in *L,* namely the two epigrams by John and the other Latin poems that Leonardi edits from this manuscript? As noted above, *V* was made up originally of two leaves of Vat. Reg. lat. 1625 along with the final folio of Paris, BnF, lat. 10307. The Paris portion of *V* contains a Greek glossary, also based on material in Laon 444,[109] a mutilated Greek verse by Sedulius Scottus to Fergus (see below, p. XLIX), and some other verses that are no longer legible. The Greek verse by Sedulius, to my knowledge, is not in Laon 444, and neither are the epigrams. This leads to the conclusion that the scribe of *V* used, in addition to *L,* a collection of epigrams and other verses emanating from an Irish circle that included Sedulius and John, and possibly Fergus as well.[110]

Ω therefore contained complete versions of all the poems in R, all the poems of part 2 of L^{II} in their complete form, and the lost

---

[108] LEONARDI, 'Nuove voci', p. 146–148.
[109] CONTRENI, *Cathedral School,* p. 141.
[110] CONTRENI, 'Irish "Colony"', p. 60–61.

poems indicated by the yet 'unattached' lemmata of L^I (Frs. 1–3). It is not clear whether Ω gave the items that are not in L, but are given by V. Ω did not contain *Aulae sidereae* (no. 25), which had not yet been composed. In the edition that follows, nos. 1–17 plus Frs. 1–3 constitute a reconstruction of Ω as far as this is possible.

There is another important characteristic of Ω that must be mentioned here. The VERSVS AD KAROLVM – as represented by R – contain three authorial colophons that almost certainly could not have stood in the copies presented to the king himself. Traube, rightly, set these colophons apart from the main verses in his typography. The two colophons read:

> Christe, tuis famulis caelestis praemia uitae
>   Praesta; uersificos tute tuere tuos.
> Poscenti domino seruus sua debita soluit,
>   Mercedem serui sed uideat dominus. (1, 79–82)

> Hos uersus cecini sex denos bisque quaternos
>   Iohannes, uester seruulus indiguus.
> ΜΕΛΠΩ dum, laetus regi mea debita soluo:
>   Soluere curarim, si sibi grata foret. (2, 69–72)

> Sat sat perpaucos ingratos ponere uersus
>   Molestos regi quid ualet astruere?
> Quod plane perhibet iam nuper dedita Musa:
>   Expers mercedis tristis, inanis erat. (6, 37–40)

Ω, therefore, apparently preserves John's poems with the author's comments in verse on their reception. It seems that we have to do with a collection meant for publication and circulation among friends, but not for the eyes of the king. The existence of Ω is guaranteed by the almost complete agreement of the glosses and by common 'errors' in Greek in R and L. The most significant of these are:

2, 67. A spondaic foot was omitted at the end of this line in both L^{II} and R. This was successfully restored by Floss.

2, 68. ΣΟΒΡΟΝ for ΣΟΦΡΟΝ in L^{I-II} and R.

3, 14. *Osana* (R) and ΟΣΑΝΑ (L^I) represent a common error for *oscina = oscines*. The gloss word is *aues* in R and L^I.

3, 45. *Id almata* (R) and ΔΑΛΜΑΤΑ (L^I) point to archetypal ΙΔΑΛΜΑΤΑ written as two words: Ι ΔΑΛΜΑΤΑ.

8, 20. The omission of -ΦΟΡΟΣ in ΦΟΣΦΟΡΟΣ by L (L^I and L^{II}) and R.

8, 35. ΜΟΡΦΩ for ΜΟΡΦΩΝ in L (L[I] and L[II]) and R. The error was corrected independently by R.

There are two short fragments of no. 8 (*Si uis* ΟΥΡΑΝΙΑΣ) that descend from this collection. They occur in the following manuscripts:

P1 Paris, BnF, lat. 12949 (s. IX/X), f. 24r
P2 Paris, BnF, lat. 10307 (s. IX[ex.]), f. 95v [111]

P1 cites lines 1 and 3 of no. 8 in the context of a tiny poetic *florilegium* that includes, besides John, Bede, Prudentius, Vergil, Persius, and an anonymous epitaph of St Augustine. This is written out on the reverse side of a strip of parchment about 10 cm high inserted into the manuscript between f. 23v and 24r. The other side contains glosses, including glosses to Greek words. The manuscript belonged to Hucbald of Saint-Amand and Remigius of Auxerre.[112] *P2* cites lines 1–3 of no. 8 in the left margin of f. 95r. The manuscript, a text of Vergil with Servius, may be connected to Auxerre.[113]

It is now possible to give the stemma of Ω:

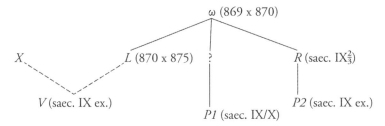

2. The dedicatory poems (nos. 20–22)

John wrote groups of prefatory poems to his translations of the pseudo-Dionysian corpus and the *Ambigua* of Maximus the Confessor. These are edited here, respectively, as nos. 20–21 and 22–24. These groups have separate traditions.

The prefatory poems to John's translation of the pseudo-Dionysian corpus (nos. 20–21) are preserved in numerous manuscripts, of which the later copies tend to be heavily corrupt. The

---

[111] I have given *P2* a separate siglum from the Paris portion of *V*.
[112] CONTRENI, *Cathedral School*, p. 87–88.
[113] CONTRENI, *Cathedral School*, p. 141, with n. 21.

edition here is based on the four manuscripts used by Traube plus selective readings from a group of Vatican manuscripts:[114]

- *Ph*   Berlin, Deutsche Staatsbibliothek, 46 (= Phillipps 1668) (s. x), f. 3v, 6r
- *F*   Florence, Biblioteca Laurenziana, Medicea, plut. lxxxix, sup. (s. xi$^{ex.}$), f. 2r, 3v
- *O*   Munich, Bayerische Staatsbibliothek, clm 14137 (s. xi), f. 1r, 4v–5r, written by Otloh of St Emmeram
- *B*   Bamberg, Staatsbibliothek, Patr. 66B (B. IV. 8) (s. xi), f. 1r, 4r
- *β*   *consensus codicum* of Vat. Urb. lat. 62, Vat. lat. 176, and Vat. lat. 177

The prefatory poems to the translation of the *Ambigua* of Maximus the Confessor (nos. 22–24) are preserved in the two principal ninth-century manuscripts that contain the translation itself:

- *Ar*   Paris, Bibliothèque de l'Arsenal, 237 (s. ix$^{ex.}$), f. 7r–8v
- *Ma*   Paris, Bibliothèque Mazarine, 561 (s. ix$^{ex.}$), f. 6r–7v

The manuscripts agree closely with one another, and both preserve the acrostic KAROLVS REX, lines 1–10 in the poem *Kyrrie, caeligenae* (no. 22), followed by a visual break before the rest of the poem.

3. *Aulae sidereae* (no. 25)

As already noted, this poem has a separate tradition because it was written too late for inclusion in the main collection (on the date of this poem, see below, p. XLI). It is preserved in a *codex unicus*:

- *C*   Cambridge, Corpus Christi College, 223 (s. ix/x), p. 342–344

4. The poems of the appendix (App. 1–17)

The appendix contains poems that are plausibly by John, but whose authenticity cannot be corroborated by manuscript attributions. These poems will be discussed on a case-by-case basis in Section C. They are arranged in chronological order – to the extent that this can be established.

---

[114] O. SZERWINIACK, 'Liste provisoire des manuscrits contenant les poèmes "Hanc libam" and "Lumine sidereo" de Jean Scot Érigène', *Sciptorium* 54, 1 (2000), p. 87–91, lists fifty-seven manuscripts that transmit one or both poems. The article does not inform us if any of the manuscripts present a substantially different text from that of the MGH or Dublin editions.

App. 1, a poem of two distichs prefacing John's treatise on predestination, is transmitted in the sole manuscript that preserves the treatise:

P3 Paris, BnF, lat. 13386 (s. IX$^{ex.}$), f. 104r; formerly at Corbie[115]

App. 2 is a glossator's colophon to a copy of the Greek gospels with a Latin interlinear translation and prefatory material. This metrical colophon is preserved in:

S St Gallen, Stiftsbibliothek, 48 (s. IX$^{2/3}$), p. 395[116]

The biblical majuscule of the Greek text is written in an obviously Irish hand;[117] the Latin gloss is in Irish minuscule. The order and uniformity of the book, neatness and paucity of corrections argue that it is a copy, not an original. The biblical text and the glosses were written contemporaneously,[118] and I believe that the same holds for the colophon. The marginal glosses, with references to Irish scholars and prominent figures of the ninth century such as Gottschalk, connect this book closely to the manuscripts of the circle of Sedulius.[119] It is clear that the poem was written in two stretches (see **Plate V**). It is difficult to decide whether a second scribe wrote lines 5–18, or the same scribe finished the poem using a different pen.[120]

Various scholars believe that St Gallen 48 was written in Northern Italy.[121] Without questioning this attribution, it should be reiterated that this gospel book was copied by an Irish scribe or

---

[115] BISCHOFF, *Katalog*, III, 207, no. 13386; D. GANZ, *Corbie in the Carolingian Renaissance*, Sigmaringen, 1990, p. 156

[116] BISCHOFF, *Katalog*, III, 302, dating slightly earlier; see M. W. HERREN, 'St Gall 48: A Copy of Eriugena's Glossed Greek Gospels', in *Tradition und Wertung: Festschrift für Franz Brunhölzl zum 65. Geburtstag* – ed. G. Bernt – F. Rädle – G. Silagi, Sigmaringen, 1989, p. 97–105.

[117] For a cautious judgement on the palaeographical relationship between St Gallen 48 and the 'Basel Psalter', see the introduction by L. BIELER, *Psalterium Graeco-Latinum: Codex Basil. A. VII. 3* (*Umbrae codicum Occidentalium*, 5), Amsterdam, 1960, p. xix–xxi.

[118] BISCHOFF, 'Irische Schreiber', *Mittelalterliche Studien*, III, 46.

[119] L. TRAUBE, 'O Roma Nobilis: Untersuchungen aus dem Mittelalter', separately published from the *Abhandlungen der Königlichen Bayerischen Akademie der Wissenschaften*, 29, 2, Munich, 1891, p. 52.

[120] Thus Bernhard Bischoff, orally. HERREN, 'St Gall 48', p. 100–101 advanced the view that two scribes were involved.

[121] For a discussion and summary of the scholarship, see B. M. KACZYNSKI, *Greek in the Carolingian Age: The St Gall Manuscripts* (Cambridge, MA, 1988), p. 85–86.

scribes from an exemplar written in Northern France (or Lotharingia) in an Irish milieu.[122]

App. 3–6 is a small collection of epigrams written in the bottom margins of the opening pages of the so-called 'Leiden Priscian', a copy of the *Institutiones grammaticae* written in 838 by a certain Dubthach, later corrected and glossed in the hand of i[1] (John Scottus). This manuscript is:

So   Leiden, Universiteitsbibliotheek, BPL 67 (a. 838, with additions from c. 860), f. 2r–3r[123]

In addition to the poems printed here, the *tituli* on a decorated robe presented to Pope Nicholas (the handwork of Irmintrude) are also given in the same part of the manuscript, thus bringing the transmitted material into the 860s.[124]

App. 7 is a distich addressed to a certain Winibert. It is transmitted as follows:

La   Laon, Bibliothèque municipale, 24, flyleaf (Northern France, s. IX$^{3/4}$)[125]

The poem is transmitted with a brief letter asking for the loan of a book. Both are written in the hand of i[1], and on this basis John Contreni has argued for John's authorship.[126] The full circumstances of the transmission of this poem and letter are worth reporting here, as they involve an audacious scribal prank. The text of the letter is as follows:

> Domine Winiberte, commodate nobis Felicem Capellam paruo tempore, et si uultis, illum emendabo in illis partibus quas dum simul eramus praetermissimus. Vtinam in uno loco essemus etiam paruo tempore.

An interlinear gloss by another hand, inserted in such a way as to comment on the final sentence, wrote: 'Probatio pennae: et bonae puellae; Outinam (*sic*) in thalamos inuisi cetaris (*i.q.* ceteris) isse-⟨mus⟩'.

---

[122] BISCHOFF, 'Irische Schreiber', p. 45–46 confirmed Traube's hypothesis that this gospel book emanated from the circle of Sedulius, which included John Scottus.
[123] BISCHOFF, *Katalog*, II, 40, no. 2139, confirming the hand of John Scottus.
[124] The *tituli* are printed by TRAUBE (*MGH, Poetae*, 3), p. 687–688 (no. 5); see DUTTON, 'Royal Poet', p. 67–68; DUTTON, 'Dubthach's Priscian Codex'.
[125] BISCHOFF, *Katalog*, II, 20, no. 2045
[126] CONTRENI, 'Irish Colony', p. 60.

App. 8 is a poem in praise of Dionysius the Areopagite written entirely in Greek, preserved in Roman characters. It is preserved in a single manuscript:

G   Brussels, Bibliothèque royale, 10078 (s. xi/xii), additional folio; formerly Gembloux

App. 9a–c consists of three separate versions of the well-known epitaph of Hincmar attributed to John. There is no sure basis on which to establish an original or authentic version. The three versions are transmitted in four manuscripts:

9a

At   Attendorn (Sauerland), Kreisheimatsmuseum, s.n. (s. $ix^{2/3}$), two leaves in damaged condition [127]

Mo   Munich, Staatsbibliothek, clm 14569 (s. xi), f. 72v; formerly at Regensburg

9b

Va   Vatican City, Biblioteca Apostolica Vaticana, Reg. lat. 240 (s. x), f. 121v

9c

H   London, British Library, Harley 2688, f. 18v (s. ix/x); originally part of Harley 3095 (Boethius) [128]

It is interesting that the epigram occurs in two manuscripts (*At* and *H*) that transmit Boethius's *Consolation of Philosophy*. The epigram in the bifolium in *H* is followed by a Greek grammar and glossary with the name ΙΟΑΝΗΣ at the end. [129]

App. 10–16 consists of a collection of *tituli* to manuscript illustrations. These *tituli* are preserved in:

E   Munich, Bayerische Staatsbibliothek, clm 14000, 'Codex Aureus of St Emmeram' (a. 870), written by the scribes Beringar and Liut-

---

[127] BISCHOFF, *Katalog*, I, 31, no. 118.
[128] The hand of the epigram itself is s. ix/x (thus Bischoff, orally). The material in the bifolium inserted into the Harley manuscript is of various dates. The connection between the two Harley manuscripts was first pointed out by David Ganz, reported by DIONISOTTI, 'Greek Grammars', p. 17, with n. 40. See BISCHOFF, *Katalog*, III, 249, no. 3124.
[129] Unedited.

hard; formerly at St Emmeram, Regensburg; written in northeastern France at Saint-Denis or Compiègne.[130]

A number of verses from these *tituli* was copied out in Paris, BnF, lat. 5577 (s. XI), f. 18v–19r. However, as this manuscript is demonstrably a copy of *E*, it is of no value to the text and has not been used here. The literature surrounding both these manuscripts, including art-historical material, has been admirably surveyed by Dutton and Jeauneau, 'The Verses'.

App. 17, Fr. 1 is a list of thirty-six Greek words with Latin definitions in L1, f. 294v, introduced by the title 'Graeca ad Versus'.

C. The corpus of John's poems and problems of authenticity

1. Overview

The corpus that follows has been established on the basis of textual transmission. Poems 1–25 are works that may be regarded as genuine because they are attributed by the manuscripts to John. The poems numbered App. 1–16 are poems with a claim to authenticity but lack clear manuscript proof thereof. The genuine poems are arranged according to the divisions of the previous section: poems and fragments in Ω (nos. 1–19 + Frs. 1–3); prefatory poems to John's translations from the Greek (nos. 20–24); *Aulae sidereae* (no. 25). Likewise, the arrangement of the poems in Ω is based on their transmission. Poems 1–10 constitute the collection of *R* corroborated by the στίχοι, or selections of complete verses in Greek, given in the first part of L^{II}. Poems 11–17 are Greek poems or partial poems given in the same order as they are in the second part of L^{II} (see above, p. XXX–XXXI). Poems 18–19, given by *La*, have clear attributions in that manuscript. The fragments (Greek word lists with Latin glosses), which are given only in L^{I}, are placed at the end of the poems in Ω for the sake of clarity.

To a certain extent, a dating order has been maintained in the arrangement of Ω. The poems of *R* (1–10) seem to have been edited in an approximate chronological order, either by the editor-

---

[130] Saint-Denis: B. BISCHOFF, *Die südostdeutschen Schreibschulen*, I, Wiesbaden, 1960, p. 225; Compiègne: W. KOEHLER – F. MÜTTHERICH, *Die Karolingischen Miniaturen, V: Die Hofschule Karls des Kahlen,* Berlin, 1982, p. 70–71.

scribe of Ω or by the scribe of R. This hypothesis is substantiated by the fact that no. 1 is datable to 859, no. 4 was written for an occasion in 864, while no. 10 celebrates an event in 867. Yet caution must be exercised here, as the dating of no. 8 (*Si uis* ΟΥΡΑΝΙΑΣ) is problematic. There is much about the poem that argues for a place in the middle of the collection, where it indeed stands, but a case can be made for dating it either very early (a. 859) or very late (a. 870). It is difficult to establish a dating order for the poems of part 2 of L^{II} (nos. 11-17); however, the final poem in L^{II} was almost certainly written in 869, providing yet another indication for an approximate dating order for the whole collection. The prefatory poems (nos. 20-24) overlap chronologically the collection of Ω. *Aulae sidereae* (no. 25) is given last in this edition, as it was written at the end of 869 or, more likely, the beginning of 870 and is thus John's latest genuine poem.

The poems of the Appendix are also given in a dating order as far as this can be established. App. 1 prefaces John's treatise on predestination and is therefore datable to 851. App. 2 is a colophon to a Greek gospel book possibly written in the second half of the 850s. The collection of epigrams represented by App. 3-6 was probably written at Saint-Médard at Soissons during the abbacy of Wulfad, 858-860. App. 7 cannot be placed. App. 8 may relate to the same occasion as no. 10 (the opening of the refurbished church of Saint-Denis in 867; however, see the caveats noted in the *Addendum*, p. LXXVII-LXXVIII. It is impossible to say much about App. 9 (*Hic iacet Hincmarus*). The authorship question is as vexed as the problem of the identity of the recipient. Furthermore, the obits of the two Hincmars are of no help, as the epigram may have been meant to be read by the recipient before his death. App. 10-16, the *tituli* of the 'Codex Aureus', were written in 870, almost certainly after the composition of *Aulae sidereae* in the same year, as is shown by the dependence of the *tituli* on that poem.[131]

John's poems can be classified into three fairly discrete types: (1) 'long poems' (nos. 1-10 and 25) addressed to the king on the occasion of an important feast or event; these poems skilfully interweave theological themes with topics of current interest; (2) metrical prefaces, colophons, and *tituli* meant to accompany

---

[131] DUTTON – JEAUNEAU, 'The Verses', p. 99-101; HERREN, 'Eriugena's "Aulae sidereae"', p. 607.

John's own writings and translations and perhaps manuscript illustrations (nos. 20-24; App. 1, App. 2, App. 10-16); (3) short poems in Greek, Latin, or a mixture thereof, often in epigrammatic form, addressed to or dealing with a variety of individuals: the king (nos. 11, 14, 17, App. 8), one or both of the Hincmars (nos. 12a-b, App. 9a-c [by John?]), a certain Winibert (App. 7), Abbot Wulfad and Karloman (App. 5), an unnamed teacher accused of arrogance (no. 16), a successful pupil of Greek named Liuddo (no. 15). The Greek distich ΙΔΕ ΒΑΘΟΥ (no. 13) is hard to classify: it may, in fact, have been meant as a *titulus* to accompany an illustration of the resurrection.[132]

John wrote no long poems in Greek. He employed Greek distichs in nos. 2 and 5, and groups of στίχοι in no. 8: lines 20-22, 34-35, 85-86; otherwise he confined himself to individual Greek words and short phrases in the poems to Charles the Bald collected in R. The poems written entirely in Greek are contained in the collection that constitutes the second part of L^{II}: nos. 11-17. The longest of these is no. 17, a poem of fourteen lines. Interestingly, partial or complete *metrical* translations in Latin to nos. 12a-b, 14, and 15 are provided – probably by John himself. Although John did attempt to deal with serious themes in Greek (e.g. nos. 11, 13, 14, 17, App. 8), he was also effective in using this language for satirical or witty themes (nos. 12a-b, 15, 16).

The poems of R (nos. 1-10) form a coherent collection not only because they are 'long' and addressed to Charles the Bald, but also because many of them deal with theological matters which the poet associates closely with the celebration of a liturgical feast. References to a liturgical occasion are given in nos. 1, 43-44; 3, 61-74; 5, 43-50 (participation of Charles); 8, 68-69, 81-82; 10, 5-6, 14-20; 25, 20-21. The poems of R, therefore, are truly 'occasional poems'. As most of the poems (nos. 1-3, 5-7, 9-10) celebrate the death, resurrection, and descent of Christ into hell, it is possible that the collection was meant to commemorate the king's presence at Easter mass in different years and thus mark his Easter itinerary in the years 859-867. Yet caution should again be exercised. No. 4, addressed principally to Irmintrude, is non-liturgical, and no. 8 lays stress on the incarnation (with secondary emphasis on the redemption). Curiously, no. 9 is not addressed to the king nor does it mention him by name.

---

[132] BERNT, *Epigramm*, p. 281.

Poems in Ω, but not in R, were also written for specific occasions at which the king was present. No. 17, the final poem in L^{II} and the latest datable poem in Ω, is written entirely in Greek. It appears to have been composed to celebrate Charles's coronation at Reims by Archbishop Hincmar in 869, after the king annexed Lotharingia on the death of his brother Lothair.

The poem *Aulae sidereae* (no. 25) is also an occasional poem. It conflates the construction of Charles's new church (at Compiègne) with Charles' celebration of Christmas at the ancestral church at Aachen in 869, written in 870.[133]

Although it is fair to say that John's poems are dominated by theological themes, they are not without political interest. *Hellinas Troasque* (no. 1) is clearly a partisan effort by the royal poet to champion his patron's cause in the fraternal war that broke out in 858. *Postquam nostra salus* (no. 9), which does not mention the sovereign by name, contains an implicit attack on Charles's pro-Jewish policies and champions the position of the clerical party.[134] *Graculus Iudaeus* (no. 10) gives tacit approval to the monarch's assumption of the abbacy of Saint-Denis in 867. Poems 12a-b, which contain overlapping content, are distinguished by line 1 in 12a, which differentiates between a good and a bad Hincmar (H. of Laon, H. of Reims), and appear to touch on the jurisdictional conflict between the two. ΘΑΥΜΑΣΤΩ ΒΑΣΙΛΕΙ (no. 17) vindicates Charles's claim to an enlarged kingdom and an additional crown. *Aulae sidereae* (no. 25), which celebrates Charles's most ambitious ecclesiastical building project (the palatine church of St Mary at Compiègne) and is patently an encomium of the king's munificence, is a complex poem replete with ambiguous symbolism.

John's shorter poems and epigrams reveal a different facet of the poet's personality and artistry. Whereas the long poems may contain irony and ambiguity, they are not meant to be witty. The author appears to strive for a high seriousness and dignified beauty – ideals that are usually within his grasp. By contrast, the short pieces are, by turns, charming or caustic. The poems on wine-drinking (no. 19, App. 3-4) show John's penchant for conviviality, as does App. 5, which apparently describes John in animated conversation with Karloman and Wulfad in the abbot's quarters. App. 7, addressed to Winibert, is an expression of admi-

---

[133] HERREN, 'Eriugena's "Aulae sidereae"', p. 603.
[134] HERREN, 'Gli ebrei', p. 550–552.

ration and warm friendship. However, John was capable of scathing sarcasm when the occasion warranted. His poem on a prattling teacher (no. 16) is both funny and biting; it is surely the most successful Greek poem of the Carolingian age. The famous or infamous epitaph on Hincmar (App. 9a–c) does not permit a clear interpretation, as we can be positive neither as to authorship nor as to the recipient (though I think that Hincmar of Reims is likelier).[135] The poem must be allowed to stand as one of the most tantalizing literary puzzles of the later Carolingian world.[136]

2. Problems of authenticity in Ω

As noted above, the second part of L^{II}, which contains the material (all in Greek) that is not in R, was edited by Martinus Hiberniensis in a somewhat unclear fashion. This can be seen at a glance by a reference to plates II–III. Part 2 of L^{II} begins at the bottom of f. 297r (plate II), with no. 11 (ΖΗΣ ΝΥΝ ΖΗΣ) and continues to the end of no. 17 at a point near the bottom of f. 298r (plate III). There are no new attributions after the inscription to no. 11, ΤΟΙ ΙΟΑΝΝΟΙ ΤΩ ΚΙΡΡΙΩ ΚΑΡΟΛΩ and prior to no. 16; however, each separate item is noted by the word *uersus* or *prosa* in the left margin. The final item in the collection (no. 17, addressed to Charles) is prefaced by an inscription assigning the poem to John.

Traube adopted a solution to the problem that strikes me as unsatisfactory. He accepted as genuine the poems ΖΕΣ ΝΥΝ ΖΗΣ (here no. 11; Traube no. 3, 3), ΙΔΕ ΒΑΘΟΥ (here no. 13; Traube no. 3, 5), and ΕΡΗΝΗ ΠΙΣΤΩ (here no. 14; Traube no. 3, 6). He printed only the second version of ΛΑΜΠΡΟΤΑΤΟΣ (here no. 12b; Traube no. 3, 10), but omitted 12a. He also printed ΘΑΥΜΑΣΤΣ ΒΑΣΙΛΕΙ (here no. 17; Traube no. 5, 4). Nos. 15–16, which I include among the *genuina*, were printed by Traube in the section of the same volume entitled 'Carmina Scottorum': nos. 12, 3 and 12, 5 (p. 697).

Not all poems in the second part of L^{II} are represented in L^{I}. Indeed, the *graeca* of only nos. 12a and 13 are glossed in L^{I}. This fact, however, does not impugn the authenticity of those poems

---

[135] Dutton, 'Royal Poet', p. 57–59, assumes Eriugenian authorship of the epigram. He favours Hincmar of Reims as the probable recipient of the poem, but admits that the point can be argued either way.

[136] For a detailed discussion of the versions see G. Bernt, *Das lateinische Epigramm im Übergang von der Spätantike zum frühen Mittelalter*, Munich, 1968, p. 281–286.

not glossed in L^I, especially as nos. 11 and 17, lacking in L^I, bear inscriptions in L^{II} assigning the works to John. No. 12a, which *is* glossed in L^I, also exhibits two lines of metrical glossing. These lines must surely be authorial, as we have no independent evidence of Latin poetry written by Martin, the editor of the collection. There are also metrical glosses for nos. 12b, 14, and 15. It is a reasonable assumption that John wished to give further evidence of his own poetic versatility by providing his Greek hexameters with Latin translations in the same metre.

There is, *prima facie,* a good reason for excluding ΕΙΣΧΡΕ ΑΝΑΓΙΝΟΣΤΣΗΣ (no. 16) from the genuine poems, as this poem is preceded by the inscription ΣΤΙΧΟΣ ΠΡΕΠΟΣ ΔΙΔΑΣΚΑΛΟΥ ΜΑΡΤΙΝΟΥ. I shall come to this matter presently. However, it is hard to see on what basis Traube excluded nos. 12a and 15.[137] It would seem logical either to accept as genuine all the poems in part 2 of L^{II}, with the exception of no. 16, which is allegedly Martin's, or else to regard nos. 12–15, which have no separate attributions as *dubia* and to exclude no. 16 for the reason stated above.

If it were not for the 'Martin-inscription' written at the bottom of the page preceding no. 16, there would be little reason for casting doubt on other poems in the collection. Until fairly recently, no one queried the ascription of ΕΙΣΧΡΕ ΑΝΑΓΙΝΟΣΤΗΣ (no. 16) to Martin. However, A. C. Dionisotti expressed scepticism towards the attribution, arguing that Martin's Greek (as we know it from his editorial work in Laon 444) was too weak to enable him to compose a poem of this quality.[138] Dionisotti's contention led me to a minute re-examination of the Laon manuscript *in situ.*

The attribution of the poem occurs in an inscription at the bottom of f. 297v (plate II) just above the ruling of the lower margin: ΣΤΙΧΟΣ ΠΡΕΠΟΣ ΔΙΔΑΣΚΑΛΟΥ ΜΑΡΤΙΝΟΥ. As can be seen from the plate, the inscription commences with three letters – ΣΤΙ – outside the outermost left vertical ruling. Directly below the inscription two lines have been expunged. One line contained the text, another just above it contained one or more glosses. The letters are written in the same light brown ink as that of the preceding and following text. The erasure was done so thoroughly that

---

[137] A case could be made for excluding no. 15 because John is mentioned in the third person, and that an otherwise unknown Liuddo is celebrated for surpassing John in his knowledge of Greek. However, it is equally plausible that John is simply employing the modesty topos to praise one of his own students.

[138] DIONISOTTI, 'Greek Grammars', p. 47.

hardly anything is visible except traces of the light brown ink (faintly discernible in plate II). The final two letters of the text line look like majuscules, so one may tentatively conclude that it constitutes an attempt to write Greek verse. The positioning of the poem outside the vertical and horizontal rulings points to the likelihood that it had not been planned for inclusion in the main collection.

The inscription is written in a darker ink than that used for the main text and with a finer pen. However, the Greek letters are formed according to Martin's fashion: T slightly below the line, Δ with a long horizontal bar at the bottom, Λ with a long left 'leg'. To the left of the inscription a scribe (presumably Martin) put an X, using the same ink as that of the inscription. The sign is repeated in the same ink in the top left margin of the next folio (f. 298r, plate III). Beneath that sign is the sign in the light brown ink of the text: it is the same sign used throughout this section by Martin to indicate a change of text, hence a type of coronis. A dark-ink X is also employed above the same form of coronis in light ink at the start of the next poem, identified as a poem by John to Charles (no. 17) on the same folio, which is the concluding poem of the section.

I think it is a fair conclusion that Martin went back over his section and corrected it in dark ink. The same dark ink is used in his Greek scribal colophon on f. 296r. Other traces of this ink are visible, e.g. on the bottom of f. 297r, where the B and ΩN of ΣΤΙΛΒΩN are written over, as is the N of ZΩNTOΣ in the next line. When he came to his verse on f. 297v, Martin felt obliged to give it a proper inscription, if only to mark it off from the other poems in the section. It was at this stage that he added the Xs to emphasize the textual breaks already indicated by a coronis. At a later stage Martin or another scribe erased the lines of Martin's poem, but curiously not the inscription.

Martin's Greek was good enough to distinguish between singular and plural forms. Aptly, ΣΤΙΧΟΣ ΠΡΕΠΟΣ, glossed *uersus pulcher*, points to a single line of poetry (ΣΤΙΧΟΙ is used elsewhere to indicate multiples lines), and indeed it is a single line (plus traces of a gloss) that has been erased. Martin's verse is therefore irretrievably lost, unless it just happens to be the Greek prayer in what resembles verse written out in Martin's hand on f. 298v (plate IV) and copied by *V* (cited above, p. XXXVI). At all events, the remaining inscription was demonstrably not intended to introduce the poem ΕΙΣΧΡΕ ΑΝΑΓΙΝΟΣΤΗΣ. With the disposal of the argument for Martin's authorship of no. 16, there is every reason to assume that the was included as the work of John Scottus; indeed, it is followed by a work that is demonstrably his. All the verses and the prose text in L^{II}, concluding with no. 17, were intended to represent the work of Eriugena.

3. Poems of the appendix

As noted in Section B, the poems of the Appendix are works that have some claim to authenticity but lack certain manuscript proof thereof. It is therefore necessary to examine each poem or group of poems on a case-by-case basis.

App. 1, *Caesare sub Karolo,* was printed with misgivings by Traube in his main collection (as no. I). These verses occur at the end of the preface to Eriugena's treatise *De praedestinatione* in Paris, BnF, lat. 13386. Traube rightly observed that John never referred to Charles the Bald as 'Caesar'; moreover, it was John's practice to address the king directly. One stylistic feature, however, favours the authenticity of the verses. This is the use of three-word alliteration in line 3 (on this feature, see below, p. LXXII). On balance, there is no basis for including the verses in the main collection, but it does not seem possible to reject them absolutely.

App. 2, ΓΡΑΜΜΑΤΑ ΓΡΑΙΥΓΕΝΩΝ is, as noted in section B, a metrical colophon to the Greek gospels with a Latin interlinear translation contained in St Gallen 48. Traube published this poem among his 'Carmina Scottorum' (*MGH Poetae,* 3, p. 686–687, no. 4). I have given detailed reasons elsewhere for regarding this poem as a genuine work by John.[139] But because so much depends on the attribution of this poem (chiefly the authorship of the interlinear gloss of a biblical text), it is necessary to restate some of these arguments here and to provide additions and modifications based upon subsequent research.

In line 2 of the poem the author claims to have clarified the Greek text:

Cerne labore meo lingua Pelasga patet.

It is therefore necessary to assume that the author of the poem was also the author of the Latin interlinear translation, even if he was

---

[139] HERREN, 'St Gall 48'.

not the scribe of St Gallen 48. In fact, the translator was almost certainly not identical with the scribe. As has been noted, Bischoff has shown convincingly that St Gallen 48 is a *copy* of one of the biblical manuscripts made by the 'circle of Sedulius', not an original.[140] Thus, if the Irishman Fergus, a close friend of Sedulius, was the scribe of the poem as well as other material in the book, as Traube alleged,[141] this proves nothing about the authorship of the poem itself and hence nothing about the authorship of the interlinear gloss.

The original of St Gallen 48 had to have been written at some time between c. 850 and c. 870,[142] thus coinciding with John's *floruit*. John himself was involved with the glossing of the manuscripts connected with the circle of Sedulius, as is shown most clearly in the case of Bern 363.[143] The glossing of St Gallen 48 thus brings us into the immediate time and milieu of John. Was John the author of the gloss and colophon?

Other Irishmen besides John living in Northern France in the second third of the ninth century knew some Greek, notably Sedulius, Martin, and Fergus; yet as far as we know, none could rival John's achievement in this tongue. The Latin gloss to the Greek text of St Gallen 48 is by no means a mechanical piece of work. The translator employed known versions of the Latin Bible where possible, but elsewhere adjusted the Latin to the demands of the Greek syntax, so that the resulting Latin version defies classification.[144] The translator's purpose, therefore, was to supply a crib to the Greek with the implicit purpose of encouraging the study of the gospels in their original tongue. This purpose is made explicit in lines 1–4 of the colophon.

---

[140] Above, p. XXXV, n. 118; BISCHOFF, *Katalog*, III, 302, no. 5534 ('anscheinend Oberitalien').

[141] TRAUBE, 'O Roma Nobilis', p. 52.

[142] The *Vorlage* of St Gallen 48 must post-date the predestination controversy (850–851), as there are several mentions of Gottschalk – mostly critical – in the margins. Aganon (probably bishop of Bergamo, 837–867) is also mentioned. The Irish scholars Sedulius, Dubthach, Kathasach and Dongus, whose names also appear, are hard to date precisely. For these figures, see the indices to CONTRENI, *Cathedral School* and to LAPIDGE – SHARPE, *A Bibliography of Celtic-Latin Literature*; Ó CORRÁIN, *Clauis litterarum Hibernensium*, III.

[143] J. J. CONTRENI, 'The Irish in the Western Carolingian Empire', in *Die Iren und Europa im früheren Mittelalter* – ed. H. Löwe, Stuttgart, 1982, II, 758–798, especially p. 766–798.

[144] F. J. KENYON, *The Text of the Greek Bible*, London, 1937, p. 102.

No Carolingian scholar was more intent on promoting the study of Greek than John Scottus. An egregious example of John's Hellenistic fervour is to be found in no. 20, which prefaces the translation of the pseudo-Dionysian corpus. In lines 5–6 the poet goes so far as to urge his patron to take up the study of Greek himself. Elsewhere he alludes with pride to his accomplishments in the sphere of Greek studies: he even compares himself to Jerome (20, 15–16).

While we know that Sedulius knew some Greek,[145] it is unlikely that this scholar was responsible for the exemplar of St Gallen 48 – despite the association of this gospel book with Sedulius's circle. To be sure, we possess a Greek psalter written in Sedulius's own hand. This is Paris, Bibliothèque de l'Arsenal 8407.[146] Because of an error (*rarus sed egregius*) by J. F. Kenney,[147] modern scholars have assumed that this psalter was likewise an interlinear bilingual book in the style of the other biblical books associated with the circle, notably the 'Basel Psalter' and the 'Codex Boernerianus'.[148] But this is simply wrong. The Greek psalter written in Sedulius's hand and bearing his 'signature' in a Greek colophon[149] contains neither interlinear nor parallel-column Latin text, at least in the psalter section (f. 1–55). The remaining portion of the manuscript contains Greek prayers, liturgical texts, biblical texts possibly intended for liturgical use and a patristic florilegium. The final item is a Greek poem with the Latin inscription *Apollo dicit*.[150] All these Greek texts are given with Latin translation *in parallel columns*. If we are prepared to believe that Sedulius was responsible for interlinear glossing elsewhere, then we must work from the hypothesis that he departed radically from the method we know he employed in the appendix to his autograph psalter.

---

[145] M. W. HERREN, 'Sedulius Scottus and the knowledge of Greek', in *Early Medieval Ireland and Europe: Chronology, Contacts, Scholarship. A Festschrift for Dáibhí Ó Cróinín* – ed. P. Moran, I. Warntjes, Turnhout, 2015, p. 515–535.

[146] The Bibliothèque nationale de France has published photographs of the manuscript online. A facsimile of a single page containing Sedulius's subscription in Greek was given by B. DE MONTFAUCON, *Palaeographia graeca*, Paris, 1708, p. 237.

[147] KENNEY, *Sources*, p. 557.

[148] Dresden, Sächsische Landesbibliothek, MS A 145b.

[149] The colophon reads: ΣΗΔΥΛΙΟΣ ΣΚΟΤΤΟΣ ΕΓΩ ΕΓΡΑΨΑ. Above the signature in the same hand: ΕΥΧΑΣ ΘΕΩ ΕΓΩ ΑΜΑΡΤΩΛΟΣ ΠΡΑΞΟ.

[150] This is a fragment of the *Oracula sibyllina* in the translation of Lactantius. See the discussion by HERREN, 'Sedulius Scottus and the knowledge of Greek', p. 524–529.

John Scottus, however, favoured the use of interlinear translation in his work on the grammar of Priscian. The so-called 'Leiden Priscian' (see above, p. XIX–XX) contains numerous corrections and additions to the text of Priscian in the hand of i¹, implying that John edited Priscian in his own hand. On several folios one finds Priscian's quotations from classical Greek authors, notably Homer, recopied in the hand of i¹ in the bottom margin and supplied with a Latin interlinear gloss.[151] Thus the available evidence shows that John favoured the interlinear format, whereas Sedulius employed parallel columns for the translation of Greek texts.

In deciding the question of authorship between John and his Irish contemporaries, we must keep in mind that the opening line of the colophon is a Greek hexameter:

ΓΡΑΜΜΑΤΑ ΓΡΑΙΥΓΕΝΩΝ ΚΑΤΑ ΣΚΗΜΑΤΑ ΣΟΦΕ ΓΥΝΟΣΚΕΙΣ

The verse is far from perfect. The first syllable of σοφέ, which is short, is in a raised metrical position, and γυνόσκεις is a misspelling of the *koine* form γινώσκεις (Attic γιγ-). Practically all westerners who attempted to write Greek (and some Greeks as well) had difficulty with the long and short vowels ω and ο, η and ε. However, there are no serious syntactical or morphological problems in the line.

By contrast, Martin, whose inscription at the end of *L¹* does in fact constitute a Greek hexameter,[152] had difficulties with the basics of Greek:[153]

ΕΛΛΗΝΙΣ ΓΡΑΨΕΝ ΜΑΡΤΙΝΟΣ ΓΡΑΜΜΑΤΑ ΑΥΤΑ

A morphological problem (ΠΡΕΠΟΣ for πρέπων) also occurs in the inscription to his expunged verse or verses:

ΣΤΙΧΟΣ ΠΡΕΠΟΣ ΔΙΔΑΣΚΑΛΟΥ ΜΑΡΤΙΝΟΥ

There are no complete hexameter verses among the edited genuine poems by Sedulius. However, Sedulius did write one Greek

---

[151] Examples: f. 32v (Homer), 56r (Homer), 65r (Homer), 74r (Anacreon).
[152] LAPIDGE, 'L'influence stylistique', p. 444.
[153] DIONISOTTI, 'Greek Grammars', p. 47. It may be that Martin's knowledge of Greek was influenced by the spoken language: see M. W. HERREN, 'Evidence for "Vulgar Greek" in Early Medieval Latin Texts and Manuscripts', in *Sacred Nectar*, p. 72.

verse, of which I have recently been able to recover a portion.[154] This occurs on the last folio of Paris, BnF, lat. 10307 (*La*):

    Vers. ferg.... dic.... ...ψλιος sco.... uel ΣΟΦΕ
    ΣΟΦΙΑ ..... ΛΙΚΝΟΝ ...... ΛΑΜΠΡΟΝ

I reconstruct the inscription as follows:

    Vers⟨um⟩ Ferg⟨o⟩ dic⟨tauit Sed⟩ulios Sco⟨ttus⟩

However, even if Sedulius was capable of writing Greek verse as well as a grammatically correct Greek subscription to his psalter (see above, p. XLVII, n. 145), he was probably not responsible for the gloss and colophon of St Gallen 48 for reasons already stated.[155]

The elimination of Martin and Sedulius as possible authors of our poem and the translation to which it is a colophon is not sufficient to establish John's authorship, even if it narrows the field. There were other authors of Greek verse written in the reign of Charles the Bald, some of whom have been identified (e.g. Heiric of Auxerre), others not. Moreover, there may well have been contemporaries of John (such as the Liuddo praised in no. 15) who could have managed a Latin crib to the Greek of the gospels.

It must therefore be admitted that the question of authorship cannot be decided on the knowledge of Greek alone. If we consider the poem by itself, we must judge it on the basis of style, content and structure. I have already adduced several textual parallels between this poem and Eriugena's firmly attested poems in my article 'St Gall 48'; these are repeated here in the *apparatus fontium* to the poem at lines 7, 11, 12. Moreover, a close reminiscence of the *Periphyseon* is recorded in the note to line 9.[156] In addition to modes of phrasing, the metrical colophon closely resembles the genuine poems in the manner of alliteration.[157]

Ultimately, however, it is the themes and their organization that are decisive. The poet begins by contrasting his ability to clar-

---

[154] BISCHOFF, 'Das griechische Element', p. 267, n. 107 gives the inscription and verse. He deciphered the inscription as follows: "Versus ... Ferg ... sco**(ott ...?)," and understood the Greek verse to be the work of Fergus. I discuss this matter at greater length in M. W. HERREN, 'Sedulius's Knowledge of Greek'.

[155] Above, p. XLVII–XLVIII.

[156] I am grateful to Professor Gustavo Piemonte of Buenos Aires for pointing this out to me. See now his 'Acotaciones 2', p. 42, n. 177.

[157] HERREN, 'St Gall 48', p. 102. On John's alliterative style, see below, p. LXXI–LXXII.

ify the sense of a Greek text with the common capacity to recognize letter shapes (lines 1–2). This is followed by an exhortation to the study of (Greek) grammar (lines 3–4). The implied boast of the rare achievement in Greek and the promotion of Greek study are Eriugenian *topoi,* as noted above. The next ten lines (5–14) deal with theological themes: the creation, incarnation, redemption, and their interconnection: Christ who made the world was made man through the agency of a virgin; the *Word* of God came into the world to bring to it the *words* of God. These great paradoxes form the centrepiece of virtually all the major Eriugenian poems. In the last part of the poem (lines 15–22) the writer begs Christ's mercy and claims himself to be the cause of his own sorrow. The allusion to man as the self-willing cause of misery (line 20) and a God who shows mercy to those of good will (*dolentis,* line 19) reflects an Eriugenian doctrine known not only from the *De praedestinatione* but also from the genuine poetry: see especially 8, 74–78. In the context of the gospel book, with its references in the margins to Gottschalk and the predestination controversy,[158] these lines are particularly apt.

Finally, the themes are structured in a fashion that is strongly reminiscent of John's poetry. The poet begins with a reference to letters which, as symbols, communicate to men the great mysteries of faith: the creation, incarnation, and redemption. These mysteries in their turn, are related to the existential situation of particular human beings and times – in this case, the plight of the poet/translator. This tripartite structure is to be found in several of John's major poems.[159]

Let us conclude the present discussion with some observations on the textual unity of ΓΡΑΜΜΑΤΑ ΓΡΑΙΥΓΕΝΩΝ. The verses make excellent sense as a single poem, just as Traube published them originally. As Bischoff observed, what appears to be a break in hands at line 5 (see plate V) may in fact reveal nothing more than a change of pen. But even if a second scribe did finish the poem, this scribe was a close contemporary of the first (so Bischoff, orally). There is therefore no basis for assuming that two separate colophons have been artificially joined. There is every reason to think that this single poem (and therefore the gloss which it accompanies) was the work of John Scottus.

---

[158] Herren, *ibid.,* p. 104, n. 26.
[159] Herren, 'Johannes Scottus Poeta', p. 102–106.

App. 3-6 is a small collection that comes from the same manuscript that contains the 'Leiden Priscian' (BPL 67). The continental hand of the poems is contemporary with the i¹ glosses and corrections to Dubthach's text of Priscian. Traube printed the four poems as part of his 'Carmina Scottorum' without attribution (*MGH, Poetae,* 3, p. 690, nos. 7, 1-4). The first two poems, both distichs on the joys of Bacchus, remind us unambiguously of no. 19, a genuine poem that Traube did not know. App. 5 must have been written at Soissons when Karloman was a monk there and Wulfad was the abbot, hence 858-860.[160] Wulfad was particularly close to Eriugena, as the *Periphyseon* was dedicated to him. Thus *tempus, locus et personae* are all consistent with John's life and associations. App. 6 contains two reminiscences of the *genuina: flatibus austri* (4, 49, but also Ovid, *Trist.* 1, 10, 33) and *prosilit ex Erebo* (6, 1). Line 3 of the poem, ... *praedicens luminis ortum,* referring simultaneously to the rising sun and the resurrection, strikes me as characteristically Eriugenian. There are two purely Greek words in the collection: *tragos* in App. 4 and *allector* in App. 6.

The coalescence of the text-tradition evidence with the setting, content and style of the poems argues strongly in favour of Eriugenian authorship. The fact that these poems connect John closely with Soissons cannot constitute an objection, given the evidence assembled in favour of his long-term residence there (see above, p. XII).

App. 7 has been regarded as genuine because it is written in the hand known as i¹, which most scholars now accept as the autograph of John Scottus.[161] However, the authenticity of the poem can be supported on other grounds. It strikes me that there are independent reasons for accepting the verses as genuine. The letter to Winibert that accompanies the poem (cited above, p. XXXVI) refers to glossing the portions of Martianus Capella's text that had been overlooked. This implies that the author of the letter had already written one set of glosses to Martianus and was planning a second set. I have argued elsewhere that Eriugena wrote not one, but two versions of a commentary on the *De nuptiis.*[162] This con-

---

[160] See Traube's notes, *ibid.;* KENNEY, *Sources,* p. 562 (no. 366); CAPPUYNS, p. 166; DUTTON, 'Dubthach's Priscian Codex', p. 21-28.

[161] See above, p. XIX-XX with n. 57.

[162] M. W. HERREN, 'The Commentary on Martianus Attributed to John Scottus: Its Hiberno-Latin Background', in *Jean Scot écrivain,* p. 265-286, especially 267-271.

clusion would exclude other known commentators on Martianus, such as those by Remigius and pseudo-Dunchad. The transmission of the poem in the flyleaf of a Laon manuscript (Laon, Bibliothèque municipale, MS 24), for which Martinus Hiberniensis provided the table of contents and other entries,[163] places the poem firmly in John's time and milieu. Martin himself can be excluded on the basis of the hand, as Martin's autograph has been identified.[164] The distich is in all probability by John.[165]

App. 8, the Greek poem *Semeron autokrator*, is a poem on the legendary St Denis, who is associated with Dionysius the Areopagite. Traube believed that there were good reasons for regarding the work as genuine, but made allowance for doubts, as the poem stands outside the main collection and none of its *graeca* was excerpted by Martin. Traube's misgivings were echoed recently by Dutton, who adds that the term *autokrator* need not apply to Charles the Bald alone, that there was more than one king named Charles in the later Carolingian period, and that the interest in Dionysius was the common intellectual property of western thinkers of the times.[166]

But, perhaps, these scruples have been carried too far. Eriugena addressed two other poems to Charles on the subject of Dionysius: no. 10, *Graculus Iudaeus*, which celebrates Charles's refurbishment of a church dedicated to this saint, and no. 21, *Lumine sidereo*, which recounts the legend of Dionysius the Areopagite. *Semeron autokrator* picks up both themes: a liturgical occasion connected with the patron of the church and the legend of the saint.

More decisive, in my view, is the evidence of the use of Greek (however badly preserved in the manuscript). Traube (p. 525) wrote of Floss's decision to include the poem: 'neque immerito, cum versus in Dionysii laude versentur et facti sint ad leges, quas Iohannes exerceret'. The question therefore becomes: how many western scholars were there between the late ninth century and c. 1100 who could write eight lines in continuous Greek, and not only that, but in hexameter verses following the same metrical

---

[163] CONTRENI, *Cathedral School*, p. 96.
[164] *Ibid.*, plate II.
[165] See BISCHOFF, *Katalog*, I, 20, no. 2045, confirming the letter to Winibertus as an autograph by John.
[166] DUTTON, 'Royal Poet', p. 61, n. 42.

laws observed by John Scottus?[167] And of this group, how many of them would have addressed their verses to a Charles *autokrator* on the subject of Dionysius the Areopagite on a liturgical occasion? One other point, albeit a small one, tells in favour of the poem's authenticity: the *codex unicus* (G) preserves the (mis)spelling *kyrrios,* with two *r*'s. This is the spelling regularly given by the manuscripts of John's genuine poems.

The content of the poem is also of interest, as it points to John's use of either the prose or the metrical *Passio S. Dionysii* by Hilduin of Saint-Denis. App. 8, lines 4–8, records the detail that Dionysius experienced from afar the darkness that had settled over the world at the time of the crucifixion, and knew that the redemption had been accomplished. This narrative is recorded in both versions of the *Passio;* see the *apparatus fontium* ad loc. When all these factors are taken together, the possibility that someone other than John Scottus wrote this poem is remote.

App. 9a–c, the infamous epitaph for Hincmar, occurs in three irreconcilable versions, one of which is repeated in two manuscripts. Traube knew only two manuscripts of the poem, but these give different versions; I believe that he was in error in attempting to reduce them to one. Lehmann's discovery of a third manuscript,[168] producing a third version with its awkward addition of a second hexameter line before the pentameter verse, made the situation even more complex. Finally, Bernhard Bischoff discovered and communicated to me yet another manuscript (*At*), which, but for its curious attribution, the variant *gestit* for *gessit,* and interesting glosses, gives the same version as *Mo*. It may be useful here to give all the manuscript readings together with surrounding inscriptions and glosses:

At:

GOTISCALT

Hic iacet igma... cleptes uehementer auarus
   Hoc tantum gestit nobile quod periit.

---

[167] Traube refers to the fact that John regularly places a long syllable just before the caesura, where the Greek (as well as the Latin) hexameter requires a long syllable. This practice stands in contrast to that of the author of what is perhaps the longest known Carolingian Greek poem *not* written by John, namely the poem, beginning ΥΨΥΛΟΣ ΚΥΡΙΟΣ, printed by Traube in the 'Carmina Scottorum' (*MGH, Poetae,* 3), p. 698.

[168] LEHMANN, 'Mitteilungen', p. 18–20.

Gloss: clepit .i. foromat dr̄ cleptes et clepus
H:

> Vt cito sis uerax. tibi mandat nuncius audax.
> Hic iacet incmarus cleptes uehementer auarus
> Sordidus instabilis madescit rore pericli
> Hoc solum fecit nobile quod periit.

Glosses: none; scansion marks over lines 2 and 3.
Mo:

> Mausolea sunt sepulchra seu monumenta regum a mausoleo rege dicta.
> Hic iacet hincmarus clepthes uehementer auarus
>   Hoc solum gessit nobile quod periit.
> Remis misit equum mulum burdegula nullum
>   Aut mulus ueniat aut equus huc redeat.

Gloss in right margin: a charm beginning *In x̄p̄ī nomine incipit ratio.*
V:

> Hoc epitaphium composuit Iohannes Scotus licet sapiens hereticus. Hic iacet. igcmarus cleptes. et semper auarus. Hoc solum fecit nobile ut (*del.*) quod periit.

It seems fairly clear that *H* contains a line of verse that is meant to introduce the epigram and thus does not belong to it.[169] *Mo* contains, in addition to the scholion on *mausoleum* (Isidore, *Etym.* 15, 11, 3), two lines of an epigram identified as the work of Hincmar, archbishop of Reims.[170] If we remove this material and the inscription in *V*, we are left with three versions of the poem. If any or all of these versions are by John, the editorial situation is analogous to that of the Greek verses addressed to an unidentified *doctor* and to one of the Hincmars (12a–b).

But who wrote the epitaph for Hincmar – a cruel epigram doubtless intended to be read by the recipient prior to his interment? *Mo* and *H* are silent; *V* ascribes the poem unequivocally to John Scottus; *At* ascribes the work to Gotiscalt, presumably Gottschalk of Orbais, the opponent of Eriugena in the predestination controversy. As Dutton has noted of *V*, 'The Vatican copy

---

[169] This point was noted earlier by DUTTON, 'Royal Poet', p. 57, n. 25. The introductory verse was written in a different hand from that of the main epigram.
[170] Identified and printed by Traube (*MGH Poetae,* 3), p. 415 (no. 5).

is found at the end of a manuscript that contains Florus of Lyon's treatise against the predestination doctrines of Eriugena.'[171] Can the rival claims to authorship of this poem be resolved?

The evidence of *H* has not yet been considered in its entirety. The relevant portion of the manuscript containing the poem is a bifolium that belonged originally to Harley MS 3095, a manuscript of the *Consolatio* of Boethius with extensive commentary. On fol. 19r and 22r is to be found a Greek glossary and grammar. It has been noted above that the name ΙΟΑΝΗΣ stands at the end of the Greek grammar and glossary on f. 22r, leaving little doubt that the Greek textbook material was excerpted from some work of Eriugena's. The Hincmar epitaph on f. 18v is thus placed opposite the beginning of a grammatical text of Eriugena's.

Several factors thus favour Eriugenian authorship: the unambiguous attribution in *V*, the circumstances of transmission in *H*, and the sophisticated level of Greek glossing in *At* pointing to a person highly skilled indeed in Greek, if the glosses are authorial. One notes the corrupt *foromat*, which doubtless contains φώρ, another Greek word for 'thief', and ὀνόμαται; thus, the glossator glosses Greek with Greek. That the author knew something of Greek orthography is shown by the initial IG in the name *Hincmar* in both *At* and *V*.[172]

In favour of Gottschalk is the solitary testimony of *At*, but this must be taken seriously, as the fragment dates from the second third of the ninth century (thus Bischoff, orally) and thus falls directly into the lifetimes of Eriugena and Gottschalk. There is also a stylistic factor of singular importance which, I believe, tips the balance in favour of Gottschalk, namely the use of double leonine rhyme in the first line of the couplet, followed by single leonine rhyme in the second. John uses single leonine sparingly in his genuine verses and never employs double leonine in his hexameters, albeit there is a solitary example of double leonine in a pentameter verse (6.30). By contrast, leonine is a trademark of Gottschalk's poetry, whether of the rhythmical or metrical variety. In the metrical portion of Gottschalk's *Carmen ad Rathramnum*,[173] which comprises 154 hexameter lines, leonine rhyme occurs in every verse. Most examples are single leonine, but double leonine is not

---

[171] DUTTON, 'Royal Poet', p. 58.
[172] Observed by BERNT, *Epigramm*, p. 284.
[173] TRAUBE (*MGH, Poetae*, 3), p. 733–737.

infrequent. At one place in the poem it occurs in three successive lines (55-57):

> Quae sancto flatu, non uili inflata boatu,
> Dulciloquo affatu, celebri rutiloque relatu
> Demulcet mentem modulaminis huius egentem.

Sometimes the double rhymes are mingled with clever plays of sound and sense, as at line 95:

> Sensibus arguto, lingua uehementer acuto.

If we consider only versions *a* and *b,* the above analysis favours Gottschalk's authorship. However, the introduction of a second hexameter line into the poem in version *c* raises a new problem. The line 'Sordidus, instabilis, madescit rore pericli' contains no caesural rhyme. Moreover, it is inconceivable that it belonged to the 'original' poem, as it interrupts the regular alternation of hexameter verse and pentameter.[174] I propose as a possibility that Gottschalk wrote the 'original' couplet (allowing for the verbal variant in the second line). John may have written a separate epigram on one of the Hincmars – he was certainly believed to have done so by the scribe of *V*. The two epigrams may have been conflated later. In this case, the line beginning 'Sordidus, instabilis' may be the only genuine bit of John's work that is transmitted. Yet even this supposition is unprovable.

In the final analysis, the puzzle may be unsolvable. Manuscript attributions here are of little help not only because they conflict, but also because, in the present instance, the attribution of a poem is tantamount to an accusation. I do not believe that anyone would have signed his name to these verses. The unstable character of the manuscript tradition suggests that the epigram may have circulated orally and 'fathered upon' at least two different writers, persons known to have had good motives for attacking one or the other Hincmar. We must conclude here with a *non liquet*.

App. 10-16, as noted above, form a collection of *tituli* to paintings in the 'Codex Aureus of St Emmeram' written in 870. Dutton and Jeauneau have put forward an excellent case to show that these *tituli* closely reflect the genuine poetry of Eriugena both in

---

[174] BERNT, *Epigramm,* p. 284-285. Bernt records *mandescit* as the reading of *H* – a misreading owed to the confusion of a suspension mark with a scansion mark.

verbal parallels and in content.[175] At the same time, these scholars were able to show convincingly that the *tituli* were not composed by Alcuin, to whom Dümmler had assigned them.[176] The reason for their earlier ascription to Alcuin is that excerpts from them occur in an important Alcuin manuscript: Paris, BnF, lat. 5577. The *tituli* excerpts, which are written on f. 18v, are intermingled with Alcuinian material. On f. 18r there is a metrical epitaph for Alcuin, and on f. 19r we find the *Versus Alquini ad mensam*, followed by another set of verses found also in the 'Codex Aureus'. But the Alcuinian verses are clearly labelled and demarcated from the other verses which are not ascribed to anyone. Moreover, the inscriptions to the *tituli* in Paris, BnF, lat. 5577 make it possible to identify the pictures in the 'Codex Aureus' for which the verses were written.

Dutton and Jeauneau contented themselves with removing the verses from Alcuinian authorship and showing their close relation to the style and content of verses written by John, stopping short of claiming Eriugenian authorship. I should like to view the *tituli* of the 'Codex Aureus' as 'atelier poems' in which more than one poet was involved. It is possible, for example, that the two scribes, the brothers Beringar and Liuthard, who presumably wrote their own metrical colophons,[177] had a hand in composing parts of the *tituli*. The sections seem to be of uneven quality. App. 16, *Cum sancto penitras*, is first-rate and reflects closely Eriugena's style and thought. At the other extreme, App. 15, *Lucas Achaicis*, is hackneyed and shows a weak connection of ideas. On the whole, it seems best to view these poems as the work of a master and his apprentices. As it is not possible to demonstrate formally which lines belong to the master, which to the apprentices, it seems best to regard the entire collection as 'workshop of John Scottus'.[178]

App. 17, Fr. 1 is a list of thirty-six Greek words with Latin definitions in L¹, f. 294v, introduced by the title 'Graeca ad Versus'. Most words in the list are found in the genuine poems of John Scottus and are followed by the same definitions: ΔΙΚΑΙΟΣ iustus,

---

[175] DUTTON – JEAUNEAU, 'The Verses', p. 97–102.

[176] *MGH, Poetae,* 1, p. 292–293; see also E. DÜMMLER, 'Die handschriftliche Überlieferung der lateinischen Dichtungen aus der Zeit der Karolinger', *Neues Archiv,* 4 (1879), 128.

[177] Printed by TRAUBE *MGH, Poetae,* 3), p. 254; by DUTTON – JEAUNEAU, 'The Verses', p. 96–97. On these scribes, see BISCHOFF, *Schreibschulen,* I, 225.

[178] See DUTTON – JEAUNEAU, 'The Verses', p. 98.

ΑΓΑΘΟΣ bonus, ΜΕΓΑΛΟΣ magnus, ΤΙΜΙΟΣ pretiosus, ΑΚΡΟΣ summus. We also see what are taken to be John's misspellings of certain Greek words: ΚΛΕΟΡ (for ΚΛΕΟΣ), ΦΟΜΕΝΟΡ (for ΦΟΜΕΝΟΣ). It is possible that words in the list that are not attested in the genuine poems might belong to one or more of his lost poems that may later be identified.

4. Spurious poems

Traube appended two poems to his canon of the genuine poems of John, namely some verses published by Floss beginning 'Ornat (acus mi)ro sabanum molimine fulta' and the so-called 'Versus Romae'. Traube showed that the second poem was spurious and included the first only 'ne quid uersuum, qui in Flossii editione habeatur ab eoque adscribantur Iohanni, apud nos frustra quaeratur'.[179] Those wishing to read these works are advised to consult them in the editions of Floss and Traube.

III. John as a poet

This section will deal, albeit briefly, with John's work as a poet: his reading and methods of citation, diction, prosody, poetic techniques, and – I think most importantly – his method of structuring his poems. I have not seen it as my task to exhaust these topics, but rather to point in certain directions where further research would be of profit. Ultimately, the aim should be to place John's work in the broader context of Carolingian poetry. Despite recent progress, work on Carolingian poetry, other than textual, is still in its beginnings.

A. John's poetic reading and citation

John's reading of classical, late antique and early Carolingian poets was wider than has been suspected heretofore. This fact in turn points to his enduring interest in the liberal arts and perhaps to the conclusion that the most advanced representative of Carolingian philosophy did not regard the study and commentary of po-

---

[179] Traube (*MGH, Poetae,* 3), p. 554–556.

etry as propaedeutic to philosophy, but rather as a central activity that one continues to pursue alongside philosophy. Indeed, we see in John's serious poetic work that poetry and philosophy are highly compatible entities.[180] Such a happy synthesis is only possible when the poet-philosopher refreshes himself continually at the wells of the muses, as John seems to have done.

Unlike some Carolingian poets, John does not cite extensively.[181] If we make an exception of the 'atelier poems' and confine ourselves to works written entirely by him, it is not possible to cite an instance where a whole line has been borrowed from another poet. John's borrowings are usually limited to a suggestive phrase, most often a metrical line ending, sometimes a line beginning. These borrowed phrases rarely consist of more than three words. In a good many cases it is impossible to tell from whom John borrowed a particular reminiscence, since it is attested in the works of several poets. On the whole, John strove for freshness and originality in his poetic expression.

Despite this love of originality, it is still possible to identify a good many borrowings and reminiscences. To begin with the classical sources, it comes as no surprise that John's principal poetic source was the corpus of Vergil. Vergil was a major source not only for John's poetry, but for his philosophical works as well.[182] Moreover, a selection of John's notes to Vergil survives in Bern 363, a monument to Irish classical scholarship in the Carolingian period.[183] These notes deal with Books 1-6 of the *Aeneid,* with a not surprising concentration of scholia to the 'philosophical' sections of Book 6. Nonetheless, John's knowledge of the *Aeneid* seems to have been comprehensive; he also knew the *Georgics*. It is striking that John's Vergilian borrowings are not the usual poetic plunderings – phrases taken over from one poem to the next without regard to context. Several of the Vergilian reminiscences are strikingly apt and demand of the reader a knowledge of the Vergilian setting. Some examples:

At 1, 59, John describes the rout of Louis and his troops by Charles. The former are described:

---

[180] See COLNAGO, *Poseia e teologia*, p. 129.
[181] See the *Index scriptorum* for a full listing of the poetic sources given in the notes.
[182] G. MADEC, 'Jean Scot et ses auteurs', in *Jean Scot écrivain,* p. 144-186, especially 185-186. With respect to the use of Vergil, Madec's article is now superseded by P. E. DUTTON, 'Eriugena and Virgil', in *Eriugena and Creation,* p. 3-30.
[183] CONTRENI, 'The Irish in the Western Carolingian Empire', p. 774-798.

> Qui laeti fuerant quaerentes extera regna.

Eriugena expects that his more learned readers will remember Vergil's words at *Aen.* 4, 350:

> et nos fas extera quaerere regna.

An especially skilful borrowing of Vergil occurs in no. 9, *Postquam nostra salus,* where the Satanic protagonist – a precursor of Milton's Lucifer in *Paradise Lost* – is given an heroic soliloquy, in which he pours out all his bitterness at the sight of the released souls flying to paradise, a feat that he is incapable of preventing. As he sees the flying spirits (line 53):

> Suspicit et nutrit tristi sub pectore uulnus.

one cannot help thinking of Juno in a similar plight (*Aen.* 1, 36):

> Cum Iuno aeternum seruans sub pectore uulnus.

The *tituli* of the *Codex Aureus* show the skilful use of Vergil for panegyric (App. 10, 5):

> Hludouuic iustus erat, quo rex non iustior alter.

This is a clear reminiscence of *Aen.* 1, 544–545:

> Rex erat Aeneas nobis, quo iustior alter
> Nec pietate fuit ...

The learned reader of the *tituli* will note the comparison between Aeneas and Louis the Pious in respect of justice, but he may also be prompted to recall the rest of the Vergil line that speaks of Aeneas's *pietas.*

Examples of this sort could be extended. Vergil may have been the only classical poet whom John knew directly and cited to good effect. There are, however, several Ovidian echoes. These seem on the whole derivative and generally unrelated to poetic context. The most striking Ovidian image is *cornua lunae* (*Met.* 8, 11; 10, 479; 12, 264). This occurs once in John's poetry at 3, 13:

> Aereum spatium tangebant cornua lunae.

A Lucretian echo occurs twice (8.49 and 9.51): 'uolitare per auras' (LUCR. 4.221); another occurs at 3, 5: 'machinae mundi' (LUCR., 5, 96). A sign of direct use of Lucretius by John is his occasional practice of treating a short vowel followed by *s* at the end of a word as *u'*; see the discussion of prosody below, p. LXIX–LXXI.

Of the late Latin poets, both pagan and Christian, John knew and used the poetic portions of Martianus Capella's work; he also cites the poems of Paulinus of Nola, apparently at first hand. Other possible late Latin poets known to Eriugena are Iuvencus and Venantius Fortunatus. The Iuvencus citations, however, are uncertain as they coincide with similar patterns in Aldhelm – note that Aldhelm knew and used Iuvencus.[184] John was also reliant on Avitus, as was brought to my attention in 2002.[185] Finally, I have noted several echoes from the poems of Corippus, most from the *Iohannis,* but one from the *In laudem Iustini* (see the *Index scriptorum*). These are hard to explain, as the *Fortleben* of Corippus was tenuous.[186] It is noteworthy that there is no clear citation of Caelius Sedulius apart from one line from the *Carmen paschale* cited almost *verbatim* in the *tituli* (App. 1, 2 and *Carm. pasch.* 5, 357):

Discedat synagoga sui fuscata colore.

This paucity of citation is surprising given the great popularity of Caelius Sedulius in the Carolingian period. But perhaps the explanation lies in the fact that Eriugena too wrote paschal poetry and strove mightily to ensure that his verses did not appear derivative.

Of the pre-Carolingian and Carolingian poets, four merit close attention: Aldhelm, Alcuin, Theodulf, and Sedulius Scottus. Aldhelm, to be sure, was one of the best known and most widely cited poets (after, perhaps, Vergil and Caelius Sedulius) prior to the Carolingian period.[187] There are several echoes and some definite quotations from Aldhelm throughout Eriugena's poems. These,

---

[184] See the *Index locorum* in the edition of Aldhelm's poems by R. Ehwald (*MGH, Auct. ant.,* 15), p. 545.

[185] See T. Gärtner, 'Zum spätantiken und mittelalterlichen Nachwirkung der Dichtungen des Alcimus Avitus', *Filologia mediolatina* 9 (2002), 171–176. The present edition cites most suggested parallels.

[186] This applies to the *Iohannis* in particular, from which a number of Eriugena's citations is drawn: see the introduction to *Flavii Cresconii Corippi Iohannidos libri viii* – ed. J. Diggle, F. D. R. Goodyear, Cambridge, 1970, p. vii. There is, however, an extant early ninth-century manuscript of *In laudem Iustini*: Paris, BnF, lat. 8093 + Leiden, Voss. lat. F. 111, probably written at Lyon; see *Texts and Transmission: A Survey of the Latin Classics* – ed. L. D. Reynolds, Oxford, 1983, p. xviii–xix. The poetic anthology is dated by B. Bischoff 'IX Jh., 1. Viertel (wohl vor 821)': *Katalog,* III, 139, no. 4529.

[187] See the index to Manitius, *Geschichte,* I, 726. Additional references are given by F. Brunhölzl, *Geschichte,* I, 577. Parallel diction between Aldhelm and his Anglo-Saxon heirs (Boniface, Tatwine, Eusebius, et al.) is recorded by A. Orchard, *The Poetic Art of Aldhelm,* Cambridge, 1994, p. 284–292.

however, seem to be largely verbal, such as the striking phrase *mirabile fatu* (modelled on the Vergilian *mirabile dictu*).

Although there is no evidence that Eriugena read widely in Alcuin's poetic corpus, one Alcuinian poem, at least, captured our poet's attention: the *Versus de patribus, regibus, et Euboricensis Ecclesiae*.[188] This poem was used in the earliest poems dedicated to Charles the Bald (nos. 1 and 2) and the very last (25). I believe that the following collection of reminiscences shows John's first-hand knowledge of this poem. At 1, 79 John writes:

> Christi tuis famulis caelestis praemia uitae.

Aldhelm, in his *Aenigmata* (91, 5) has:

> Edita caelestis prensant et praemia uitae,

Alcuin, *carm*. 1. 1255 reads:

> peruigil exspectans caelestis praemia uitae.

How do we decide between Aldhelm and Alcuin for this borrowing? First of all, only Alcuin has the continuous three-word ending *caelestis praemia vitae;* secondly, the Aldhelm line comes from the *Aenigmata,* not the *De laudibus uirginum,* whereas all of our definite Aldhelm borrowings in Eriugena come from the latter work rather than the former (see the *Index fontium*). A rare example of John's borrowing most of a line from another poet occurs at 2, 57:

> Christe, dei uerbum, uirtus sapientia patris.

This line is a very close imitation of line 1 of Alcuin's 'York poem' (echoing I Cor. 1, 24):

> Christe, Deus, summi uirtus sapientia patris.

Interestingly, even in this case of a close imitation, Eriugena has sealed the line with his own monogram – the impression of the ΛΟΓΟΣ, the Word of God. Line 25 of the same poem by John appears to be based on line 641 of Alcuin's poem:

> John: Te sequitur uirtus omnis, te uita salusque.
> Alcuin: Angelicos sequitur monitus, mox uita salusque.

---

[188] *Alcuin: The Bishops, Kings, and Saints of York* – ed. P. Godman, Oxford, 1982.

Finally, it appears that Eriugena has turned to Alcuin for inspiration in constructing his famous poem on the church at Compiègne (no. 25). Alcuin wrote at I, 1508:

> Haec nimis alta domus solidis suffulta columnis.

This appears to be the source of two lines in *Aulae sidereae:*

> 74. Cuique remota domus septenis fulta columnis.
> 87. Alta domus pulcre centeno normate facta.

The use of Theodulf in the *tituli* of the *Codex Aureus* is consistent with John's use of this poet in his other poems.[189] Perhaps of greater interest is the question of the poetic relationship between John and his great Irish contemporary Sedulius. These two men seem to have been close contemporaries, and therefore it is difficult to determine a relationship of poetic influence one way or the other. However, in one case it appears that John borrowed one significant phrase from Sedulius. At the opening of John's last major poem, no. 25, the poet writes:

> Aulae sidereae paralelos undique circos.

This seems to have been borrowed from Sedulius, *carm.* I, 1, 24:

> Donec sideream uos ascendatis in aulam.

The foregoing supports the notion that John did not borrow extensively, and when he did, the borrowings are seldom more than echoes. On the other hand, Eriugena knew how to quote to good effect, and his reading of the poets was wider than has been assumed. But it also seems clear that while John knew a small number of poets or specific works extremely well, in the majority of cases his acquaintance was indirect or superficial – at least such is the conclusion to be reached from the available evidence.

B. The diction of John's poetry

1. Greek

The most striking feature of Eriugena's poetry is the use of Greek. The evidence of the manuscripts shows that most of the Greek words occurring in the poems were written in Greek characters in

---

[189] See DUTTON – JEAUNEAU, 'The Verses', p. 97–98, and the *Index scriptorum*.

the archetype, and therefore almost certainly by John himself. Greek words occur individually, as phrases, as whole lines, and as groups of lines within poems written predominantly in Latin. Moreover, several poems are written entirely in Greek, the longest comprising fourteen lines (no. 17).

The use of Greek may be regarded simply as a form of ornamentation or as an artifice employed to show the writer's linguistic skill and intellectual superiority over his contemporaries.[190] This certainly played a role. Yet I think a case can be made that John's use of Greek in his poems was motivated by other concerns than the simple desire to show off. First, as already noted (above, p. XXIV), John genuinely loved Greek and believed it to be a language superior to Latin in its powers of expression. He was very much aware that he lived in an intellectual milieu that was largely indifferent to the Greek world, if not hostile to it. A certain amount of lip-service was accorded to Greek as one of the *tres linguae sacrae*,[191] and a tiny handful of scholars may have been aware of its importance for the proper study of the Bible. However, in the Carolingian period, the study of Greek north of the Alps was limited largely to the Irish colonies in north-eastern France and Belgium and to the Alemannian centres of Reichenau and St Gallen.[192] Although there is some limited evidence for the presence of Greek-speaking teachers in the Frankish kingdoms,[193] we know little about them (our knowledge of their activity in the Ottonian kingdom is more precise).[194] As suggested above, the possibility of a contact between John and Hilduin of Saint-Denis while John was at Saint-Médard raises the possibility that Hilduin put John in contact with one or more Greek-speaking teachers. But for the present that idea remains an unproven hypothesis, and we still do

---

[190] Raby's judgement of the Greek used by the Irish *peregrini* seems particularly harsh (*Secular Latin Poetry*, I, 236): 'The influx of Irish scholars in the ninth century left its mark on the poetry of monastic schools. They came, bringing with them, besides an acquaintance with Greek, which in most of them did not go very far, the desire to create a favourable impression by a parade of learning, which was tempered by an easy-going attitude on non-essentials and a willingness to take whatever their patrons could provide'.

[191] BISCHOFF, 'Das griechische Element', p. 248–251.

[192] For a judicious evaluation of the respective roles of Irish and Germanic scholars in the transmission of Greek at St Gallen, see KACZYNSKI, *Greek in the Carolingian Age*, p. 23–25.

[193] For the evidence, see JEAUNEAU, 'Jean Scot Erigène et le grec', p. 15.

[194] The earliest teacher of Greek in the West (outside the Canterbury School) known by name is the Calabrian Philagathos, teacher of Otto III (late tenth century); see P. RICHÉ, 'Le grec dans les centres de culture d'occident', in *Sacred Nectar*, p. 156.

not know how Eriugena was able to acquire as much of the language as he did.

John speaks frankly in his poems of the effort expended in learning Greek and of the great difficulty of translating Greek texts into Latin for his royal patron (20, 21, 22, 21). This is no idle *topos* when one considers how difficult it must have been for a westerner at this time to acquire anything of this difficult language.[195] Despite these hardships, John was an ardent proselytizer of Greek studies. He urged Charles himself to undertake the subject (20, 5–6). The Greek in the poems, therefore, was employed to challenge not only his royal patron, but all who came into contact with John's verses. They stand as living proof that a westerner might attain a command of the Greek language such as to enable him to think and write in it – however harshly modern scholars may have judged the fruits of that effort.

The quality of the Greek of John's poems, as transmitted, has been commented upon negatively by earlier scholars. Moreover, recent and careful investigations have shown that John's knowledge of the Greek language was far from secure.[196] However, in assessing the level of John's 'Hellenism' as exhibited in the poems, it is important to take into account several factors. First of all, there is the probability that some, even much, of the *graeca* of John's poems has been corrupted in transmission.[197] Second, it was virtually impossible for a westerner in the Carolingian Empire to learn correct classical vowel quantities. A glance at the extant eighth and ninth-century Graeco-Latin lexicons and word-lists used in the West quickly reveals numerous confusions of E and H, O and Ω. If occidental writers did not have access to accurate information regarding vowel quantities, they could hardly be expected to write quantitative Greek poetry at a level close to classical standards (as they did in the case of Latin poetry). Third, and most surprising, westerners who aspired to this goal could expect little help from native speakers of Greek. We recall the egregious case of Lupus of Ferrières, who was misled by a Greek whom he consulted on the Greek vowel quantities in *blasphemus*.[198] The ignorance of Lupus's source may well be ascribed to the fact that

---

[195] DIONISOTTI, 'Greek Grammars', p. 1–6.

[196] JEAUNEAU, 'Jean Scot Erigène et le grec', p. 13–14; J. PÉPIN, 'Jean Scot, traducteur de Denis', in *Jean Scot écrivain,* p. 129–141.

[197] See especially App. 8 with Traube's reconstruction.

[198] DIONISOTTI, 'Greek Grammars', p. 3.

quantitative Greek poetry was very little practised in the ninth century, even in Constantinople. This makes a surprising contrast to the Latin West, where there was an unbroken tradition from antiquity in the study and writing of quantitative verse in Latin. (One must allow, of course, for a range of deviations from classical practice.)

This raises the central problem: where did John receive the impetus to write quantitative verse in Greek and what were his models? Obviously, contemporary Greek panegyric would not have yielded a pattern for a Greek work such as John's Poem 17 (ΘΑΥΜΑΣΤΩ ΒΑΣΙΛΕΙ).[199] I am convinced that the answer lies in large part with the Irish tradition of the close study of Priscian's *Institutiones,* Martianus Capella's *De nuptiis Philologiae et Mercurii,* and Macrobius's *Saturnalia,* all of which are rich in classical Greek quotations, especially of the poets.[200] Priscian's work, which was studied by the Irish beginning in the seventh century,[201] was replete with quotations of excerpts of the hexameter verses of Homer and Hesiod. In the same ninth-century copy of the *Institutiones* in which poems App. 3–6 appear, there are several examples of Homeric excerpts, recopied and corrected in the bottom margin of the page and provided with a *verbatim* Latin interlinear gloss. These glossed excerpts are written in the hand of i¹.[202] The existence of these excerpts attests to John's close interest in the text of Homer in the form in which it was available to Carolingian scholars. Equipped with examples of Homeric verse, a clever scholar might deduce the principles of their composition from his knowledge of Latin prosody.

It should also not be overlooked that the Irish already possessed a relatively long tradition of writing macaronic verses employing Greek. The poetically-conceived *Hisperica famina* (mid-seventh century) contain numerous Greek words, and other poems written by the Irish (though not necessarily composed in Ireland) con-

---

[199] See T. VILJAMAA, *Studies in Greek Encomiastic Poetry of the Early Byzantine Period* (*Commentationes humanarum litterarum, Societas scientiarum Fennica,* 42, 4), Helsinki, 1968.
[200] See M. W. HERREN, 'Commentary on Martianus', p. 283–286.
[201] KENNEY, *Sources,* p. 676; see A. AHLQVIST, 'Notes on the Greek Materials in the St Gall Priscian (Codex 904)', in *Sacred Nectar,* p. 195–214.
[202] Discussed above, p. XIX–XX, with n. 57.

tain phrases and whole lines in Greek.²⁰³ While we see the same phenomenon in the poems of Ausonius,²⁰⁴ it is not clear that John had any acquaintance with this poet, as the one certain echo of Ausonius occurs in App. 9, an epigram also attributed to Gottschalk.²⁰⁵

John's Greek vocabulary is curiously eclectic. Many words, of course, are the common stock of the Greek language. Other words strike one as more specifically classical, biblical, or patristic. None of it reflects the Greek idiom of John's own time.²⁰⁶ Some of the elements that compose this strange idiom are directly traceable to John's reading. Thus ΘΕΟΣΙΣ (Fr. 1, 13) probably comes from Maximus the Confessor. The words for the angelic orders in their Greek form come from Pseudo-Dionysius. But other words and forms are peculiarly Homeric: ΑΝΑΞ (2, 67; 17, 2; Fr. 1, 22), ΑΙΓΛΕ (8, 18), ΒΑΛΗΝ, without augment (Fr. 3, 5), and ΦΑΟΣ rather than 'standard' ΦΩΣ (17, 1).²⁰⁷ Then there are words of a classical (but not specifically Homeric) flavour: ΠΝΥΞ (2, 13; 13, 2), 'the place where the assembly was held', used by John as a substitute for ΕΚΚΛΗΣΙΑ; ΚΟΡΥΠΦΗΝ (8, 6; 17, 8), 'head, summit'; and ΟΜΜΑ, 'eye' (8, 3), favoured by the tragic poets and used rather than the more common ΟΦΘΑΛΜΟΣ.

In fine, the Greek of John's poems constitutes an idiom that has no basis in time or place; it is an uncritical amalgam of words drawn from texts known sometimes at first hand (pseudo-Dionysius, Maximus the Confessor, the Gospels), sometimes from secondary sources (Priscian, Martianus, Macrobius), and possibly from glossaries as well. Its eclecticism can be demonstrated by citing the first two words of 2, 67: ΟΡΘΟΔΟΞΟΣ ΑΝΑΞ! One is led to imagine Agamemnon receiving communion from the patriarch of

---

²⁰³ *The Hisperica famina* – ed. M. W. Herren, I, Toronto, 1974, p. 45, 191–193; II, Toronto, 1987, p. 67–71, 193–195.

²⁰⁴ LAPIDGE, 'L'influence stylistique', p. 442–443.

²⁰⁵ See above, p. LV–LVI.

²⁰⁶ The generally bookish character of John's Greek may be reflected in the little 'conversation manual' from Laon 444, cited by JEAUNEAU, 'Jean Scot Érigène et le grec', p. 39. For the transmission of the contemporary Greek idiom to the West, see M. W. HERREN, 'Evidence for "Vulgar Greek"', *Sacred Nectar*, p. 69–70. See now HERREN, 'An Eleventh-Century Travel Phrase Book in Demotic Greek', in *Teaching and Learning in Medieval Europe: Essays in Honour of Gernot R. Wieland* – ed. G. Dinkova-Bruun, T. Major (Publications of *The Journal of Medieval Latin*, 11), Turnhout, 2017, p. 203–210.

²⁰⁷ See the entries in G. AUTENRIETH, *A Homeric Dictionary* – transl. R. P. Keep, London, 1876.

Constantinople. For all this, John's Greek verses represent a remarkable achievement. They stand as a monument to the determination of one early medieval westerner to master the language that provided the key to the riches of the East.

2. Latin

John's Latin vocabulary was supple and rich. It was formed by direct study of the classical and Christian poets as well as the Bible and the Latin Church Fathers. Ludwig Bieler's general evaluation of John's Latinity is worth repeating here:

> The first thing about Eriugena's Latin that strikes the reader is its overall normality. His grammar is that of an educated writer of late Christian antiquity, an Augustine or Boethius. His style also is evidently modelled on theirs.[208]

Bieler's evaluation, which was based on Eriugena's original prose compositions, applies as well to the poems, *once we remove the Greek element from consideration*. Yet even within the Greek element, there are a number of ordinary words in the poems that had long been the common property of Christian Latin writers: *sophia, dogma, symbolicus, hymnizare, psallere,* and the like.[209] Thus the main reason that John's poetic vocabulary seems strange is the use of Greek words (whether in the Greek or Roman alphabet) that had *not* become part of the Latin lexicon.

There were, however, two major types of abstruse vocabulary which John might have utilized. These were archaism and neologism. The latter feature, in particular, found a place in Irish Latinity, especially in the *Hisperica famina* and the works related to them.[210] John, however, avoided archaism altogether and was sparing in his employment of neologism. There is only a tiny handful of words in the poems that appear to have been coined by John. I have noted *glauciuido,* 'gleaming' (lit. 'bright-seeing') (8, 3), *uatiuomi,* 'prophet-spewing' (9, 7), and possibly *umbramine* (25, 25). Besides these there are a few words that reflect the tendency of late Latin poets to form new nouns in *-amen* such as *peccamen* (1, 27), *modulamen* (1, 15; 8, 23); adjectives in *-ger, -genus,*

---

[208] L. BIELER, 'Remarks on Eriugena's Original Latin Prose', in *The Mind of Eriugena*, p. 141.
[209] See E. LÖFSTEDT, *Late Latin,* Oslo, 1959, p. 68–119.
[210] HERREN, *Hisperica famina,* I, 48–49.

and *-ficus* such as *astriger* (8, 18), *caeligenus* (1, 3; 22, 1), *uersificus* (1, 80); and adverbs in *-im, -tim* such as *dispersim* (3, 44) and *cumulatim* (3, 44).

Bieler noted the absence of 'Hibernian' influences on John's Latinity.[211] Although this is generally right, I have been able to detect several hisperic words in John's vocabulary.[212] One example occurs in the poems: *toli* (2, 40), from a nominative *tolus*, most probably based on Old Irish *tolae*, 'flood'.[213] John's Latin lexicon, therefore, is 'conservative' not only by the standards of his countrymen of an earlier generation, but also when compared to some of the more 'precious' poets of late antiquity and the early Middle Ages.

C. Prosody

John had a strong interest in prosody, as is clear from a number of notes in his scholia on Martianus and Vergil.[214] Nonetheless, his own practice was restricted to the familiar heroic and elegiac forms. (Interestingly, nos. 1–7 are written in the elegiac form, while nos. 8–10 and 25 are in hexameters. This may reflect a change in John's conception of the function of poetry.[215]) It should perhaps also be noted that John showed no interest in the non-metrical poetry which had characterized the Hiberno-Latin verse of an earlier time and was still practised in his own day.[216]

Despite John's study of metrics and an apparently strong theoretical interest in the subject, his prosody was in some respects deficient, in others, eccentric. We know, of course, that the 'Silver Age' and later Latin poets departed from the established practices of the 'Golden Age' in various respects. But John makes a number of simply careless errors in scansion, e.g. at 3, 53, *mactat ipse*, where the second *a* is treated as long, though it is short by nature and 'by position'. A similar error occurs at the beginning of 5, 25, 'Hic fuerat aries', where the final syllable of *fuerat*, treated by John as

---

[211] BIELER, 'Eriugena's Original Latin Prose', p. 141–143.

[212] HERREN, 'Commentary on Martianus', p. 277–279.

[213] *Ibid*. This *tolus* is not to be confused with *tolus* = θόλος; see HERREN, *Hisperica famina*, I, 134.

[214] See, for example, the *apparatus fontium* at 1, 33.

[215] See M. W. HERREN, 'Johannes Scottus Poeta', p. 104–106.

[216] For a contemporary rhythmical poem by an Irish writer, see SEDULIUS SCOTTUS, 'Item rithmici versiculi' (*MGH, Poetae,* 3), p. 215.

long, is actually short. Another elementary mistake of the same type occurs at the start of 8, 37: 'Inde ΓΝΟΦΟΣ', where the rules demand that the *e* of *Inde* be treated as long 'by position' because of the following two successive consonants in ΓΝΟΦΟΣ.

Besides errors of this type attributable to inattentiveness, John makes mistakes that must be ascribed to ignorance, as the same mistake occurs in more than one place. Thus, we find *plăcens* (3, 54) for *plăcens* and *plăcita* (4, 40) for *plăcita*. Similarly, *potitur* is scanned twice (2, 41 and 6, 32) with long *o* in the first syllable. *Molestus* was another word that was bothersome for John: he scans it twice (1, 77 and 6, 37) with long *o*, an understandable mistake, since *moles,* from which *molestus* is derived, shows long *o* in the root syllable. A curious error is *dēdicans* (3, 52 and 4, 35), possibly to be explained by a putative association with *dĕdi,* the perfect active of *do*. Other errors are noted in the *Index metricus*.

Most poets showed some form of prosodical inconsistency, but John's treatment of *h* is noteworthy: at some places it prevents elision, at other places it does not. In poem 5, within the space of some twenty-six lines, *h* prevents elision four times (lines 13, 18, 22, 43) but permits it twice (27, 39). It is this inconsistent treatment of *h* that is responsible for most instances of hiatus (see the *Index metricus*). Another inconsistency is the treatment of the syllable quantity before the enclitic *-que*. According to Latin rules, *-que* affects only the accent of the syllable it follows, not the quantity of the syllable. But at 4, 5 and 6, 14 we see lengthening before *-que*, whereas at 1, 55 this does not occur.

One type of apparent metrical error turns out not to be an error at all. This is the treatment of final *-s* after a short vowel. From the Golden Age onwards, *s* in this situation was treated metrically no differently from any other final consonant. But the earlier poets, including Lucretius, regularly treated words such as *amicus* as *amicu'*.[217] This same phenomenon occurs three times in John's genuine poems: *mentibu'* (3, 62), *aedibu'* (3, 70), and *Graculu'* (10, 1).[218] Whether John learned this device from reading Lucretius or from a handbook is hard to say.

While hiatus is more frequent than one would expect, the occurrence of elision is relatively infrequent. This fact seems to re-

---

[217] W. M. LINDSAY, *Early Latin Verse,* Oxford, 1922, p. 126–135.
[218] The first two examples were observed by TRAUBE (*MGH, Poetae,* 3), p. 553n.

flect a trend in Carolingian poetry: in late antiquity and afterwards elision becomes increasingly rare.[219]

Our overall impression of John's prosodic abilities is that of a man who came to metrical studies relatively late in life. John knew a great deal about the *minutiae* of metrics, but he lacked the natural familiarity with quantities possessed by those who begin the study of metrical poetry in early youth, or learn the correct quantity of vowels from childhood. The task of editing John's poems confirms my earlier assessment that he acquired most of his knowledge of metrics on the continent rather than in his native Ireland.[220]

D. Poetic techniques

While John's prosody is somewhat shaky, his command of the techniques of alliteration and assonance show a high degree of verbal artistry. John appears to have patterned himself on Vergil, whose hexameter lines are famous for their rich sound effects.

First, alliteration is very common in John's poems.[221] Although this can occur in virtually every part of the line, one is struck by the fact that it seems often to be used as a device to link the pre- and post-caesural portions of the hexameter line, as in 1, 43:

    Te Christum *c*olimus / *c*aeli terraeque potentem.

The same technique is used in the pentameter to join the two metrically equal hemistichs, as in 1, 12:

    Ymnizare *l*icet / *l*audibus eximiis.

Next, alliteration is used to link the first word of the hexametrical cadence (the dactyl-spondee combination at the end of each line) with a word that occurs before the cadence,[222] as in 2, 51:

---

[219] D. Norberg, *An Introduction to the Study of Medieval Latin Versification* – ed. J. M. Ziolkowski, trad. G. C. Roti, J. de La Chapelle Skubly, Washington, DC, 2004, p. 26. Frequency rates for elision for classical poets and a selection of late antique and Insular poets are given by A. Orchard, *The Poetic Art of Aldhelm*, Cambridge, 1994, p. 79–83.

[220] Herren, 'Commentary on Martianus', p. 274–275.

[221] See the discussion of this feature by Piemonte, 'Acotaciones 1', p. 31–33.

[222] This type is also frequent in Aldhelm, as is shown by Michael Lapidge, who established a typology for Aldhelm's alliterative practice: 'Aldhelm's Latin Poetry and Old English Verse', *Comparative Literature*, 31 (1979), 209–231, especially p. 221. An important difference, however, is the fact that John only sometimes links the first word in the

> *M*agdaline, quaeris dominum quod *m*aesta sepultum.

Sometimes double alliteration occurs between words in the cadence and words in the pre-cadence portion of the line, as in 1, 61:

> Atque *p*auor ualidus *t*itubantia *p*ectora *t*urbans.

John also employs three-word alliteration in virtually all places in a line. This alliterative pattern may be either consecutive or allow for separation between words. Occasionally, three-word alliteration occurs in consecutive lines, as in 20, 22–23:

> Forsan *u*irtutem *u*ilia *u*erba tenent.
> *S*aepe *s*olent *s*pinis redolentes crescere flores.

Assonance is also a principle feature of John's verses. Indeed, John was a veritable master of the art of harmonizing vowel sounds. The following line illustrates his technique (1, 5):

> Illis Iliacas flammas subitasque ruinas.

The opening *i*-sounds shift to *a*, then *u*, with a resolution in the last word, which blends all three vowels. Note, too, the effective combination with the liquid in the first three words of the line. Alliteration is effectively combined with assonance to produce the musical effects of 8, 80:

> Nu*ll*um ue*ll*e boni depe*ll*it *l*umine *l*ucis.

One could multiply examples of John's art of harmonizing sounds. Nearly every line shows the effects of careful craftsmanship. John's poetic production was small – probably no more than one major poem per year. He must have composed slowly and revised much. One is reminded of Donatus's famous description of Vergil's method of composing:

> cum Georgica scriberet, traditur cotidie meditatos mane plurimos uersus dictare solitus ac per totum diem retractando ad paucissimos redigere, non absurde carmen se ursae more parere dicens et lambendo demum effingere.[223]

---

line with the first word in the cadence, a practice which Lapidge believes to reflect the influence of Germanic alliteration.

[223] *Vita Donati* 22, in *P. Vergilii Maronis Appendix Vergiliana* – ed. C. Hardie, Oxford, 1907, p. 7.

E. Structure

One of the most remarkable features of John's poems is their structure. Few of his poetic compositions could be described as rambling or loosely organized. Perhaps the only 'long poem' that shows sign of careless organization is no. 4, addressed to Irmintrude. Here John seems to content himself with the enumeration of female virtues; the poem reads like a catalogue. By contrast, most of the other 'long poems' show close attention to the nexus of ideas contained in them. The 'typical' poem begins with an invitation to consider the meaning of a symbol. This can take the form of a concrete object such as the cross (no. 2), the origin of a word (no. 3), holy scripture (no. 5), the heavenly order (no. 8), or the significance of a number (no. 25). The same kind of proemium is found in App. 2 (see above, p. L), which invites the reader to contemplate the letters of the Greek alphabet. All such symbols lead the reader directly to the contemplation of the *mysteria Christi* – his Incarnation, birth, death, resurrection, and descent into hell – which provide the only proper matter of true Christian poetry (cfr 1, 1–16). These mysteries, in turn, find concrete expression in liturgy, in which all people can participate. Through the mediation of the liturgy we are led from divine history, which is eternal and immutable, to the vicissitudes of human history. Liturgy expresses the divine, but it is made operational by the human.

John's great poems invariably end in human history, made concrete in the person of the king and his actions. The prayers for Charles, with which many of the poems are concluded, are not simply formulaic orisons for royal well-being. Rather, they are intended to remind us of the real dangers which Charles and his kingdom faced: civil war and barbarian incursions. Thus, a fair number of the 'long poems' exhibit a 'top-down' structure. For the reader, the journey begins with the heavens and the divine mysteries and descends to earth along the axis of the liturgy, which joins the two realms. Because the reader begins his journey in heaven, he is privileged to view human history *sub specie aeternitatis*.

In the final analysis, it is the structure of John's poems that makes them unique in their time. No other Carolingian poet attempted anything like them.

F. Conclusion

John Scottus was a better poet, certainly a more interesting poet, than earlier critics thought. The ostentatious and not always happy use of Greek has led readers to concentrate on the flaws of these works – flaws which have obscured their virtues. But allowing for some lapses of prosody, John was an excellent versifier. He possessed a formidable ability to harmonize sounds, through assonance and alliteration, into lines of grave beauty. His lines, particularly the hexameters, avoid monotony in their metrical structure. Numerous lines show the capacity to carry a thought beyond the confines of a single hexameter. John's Latin vocabulary is large and supple. Above all, there is tight control over the progression of ideas and a clear structure that shows the relation of the parts. While some phrases, especially line-endings, show familiarity with a number of poets, John's verses reveal considerable freshness and originality. When one compares his verse to that of his contemporaries, one gains the impression that John was as daring and innovative in his writing of poetry as he was in all his other endeavours.

IV. Editorial Principles

Given that the poems in Ω are preserved only by R and L^{I-II}, it is obvious that one must follow R for readings of Latin words. However, I have normalized non-standard spellings in R and Latin spellings of Greek words, e.g. *Cypris* (4, 14) rather than *Cipris*).

I have taken an entirely different approach to the spellings of Greek words written in Greek letters. I follow L as the 'best manuscript'. L often gives words in Greek letters which R transliterates, e.g. *Eklypsis* (1, 33), 1, 39 (*oplistes*), 2, 23 (*Erytreas*), 2, 49 (*Chalceus*), 3, 26 (*Isidam*), and more. In one case I follow R, where R's reading could not have been derived from an exemplar in which a word was written in Greek characters. The instance is 1, 32, where I print *Stygis* (with Traube) in place of R's *fagis* and L^P's ΣΤΥΚΙΣ.

There are also instances of apparent conflation of Greek and Latin words. ΕΝΚΛΥΤΟΣ (cfr κλυτός) occurs for *inclitus* (2, 67), also ΗΝΚΛΥΤΟΣ at 17, 10.[224] As these forms occur in lines written entirely in Greek, I have not emended them to the Latin forms. More difficult cases are ΣΟΒΡΟΝ for σώφρων (2, 68), which shows confusion with Latin *sobrius*, and ΙΝΔΥΣΙΑΣ for ἐνδύσιας (4, 10),[225] which retains the initial *i* of Latin *indutias*, which has the identical meaning. In the first case, I retain ΣΟΒΡΟΝ, which is attested by the *consensus codicum*; in the second, I retain ΙΝΔΥΣΙΑΣ (*L¹*) against *indusias* (*R*), or, potentially, Latin *indutias*, because it is apparent that John intended a Greek word. It is possible, then, that we are dealing not with confusions caused by ignorance, but with a playful attempt to interweave Greek and Latin words that have common etyma.

Establishing Eriugena's spelling of Greek words is a distinct challenge. In following *L* one cannot be sure in every instance if one is following John's or Martin's orthographical practice. However, a few peculiarities stand out: ΚΛΕΟΡ (for κλέος) 14, 1, 15, 1, ΦΟΜΕΝΟΡ (for *φαόμενος ⟨ φάω, 'shine'). The final *rho* in place of *sigma* indicates that John had acquired these words from Latin transliterations in which final *s* and *r* are frequently confused. The spelling ΚΙΡΡΙΟΣ or ΚΥΡΡΙΟΣ with two *rho*'s for κύριος is authorial. It occurs without variant in both *R* and *L*: 2, 68; 8 (inscription); 8, 29; 11 (inscription); 17 (inscription): 17, 7, and in the transliteration *kyrrie* (App. 8, 4). There is also ΦΙΣΙΣ for φύσις. The word appears three times in *carmen* 8. At 8, 52 *R* and *L¹* agree on ΦΙΣΙΣ. At 8, 74 the readings are divided, with only *R* giving ΦΥΣΙΣ; in the next line *R* gives ΦΙΣΙΣ (omitted in *L¹* since it is unnecessary to repeat the gloss twice). Fr. 1, 3 has ΦΙΣΕΟΣ. The *consensus codicum* thus favours ΦΙΣΙΣ as the authorial spelling.

Another matter that requires comment is the manuscript base of poems 20 and 21, which introduce John's translation of the Pseudo-Dioynisian corpus. For the manuscripts used here see p. XXXIII–XXXIV. The choice of manuscripts and the editions based on them are essentially the work of Traube with only trifling interventions. A future editor of these verses may wish to explore the list of manuscripts containing these poems, established by the

---

[224] Cfr *Lateinisches etymologisches Wörterbuch* – ed. A. Walde, J. B. Hofmann, Heidelberg, 1965⁴, I, 690–691, s.v. *inclutus*.

[225] For ἔνδυσις in the extended sense of 'clothing, dress', see the references in *A Greek-English Lexicon of the New Testament and Other Early Christian Literature* – ed. W. F. Arndt, F. W. Gingrich, Chicago – London, 1958², p. 263.

praiseworthy efforts of Olivier Szerwiniack,[226] and construct a new *recensio codicum*. This may very well prove useful. For the present, Traube's work on these poems looks to be solid enough, as it fairly represents John's Scottus' practices and abilities as a poet.

There are a few departures from the Dublin edition that should be noted. I have striven to keep enumeration in the present work consistent with the earlier one. I believed that the prose pieces in Greek addressed to Irmintrude and Charles should be included for the sake of having a full record of John's extant compositions in Greek. Accordingly, I labelled them 15* with the intent of marking their difference from the poems and simultaneously preserving the enumeration. I also added the 'Graeca ad uersus' given in L^I to the end of the Appendix, as many of the words in the list are typically Eriugenian, and in the hope that the list might serve to identify lost poems. As noted in the apparatus criticus to the relevant pieces, I transposed the Greek verses 28-29 in poem 8 to the end of the work and adjusted the numbering. In poem 12a I inserted line 2 from a list of words in L^I. I believe that the poem is now complete except for the first part of line 5. I retreat from one emendation made in the Dublin edition. I accept the reading of the manuscript (*R*) at 9.32, keeping *fragilem* against the emendation ΦΡΑΚΤΟΝ. In App. 5, line 2, I retain *So*'s reading *frigora lusqua domus* ('the dusky chill of the house'). New changes include 3, 11, emending *R*'s *Neptuni Nerea* to *Neptunum et Nerea*; at 5, 43, I emend *R*'s *canoros* to *canoro*.

---

[226] SZERWINIACK, 'Liste provisoire'.

ADDENDUM

John Scottus Eriugena's last datable poem composed in Latin is *Aulae sidereae* (no. 25), written in 870. It cites Charles the Bald's celebration of Christmas at Aachen in 869 and his plans to build a royal church at Compiègne.[1] However, it is not, as previously claimed, the last evidence of his poetic activity.[2]

It can be argued that John was careful in his application of titles to his king. Imperial titles are used only in no. 14 (ΔΕΣΠΟΤΑ), and App. 8 (*autocrator*), both written in Greek. *Princeps* occurs in App. 11, 9 (a. 870). Although that poem is very likely from Eriugena or his circle, *princeps* meaning 'emperor' would probably not have retained its imperial connotation in ninth-century western Europe. Royal titles include ΑΝΑΞ (2, 67; 3, 26; 8, inscription; 17, 2; note the equivalence ΑΝΑΞ and *rex* at Fr. 1, 21). ΑΡΧΟΣ ('ruler') is found at 2, 67 (a conjecture supported by 17, 10). ΒΑΣΙΛΕΥΣ, the usual Greek equivalent of *rex* (cfr App. 17, Fr. 1, 13) occurs at 5, 49; 7, inscription; 11, 1; 14, 1; 17, 1. ΜΟΝΑΡΧΟΣ occurs once at 17, 3. It, of course, means 'monarch' or 'one who rules alone'; however, it has no certain imperial connotation. Other terms used include ΚΥΡΙΟΣ, spelled invariably with two rho's (2, 68; 8, inscription; 8, 86; 11, inscription; 17, inscription; 17, 7; 22, 1; App. 8, 4) and ΚΟΡΥΦΗΝ (17, 8). However, neither of these terms is precise enough to be probative on the issue of a royal versus imperial designation. John's usual Latin title for Charles is *rex* (1, 47; 2, 71; 4, 27; 4, 37; 6, 38; 14, 1 [in the Latin translation]; 22, 7; 25, 8; 25, 98). *Vertex* (22. 7) matches the Greek ΚΟΡΥΦΗΝ (17, 8). *Imperator* does not occur, and *Caesar*, its equivalent, is found only in App. 1, which, despite its placement at the end of the *De praedestinatione*, is almost certainly spurious. The phrase *Caesareos ... uultus* occurs at 22, 2, but the line seems to refer to Charles's imperial ancestors: 'For whom starry crowns gird imperial faces'.[3]

Whereas ΔΕΣΠΟΤΑ has only a few attestations to the meaning 'emperor', *autocrator* carries that sense unambiguously. It occurs

---

[1] Herren, 'Eriugena's Aulae sidereae', p. 600-608.
[2] Herren, 'Eriugena's Aulae sidereae', p. 601.
[3] Revising the translation of the Dublin edition, p. 113.

only in App. 8 (*Semeron autocrator*), a poem that Traube regarded as genuine (no. VI), and which I consigned to the appendix only because of its missing attribution (see discussion, p. LII-LIII). It is not included in L^{II}, the collection of Greek poems prepared by Martin Hiberniensis. The latest datable poem in this collection is no. 17, written in 869 to celebrate Charles's coronation at Metz in 869, when Charles added the crown of Lotharingia to his own.[4] This leaves open the possibility that App. 8 was written later than 869, or even later than 875, the year assigned to Martin's death. The poem was doubtless written to celebrate a liturgical occasion when the king was present. Although at first glance it appears to refer to the feast of St Denis, the emphasis of the poem is on the crucifixion of Christ and Dionysius's prescience of that event. It is therefore likely that it marks Good Friday of 876 when Charles was in attendance at St Denis in advance of the Easter celebration.[5] At that time, Charles could be legitimately addressed as *autocrator*, as he had been crowned emperor by Pope John VIII at Pavia on 29 December 875. *Carm.* App. 8, assuming that it is genuine, shows that John continued his activity as a poet and his close association with the king after the year 870.

Acknowledgements

I should like to record my own thanks to Édouard Jeauneau, who graciously invited me to edit Eriugena's poems for the *Corpus Christianorum*, although it had been his lifelong intention to edit them himself. During his years in Toronto, Édouard was an inspiration to me not only in my work on Eriugena, but as a scholar *tout court*. It is a matter of particular regret that he did not live to see the publication of this volume. A good friend, he graced our family table many a time with his wit and charm. I should also like to thank Andrew Dunning for his valued assistance in formatting this work and making it conform to the demands of the *CC CM* stylesheet, as well as providing some of the references in the apparatus biblicus and apparatus fontium. I should also like to acknowledge the late Anders Ahlqvist, who, as chair of the publications committee of the Dublin Institute for Advanced Studies, facilitated permission from the Institute to re-edit the *Iohannis*

---

[4] Dutton and Jeauneau, 'The Verses', p. 114 with n. 31.
[5] Dutton, 'Eriugena, the royal poet', p. 67.

Scotti Eriugenae Carmina for publication in the *CC CM* series. My gratitude also to Bart Janssens of Brepols Publishers for his keen editorial eye, efficiency, and courtesy during the process of publication. Last but not least, I pour libations dis manibus Donnchadh Ó Corráin, whose monumental *Clavis Litterarum Hibernensium* significantly eased the task of identifying the relevant publications that appeared between 1993, the date of the Dublin edition, and the present.

PLATE I

297

                                                                          Karolus
        recce credens rex pius   gloriosus temerans xpm foues Karolus
ΟΡΘΩΔΟΞΟΣ ΑΝΑΞ ΕΥΣΗΒΗΣ· ΕΝΚΑΥΤΟΣ ΣΩΦΡΟΝ· ΧΡΙΣΤΟΦΟΡΟΣ ΚΙΡΡΙΟC
            regis karoli   ημῶν tu   saue
versus ΒΑΣΙΛΕΩΣ ΚΑΡΟΛΟΙ ΗΜΩΝ CY· ΧΡΕ ΒΟCΟΙ·
    ut possidere   choros   possit   caelestes
ως κλειρεισθε ΧΟΡΟΙC ΔΙΝΑΤΟC ΟΥΡΑΝΙΟΥC;

        ΤΟΥ· CΤΟΙΧΟΙ· ΙΩΑΝΝΟΥ· ΤΩ ΒΑCΙΛΕΙ ΚΑΡΟΛΟ;
            versus   domino suo regi
        ΟΙ CΤΙΧΟΙ· ΤΟΙ ΙΩΑΝΝΟΥ· ΤΩ ΚΙΡΡΙΩ· ΚΑΙ ΤΟΥΤΟ ΑΝΑΚ ΤΟ ΚΑΡΟΛΩ.
        luna   et mercurius et lucifer sol   mars iouis
versus ΦΟΕΒΗ· ΚΑΙ ΙCΤΙΛΒΟΝ· ΚΑΙ ΦΟCΗΛΙΟC· ΑΡΗC; ΦΟΕΤΟΝ·
    et saturni   summi   circu plagas   pruina
ΚΑΙ ΦΑΙΝΟΝΟC ΑΚΡΟΙ ΠΕΡΙ ΚΛΙΜΑΤΑ ΠΑΧΗΝ
    deinde   mundi medium oceanus immensurabile salum
Ε ΞΗC ΤΟΥ ΚΟCΜΟΥ ΚΕΝΤΡΟΝ ΤΕΘΙC· ΑCΧΕΤΟC ΑΛΑC;

      dne   uitam   aeterna det tibi semp
    ΚΥΡΡΙΕ ΚΑΡΟΛΕ ΖΩΗΝ· ΑΟΙΝΙΟΝ ΔΩCΕΙ CΟΙ ΠΑΝΤΟΤΕ ΧΡC·
            dne uiuas multos   annos   hic essas
versus ΚΥΡΡΙΕ· ΖΗC ΠΟΛΛΟΥC ΕΝΙ ΑΥΤΟΥC· ΩΔΕ CΕΒΑCΤΕΙC·
    ens finis   principiū omniū   quies qē q substistunt
ΩΝ ΤΕΛΟC· ΩΝ ΑΡΧΗ ΠΑΝΤΟΝ Ω ΝΟΝΤΑ ΤΛΕΙCΙΝ
    ens oramus te bonus   pulchritudo·formam q   exemplar
ΩΝ ΑΓΑΘΟC ΚΑΙ ΚΑΛΟC ΚΑΛΛΟC ΜΩΡΦΩ ΤΕ ΧΑΡΑΚΤΗΡ;

        CΤΙΧΟΙ ΙΩΑΝΝΙC GLORIOSO REGI KAROLO;

        ΤΟΙ ΙΩΑΝΝΟΙ ΤΩ ΚΙΡΡΙΩ ΚΑΡΩΛΩ;
            uiuas nunc uiuas   plures an. in annos
versus ΖΕC ΝΥΝ· ΖΗC ΒΑCΙΛΗC ΠΑΙC· ΤΟΥ CΕΙC ΤΟΙC ΕΝΙ ΑΥΤΟΥC·
    af futurus   xpo congregare   in multa seta
Ο ΜΕΛΛΟΜΕΝΟC ΧΩ CΥΝ· ΖΗΝ ΕΙC· ΠΟΛΛΑC ΑΙΩΝΑC·
                  saluat   cui af regnum   dedisti
ΧΡΕ CΟCΟΝ ΚΑΡΟΛΟΝ ΤΟ ΤΗΝ ΒΑCΙΛΕΙΑΝ ΕΔΟΚΑC;

            malus   bonus   magnusq   paruus q
versus Ν am ΚΑΚΟC ΑΤΑ· ΑΓΑΤΟC prorsus ΜΕΓΑΛΟC ΤΕ· ΜΙΚΡΟC ΤΕ·
    prælucens   splendens   præmina   summo
ΛΑΜΠΡΟΤΑΤΟC doctor CΤΙΛΒΩΝ ΚΗΡΥΓΜΑΤΟC ΑΚΡΟΥ·
        uerbi   tota di uiuentis in ore   tenendo
ΡΗΜΑΤΟC· ΟΠΑΛ ΘΥ ΖΩΝΤΟC ΤΟΥ· CΤΟΜΑΤΟC· ΕΧΩΝ·
    ima tenera musitas ti   confirmit conclusio
ΚΡΥCΜΑΤΑ non nosens πε· CΥΜΠΛΕΡΑCΜΑ requirens.

Laon, Bibliothèque municipale, ms. 444, f. 297r
(siglum L^{II}, see p. XXIX of the introduction)

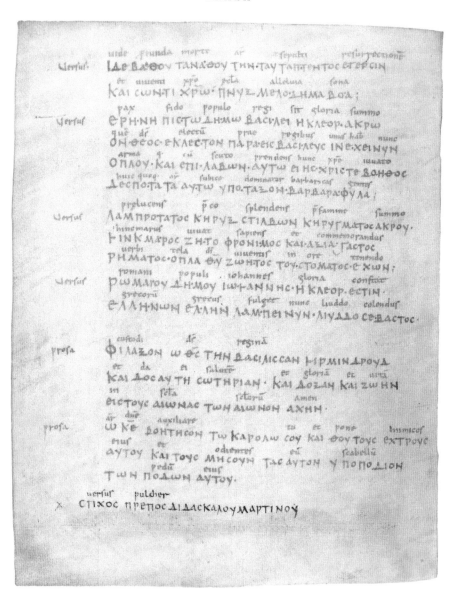

LAON, Bibliothèque municipale, ms. 444, f. 297v
(siglum L^{II}, see p. XXIX of the introduction)

PLATE III

⳨ ειςκρε ΑΝΑΓΙΝΟϹΤΗϹ ΕΝΤΕΥΘΕΝΔ· ΥΠΑΓΕ ΦΕΥΓΕ·
 improbe   lector   hinc   uade   fuge

ΜΗΔ ΕΛΕΛΥΘΑ ΛΟΓΩ ϹΟΥ ΚΑΙ ΤΑΧΑ ΜΗΔΕ ΠΟΡΕΥΩ·
 neq. ueni uerbo tuo et forsan neq. uada

ΑΡΝΕΤΕ ϹΕ ΗΛΙΚΙΑ ΚΡΟΤΑΦΩΝ ΑΠΑΛΩΝΤΕ ΝΕΩΝΤΕ·
 negat te aetas pueror.   pudium nouorūq.

ΙΔΕ ΛΑΛΕΙΝ ΤΙΘΟΜΑΙ ΝΥΝ ΩϹ ΠΑΡΑΚΑΛΕΤΕ ΠΕΡΑΝ·
 ecce loquendi pono nunc sic iubens fine

ΝΥΝ ΛΗΓΕ ΝΕΑΝΙϹΚΕ ΛΕΓΕΙΝ ΔΟϹ ΔΕϹΜΑΤΑ ΧΙΛϹΙΝ·
 nunc desine o iuuenis dicere da uincula labiis·

§ ΤΩ ΚΙΡΡΙΩ ΚΑΡΟΛΩ ΙΩΑΝΝΗϹ ΧΑΙΡΕΙΝ ΘΑΥΜΑϹΤΩ ΒΑϹΙΛΕΙ
ΚΑΡΟΛΩ ΖΩΗ ΤΕΦΛΟϹ· ΤΕΟΝΤΟϹ ΔΟΞΟϹ ΑΝΑΞ ΦΡΑΤΤΩΝ· ΤΩ ΔΟΞΑ
ΤΙΜΕ ΤΕ ΘΕϹΠΕϹΙΟϹ ΚΑΙ ΑΓΑΘΟϹ ΠΙϹΤΟϹ Κ᾽ ΑΚΡΟϹ ΤΕ ΜΟΝΑΡΧΟϹ
ΕΛΠΙϹΤΗϹ ΠΑΤΡΙΔΟϹ ΤΗϹ ΑΞΙΟϹ ΑΘΑΝΑϹΙΑϹ ΩΝ ΔΕ ΦΟΡΩΝ ϹΤΕΦΑΝΩΝ
ΧΡΙϹΙΟΝΤΑ ΔΕϹ ΤΕΜΜΑΤΑ ΠΑΤΡΩΝ ΕΝ ΧΕΥΡΟϹ ϹΚΕΠΤΡΟΝ
ΡΑΒΔΟϹ ΓΑΡ ΤΗϹ ΒΑϹΙΛΙΑϹ· ΧΡΕ ϹΩϹΟΝ ΔΟΥΛΟΝ ϹΟΝ ΤΩΝ· ΜΟΙ
ΚΥΡΡΙΟΝ ΕΙΠΩ ΤΟΝ ΚΑΡΟΛΟΝ ΜΗ ΓΑΛΗΝ ΕΜΟΝ ΠΟΛΛΟΝ
ΤΕ ΚΟΡΥΦΗΝ ΟϹϹΟΦΟϹ ΟϹ ΔΥΝΑ ΤΟϹ ΠΑΝΥ ϹΟΦΡΩΝ ΤΕ ΚΡΑΤΟϹ
ΤΕ ΕΙΠΡΕΠΗϹ ΕΥ ΜΟΡΦΟϹ ΦΑΥΝΩΝ Ω ϹΗΝ ΚΑΥΤΟϹ ΑΡΧΟϹ Ω ΘΙΟΝ
ΟΥΡΑΝΙΟΝ ϹΤΙΛΒΩΝ ΔΙΑΔΕΜΑΤΟϹ ΑϹΤΡΟΝ· ΗΛΙΟϹ ΟϹ ΛΑΜΠΡΟϹ
ΔΟϹ ΦΟϹ ΦΩΡΟϹ ΟϹϹΑ ΔΝΗ ΚΕ ΔΩϹΕΙΩ ΚΑΡΩΛΩ ΖΩΗ ΝΕϹ
ΤΟΙϹ ΠΑΝΤΑϹ ΑΙΩΝΑϹ ΕΥΧΕΤΕ ΤΑΙ ΤΑΔΑ ΟΙ ΝΥΝ ΕΥΧΕ ϹΥΦΡΑΓΓΑ ΠΑϹϹΑ

§ ΖΥΜΗ i. *fermentū. ūt et* ΖΥΜΩ i. *fermēto.* ΕΚΠΟΕΛΛΩ ΖΥΜΗ *coponit*
  † sincerus purus.
 ΑΖΥΜΟϹ i. *infermentatus.* Δ *ħ negatiue ponit*

LAON, Bibliothèque municipale, ms. 444, f. 298r
(siglum L^{II}, see p. XXIX of the introduction)

PLATE IV

ⵑ ⲤⲨⲘⲠⲞⲤⲒⲞⲚ ⳽ conuiuiu̅ · exq̅ uɢ ⲤⲨⲘⲠⲞⲤⲒⲀⲔⲞⲤ ⳽ conuiua·
⳽ conuiuncula·

ⵑ ⲠⲢⲞⲂⲖⲎⲘⲀ ⳽ questio ⳽ ppositio · un̅ et ⲠⲢⲞⲂⲖⲎⲘⲀⲦⲒⲞⲚ

ⵑ Ut dyonisius ariopagita dc̅ dr̅ ⲨⲠⲈⲢⲐⲈⲞⲤ ē ⳽ sup dr̅·
et ⲨⲠⲈⲢⲀⲄⲀⲐⲞⲤ ⳽ sup bonus · et ⲨⲠⲈⲢⲀⲖⲎⲐⲎⲤ ⳽ sup uerus·

ⵑ I̅n sc̅do libro paralipomenon · fec̅ aut̅ hy̅rā lebetas quoq̅ ·et
creagras · ꝫ fialas · In sc̅do libro regu̅ · fecit ꝫ hy̅rā lebetas · et
scutras · ꝫ amulas · It̅e m eode̅ · duo ordines sculptaru̅ historiaru̅
erant fusiles · Creagrae tridentes ut fuscinulae ad
carnes decaldariis p̅ferendas · ⲔⲢⲈⲀ # grece · caro latine
et ⲀⲄⲢⲀ · captio · atq̅ ex his co̅ponitur ⲔⲢⲈⲀⲄⲢⲀ·

ⵑ ⲀⲚⲐⲢⲞⲠⲞⲘⲞⲢⲪⲒⲦⲀⲒ · ⳽ heretici qui humana̅ forma̅
in d̅o fingu̅nt·

ⵑ domine iube benedicere
ⲔⲨⲢⲒⲈ ⲒⲦⲞⲚ ⲈⲨⲖⲞⲄⲒⲤⲈ·
filius d̅i nos benedicat
ⲨⲒⲞⲤ ⲐⲨ ⲒⲘⲀⲤ ⲈⲨⲖⲞⲄⲒⲤⲞⲚ· ⲀⲘⲎⲚ·
tu aut d̅n̅e miserere n̅r̅i
ⲤⲨ ⲆⲈ ⲔⲨⲢⲒⲈ ⲈⲖⲈⲒⲤⲞⲚ ⲒⲘⲀⲤ·
d̅o statuas
ⲐⲈⲞ· ⲔⲀⲢⲒⲤ·

in nomine p̅r̅s et filii et s̅p̅s̅ s̅c̅i in no
ⲈⲚ ⲞⲚⲞⲘⲀⲦⲒ ⲦⲞⲨ ⲠⲀⲦⲢⲞⲤ· Ⲕꝫ ⲦⲞⲨ ⲨⲒⲞⲨ· ⲔⲀⲒ ⲦⲞⲨ ⲠⲚⲈⲨⲘⲀⲦⲞⲤ ⲀⲄⲒⲞⲨ· ⲈⲚ ⲞⲚⲞ
mine d̅n̅i
ⲘⲀⲦⲒ ⲦⲞⲨ ⲔⲨⲢⲢⲒⲞⲨ
p
ⲠⲞⲤⲦⲀⲌⲈ ⲔⲨⲢⲢⲒⲈ ⲈⲨⲖⲞⲄⲈⲒⲚ· ⲈⲨⲖⲞⲄⲈⲦⲞⲤ ⲞⲒ Ⲟ ⲐⲤ·
ⲤⲨ ⲆⲈ Ⲕ̅Ⲥ̅ ⲈⲖⲈⲎⲤⲞⲚ ⲎⲘⲰⲚ·

Laon, Bibliothèque municipale, ms. 444, f. 298v
(see p. XXXI of the introduction)

PLATE V

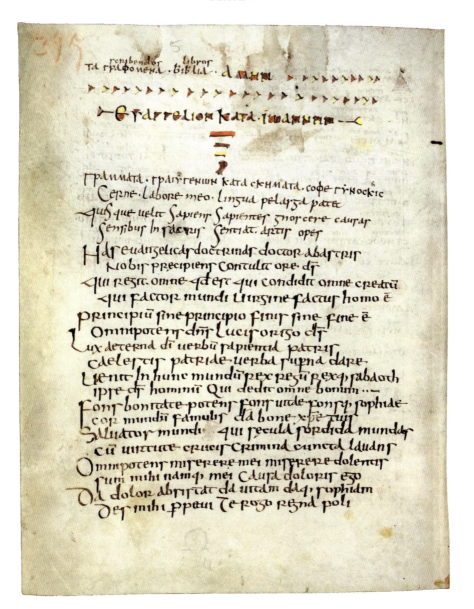

Sankt Gallen, Cod. Sang. 48, p. 395
(siglum *S*, see p. XXXV of the introduction)

BIBLIOGRAPHY

Primary sources

A. Editions of the Poems of John Scottus Eriugena

J. Ussher, *Veterum epistolarum Hibernicarum sylloge,* Dublin, 1632.

A. Mai, *Classici auctores e codicibus Vaticanis editi.* 5 vols., Rome, 1833–1838, V (1838), 426–448.

H. J. Floss, *Johannis Scoti opera quae supersunt omnia* (*PL,* 122), Paris, 1853, col. 1221–1234, 1237–1240.

E. Miller, 'Glossaire grec-latin de la bibliothèque de Laon', *Notices et extraits des manuscrits de la Bibliothèque nationale et autres bibliothèques* 29, 2 (1880), 194–200.

L. Traube, *Poetae latini aevi Carolini* (*MGH, Poetae,* 3, 2), Berlin, 1896, 518–556.

M. Foussard, '*Aulae sidereae:* Vers de Jean Scot au Roi Charles', *Cahiers archéologiques,* 21 (1971), 79–88.

M. W. Herren, *Iohannis Scotti Eriugenae Carmina* (*Scriptores latini Hiberniae,* 12), Dublin, 1993.

F. Colnago, *Giovanni Scoto Eriugena Carmi. Un Capolavoro nell'epoca carolingia* (*Biblioteca di cultura medievale*), Milan, 2014.

B. Editions of works cited

Alc. Avit., *Carm.* = Alcimus Ecdicius Avitus, *Carmina,* in *Alcimi Ecdicii Auiti Viennensis episcopi Opera quae supersunt* – ed. R. Peiper (*MGH, Auct. ant.,* 6, 2), Berlin, 1883, p. 203–294.

Alcvin., *Carm.* = Alcuinus, *Carmina,* in *Poetae latini aeui Carolini* – ed. E. Dümmler (*MGH, Poetae,* 1), Berlin, 1881, p. 186–351.

Aldh., *Aenig.* = Aldhelm, *Aenigmata,* in *Aldhelmi opera omnia* – ed. R. Ehwald (*MGH, Auct. ant.,* 15), Berlin, 1919, p. 59–149.

Aldh., *Carm. eccles.* = Aldhelm, *Carmina ecclesiastica,* in *Aldhelmi opera omnia* – ed. R. Ehwald (*MGH, Auct. ant.,* 15), Berlin, 1919, p. 11–32.

ALDH., *Laud. uirg.* = ALDHELM, *De laude uirginitatis,* in *Aldhelmi opera omnia* – ed. R. Ehwald (*MGH, Auct. ant.*, 15), Berlin, 1919, p. 228–323.

AMARC., *Serm.* = SEXTUS AMARCIUS, *Sermones* – ed. K. Manitius (*MGH, Quellen zur Geistesgeschichte des Mittelalters,* 6), Weimar, 1969.

ANON. BOBB. = ANONYMUS BOBIENSIS, in *Die lateinischen Dichter des deutschen Mittelalters* – ed. K. Strecker (*MGH, Poetae,* 5), Leipzig, 1937, p. 410–412.

ANTH. LAT. = *Anthologia latina siue poesis latinae supplementum, pars prior: Carmina in codicibus scripta* – ed. A. Riese (*Biblioteca Teubneriana*) Leipzig, 1869.

ANTIPH. BANG. = *The Antiphonary of Bangor,* 2 vols. – ed. F. E. Warren (*Henry Bradshaw Society,* 4, 10), London, 1893–1895.

ARATOR, *Act.* = *Aratoris subdiaconi Historia apostolica* – ed. A. P. Orbán (*CC SL,* 130), Turnhout, 2006.

AVG., *Ciu.* = *Sancti Aurelii Augustini episcopi De ciuitate Dei* – ed. B. Dombart, A. Kalb (*Bibliotheca Teubneriana*), Stuttgart, 1981^5.

AVSON. = *Decimi Magni Ausonii opera* – ed. R. P. H. Green (*Oxford Classical Texts*), Oxford, 1999.

BEDA, *Cuth.* = BEDA VENERABILIS, *Vita Cuthberti metrica,* in *Bedas metrische Vita sancti Cuthberti* – ed. W. Jaager, Leipzig, 1935.

BEDA, *Iud.* = BEDA VENERABILIS, *De die iudicii,* in *Bedae Venerabilis Liber hymnorum, rhythmi, uariae preces* – ed. J. Fraipont (*CC SL,* 122), Turnhout, 1955, p. 439–444.

PS. BEDA, *Quat. temp.* = BEDA VENERABILIS, *De celebritate quatuor temporum* (*PL,* 94), Paris, 1850, col. 606–615.

CAND. FVLD., *Vita Aegil. II* = CANDIDUS FULDENSIS, *Vita Aegil abbatis Fuldensis a Candido ad Modestum* – ed. G. Becht-Jördens, Marburg, 1994, p. 31–77.

CHALC., *Transl.* = CALCIDIUS, *On Plato's Timaeus* – ed. and transl. J. Magee (Dumbarton Oaks Medieval Library, 41), Cambridge, MA – London, 2016.

CORIPP., *Ioh.* = *Flavii Cresconii Corippi Iohannidos libri VIII* – ed. J. Diggle, F. R. D. Goodyear, Cambridge, 1970.

CORIPP., *Iust.* = FL. CRESCONIUS CORIPPUS AFER, *In laudem Iustini Augusti minoris* – ed. A. Cameron, London, 1976.

Ecbas. capt. = *Ecbasis cuiusdam captivi per tropologiam,* ed. K. Strecker (*MGH, SS rer. Germ.*, 24), Hanover, 1935.

Ermold. Nigel., *Ludow.* = Ermoldus Nigellus, *Carmen elegiacum in honorem Ludowici*, in *Poetae latini aeui Carolini* – ed. E. Dümmler (*MGH, Poetae*, 2), Berlin, 1884, p. 4–79.

Flor. Lvgd., *Carm.* = Florus Lugdunensis, *Carmina*, in *Poetae latini aeui Carolini* – ed. E. Dümmler (*MGH, Poetae*, 2), Berlin, 1884, p. 509–556.

Greg. M., *In Ezech.* = *Sancti Gregorii Magni Homiliae in Hiezechihelem Prophetam* – ed. M. Adriaen (*CC SL*, 142), Turnhout, 1971.

Heric., *Vita Germ. metr.* = Hericus Autissiodorensis, *Vita metrica s. Germani, episcopi Autissiodorensis*, in *Poetae latini aeui Carolini* – ed. L. Traube (*MGH, Poetae*, 3), Berlin, 1896, p. 428–517.

Hier., *Adu. Rufin.* = Hieronymus Stridonensis, *Contra Rufinum* – ed. P. Lardet (*CC SL*, 79), Turnhout, 1982.

Hildvin., *Dion. metr.* = Hilduinus, *Passio metrica s. Dionysii*, in *Hilduin of Saint-Denis: The Passio s. Dionysii in Prose and Verse* – ed. M. Lapidge (*Mittellateinische Studien und Texte*, 51), Leiden, 2017, p. 305–446.

Hildvin., *Dion. prosa* = Hilduinus, *Passio s. Dionysii*, in *Hilduin of Saint-Denis: The Passio s. Dionysii in Prose and Verse* – ed. M. Lapidge (*Mittellateinische Studien und Texte*, 51), Leiden, 2017, p. 229–303.

Hor., *Sat.* = Q. Horatius Flaccus, *Saturae*, in *Q. Horatii Flacci opera* – ed. D. R. Shackleton Bailey (*Bibliotheca Teubneriana*), Leipzig, 2001[4], p. 165–250.

Hraban., *Carm.* = Hrabanus Maurus, *Carmina*, in *Poetae latini aeui Carolini* – ed. E. Dümmler (*MGH, Poetae*, 2), Berlin, 1884, p. 159–244.

Hymn. Nynie = *Hymnus Nynie*, in *Poetae latini aeui Carolini* – ed. K. Strecker (*MGH, Poetae*, 4.3), Berlin, 1923, p. 943-962.

Ioh. Scot., *Gloss. Div. Hist.* = *Glossae divinae historiae. The Biblical Glosses of John Scottus Eriugena* – ed. J. J. Contreni – P. Ó Néill, Florence, 1997.

Ioh. Scot., *Gloss. Mart. Cap.* = *Iohannis Scotti Annotationes in Marcianum* – ed. C. E. Lutz, Cambridge, MA, 1939.

Ioh. Scot., *Homil. Ioh.* = Iohannes Scotus Eriugena, *Homilia super 'In principio erat uerbum'*, in *Iohannis Scotti seu Eriugenae Homilia et commentarius in euangelium Iohannis* – ed. É. A. Jeauneau (*CC CM*, 166), Turnhout, 2008, p. 3–43.

Ioh. Scot., *Ier. Dion.* = *Iohannis Scoti Eriugenae Expositiones in hierarchiam coelestem* – ed. J. Barbet (*CC CM*, 31), Turnhout, 1975.

Ioh. Scot., *Periphys.* = *Iohannis Scotti Eriugenae Periphyseon* – ed. É. A. Jeauneau (*CC CM*, 161–165), Turnhout, 1996–2003.

Ioh. Scot., *Praedest.* = *Iohannis Scotti Eriugena de praedestinatione* in *Giovanni Scoto Eriugena De praedestinatione liber. Dialettica e teologia all' apogeo della renascenza carolingia* – ed. and transl. E. S. N. Mainoldi, Florence, 2003.

Ioh. Scot., *Versio Dion. Ar.* = Iohannes Scotus Eriugena, *Versio operum s. Dionysii Areopagitae*, in *Hugonis de Sancto Victore Super Ierarchiam Dionisii* – ed. D. Poirel (*CC CM*, 178), Turnhout, 2015, p. 361–396.

Ioh. Scot., *Versio Max.* = *Maximi confessoris Ambigua ad Iohannem iuxta Iohannis Scoti Eriugenae latinam interpretationem* – ed. É. A. Jeauneau (*CC SG*, 18), Turnhout, 1988.

Isid., *Expos. in gen.* / *Expos. in exod.* = Isidorus Hispalensis, *Mysticorum expositiones sacramentorum*, in *Sancti Isidori Hispalensis episcopi opera omnia* – ed. J.-P. Migne (*PL*, 83), Paris, 1850, col. 207–424.

Ivvenc. = *Gai Vetti Aquilini Iuuenci Euangeliorum libri quattuor* – ed. J. Huemer (*CSEL*, 24), Vienna, 1891.

Lvcr. = T. Lucretius Carus, *De rerum natura* – ed. M. Deufert (*Bibliotheca Teubneriana*), Berlin, 2018.

Macr., *Somn.* = Macrobius Ambrosius Theodosius, *Commentarii in Ciceronis somnium Scipionis* – ed. J. Willis (*Bibliotheca Teubneriana*), 1970².

Mart. = *M. Valerii Martialis Epigrammata* – ed. D. R. Shackleton Bailey (*Bibliotheca Teubneriana*), Stuttgart, 1990.

Mart. Cap. = Martianus Minneius Felix Capella Carthaginiensis, *De nuptiis Philologiae et Mercurii* – ed. J. Willis (*Bibliotheca Teubneriana*), Leipzig, 1983.

Ov., *Am.* = *P. Ovidii Nasonis Amores* – ed. E. J. Kenney (*Oxford Classical Texts*), Oxford, 1961.

Ov., *Ex Pont.* = *P. Ovidii Nasonis Ex Ponto Libri Quattuor* – ed. S. G. Owen (*Oxford Classical Texts*), Oxford, 1915.

Ov., *Fast.* = Ovidius, *Fasti* – ed. J. G. Frazer, rev. G. P. Goold, Cambridge, MA, 2014.

Ov., *Her.* = *P. Ouidii Nasonis Epistulae heroidum* – ed. H. Dörrie, Berlin, 1971.

Ov., *Met.* = *P. Ouidi Nasonis Metamorphoses* – ed. R. J. Tarrant (*Oxford Classical Texts*), Oxford, 2004.

Ov., *Trist.* = *P. Ouidi Nasonis Tristia* – ed. J. B. Hall (*Bibliotheca Teubneriana*), Stuttgart, 1995.

PAVL. NOL., *Carm.* = *Paulini Nolani Carmina* – ed. F. Dolveck (*CC SL*, 21), Turnhout, 2015.

PAVL. PETRIC., *Mart.* = PAULINUS PETRICORDIAE, *De uita Martini episcopi*, in 'Paulini Petricordiae Carmina' – ed. M. Petschenig, in *Poetae christiani minores* (*CSEL*, 16, 1), Vienna, 1888, p. 17–159.

PRISC., *Inst.* = *Prisciani grammatici Caesariensis Institutionum grammaticarum libri XVIII* – ed. M. Hertz (*Grammatici latini*, 2–3), Leipzig, 1855.

PROSP., *Epigr.* = PROSPER AQUITANUS, *Liber epigrammatum* – ed. A. G. A. Horsting (*CSEL*, 100), Berlin, 2016.

SEDVL., *Carm. pasch.* = SEDULIUS, *Carmen paschale*, in *Sedulii opera omnia* – ed. J. Huemer (*CSEL*, 10), Vienna, 1885, p. 14–146.

SEDVL. SCOT., *Carm.* = *Sedulii Scotti Carmina* – ed. J. Meyers (*CC CM*, 117), Turnhout, 1991.

SERV., *Aen.* = SERVIUS, *Commentarius in Vergilii Aeneida*, in *Servii grammatici qui feruntur in Vergilii carmina commentarii* – ed. G. Thilo, H. Hagen (*Bibliotheca Teubneriana*), Leipzig, 1878–1902.

STAT., *Theb.* = *P. Papini Stati Thebaidos libri XII* – ed. D. E. Hill, Leiden, 1996².

THEODVLF., *Carm.* = THEODULFUS AURELIANENSIS, *Carmina*, in *Poetae latini aeui Carolini* – ed. E. Dümmler (*MGH, Poetae*, 1), Berlin, 1881, p. 443–569, 573–581, app. p. 629–630.

VEN. FORT., *Carm.* = VENANTIUS FORTUNATUS, *Carmina*, in *Venanti Honori Clementiani Fortunati presbyteri Italici opera poetica* – ed. F. Leo (*MGH, Auct. ant.*, 4, 1), Berlin, 1881, p. 3–270.

VEN. FORT., *Mart.* = VENANTIUS FORTUNATUS, *Vita Martini*, in *Venance Fortunat, œuvres*, IV, *Vie de Saint Martin* – ed. S. Quesnel (*Collection des universités de France*), Paris, 1996.

VERG., *Aen., Ecl., Georg.* = *P. Vergili Maronis opera* – ed. R. A. B. Mynors (*Oxford Classical Texts*), Oxford, 1969, p. 1–28.

SECONDARY LITERATURE

ALARD, G.-H., ed., *Jean Scot écrivain: Actes du IVe colloque international, Montréal 28 août – 2 septembre 1983*, Montreal – Paris, 1986.

G. BERNT, *Das lateinische Epigramm im Übergang von der Spätantike zum frühen Mittelalter*, Munich, 1968, p. 279–286.

W. BEIERWALTES, *Denken des Einen: Studien zur neuplatonischen Philosophie und ihrer Wirkungsgeschichte*, Frankfurt am Main, 1985.

W. BEIERWALTES, 'Sprache und Sache. Reflexionen zu Eriugenas Einschätzung von Leistung und Funktion der Sprache', *Zeitschrift für philosophische Forschung*, 38.4 (1984), p. 523–543.

W. BERSCHIN, *Griechisch-lateinisches Mittelalter: Von Hieronymus zu Nikolaus von Kues*, Bern – Munich, 1980, p. 145–152, *passim*. [English translation of the revised edition: *Greek Letters and the Latin Middle Ages: from Jerome to Nicholas of Cusa* – transl. J. C. Frakes, Washington, DC, 1988.]

B. BISCHOFF, *Die Südostdeutschen Schreibschulen und Bibliotheken in der Karolingerzeit. I. Die Bayerischen Diözesen*, Wiesbaden, 1960.

B. BISCHOFF, 'Irische Schreiber in der Karolingerzeit', in *Mittelalterliche Studien: Ausgewählte Aufsätze zur Schriftkunde und Literaturgeschichte* – ed. B. Bischoff, Stuttgart, 3 vols, 1966–1981, III (1981), 39–54.

B. BISCHOFF, *Katalog der festländischen Handschriften des neunten Jahrhunderts (mit Ausnahme der wisigotischen)*, 3 vols., Wiesbaden, 1998–2013.

F. BRUNHÖLZL, *Geschichte der lateinischen Literatur des Mittelalters*, 2 vols., Munich, 1975–92, I, 473–474.

M. CAPPUYNS, *Jean Scot Érigène, sa vie, son œuvre, sa pensée*, Paris – Louvain, 1933, p. 76–78, 233–237.

Y. CHRISTE, 'Sainte-Marie de Compiègne et le temple d'Hézéchiel', in *Jean Scot Érigène et l'histoire de la philosophie: Laon, 7–12 juillet 1975*, Paris, 1977, p. 477–481.

Clavis Litterarum Hibernensium: Medieval Irish Books & Texts (c. 400– c. 1600) – ed. D. Ó Corráin (*CC Claves*), 3 vols, Turnhout, 2017, I, 510–511.

F. COLNAGO, *Poesia e teologia in Giovanni Scoto Eriugena* (*Biblioteca di cultura romanobarbarica*), Rome, 2009.

J. J. CONTRENI, 'A propos de quelques manuscrits de l'école de Laon au IXe siècle', *Le Moyen Age*, 78 (1972), p. 5–39, esp. p. 9–14.

J. J. CONTRENI, *The Cathedral School of Laon from 850 to 930: Its Manuscripts and Masters*, Munich, 1978, p. 86, 89–90, 120.

J. J. CONTRENI, 'The Irish in the Western Carolingian Empire (according to James F. Kenney and Bern, Burgerbibliothek 363)', in *Die Iren und Europa im früheren Mittelalter* – ed. H. Löwe, 2 vols, Stuttgart, 1982, p. 758–798.

J. J. CONTRENI, 'The Study and Practice of Medicine in Northern France During the Reign of Charles the Bald', *Studies in Medieval Culture*, 6–7 (1976), p. 43–54.

P. Dronke, '"Theologia veluti quaedam poetria": quelques observations sur la fonction des images poétiques chez Jean Scot', in *Jean Scot Érigène et l'histoire de la philosophie* – ed. R. Rocques, Paris, 1977, p. 243–252.

E. Dümmler, 'Die Überlieferung der lateinischen Dichtungen aus der Zeit der Karolinger', *Neues Archiv der Gesellschaft für ältere deutsche Geschichtskunde,* 4 (1879), p. 128, 531–533.

P. E. Dutton, 'Eriugena the Royal Poet', in *Jean Scot écrivain: Actes du IVe colloque international, Montréal, 28 août–2 septembre 1983* – ed. G.-H. Allard, Montreal – Paris, 1986, p. 51–80.

P. E. Dutton – É. A. Jeauneau, 'The Verses of the "Codex Aureus" of Saint-Emmeram', *Studi Medievali,* 3rd ser., 24 (1983), p. 75–120.

P. E. Dutton, 'Eriugena and Virgil', in *Eriugena and Creation. Proceedings of the Eleventh International Conference on Eriugenian Studies, held in honor of Édouard Jeauneau, Chicago, 9–12 November 2011* – ed. W. Otten, M. I. Allen (*Instrumenta patristica et mediaevalia,* 68), Turnhout, 2014, p. 3–30.

P. E. Dutton, 'Evidence that Dubthach's Priscian Codex Once Belonged to Eriugena', in *From Athens to Chartres: Studies in Honour of Édouard Jeauneau* – ed. H. J. Westra, Leiden, 1992, p. 15–45, esp. p. 21–28.

P. Godman, 'Latin Poetry under Charles the Bald and Carolingian Poetry', in *Charles the Bald: Court and Kingdom* – ed. M. Gibson, J. Nelson (*British Archaeological Reports,* 101), Oxford, 1981, p. 293–309.

P. Godman, *Poetry of the Carolingian Renaissance,* London, 1985, p. 58–60, 300–306.

P. Godman, *Poets and Emperors: Frankish Politics and Carolingian Poetry,* Oxford, 1987, p. 169–73.

M. W. Herren, 'The Commentary on Martianus attributed to John Scottus: Its Hiberno-Latin background', in *Jean Scot écrivain: actes du IVe colloque international, Montréal, 28 août–2 septembre 1983* – ed. G.-H. Allard, Montréal, 1986, p. 265–286.

M. W. Herren, 'Eriugena's *Aulae sidereae,* the "Codex Aureus", and the Palatine Church of St Mary at Compiègne', *Studi Medievali,* 3rd ser., 28 (1987), p. 593–608.

M. Herren, S. A. Brown, eds., *The Sacred Nectar of the Greeks: The Study of Greek in the West in the Early Middle Ages* (*King's College London Medieval Studies,* 2), London, 1988.

M. W. Herren, 'St Gall 48: A Copy of Eriugena's Lost Greek Gospels', in *Tradition und Wertung: Festschrift für Franz Brunhölzl* – ed. G. Bernt, F. Rädle, G. Silagi, Sigmaringen, 1989, p. 97–105.

M. W. HERREN, 'Gli ebrei nella cultura letteraria al tempo di Carlo il Calvo', in *Giovanni Scotto nel suo tempo: l'organizzazione del sapere in età carolingia* – ed. C. Leonardi, E. Menestò, Spoleto, 1989, p. 537–552, esp. p. 549–552.

M. W. HERREN, 'Johannes Scottus Poeta', in *From Augustine to Eriugena: Studies on Neoplatonism and Christianity in Honour of John O'Meara* – ed. F. X. Martin, J. Richmond, Washington, DC, 1991, p. 92–106.

M. W. HERREN, 'John Scottus and the Biblical Manuscripts Attributed to the Circle of Sedulius', in *Iohannes Scottus Eriugena: The Bible and Hermeneutics. Proceedings of the Ninth International Colloquium of the Society for the Promotion of Eriugenian Studies Held at Leuven and Louvain-la-Neuve June 7–10, 1995* – ed. G. Van Riel, C. Steel, J. J. McEvoy, Leuven, 1996, p. 303–320.

M. W. HERREN, 'Sedulius Scottus and the knowledge of Greek', in *Early Medieval Ireland and Europe: Chronology, Contact, Scholarship. A Festschrift for Dáibhí Ó Cróinín* – ed. P. Moran, I. Warntjes (Studia Traditionis Theologiae, 14), Turnhout, 2015, p. 515–535.

É. A. JEAUNEAU, 'Les écoles de Laon et d'Auxerre au IXe siècle', in *La scuola nell'Occidente latino dell'alto medioevo* (*Settimane di studio del Centro italiano di studio sull'alto medioevo*, 19), Spoleto, 1972, p. 495–522 and 555–560. Reprinted in *Études Érigéniennes*, Paris, 1987, p. 57–84.

É. A. JEAUNEAU, 'Jean Scot Erigène et le grec', *Archivum Latinitatis Medii Aevi* (*Bulletin du Cange*), 41 (1979), p. 5–50, esp. p. 19–21. Reprinted in *Études Érigéniennes*, Paris, 1987, p. 85–132.

É. A. JEAUNEAU, 'Jean Scot et l'ironie', in *Jean Scot écrivain: actes du IVe colloque international, Montréal, 28 août–2 septembre 1983* – ed. G.-H. Allard, Montréal, 1986, p. 13–27. Reprinted in *Études Érigéniennes*, Paris, 1987, p. 321–337.

J. F. KENNEY, *The Sources for the Ecclesiastical History of Ireland I. Ecclesiastical*, New York, 1966[2], p. 587–588.

M. LAPIDGE, 'L'influence stylistique de la poésie de Jean Scot', in *Jean Scot Erigène et l'histoire de la philosophie* – ed. R. Roques (*Colloques Internationaux du Centre National de la Recherche Scientifique*, 561), Paris, 1977, p. 441–452.

M. LAPIDGE and R. SHARPE, *A Bibliography of Celtic-Latin Literature 400–1200*, Dublin, 1985.

P. LEHMANN, 'Mitteilungen aus Handschriften II', *Sitzungsberichte der bayerischen Akademie der Wissenschaften, philologisch-historische Abteilung*, 1930, Heft 2, p. 1–47, at p. 18–20.

C. Leonardi, 'Nuove voci poetiche tra secolo IX e XI', *Studi Medievali*, 3rd ser., 2 (1961), 139–168.

M. Manitius, *Geschichte der lateinischen Literatur des Mittelalters*, 3 vols., Munich, 1911–31, I, 332.

P. Moran, 'Greek in Early Medieval Ireland', in *Multilingualism in the Graeco-Roman World* – ed. A. Muller and P. James, Cambridge, 2012, p. 172–192.

B. Münxelhaus, 'Aspekte der Musica Disciplina bei Eriugena', in *Jean Scot Érigène et l'histoire de la philosophie: Laon, 7–12 juillet 1975*, Paris, 1977, p. 253–262.

J. J. O'Meara, L. Bieler, eds., *The Mind of Eriugena: Papers on a Colloquium in Dublin 14–18 July 1970*, Dublin, 1973.

J. J. O'Meara, *Eriugena*, Oxford, 1988, p. 177–197.

W. Otten, M. I. Allen, eds., *Eriugena and Creation: Proceedings of the Eleventh International Conference on Eriugenian Studies, held in honor of Edouard Jeauneau, Chicago, 9–12 November 2011* (*Instrumenta patristica et mediaevalia*, 68), Turnhout, 2014.

G. A. Piemonte, 'Acotaciónes sobre algunos poemas de Eriúgena', *Patristica et Mediaevalia*, 10 (1989), 21–48 (I); 11 (1990), 27–67 (II).

G. A. Piemonte, 'L'expression "Quae sunt et quae non sunt": Jean Scot et Marius Victorinus', in *Jean Scot écrivain: actes du IVe colloque international, Montréal, 28 août–2 septembre 1983* – ed. G.-H. Allard, Montréal, 1986, p. 81–113.

La poesia carolingia – ed. F. Stella, Florence, 1995, p. 246–263

F. J. E. Raby, *A History of Secular Latin Poetry in the Middle Ages*, 2 vols., Oxford, 1957^2, I, 237–238.

R. Roques, ed., *Jean Scot Erigène et l'histoire de la philosophie* (*Colloques internationaux du Centre national de la recherche scientifique*, 561), Paris, 1977.

O. Schumann, *Lateinisches Hexameter-Lexikon: Dichterisches Formelgut von Ennius bis zum Archipoeta*, 6 vols, München, 1979–1983.

F. Stella, *La poesia carolingia latina a tema biblica* (*Biblioteca di 'Medioevo latino'*, 9), Spoleto, 1993, p. 271–299.

O. Szerwiniack, 'Liste provisoire des manuscrits contenant les poèmes "Hanc libam" et "Lumine sidereo" de Jean Scot Érigène', *Scriptorium* 54.1 (2000), p. 87–91.

J. Szövérffy, *Weltliche Dichtungen des lateinischen Mittelalters, ein Handbuch. I. Von den Anfängen bis zum Ende der Karolingerzeit*, Berlin, 1970, p. 653–655.

L. Traube, 'O Roma Nobilis. Philologische Untersuchungen aus dem Mittelalter', (*separatum* of the *Abhandlungen der philosophisch-philologischen Klasse der königlichen bayerischen Akademie der Wissenschaften,* 19), Munich, 1892, p. 299-395.

IOHANNIS SCOTTI ERIVGENAE

DE IMAGINE

Introduzione a cura di
Chiara Ombretta Tommasi

Edizione a cura di
Giovanni Mandolino

INTRODUZIONE

a cura di
Chiara Ombretta Tommasi

Il *De imagine* di Giovanni Scoto Eriugena costituisce la traduzione latina dello scritto περὶ κατασκευῆς ἀνθρώπου (*De opificio hominis*) di Gregorio di Nissa.[1] Esso rientra in un più ampio progetto di traduzione di scritti teologici e filosofici di Padri greci, condotto dall'Eriugena alla corte di Carlo il Calvo, grazie all'ammirazione per la cultura greca e alla non comune conoscenza della lingua, appresa verosimilmente tramite i contatti della corte carolingia con dotti e diplomatici bizantini.[2] Da collocarsi forse nella

---

[1] Un tale "titre évocateur" (così É. JEAUNEAU, in *Iohannis Scotti seu Eriugenae Periphyseon*, vol. 4, Turnhout, 2000 [*CC CM*, 164], p. IX) è chiaramente ispirato da Gen. 1, 26-27, il versetto sulla creazione dell'uomo a immagine di Dio e sulla differenza sessuale, centrale per la speculazione del Nisseno. Il titolo attuale è invalso a partire dall'edizione di Johannes Leunclavius, pubblicata a Basilea nel 1567. Già alcuni codici (tra cui il Monacensis gr. 192, il Monacensis gr. 206, il Vindobonensis theologicus gr. 113, e il Maritensis 4861) recano tuttavia il titolo περὶ εἰκόνος ἀνθρώπου, un dato presente in G. H. FORBES, *Sancti Patris Nostri Gregorii Nysseni Basili Magni fratris opera quae supersunt omnia*. Tomus primus, Burntisland, 1855, p. 97, e recentemente valorizzato da Ch. ERISMANN, 'On the Significance of the Manuscript Parisinus graecus 437. The Corpus Dionysiacum, Iconoclasm, and Byzantine-Carolingian Relations', in *Menschen, Bilder, Sprache, Dinge. Wege der Kommunikation zwischen Byzanz und dem Westen* – ed. F. Daim – C. Gastgeber – D. Heher – C. Rapp, Mainz, 2018, p. 95-101, in part. 99.

[2] Su tutto ciò rimandiamo alle considerazioni di M. CAPPUYNS, *Jean Scot Érigène. Sa vie, son oeuvre, sa pensée*, Louvain, 1933 (rist. Bruxelles, 1969), ma soprattutto all'articolo di É. JEAUNEAU, 'Jean Scot Érigène et le grec', *Archivum Latinitatis Medii Aevi (Bulletin Du Cange)*, 61 (1979), p. 5-50 (= *Études érigéniennes*, Paris, 1987, p. 85-132). Cappuyns è dell'avviso (p. 13) che la prodigiosa conoscenza del greco da parte dell'Eriugena sia da ascrivere a una fase posteriore rispetto alla sua formazione irlandese, ove le scuole stavano subendo un progressivo declino (a favore dell'apprendimento, almeno parziale, già nella madrepatria può far pensare il fatto che nelle *Glossae diuinae historiae* siano chiosati dei termini greci; non è però certo che l'opera sia stata composta prima dell'arrivo in Gallia, tanto che alcuni studiosi la datano al decennio 850-60). Jeauneau nota come fossero comunque presenti degl'Irlandesi in quei centri sul continente ove il greco era praticato (Laon, Liegi, San Gallo, o anche alla Scuola Palatina) e che irlandesi furono anche intellettuali di spicco quali Sedulio Scotto o Martino di Laon, mettendo parimenti in rilievo come l'*imitatio imperi* fosse un tratto comune alla corte di Carlo e che il sovrano venisse spesso apostrofato con termini greci: il greco non era dunque soltanto la lingua delle controversie teologiche con l'Oriente, ma aveva anche aspetti che la rendevano attraente e, per così dire, 'di moda'. L'ipotesi più verisimile sembra quindi che Eriugena avesse ap-

più matura fase della carriera dell'Eriugena, dunque intorno agli anni '60 del nono secolo, e parallelamente alla stesura dell'opera maggiore, il *Periphyseon*, la versione del *De opificio hominis* si pone a fianco della fondamentale traduzione del *corpus* dello Pseudo-Dionigi Areopagita e di due opere (*Ambigua ad Iohannem* e *Quaestiones ad Thalassium*) di Massimo il Confessore,[3] testi che sembrano interessanti anche da una prospettiva metodologica per quanto attiene alla ripresa del dibattito, inauguratosi già in epoca tardoantica con Gerolamo e Rufino, sul modo di tradurre. Le tra-

---

preso il greco sul continente, alla corte di Carlo, per mezzo di strumenti come glossari, opere grammaticali e salteri bilingui ed eventualmente anche grazie a contatti diretti con diplomatici bizantini. Per altri dettagli sulla biografia di Eriugena cfr J. J. O'MEARA, *Eriugena*, Oxford, 1988. Sulla formazione dell'Eriugena si veda anche J. J. CONTRENI – P. P. Ó NÉILL, 'The Early Career and Formation of John Scottus', in J. J. Contreni, *Learning and Culture in Carolingian Europe: Letters, Numbers, Exegesis, and Manuscripts* (*Variorum Collected Studies series*, 974), Farnham, 2011, n. VI (p. 1-24), saggio che rivede e amplia, degli stessi autori, Divinae Historiae. *The Biblical Glosses of John Scottus Eriugena*, Firenze, 1997. Sulla questione delle conoscenze del greco in Occidente cfr anche B. M. KACZYNSKI, *Greek in the Carolingian Age: The St. Gall Manuscripts*, Cambridge Mass., 1988. Ulteriori dettagli si possono leggere nella Introduzione di M. Herren ai *Carmina*, p. XV-XVIII.

[3] Cfr *Maximi Confessoris Quaestiones ad Thalassium I. Quaestiones I-LV una cum Latina interpretatione Iohannis Scotti Eriugenae iuxta posita*, ed. C. LAGA – C. STEEL, Turnhout, 1980 (*CC SG*, 7); *Maximi Confessoris Ambigua ad Iohannem iuxta Iohannis Scotti Eriugenae latinam interpretationem*, ed. É. JEAUNEAU, Turnhout 1988 (*CC SG*, 18). All'Eriugena si ascrive inoltre la traduzione di un'opera di storia naturale di Prisciano: cfr M.-Th. D'ALVERNY, 'Les *Solutiones ad Chosroem* de Priscianus Lydus et Jean Scot', in *Jean Scot Érigène et l'histoire de la philosophie (Colloques internationaux du Centre national de la Recherche scientifique, n° 561, Laon 7-12 juillet 1975)* – ed. R. Roques, Paris, 1977, p. 145-160, opera che si accorderebbe con gl'interessi per la fisiologia e la storia naturale testimoniati dal *De imagine* (si noti inoltre che recentemente è stato attribuito a Eriugena anche un commento a Prisciano: cfr P. E. DUTTON – A. LUHTALA, 'Eriugena in Priscianum', *Medieval Studies*, 56 (1994), p. 153-163). Su alcune delle caratteristiche di Eriugena traduttore cfr É. JEAUNEAU, 'Jean Scot Érigène et le grec', cit., p. 41s. (= p. 123s.); ID., 'Jean Scot Érigène: grandeur et misère du métier de traducteur', in *Traductions et traducteurs au Moyen Âge. Actes du Colloque international du CNRS organisé à Paris (IRHT) les 26-28 mai 1986* – ed. G. Contamine, Paris, 1989, p. 99-108 (= 'Tendenda Vela': Excursions littéraires et digressions philosophiques à travers le *Moyen Âge*, Turnhout, 2007, p. 231-242), con bibliografia; ID., 'L'influence des traductions érigéniennes sur le vocabulaire philosophique du Moyen Âge: simples remarques', in *L'élaboration du vocabulaire philosophique au Moyen Âge. Actes du Colloque international de Louvain-la-Neuve et Leuven, 12-14 septembre 1998* – ed. J. Hamesse – C. Steel, Turnhout, 2000, p. 157-169; P. CHIESA, 'Ad verbum o ad sensum? Modelli e coscienza metodologica della traduzione tra tarda antichità e alto medioevo', *Medioevo e Rinascimento*, 1 (1987), p. 1-51; ID., 'Traduzioni e traduttori dal greco nel IX secolo: sviluppi di una tecnica', in *Giovanni Scoto nel suo tempo. L'organizzazione del sapere in età carolingia*, Spoleto, (1989), p. 171-200; E. S. MAINOLDI, 'Le citazioni dei Padri orientali nelle opere di Giovanni Scoto. Nuove osservazioni sul metodo dell'Eriugena traduttore', *Schede Medievali*, 52 (2014), p. 255-271.

duzioni eriugeniane sono volutamente improntate a un sostanziale letteralismo, in nome della fedeltà al modello: una norma che ammette deroghe soltanto laddove la resa *uerbum de uerbo* tradisca la *proprietas* del senso del testo di partenza. [4] Oltre a questi Padri greci, l'Eriugena conosce e cita anche l'*Ancoratus* di Epifanio di Salamina – ma non sappiamo se lo tradusse mai per intero – e una traduzione, di paternità incerta e ancora da identificare (in quanto differisce da quella di Eustazio), dell'*Hexaemeron* di Basilio di Cesarea; [5] mentre l'Origene a lui noto è certamente quello tradotto da Rufino. A completare il quadro degli autori greci noti ad Eriugena (come si vede, solo cristiani, e non prendendo in considerazione la traduzione da Prisciano delle *Solutiones ad Chosroem regem*, di dubbia paternità), [6] egli cita da due omelie di Giovanni Crisostomo, di cui una spuria. [7] Verisimilmente, Eriugena poté consultare almeno parte della Bibbia greca, forse un Salterio bilingue e forse le Epistole paoline, quasi certamente il Vangelo di Giovanni. [8]

In questo quadro, la traduzione eriugeniana da Gregorio di Nissa, sia per le dimensioni che per l'influenza esercitata sulla successiva tradizione culturale, è certamente un lavoro minore, [9] sfavorita peraltro dall'esistenza di una precedente traduzione della medesima opera, effettuata nel VI secolo da Dionigi il Piccolo, con assai più compiuta padronanza della lingua greca e destinata, forse anche in virtù delle lodi ricevute da Cassiodoro, ad avere

---

[4] Per una dichiarazione di metodo particolarmente significativa, si veda la prefazione alla *Versio Dionysii* in *MGH, Ep.* VII, p. 158-161, con gli studi citati alla nota precedente. Il metodo eriugeniano, improntato a stretto letteralismo, non sarà comunque esente da critiche, come dimostra, pochi anni dopo, il giudizio di Anastasio Bibliotecario, a sua volta traduttore, diplomatico e uomo politico di spicco della curia pontificia, che, malgrado gli elogi iniziali, riterrà la *Versio Dionysii* bisognosa di un traduttore (*quem interpretaturus susceperat, adhuc redderet interpretandum*: *MGH, Ep.* VII, p. 430-434): cfr É. Jeauneau, 'Jean Scot Érigène et le grec', cit., p. 42 (= p. 124).

[5] Jeauneau, 'Jean Scot Érigène et le grec', cit., p. 26 (= p. 108).

[6] M.-Th. D'Alverny, 'Les *Solutiones*', cit.

[7] Cfr l'introduzione di É. Jeauneau, in Jean Scot, *Homélie sur le Prologue de Jean*, Paris, 1969 (*SC*, 151), p. 38-42 (= É. Jeauneau, *Études érigéniennes*, Paris, 1987, p. 42-46).

[8] É. Jeauneau, 'Jean Scot Érigène et le grec', cit., p. 29.

[9] É. Jeauneau, 'La division des sexes chez Gregoire de Nysse et chez Jean Scot Érigène', in *Eriugena: Studien zu seinen Quellen* – ed. W. Beierwaltes, Heidelberg, 1980, p. 33-54 (rist. in *Études érigéniennes*, cit., p. 343-364), p. 35 (= 345) avanza anche l'ipotesi che Eriugena possa aver affidato a un suo discepolo il compito di tradurre l'opera del Nisseno.

maggior fortuna e più ampia diffusione manoscritta.[10] Il rilievo secondario che il *De imagine* eriugeniano assume nell'ambito della sua ricca produzione di pensatore originale e di traduttore, malgrado l'ampio numero di citazioni e parafrasi nel *Periphyseon*, rende ragione anche dell'assenza di una ricostruzione filologica complessiva intorno a questo testo.

A oggi, l'unica edizione di quest'opera si deve a Maïeul Cappuyns, il quale pubblicò nel 1965 la trascrizione diplomatica del solo manoscritto allora noto (il Bambergensis Misc. Patr. 78),[11] del quale aveva annunciato la scoperta nella monografia dedicata a Eriugena.[12] Nel 1980 fu identificato, tra le nuove acquisizioni della Bibliothèque Nationale di Parigi, un altro manoscritto contenente il testo del *De imagine*, che fu poi descritto e parzialmente collazionato, da Édouard Jeauneau nella sua edizione del libro 4 del *Periphyseon*, dove si trova la maggior parte delle citazioni dal *De imagine*.[13]

---

[10] La versione dionisiana è leggibile in *PL*, 67, 347-408. Cfr A. Cacciotti, 'La Fortuna del *De Opificio hominis* di Gregorio di Nissa in occidente', *Studi sull'Oriente Cristiano*, 1 (2002), p. 19-29 e, precedentemente, P. Levine, 'Two Early Latin Versions of St. Gregory of Nyssa's περὶ κατασκευῆς ἀνθρώπου', *Harvard Studies in Classical Philology*, 63 (1958), p. 473-492, che, dopo aver evidenziato ancora una volta il letteralismo eriugeniano, conclude (p. 481-482): "since both scholars [cioè Dionigi ed Eriugena rispettivamente] were held in highest esteem for their linguistic talents in their respective times, the striking contrast between the two versions of St. Gregory of Nyssa's περὶ κατασκευῆς ἀνθρώπου may be taken as eloquent testimony to the marked decline in the standard of learning during the three turbulent centuries that separated Dionysius Exiguus from John Scotus". Levine ricorda inoltre altre due traduzioni latine, del XVI secolo, quella di Ambrogio Ferrari (1553) e quella del Leunclavius (1567). Giova rammentare che l'opera di Gregorio circolò anche in versioni armene, georgiane, siriache, forse arabe, e slave: cfr L. Sels, De hominis opificio. *The Fourteenth-Century Slavonic Translation. A Critical Edition with Greek Parallel and Commentary*, Wien-Köln-Weimar, 2009, in part. p. 10. La versione siriaca, trasmessa nel ms. Vat. Syr. 106 (datato da Assemani all'VIII secolo, ma ora ritenuto ascriversi alla fine del VI), è stata solo parzialmente edita in tempi recenti, a cura di diversi studiosi in varie annate di *Studi sull'Oriente Cristiano*. Sulla vita e l'opera di Dionigi rimandiamo alla voce redatta da H. Mordek per il *Dizionario Biografico degli Italiani* (vol. 40 [1991], p. 199-204).

[11] 'Le *De imagine* de Grégoire de Nysse traduit par Jean Scot Érigène', *Recherches de Théologie Ancienne et Médiévale*, 32 (1965), p. 205-262.

[12] M. Cappuyns, *Jean Scot Érigène*, cit., p. 127-128.

[13] Per le circostanze della scoperta cfr É. Jeauneau, 'Pseudo-Dionysius, Gregory of Nyssa, and Maximus the Confessor in the Works of John Scottus Eriugena', in *Carolingian Essays. Andrew W. Mellon Lectures in Early Christian Studies* – ed. U.-R. Blumenthal, Washington, 1983, p. 137-149, in part. 142-143 (= *Études érigéniennes*, cit., p. 180-181); Id., 'La Bibliothèque de Cluny et les oeuvres de l'Érigène', in *Pierre Abélard, Pierre le Vénérable. Les courantes philosophiques, littéraires et artistiques en occident au milieu du XIIe siècle. Abbaye de Cluny, 2-9 juillet 1972*, Paris, 1975, p. 703-725 (= *Études érigéniennes*,

La presente nuova edizione ha tentato di completare il lavoro di ricostruzione, anzitutto fornendo un testo critico basato su una collazione sistematica dei testimoni noti, e parimenti confrontato con il testo originale del Nisseno. Si sono inoltre considerati i brani del *De imagine* citati nel *Periphyseon*, al fine di osservare un eventuale grado di rielaborazione, che ha, in qualche caso, influito nella costituzione del testo; il medesimo confronto è stato effettuato anche rispetto al *De natura corporis et animae* di Guglielmo di Saint-Thierry (XII sec.), l'unica altra opera che ha certamente tra le sue fonti il *De imagine*. Parallelamente, infine, si è cercato di corredare il testo critico del *De imagine* con quanti più riferimenti possibili alle ancora poco esplorate fonti patristiche e non del testo greco originale (inclusi i riscontri contenutistici con altre opere di Gregorio di Nissa), nonché con rinvii a passi di altre opere eriugeniane contenenti riferimenti certi o probabili al testo del *De imagine*. Tanto i rimandi del greco che la tradizione indiretta (Eriugena stesso e Guglielmo) sono state raggruppate in un unico apparato di fonti e passi paralleli. Le considerazioni introduttive che seguono hanno inteso altresì esporre alcune ipotesi circa il momento di composizione e la circolazione della traduzione eriugeniana.

Nella costituzione del testo non di rado è stato necessario confrontarsi con un dettato e uno stile non particolarmente semplici, dovuti all'estremo letteralismo della traduzione, in qualche caso persino inintelligibili e sintatticamente scorretti, molto probabilmente come risultato di un'errata lezione sull'esemplare greco o di un fraintendimento di Eriugena (eclatante, ad esempio, il caso della frase di apertura del prologo): abbiamo cercato di ricostruire in apparato cosa probabilmente avesse letto o compreso Eriugena, ma abbiamo rinunziato a emendare il testo. Per quanto riguarda le consuetudini ortografiche e la punteggiatura, si sono seguiti i criteri già stabiliti e discussi da Édouard Jeauneau nella premessa al *Periphyseon*, ai quali rimandiamo, in particolare l'uso delle parentesi tonde per quanto riguarda le glosse esplicative di certi concetti o termini greci.[14] È stata modificata la punteggiatura rispetto ai codici e al testo stampato da Cappuyns, tenendo conto dell'origi-

---

cit., p. 397-421). Cfr anche E. S. MAINOLDI, 'Iohannes Scottus Eriugena', in *La trasmissione dei testi latini del medioevo. Medieval Latin Texts and their Transmission* – ed. P. Chiesa – L. Castaldi, vol. 2, Firenze – Impruneta, 2005, p. 250-252.

[14] É. JEAUNEAU, in *Iohannis Scotti seu Eriugenae Periphyseon*, vol. 1, Turnhout, 1996 (*CC CM*, 161), p. LXXXVII.

nale greco e delle traduzioni moderne. Per comodità del lettore, si è scelto di riportare a margine la paginazione di Cappuyns e dei due manoscritti, come anche si è indicata la scansione in colonne del testo greco stampato nel Migne (vol. 44, col. 124C-256C). La divisione in capitoli e paragrafi, non presente in Cappuyns, si conforma a quella operata da Forbes nella sua edizione del testo di Gregorio. Abbiamo, infine, ricollazionato e segnalato alcune varianti peculiari del manoscritto greco Coisl. 235 (*q*), che, allo stato attuale delle conoscenze, risulta essere l'esemplare più affine a quello utilizzato da Eriugena (cfr *infra*), anche laddove esse si discostino dalla resa di Eriugena. Nel citare il greco, quindi, l'apparato fa riferimento tanto alla Patrologia (*PG*) e a Forbes (*Forb.*), quanto a *q*. In qualche altro caso abbiamo altresì riportato ulteriori varianti di un qualche interesse, ricavandole dall'apparato di Forbes e indicandole con la sigla generale di *Forb.*$^{u.l.}$.

Per quanto riguarda il dettato ortografico, considerando ove possibile la grafia eriugeniana attestata nel ms. *R* del *Periphyseon* e basandoci sull'edizione di Jeauneau, abbiamo inoltre uniformato le consuetudini di scrittura, laddove i testimoni presentavano varianti e oscillazioni anche all'interno dello stesso codice e per il medesimo vocabolo: ad esempio, *B* alterna, talvolta a poca distanza, *intellegentia*/*intelligentia* o *intellego*/*intelligo*, con netta prevalenza per la forma con -*e*; *elimentum* o *elementum* (cfr cap. XXVII); *inmaterialis* o *immaterialis* (cfr cap. XXIII); *ingero* o *iggero* (cfr cap. XXX). Trattandosi di un testo critico e non di una trascrizione diplomatica, tale scelta ci è parsa necessaria per ragioni di coerenza e uniformità[15]. Abbiamo scelto in molti casi di adeguarci all'*usus scribendi* classico, considerando che di norma il codice *C* è abbastanza regolare e attesta nella maggior parte dei casi tale tendenza conservativa: per esempio, il più delle volte ha *intelligentia* rispetto a *intellegentia* di *B*; *character* rispetto a *caracter*; *umidus*, rispetto a *humidus*; *phantasia* rispetto a *fantasia* (cfr cap. XIV; ma si veda *teophania* di *B*, p. 105, 155); *administro* in luogo di *amministro*; il nesso -*tio* su *C* è di norma -*cio* su *B* (cfr *pretiosior*, p. 75, 2 [ma *preciosa* è attestato su *B* e *C*, p. 74]; *enuntiatio*, p. 83, 23; *otium*, p. 104, 121). In qualche caso, invece, *C* è meno

---

[15] Cfr anche quanto scrive Jeauneau in *Iohannis Scotti seu Eriugenae Periphyseon*, vol. 1, Turnhout, 1996 (*CC CM*, 161), p. LXXXVII: "je me suis permis aussi de régulariser certaines graphies là où leur divergence ne reflète rien d'autre que la fantaisie de l'auteur ou la négligénce de ses copistes".

regolare rispetto a *B*: per esempio attesta forme quali *habundantia* (p. 97, 112) o *misterium* (p. 118, 28). Sulla base di queste considerazioni, abbiamo corretto e normalizzato il testo di *B* anche laddove esso rimaneva l'unico esemplare, essendo *C* mutilo (cfr *tertius*, p. 155, 26; 156, 53; 163, 271). Per non appesantire l'apparato ci siamo limitati a segnare tacitamente le diverse lezioni, senza specificare (nei casi di dette correzioni ortografiche) che si trattava di nostri interventi; così come non abbiamo quasi mai indicato le corrispondenze tra Cappuyns e *B*, giacché tale edizione è quasi sempre trascrizione diplomatica del codice di Bamberg. Più complessa la questione dell'uso del dittongo, che abbiamo corretto per esigenze di uniformità: *B* tende spesso a scrivere nella forma *-ae* gli avverbi in *-e*, che sono invece regolari su *C* (cfr *conspicue*, p. 86, 6; *uarie*, p. 88, 69; *mensurate*, p. 101, 25; *obscure*, p. 104, 133; *curiose*, p. 134, 55; *inconfuse*, p. 135, 14; *inoperose spontaneeque*, p. 146, 73; *informe*, p. 146, 84; *fabulose*, p. 147, 28; *aeque*, p. 152, 44; *proprie*, p. 157, 107; *exanime*, p. 164, 304); del pari, in qualche caso, sono rese nella forma monottongata le desinenze *-ae* della prima declinazione (*capreole*, p. 81, 16; *plante*, p. 82, 59; *aspereque*, p. 87, 22; *cetere*, p. 108, 2; *pulcherrime*, p. 156, 70; *solide*, p. 157, 79; *dispertite*, p. 90, 42; per non dire dell'alternanza tra *queris* e *quaeris* a poche righe di distanza, p. 141, 166 e 175). In tal modo, sempre per esigenze di uniformità e per coerenza, abbiamo ritenuto opportuno correggere queste lezioni isolate; viceversa, abbiamo mantenuto forme quali *Manicheus* o *Grecus* (rispettivamente p. 134, 51; e 126, 6; 148, 38; 150, 99); il caso di *heretice impietatis* (p. 112, 57) è abbastanza interessante e abbiamo pensato di normalizzare solo la desinenza.

*
* *

I. La tradizione manoscritta

Come già anticipato, i testimoni diretti che tramandano il testo del *De imagine* eriugeniano sono due:

B Bamberg, Staatsbibliothek, Misc. Patr. 78 (*olim* B.IV.13), pergamenaceo, di dimensioni 33 × 24 cm., con specchio di scrittura 25,5 × 17 cm., e mancante del primo foglio. Si tratta del manoscritto pubblicato da Cappuyns, che vi aveva scoperto ed identificato il *De imagine* eriugeniano: lo studioso è propenso a datarlo alla fine del IX secolo, mentre i cataloghi propongono una data intorno al 1000; secondo Cappuyns, inoltre, il manoscritto subì le medesime vicende postulate da Ludwig Traube per i testimoni di altre opere eriugeniane: provenienti da Reims, essi sarebbero stati donati da Gerberto d'Aurillac al suo pupillo Ottone III, e sarebbero poi stati lasciati in dono alla biblioteca della cattedrale di Bamberg dall'imperatore Enrico II († 1024).[16] Anche in questo caso, i cataloghi sembrano suggerire un diverso luogo di provenienza, ossia Cluny, sulla base di somiglianze con altri esemplari.[17] Su questa eventualità e sulla questione della circolazione dei contenuti di *B* occorrerà tornare più avanti.

Il codice contiene le orazioni di Gregorio di Nazianzo nella traduzione di Rufino (f. 2^v-53^v): *Incipit praefatio gregorii nanzanzeni episcopi uel rufini presbyteri* (si tratta di otto orazioni, ciascuna corrispondente a un libro); segue (f. 53^v-87^v) il *De sacerdotio* di Giovanni Crisostomo, in sei libri: *Incipit dialogus basilii et iohannis libri sex*. Il testo del *De imagine* è il terzo e ultimo di questa miscellanea, riportato ai f. 88^r-114^r, con il titolo (lacunoso): *Sermo Gregorii Episcopi Nysae De ⟨imagine⟩ in ea quae relicta sunt in Examero a Beato Basilio suo fratre*.

C Paris, BNF n.a.lat. 2664, pergamenaceo, di dimensioni 30 × 23,5 cm, siglato *C* da Jeauneau.[18] Il codice, miscellaneo, è composto di parti provenienti da manoscritti diversi, datati tra la fine del X secolo e la prima metà dell'XI. Esso contiene il *De musica* di Boezio (f. 2^r-31^v); una *Vita Karoli magni* erroneamente attribuita ad Alcuino (f. 32ra-41ra); la *Revelatio quemadmodum caput sancti Iohannis precursoris Domini de civitate Herodis Emessa sit delatus*

---

[16] L. TRAUBE, 'Palaeographische Forschungen IV. Bamberger Fragmente der vierten Dekade des Livius. Anonymus Cortesianus', *Abhandlungen der Königlich Bayerischen Akademie der Wissenschaften*, München, 1904, p. 7-10.

[17] Cfr F. LEITSCHUH – H. FISCHER, *Katalog der Handschriften der Königlichen Bibliothek zu Bamberg*, vol. 1, Bamberg, 1887 (rist. 1966), p. 450; G. SUCKALE-REDLEFSEN, *Die Handschriften des 8. bis 11. Jahrhunderts der Staatsbibliothek Bamberg*, vol. 1.1, Wiesbaden, 2004, p. 66.

[18] Agli studi citati precedentemente (n. 13) si aggiunga la breve scheda redatta da D. BLOCH, in *Cinq années d'enrichissement du patrimoine national: 1975-1980, donations, dations, acquisitions*, Paris, 1980, p. 315-316. Cfr inoltre la scheda http://archivesetmanuscrits.bnf.fr/ark:/12148/cc716502 (ultimo accesso marzo 2019), con ulteriori informazioni.

di Dionigi il Piccolo (f. 41ra-44va); una *Passio sancti Clementis* (f. 44va-47rb); un breve testo di Gregorio di Tours (f. 47rb-47vb, *Ex libro Gregorii Miraculorum. Clemens martyr* [= *In gloria martyrum*, 36-37]); le *Recognitiones s. Clementis* nella traduzione di Rufino (f. 48ra-117vb); una *Epistola s. Clementis ad Jacobum de obitu Petri et de ordinatione sua* (f. 117vb-119va); il *Libellus de informatione episcoporum seu de dignitate sacerdotali*, edito sotto il nome di Ambrogio (*PL* 17, 567-580), o di Gilberto di Aurillac (*PL* 139, 169-178) (f. 119va-121rb); e infine il *De imagine* eriugeniano (f. 122^{r}-139^{v}).

Le note di computo ai f. 1^{v} e 140^{v} indicano che la raccolta fu assemblata a partire dalla metà dell'XI sec.; con questo dato si accorda il fatto che in alcune di queste opere è stata riconosciuta la mano del notaio *Giraldus leuita*, attivo presso la cancelleria di Cluny fra il 1019 e il 1030.[19]

La provenienza cluniacense sembra attestata anche dal fatto che nel catalogo medievale della biblioteca di Cluny questo codice si trova rubricato insieme ad altre cinque opere di Eriugena:[20] nel catalogo di Delisle esse sono il *De imagine* (n. 24); il *De praedestinatione* (n. 199); una versione del *De caelesti Hierarchia* dello Pseudo-Dionigi (n. 278); il *Periphyseon* (n. 455); le *Expositiones in ierarchiam coelestem* (n. 25) e infine gli *Ambigua ad Iohannem* (n. 298). Fino al ritrovamento di *C* e alla sua acquisizione da parte della Bibliothèque Nationale, solo i manoscritti di queste ultime due opere erano conservati e noti: essendosi gli altri perduti in vari momenti nell'età moderna. Il *Periphyseon* era già mancante nel catalogo del 1644-45 redatto da dom Anselme Le Michel; il ms. *C* e la versione del *De caelesti Hierarchia* risultavano assenti quando negli anni della Rivoluzione francese fu steso un inventario dettagliato dei beni dell'abbazia (1790); il ms. del *De praedestinatione* invece vi figurava ancora, e si troverà anche in un ulteriore catalogo del 1801, mentre nel 1881 risulta sparito.[21]

---

[19] M.-C. GARAND, 'Giraldus levita, copiste de chartes et de livres à Cluny sous l'abbatiat de saint Odilon († 1049)', in *Calames et cahiers. Mélanges de codicologie et de paléographie offerts à Léon Gilisen* – ed. J. Lemaire – E. Van Balbergh, Bruxelles, 1985, p. 41-48.

[20] Secondo L. DELISLE, *Inventaire des manuscrits des fonds de Cluni*, Paris 1884, p. 337 s., il catalogo fu redatto nel XII secolo sotto l'abate Ugo III (1158-1161).

[21] Le vicende di questi manoscritti sono esaurientemente riassunte da É. JEAUNEAU, 'La bibliothèque de Cluny', cit. Cfr anche P. GASNAULT, 'Dom Anselme Le Michel et les manuscrits de l'abbaye de Cluny', *Bibliothèque de l'École des chartes* 131 (1973), p. 209-219.

Il testo del *De imagine* si presenta acefalo, per la caduta certamente di un solo foglio (mancano la prefazione e le prime righe del cap. I: il testo conservato incomincia al f. 122ʳ con le parole *ac firmitas*: *De imag.* I, 1, p. 210, 37 Capp. = p. 71, 10), e privo della parte finale: si interrompe al cap. XXIII dell'opera (secondo la numerazione eriugeniana, differente da quella usuale del testo greco); l'ultima parola (al f. 139ᵛ) è *matherie* (ossia *materiem*: *De imag.* XXIII, 4, p. 245, 5 Capp. = p. 134, 50). Dal momento che il testo si interrompe nel mezzo della pagina senza indicazioni di alcun genere, occorrerà pensare verisimilmente a una caduta di fogli nell'antigrafo, piuttosto che a un meno probabile abbandono del lavoro di copiatura.

Di conseguenza, il testo completo del *De imagine*, se si eccettua la mancanza del cap. XXII e una omissione non segnalata dal ms. a poche righe dalla fine dell'opera, sulle quali torneremo più avanti, è tramandato dal solo *B*.

A una collazione sistematica, i testimoni *B* e *C* si sono rivelati indipendenti l'uno dall'altro. *C*, ad esempio, non presenta alcune omissioni di *B*: così in *De imag.* I, 5 (p. 211, 42-43 Capp. = 73, 73-74), dove *B* riporta *et omne quodcumque in conuallibus uirescit in pabulum*, *C* ha un segmento in più, omesso da *B* per un *saut du même au même*: *et omne quodcumque est procliuum et sopinum et omne quodcumque in conuallibus uirescit in pabulum*.
Altre omissioni di una parola sola avvenute in *B* sono estranee a *C*, che concorda con l'originale greco: in *De imag.* I, 4 (p. 211, 31-32 Capp. = 73, 59) fra *ut in natura stabili conuersionem* e *inconuersibili motum*, *B* lascia uno spazio, mentre *C* reca *ut in natura stabili conuersionem inuero* (δέ) *inconuersibili motum*; in VIII, 5 (p. 217, 16 Capp. = 84, 52) *sectio cum suis*, *C* ha *sectio nunc* (νῦν) *cum suis*; in XXIII, 3 (p. 244, 26 Capp. = 133, 24) a fronte di *B materiam, talibus*, *C* legge *materiam conformant* (κατασκευάζουσι), *talibus*.
C presenta anche alcune lezioni divergenti e in qualche caso migliori rispetto a *B* (come in *De imag.* VII, 3, p. 216, 10 Capp. = 82, 49, dove *B* ha *pro cor quod illis quam is* e *C* restituisce il testo originario, *pro crocodili squamis*); al contrario, in IX,3a (p. 219, 30 Capp. = 88, 68) *mentorum* di *B* è *meritorum* su *C*. Come si è accennato, *C* conserva un certo numero di grafie medievali in luogo di quelle classiche, ma di norma il suo dettato è più regolare.

L'impressione complessiva è che *B*, benché cronologicamente anteriore, si comporti in modo più libero, talora modificando, sia pur lievemente, il testo per renderlo stilisticamente più accettabile; di fronte alle parole greche traslitterate in latino o ai nomi è più facile che *B* si sia preso la libertà di alterare la grafia del termine rispetto a quanto accade in *C* (ad es. mentre in *B* la grafia oscilla fra *Moses/Moyses*, *C* ha regolarmente *Moyses*).
I due testimoni presentano inoltre alcune innovazioni in comune: queste fanno pensare a un archetipo che sarebbe stato l'anello intermedio fra questi due testimoni e l'autografo eriugeniano dell'opera (perduto, ma in parte ricostruibile sulla base delle citazioni presenti nel *Periphyseon*). Ad esempio, una innovazione prodottasi nell'archetipo di *B C* e certamente assente dall'autografo, è il caso in *De imag.* III, 1 dove, verosimilmente per un salto da pari a pari, *B C* omettono una riga circa di testo, presente però nella citazione corrispondente sul *Periphyseon*. Altre due omissioni di *B C* più brevi vengono restituite nel *Periphyseon* (*De imag.* XXI, 1, cfr *Periphys.* 4, 820B; *De imag.* XXII, 2: cfr *Periphys.* 4, 917B). Altrove (*De imag.* I, 4, p. 211, 26 Capp. = p. 73, 53), il copista di *B* (f. 89ʳ) trascrive in margine le parole *et immutabilitas* (la sequenza di parole da leggersi a testo è perciò *inconuersibilitas et immutabilitas in aliqua creatura uideretur deum faceret*); *C* ha le parole *et immutabilitas* a testo, ma nel punto sbagliato e sostituendole a un'altra parola che faceva parte del testo (dando luogo alla sequenza: *inconuersibilitas in aliqua creatura uideretur et immutabilitas faceret*, con l'omissione di *deum*). *B* e *C* avranno dunque reagito diversamente a uno stesso archetipo in cui le parole *et immutabilitas* erano scritte in interlinea.
Rappresentando graficamente la situazione ricostruita in base ai casi stemmatici sopra presentati, si ottiene una situazione di questo genere (dove ε indica l'autografo del *De imagine* dell'Eriugena, utilizzato per le citazioni nel *Periphyseon*.):

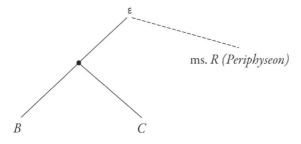

Infine, entrambi i manoscritti, se confrontati col testo a stampa del *De opificio hominis* presentano in alcuni punti una differente divisione in capitoli: nel cap. IX del testo latino confluiscono quelle che nel testo greco sono la parte finale del capitolo precedente e la prima parte di quello seguente. Questa modifica non sembra essere opera di Eriugena, né è frutto di una innovazione nell'archetipo di *B C*, bensì si direbbe dovuta all'esemplare greco a partire dal quale venne effettuata la traduzione: anche la traduzione di Dionigi il Piccolo, infatti, presenta la stessa situazione nella divisione del testo; d'altra parte, alcuni manoscritti greci dell'opera attestano l'inclusione all'interno del cap. IX greco di quello che nel testo della *Patrologia* è l'inizio del cap. X. Nel testo latino di Eriugena, inoltre, il cap. XII del testo greco è spezzato in due capitoli distinti, i capp. XII e XIII della versione latina; anche il titolo greco di questo capitolo è stato spezzato in due titoli latini distinti, ciascuno premesso alla parte di capitolo corrispondente. Questa modifica era pure già presente in parte della tradizione manoscritta greca dell'opera (tra cui in *q*) e nella versione di Dionigi il Piccolo. Perciò da questo punto del testo fino al cap. XXII latino incluso (= cap. XXI del testo greco) la numerazione dei capitoli del testo latino procede sfasata di una cifra (in più) rispetto all'originale greco. Dopodiché, però, i mss. *B C* mancano del cap. XXII del testo greco: da questo momento, quindi, le numerazioni dei capitoli del testo greco e di quello latino tornano a combaciare.

Per quanto riguarda la conclusione, *B*, l'unico esemplare che tramandi il testo nella sua interezza, nel trascrivere l'ultimo capitolo omette senza segnalazioni una consistente porzione di testo (*De imag.* XXX, 31-33, corrispondente a *PG* 44, 253D-256C: da dopo τελειότερον δὲ fino a prima di ὅπως ἂν τοῦ σπουδαζομένου), riprendendo la trascrizione a poche righe dalla fine dell'opera.

Come si è detto, entrambi i manoscritti sono privi del cap. XXII del testo greco:[22] non è dato sapere se questa mancanza fosse dovuta all'esemplare greco utilizzato per la traduzione oppure se la ragione di tale omissione sia da ricercarsi in altre cause, quali una distrazione del copista. Sembra tuttavia poco probabile che que-

---

[22] Questo capitolo contiene una spiegazione del perché la resurrezione, pur essendo un mutamento positivo per l'uomo in quanto consiste nella liberazione definitiva dalla condizione attuale, segnata dal peccato, debba compiersi alla fine dei tempi (donde il titolo: Πρὸς τοὺς λέγοντας, εἰ καλόν τι καὶ ἀγαθὸν ἡ ἀνάστασις, τί οὐχὶ ἤδη γέγονεν, ἀλλὰ χρόνων τισὶ περιόδοις ἐλπίζεται).

DE IMAGINE   CV

sto capitolo non figurasse nell'esemplare greco, ma è altresì poco
verisimile supporre che l'assenza del capitolo in questione dai testimoni latini *B C* sia dovuta a un guasto meccanico del loro archetipo, in quanto ciò presupporrebbe l'ipotesi quantomai rara di
una caduta di fogli corrispondente esattamente a un capitolo.[23]
L'edizione di Cappuyns integrava tale omissione utilizzando una
traduzione latina, anonima, contenuta in un florilegio patristico
V trasmesso dal codice Vat. Reg. lat. 195 (*V*).[24] Risalente al IX-X
secolo e probabilmente copiato nel nord-Italia, il codice contiene
una miscellanea omiletica, un sermone di Fulgenzio, parte del *De
duodecim abusiuis saeculi*, e infine una miscellanea patristica, fra
cui l'estratto del *De imagine* (f. 61^v-62^r), introdotto dalla titola-
tura: *sancti gregorii episcopi niseni*. Il frammento in questione, di
senso compiuto, corrisponde in greco alla porzione di capitolo
che va da τελεσθείσης δὲ τῆς τῶν ἀνθρώπων γενέσεως fino a καὶ
οὕτως πάντοτε συν Κυρίῳ ἐσόμεθα (*PG* 44, 205C-208A).
Cappuyns propose dubitativamente di attribuire la paternità della
traduzione a Eriugena, giacché essa non corrisponde all'unica altra traduzione nota del *De opificio hominis*, quella di Dionigi il
Piccolo, per quanto l'appartenenza di questo frammento al *De
imagine* eriugeniano non possa dirsi in alcun modo certa: la sua
brevità non permette di basarsi solidamente su fattori lessicali, né
il brano figura fra le citazioni incluse in altre opere di Eriugena, o
in altre opere da lui tradotte.[25] Se però essa si rivelasse corretta, ciò
dimostrerebbe che il capitolo omesso dai due testimoni *B C* si trovava nel testo greco accessibile al filosofo.
Anche per quanto riguarda il cap. XXII, i testimoni si sono accre-
sciuti rispetto all'edizione di Cappuyns. In particolare si deve se-

---

[23] Per tentare di dimostrare la corretta attribuzione del frammento ad Eriugena, abbiamo provato ad attuare un confronto col testo greco dell'edizione Forbes, se mai la
traduzione riflettesse varianti del testo greco presenti su *q*, che tuttavia, per questo brano,
non offre lezioni importanti. L'unica piccola variante significativa sembra anzi divergere
da *q*, ove si legge (insieme ad altri mss.) ἀλλαγήν, mentre il frammento latino ha *immutationem* (riga 3 del f. 62^r), che sembra riflettere piuttosto la lezione diffusa ἐναλλαγήν (*PG*
44, 205D11). Inoltre, il frammento in latino omette una parte di frase (καὶ τῇ μεταβολῇ
τοῦ ὅλου συναμειφθῆναι, *PG* 44, 205C13-4), ma l'omissione non si trova su nessuno dei
testimoni impiegati da Forbes e del resto essa potrebbe anche essere semplicemente dovuta ad una svista del copista del testo latino.

[24] M. CAPPUYNS, 'Le *De imagine*', cit., p. 205-206, n. 1. Per una descrizione del ms.
Reginense, cfr A. WILMART, *Codices Reginenses Latini*, Roma, 1937, p. 465-468.

[25] Scettico sull'attribuzione si mostra ad esempio É. JEAUNEAU, 'La division des sexes',
cit., p. 35 (= p. 345). A questo stesso studio dobbiamo la menzione del cod. BNF lat.
18095.

Q gnalare la sua presenza ai f. 186ʳ-186ᵛ del codice berlinese, Lat. Qu. 690 (Görres 87).²⁶ Il codice risale al IX-X secolo e proviene dall'abbazia di St. Maximin di Trier. Si tratta di due parti originariamente separate e assemblate già in età umanistica (XV sec.). La seconda, più antica e contenente anche il frammento del *De imagine*, risale al IX secolo. Il brano del *De imagine* si trova fra altri *excerpta* che, sia pure pochi e in ordine diverso, compaiono anche nel florilegio vaticano *V*. Schillmann, descrivendo nel suo catalogo questa seconda e più antica parte del ms. berlinese, vi individua otto mani differenti, di cui l'ultima, quella relativa alla parte di nostro interesse, verga i f. 175ᵛ-187ᵛ (cioè le ultime pagine del ms.). Secondo Schillmann, queste mani, pur nella loro varietà, sono accomunate da un forte "influsso insulare". All'*Enchiridion* di Agostino (f. 65ʳ-115ᵛ) sono apposte glosse irlandesi, che risalirebbero al X secolo e che potrebbero provenire da Reichenau o da St. Maximin,²⁷ tanto che Schillmann suggerisce di indicare l'origine del codice proprio nell'abbazia di Reichenau (altri hanno pensato a Mainz):²⁸ le note di possesso informano che dal XII secolo il ms. si trovava a St. Maximin di Trier.²⁹

L'esame di questi due florilegi potrebbe forse apportare qualcosa di più sulla tradizione e la circolazione del *De imagine*, e la ragione della sopravvivenza dell'estratto esclusivamente a sé è da ricercarsi nella particolare scelta antologica di tali codici, che presenta una sezione miscellanea di brani patristici, con speciale attenzione alla

---

²⁶ Questo nuovo testimone del frammento è menzionato nel *Catalogus Translationum et Commentariorum: Medieval and Renaissance Latin Translations and Commentaries –* ed. F. E. Cranz – P. O. Kristeller, vol. 5, Washington, 1984, p. 126-127. Un estratto del solo cap. XXII si legge ai fogli 40v-41 del codice BNF Lat. 18095, codice miscellaneo del nono

F secolo, originariamente posseduto dalla Biblioteca di Notre Dame, da noi siglato *F* su cui cfr https://archivesetmanuscrits.bnf.fr/ark:/12148/cc69025m (ultimo accesso marzo 2019).

²⁷ L. C. Stern, 'Altirische Glossen zu dem Trierer Enchiridion Augustins in der Königlichen Bibliothek zu Berlin', *Zeitschrift für celtische Philologie* 7 (1910), p. 475-497; B. Bischoff, 'Irische Schreiber im Karolingenreich', in *Jean Scot Erigène et l'histoire de la philosophie (Colloques internationaux du Centre national de la Recherche scientifique, n° 561, Laon 7-12 juillet 1975)* – ed. R. Roques, Paris, 1977, p. 47-58.

²⁸ A. Fingernagel, *Die illuminierten lateinischen Handschriften deutscher Provenienz der Staatsbibliothek Preussischer Kulturbesitz Berlin: 8-12. Jahrhundert*, Wiesbaden, 1991, p. 88.

²⁹ Per una descrizione generale di questo manoscritto berlinese, cfr F. Schillmann, *Die Handschriften-Verzeichnisse der Preussischen Staatsbibliothek zu Berlin. Verzeichnis der lateinischen Handschriften*, vol. 14.3, Berlin, 1919, p. 89-93.

tematica della resurrezione in riferimento alla prima Epistola paolina ai Corinzi (I Cor. 15, 51-54).[30] I due testimoni recanti questo frammento riportano a breve distanza anche altri due estratti di contenuto simile, seppure disposti in ordine diverso. Si tratta di un estratto da Giovanni Crisostomo e di uno da Atanasio di Alessandria (in realtà da Basilio di Seleucia):

Reg. lat. 195 (catalogo Wilmart)

f. 59^r-60^r: *sancti iohannis chrisostomi de epistola beat*(i) *pauli ap*(ostoli) *ad corinthios prim*(a) (cap. 15, 51-4: v. *PG*, 61, 364, par. 21.4 – 365 r. 11); inc. *In loco ubi dicit. Omnes quidem* [*non*] *dormiemus* etc. *Quod autem dicit hoc est non omnes quidem moriemur*, des. *Et corruptibile. hoc induerit incorruptionem. Tunc fiet sermo* etc. *in uictoria.*
f. 60^r-60^v: *sancti* ⟨*a*⟩*thanasi archiepiscopi alexandriae*; inc. *Saluatoris quidem resurrection*(is?) *communis est omnium reparatio*, des. *O magni luctus in gaudio consummatio.*
f. 61^v-62^r: *sancti gregorii episcopi niseni*; inc. *Peracta quidem hominum genitura eius quae termino conterminari tempus*, des. *Sed sublime possit in aerem permeare. Rapiemur enim inquid* etc. *cum deo erimus.*

Lat. Qu. 690 (Görres 87) (catalogo Schillmann)

f. 185^v: *Sancti Iohannis Chrisostomi de epistola beati pauli apostoli ad corintheos prima*; inc. *in loco ubi dicit. Omnes quidem Non dormiemus omnes autem...*

f. 186^r: *Sancti Gregorii episcopi Niseni*; inc. *Per acta quidem hominum genitura eiusque termino...*

f. 186^v: *Sancti Athanasii Archiepiscopi Alexandriae*; inc. *Saluatoris quidem resurrectio communis est omnium reparatio...*

*
* *

---

[30] *Ecce mysterium uobis dico: Non omnes quidem dormiemus, omnes autem immutabimur, in momento, in ictu oculi, in nouissima tuba; canet enim, et mortui suscitabuntur incorrupti, et nos immutabimur. Oportet enim corruptibile hoc induere incorruptelam, et mortale induere immortalitatem. Cum autem corruptibile hoc induerit incorruptelam, et mortale hoc induerit immortalitatem, tunc fiet sermo, qui scriptus est: Absorpta est mors in uictoria.*

II. Il *De imagine* nelle opere di Eriugena

A. *Le citazioni del* De imagine *nel* Periphyseon

Il *De imagine*, come già accennato, è largamente impiegato nel *Periphyseon*, specie nel libro 4, dove l'autore intraprende la riflessione antropologica a conclusione dell'esegesi sui sei giorni della creazione incominciata nel libro 3, servendosi, oltre che dell'opuscolo del Nisseno, del *De Paradiso* di Ambrogio e degli *Ambigua* di Massimo.[31] La sede è del resto quantomai appropriata, dato che Gregorio stesso aveva esplicitamente proposto la sua operetta come suggello all'*Hexaemeron* di Basilio di Cesarea, di cui pure il *Periphyseon* utilizza parti. All'incirca un quarto della traduzione nissena confluisce nell'opera eriugeniana maggiore,[32] il che la rende una possibile risorsa per la costituzione del testo del *De imagine*, ma obbliga altresì ad un confronto che renda ragione delle modalità del riutilizzo. Il fatto che Eriugena reimpieghi parti delle sue traduzioni nel *Periphyeson* presenta infatti delle implicazioni particolari, legate spesso alle complesse vicende della sua redazione, così come documentate dalla recente edizione di Édouard Jeauneau.[33]

---

[31] É. Jeauneau, 'Le *De Paradiso* d'Ambroise dans le livre IV du *Periphyseon*', in ΣΟΦΙΗΣ ΜΑΙΗΤΟΡΕΣ *(Chercheurs de sagesse). Hommage à Jean Pépin* – ed. M.-O. Goulet-Cazé – G. Madec – D. O'Brien, Paris, 1992, p. 561-571 (= 'Tendenda vela', cit., p. 217-229).

[32] A una stima quantitativa, le citazioni dal *De imagine* occupano all'incirca quattro colonne della *Patrologia* per i libri 1, 3 e 5 del *Periphyseon*, mentre ne occupano undici per il solo libro 4. Dobbiamo la gentile segnalazione a Édouard Jeauneau.

[33] Per riassumere le note conclusioni di Jeauneau (che tengono conto, tra l'altro di T. A. M. Bishop, 'Autographa of John the Scot', in *Jean Scot Erigène et l'histoire de la philosophie (Colloques internationaux du Centre national de la Recherche scientifique, n° 561, Laon 7-12 juillet 1975)* – ed. R. Roques, Paris, 1977, p. 89-94), del *Periphyseon* possediamo quattro versioni differenti, ciascuna delle quali è una "edizione riveduta" della precedente. Le prime due versioni sono tramandate per i libri 1-4 (il 4 è incompleto) dal ms. *R* (Reims, Bibliothèque municipale 875). La versione I vi è costituita dal nudo testo; la versione II è il frutto di modifiche e correzioni effettuate di suo pugno dall'autore (la mano i^1) e da un collaboratore sottoposto al suo controllo (la mano i^2), nonché da interventi in minuscola carolina (R^c), anch'essi presumibilmente controllati dall'Eriugena. Gli interventi di i^2 su *R* sembrano quelli di uno scriba che dietro indicazione di Eriugena copia dei brani che presumibilmente il filosofo gli aveva approntato. Abbiamo dunque su *R* correzioni autografe di Giovanni Scoto, che ci assicurano di trovarci di norma in presenza di una versione (II) sorvegliata dall'autore. La versione III, tramandata da *B* (Bamberg, Staatsbibliothek Philos. 2/1), è frutto di modifiche della versione II ad opera del solo collaboratore di Eriugena i^2. Gli interventi di i^2 sembrano ora quelli di un editore che

Abbiamo perciò confrontato il testo dei mss. *B C* con le varianti
R presenti nel ms. Reims 875 del *Periphyseon* (pubblicato nella *synopsis uersionum* di Jeauneau, contenente le versioni I-II dell'opera, ossia quelle ancora sotto il controllo autoriale e corredate di note autografe eriugeniane). Verso la fine del libro 4 del *Periphyseon* (855D) *R* viene meno: testimoni della versione II dell'opera restano perciò due mss. risalenti al XII secolo, *H* e *M* (rispettivamente Avranches, Bibliothèque municipale, 230 e Cambridge, Trinity College, O.5.20), nonché la *Clauis Physicae* di Honorius Augustodunensis, della quale, per la costituzione del testo, Jeauneau sceglie di riportare un codice siglato *A* (Paris, Bibliothèque Nationale, Lat. 6734). Relativamente al libro 5 dell'opera, perciò, le citazioni del *De imagine* contenute nel *Periphyseon* non corrispondono più necessariamente alle intenzioni di Eriugena: anche se le modifiche appaiono di norma minute, è bene menzionare questa differenza del libro 5 rispetto al resto dell'opera e tenerla presente nel confronto.[34]

---

lavora per suo conto su un testo ormai non più controllato dall'autore: i^2, cioè, non ricopia passi, bensì aggiunge glosse, titoli dei capitoli, rimandi interni; ma, in più, interpola anche maldestramente il testo del maestro, a volte giungendo a falsarne il pensiero in passaggi concettualmente delicati. Aggiunte di questo genere fatte da i^2 si trovano anche su *R*, e non è detto che anche lì non distorcano il senso del testo voluto dall'autore. È probabile che i^2 abbia fatto in un primo momento da scriba per conto di Eriugena, poi autonomamente da suo editore, giungendo a modificarne il testo su *R* e su *B*. Visto questo comportamento, si tratta di aggiunte che non possono essere considerate "autentiche", ossia volute dall'autore. La versione III, quindi, costituisce l'"edizione" dell'opera da parte di i^2 il quale, libero dal controllo autoriale, non esita ad intervenire con modifiche sostanziali sul testo voluto dall'autore. Infine, la versione IV è quella conservata sul ms. *P* (Paris, Bibliothèque nationale, Latin 12964), consistente nel testo della versione III, più aggiunte non riconducibili a nessuna delle due mani irlandesi e di solito decisamente inautentiche e deteriori. Cfr anche P. E. DUTTON, 'Eriugena's Workshop: The Making of the *Periphyseon* in Rheims 875', in *History and Eschatology in John Scottus Eriugena and His Time* – ed. M. Dunne – J. McEvoy, Leuven, 2002, p. 141-167, in part. 107-16; si veda anche É. JEAUNEAU, 'Le Periphyseon: son titre, son plan, ses remaniements', *Les Études philosophiques*, 104 (2013), p. 13-28, p. 24: "On s'accorde à reconnaître dans i^1 la main de Jean Scot et dans i^2 celle d'un de ses collaborateurs, que j'ai appelé Nisifortinus". Sull'ed. Jeauneau, cfr anche D. C. GREETHAM, 'Édouard Jeauneau's Edition of the *Periphyseon* in Light of Contemporary Editorial Theory', *American Catholic Philosophical Quarterly* 79 (2005), p. 527-548.

[34] In particolare, va tenuto presente che la *Clauis* per i primi quattro libri dell'opera e fino a V, 881B costituisce una riduzione del *Periphyseon*, con inserzioni di frasi di raccordo da parte di Onorio. Dopodiché, essa cita in modo più fedele, eccettuati piccoli adattamenti (omissione di rinvii interni ad altri libri del *Periphyseon*; la *Clauis* non è divisa in libri; la grafia non è più specchio delle abitudini di età carolingia, per cui ad esempio c'è la tendenza a sostituzioni come *sensilis* per *sensibilis*, *rationalis* per *rationabilis*). Sui debiti di Onorio nei confronti di Eriugena cfr D. YINGST, '*Quae Omnia Conco*r*diter Consonant*:

Nella presente edizione, il testo del *De imagine* è stato corretto sulla base di quello del *Periphyseon* soltanto nei casi in cui certamente è occorsa una svista o un'omissione sull'archetipo dei mss. *B C*, oppure nei casi in cui *B* e *C* divergevano e soltanto uno dei due si accordava con la lezione presente nel *Periphyseon*: in questo modo si è voluto evitare di trasferire indebitamente sul testo della traduzione a sé stante modifiche apportate solo successivamente nel *Periphyseon*.

La presenza di citazioni del *De imagine*, a volte modificate, all'interno del *Periphyseon*, pone infatti il problema di capire se vi sia stata da parte di Eriugena una revisione della traduzione (come nel caso della sua traduzione dello Pseudo-Dionigi Areopagita), e se questa revisione sia stata sistematica oppure relativa solamente alle parti confluite nel *Periphyseon*.

Sono stati distinti i seguenti casi:

1) su *R* la mano i^1 (= Eriugena) corregge sviste minute o errori del copista: in tal modo le citazioni dal *De imagine* risultano identiche a quelle tramandate dai testimoni diretti. Non si tratta perciò di interventi rilevanti sotto il profilo editoriale;

2) più significativi e complessi sono i casi in cui il *Periphyseon* si discosta dal testo di *B C*. Occorre distinguere in primo luogo fra le modifiche operate sul testo di *R* (versione II), e quelle presenti già nella versione I dell'opera (*R**, ossia *R* anteriormente a qualunque correzione o aggiunta).[35]

La versione II presenta modifiche dovute tanto a Eriugena quanto al suo segretario-editore. Si tratta evidentemente di modifiche introdotte nel *Periphyseon*, talora *supra lineam* o a margine, e non sull'autografo del *De imagine*. Esse appaiono per lo più miglioramenti stilistici, come ad esempio il cambiamento di modi e

---

Eriugena's Universe in the Thought of Honorius Augustodunensis', in *Eriugena and Creation: Proceedings of the Eleventh International Conference on Eriugenian Studies, held in honor of Edouard Jeauneau, Chicago, 9-12 November 2011* – ed. W. Otten – M. Allen, Turnhout, 2014, p. 427-461, con bibliografia.

[35] I casi tratti dal libro 5 sono stati esclusi in quanto, venendo meno il ms. *R* controllato dall'autore, non è più possibile distinguere al suo interno il testo "base" (versione I) dalle modifiche intervenutevi in un secondo momento, ad opera dell'autore o di altre mani (versione II). Non si può più distinguere, cioè, se una modifica nel testo del *Periphyseon* rispetto al testo del *De imagine* è stata introdotta fin dalla prima stesura (e quindi potrebbe rifarsi a una revisione della copia di lavoro del *De imagine*), oppure se è stata introdotta direttamente sul testo del *Periphyseon*; non è inoltre più possibile distinguere le mani all'opera nella revisione del *Periphyseon*.

tempi verbali (*De imag.* XI, 3-4), l'inserzione di particelle tipo *autem* o *vero*, oppure la sostituzione di *nonne* a *non* in un'interrogativa retorica (*De imag.* XVII, 7), presenza di glosse.

Tra questi casi possiamo segnalare:

p. 221, 23 Capp. = 92, 31 (= *Periphys.* 4, 788B-789A), *necessarium est* corretto in *necessarium erit*;

p. 221, 25 = 92, 33-34 (= 4, 788B-789A) *comprehenderet* corretto in *comprehenderit*;

p. 221, 26 = 92, 34 (= 4, 788B-789A) *esset* corretto in *erit*;

p. 224, 29 = 98, 25-26 (= 4, 789A-790B) *informitati* corretto *in informitate* (cfr καὶ τῇ ἀμορφίᾳ ταύτης συνδιεφθάρη τὸ κάλλος τῆς φύσεως, *PG* 44, 161D11-2);

p. 225, 10 = 99, 39 (= 4, 789A-790B) *ex his ostenditur* corretto in *ex his autem ostenditur*;

p. 225, 29 = 99, 62 (= 4, 790B) *in natura manet*, che diviene *in natura (hoc est in imagine animi) manet.*

p. 225, 29 = 99, 62 (= 4, 790B) *cum* corretto in *dum*;

p. 230, 21 = 108, 24 (= 4, 792A-D) *etsi intellectuali*, che diviene *si in intellectuali*;

p. 231, 12 = 109, 22 (= 3, 737A) *sic igitur anima est dum intellectuali*, modificato in *si uero in "anima intellectuali"*;

p. 231, 32 = 110, 45 (= 4, 792D-793A) *comprehendens* corretto in *comprehensus*;

p. 233, 7 = 112, 49 (= 4, 793C-797C) *igitur* corretto in *itaque*;

p. 233, 18 = 113, 66 (= 4, 793C-797C) *non* corretto in *nonne*;

p. 234, 20 = 114, 109 (4, 793C-797C) *participationi*, corretto in *suae participationi*;

p. 234, 28 = 115, 119 (4, 793C-797C) *non est igitur*, corretto in *non ergo est*;

p. 245, 33 = 135, 17 (1, 502B-503A) *eorum* modificato in *earum* (forse per il senso);

p. 245, 37 = 135, 25 (1, 502B-503A) *soluitur* corretto in *soluetur*;

p. 245, 39 = 135, 27 (1, 502B-503A) *res (oycia)* corretto in *res id est OYCIA*.

Di un certo interesse è il caso di p. 231, 33-34 = 110, 47 (4, 792D-793A), ove *intelligibilem* è corretto in *inintelligibilem*.

Oltre alla mano *Ri¹* di Eriugena, il ms. *R* del *Periphyseon* ha un testo su cui intervengono con varianti redazionali anche una seconda mano irlandese, denominata *Ri²*, e una mano che scrive in carolina, *Rᶜ*; si tratta di pochi casi, plausibilmente autorizzati da Eriugena, che pure lavorava su questo manoscritto. Anche qui le modifiche sono certamente intervenute sul testo del *Periphyseon*, e non sull'autografo del *De imagine*. Parimenti, si ha a che fare con miglioramenti stilistici volti a rendere più piana la traduzione, ad esempio attraverso l'esplicitazione di alcuni punti (*De imag.* XX, 5; XXI, 3), oppure tramite la sostituzione di *per* più accusativo con un ablativo semplice (*De imag.* XIIII, 1; XVIII, 4):

p. 226, 3 Capp. = 100, 4 (= *Periphys.* 4, 791C-792A) *per motum* è corretto in *motu* da R^c;
p. 237, 26 = 120, 63 (= 4, 797D-799A; 4, 812A) *per prognosticam operationem* è corretto in 4,812A in *prognostica operatione* da R^c;
p. 240, 33 = 126, 42 (4, 819A-820A) *uitae ligno omne lignum*, corretto in *lignum uitae et 'omne lignum'* da Ri^2 (cfr gr. τῷ τῆς ζωῆς ξύλῳ τὸ πᾶν ξύλον: *PG* 44, 197B3-4);
p. 242, 19 = 128, 46 (4, 820A-821D) *alicui* è corretto in margine da Ri^2 in *alicui bono*.

Più difficile è stabilire se le modifiche presenti fin dalla versione I dell'opera (R^*) possano essere state introdotte o ancora sull'autografo del *De imagine*, ovvero come varianti redazionali sul ms. del *Periphyseon* che doveva costituire l'antigrafo di R^* (vale a dire su un anello intermedio non verificabile fra l'autografo eriugeniano del *De imagine* e il ms. *R* del *Periphyseon*). In breve, è incerto se queste modifiche siano state effettuate ancora sul testo del *De imagine* o già su una prima copia, precedente a R, della versione I del *Periphyseon*. Un primo gruppo di casi, appartenenti a varie citazioni, sembra aver subito anche qui solo dei piccoli ritocchi di forma. Oltre a questi, però, si segnala come caso particolare quello di una lunga citazione in *Periphys.* 4 819A-821D, che riporta integralmente i capitoli XX-XXI del *De imagine*, omettendone solo i titoli (al posto del titolo del cap. XXI Eriugena segnala il passaggio da un capitolo all'altro con una frase di raccordo: *Idem in uicesimo primo eiusdem sermonis capitulo*: *Periphys.* 4, 820A). Nella citazione di questi due capitoli colpisce l'abbondanza di discrepanze del testo citato nel *Periphyseon* rispetto al testo del *De imagine*. Questi casi, quando non sono anch'essi miglioramenti stilistici, consistono in delle esplicitazioni della resa latina di Eriugena, che qui però tendono con frequenza ad assumere l'aspetto di vere e proprie brevi glosse lessicali: così *pan* (πᾶν) viene chiarito nel testo del *Periphyseon* con *id est omne*; il pronome *illud* col suo referente *lignum*; *diiudicationis* con *hoc est discretionis*; e così via. Si tratta probabilmente di glosse introdotte dall'autore, simili a quelle già evidenziate.

Tali ad esempio:

p. 226, 4 Capp. = 100, 5 (= *Periphys.* 4, 791C-792A) *stanti*, corretto in *stante*;

p. 226, 10 = 100, 12 (= 4, 791C-792A) *mutabilitate*, che diviene *post mutabilitatem*;

p. 231, 15 = 109, 25 (= 3, 737A) *coutens*, corretto in *utens*

p. 231, 22 = 109, 33 (= 3, 739C) *talibus* (*gr.* ἐν τούτοις; *PG* 44, 177A14), modificato in *hominibus* (forse per il senso)

p. 231, 26-7 = 109, 38-39 (4, 792D-793A) *non in parte... comprehenditur*, modificato in *in parte... non comprehenditur*;

p. 234, 23 = 114, 112 (= 4, 793C-797C) *percipere*, corretto in *perficere*;

p. 235, 15 = 116, 151 (= 4, 793C-797C) *erat*, corretto in *est*;

p. 236, 35 = 119, 31 (= 4, 797D-799A) *autem* è omesso su *R**;

p. 237, 5 = 119, 38 (= 4, 797D-799A) *sic in*, corretto in *sic enim in*;

p. 237, 22 = 120, 59 (= 4, 797D-799A; 4, 812A) *qui enim omnia*, corretto in *qui omnia*.

Il caso dei capitoli XX-XXI rientra inoltre in una ampia parte di testo in cui il ms. *R* sembra non essere stato riveduto dall'autore: a partire da *Periphys.* 4, 810D, infatti, le note della mano *i¹* scompaiono, per ricomparire soltanto in un punto ormai vicino alla fine del libro 4 (854B-C). Forse Eriugena non ha rivisto questo testo su *R* perché aveva già lavorato su di esso in qualche momento fra la traduzione del *De imagine* e la prima stesura del *Periphyseon*, di cui la versione I del ms. *R* costituisce già una copia.

Resta da domandarsi in quale momento queste modifiche furono apportate da Eriugena, se già sul testo del *De imagine* oppure solo al momento della trascrizione di suoi estratti nel *Periphyseon*.

Il *De imagine* contiene un passo (XVII, 5) che si trova citato in due luoghi diversi del *Periphyseon* (801A-C; 4, 802C): nel *De imagine* il ms. *B* (*C* termina prima di questo punto) reca *ab ea uidelicet anima ignorantur*; così riporta anche la prima delle due citazioni nel *Periphyseon*; la seconda, invece, ha solamente *ab ea ignorantur* (così anche il testo greco). Si direbbe che nell'archetipo di *B C* le parole *uidelicet anima* non fossero a testo, ma, ad esempio, in posizione interlineare, donde il differente trattamento nelle due citazioni nel *Periphyseon*. Tuttavia, il testo del *De imagine* contiene alcune brevi glosse esplicative che sono state verosimilmente introdotte da Eriugena nell'archetipo di *B C*, dunque la presenza di un'aggiunta come quella appena menzionata non dimostra la volontà di una vera e propria revisione del *De imagine*, ma soltanto l'intento di Eriugena di chiarire in alcuni punti la propria traduzione. Questo stesso intento plausibilmente ha motivato anche le aggiunte nelle citazioni dei capitoli XX-XXI del *De imagine* al momento della loro trascrizione sull'antigrafo del ms. *R* del *Periphyseon*.[36]

Infine, un altro passo del *De imagine* (XV, 2) viene citato due volte nel *Periphyseon*, una volta nel libro 3 (736B) e una nel libro 4 (792C). Eriugena nel *De imagine* era incorso in una svista di traduzione, lasciando in latino al nominativo un participio che era accusativo nell'originale greco: *perque omnem uirtutem penetrans* (τὴν δὲ λογικὴν καὶ τελείαν δι' ἁπάσης διήκουσαν τῆς δυνάμεως). Nella prima citazione di questo passo all'interno del *Periphyseon* la svista si trova già corretta sul ms. *R*, la seconda volta invece no, rimanendo così uguale a come figurava nel *De imagine*. La differenza di trattamento della svista nel testo del *Periphyseon* fa verosimilmente pensare che essa sia stata modificata solamente al momento della sua trascrizione all'interno di quest'ultima opera.

Concludendo, l'impressione complessiva è che l'interesse di Eriugena fosse focalizzato sul testo del *Periphyseon*, piuttosto che sulla traduzione a sé stante. Quest'ultima sarà rimasta allo stadio di autografo provvisorio, sul quale l'autore potrebbe anche non essersi curato di correggere i propri errori di traduzione. Con questa situazione collima del resto la presenza, sull'archetipo di *B C*, di glosse presumibilmente in posizione ancora interlineare o comunque non ancora a testo, e l'aggiunta di ulteriori note esplicative minime inframmezzate alla citazione dei capitoli XX-XXI della traduzione all'interno del *Periphyseon*. Insieme all'assenza di dedica in testa alla traduzione e al numero ridotto dei testimoni dell'opera, questi dati fanno propendere per traduzione rimasta limitata all'utilizzo privato da parte del suo autore, principal-

---

[36] Tra le aggiunte fatte a questi capitoli, soltanto quella di *illud (lignum uidelicet)* nel citare da *De imag.* XXI, 1, è senz'altro avvenuta al momento della trascrizione sul *Periphyseon*. Infatti la menzione del *lignum*, referente di *illud*, si trovava nell'unica parte del testo dei capitoli XX-XXI che non è stata citata: il titolo del cap. XXI (*Qualis in paradiso uita et quid uetitum illud lignum*). Occorre perciò pensare che questa sia una glossa eriugeniana introdotta durante la stesura della versione I del *Periphyseon*, cioè soltanto al momento del riutilizzo del *De imagine* nell'opera maggiore. Questo caso, tuttavia, non comporta naturalmente una revisione del testo: sarà semplicemente stato inserito per chiarimento quando i due capitoli del *De imagine* sono stati introdotti nell'antigrafo del ms. *R* del *Periphyseon*.

mente in vista dei suoi reimpieghi nel quadro del *Periphyseon*, sua opera originale.[37]

Benché lavoro minore, perciò, questa versione dal greco assume una sua rilevanza: come testimonianza da un lato del lavoro di Giovanni Scoto traduttore, dall'altro della sua ricezione dei contenuti concettuali del testo di partenza, nonché della sua attenzione e riflessione intorno ad essi. Del resto, come rileva Édouard Jeauneau, proprio in questo doppio ruolo di traduttore e di pensatore (o, se preferiamo, di "ripensatore") consiste il tratto forse più singolare di questo autore.[38]

B. *Presenza del* De imagine *in altre opere opere eriugeniane*

La cronologia delle opere di Eriugena è molto incerta e ampiamente ipotetica. Le sue traduzioni vengono di solito datate all'incirca agli stessi anni della stesura del *Periphyseon*, per la cui composizione il *terminus ante quem* di norma accettato è l'866, sulla base dell'epistola di Eriugena all'amico Wulfad apposta in chiusa all'opera.

Citazioni letterali e ampi stralci del *De imagine* si ritrovano soltanto nel *Periphyseon*; tuttavia, fra le altre opere originali di Eriugena si possono forse ravvisare reminiscenze e riproposizioni *ad sensum* di passi argomentativi del *De opificio hominis*. Nella prima

---

[37] Altre osservazioni sulle modifiche apportate da Eriugena nelle sue citazioni dal *De imagine* (in part. sui capp. XII, XIII e XIV) e da altre sue traduzioni si trova nell'articolo di E. S. MAINOLDI, 'Le citazioni filosofiche dei Padri orientali', cit., per il quale (p. 263): «Eriugena ritorna sovente sul testo tradotto per renderlo più comprensibile; probabilmente egli non dispone più del testo greco, cosa che indicherebbe lo stacco cronologico tra la traduzione e la sua citazione nel *Periphyseon*; la IV versione del dialogo eriugeniano evidenzia la tendenza a un'ulteriore revisione del testo del Nisseno, evidentemente perché la sua resa in latino appariva oscura a chi si applicò a questa redazione, ma i risultati di questi interventi legittimano il dubbio che non siano riconducibili *in toto* alla penna di Giovanni Scoto».

[38] É. JEAUNEAU, 'Pseudo-Dionysius, Gregory of Nyssa', cit., p. 139 (= *Études érigéniennes*, p. 177). Cfr anche quanto osservato a p. XIX e XXII di *Iohannis Scotti seu Eriugenae Periphyseon*, vol. I, Turnhout, 1996 (CC *CM*, 161): si tratta «non d'un produit fini, mais d'une matière en fusion, non point d'un texte établi et fixé de façon canonique, mais d'un texte en perpetuel devenir». T. BUDDE, 'The Three Recensions of the *Versio Dionysii*', *Journal of Medieval Latin* 17 (2008), p. 253-272 e M. CUPICCIA, 'Le sorti di un testo tradotto, rivisto e commentato. Il corpus pseudo-dionysiacum nella versione latina di Giovanni Scoto (secc. IX-XII)', *Filologia mediolatina* 16 (2009), p. 57-80, dimostrano come un analogo processo di riscrittura subì la versione delle opere dello pseudo-Dionigi Areopagita.

opera eriugeniana sicuramente databile, il *De praedestinatione* (composto nell'850-51 per contrastare le tesi di Godescalco d'Orbais), sono riscontrabili alcuni passi, per quanto non molto estesi e spesso parafrasati, i cui contenuti corrispondono ad argomentazioni del *De opificio hominis*: in tal caso, Eriugena dovrebbe aver avuto conoscenza dell'opera diversi anni prima di quanto normalmente si ritiene: anche la sua traduzione potrebbe essere allora retrodatata, a meno di non supporre che egli leggesse o utilizzasse anche la traduzione di Dionigi il Piccolo.[39]

Un primo punto di contatto del *De praedestinatione* con i contenuti del *De opificio hominis* riguarda il libero arbitrio dell'uomo. In Gregorio (*hom. opif.* XVI = *De imag.* XVII), l'argomentazione mostra che l'uomo è stato fatto ad immagine di Dio nel senso che Dio lo ha reso partecipe della pienezza dei suoi beni, fra i quali la libertà. Eriugena riprende quest'idea, dopo aver dimostrato che la libera volontà divina è identica con Dio stesso, spiegando che, proprio *in quanto* Dio ha fatto l'uomo a sua immagine, gli ha fornito come parte di quest'immagine il libero arbitrio, che risulta perciò parte ineliminabile dell'immagine divina nell'uomo, anche dopo il peccato originale (*De praed.* 4, 5, 373A; cfr *De imag.* XVII, 10-2). Un secondo punto di contatto è da ravvisare nell'idea della predeterminazione del numero complessivo delle anime da parte di Dio al momento della creazione del primo uomo (*De praed.* XVII, 8, 434C-D; cfr *De imag.* XVIII, 4).

Un ulteriore argomento di Gregorio di Nissa che sembra essere stato riproposto da Eriugena nel contesto del *De praedestinatione* è quello relativo alla limitatezza del male rispetto all'infinità del bene, e la necessaria soggezione del primo alle leggi del secondo. Nel cap. XXI del *De opificio hominis*, infatti, Gregorio argomentava l'impossibilità umana di esaurire la progressione verso il bene: il male è al contrario racchiuso dentro confini necessari. Per la natura creata, che è in costante movimento, questo comporta la necessità, una volta percorsa per intero ed esaurita l'estensione del male, di rivolgersi poi all'infinità del bene (come uscendo alla luce da una zona d'ombra). Anche quest'argomento si ritrova nel *De praedestinatione* (XVIII, 7-8, 434AD; cfr *De imag.* XXII).[40] A

---

[39] Come è incline a pensare ad es. É. JEAUNEAU, in Jean Scot, *Homélie*, cit. p. 35 (= *Études érigéniennes*, cit., p. 39).

[40] Altri cenni sono probabilmente da ravvisarsi relativamente al modo della resurrezione finale: cfr *De imag.* XXVI, 2 e XXVII, 2 con *praed.* XIX, 436D-437A (sulla riu-

confermare che Eriugena avesse in mente il *De opificio hominis* può concorrere il fatto che proprio quest'ultimo cenno di Gregorio viene esplicitamente ripreso nelle *Expositiones in Ierarchiam Coelestem*, datata indicativamente agli anni fra l'865 e l'870 (qui l'accento è spostato sulla nozione dell'infinità del bene e, conseguentemente, sull'infinità della ricerca della divinità):

> ... quamuis beatus Gregorius Theologus, [41] in sermone *De imagine*, patenter asseruerit omnem rationalem et intellectualem creaturam eternaliter ac sine fine Deum suum uidere desideraturam et quesituram. Quoniam infinitum est quod querit, necesse est ut infinite querat, et quodammodo inueniat et quodammodo non inueniat: inueniat quidem ipsius theophaniam, non inueniat ipsius substantiam. Scriptum est enim: "Dei occultum nemo uidit, neque uidebit".
> (Eriugena, *Expositiones in Ierarchiam Coelestem* VI, 1)

Oltre ai richiami presenti nel *De praedestinatione*, il *De imagine* ha lasciato tracce di sé anche in materiale esegetico di provenienza eriugeniana. Édouard Jeauneau, infatti, ha pubblicato delle glosse al I libro del *De nuptiis* di Marziano Capella, tramandate dal ms. Oxford, Bodl. Lib., Auct. T. 2.19, che costituiscono con tutta probabilità la trascrizione o comunque una rielaborazione di un commento eriugeniano a tale opera. [42] Un passo di queste glosse ha verosimilmente come fonte i contenuti del *De imagine*:

> Hymeneus: Isidorus dicit membranulam in lumbis possitam. Qui autem de natura rerum disputant aiunt duas membranulas esse, una quae est circa cerebrum quae grece uocatur ΜΗΝΙΚΑ, altera uero quae est in lateribus, quae gr(ece) dicitur ΦΡΕΝ, inde frenetica passio.
> (ms. Oxford, Bodl. Libr. Auct. T. 2. 19, f. 1ᵛ; ed. Jeauneau, p 102-103)

---

nione dei quattro elementi a formare i corpi dei defunti al momento della resurrezione); e cfr *De imag.* XXX, 20 con *praed.* XIX, 437A-B (sull'elemento igneo che attira in sé le qualità degli elementi inferiori come nutrimento). Cfr forse anche *De imag.* I, 2 con *praed.* XVII, 8, 429B (sul riferimento al fuoco incorporeo, non chiaro se attribuito a Gregorio Nisseno o a Gregorio Magno: in merito si veda E. S. MAINOLDI, 'Le fonti del *De praedestinatione liber* di Giovanni Scoto Eriugena', *Studi Medievali* 45/2 (2004), p. 651-698, in part. 657-659).

[41] Sulla confusione presente talora nell'Eriugena tra Gregorio di Nissa e Gregorio di Nazianzo (designato correntemente in età bizantina come 'Teologo') cfr n. 58.

[42] Le glosse del ms. oxoniense sono edite in É. JEAUNEAU, *Quatre thèmes érigéniens*, Montréal-Paris 1978 (*Conférence Albert-le-Grand 1974*), p. 91-166.

Queste brevi righe si possono confrontare con *De imag.* XII, 2-4, dove si ritrova la menzione del "pensiero di quelli che disputano cose del genere sulla natura", nel testo greco di Gregorio κατὰ τὸν λόγον τῶν τὰ τοιαῦτα φυσιολογούντων (*hom. opif.* 157C), tradotto con *iuxta rationem talia philosophantium de natura*. Anche il *De imagine* ricorda inoltre la *frenecin*, malattia delle membrane dette *frenes*.

Il secondo passo delle glosse nomina Gregorio esplicitamente, riferendosi senz'ombra di dubbio al cap. XXVIII del *De opificio hominis*. Nell'originale greco, si tratta della menzione della dottrina di Empedocle (fr. B117 Diels):

> Gregorius Nyseus, germanus Basilii, ait quia iuuenis quidam dicebat se esse aliquando sicut uir, aliquando sicut femina, uel etiam sicut uolatile, uel sicut piscis, uel sicut rana. Ideo dicit hoc propter nimiam miseriam animarum.
> (ms. Oxford, Bodl. Libr. Auct. T. 2. 19, f. 11ᵛ; ed. Jeauneau, p. 122)

Il riferimento è a *De imag.* XXVIII, 3 (*hom. opif.* 28, 232A).[43] Eriugena peraltro sembra qui aver inteso il riferimento di Gregorio alla dottrina della trasmigrazione delle anime nel senso della mutevolezza dei pensieri dell'anima.[44]

Ad ogni modo, non conoscendo la datazione di queste glosse, è difficile ricavarne informazioni sul momento in cui Eriugena poté leggere e forse già tradurre l'opera di Gregorio.

Un piccolo indizio testuale fa pensare che Eriugena, all'epoca in cui tradusse il *De imagine*, conoscesse già le opere dello Pseudo-Dionigi: a *De imag.* XVI, 3, p. 110, 47, infatti, traduce l'aggettivo greco ἀμήχανον ("inspiegabile, incomprensibile", riferito al modo di unione dell'anima al corpo) con *superrationabilem*. Si tratta di una scelta terminologica di traduzione certo non suggerita dal vocabolo greco, ma che rimanda piuttosto per la sua morfologia ai composti con ὑπερ-/*super*- caratteristici del vocabolario dello

---

[43] Il greco non parla di uno *iuuenis*, come le glosse, ma di "un sapiente" (φασί τινα τῶν παρ' ἐκείνοις σοφῶν εἰρηκέναι, ὅτι...: 232A): siccome il testo greco difficilmente avrà dato luogo a un equivoco, si può supporre o una citazione a memoria, oppure forse che Eriugena abbia presente anche la citazione che di questo frammento fa Calcidio, *in Tim.* 197, dove si dice che il sapiente in questione assunse fra le varie forme anche quella di *puer* (su Calcidio tra le possibili fonti eriugeniane cfr É. JEAUNEAU, in Jean Scot, *Homélie*, cit., p. 41 (= *Études érigéniennes*, p. 45).

[44] *Non enim semper mens uniuscuiusque hominis in eodem statu est, sed per uices sic, per uices etiam sic: aliquando enim bona cogitat et ibi si perseueraberit felix erit, aliquando mala et in illis si perseuerauerit mergetur et non ad ripam perueniet*: f. 11ʳ (p. 122 Jeauneau).

Pseudo-Dionigi e conseguentemente della sua traduzione eriugeniana.[45]

Per quanto riguarda la presenza del *De imagine* nelle due opere più tarde di Eriugena, ovvero l'omelia sul prologo del vangelo di Giovanni *Vox spiritualis aquilae* (*Homilia super 'In principio erat Verbum'*) e il *Commentarius in Euangelium Iohannis* (forse l'ultima opera del maestro irlandese, rimasta incompiuta per la sua morte), si possono notare alcune altri riscontri. In *Hom.* IV, 1,[46] è un richiamo al *De imagine* che dirime la scelta di una lezione: nell'omelia, l'irlandese si riferisce a Giovanni Evangelista come a uno *spirituale petasum*; proprio questo termine era già stato da lui adoperato per tradurre l'espressione τῶν μουσικῶν ὀρνίθων di Gregorio di Nissa nel cap. I del *De opificio hominis* (*musicorum petasum*: *De imag.* I, 5, p. 74, 78), termine probabilmente rinvenuto nel *De nuptiis* di Marziano Capella (I, 26; II, 176, dove tuttavia è usato in senso letterale).[47]

Nel *Commentarius*, infine, Eriugena recupera un'osservazione tratta da *De imag.* XVII, 1-2). Commentando il versetto giovanneo *Sic enim deus dilexit mundum ut filium suum unigenitum daret* (Gv 3, 16), Eriugena intende l'affermazione "Dio ha amato il mondo" nel senso che il *mundus* è l'uomo, nel quale in qualche maniera tutte le cose sono state create (tema sviluppato nel libro 4 del *Periphyseon* e ripreso nell'*Homilia* – si v. ad es. il cap. XIX – oltre che nel *Commentarius*). Eriugena specifica qui che il termine *mundus* nel senso di "uomo" non deve fuorviare: l'uomo non è propriamente "mondo", ossia non è un microcosmo in quanto composto degli stessi quattro elementi corporei che compongono l'universo-macrocosmo.[48] Il greco, il cui uso linguistico è secondo Eriugena di solito più rivelatore, indirizza meglio: l'uomo è detto

---

[45] Può darsi che l'errore sia dovuto al fraintendimento di ἀ- (con valore intensivo anziché privativo), come nel caso di ἄπιστος reso con *fidelis* in *Amb.* XVII, 88: cfr É. JEAUNEAU, 'Jean Scot Érigène: grandeur et misère', cit., p. 104 (= p. 238), ovvero nel caso di ἀτεχνῶς con *valde artificialiter* (*Expos.* II, 124): cfr ID., 'Jean Scot Érigène et le grec', cit., p. 47.

[46] *Iohannis Scotti seu Eriugenae Homilia super 'In principio erat uerbum' et Commentarius in Euangelium Iohannis* – ed. É. Jeauneau, Turnhout, 2008 (CC CM, 166), p. 8.

[47] Cfr in merito la discussione in Jean Scot, *Homélie*, cit., appendice I, p. 319-322. La lezione *petasum* è peraltro confermata dall'altro testimone diretto del *De imagine*, il già visto ms. *C* (f. 122ᵛ). Per l'idea cfr A. KIJEWSKA, 'The Eriugenian Concept of Theology. John the Evangelist as the Model Theologian, in *Iohannis Scottus Eriugena. The Bible and Hermeneutics* – ed. G. van Riel – C. Steel – J. McEvoy, Leuven, 1996, p. 173-193.

[48] Sul tema in Gregorio di Nissa cfr R. CHVÁTAL, 'Der Mensch als Mikrokosmos in den Werken Gregors von Nyssa', *Revue des Études Byzantines*, 62 (2004), p. 47-70.

"mondo" nel senso del greco κόσμος, che ha per Eriugena il significato primario e più proprio di *ornatus*. L'uomo amato da Dio è cioè detto dal Vangelo "mondo", nel senso di "ornato", in quanto reca in sé l'immagine divina, consistente nell'anima:

> Sed quaeritur quem mundum dilexit deus. Non enim credendum est mundum istum, id est uniuersitatem quae constat ex caelo et terra, patrem dilexisse. Ille enim non propter se ipsum, sed propter superiorem mundum factus est. Mundum igitur superiorem, quem ad imaginem et similitudinem suam condidit, id est humanam naturam, pater dilexit ita ut filium suum pro eo traderet. Sed notandum quod mundus quem pater dilexit, id est, homo, non propterea mundus uocatur quod quattuor elementis constiterit, quod solum secundum corpus fieri in terreno adhuc homine consideratur; sed ideo homo 'cosmos' uocatur quoniam ornatus est ad imaginem et similitudinem dei quae, uel solum uel maxime, in anima intelligitur. 'Cosmos' quippe graece ornatus proprie interpretatur, non mundus.
> (Eriugena, *Commentarius in euangelium Iohannis*, 3, 6, p. 88, 8-89, 20 = 320D-321A)

La medesima idea dell'"uomo-mondo", ossia dell'uomo microcosmo in quanto composto, nella sua parte corporea, degli stessi quattro elementi (aria, acqua, fuoco, terra) che compongono il creato, era già stata respinta da Gregorio di Nissa (*hom. opif.* 16): proprio in polemica con questa concezione il Cappadoce aveva additato nell'immagine di Dio la vera ragione della preminenza dell'uomo sulle altre creature. Eriugena, pur brevemente, ripropone la stessa considerazione.

Da questi riscontri, selezionati fra altri possibili, si possono dedurre la conoscenza e l'utilizzo del *De opificio hominis* di Gregorio da parte di Eriugena già dall'851 col *De praedestinatione*, pur senza avere la certezza che ne avesse già allora effettuata la traduzione, fino alle opere più tarde, normalmente datate agli anni '70 del IX secolo. L'utilizzo maggiore, tuttavia, rimane naturalmente quello testimoniato nel *Periphyseon*.

*
* *

III. L'ESEMPLARE GRECO

A differenza della versione eriugeniana del *corpus* dello Pseudo-Dionigi Areopagita, per la quale è noto il manoscritto greco che servì da esemplare per la traduzione (BNF Gr. 437), nel caso del *De imagine* non è stato possibile identificare il testimone greco sul quale lavorò Eriugena.

Non ultima delle ragioni è l'assenza di un'edizione critica soddisfacente del testo greco del *De opificio hominis* di Gregorio, su cui basarsi per un tentativo definitivo di identificazione del testimone in questione. L'unica edizione con apparato critico, fondata soltanto su un campione incompleto di testimoni, è quella ottocentesca curata da George Hay Forbes,[49] mentre, come è noto, il testo stampato nella *Patrologia* del Migne riprende l'edizione compiuta nel XVI secolo da Johannes Leunclavius. È stato quindi necessario fare riferimento al testo di Forbes: la divisione in capitoli e paragrafi del testo del *De imagine* fornito nella presente edizione corrisponde a quella dell'edizione di Forbes; fra le varianti riportate nel suo apparato, inoltre, sono state scelte e indicate nell'apparato al testo del *De imagine* quelle che rendevano conto di determinate traduzioni eriugeniane.

Édouard Jeauneau si era già servito dell'edizione Forbes per individuare quella che finora rimane la migliore approssimazione all'esemplare greco utilizzato da Eriugena: si tratta del ms. Paris, BNF Coislin 235 (fine X – inizio XI sec.),[50] da Forbes siglato *q* e da Jeauneau nella sua edizione del *Periphyseon G*; nell'apparato della presente edizione esso figura come *q*, per consentire di individuarlo più agevolmente sull'edizione Forbes (da tale apparato si ricava un altro codice che presenta lezioni singolari, talora affini

---

[49] *Sancti Patris Nostri Gregorii Nysseni Basili Magni fratris opera quae supersunt omnia*, I, 1-2 – ed. G. H. Forbes, Burntisland, 1855-1861, p. 96-319. L'edizione presenta a fronte anche il testo critico della traduzione di Dionigi il Piccolo.

[50] Come gli altri manoscritti appartenenti al fondo Coislin della Bibliothèque Nationale, anche questo giunse dall'Oriente in Europa in età moderna, procurato al cancelliere francese Séguier († 1672) da un sacerdote greco, il padre Atanasio: cfr R. Devreesse, *Catalogue des Manuscrits grecs*, II: *Le Fonds Coislin*, Paris 1945, p. VI. Coislin 235 contiene le *Homiliae in Hexaemeron* di Basilio (f. 1^r-121^r), seguite dal *De opificio hominis* (f. 121^r-208^v). Le ultime pagine del ms. (f. 209^r-219^v), contenenti frammenti dell'*Apologia in Hexaemeron* di Gregorio di Nissa, sono state inserite da un altro codice più tardo (XIII-XIV sec.).

alle scelte di Eriugena, ossia il Marcianus Graecus 58 [coll. 499], della fine del IX – inizi del X secolo, siglato *n*).[51]

Il ms. *q*, insieme ad alcuni altri testimoni greci, presenta diverse particolarità che lo accomunano al testo del *De imagine* eriugeniano: nonostante il cap. XXII sia presente (f. 174ᵛ-178ᵛ), anche *q* spezza in due capitoli distinti il cap. XII, e ha una lacuna finale, sebbene non perfettamente coincidente con l'omissione del *De imagine* (da poco dopo il punto in cui nel *De imagine* si trova l'omissione fino alla fine; la lacuna inizia dopo le parole ἀτελὲς ἐν τῷ ἀτελεῖ, καὶ ἐν τῷ...: *PG* 44, 253D); le prime parole del cap. XXII (XXIII), Ἀλλὰ τῆς ἀκολουθίας τῶν ἐξητασμένων ἐχώμεθα (*PG* 44, 204b3), sono invece attestate come ultime del cap. XXI (XXII). La corrispondenza fra le scelte di traduzione di Eriugena e singole varianti testuali del ms. greco rafforzano la somiglianza. Tra queste Jeauneau ha notato:

PG 44, 176B3 ὥστε συγκρότημά τι πολλῶν ψυχῶν τὴν ἀνθρωπίνην φύσιν νομίζειν, che viene reso (XV, 2, p. 230, 23-24 Capp. = 108, 27-28) *ita ut conformatione multarum animarum humanam esse arbitretur*: ciò farebbe pensare ad una lettura συγκροτήματι e all'omissione di φύσιν, come accade nel ms. *q*.

PG 44, 188D2-3 ὁ πρὸ τῆς παραβάσεως βίος ἀγγελικός τις ἦν: Eriugena scrive (XVIII, 2, p. 237, 2-3 Capp. = 119, 35) *ante ruinam angelus quidam erat*, il che ben si accorda con la lezione di *q*, ὁ πρὸ τῆς καταπτώσεως ὡς ἄγγελος τις ἦν.

PG 44, 200B3 τὴν διαφθοράν è reso da Eriugena (XXI,3 p. 242, 7 Capp. = 128, 32) *differentiam*, che corrisponde a τὴν διαφοράν di *q*.

Si deve tuttavia osservare che *q*, insieme ai codici siglati *a b c i k m n r t*, appartiene ad una delle due famiglie della tradizione così come identificata da Forbes e che a questa stessa famiglia dovette appartenere anche il testo impiegato da Dionigi il Piccolo;[52] si deve poi tener presente che in altri casi, viceversa, le lezioni peculiari di *q* non sembrano accordarsi con il testo eriugeniano: tanto delle somiglianze quanto delle divergenze più significative ab-

---

[51] É. JEAUNEAU, 'Érigène et Grégoire de Nysse', in *Du copiste au collectionneur: mélanges d'histoire des textes et des bibliothèques en l'honneur d'André Vernet* – ed. D. Nebbiai-Dalla Guarda – J. F. Genest, Turnhout, 1998, p. 57-69 (= 'Tendenda vela', cit., p. 201-215); l'ipotesi è riproposta con dettagli su singole varianti del testo greco in *Iohannis Scotti seu Eriugenae Periphyseon* – ed. É. Jeauneau, vol. 4, Turnhout 2000 (CC CM, 164), p. XLI

[52] É. JEAUNEAU, 'Érigène et Grégoire de Nysse', cit., p. 66 s. (= 212 s.).

biamo dato ragione in apparato. Inoltre, il testo del *De imagine* è privo, su entrambi i testimoni *B C*, di quello che nell'edizione Forbes è il paragrafo 3 del capitolo I: può darsi che anche questa omissione sia dovuta all'esemplare greco.

Solo una futura edizione del testo greco di Gregorio di Nissa potrà dunque apportare qualche nuova conoscenza riguardo al codice greco impiegato da Eriugena, oppure quantomeno testimoniare la presenza di ulteriori varianti o lezioni peculiari, come anche caratteristiche testuali analoghe a quelle della versione latina (titolo; assenza del capitolo omesso dal *De imagine*, lacuna in prossimità della fine dell'opera, e simili).[53]

Infine, sembra necessario segnalare che probabilmente ancora non siamo a conoscenza di tutto il materiale greco a disposizione di Eriugena: questi, infatti, nel suo *Periphyseon* cita alcuni brani dalle *Homiliae in Hexaemeron* di Basilio di Cesarea, l'opera a cui Gregorio di Nissa aveva voluto esplicitamente ricongiungersi con il *De opificio hominis*: alla sua morte nel 379, infatti, Basilio lasciò incompiuta la sua esegesi dei sei giorni della creazione prima di poterne esaminare l'ultima creatura, l'uomo: di qui la ripresa di Gregorio, e di qui anche una tradizione manoscritta spesso congiunta delle due opere, a volte insieme anche ad altre due omelie

---

[53] Martin Reinfelder (Frankfurt a.M.) collabora con Hadwig Hörner ad una edizione del testo gregoriano per i *GNO*, ma, a quanto ci comunica *per litteras*, la pubblicazione non è imminente, e verisimilmente supponiamo che il lavoro subirà ulteriori ritardi, a causa del decesso della studiosa nel giugno 2019. Lo ringraziamo, comunque, per averci messo a disposizione alcuni risultati preliminari. Da una ricerca sul repertorio *Pinakes* dell'IRHT si ricava la presenza di 166 manoscritti (completi o parziali) dell'opera gregoriana, senza che si possano identificare altre caratteristiche utili a restringere l'indagine (presenza di lacune, divisioni di capitoli, etc.). Pertanto, ci limitiamo a rinviare, con M. CAPPUYNS ('Le *De imagine*', cit., p. 207 n. 8), a H. DIELS, 'Die Handschriften der antiken Ärzte. II. Teil. Die Übrigen Griechischen Ärzte ausser Hippokrates und Galenos', *Abhandlungen der Königl. Preuß. Akademie der Wissenschaften*, Berlin, 1906, p. 39-40. Importante è anche lo studio di W. JAEGER, 'Greek Uncial Fragments in the Library of Congress in Washington', *Traditio*, 5 (1947), p. 79-102, che identifica come frammenti del *De Opif. Hom.* (parti del cap. XVI e dei cap. XVIII-XIX) i due fogli di un codice in onciale posseduti dalla Library of Congress di Washington, identificandoli altresì come fogli mancanti dal codice Vat. Graec. 2066; proveniente da Rossano, ma probabilmente di fattura costantinopolitana, il codice è dallo stesso Jaeger messo in relazione con un'altra serie di codici in onciale databili al nono secolo prodotti a Costantinopoli, tra cui Par. Gr. 437 (ossia il codice di Dionigi l'Areopagita offerto in dono a Ludovico il Pio). Tanto le vicende della sua circolazione, quanto un confronto delle lezioni non permettono di affermare che Vat. Gr. 2066 sia l'esemplare su cui lavorava Eriugena. Per la questione del titolo, cfr ERISMANN, 'On the Significance', cit.

sulla creazione dell'uomo, di attribuzione controversa, ora a Basilio, ora al Nisseno.[54]

Jeauneau, nell'*Index auctorum* al libro 5 del *Periphyseon* (*CC CM*, 165, p. 908-9), indica numerosi riferimenti alle omelie sull'esamerone di Basilio, ma per lo più si tratta di rimandi *ad sensum* (per i quali lo studioso richiama nel suo apparato delle fonti la traduzione latina di queste omelie ad opera di Eustazio l'Africano nel V secolo).[55] Vi sono però anche alcune citazioni dirette (spesso di non trascurabile estensione), che si trovano tutte nel libro 3 del *Periphyseon*, da ritenersi probabilmente opera dello stesso Eriugena.[56]

Si può forse ipotizzare, con tutte le cautele del caso, che questo materiale, se non tutte le omelie di Basilio, si trovasse sul manoscritto greco del *De opificio hominis* a disposizione di Eriugena. Del resto, l'ipotesi non sembra contraddire i (pochi) dati noti: il testo dell'*Hexaemeron* basiliano si trova anch'esso sul nel ms. *q* individuato da Jeauneau.[57]

È notevole infine che tutte le citazioni letterali dell'*Hexaemeron* tradotto si trovino già a testo (la cosiddetta *Versio I* dell'edizione Jeauneau) nel ms. *R* (Reims, Bibliothèque Municipale 875) del *Periphyseon*, sottoposto al controllo diretto dell'autore e arricchito di numerose sue notazioni autografe: le varie mani all'opera nella revisione del ms. *R* vi apportano solo alcune correzioni di scarso peso. Questa presenza già a testo in *R* farebbe presupporre

---

[54] Cfr Basile de Césarée, *Sur l'origine de l'homme* – ed. A. Smets – M. van Esbroeck, Paris, 1970 (*SC*, 160), p. 36-37; *Auctorum incertorum uulgo Basilii uel Gregorii Nysseni Sermones de creatione hominis, Sermo de paradiso* – ed. H. Hörner, Leiden, 1972 (Gregorii Nysseni Opera Supplementum).

[55] Sono le citazioni in *Periphys.* 2, 521A-B (Basil., *Hex.* II, 7; VI, 8); *Periphys.* 2, 545C-546A (*Hex.* I, 7); *Periphys.* 2, 548C (*Hex.* II, 1); *Periphys.* 2, 553D (*Hex.* II, 6); *Periphys.* 3, 715B (*Hex.* VI, 2). Nel complesso, soltanto alcune citazioni sembrano presentare una qualche somiglianza con la versione di Eustazio: essa non sembra quindi la fonte primaria di Eriugena per il testo di Basilio. Di questo stesso parere appare anche M. Cappuyns, *Jean Scot Érigène*, cit., p. 389.

[56] Di seguito i riferimenti alle *Homiliae in Hexaemeron* di Basilio e ai corrispondenti passi del *Periphyseon*: *Hex.* VIII, 1 = *Periphys.* 3, 685B-C; *Hex.* IV, 3-4 = *Periphys.* 3, 707B-708A; *Hex.* IX, 2 = *Periphys.* 3, 709B-C; *Hex.* VII, 1 = *Periphys.* 3, 735C-D (seguita da due citazioni dal *De imagine*, capp. XV e XVI, quest'ultima aggiunta in margine sul ms. R); *Hex.* VIII, 2 = *Periphys.* 3, 736C-737A (seguito da una citazione dal *De imagine*, cap. XVI); *Hex.* VIII, 1 = *Periphys.* 3, 739D.

[57] Forse nuova luce sulla provenienza di questo materiale potrebbe anche chiarire il problema del frammento di capitolo omesso, eventualmente confermandone o smentendone l'appartenenza eriugeniana.

che, prima della prima stesura attestata dell'opera, al maestro carolingio fosse già noto, in qualche maniera, fra i Padri greci anche Basilio.[58]

*
* *

---

[58] Non discutiamo la questione della presunta confusione tra Gregorio di Nazianzo e Gregorio di Nissa che sembra talora affiorare nel *Periphyseon*: essa, più che a Eriugena, sembra da imputare al suo "segretario-editore", i^2, e deriverebbe da un fraintendimento della traduzione latina della *Historia Tripertita* di Sozomeno, come suggerisce É. JEAUNEAU, 'Érigène et Grégoire de Nysse', cit., p. 69 (= p. 215).

IV. La circolazione del *De imagine*

A. *Il* De imagine *a Bamberg*

Il numero esiguo di testimoni manoscritti permette di supporre che il *De imagine* ebbe quasi certamente una scarsissima diffusione: sarà stato disponibile praticamente soltanto nella cerchia di Eriugena, del suo amico Wulfad e dell'ignoto collaboratore di Eriugena, ossia la mano siglata come i^2. Ricostruire le vicende della sua trasmissione è altamente problematico, perché manca ogni notizia sulla circolazione dell'opera. Di conseguenza, si possono formulare solo ipotesi.

Le informazioni più vicine all'epoca di Eriugena e alla sua cerchia non menzionano il *De imagine*, che, vista anche l'assenza di un'epistola dedicatoria o di una prefazione, dovette rimanere opera di tipo privato, e non è da ritenersi commissionata dalla corte.

Per quanto riguarda il ms. *B*, la ricostruzione più verosimile rimane probabilmente quella originariamente avanzata da Traube, che collega l'ambiente di Eriugena a Bamberg.

Wulfad, l'amico a cui Eriugena dedicò il *Periphyseon*, fu proprietario di una biblioteca personale, il cui catalogo ci è stato conservato al f. 219^v in un manoscritto di sua proprietà, l'attuale ms. Paris, Bibliothèque Mazarine 561 (*M*), risalente al terzo quarto del IX secolo e copiato a Saint-Médard di Soissons che contiene anche una copia degli *Ambigua ad Iohannem*.[59] Il luogo di copiatura fa ritenere che il catalogo sia anteriore all'866, anno in cui Wulfad lasciò Soissons, dove era abate, per diventare arcivescovo di Bourges (carica che deterrà fino alla morte nell'876). Il ms. Mazarine 561 contiene inoltre (f. 67^v) una glossa di una mano riconosciuta come i^2, lo stretto collaboratore di Eriugena che interviene sotto la sua supervisione anche nel ms. Reims 875 del *Periphyseon*. L'ignoto i^2 perciò verosimilmente conosceva Wulfad ed era forse una sorta di intermediario fra Eriugena e l'abate di Saint-Médard.[60] Il *De imagine* non è menzionato nel catalogo dei libri di

---

[59] Il catalogo è stato pubblicato da M. Cappuyns, 'Les "Bibli Vulfadi" et Jean Scot Érigène', *Recherches de Théologie Ancienne et Médiévale* 33 (1966), p. 137-139.

[60] J. Marenbon, 'Wulfad, Charles the Bald and John Scottus Eriugena', in *Charles the Bald: Court and Kingdom. Papers based on a Colloquium held in London in April 1979* – ed. M. Gibson – J. Nelson, Oxford, 1981, p. 375-383.

Wulfad, che pure comprende varie altre opere eriugeniane; neppure si sa che cosa avvenne di questa biblioteca privata.

È comunque possibile che il *De imagine* abbia accompagnato altri manoscritti di opere eriugeniane più note, partendo dall'ambiente del suo autore per pervenire a Bamberg, dove un suo testimone, appunto *B*, è conservato. Così Cappuyns propose in un primo momento che *B* avesse seguito la medesima trafila proposta da Traube per diversi manoscritti eriugeniani conservati a Bamberg, in particolare per i mss. Bamberg, Staatbibliothek Philos. 2/1 e 2/2 (già H.J.IV.5-6), che contengono rispettivamente i libri I-III e IV-V del *Periphyseon* e costituiscono i testimoni della versione III dell'edizione di Jeauneau, ossia la versione dell'opera curata dal solo i^2. Come già detto, Traube riteneva che questi manoscritti del *Periphyseon* provenissero da Reims e che successivamente, passando per le mani di Gerberto d'Aurillac e di Ottone III, entrassero a far parte dei volumi lasciati in dono dall'imperatore Enrico II alla biblioteca della cattedrale di Bamberg all'inizio dell'XI secolo. Oggi si pensa che i due mss. bambergensi del *Periphyseon* provengano non da Reims, ma da Soissons: anche Cappuyns ha sostenuto che appartenessero proprio a Wulfad, nel cui catalogo trovano in effetti corrispondenza. Forse allora anche il *De imagine*, malgrado la sua assenza dal catalogo di Wulfad, ha seguito questo percorso insieme al *Periphyseon*.[61]

Un altro manoscritto di Bamberg, Misc. Patr. 64 (*olim* B.IV.6), consistente in una raccolta di opere copiate in periodi diversi, dall'XI al XIII secolo, fornisce ulteriori elementi. Nella sua prima parte, copiata nell'XI secolo, esso contiene le stesse due opere contenute dal ms. *B* del *De imagine* accanto alla traduzione eriugeniana. Sul ms. Bamberg Misc. Patr. 64, infatti, si trovano le orazioni di Gregorio di Nazianzo nella versione di Rufino (f. 38^r-75^r) e, di seguito, il *De sacerdotio* di Giovanni Crisostomo (f. 75^r-100^v, anche qui – come su *B* – indicato come *dialogus Basilii et*

---

[61] Ad esempio, a Bamberg sono presenti anche due copie della *Versio Dionysii* eriugeniana, contenute sui mss. Bamberg Misc. Patr. 66 (B.IV.8) e 67 (B.IV.7): stando ai cataloghi, il primo ms. è dell'inizio dell'XI secolo, il secondo, verosimilmente un suo *descriptus*, dell'inizio del XIII secolo (F. LEITSCHUH – H. FISCHER, *Katalog*, cit., p. 433-434; G. SUCKALE-REDLEFSEN, *Die Handschriften*, cit., p. 6). La presenza di quest'opera a Bamberg non è tuttavia determinante: essa era piuttosto diffusa nel medioevo e conta numerosi testimoni manoscritti.

Iohannis libri VI).⁶² Engelbrecht, l'editore della versione rufiniana dalle omelie di Gregorio,⁶³ ritiene che questo manoscritto e il manoscritto *B* del *De imagine* siano imparentati, ma non fornisce ulteriori indicazioni in merito.

Infine, anche la ricostruzione di Traube e Cappuyns è resa plausibile dalla vicinanza geografica tra Laon (centro culturale in cui Eriugena probabilmente operò), Soissons (dove si trovava la cerchia di Wulfad e dove sono conservati anche alcuni autografi eriugeniani) e Reims. Una localizzazione che rimanga all'interno di quest'area meglio si accorda con la circolazione limitata dell'opera.

B. *Il* De imagine *nel catalogo di Cluny*

Vengono qui di seguito menzionati quanti più dati possibili per spiegare la presenza del testimone *C* del *De imagine* a Cluny: anche di questo codice, infatti, non si conoscono le vicende in età medievale. Quanto da noi formulato in proposito resta dunque ipotetico.

Il catalogo medievale della biblioteca di Cluny (metà del XII sec. ca.) designa così *C* (n. 24 del catalogo nella versione pubblicatane da Delisle):⁶⁴

> 24. Volumen in quo continentur gesta Clementis, cum epistolis ejusdem ad Jacobum, fratrem Domini, et opus Gregorii Nisseni de his quae relicta sunt in exameron a Basilio fratre, praemissis in initio musica Boetii, vita Karoli, revelatione capitis precursoris Domini, et passione ipsius Clementis.

Il titolo fa pensare che il testo del *De imagine* tramandato da *C*, benché oggi acefalo (privo probabilmente del primo foglio, come già detto), possedesse un titolo analogo a quello di *B*, del tipo: *Sermo Gregorii Episcopi Nysae De ... in ea quae relicta sunt in Examero a Beato Basilio suo fratre*, in cui per correggere la lacuna si utilizzò la formula *de his quae relicta sunt* ecc.

---

⁶² F. LEITSCHUH – H. FISCHER, *Katalog*, cit., p. 437-439; G. SUCKALE-REDLEFSEN, *Die Handschriften*, cit. p. 156.

⁶³ *Tyrannii Rufini orationum Gregorii Nazianzeni novem interpretatio*, ed. A. Engelbrecht, Leipzig, 1910 (rist. New York, 1965), p. XXXVII.

⁶⁴ L. DELISLE, *Inventaire*, cit., p. 339.

DE IMAGINE CXXIX

C'è un altro riscontro, nel catalogo di Cluny, in cui il *De imagine* sembra addirittura comparire due volte:

> 69. Volumen in quo continentur libri Basilii IX de principio celi et terre, et liber Gregorii episcopi Niseni de hominis conditione ad fratrem suum Petrum, et opus ejusdem de his que relicta sunt a Basilio, fratre suo, in exameron.[65]

L'apparente sdoppiamento si può spiegare o come errore o, forse più probabilmente, con l'ipotesi che il primo *De imagine* menzionato sia quello di Dionigi il Piccolo, cui viene affiancato quello eriugeniano. In effetti, la prima menzione (dove l'argomento dell'opera è indicato con *de hominis conditione*) sembra corrispondere meglio al titolo tramandato per la versione dionisiana (es. *Incipit liber scti Gregorii niseni epi quam misit ad fratrem suum PETRUM prbum de ymagine. id est hominis conditione que a fre eorum sco basilio epo in hexâmeron omissa*).[66] La seconda menzione, invece, corrisponde piuttosto al titolo della versione eriugeniana, attestato in *B* (*Sermo Gregorii Episcopi Nysae De ⟨imagine⟩ in ea quae relicta sunt in Examero a Beato Basilio suo fratre*) e verosimilmente anche in *C*, stando al n. 24 del catalogo. L'*opus ejusdem de his que relicta sunt a Basilio, fratre suo, in exameron* menzionato al n. 69 del catalogo cluniacense, per quanto ne sappiamo, potrebbe essere il testo dell'antigrafo di *C*, oppure anche di *C* medesimo, prima che venisse scorporato dal codice catalogato al n. 69 per venire assemblato nella raccolta che costituisce l'attuale ms. *C*.

Diversi altri codici di questo catalogo cluniacense del XII secolo corrispondono ad alcuni dei libri presenti nel catalogo di Wulfad. Vengono qui sotto riportati a confronto quei *bibli Vulfadi* (con la numerazione di Cappuyns[67]) che sembrano trovare riscontro nel catalogo di Cluny pubblicato da Delisle:

---

[65] L. DELISLE, *Inventaire*, cit., p. 341. Cfr anche É. JEAUNEAU, 'La Bibliothèque de Cluny', cit., p. 709 (= *Études érigéniennes*, cit., p. 405), il quale segnala anche la porzione frammentaria rubricata al n. 259 (Delisle, p. 352).

[66] Questo titolo di ms. è ricavato da: G. H. FORBES, *Sancti Patris Nostri Gregorii Nysseni Basili Magni fratris opera quae supersunt omnia*. Tomus primus, Burntisland, 1855, p. 101 (introd. al *De hominis opificio*). Un parallelo potrebbe essere fornito ad esempio da un ms. di ambiente benedettino, catalogato nella biblioteca di Vendôme, riportante un *Gregorius Nyssenus de imagine et conditione hominis* (dunque con il titolo che sembra "specifico", se non unico, della versione di Dionigi il Piccolo), preceduto anche in questo caso dal *Basilii hexaemeron* (XI sec.): la descrizione è in G. HAENEL, *Catalogi librorum manuscriptorum*, Leipzig, 1830, p. 495 n. 118.

[67] M. CAPPUYNS, 'Les *Bibli Vulfadi*', cit.

Catalogo di Cluny	*bibli Vulfadi*
23. Volumen in quo continetur historia tripartita	3. Historia tripertita.
25. Volumen in quo continentur historia Egesippi et expositio hierarch[i]arum sancti Dionysii. (n.a.lat. 1490)	1. Historiae iosephi.
26. Volumen in quo continentur Josephus Antiquitatum et historia Egesippi.	2. Historia. aegesyppi.
Lucentes apices notat aurea bucca Johannes.	14. Omeliae iohannis chrisostomi. in matthaeum XXV
106. Volumen in quo continentur homilie in Mattheum XXV.	
Ingenium vivax Hieronimus perarat. [...]	25. Explanatio hieronimi in danielem.
199. Volumen in quo continentur in Danielem, et Johannes Scotus de predestinatione.	
Origenes varios praeclaros conserit actus.	10. Item [*sc.* Origenis]. in genesi. In exodo. in leuitico. in lucam in ihesum filium naue.
220. Volumen in quo continentur XV homilie sive oratiuncule in Leviticum.	
221. Volumen in quo continentur XXVI homilie in [Jhesu] Nave.	
224. Volumen in quo continentur X libri explanationum in epistolam ad Romanos.	9. Origenis. in epistulis pauli ad romanos
278. Volumen in quo continentur libri Dionysii Areopagite de celesti hierarchia, quos Johannes Erigena transtulit de greco in latinum, jubente ac postulante Carolo rege, Ludovici imperatoris filio, habens in principio prefationem Anastasii, apostolice sedis bibliothecarii, ad eundem regem, et in fine de sermone beati Augustini quod Dominus finxit se longius ire, et quan-	5. Sancti dionysii ariopagitae 6. Item eiusdem.

dam expositionem psalmi in..... martyrum.

298. Volumen in quo continetur ex-   30. Scoliarum Maximi
planatio Maximi monachi de ambi-
guis sententiis Gregorii theologi.

455. Volumen in quo continetur dia-   16-17. Libri perifiseon.. II.
logus Johannis Scoti de hiis que sunt
et que non sunt, de distinctionibus,
divisionibus et differentiis et ceteris
rationationibus.

Ci sono anche altre coincidenze, relative però ad opere molto diffuse e la cui compresenza in entrambi i cataloghi è perciò meno cogente: queste opere sono state escluse dal prospetto sopra riportato,[68] ad eccezione della *Historia tripertita* di Cassiodoro che, per quanto diffusa, è stata comunque inclusa perché è la prima di una serie di tre opere consecutive del catalogo cluniacense (nn. 23, 24, 25) che trovano una loro corrispondenza nella biblioteca di Wulfad oppure, nel caso del *De imagine* (n. 24 Cluny, non attestato fra i libri di Wulfad), fra le opere eriugeniane.

Oggi sopravvivono soltanto due dei manoscritti di Cluny che hanno un riscontro nella biblioteca di Wulfad: quello delle *Expositiones in hierarchiam caelestem* (Paris, Bibliothèque Nationale, n.a.lat. 1490), della prima metà del X secolo, e quello già citato degli *Ambigua*, su cui si trova il catalogo di Wulfad (Paris, Bibliothèque Mazarine 561). Non si può trattare dei manoscritti stessi posseduti da Wulfad ma, se la corrispondenza fra i due cataloghi ha un qualche valore, si potrebbe forse ipotizzare che si tratti di testimoni con essi imparentati.

Nel caso del manoscritto cluniacense n.a.lat. 1490 delle *Expositiones in hierarchiam caelestem*, presente a Cluny almeno fin dall'epoca del nostro catalogo, l'editrice più recente ritiene che questo esemplare, incompleto, sia separato da almeno due copie, una lacunosa e una incompleta, dal subarchetipo in cui figurava il

---

[68] Così il n. 4 Wulfad (*Liber Paterii*), che potrebbe corrispondere al n. 50, 51, 52 o 82 del catalogo di Cluny; il n. 7 Wulfad (*Epistulae gregorii ex registro*), che potrebbe corrispondere al n. 40 del catalogo di Cluny; e i n. 18-19 di Wulfad, *Ambrosii de officiis* e *Ambrosii de psalmo CXVIII.*, che potrebbero corrispondere rispettivamente al n. 97 e al n. 92 (n.a.lat. 1437) o 99 di Cluny.

testo completo.⁶⁹ Alla luce delle corrispondenze fra i due cataloghi, potrebbe perfino darsi che questo subarchetipo, o addirittura l'archetipo, fosse la copia appartenuta a Wulfad (che il ms. cluniacense non possa essere esso stesso l'esemplare posseduto da Wulfad, del resto, è suggerito dal fatto stesso che il suo testo sia incompleto: difficile pensare che l'amico di Eriugena leggesse una versione già mutila di un'opera che gli sarà stata inviata dall'autore in persona).⁷⁰

Il ms. degli *Ambigua*, cioè Paris, Bibliothèque Mazarine 561 (*M*), risalente come già detto all'850-75 e copiato a Saint-Médard di Soissons, alla morte di Wulfad passò per vie ignote alla biblioteca di Saint-Bénigne de Dijon, dove arrivò entro la metà dell'XI secolo, quando vi fu catalogato. Da allora le tracce del manoscritto si perdono fino all'età moderna:⁷¹ è perciò possibile che esso sia passato per Cluny entro la metà del sec. XII, anche se probabilmente è più prudente ipotizzare che il manoscritto cluniacense ne sia una copia, diretta o con copie intermedie.

Anche a Cluny, infine, si potevano trovare le opere presenti insieme al *De imagine* su *B*; anche nel catalogo di Cluny, come a Bamberg, esse figurano affiancate, e anche i titoli sono assai simili:

> Rethor Gregorius serit ac doctor Ciprianus.
> 65. Volumen in quo continentur VIII libri Gregorii Nazanzeni de diversis causis et aliquibus festivitatibus, et dialogus Basilii et Johannis, et liber contra Adamantum Manicheum.

Infine, neppure il fatto che il *De imagine* sia assente dal catalogo di Wulfad può smentire quest'ipotesi: non tutto ciò che era contenuto nei codici appartenuti a Wulfad dev'essere stato necessariamente catalogato. Può costituire un esempio in tal senso il caso del manoscritto di Wulfad contenente il commento di Gerolamo a

---

⁶⁹ Per la tradizione manoscritta delle *Expositiones* eriugeniane, cfr *Iohannis Scoti Eriugenae Expositiones in ierarchiam coelestem* – ed. J. Barbet, Turnhout, 1975 (*CC CM*, 21).

⁷⁰ L'unico ms. riportante il testo integrale delle *Expositiones* di Giovanni Scoto è il ms. Douai Bibl. mun. 202 (D), risalente alla metà del XII sec., con tutta probabilità una copia di un ms. di proprietà di Rodolfo il Verde (Radulphus), arcivescovo di Reims dal 1106 al 1124 (cfr *Iohannis Scoti Eriugenae Expositiones*, cit., p. XVII). Si dovrebbero cercare eventualmente ulteriori legami di questo personaggio con Soissons, testimoniati ad esempio nel fatto che fu Rodolfo a presiedere il concilio di Soissons che nel 1121 condannò Pietro Abelardo.

⁷¹ Sulla storia di questo ms., cfr *Maximi Confessoris Ambigua ad Iohannem iuxta Iohannis Scotti Eriugenae latinam interpretationem*, ed. É. Jeauneau, Turnhout 1988 (CC SG 18), p. XXVI-XXIX.

Daniele, opera posseduta anche a Cluny (riportata nel prospetto più sopra: n. 25 Wulfad, n. 199 del catalogo di Cluny). Se questo manoscritto di Cluny è il codice appartenuto a Wulfad o una sua copia, occorre pensare che nel catalogo di Wulfad il suo contenuto sia stato indicato sommariamente con la menzione soltanto della prima opera che vi figurava, ossia appunto il commento geronimiano, mentre non è stato annotato il *De praedestinatione*. Forse, dunque, anche il *De imagine* poteva trovarsi nella biblioteca dell'abate di Soissons, sebbene non sia menzionato nel suo catalogo.

Si tratta naturalmente di un'ipotesi: in una biblioteca ricca come quella di Cluny, fornita di diverse centinaia di volumi, la pregnanza delle corrispondenze con alcuni dei libri di Wulfad non va sopravvalutata. Posto quindi che le corrispondenze fra il catalogo dei libri di Wulfad e quello di Cluny offrano effettivamente un indizio e non si tratti di pure coincidenze, i dati disponibili non smentiscono l'ipotesi che alcune opere presenti a Cluny nel XII secolo vi siano pervenute proprio a partire dalla biblioteca personale di Wulfad. Fra queste, sebbene non menzionato nel catalogo di Wulfad, potrebbe essere anche il *De imagine*.

Può infine darsi, come proposto da Ernesto Mainoldi, che sia stata la scuola di Auxerre, fra IX e X secolo, il tramite del passaggio dalla biblioteca di Wulfad, o comunque dalla cerchia eriugeniana, a Cluny, giungendo fra le mani di Remigio d'Auxerre e da questi ad Oddone, abate di Cluny.[72]

*
* *

---

[72] Tale proposta è formulata da E. S. MAINOLDI, *L'influenza letteraria e dottrinale del pensiero e dell'opera di Giovanni Scoto Eriugena nel medioevo (secc. IX-XV)*, in corso di stampa.

V. Il *De imagine* in Guglielmo di Saint-Thierry

Il principale testimone di tradizione indiretta per il *De imagine* eriugeniano, dopo il *Periphyseon* stesso, è il *De natura corporis et animae* di Guglielmo di Saint-Thierry (1075/1080 ca.-1148).[73] L'opera è costituita da un centone di citazioni, la cui originalità sta nell'assemblaggio di materiali precedenti a formare un discorso nuovo. Fra le opere di Guglielmo, questa modalità compositiva si trova non solo nel *De natura corporis et animae*, ma anche in quella che probabilmente è la sua prima opera, il *Liber de corpore et sanguine Domini*, scritto contro il *De divinis officiis* di Ruperto di Deutz sul problema del modo della presenza di Cristo nel sacramento eucaristico e successivamente unito all'epistola a Ruperto e a quella dedicatoria a san Bernardo a formare il *De sacramento altaris*, e nella *Expositio in Epistolam ad Romanos*.

Il *De natura corporis et animae* di Guglielmo è diviso in due sezioni, *De physica humani corporis* e *De anima*. Guglielmo in quest'opera, nella sola sezione *De anima*, cita il *De imagine* ampiamente e direttamente (l'eventualità che Guglielmo citi il *De imagine* tramite il *Periphyseon* è certamente da escludersi, in quanto riporta anche brani della traduzione eriugeniana non confluiti nel *Periphyseon*). Per quanto riguarda la prima sezione, relativa al corpo umano, le due fonti quasi esclusivamente utilizzate sono il *Liber Pantegni* nella traduzione di Costantino l'Africano e il *Premnon Physicon* di Nemesio di Emesa;[74] per la sezione sull'anima, il *De imagine* eriugeniano e il *De statu animae* di Claudiano Mamerto. In ciascuna delle due sezioni la distribuzione del materiale citato è disomogenea: nella sezione fisica le citazioni dal *Liber Pantegni* e da Nemesio sono inizialmente, per così dire, intrecciate, alternandosi grosso modo una di seguito all'altra, ma dopo alcune pagine Costantino diventa il riferimento pressoché

---

[73] Come già si avvide J.-M. DÉCHANET, *Aux sources de la spiritualité de Guillaume de Saint Thierry*, Bruges 1940. Su Guglielmo e la traduzione eriugeniana cfr anche A. SAWORD, 'Man as the Image of God in the Works of William of St Thierry', *Cistercian Studies Quarterly* 9 (1974), p. 309-327.

[74] Per i temi portanti dell'opera di Nemesio cfr B. MOTTA, *La mediazione estrema. L'antropologia di Nemesio d'Emesa fra platonismo e aristotelismo*, Padova, 2004. Segnaliamo che quest'opera nel medioevo andava spesso proprio sotto il nome di Gregorio di Nissa; tuttavia, non siamo riusciti a rintracciare legami fra la diffusione del *Premnon* (su cui cfr *Premnon Physicon. Versione latina del* περὶ φύσεων ἀνθρώπου *di Nemesio* – ed. I. CHIRICO, Roma, 2011) e la trasmissione del *De imagine*.

unico; nella sezione sull'anima, invece, vengono prima per lo più le citazioni dal *De imagine*, poi quelle da Claudiano Mamerto.

Si ritiene che le due sezioni dell'opera siano state composte in due tempi differenti e aggregate così come le possediamo solo in un secondo momento. Anche se gli spostamenti di Guglielmo di Saint-Thierry nel corso della sua vita sono per lo più noti, è sconosciuta la data di stesura di ciascuna delle due parti, così come quella della loro aggregazione in uno scritto unico, né è possibile determinare il luogo in cui Guglielmo potè leggere il *De imagine* eriugeniano per riutilizzarlo nel *De natura corporis et animae*.

Le proposte di datazione per quest'ultima opera, infatti, oscillano di quasi cinquant'anni, dalla giovinezza alla morte dell'autore. Guglielmo, nativo di Liegi, studiò verso la fine dell'XI secolo, probabilmente a Reims, certamente in una scuola cattedrale; all'inizio del XII secolo entrò nell'ordine benedettino presso il monastero di Saint-Nicaise a Reims, dove rimase per circa un ventennio (1100-1120 ca.); quindi, ancora a Reims, fu abate benedettino di Saint-Thierry (1121-1135); ricoprì questa carica malvolentieri, finché riuscì a rinunciare alla carica abbaziale e a ritirarsi come semplice monaco fra i cistercensi di Signy, dove trascorse i suoi ultimi anni (1135-1148). Molto probabilmente Guglielmo non scrisse nulla prima del periodo a Saint-Thierry: sembra pertanto da escludere l'attribuzione del *De natura corporis et animae* al periodo "giovanile" di Saint-Nicaise.[75]

Qualche traccia può supportare l'ipotesi della stesura della sezione *De anima* nel periodo dell'abbaziato a Saint-Thierry. In primo luogo, a Reims è conservato un manoscritto del XII secolo contenente, dopo un vangelo di Giovanni *cum glossa vulgari*, anche una delle fonti del *De natura corporis et animae*, ovvero il *De statu animae* di Claudiano Mamerto. Questo manoscritto reca più volte l'*ex libris* di Saint-Thierry, vergato sempre da una stessa mano contemporanea. Guglielmo potrebbe dunque averlo letto lì.[76] Per contro, a Signy (per quanto verificabile dal catalogo della

---

[75] *Guillelmi a sancto Theodorico opera omnia III. De sacramento altaris; De natura corporis et animae; De contemplando Deo; De natura et dignitate amoris; Epistola ad fratres de Monte Dei* – edd. P. Verdeyen – S. Ceglar, Turnhout, 2003 (*CC CM*, 88), p. 95.

[76] Questo manoscritto potrebbe anche essere l'esemplare utilizzato da Guglielmo (H. LORIQUET, *Catalogue général des Manuscrits des Bibliothèques Publiques de France*, t. 38, Paris, 1904, p. 175-176); ed è più logico pensare, per ragioni di vicinanza rispetto a Reims, che egli potrebbe avervi avuto accesso mentre ancora si trovava a Saint-Thierry.

biblioteca di Charleville) non era presente alcuna delle opere utilizzate per il *De natura corporis et animae*.[77]

In secondo luogo, come nota Jean Déchanet,[78] il manoscritto del *De natura corporis et animae*, Charleville, Bibliothèque Municipale 172, proveniente da Signy e testimone più vicino all'autore, riporta in testa al *De natura corporis et animae* e nel margine in basso della medesima pagina (f. 113^r) il nome di Guglielmo col titolo di abate (*Abbatis Sancti Theoderici*), laddove le opere del periodo di Signy sono generalmente accompagnate dalla qualifica di *monachi signiacensis*.[79]

Le citazioni di Guglielmo non sono sempre letterali, ma spesso consistono in vere e proprie parafrasi. Questo complica l'individuazione del testimone del *De imagine* più vicino a quello utilizzato da Guglielmo. Almeno un caso, tuttavia, sembra avvicinare questo testimone al manoscritto C. Infatti, laddove il ms. *B* del *De imagine* presenta al cap. VII, 3 una corruttela – il già citato caso di *pro cor quod illis quam is* – Guglielmo cita parafrasando inequivocabilmente la lezione esatta tramandata da *C* (*pro crocodili squamis*): *Habet etiam ex ipso ferro munimenta corporis fortiora squamis cocodrilli...* (*De natura corp. et an.* 84).

Il testimone utilizzato da Guglielmo, tuttavia, non può essere nessuno dei due oggi conservati. Guglielmo, infatti, cita anche dall'ultimo capitolo (XXX, 30) del *De imagine*. Questo capitolo era

---

D'altronde, anche le altre opere rare a disposizione di Guglielmo nello scrivere il *De natura corporis et animae* circolarono in ambiente benedettino (cfr *CC CM*, p. 96-97).

[77] Per la sezione *De physica humani corporis*, invece, l'editore dell'opera, Michel Lemoine, ritiene che Guglielmo potrebbe aver sviluppato interessi per talune delle sue fonti a partire dalla polemica contro Guglielmo di Conches, sorta intorno al 1141 in conseguenza di quella (assai più nota) contro Abelardo (cfr Guilelmus de Sancto Theoderico, *De natura corporis et animae* – ed. M. Lemoine, Paris, 1988, p. 29). Guglielmo di Saint-Thierry dichiara nel *De erroribus Guillelmi de Conchis* (cap. 1; ed. *CC CM*, 89A), risalente dunque al periodo di Signy, di essere da poco venuto a conoscenza della *Summa philosophiae* di Guglielmo di Conches. Perciò, se la sezione fisica sul corpo umano è stata composta dietro influenza delle fonti scoperte tramite Guglielmo di Conches, e se l'ipotesi della datazione della sezione *de anima* al periodo di Saint-Thierry è corretta, la prima delle due sezioni dell'opera dovrebbe essere posteriore.

[78] J. Déchanet, *Guillaume de Saint-Thierry. Aux sources d'une pensée*, Paris, 1978, p. 66 n. 8.

[79] Il fatto che questo ms. provenga da Signy, come i manoscritti principali di quasi tutte le opere della vecchiaia di Guglielmo, malgrado una composizione dell'opera precedente il periodo signiacense, si può forse spiegare ipotizzando una prima stesura nel periodo dell'abbaziato a Saint-Thierry, poi approntata nella sua forma attuale (es. unificando le due sezioni separate, aggiungendo passi, modificando lo stile ecc.) soltanto più tardi a Signy.

assente in *C* (il cui testo termina al cap. XXIII); il testo di *B* arriva fino alla fine dell'opera ma, come è stato anticipato, a poche righe dalla fine (f. 114ʳ) il manoscritto contiene un'omissione non segnalata (il testo è continuo): [80]

> Obscuriorem quidem primo[81] per quoque ut sollicitudinem consequerentur suggerit dicens spoliari oportere ueterem hominem, et indui renouatum ad imaginem creantis ut redeamus iterum in diuinam gratiam illam in qua creauit ab initio hominem dicens deus, faciamus hominem ad imaginem et similitudinem nostram, cui gloria et potentia patri et filio et sancto spiritui in saecula amen.
> (ms. Bamberg, Staatsbibliothek, Misc. Patr. 78, f. 114ʳ)

Fra le parole *primo per quoque* e *ut sollicitudinem* si trova l'omissione. Guglielmo di Saint-Thierry cita questa parte proprio a partire da poche parole prima dell'omissione, proseguendo la citazione e restituendo parte del testo omesso da *B*, per giunta in una forma piuttosto aderente al testo eriugeniano, come si evince dal confronto col greco originale del *De opificio hominis*:

... obscuriorem quidem in primo, euidentiorem uero et perfectiorem post operis consummationem. Sic ergo in sculptura organi animae species secundum subiecti analogiam praemonstratur, imperfecta in imperfecto, in perfecto perfecta futura. Quae ex principio perfecta esset, si in suo principio corrupta natura per malitiam non fuisset. Propterea nascimur ut pecudes, nec continuo nec nisi cum magnis et diuturnis laboribus relucere potest in nobis factoris imago, sed longa quadam uia per materiales et pecuales animae proprietates ad perfectionem suam homo ducitur. (Guilelmus de Sancto Theodorico, *De natura corporis et animae* 57-8)[82]	... ἀμυδρότερον μὲν παρὰ τὴν πρώτην, τελειότερον δὲ μετὰ τὴν τοῦ ἔργου συμπλήρωσιν· οὕτω καὶ ἐν τῇ τοῦ ὀργάνου γλυφῇ τὸ τῆς ψυχῆς εἶδος κατὰ τὴν ἀναλογίαν τοῦ ὑποκειμένου προφαίνεται, ἀτελὲς ἐν τῷ ἀτελεῖ, καὶ ἐν τῷ τελείῳ τέλειον. Ἀλλ' ἐξ ἀρχῆς ἂν τέλειον ἦν, εἰ μὴ διὰ τῆς κακίας ἡ φύσις ἐκολοβώθη. Διὰ τοῦτο ἡ πρὸς τὴν ἐμπαθῆ καὶ ζωώδη γένεσιν κοινωνία, οὐκ εὐθὺς ἐκλάμπειν τὴν θείαν εἰκόνα ἐν τῷ πλάσματι ἐποίησεν, ἀλλ' ὁδῷ τινι καὶ ἀκολουθίᾳ διὰ τῶν ὑλικῶν καὶ ζωωδεστέρων τῆς ψυχῆς ἰδιωμάτων ἐπὶ τὸ τέλειον ἄγει τὸν ἄνθρωπον. (Gr. Nyss. *hom. opif.* 30; *PG* 44, 253D-256A)

---

[80] La lacuna non è stata segnalata da Cappuyns (p. 262, 32 Cappuyns); gli editori del *De natura corporis et animae* segnalano solo la citazione delle poche parole precedenti l'omissione.

[81] Cappuyns erroneamente leggeva *obscurioremque de primo*.

La lezione *per quoque* del ms. *B* corrisponderà perciò a una corruzione dell'aggettivo *perfectiorem* restituito da Guglielmo, in una forma del tipo *perfectioremque*. Questa citazione di Guglielmo restituisce una breve porzione, altrimenti perduta, dell'opera.

Si segnala infine che nella presente edizione, vista la prassi alquanto libera di citazione in Guglielmo, anche questo passo dal *De natura corporis et animae*, come il frammento del capitolo omesso da *B C* e tramandato dai due florilegi visti più sopra, è stato inserito nel corpo del testo del *De imagine* fra segni di integrazione, a segnalarne la differente provenienza.

*
* *

---

[82] Citazione dall'edizione critica già menzionata di Lemoine, dove il brano si trova a p. 139; il testo critico di Lemoine si trova ristampato con numerazione di righe in *Guillelmi a sancto Theodorico opera omnia III. De sacramento altaris, De natura corporis et animae, De contemplando Deo, De natura et dignitate amoris, Epistola ad fratres de Monte Dei* – ed. P. Verdeyen – S. Ceglar, Turnhout, 2003 (*CC CM*, 88), dove il passo interessato è a p. 123 (57,698-58,708).

VI. La destinazione dell'opera

Il *De hominis opificio* è la sola opera di Gregorio di Nissa nota ad Eriugena e da essa l'irlandese deriva gran parte della sua antropologia filosofica.[83] In quest'opera, che sembra per alcuni aspetti legarsi a quanto più ampiamente espresso nel *De anima et resurrectione*, Gregorio sottolinea, sulla scia di larga parte della tradizione greca, la bellezza e perfezione del cosmo e l'eccelsa dignità dell'uomo, richiamandosi alla tradizione alessandrina (da Filone in poi), secondo cui la creazione a immagine di Dio riveste un chiaro senso morale, mediante la scelta di un termine quale ἀρχέτυπος, utilizzato dai filosofi platonici con riferimento al rapporto tra la natura divina e la natura umana;[84] seguendo Plotino, che aveva interpretato anche in senso etico la dottrina della conoscenza del simile da parte del simile, Gregorio (e prima di lui Basilio e Gregorio di Nazianzo) opera una trasformazione in senso cristiano, impiegando il concetto nuovo dell'amore tra il creatore e la creatura. In tal modo, la corrispondenza tra realtà umana e archetipo divino permette all'uomo di avere un'immagine di Dio,

---

[83] Sull'antropologia eriugeniana cfr W. Otten, *The Anthropology of Johannes Scottus Eriugena*, Leiden, 1991. Per l'aspetto della creazione, C. Riccati, *Processio et Explicatio. La doctrine de la création chez Jean Scot et Nicolas de Cues*, Napoli, 1983.

[84] Per le considerazioni che seguono si sono tenuti presenti soprattutto gli studi di K. Gronau, *Poseidonios und die jüdisch-christliche Genesisexegese*, Berlin, 1914, cap. III ("Gregors von Nyssa περὶ κατασκευῆς ἀνθρώπου"), p. 141-219; J. Zachhuber, *Human Nature in Gregory of Nyssa. Philosophical Background and Theological Significance*, Leiden, 2000 (che evidenziano soprattutto richiami e influssi stoici); E. Peroli, *Il Platonismo e l'antropologia filosofica di Gregorio di Nissa. Con particolare riferimento agli influssi di Platone, Plotino e Porfirio*, Milano, 1993; C. Desalvo, *L'oltre nel presente. La filosofia dell'uomo in Gregorio di Nissa*, Milano, 1996. Sul *De opificio hominis* nello specifico, resta fondamentale il volume *Arché e Telos. L'antropologia di Origene e di Gregorio di Nissa. Analisi storico-religiosa, Atti del Colloquio Milano 17-19 maggio 1979* – ed. U. Bianchi – H. Crouzel, Milano, 1981. Utili rimandi si possono trovare anche nelle due traduzioni moderne: Grégoire de Nysse, *La création de l'homme* – ed. J. Laplace – J. Daniélou, Paris 2002² (1943) (*SC*, 6); Gregorio di Nissa, *L'uomo* – ed. B. Salmona, Roma 1982 e un buon sunto è fornito da R. Scognamiglio, 'Il *De opificio hominis*: eredità filoniana e origeniana nell'antropologia del Nisseno', in *Origene e l'alessandrinismo cappadoce (III-IV secolo). Atti del V Convegno del Gruppo Italiano di Ricerca su Origene e la Tradizione Alessandrina, Bari 20-22 settembre 2000* – ed. M. Girardi, Bari, 2002, p. 115-137. Cfr recentemente J. Behr, 'The rational Animal. A Rereading of Gregory of Nyssa's *De hominis opificio*', *Journal of Early Christian Studies* 7 (1999), p. 219-247.

che si possa contemplare nella nostra natura, qualora essa si sia purificata e ricondotta alle qualità originarie.[85]

Inoltre, uno dei principali problemi che Gregorio affronta, e che Eriugena riprende nel *Periphyseon*, è quello della divisione dei sessi e in particolare la ragione per cui se Dio, che è semplice e non composto (principio essenziale della teologia medio- e neoplatonica) e ha creato l'uomo simile a sé, abbia introdotto nella creatura una distinzione che nel creatore non sussiste. Similmente, l'anima è 'semplice' e 'non composta', in quanto essa è stata fatta a immagine di Dio, e il suo rapporto di unione con il corpo deve essere inteso come una forma di presenza e di inerenza ovverosia di comunanza tra intelletto e corpo.[86] Con un ragionamento tratto dal *Timeo* platonico, Gregorio osserva che Dio, assolutamente buono e perciò non invidioso, ha creato l'uomo senza voler porgli un limite di bontà, così che la creatura potesse avvicinarsi per quanto possibile alla bontà del suo creatore.[87] Dio ha perciò colmato l'uomo dei suoi beni, fra cui la libertà, condizione necessaria alla possibilità di praticare le virtù. Ma mentre Dio è immutabile e pertanto la sua libertà non si sostanzia in scelte, l'uomo è mutevole: il peccato originale discende precisamente dal fatto che la libertà umana implica scelte che possono essere sbagliate. L'uomo, creato pari agli angeli nel paradiso terrestre, ha scelto di rendersi uguale agli animali, perdendo così diritto a moltiplicarsi alla maniera angelica. Dio lascia che il peccato avvenga, perché ha creato l'uomo libero, ma, prevedendolo, nello stesso momento in cui crea l'uomo a sua immagine, crea anche la divisione sessuale. Particolare importanza riveste in tale contesto il motivo della doppia creazione, spesso esemplificata dal motivo delle 'tuniche di pelle' di Gen. 3,11.[88] Nel mondo postlapsario, l'uomo si trova

---

[85] J. PÉPIN, '"Image d'image", "Miroir de miroir" (Grégoire de Nysse, *De hominis opificio* xii, *PG* 44, 161C-164B)', in *Platonism in Late Antiquity* – ed. S. Gersh – C. Kannengiesser, Notre Dame, 1992, p. 217-229.

[86] E. PEROLI, 'Gregory of Nyssa and the Neoplatonic Doctrine of the Soul', *Vigiliae Christianae*, 51 (1997), p. 117-139.

[87] W. OTTEN, 'Reading Creation: Early Medieval Views of Genesis and Plato's *Timaeus*', in *The Creation of Heaven and Earth. Re-interpretations of Genesis 1 in the Context of Judaism, Ancient Philosophy, Christianity, and Modern Physics* – ed. G.H. van Kooten, Leiden, 2005, p. 225-243; EAD., 'Anthropology between *Imago Mundi* and *Imago Dei*: The Place of Johannes Scottus Eriugena in the Tradition of Christian Thought', *Studia Patristica* 43 (2006), p. 459-472.

[88] Sul problema della doppia creazione nella tradizione greca e in Gregorio Nisseno in particolare, cfr *La 'doppia creazione' dell'uomo, negli Alessandrini, nei Cappadoci e nella*

DE IMAGINE   CXLI

prigioniero della passione e, dunque, della materialità, secondo un'idea che vede i Cappadoci perfettamente integrati nella mentalità neoplatonica. Sono, in breve, questi i contenuti del *De hominis opificio* di Gregorio di cui Eriugena è debitore, in modo specialmente vistoso nel libro 4 del *Periphyseon*: l'irlandese vi avrà senz'altro scorto l'opportunità di recuperarli e di appropriarsene per la propria opera originale, passando per la traduzione che stiamo esaminando.

È possibile tuttavia avanzare un'ulteriore ipotesi su un'altra ragione per cui l'opera greca potrebbe aver attirato l'attenzione di Giovanni Scoto al punto da convincerlo ad approntarne una traduzione. Il *De imagine*, infatti, non contiene soltanto riflessioni di antropologia filosofica, ma anche diversi brani di carattere "anatomico" o "fisiologico". È il caso, ad esempio, dei capitoli 10 (*Quia per sensus operatur intellectus*) e soprattutto 12 (*Exquisitio in qua*

---

gnosi – ed. U. Bianchi, Roma, 1978; P. Pisi, Genesis *e* phthora*. Le motivazioni protologiche della verginità in Gregorio di Nissa e nella tradizione dell'*enkrateia, Roma, 1983; P.F. Beatrice, 'Le tuniche di pelle. Antiche letture di Gen. 3,21', in *La tradizione dell'Enkrateia. Motivazioni ontologiche e protologiche* – ed. U. Bianchi, Roma, 1985, p. 433-484. Cfr recentemente G. Mandolino, '"Come un indovinello": doppia creazione e immagine di Dio nel *De opificio hominis* di Gregorio di Nissa', *Adamantius* 24 (2018), p. 416-434; C. Moreschini, 'Né maschio né femmina: la creazione dell'uomo secondo Gregorio di Nissa e Massimo il Confessore', in corso di stampa in *"Masculum et feminam creavit eos" (Gen. 1,27) Paradigmi del maschile e femminile nel cristianesimo antico. XLVII Incontro di Studiosi dell'Antichità Cristiana*, Istitutum Patristicum Augustinianum, Roma. Per Eriugena, cfr *Periphys.* 4, 794B-799A, con le considerazioni di É. Jeauneau, 'La division des sexes', cit.; un breve ma chiaro sunto della dottrina nissena della creazione è offerto anche dallo stesso studioso in 'Érigène et Grégoire de Nysse', cit. Si veda anche M. Naldini, 'Gregorio Nisseno e Giovanni Scoto Eriugena. Note sull'idea di creazione e di antropologia', *Studi Medievali* 20 (1979), p. 501-533. Sulle interpretazioni dei primi capitoli della Genesi e in particolare di quelli che riguardano il peccato originale cfr B. McGinn, 'Exegesis as Metaphysics: Eriugena and Eckhart on reading Genesis 1-3, in *Eriugena and Creation: Proceedings of the Eleventh International Conference on Eriugenian Studies, held in honor of Edouard Jeauneau, Chicago, 9-12 November 2011* – ed. W. Otten – M. Allen, Turnhout, 2014, p. 463-499; e soprattutto D. F. Duclow, 'The sleep of Adam, the making of Eve: Sin and creation in Eriugena', *ibid.*, p. 235-261. Sul motivo (derivato piuttosto da Massimo il Confessore) del ritorno cfr É. Jeauneau, 'The Neoplatonic Themes of *Processio* and *Reditus* in Eriugena', *Dionysius* 15 (1991), p. 3-29 (= 'Tendenda vela', cit., p. 511-539); M. Zier, 'The Growth of an Idea', in *From Athens to Chartres. Neoplatonism and Medieval Thought. Studies in Honour of Édouard Jeauneau* – ed. H. Westra, Leiden, 1992, p. 71-83. Per altre questioni, afferenti soprattutto al quinto libro del *Periphyseon* cfr H. A. Mooney, 'The Notion of the Liberality of God in Gregory of Nyssa and Johannes Scottus Eriugena', *Studia Patristica* 37 (2001), p. 207-211. Una buona sintesi in I.-P. Sheldon-Williams, 'The Greek Platonist Tradition from the Cappadocians to Maximus and Eriugena', in *The Cambridge History of Later Greek and Early Medieval Thought* – ed. A.H. Armstrong, Cambridge, 1970, p. 425-501.

parte corporis principale animi esse aestimandum in quo etiam de lacrimis ac risu fysiologia), 14 (*De somniis et oscitatione et uisione* ΑΕΤΙΟΛΟΓΙΑ *hoc est causalis ratio*) e 30 (*Speculatio quaedam medicinalis de constitutione corporis nostri, perpauca*).[89] È già stata proposta da John Contreni con buone argomentazioni l'identificazione di Giovanni Scoto con il *Johannes medicus* menzionato in un documento ufficiale e in due ricette mediche dell'epoca: egli sarebbe stato in contatto con personaggi, quali Pardulo e Incmaro e un certo *Martinus Hiberniensis*, appartenenti a Laon e a Reims, i due più importanti centri della cultura medica carolingia.[90] Due epigrammi attribuiti ad Eriugena, scoperti e pubblicati da Claudio Leonardi,[91] pure menzionano (sebbene in modo ironico e leggero) situazioni patologiche o termini medici. Nel caso che questa identificazione fosse corretta, una delle ragioni dell'interesse del *De hominis opificio* agli occhi di Giovanni Scoto potrebbe risiedere anche nelle sue parti "mediche" e più tecniche, quelle che Gregorio di Nissa aveva a sua volta ripreso da Galeno. Riportiamo a titolo d'esempio una glossa eriugeniana dalle *Annotationes in Marcianum* già citata da Contreni a dimostrazione delle conoscenze e degli interessi medici da parte del filosofo irlandese:

> Si autem uis nosse aethimologiam nominis Hymenei, cognosce tres membranulas in corporibus esse animantium, quarum quidem duas esse in uirili sexu, tres uero in femineo, medicinalis physica comprobat. Membranula quippe cerebri quam Greci μήνιγγα dicunt, ex qua diuersae fistulae quinquepertiti sensuus

---

[89] Cfr A. M. IERACI BIO, 'Gregorio di Nissa (*De hominis opificio* 30) e la fisiologia galenica del *De usu partium*', in *La cultura scientifico-naturalistica nei Padri della Chiesa (I-V sec.)*. *XXXV incontro di studiosi dell'Antichità cristiana, 4-6 maggio 2006*, Roma, 2007, p. 489-512 (*Studia Ephemeridis Augustinianum*, 101). L'unione di dottrine antropologiche e fisiologia è attestata anche nell'*Ad Gaurum* di Porfirio e nel *De Natura hominis* di Nemesio.

[90] J. J. CONTRENI, 'Masters and medicine in Northern France during the regin of Charles the Bald', in *Charles the Bald: Court and Kingdom. Papers based on a Colloquium held in London in April 1979* – ed. M. Gibson – J. Nelson, Oxford, 1981, p. 333-350 (rielaborazione di ID., 'The Study and Practice of Medicine in Northern France during the Reign of Charles the Bald', in *Studies in Medieval Culture*, 6-7, Kalamazoo, 1976 – ed. J. R. Sommerfeldt – E. R. Elder, p. 43-54. Per le testimonianze del IX sec. su Giovanni Scoto medico, cfr M. BRENNAN, 'Materials for the Biography of Johannes Scottus Eriugena', *Studi Medievali* 27/1 (1986), p. 413-460, in part. p. 416-421 (*testimonia* 1-4). Su questo punto si vedano anche le considerazioni di Herren, nella Introduzione ai *Carmina*, p. XI, n. 13.

[91] C. LEONARDI, 'Nuove voci poetiche tra secolo IX e XI', *Studi medievali*, 2 (1961), p. 139-168, in part. 148; cfr altresì Herren, p. XXXI.

profluunt, communis est omnibus siue rationalibus siue inrationabilibus animantibus. Item membranula que diuidit inter ilia, hoc est inferiora uentris uiscera et superiora pectoris, iecur cor et arterias, quam Greci φρήν dicunt, ex qua frenetici uocantur, omni sexui communis est. Membranula autem uentris in qua puerperia concipiuntur et feminei sexus proprium est, et a Grecis ὑμην uocatur, inde Hymeneus qui corporalibus presidet conceptionibus ut poeticae fabule fingunt.[92]

A questa glossa fanno bene da *pendant* un paio di luoghi del *De imagine*, uno in cui si parla di *MENHITA* e di *frenecin* (cap. XII, p. 222, 20-44 Capp. = 94-95, 30-59) e uno relativo all' *ΥΜΗΝ* (cap. XXX, p. 258, 23-32 Capp. = 157, 96-106). Non si tratterà dei luoghi che sono serviti da fonte ad Eriugena (i contenuti non sembrano perfettamente sovrapponibili, e la cronologia delle sue opere lo rende improbabile), ma è possibile che questi passi abbiano suscitato la sua attenzione e i suoi interessi per la medicina. In breve, un intellettuale che riuniva in sé interessi filosofici e scientifici, oltre ad una innegabile ammirazione per i padri greci e per la loro lingua, poteva verosimilmente sentirsi fortemente portato a fare una traduzione da un'opera come il *De hominis opificio*.[93]

Il fatto però che il testo del *De imagine* sia pervenuto anonimo perché privo di dedica, porta in ogni caso a ritenere che si tratti di una traduzione eseguita non dietro committenza, ma per ragioni personali; tanto più che l'autore, per quanto ci consta dal catalogo di Wulfad, potrebbe non averla inviata nemmeno all'amico, a cui pure aveva fatto pervenire altre sue traduzioni ad uso personale (quelle da Massimo il Confessore). Peranto, lo scopo che l'irlandese avrebbe avuto in mente nel tradurre l'opera sarebbe stato principalmente il riutilizzo della sua versione latina dell'opera nissena nel contesto del *Periphyseon*.

---

[92] *Iohannis Scotti Annotationes in Marcianum* – ed. C. E. LUTZ, Cambridge Mass., 1939, p. 3,26-4,3.

[93] Per questo tipo di contenuti nell'opera gregoriana cfr D. DE BRASI, 'Eine Neubewertung des Körpers. Anthropologie und Glauben in den Schriften zur menschlichen Natur des Nemesios von Emesa und des Gregor von Nyssa', in *Anthropologie in Antike und Gegenwart. Biologische und philosophische Entwürfe vom Menschen* – ed. D. De Brasi – S. Föllinger, Freiburg, 2015, p. 377-395; ID., 'Rhetorik, Medizin und Glauben: die Auffassung des menschlichen Körpers in Laktanzens *De Opificio Dei* und Gregor von Nyssas περὶ κατασκευῆς ἀνθρώπου', in Soma: *Körperkonzepte und körperliche Existenz in der antiken Philosophie und Literatur* – ed. Th. Buchheim – D. Meißner – N. Wachsmann, Hamburg, 2016, p. 121-141.

*
* *

La presente edizione del *De imagine* di Eriugena, per quanto abbia tentato di approfondire e completare la ricostruzione di quest'opera, presenta certamente alcuni limiti, il primo dei quali è dovuto alla natura del testo stesso: la traduzione eriugeniana rimane spesso incomprensibile se non si tiene presente l'originale greco, e a ciò si è tentato di supplire presentando in apparato citazioni volte a rendere ragione delle rese di Eriugena, come anche delle sue sviste di traduzione. Il *De imagine* si leggerebbe senz'altro più agevolmente affiancato al testo greco dell'opera, del quale, come si è più volte sottolineato, non è ad oggi disponibile un'edizione critica aggiornata.

Ai problemi di carattere testuale si aggiunga il fatto che, se si escludono le note dell'edizione francese curata da Jean Laplace e Jean Daniélou o quelle della traduzione italiana di Bruno Salmona, manca del pari un commento che fornisca esaurienti riferimenti alle fonti, o ai riscontri contenutistici del *De opificio hominis* con altre opere di Gregorio. Nell'apparato della presente edizione ne sono stati evidenziati quanti più possibile, e senza pretesa di esaustività, ma con l'idea di segnalare passi particolarmente importanti o significativi in un testo che merita ancora di essere esplorato: oltre ai rimandi ad alcuni autori classici e ai paralleli già chiaramente usati da Gregorio di Nissa, si è scelto di notare talora la peculiarità del vocabolo scelto (es. *petasum*, *uolema*, rispettivamente p. 74, 78 e 163, 272 s.); si sono indicati inoltre i rinvii ai passi del *Periphyseon* e di altre opere di Eriugena, come anche al *De natura corporis et animae* di Guglielmo di Saint-Thierry, che certamente potranno essere integrati e migliorati da ricerche future.

La speranza è quella di avere almeno in parte fatto luce o avanzato proposte di ricerca su un testo che, benché certamente minore, presenta comunque motivi di interesse, sia in quanto testimonianza dell'attività di traduzione di Eriugena, sia in quanto punto di riferimento del suo pensiero, specialmente nel campo dell'antropologia filosofica.

Il lavoro di edizione, compiuto per la massima parte da Giovanni Mandolino, è stato controllato e interamente revisionato da Chiara Ombretta Tommasi, che lo ha inoltre approntato per la pubblicazione. Per necessità editoriali, si è convenuto di attribuire la redazione dell'introduzione a Chiara Ombretta Tommasi e quella del testo a Giovanni Mandolino.

I due autori desiderano ringraziare Paolo Chiesa, che con grande disponibilità ha seguito il lavoro da cui si origina la presente edizione; Bart Janssens (e i suoi collaboratori, Christine Vande Veire e Yannick Anné), Ernesto S. Mainoldi, Claudio Moreschini, Martin Reinfelder, per i suggerimenti forniti nella preparazione del lavoro. Un ringraziamento particolare va a Édouard Jeauneau, che fin dai primi momenti, con vivace entusiasmo e rara generosità intellettuale ha messo a nostra disposizione il suo magistero e le sue eccellenti conoscenze, frutto di una vita dedicata allo studio di Eriugena, esortando a che questa ricerca vedesse la luce. La sua scomparsa, alla vigilia della pubblicazione del volume, lascia il rimpianto per non essere riusciti a mostrarglielo di persona, ma ci auguriamo che, giunto nel *deïforme regno*, possa vedere con i sensi spirituali quanto non è riuscito a vedere qui sulla terra.

BIBLIOGRAFIA

Edizioni

A. *De Imagine*

Capp. = 'Le *De imagine* de Grégoire de Nysse traduit par Jean Scot Érigène' – ed. M. Cappuyns, *Recherches de Théologie Ancienne et Médiévale*, 32 (1965), p. 205-262.

B. Altre opere di Eriugena

Comm. Ioh. = Iohannes Scottvs Erivgena, *Commentarius in Euangelium Iohannis* – ed. É. Jeauneau et A. J. Hicks (*CC CM*, 166), Turnhout, 2008, p. 47-137.

Epist. = *Epist. uar. III* 14, in *Epistole uariorum inde a saeculo nono medio usque ad mortem Karoli II (Calui) imperatoris collectae* – ed. E. Dümmler (*MGH, Epp.*, 4: *Epistolae Karolini aeui*, 2), Berlin, 1895, p. 158-161.

Gloss. in Mart. Cap. = *Iohannis Scotti Annotationes in Marcianum* – ed. C. E. Lutz (*The Mediaeval Academy of America*, 34), Cambridge (Mass.), 1939 (New York, 1970).

Gloss. in Mart. Cap. ex ms. Ox. = 'Le commentaire érigénien sur Martianus Capella (*De nuptiis*, I) d'après le manuscrit d'Oxford (Bodl. Libr. Auct. T.2.19, fol. 1-31)', in *Quatre thèmes érigéniens (Conférence Albert-le-Grand, 1974)* – ed. E. Jeauneau, Montréal – Paris, 1978, p. 101-186.

Hier. Dion. = Iohannes Scotvs Erivgena, *Expositiones in Ierarchiam coelestem* – ed. J. Barbet (*CC CM*, 31), Turnhout, 1975.

Hom. Ioh. = Iohannes Scottvs Erivgena, *Homilia super 'In principio erat uerbum'* – É. Jeauneau et A. J. Hicks (*CC CM*, 166), Turnhout, 2008, p. 3-43.

Hom. Ioh. – SC = Jean Scot, *Homélie sur le prologue de Jean* – ed. E. Jeauneau (*SC*, 151), Paris, 1969.

Periphys. = Ioannes Scotvs Erivgena, *Periphyseon, Liber primus, secundus, tertius, quartus, quintus* – ed. E. Jeauneau (*CC CM*, 161-165), Turnhout, 1996; 1997; 1999; 2000; 2003.

Praed. = GIOVANNI SCOTO ERIUGENA, *De praedestinatione liber. Dialettica e teologia all'apogeo della rinascenza carolingia* – ed. E. S. Mainoldi (*Per verba*, 18), Firenze, 2003.

C. Altri testi

ALEX. APHR., *de An.* = ALEXANDER APHRODISIENSIS, *De Anima cum Mantissa*, in *Alexandri Aphrosisiensis Praeter Commentaria Scripta Minora* – ed. I. Bruns (*Supplementum Aristotelicum*, II, 1), Berolini, 1887, p. 1-186.

BAS., *Hex.* = BASILIO DI CESAREA, *Sulla Genesi (Omelie sull'Esamerone)* – ed. M. Naldini (*Fondazione Lorenzo Valla*), Milano, 1990.

BAS., *Struct. hom.* = BASILE DE CÉSARÉE, *Sur l'origine de l'homme* – ed. A. Smets – M. van Esbroeck (*SC*, 160), Paris, 1970.

CHALC., *Comm.* = *Timaeus a Calcidio translatus commentarioque instructus* – ed. J. H. Waszink (*Plato Latinus*, IV), London – Leiden, 1975.

EMP., *Fr.* = EMPEDOCLES, *Fragmenta*, in: *Die Fragmente der Vorsokratiker* – ed. et trans. H. Diels, W. Kranz, Berlin, 1952 (rist. 1960).

GAL., *Nat. Fac.* = CLAVDIVS GALENVS, *De naturalibus facultatibus* – ed. C. G. Kühn (*Claudii Galeni Opera Omnia*, II), Leipzig, 1821.

GAL., *Plac.* = CLAVDIVS GALENVS, *De Hippocratis et Platonis placitis* – ed. C. G. Kühn (*Claudii Galeni Opera Omnia*, V), Leipzig, 1823.

GAL., *Sem.* = CLAVDIVS GALENVS, *De semine* – ed. C. G. Kühn (*Claudii Galeni Opera Omnia*, IV), Leipzig, 1822, p. 512-651.

GAL., *UP* = CLAVDIVS GALENVS, *De usu partium* – ed. C. G. Kühn (*Claudii Galeni Opera Omnia*, III-IV), Leipzig, 1822, vol. III – vol. IV, p. 262.

GREG. NAZ., *Or.* = GRÉGOIRE DE NAZIANZE, *Discours*, 1-3; 32-37; 38-41 – ed. J. Bernardi (*SC*, 247); ed. C. Moreschini (*SC*, 318; 358), Paris, 1978; 1985; 1990.

GREG. NYSS., *Anim. et res.* = GREGORIVS NYSSENVS, *De anima et resurrectione* – ed. A. Spira (*Gregorii Nysseni Opera*, III: *Opera dogmatica minora*, 3), Leiden, 2014.

GREG. NYSS., *Opific.* – Forbes = *De conditione hominis*, in *Sancti Patris Nostri Gregorii Nysseni Basili Magni fratris opera quae supersunt omnia*, I, 1-2 – ed. G. H. Forbes, Burntisland, 1855-1861, p. 96-319.

GREG. NYSS., *Opific.* – *PG* = S. GREGORIVS NYSSENVS, *De Hominis Opificio* J. Lewenclaio Interprete, Basileae, 1567 (rist. in *PG*, 44, col. 124C-256C).

Greg. Nyss., *Opific.* - SC = Grégoire de Nysse, *La création de l'homme* - ed. J. Laplace - J. Daniélou (*SC*, 6), Paris 2002² (1943).

Greg. Nyss., *Opific.* - transl. ital. = Gregorio di Nissa, *L'uomo* - trad. B. Salmona, Roma 1982.

Greg. Nyss., *Opific.* - transl. sclau. = L. Sels, De hominis opificio. *The Fourteenth-Century Slavonic Translation. A Critical Edition with Greek Parallel and Commentary*, Wien - Köln - Weimar, 2009.

Greg. Nyss., *Or. catech.* = Gregorivs Nyssenvs, *Oratio catechetica* - ed. E. Mühlenberg (*Gregorii Nysseni Opera*, III: *Opera dogmatica minora*, 4), Leiden, 1996.

Greg. Nyss., *Vit. Moys.* = Gregorivs Nyssenvs, *De Vita Moysis* - ed. H. Musurillo (*Gregorii Nysseni Opera*, VII: *Opera exegetica In Exodum et Novum Testamentum*, 1), Leiden, 1991.

Gvill. S. Theod., *Nat. corp.* = Gvillelmvs a S. Theodorico, *De natura corporis et animae* - ed. P. Verdeyen (*CC CM*, 88), Turnhout, 2003, p. 93-146.

Gvill. S. Theod., *Nat. corp.* - Lemoine = Gvilelmvs de Sancto Theodorico, *De natura corporis et animae* - ed. M. Lemoine (*Auteurs latins du Moyen Âge*), Paris, 1988.

Martin. Lavd., *Prisc.* = Martinvs Lavdvnensis, '*Verba greca Prisciani*' in M. E. Miller, *Glossaire grec-latin de la bibliothèque de Laon* (*Notices et Extraits des Manuscrits de la Bibliothèque Nationale et autres Bibliothèques*, 29, 2), Paris, 1880, p. 118-175.

Meth., *Res.* = Methodivs von Olympvs, *De resurrectione*, herausgegeben im Auftrage der Kirchenväter-Kommission der Königl. Preussischen Akademie der Wissenschaften - ed. G. N. Bonwetsch (*GCS*), Leipzig, 1917, p. 217-424.

Orig., *Princ.* = Origène, *Traité des Principes*, II: *Livres I et II*; III: *Livres III et IV* - ed. H. Crouzel et M. Simonetti (*SC*, 253; 268), Paris, 1978; 1980.

Philo, *Opif.* = Philo Ivdaevs, *De opificio mundi* (Philonis Alexandrini *Opera quae supersunt*, I) - ed. L. Cohn, Berolini, 1896, p. 1-50.

Porph., *Gaur.* = Porphyrivs, *Ad Gaurum* = 'Die neuplatonische, fälschlich dem Galen zugeschriebene Schrift Πρὸς Γαῦρον περὶ τοῦ πῶς ἐμψυχοῦνται τὰ ἔμβρυα' - ed. K. Kalbfleisch, in *Abhandlungen der Königlich Preussischen Akademie der Wissenschaften, Philosophisch-Historische Klasse*, Berlin, 1895, p. 33-62.

Prisc., *Inst. gramm.* = Priscianvs Grammaticvs Caesariensis, 'Institutionum Grammaticarum Libri XVIII', in *Grammatici Latini*, II-III - ed. M. Hertz - H. Keil, Leipzig, 1961 (Nachdruck der Ausgabe Leipzig, 1855-1859).

SERV., *Aen.* = *Servii grammatici qui feruntur in Vergilii carmina commentarii* – ed. G. Thilo, H. Hagen, 2 vol., Hildesheim, 1961 (ed. stereotypa, 1881-1884).

Studi

Arché e Telos. L'antropologia di Origene e di Gregorio di Nissa. Analisi storico-religiosa (Atti del Colloquio Milano 17-19 maggio 1979) – ed. U. Bianchi – H. Crouzel, Milano, 1981.

BEATRICE, P. F., 'Le tuniche di pelle. Antiche letture di Gen. 3, 21', in *La tradizione dell'Enkrateia. Motivazioni ontologiche e protologiche* – ed. U. Bianchi, Roma, 1985, p. 433-484.

BEHR, J., 'The rational Animal. A Rereading of Gregory of Nyssa's *De hominis opificio*', *Journal of Early Christian Studies*, 7 (1999), p. 219-247.

BISCHOFF, B., 'Irische Schreiber im Karolingenreich', in *Jean Scot Erigène et l'histoire de la philosophie*, p. 47-58.

BISHOP, T. A. M., 'Autographa of John the Scot', in *Jean Scot Erigène et l'histoire de la philosophie*, p. 89-94.

BRENNAN, M., 'Materials for the Biography of Johannes Scottus Eriugena', *Studi Medievali*, 27/1 (1986), p. 413-460.

BUDDE, T., 'The Three Recensions of the *Versio Dionysii*', *Journal of Medieval Latin*, 17 (2008), p. 253-272.

CACCIOTTI, A., 'La Fortuna del *De Opificio hominis* di Gregorio di Nissa in occidente', *Studi sull'Oriente Cristiano*, 1 (2002), p. 19-29.

CAPPUYNS, M., *Jean Scot Érigène. Sa vie, son oeuvre, sa pensée*, Louvain, 1933 (rist. Bruxelles, 1969).

CAPPUYNS, M., 'Les "Bibli Vulfadi" et Jean Scot Érigène', *Recherches de Théologie Ancienne et Médiévale*, 33 (1966), p. 137-139.

Catalogus Translationum et Commentariorum: Mediaeval and Renaissance Latin Translations and Commentaries – ed. F. E. Cranz – P. O. Kristeller, vol. 5, Washington, 1984.

CHVÁTAL, R., 'Der Mensch als Mikrokosmos in den Werken Gregors von Nyssa', *Revue des Études Byzantines*, 62 (2004), p. 47-70.

CHIESA, P., 'Ad verbum o ad sensum? Modelli e coscienza metodologica della traduzione tra tarda antichità e alto medioevo', *Medioevo e Rinascimento*, 1 (1987), p. 1-51.

CHIESA, P., 'Traduzioni e traduttori dal greco nel IX secolo: sviluppi di una tecnica', in *Giovanni Scoto nel suo tempo. L'organizzazione del sapere in età carolingia*, Spoleto, 1989, p. 171-200.

Cinq années d'enrichissement du patrimoine national: 1975-1980, donations, dations, acquisitions, Paris, 1980.

CONTRENI, J. J., 'The Study and Practice of Medicine in Northern France during the Reign of Charles the Bald', *Studies in Medieval Culture*, 6-7 (1976), p. 43-54.

CONTRENI, J. J., 'Masters and medicine in Northern France during the regin of Charles the Bald', in *Charles the Bald: Court and Kingdom. Papers based on a Colloquium held in London in April 1979* – ed. M. Gibson – J. Nelson, Oxford, 1981, p. 333-350.

CONTRENI, J. J. – Ó NÉILL, P. P., Divinae Historiae. *The Biblical Glosses of John Scottus Eriugena*, Firenze, 1997.

CONTRENI, J. J. – Ó NÉILL, P. P., 'The Early Career and Formation of John Scottus', in J. J. CONTRENI, *Learning and Culture in Carolingian Europe: Letters, Numbers, Exegesis, and Manuscripts* (Variorum Collected Studies series, 974), Farnham, 2011, p. 1-24.

CUPICCIA, M., 'Le sorti di un testo tradotto, rivisto e commentato. Il corpus pseudo-dionysiacum nella versione latina di Giovanni Scoto (secc. IX-XII)', *Filologia mediolatina*, 16 (2009), p. 57-80.

D'ALVERNY, M.-TH., 'Les *Solutiones ad Chosroem* de Priscianus Lydus et Jean Scot', in *Jean Scot Erigène et l'histoire de la philosophie (Colloques internationaux du Centre national de la Recherche scientifique, n° 561, Laon 7-12 juillet 1975)* – ed. R. Roques, Paris, 1977, p. 145-160.

DE BRASI, D., 'Eine Neubewertung des Körpers. Anthropologie und Glauben in den Schriften zur menschlichen Natur des Nemesios von Emesa und des Gregor von Nyssa', in *Anthropologie in Antike und Gegenwart. Biologische und philosophische Entwürfe vom Menschen* – ed. D. De Brasi – S. Föllinger, Freiburg, 2015, p. 377-395.

DE BRASI, D., 'Rhetorik, Medizin und Glauben: die Auffassung des menschlichen Körpers in Laktanzens *De Opificio Dei* und Gregor von Nyssas περὶ κατασκευῆς ἀνθρώπου', in *Soma: Körperkonzepte und körperliche Existenz in der antiken Philosophie und Literatur* – ed. Th. Buchheim – D. Meißner – N. Wachsmann, Hamburg, 2016, p. 121-141.

DÉCHANET, J.-M., *Aux sources de la spiritualité de Guillaume de Saint Thierry*, Bruges 1940.

DÉCHANET, J., *Guillaume de Saint-Thierry. Aux sources d'une pensée*, Paris, 1978.

DELISLE, L., *Inventaire des manuscrits de la Bibliothèque nationale: fonds de Cluni*, Paris 1884.

DESALVO, C., *L'oltre nel presente. La filosofia dell'uomo in Gregorio di Nissa*, Milano, 1996.

DEVREESSE, R., *Catalogue des Manuscrits grecs*, II: *Le Fonds Coislin*, Paris 1945.

DIELS, H., *Die Handschriften der antiken Ärzte*, II: *Die Übrigen Griechischen Ärzte ausser Hippokrates und Galenos* (*Abhandlungen der Königl. Preuß. Akademie der Wissenschaften*), Berlin, 1906.

La 'doppia creazione' dell'uomo, negli Alessandrini, nei Cappadoci e nella gnosi – ed. U. Bianchi, Roma, 1978.

DUCLOW, D. F., 'The sleep of Adam, the making of Eve: Sin and creation in Eriugena', in *Eriugena and Creation*, p. 235-261.

DUTTON, P. E., 'Eriugena's Workshop: The Making of the *Periphyseon* in Rheims 875', in *History and Eschatology in John Scottus Eriugena and His Time* – ed. M. Dunne – J. McEvoy, Leuven, 2002.

DUTTON, P. E. – LUHTALA, A., 'Eriugena in Priscianum', *Medieval Studies*, 56 (1994), p. 153-163.

ERISMANN, Ch., 'On the Significance of the Manuscript Parisinus graecus 437. The Corpus Dionysiacum, Iconoclasm, and Byzantine-Carolingian Relations', in *Menschen, Bilder, Sprache, Dinge. Wege der Kommunikation zwischen Byzanz und dem Westen* – ed. F. Daim – C. Gastgeber – D. Heher – C. Rapp, Mainz, 2018, p. 95-101.

Eriugena and Creation: Proceedings of the Eleventh International Conference on Eriugenian Studies, held in honor of Édouard Jeauneau, Chicago, 9-12 November 2011 – ed. W. Otten – M. Allen (*Instrumenta Patristica et Mediaevalia*, 68), Turnhout, 2014.

FINGERNAGEL, A., *Die illuminierten lateinischen Handschriften deutscher Provenienz der Staatsbibliothek Preussischer Kulturbesitz Berlin: 8-12. Jahrhundert*, Wiesbaden, 1991.

GARAND, M.-C., '*Giraldus levita*, copiste de chartes et de livres à Cluny sous l'abbatiat de saint Odilon († 1049)', in *Calames et cahiers. Mélanges de codicologie et de paléographie offerts à Léon Gilisen* – ed. J. Lemaire – E. Van Balbergh, Bruxelles, 1985, p. 41-48.

GASNAULT, P., 'Dom Anselme Le Michel et les manuscrits de l'abbaye de Cluny', *Bibliothèque de l'École des chartes*, 131 (1973), p. 209-219.

GREETHAM, D. C., 'Édouard Jeauneau's Edition of the *Periphyseon* in Light of Contemporary Editorial Theory', *American Catholic Philosophical Quarterly*, 79 (2005), p. 527-548.

GRONAU, K., *Poseidonios und die jüdisch-christliche Genesisexegese*, Berlin, 1914.

HAENEL, G., *Catalogi librorum manuscriptorum*, Leipzig 1830.

JAEGER, W., 'Greek Uncial Fragments in the Library of Congress in Washington', *Traditio*, 5 (1947), p. 79-102.

Jean Scot Erigène et l'histoire de la philosophie (Colloques internationaux du Centre national de la Recherche scientifique, n° 561, Laon 7-12 juillet 1975) – ed. R. Roques, Paris, 1977.

JEAUNEAU, É., 'La Bibliothèque de Cluny et les oeuvres de l'Érigène', in *Pierre Abélard, Pierre le Vénérable. Les courantes philosophiques, littéraires et artistiques en occident au milieu du XIIe siècle (Abbaye de Cluny, 2-9 juillet 1972)*, Paris, 1975, p. 703-725. [= *Études érigéniennes*, p. 97-421]

JEAUNEAU, É., *Quatre thèmes érigéniens*, Montréal-Paris 1978.

JEAUNEAU, É., 'Jean Scot Érigène et le grec', *Archivum Latinitatis Medii Aevi (Bulletin Du Cange)*, 61 (1979), p. 5-50. [= *Études érigéniennes*, p. 85-132]

JEAUNEAU, É., 'La division des sexes chez Gregoire de Nysse et chez Jean Scot Érigène', in *Eriugena: Studien zu seinen Quellen* – ed. W. Beierwaltes, Heidelberg, 1980, p. 33-54. [= *Études érigéniennes*, p. 343-364]

JEAUNEAU, É., 'Pseudo-Dionysius, Gregory of Nyssa, and Maximus the Confessor in the Works of John Scottus Eriugena', in *Carolingian Essays. Andrew W. Mellon Lectures in Early Christian Studies* – ed. U.-R. Blumenthal, Washington, 1983, p. 137-149. [= *Études érigéniennes*, p. 180-181]

JEAUNEAU, É., *Études érigéniennes*, Paris, 1987.

JEAUNEAU, É., 'Jean Scot Érigène: grandeur et misère du métier de traducteur', in *Traductions et traducteurs au Moyen Âge (Actes du Colloque international du CNRS organisé à Paris (IRHT) les 26-28 mai 1986)* – ed. G. Contamine, Paris, 1989, p. 99-108. [= *Tendenda Vela*, p. 231-242]

JEAUNEAU, É., 'The Neoplatonic Themes of *Processio* and *Reditus* in Eriugena', *Dionysius*, 15 (1991), p. 3-29. [= *Tendenda Vela*, p. 511-539]

JEAUNEAU, É., 'Le *De Paradiso* d'Ambroise dans le livre IV du *Periphyseon*', in ΣΟΦΙΗΣ ΜΑΙΗΤΟΡΕΣ *(Chercheurs de sagesse). Hommage à Jean Pépin* – ed. M.-O. Goulet-Cazé – G. Madec – D. O'Brien, Paris, 1992, p. 561-571. [= *Tendenda Vela*, p. 217-229]

JEAUNEAU, É., 'Érigène et Grégoire de Nysse', in *Du copiste au collectionneur: Mélanges d'histoire des textes et des bibliothèques en l'honneur d'André Vernet* – ed. D. Nebbiai-Dalla Guarda – J. F. Genest, Turnhout, 1998, p. 57-69. [= *Tendenda Vela*, p. 201-215]

JEAUNEAU, É., 'L'influence des traductions érigéniennes sur le vocabulaire philosophique du Moyen Âge: simples remarques', in *L'élaboration du vocabulaire philosophique au Moyen Âge (Actes du Colloque international de Louvain-la-Neuve et Leuven, 12-14 septembre 1998)* – ed. J. Hamesse – C. Steel (*Rencontres de Philosophie Médiévale*, 8), Turnhout, 2000, p. 157-169.

JEAUNEAU, É., *Tendenda Vela: Excursions littéraires et digressions philosophiques à travers le Moyen Âge* (*Instrumenta Patristica et Mediaevalia*, 47), Turnhout, 2007.

JEAUNEAU, É., 'Le Periphyseon: son titre, son plan, ses remaniements', *Les Études philosophiques*, 104 (2013), p. 13-28.

JEAUNEAU, É. – DUTTON, P., *The Autograph of Eriugena* (*CC Autographa Medii Aevi*, 3), Turnhout, 1996.

KACZYNSKI, B. M., *Greek in the Carolingian Age: The St. Gall Manuscripts*, Cambridge Mass., 1988.

KIJEWSKA, A., 'The Eriugenian Concept of Theology. John the Evangelist as the Model Theologian, in *Iohannis Scottus Eriugena. The Bible and Hermeneutics* – ed. G. van Riel – C. Steel – J. McEvoy, Leuven, 1996, p. 173-193.

IERACI BIO, A. M., 'Gregorio di Nissa (*De hominis opificio* 30) e la fisiologia galenica del *De usu partium*', in *La cultura scientifico-naturalistica nei Padri della Chiesa (I-V sec.) (XXXV incontro di studiosi dell'Antichità cristiana, 4-6 maggio 2006)* (*Studia Ephemeridis Augustinianum*, 101), Roma, 2007, p. 489-512.

LEITSCHUH, F. – H. FISCHER, *Katalog der Handschriften der Königlichen Bibliothek zu Bamberg*, vol. 1, Bamberg, 1887 (rist. 1966).

LEONARDI, C., 'Nuove voci poetiche tra secolo IX e XI', *Studi medievali*, 2 (1961), p. 139-168.

LEVINE, P., 'Two Early Latin Versions of St. Gregory of Nyssa's περὶ κατασκευῆς ἀνθρώπου', *Harvard Studies in Classical Philology*, 63 (1958), p. 473-492.

LORIQUET, H., *Catalogue général des Manuscrits des Bibliothèques Publiques de France*, t. 38, Paris, 1904.

MCGINN, B., 'Exegesis as Metaphysics: Eriugena and Eckhart on reading Genesis 1-3, in *Eriugena and Creation*, p. 463-499.

MAINOLDI, E. S., 'Le fonti del *De praedestinatione liber* di Giovanni Scoto Eriugena', *Studi Medievali*, 45/2 (2004), p. 651-698.

MAINOLDI, E. S., 'Iohannes Scottus Eriugena', in *La trasmissione dei testi latini del medioevo. Medieval Latin Texts and their Transmission*, II – ed. P. Chiesa – L. Castaldi, Firenze – Impruneta, 2005, p. 250-252.

MAINOLDI, E. S., 'Le citazioni dei Padri orientali nelle opere di Giovanni Scoto. Nuove osservazioni sul metodo dell'Eriugena traduttore', *Schede Medievali*, 52 (2014), p. 255-271.

MAINOLDI, E. S., *L'influenza letteraria e dottrinale del pensiero e dell'opera di Giovanni Scoto Eriugena nel medioevo (secc. IX-XV)*, Firenze, in corso di stampa.

MANDOLINO, G., '"Come un indovinello": doppia creazione e immagine di Dio nel *De opificio hominis* di Gregorio di Nissa', *Adamantius* 24 (2018), p. 416-434.

MARENBON, J., 'Wulfad, Charles the Bald and John Scottus Eriugena', in *Charles the Bald: Court and Kingdom. Papers based on a Colloquium held in London in April 1979* – ed. M. Gibson – J. Nelson, Oxford, 1981, p. 375-383.

MORESCHINI, C., 'Né maschio né femmina: la creazione dell'uomo secondo Gregorio di Nissa e Massimo il Confessore', in corso di stampa in *"Masculum et feminam creavit eos" (Gen. 1,27) Paradigmi del maschile e femminile nel cristianesimo antico. XLVII Incontro di Studiosi dell'Antichità Cristiana*, Istitutum Patristicum Augustinianum, Roma.

O'MEARA, J. J., *Eriugena*, Oxford, 1988.

MOONEY, H. A., 'The Notion of the Liberality of God in Gregory of Nyssa and Johannes Scottus Eriugena', *Studia Patristica*, 37 (2001), p. 207-211.

MOTTA, B., *La mediazione estrema. L'antropologia di Nemesio d'Emesa fra platonismo e aristotelismo*, Padova, 2004.

NALDINI, M., 'Gregorio Nisseno e Giovanni Scoto Eriugena. Note sull'idea di creazione e di antropologia', *Studi Medievali*, 20 (1979), p. 501-533.

OTTEN, W., *The Anthropology of Johannes Scottus Eriugena*, Leiden, 1991.

OTTEN, W., 'Reading Creation: Early Medieval Views of Genesis and Plato's *Timaeus*', in *The Creation of Heaven and Earth. Re-interpretations of Genesis 1 in the Context of Judaism, Ancient Philosophy, Christianity, and Modern Physics* – ed. G. H. van Kooten, Leiden, 2005, p. 225-243.

OTTEN, W., 'Anthropology between *Imago Mundi* and *Imago Dei*: The Place of Johannes Scottus Eriugena in the Tradition of Christian Thought', *Studia Patristica*, 43 (2006), p. 459-472.

PÉPIN, J., '"Image d'image", "Miroir de miroir" (Grégoire de Nysse, *De hominis opificio* xii, PG 44, 161C-164B)', in *Platonism in Late Anti-*

quity – ed. S. Gersh – C. Kannengiesser, Notre Dame, 1992, p. 217-229.

PEROLI, E., *Il Platonismo e l'antropologia filosofica di Gregorio di Nissa. Con particolare riferimento agli influssi di Platone, Plotino e Porfirio*, Milano, 1993.

PEROLI, E., 'Gregory of Nyssa and the Neoplatonic Doctrine of the Soul', *Vigiliae Christianae*, 51 (1997), p. 117-139.

PISI, P., Genesis *e* phthora. *Le motivazioni protologiche della verginità in Gregorio di Nissa e nella tradizione dell'*enkrateia, Roma, 1983.

RICCATI, C., Processio et explicatio. *La Doctrine de la création chez Jean Scot et Nicolas de Cues*, Napoli, 1983.

SAWORD, A., 'Man as the Image of God in the Works of William of St Thierry', *Cistercian Studies Quarterly*, 9 (1974), p. 309-327.

SCHILLMANN, F., *Die Handschriften-Verzeichnisse der Preussischen Staatsbibliothek zu Berlin. Verzeichnis der lateinischen Handschriften*, vol. 14.3, Berlin, 1919.

SCOGNAMIGLIO, R., 'Il *De opificio hominis*: eredità filoniana e origeniana nell'antropologia del Nisseno', in *Origene e l'alessandrinismo cappadoce (III-IV secolo) (Atti del V Convegno del Gruppo Italiano di Ricerca su Origene e la Tradizione Alessandrina, Bari 20-22 settembre 2000)* – ed. M. Girardi, Bari, 2002, p. 115-137.

SHELDON-WILLIAMS, I.-P., 'The Greek Platonist Tradition from the Cappadocians to Maximus and Eriugena', in *The Cambridge History of Later Greek and Early Medieval Thought* – ed. A. H. Armstrong, Cambridge, 1970, p. 425-501.

STERN, L. C., 'Altirische Glossen zu dem Trierer Enchiridion Augustins in der Königlichen Bibliothek zu Berlin', *Zeitschrift für celtische Philologie*, 7 (1910), p. 475-497.

SUCKALE-REDLEFSEN, G., *Die Handschriften des 8. bis 11. Jahrhunderts der Staatsbibliothek Bamberg*, vol. 1.1, Wiesbaden, 2004.

TRAUBE, L., *Bamberger Fragmente der vierten Dekade des Livius. Anonymus Cortesianus (Abhandlungen der Königlich Bayerischen Akademie der Wissenschaften*, III. Kl.: *Philos.-Philol. Classe*, XXIV/1; *Palaeographische Forschungen*, IV), München, 1904.

WILMART, A., *Codices Reginenses Latini*, Roma, 1937.

YINGST, D., '*Quae Omnia Concorditer Consonant*: Eriugena's Universe in the Thought of Honorius Augustodunensis', in *Eriugena and Creation*, p. 427-461.

ZACHHUBER, J., *Human Nature in Gregory of Nyssa. Philosophical Background and Theological Significance*, Leiden, 2000.

ZIER, M., 'The Growth of an Idea', in *From Athens to Chartres. Neoplatonism and Medieval Thought. Studies in Honour of Édouard Jeauneau* – ed. H. Westra, Leiden, 1992, p. 71-83.

IOHANNIS SCOTTI ERIVGENAE

CARMINA

edidit
Michael W. Herren

adiuuante
Andrew Dunning

CONSPECTVS SIGLORVM

Ω   consensus codicum $R + L$ $(L_1 + L_2) + V$
R   VATICANO, Biblioteca Apostolica Vaticana, Reg. lat. 1587 (s. IX), fol. 57r–64v: *carm. 1–8*
      VATICANO, Biblioteca Apostolica Vaticana, Reg. lat. 1709 (s. IX), fol. 16v–18r: *carm. 9–10*
L^I LAON, Bibliothèque municipale, 444 (870×875), fol. 294v–296v: *uoces graecae cum glossis latinis excerptae seriatim uel fere ex uersibus Iohannis a librario Martino Laudunensi*
L^{II} LAON, Bibliothèque municipale, 444 (870 × 875), fol. 297r–298r: *uersus graeci Iohannis selecti ab eodem librario*: *carm. 11–17*
V   VATICANO, Biblioteca Apostolica Vaticana, Reg. lat. 1625 (s. IX), fol. 65r-66v + PARIS, Bibliothèque nationale, lat. 10307, f. 246v [siglum *La* in *editione Dublinensi*], *carm. 18–19*
Ar   PARIS, Bibliothèque de l'Arsenal, 237 (s. IX$^{ex.}$), fol. 7r–8v: *carm. 22–24*
At   ATTENDORN (Sauerland), Kreisheimatsmuseum, s.n. (s. IX$^{2/3}$): *app. 9a*
B   BAMBERG, Staatsbibliothek, Patr. 66B (B. IV. 8) (s. XI), fol. 1r, 4r: *carm. 20–21*
C   CAMBRIDGE, Corpus Christi College, 223 (s. IX/X), pp. 342–344: *carm. 25*
E   MÜNCHEN, Bayerische Staatsbibliothek, clm 14000, 'Codex Aureus of St Emmeram' (a. 870), fol. 5v–6v, 16r, 45v, 65r-v, 96v, 97v, *app. 10–16*
F   FIRENZE, Biblioteca Laurenziana, Medicea, plut. lxxxix, sup. (s. XI$^{ex.}$), fol. 2r, 3v: *carm. 20–21*
G   BRUXELLES, Bibliothèque royale, 10078 (s. XI/XII) *in folio additicio*: *app. 8*
H   LONDON, British Library, Harley 2688, f. 18v (s. IX/X): *carm. 9c*
La   LAON, Bibliothèque municpale, 24, flyleaf (s. IX$^{ex.}$), flyleaf: *app. 7*
Ma   PARIS, Bibliothèque Mazarine, 561 (s. IX$^{ex.}$), fol. 6r–7v: *carm. 22–24*
Mo   MÜNCHEN, Staatsbibliothek, clm 14569 (s. XI), f. 72v: *carm. 9a*
O   MÜNCHEN, Bayerische Staatsbibliothek, clm 14137 (s. XI), fol. 1r, 4v–5r: *carm. 20–21*
P_1 PARIS, Bibliothèque nationale de France, lat. 12949 (s. IX/X), f. 24r: *fragmentum carm. 8*
P_2 PARIS, Bibliothèque nationale de France, lat. 10307 (s. IX$^{ex.}$), f. 95v: *fragmentum carm. 8*
P_3 PARIS, Bibliothèque nationale de France, lat. 13386 (s. IX$^{ex.}$), f. 104r: *app. 1*
Ph   BERLIN, Deutsche Staatsbibliothek, 46 (s. X), fol. 3v, 6r: *carm. 20–21*
S   ST GALLEN, Stiftsbibliothek, 48 (s. IX$^{2/3}$), p. 395, *app. 2*
So   LEIDEN, Universiteitsbibliotheek, BPL 67 (a. 838, with additions from c. 860), fol. 2r--3r: *App. 3-6*
Va   VATICANO, Biblioteca Apostolica Vaticana, Reg. lat. 240 (s. X), f. 121v: *carm. 9b* [siglum *V* in editione Dublinensi]
β   *consensus codicum* Vat. lat. 176 et 177 cum Urb. lat. 62: *carm. 20–21*

I

    Hellinas Troasque suos cantarat Homerus,
        Romuleam prolem finxerat ipse Maro;
    At nos caeligenum regis pia facta canamus,
        Continuo cursu quem canit orbis ouans.
5   Illis Iliacas flammas subitasque ruinas
        Eroumque ΜΑΧΑΣ dicere ludus erat;
    Ast nobis Christum, deuicto principe mundi,
        Sanguine perfusum psallere dulce sonat.
    Illi, composito falso sub imagine ueri,
10   Fallere condocti uersibus Arcadicis;
    Nobis uirtutem Patris ueramque sophiam
        Ymnizare licet laudibus eximiis.
    Moysarum cantus, ludos satyrasque loqua⟨ces⟩
        Ipsis usus erat plaudere per populos;
15   Dicta prophetarum nobis modulamine pulchro
        Consona procedunt cordibus, ore, fide.
    Nunc igitur Christi uideamus summa tropea
        Ac nostrae mentis sidera perspicua.
    Ecce crucis lignum quadratum continet orbem,
20   In quo pendebat sponte sua dominus
    Et Verbum patris dignatum sumere carnem,
        In qua pro nobis hostia grata fuit.
    Aspice confossas palmas humerosque pedesque.
        Spinarum serto tempora cincta fero.

---

23 cfr Ioh. 19, 37: uidebunt in quem transfixerunt

---

7 cfr VEN. FORT., *Carm.* 2, 15, 15: uictus amore dei contempto principe mundi

---

Trad. text.: *R L¹*

Inscriptio: VERSVS IOHANNIS SAPIENTISSIMI AD KAROLVM CALVVM FILIVM LVDOVICI PII CVIVS AVVS FVIT KARLVS MAGNVS *R*
  6 ΜΑΧΑΣ *L¹*] machas *R*   13 ludos *Mai*] ludas *R*   22 qua *R*] quo *Traube*
23 confossas *Mai*] cnfosˢas *R*   24 serto *Mai*] sorte *uel* serte *R*

  Gloss.: 6 ΜΑΧΑΣ] pugnas *R L¹*

In medio lateris, reserato fonte salutis,
V⟨ital⟩es haustus, sanguis et unda, fluunt.
Vnda lauat totum ueteri peccamine mundum,
Sanguis mortales nos facit esse deos.
Binos adde reos pendentes arbore bina:
Par fuerat meritum, gratia dispar erit.
Vnus cum Christo paradisi limina uidit,
Alter sulphureae mersus in ima Stygis.
ΕΚΛΥΨΙΣ solis, lunae redeuntis Eoo,
Insolito cursu sideris umbra fuit;
Commoto centro, tremulantia saxa dehiscunt:
Rupta cortina, sancta patent populis.
Interea laetus solus subit infera Christus,
Committens tumulo membra sepulta nouo.
ΟΠΛΙΣΤΕΣ fortis reserauit claustra profundi;
Hostem percutiens uasa recepta tulit.
Humanumque genus nolens in morte perire
Eripuit totum faucibus ex Erebi.

---

38 cfr Ioh. 19, 41   40 Matth. 12, 29; cfr Marc. 3, 27

---

25 cfr VEN. FORT., *Carm.* 3, 6, 17: quorum uos refluens de fonte salutis   27 cfr ALDH., *Laud. uirg.* 1317: sanguine purpureo demens peccamina mundi   28 facit esse deos] cfr 2, 60 Electis tuis praestitit esse deos; IOH. SCOT., *Homil. Ioh.* 21, 20: Si filius dei factus est homo ... quid mirum si homo, credens in filium dei, filius dei futurus sit?; 25-29: Non propter seipsum uerbum caro factum est, sed propter nos, qui non nisi per uerbi carnem potuissemus in dei filios transmutari. Solus descendit, cum multis ascendit. De hominibus facit deos qui de deo fecit hominem.   32 SERV., *Ad Aen.* 6, 134   33 Eoo] cfr IOH. SCOT., glossa ad VERG., *Aen.* 2, 417 in Bern, Burgerbibliothek 363, f. 88r, CONTRENI, 'The Irish in the Western Carolingian Empire', p. 779: ioh q: Nota quod 'EOUS' 'e' naturaliter sit longum metri necessitate correptum est propter sequentem uocalem   39 cfr SEDVL., *Carm. pasch.* 5, 230: ille profunda sequens penetrauit claustra gehennae   41 cfr CAND. FVLD., *Vita Aegil* 18, 4: qui non uult quemquam peccati morte perire

---

Trad. text.: *R L*^I

---

26 Vitales] *suppl. Mai*   32 Stygis] ΣΤΥΚΙΣ *L*^I, fagis *R*   33 ΕΚΛΥΠΣΙΣ *L*^I] Eclypsis *R*   37 Christus *edd.*] Christo *R*   39 ΟΠΛΙΣΤΕΣ *L*^I] oplistes *R; librarius codicis Vaticani 1587 (R) in margine inferiore folii 59r* ΟΠΛΙΣΤΕΣ *apicibus graecis cum glossa* armatus *posuit*

Gloss.: 32 Stygis] palus inferni *R L*^I   33 ΕΚΛΥΨΙΣ] defectus *L*^I   39 ΟΠΛΙΣΤΕΣ] armatus *R L*^I

CARMEN 1

Te Christum colimus caeli terraeque potentem:
    Namque tibi soli flectitur omne genu.
45 Qui tantum largire uides quod rite rogaris
    Et quod non recte rite negare soles,
Da nostro regi Karolo sua regna tenere,
    Quae tu donasti patribus almigenis.
Fonte tuo manant ditantia regna per orbem:
50   Quod tu non dederis, quid habet ulla caro?
Inuidiam miseram fratrum saeuumque furorem
    Digneris pacto mollificare pio.
At ne disturbent luctantia fraude maligna,
    Aufer de uita semina nequitiae.
55 Hostiles animos paganaque rostra repellens
    Da pacem populo, qui tua iura colit.
Nunc reditum Karoli celebramus carmine grato:
    Post multos gemitus gaudia nostra nitent.
Qui laeti fuerant quaerentes extera regna,
60   Alas arripiunt, quas dedit ipsa fuga.
Atque pauor ualidus titubantia pectora turbans
    Compellit Karolo territa dorsa dare.
Heheu, quam turpis confundit corda cupido,
    Expulso Christo sedibus ex propriis.
65 O utinam, Hluduwice, tuis pax esset in oris,
    Quas tibi distribuit qui regit omne simul.
Quid superare uelis fratrem? quid pellere regno?
    Numquid non simili stemmate progeniti?
Cur sic conaris diuinas soluere leges?
70   Ingratusque tuis cur aliena petis?
Quid tibi baptismus, quid sancta sollempnia missae?
    Occultis semper nutibus insinuant?

---

45 cfr ALDH., *Laud. uirg.* 819: *et fidum tremuli patronum rite rogabant*   **51** cfr IVVENC., 1, 455: *animae ipsius morbi saeuique furores*   **53** fraude maligna] cfr IVVENC., 2, 112; 4, 2; ALDH., *Laud. uirg.* 316, 585, 1007, 1639, 2247, *et passim apud poetas saec. IV-X*: cfr SCHUMANN, *Lateinisches Hexameter-Lexikon*, II, p. 348-349   **59** VERG., *Aen.* 4, 350: *fas extera quaerere regna*   **59/62** cfr JEAUNEAU, 'Jean Scot et l'ironie', p. 19   **61** VERG., *Aen.* 2, 200: *obicitur magis atque improuida pectora turbat*   **67** VERG., *Aen.* 3, 249: *et patrio Harpyias insontis pellere regno?*   **71** cfr Ps. BEDA, *Quat. temp.* (col. 615B): *more dehinc solito fiunt solemnia missae*

Trad. text.: *R L¹*

---

67 fratrem *Traube*] fratres *R*   **69** sic *Mai*] si *R*

Numquid non praecepta simul fraterna tenere,
  Viribus ac totis uiuere corde pio?
75 Ausculta pauidus, quid clamat summa sophia,
  Quae nullum fallit dogmata uera docens:
'Si tibi molestum nolis aliunde uenire,
  Nullum praesumas laedere parte tua'.

Christe, tuis famulis caelestis praemia uitae
80 Praesta; uersificos tute tuere tuos.
Poscenti domino seruus sua debita soluit,
  Mercedem serui sed uideat dominus.

---

78 Matth. 7, 12; cfr Luc. 6, 31   82 cfr Matth. 25, 19

---

79 cfr ALCVIN., *Carm.* 1, 1244: peruigil expectans caelestis praemia uitae; ALDH., *Aen.* 90, 5: edita caelestis prensant et praemia uitae   81 debita soluent] cfr 2, 71; 25, 28

Trad. text.: *R L¹*

---

73 non *Mai*] nam *R*

Gloss.: 74 Sedulius] *R^(in marg.)*

2

Aspice praeclarum radiis solaribus orbem,
   Quos crux saluiflua spargit ab arce sua.
Terram Neptunumque tenet flatusque polosque
   Et siquid supra creditur esse procul.
Dum reuocat miseros humanae gentis ab imo,
   Cuspide Tartaream percutit ipsa Stygin.
O crux alma, nites ultra Seraphynque Cerybque:
   Est ⟨quod⟩, quod non est, te colit omne super.
Te domini rerum, uirtutes atque potestas,
   Ordo colit medium iure tenendo locum;
Aggelus, archagelus, princeps, totusque supremus
   Caelestis numerus te colit alta petens.
Te ΠΝΥΞ nostra dehinc iusto modulamine laudat:
   Per te, Christifera, namque redempta fuit.
Tene manu Moyses magnus gestauerat olim,
   Dum dux diuini factus erat populi?
Te Pharao stupidat uestitam pelle draconis,
   Dum sorbes alios, quos dedit arte magus.

15/18 cfr Ex. 4, 1-10; 7, 8-13

8 cfr 8, 15: quae sunt, quae non sunt, sensu seu mente uidentur; 8, 29: est, non est, super est, qui praestitit omnibus esse; 24, 20: ON quod, quod non ON, denegat omne simul; cfr PIEMONTE, 'L'expression "Quae sunt et quae non sunt": Jean Scot et Marius Victorinus' 9/11 cfr 21, 17-21 10 cfr IOH. SCOT., *Ier. Dion interp.*, 8, 1: transeundum nunc nobis in mediam caelestium intellectuum expositiones, Dominationes illas supermundanis oculis, quantum possibile, explorantibus, et uere potentia speculamina diuinarum Potestatum et Virtutum 11 Aggelus] cfr PRISC., *Inst.* 1, 39: sequente 'g' uel 'c', pro ea 'g' scribunt Graeci et quidam tamen uetustissimi auctores Romanorum euphoniae causa bene hoc facientes 'Agchises', 'agceps', 'aggulus', 'aggens' 13 cfr CAND. FVLD., *Vita Aegil* 17, 93: altithrono cantans alto modulamine laudem 14 cfr 2, 68

Trad. text.: R L*I-II*

7 Seraphimque R*a.c.* 8 quod] *suppl. Traube* 13 ΠΝΥΞ R] ΤΠΝΥΞ L*¹* 16 Dum dux *Mai Floss*] Dux dum R *Traube* 17 uestitam *Mai*] uestita R

Gloss.: 3 Neptunumque] oceanum R 6 Stygin] paludem inferni R L*¹*, tristitia inferni R*in marg.*; cfr 1, 32 13 ΠΝΥΞ] ecclesia R L*¹*

O mons uirtutis, descendens carnis ad ima
  Figeris in ligno, septa subis Erebi.
Morte tua simpla nostram consumere duplam
  Ausus eras, totum dum renouas hominem.
O crux, ΕΡΥΤΡΕΑΣ tu scindis marmoris undas,
  Victrix praecedis dasque uiam populo.
Te sequitur uirtus omnis, te uita salusque;
  Te fugiunt fluctus: crimina dico mea.
Tu das arenosis currentia flumina saxis;
  Ebibat hunc fontem uiuere quisquis amat.
In sapidos fluctus populo conuertis amaros:
  Lex depulsa grauis, gratia sola manet.
Est quoque non dispar sensus praefatibus actis,
  Si quis ΣΙΜΒΟΛΙΚΑΣ discit amare notas.
Mysticus est Moyses Christus, rex atque sacerdos,
  Qui nos Aegypto liberat edomita.
Ipse subit mortem primus mortemque resoluens
  Prosilit in uitam; uirga recepta regit.
Quid, Pharao, sequeris populum? fuge mersus in ima
  Carceris aeterni, te tegat atra palus.
Nos uirtutis iter medium dum carpimus, altae
  Instant phantasiae nequitiaeque toli.
Quas uincens animus laeta potitur harena
  Et peccata procul mersa subacta uidet.

37/41 cfr Ex. 14, 26-28

23 cfr Ivvenc., 1, 424: piscibus insidias disponere marmoris undis   25 Alcvin., *Carm.* 1, 640: angelicos sequitur monitus mox uita salusque   33 cfr Isid., *Expos. in exod.* 12-21 (col. 292-297): Moyses typum Christi gestauit, qui populum Dei a jugo diabolicae seruitutis eripuit, et ipsum diabolum in aeterna poena damnauit   40 toli] cfr Herren, 'The Commentary on Martianus attributed to John Scottus', p. 277-279   41 cfr Ov., *Met.* 12, 38: multaque perpessae Phrygia potiuntur arena   42 cfr Alc. Avit., *Carm.* 4, 655: ne redeant peccata tibi, ne mersa leuentur

Trad. text.: *R L*^{I-II}

21 tua *Traube*] sua *R*   22 renouaes *R*   23 ΕΡΥΤΡΕΑΣ *L*^I] Erytreas *R*   27 arenosis] *post* arenosis *inseruit* moneis tum *deleuit R*   32 ΣΙΜΒΟΛΙΚΑΣ *L*^I, ΣΥΜΒΟΛΙΚΑΣ *R*

Gloss.: 20 septa] claustra *R*   23 ΕΡΥΤΡΕΑΣ *L*^I] rubeas *R L*^I; Eritryum mare .i. rubrum mare *R*^{in marg.}   32 ΣΙΜΒΟΛΙΚΑΣ] significatiuas *R L*^I   40 toli] testudines *R*

CARMEN 2

    Tunc ΑΛΑΛΑΓΜΑ canit gaudens multumque triumphans,
        Laudibus amplificat tunc ΠΑΡΑΔΟΞΑ Dei.
45 Litora uirtutum lustrans tunc intrat heremum,
        Mundi contempti qua silet omnis amor,
    Spiritus inmundus nullam reperire quietem
        Qua numquam potuit, sed redit unde uenit.
    ΧΑΛΚΕΥΣ ex alto pendens ibi sibilat anguis:
50   Extinctum uirus, liber erit populus.
    Magdaline, quaeris Dominum quid maesta sepultum?
        Funere deuicto, respice laeta deum.
    Desine ΚΑΙΠΥΡΙΚΟΥΣ meditari, cernere uultus;
        Viuus adest Dominus; quem gemis ipsa uide.
55 Tersa pios uultus cursim solabere fratres;
        Euaggelistes, prima beata, uale.
    Christe, Dei Verbum, uirtus, sapientia Patris,
        Sanguinis unda tui, qua madet ara crucis,
    Nos purgat, redimit, soluit, uitamque reducit,
60   Electisque tuis praestitit esse deos.
    Da nostro Karolo pacem, cui sceptra dedisti,
        Atque suus pereat hostis ubique ferox.
    Vtque tibi placeat cunctis, quis uixerit, annis
        Semina uirtutum sparge tuo famulo.
65 Quarum perspicue uis surgat, crescat in actus,
        Vt merito tecum semper ubique regat.

---

49 Num. 21, 7-9; cfr IV Reg. 18, 4   53 Ioh. 20, 15   56 euaggelistes] cfr Marc. 16, 10; Ioh. 20, 18   57 uirtus, sapientia patris] I Cor. 1, 24: Christum Dei uirtutem et Dei sapientiam

---

57 ALCVIN., *Carm.* 1, 1: Christe deus, summi uirtus, sapientia patris; cfr FLOR. LVGD., *Carm.* 3, 5: hic lux, hic uirtus, hic est sapientia patris; cfr App. 2, 11: lux aeterna, dei Verbum, sapientia patris   61 cfr 8, 85; 25, 78; THEODVLF., *Carm.* 39, 3: qui tibi sceptra dedit, uitae det tempora longa, / Gaudia concedat, qui tibi sceptra dedit

---

Trad. text.: *R L*^{I-II}

---

43 ΑΛΑΛΑΓΜΑ *L*^I] alalagma *R*   44 ΠΑΡΑΔΟΞΑ *L*^I] paradoxa *R*   49 ΧΑΛΚΕΥΣ *L*^I] Chalceus *R*   53 ΚΑΙΠΥΡΙΚΟΥΣ (i.q. καιπουρικούς) *scripsi*] ΚΑΙΠΑΡΙΟΥΣ *L*^I, caeparios *R*, caepuarios *R*^{p.c.}   60 praestitet *R*] praestitit *R*^{p.c.}   61 cui *scripsi*] qui *R*, cfr 8, 85; 11, 3; 25, 78

Gloss.: 43 ΑΛΑΛΑΓΜΑ] hymnus victoriae *R L*^I   44 ΠΑΡΑΔΟΞΑ] miracula *R L*^I   49 ΧΑΛΚΕΥΣ] aeneus *R L*^I   53 ΚΑΙΠΥΡΙΚΟΥΣ (*ex emend.*)] ortulanos *R*, ortulanus *L*^I; caepos ortus. caeparius ortulanus *R*^{in marg.}   62 autum non (*sic*) *R*^{in marg.}

ΟΡΘΩΔΟΞΟΣ ΑΝΑΞ, ΕΥΣΗΒΗΣ ΕΝΚΛΥΤΟΣ ⟨ΑΡΧΟΣ⟩,
ΣΟΒΡΟΝ, ΧΡΙΣΤΟΦΟΡΟΣ, ΚΙΡΡΙΟΣ Ω ΚΑΡΟΛΟΣ.
Hos uersus cecini sex denos bisque quaternos
70   Iohannes, uester seruulus indiguus.
ΜΕΛΠΟ dum, laetus regi mea debita soluo:
Soluere curarim, si sibi grata forent.

69/72 cfr Dutton, 'Eriugena, the royal poet', p. 64-65.   71 debita soluo] cfr 1, 81: debita soluit

---

Trad. text.: R L^{I-II}

---

67 ΕΥΣΗΒΗΣ R L^{II}] ΕΥΣΙΒΗΣ L^{I} ΕΝΚΛΥΤΟΣ R L^{II}] ΕΝΚΛΙΤΟΣ L^{I} ΑΡΧΟΣ] suppl. Floss, cfr 17, 9   68 ΣΟΒΡΟΝ R L^{I-II} Traube] ΣΟΦΡΟΝ Mai; cfr autem 17, 9 (ΚΑΡΟΛΟΣ) ΟΣ ΣΟΦΟΣ, ΟΣ ΔΥΝΑΤΟΣ, ΠΑΝΥ ΣΟΦΡΩΝ ΤΕ ΚΡΑΤΟΣ ΤΕ   69 sic Mai] si R   71 ΜΕΛΠΟ L^{I}] ΜΕΛΠΩ edd., melpo R

Gloss.: 67 ΟΡΘΩΔΟΞΟΣ recte credens R L^{I-II} ΑΝΑΞ] rex R L^{I-II} ΕΥΣΗΒΗΣ] pius R L^{I-II} ΕΝΚΛΥΤΟΣ] gloriosus R L^{I-II} 68 ΣΟΒΡΟΝ (i. q. ΣΩΦΡΩΝ)] temperans R L^{I-II} ΧΡΙΣΤΟΦΟΡΟΣ] Christum ferens R L^{I-II} ΚΙΡΡΙΟΣ] dominus R L^{I-II} Ω] ipse R L^{I-II} ΚΑΡΟΛΟΣ] Karolus L^{I-II} 71 ΜΕΛΠΟ] canto L^{I}

3

Auribus Aebraicis notum si dixero pascha,
 Vsibus Ausoniae 'transitus' est habilis.
Primum naturae si uis cognoscere Pascha,
 Quaerito quis primus fulsit in orbe dies,
5 Quo machinae mundi cumulatim dicitur esse
 In species proprias transitus ex nihilo,
Conditor et causas, quas secum semper habebat,
 Prodidit in formas lumine conspicuas.
Sperica tunc tellus artatur limine certo
10 Vestiturque suis frondibus et ΛΑΧΑΝΙΣ.
Cincxit litorius Neptunum et ΝΕΡΕΑ limbus,
 Quem superare nequit cerula crine tumens.
Aerium spatium tangebant cornua lunae,
 Quod ualidis pennis oscina ΚΟΛΑ secant.
15 Aetherios cyclos ambibat stelliger orbis,
 Mundum circuiens motibus assiduis.
Processu uario ferebatur consona turma
 Errantum, dulces edidit ipsa tonos

---

4 cfr *Antiph. Bang.* II, 5-7 Hic enim dies quasi primogenitus   5 machinae mundi] cfr Lvcr., 5, 96   6 cfr Ioh. Scot., *Periphys.* 4, 12 (col. 796C): nam ipse ex non existente in esse transitus motus quidam est, et mutatio non existentis in esse secundum diuinam uoluntatem transmutati   7/8 cfr Chalc., *Transl.* 27c-28b (p. 40): Omne autem quod gignitur ex causa aliqua necessaria gignitur; nihil enim fit cuius ortum non legitima causa et ratio praecedat. Operi porro fortunam dat opifex suus; quippe ad immortalis quidem et in statu genuino persistentis exempli similitudinem atque aemulationem formans operis effigiem honestum efficiat simulacrum necesse est   13 cornua lunae] cfr Ov., *Met.* 8, 11; 10, 479; 12, 264

Trad. text.: *R L^I*

10 ΛΑΧΑΝΙΣ *L^I*] lachanis *R*   11 Neptuni et *scripsi*] Neptuni *R*   ΝΕΡΕΑ *L^I*] nerea *R*   limbus *R*] ΛΙΜΒΟΥΣ *L^I*   12 cerula *R*] ΚΕΡΥΛΑ *L^I*   14 oscina *Floss*] ΟΣΑΝΑ *L^I*, osana *R*; *cfr Glosse in Mart. Cap.* 10, 3 (p. 16): uolatus oscinum auium   ΚΟΛΑ (*i. q.* sine cornibus) *scripsi*] colla *R edd.*

Gloss.:   10 ΛΑΧΑΝΙΣ] herbis *R L^I*   11 ΝΕΡΕΑ] beluas *R* (*super* Neptunum) *L^I*   limbus] orbis *R L^I*   12 cerula] unda *R L^I*   14 oscina (*ex emend.*)] aues *R L^I*

CARMEN 3

  Sex numero septem spatiis modulantibus octo:
20   Caelestis sperae constitit armonia.
  Posthac extremus rex mundi dicitur aulam
   Possessurus eam, ni sua facta forent.
  Eheu, sed miserum decepit femina coniunx,
   Quam prius incautam perdidit astus ΟΦΙΣ.
25   Moyses, dux populi, celebrauit Pascha secundum,
   Bis quina plaga percutiens ΙΣΙΔΑΜ.
  Transiuit Dominus signatos sanguine postes,
   Dum primogenitos planxerat ipsa suos.
  Israhelites festinus uescitur agnum;
30   Ossibus illaesis mystica cena fuit.
  It populus gaudens, Aegyptus perfida luget,
   Insanit rabie; quem timet insequitur.
  Anxius Erythreas tunc Moyses aspicit undas;
   Inscia uirtutis territa plebs dubitat.
35   Nubibus obscuris Pharaonis turma retenta,
   Ne praedam caperet, feruida saeua stupet.
  Tum dux intrepidus Neptunia dissicat arua;
   Praestitit ignoti marmoris unda uiam,
  Ventus et exurens ΑΜΜΟΝΙΑ litora siccat
40   Et muro similis cerula prona tumet.
  Ingreditur populus limpharum gurgite tutus,
   Laetus et egrediens actea grata uidet.
  Obruitur pelagi cumulis Pharaonicus hostis;
   ΑΡΜΑΤΑ dispersim Tethidis ima tegunt.

---

27 Ex. 12, 12-13   **29** Ex. 12, 26: et comedetis festinantes

---

19 cfr Ioh. Scot., *Periphys.* 3, 33 (col. 718B): diapason habet enim octo sonos, septem spatia, sex tonos; cit. ex Mart. Cap., 7, 737; 9, 951: διὰ πᾶσιν autem sonos habet octo, spatia septem, tonos sex   **27** cfr Alc. Avit., *Carm.* 5, 241: signabit sanguis nitido de corpore postem

---

Trad. text.: *R L*^{*I*}

---

20 constitit] *coniec. Traube in app.,* condidit *R*   **24** ΟΦΙΣ *L*^{*I*}] ophis *R*; *sed librarius eandem uocem exaratam litteris graecis cum glossa in margine inferiore f. 59r posuit*   **26** ΙΣΙΔΑΜ *L*^{*I*}] Isidam *R*, ΙΣΙΔΑ *R in marg. inferiore f. 59r*   **30** caena *R*   **35** Pharaonis *edd.*] Faraonis *R*   **38** marmoris unda uiam *Mai*] uiam marmoris unda *R*   **39** ΑΜΜΟΝΙΑ *L*^{*I*}] ammonia *R*   **44** ΑΡΜΑΤΑ (*i. q.* ἅρματα) *Mai Floss*] armata *R Traube*

Gloss.: **24** ΟΦΙΣ] serpens *R L*^{*I*}   **26** ΙΣΙΔΑΜ] Aegyptum *L*^{*I*}, Egyptum *R*   **33** Erythreas] rubeas *R*; cfr 2, 23   **39** ΑΜΜΟΝΙΑ] arenosa *R L*^{*I*}

CARMEN 3

45 Haec quondam fuerant uenturi ΙΔΑΛΜΑΤΑ Christi,
     In quo conlucent, quae latuere diu.
   Qui solus uictor, prostrato principe mundi,
     Transacto triduo prosilit ex Erebo.
   Ac primum calcans mortem transiuit in alta:
50   Solus nam liber numine Tartareo.
   Sanguinis et proprii fundens libamina pura
     Mundo saluato Pascha nouum dedicat.
   Sponte sua Dominus se mactat ipse sacerdos,
     Quae Patri placens hostia sola fuit,
55 Hostia quae totum purgauit crimine mundum,
     Mundum quem potuit perdere primus homo.
   Ex uno ueniens mors est expulsa per unum;
     Morte bona uitae mors mala uicta perit.
   Primitiae Christus reserauit septa sepulchri,
60   Nostrae naturae perdita restituens.
   Harum nunc rerum celebrantur symbola sacra,
     Dum parent oculis mentibus nota prius,
   Dum corpus Christi, dum sacri sanguinis undam
     Et pretium mundi mens pia corde sapit,
65 Dum memores cenam domini reuocamus in annos,
     Dum plures odas consonat ipse chorus.
   Aeternis epulis, quas mystica signa figurant,
     Digneris Karolum pascere, Christe, tuum
   Deuotum famulum, qui te ueneratur honorat
70   Aedibus constructis aurea uasa parans,
   Cortinis patulis ⟨et⟩ longa per atria tentis,
     Vestito clero murice purpureo;
   Presbyteri sancti reboant altaria circum:
     'Perpetuis templis sic erit ipse tuus'.

---

57 I Cor. 15, 21   59 primitiae Christus] cfr I Cor. 15, 20; 15, 23

---

47 cfr 1, 7: deuicto principe mundi   48 cfr App. 6, 4: horam, qua Christus prosilit ex Erebo; 2, 7: Emicat ex Erebo   53 ipse sacerdos] cfr VEN. FORT., *Carm.* 1, 5, 9; 3, 7, 57; 4, 2, 7; 5, 5, 125   63 sanguinis undam] cfr ALC. AVIT., *Carm.* 1, 167; VEN. FORT., *Mart.* 4, 254; *Carm.* 2, 14, 13; ALDH., *Laud. uirg.* 1797   71 VERG., *Aen.* 2, 483: et atria longa patescunt; *cit.* Ecbas. capt. 603: cortinis croceis per longa palatia tensis

---

Trad. text.: *R L¹*

---

45 ΙΔΑΛΜΑΤΑ *Traube*] ΔΑΛΜΑΤΑ *L¹*, id almata *R*   49 primum *R*] primus *edd.*
61 nunc *Mai*] nec *R*   65 cenam *Mai*] caena *R*   71 et] *add. Mai Floss*

Gloss.: 45 ΙΔΑΛΜΑΤΑ] imagines *R L¹*

4

Haec nostram dominam Yrmindrudis nomine claram
  Exornant meritis laudibus apta suis:
Forma, genus, species, morum pulcherrima fama,
  Regis conubium, docta loquela decens,
5 Praeclarae sobolis donum notaque propago
  Obsequiumque bonis omnibus egregium,
Ingens ingenium, perfecta Palladis arte,
  Auro subtili serica fila parans –
Actibus eximiis conlucent pepla mariti,
10 Gemmarum series contegit ΙΝΔΥΣΙΑΣ.
Miratur fugitans numquamque propinquat arachnos,
  Quamuis Palladios aequiperat digitos.
Inclita consilio castum seruare cubile,
  Cypris ne ualeat commaculare thoros.
15 Pauperibus multis Christi iustissima cura
  Illam sollicitat rite ministra fore,
Prudentum matrum, quas laudant dogmata sacra,
  Virtutis consors enitet assidua,
Orans ac legitans libros manibusque laborans,
20 Et nullum uitiis tempus inane uacat.
Quid causas regni dicam, quas ipsa perita
  Disponit uigilans pectore praecipuo?
Si sinerent apices, quos scripserat ipse Salomon,
  Dixissem forsan quod perhibere uolunt:

---

cfr Dutton, 'Eriugena, the royal poet', p. 67-68
  1 nomine clarum] saepe inuenitur apud poetas; cfr Schumann, *Lateinisches Hexameter-Lexicon*, VI, 542-543   7 Verg., *Aen.* 2, 15: instar montis equum diuina Palladis arte

Trad. text.: *R L¹*

  10 series *Mai Traube*] serie *R*   contegit *Traube*] detegit *R*   ΙΝΔΥΣΙΑΣ *L¹*] indusias *R*   22 uigilans *Traube*] uigili *Mai,* uigilo *R*   24 quod *Traube*] quid *R*

Gloss.: 10 ΙΝΔΥΣΙΑΣ] indumenta *R L¹*   11 arachnos] aranea *R*

CARMEN 4

25 Haec nam, haec merito censetur femina fortis,
  Quam Karolus reperit fortis et almus anax.
Quem solum celebrat Francorum gloria regem
  Dignum Christicolis plebibus atque choris;
Cui gestare licet regnorum plurima sceptra,
30 Quae magni patres sustinuere sui;
Cui soli regum sapientia praeuia pollet;
  Quem purae mentis nobilitat studium;
Quem scriptura docet diuinis plena figuris,
  Ne recto Christi tramite debilitet;
35 Qui sanctas aedes dedicans ornatibus amplis
  Caelestis patriae symbola sacra uidet.
Hos ambo, regem dico dominamque potentes,
  Christe, tuere tui numinis auxilio.
Sis fidus custos, sis murus tutus in aeuum,
40 Vt tibi perpetuo placita uota ferant.
Deuotis animis semper te laudet uterque,
  Vocibus armonicis, actibus atque bonis.
Illorum tumidos inimicos sterne rebelles
  Aut his conuersos subdere colla mone.
45 Da pacem populo ⟨modo⟩ qui tibi seruit ubique;
  Omnibus Christigenis floreat alma quies.
Paganos pyratas uastantes regna per orbem
  Consumptos gladio gurgite merge maris;
In Syrtes uarias spargantur flatibus austri,
50 Illic ut pereant aestibus Oceani.
Nos uero laetos puro te corde colentes
  Ducas aetherios sidera supra choros.

---

25 cfr Prou. 31, 10

---

37 cfr VERG., *Aen.* 3, 438: iunoni cane uota libens dominamque potentem
43 sterne rebelles] cfr CORIPP., *Ioh.* 1, 144: Laguantanque acies armis prosterne rebelles
49 cfr Ov., *Trist.* 1, 10, 33: haec, precor, euincat, propulsaque flatibus austri

---

Trad. text.: *R L¹*

---

31 regum *Traube*] regnum *R* 35 Qui *Mai*] Cui *R* 43 sterne rebelles *Mai*] sternere belles *R* 44 his *Traube*] hos *R* 45 modo] *suppl. Traube* 47 paganos *Mai*] paganas *R* 52 Ducas *Mai*] ducos *R*

Gloss.: 26 anax] rex R; cfr 2, 67

5

Mystica sanctorum panduntur dogmata patrum,
   Pneumate sanctifico quae cecinere deo,
Aeterno patris uerbo, quo cuncta creantur
   Occultis sinibus ordine quaeque suis,
Fabrica quo mundi formis simul omnibus una
   Surrexit, fuerat ut ratione sua.
Quae sine praecessit non Christo tempore facta,
   Dum semper natus cuncta creata uidet.
Quam super effertur sanctus ratione regentis
   Spiritus, ut sacras uiuificaret aquas.
Angelicum numerum superorum castra tenentem
   Constituit mundo, cetera quaeque uides,
Quorum primatu hominem paradisus habebat
   Assimilem factum mente uidere deum.
Hanc homo praeclaram speciem complectere nolens,
   Corruit et prolem traxit ad ima suam.
Sed ne tanta dei penitus transiret imago,
   Hanc speciem hominis coepit habere Deus.
Hinc natus mundo, passus sub lege malorum,
   Morte sua mortem perdidit ipse meam.
Quo sunt, quo uiuunt, quo stant, quo cuncta mouentur,
   Ille Deus moritur, uiuat ut ipse homo.
Ordine multiplici signatus patribus olim
   Mactatur legi, uatibus ut canitur.
Hic fuerat aries speculo prouisus ad aram,
   Dum typicus Isaach ducitur ad iugulum.

9/10 cfr Gen. 1, 2   13 cfr Gen. 1, 27   25/26 cfr Gen. 22, 9-13

---

3 cfr Hraban., *Carm.* 4, 1, 1: summe sator rerum, qui uerbo cuncta creasti; Ioh. Scot., *Periphys.* 3, 9 (col. 642A); 3, 15 (col. 665Aff.); 3, 16 (col. 666Bff., col. 669B praesertim): simul et semel aeternaliter in uerbo domini facta sunt   5 omnibus una] cfr 6, 15; 8, 42; 25, 37   21 cfr Prosp., *Epigr.* 58, 1: principium mundi Deus est, quo cuncta mouentur   25/32 cfr Isid., *Expos. in gen.* 23 (col. 251ff.)

Trad. text.: *R L*^{I-II}

---

7 non *Traube*] in *R*   24 ut *Traube*] et *R*

     Festinans populus Aegypto hunc sumpserat agnum,
       Sanguine conspergens limina nota domus.
     Hic fons, uirga, petra, caelestis fulgor obumbrans,
30   Serpens et manna, nubs, uia, panis, aqua.
     Talia saepe Dei iussu sub tempore facta
       Aeternum Dominum significare suum.
     Hacque impleta die, sacro ueneramur honore:
       Ista dies tanta mystica facta tenet.
35   Hanc mundus prodit congaudens luce decora,
       Florigeros motus mittit in aethra suos,
     Germina producens, florentes gramine fructus:
       Nam Christus fructus dulcis ubique suis.
     Surrexit Christus: nostra hinc pia corda resultant,
40   'Alleluia' deo orbis ubique canit.
     Inclite, qui regum te rex conseruet in aeuum,
       Prospera concedat, hinc super astra uehat,
     Qui sub honore sui humili, cum corde canoro
       Alternos statuis, psallis et ipse choros.
45   Credimus: ista tibi seruantur culmine caeli,
       Heres Dauiticus efficiere pius.
     ΠΡΟΣΕΥΧΙΣ petimus, uotis et corde precamur:
       Qui dedit hoc uelle, det tibi posse Deus.
     ΒΑΣΙΛΕΩΣ ΚΑΡΟΛΟΙ ΗΜΩΝ ΣΥ, ΧΡΙΣΤΕ, ΒΟΕΘΕΙ
50   ΩΣ ΚΛΕΙΡΕΙΣΘΕ ΧΟΡΟΙΣ ΔΙΝΑΤΟΣ ΟΥΡΑΝΙΟΥΣ.

27/28 Ex. 12, 7

---

30 nubs cfr Serv. *Aen.* 10, 636

Trad. text.: *R L*^{I-II}

---

33 ueneramur *Mai*] uenerantur *R Traube*   39 nostra hinc pia corda *Mai*] nunc nostra pia corda *R*   43 canoro] *scripsi*, canoros *R, edd.*   49 ΒΑΣΙΛΕΩΣ ΚΑΡΟΛΟΙ ΗΜΩΝ ΣΥ ΧΡΙΣΤΕ ΒΟΕΘΕΙ *R L*^{II}] *om. L*^I. *Cfr* 7, *tit., quo inuenitur* ΒΑΣΙΛΕΙ ΚΑΡΟΛΟ, *id quod demonstrat aut Iohannem Scottum aut librarium incertum esse de usu casus genitiui aut datiui in locutionibus graecis; uide* R. BROWNING, *Medieval and Modern Greek*, Cambridge, 1983², p. 36-38   ΚΑΡΟΛΟΙ *L*^{II}] ΚΑΡΛΟΙ *R*

Gloss.: 47 ΠΡΟΣΕΥΧΙΣ] *lemma sine glossa apud L*^I   49 ΒΑΣΙΛΕΩΣ] regis *R L*^{II} ΚΑΡΟΛΟΙ] Karoli *L*^{II}   ΗΜΩΝ] nostri *R L*^{II}   ΣΥ] tu *R L*^{II}   ΒΟΕΘΕΙ] faue *R L*^{I-II} 50 ΩΣ] ut *R L*^{II}   ΚΛΕΙΡΕΙΣΘΕ] possidere *R L*^{I-II}   ΧΟΡΟΙΣ] choros *R L*^{II}   ΔΙΝΑΤΟΣ] possit *R L*^{I-II}   ΟΥΡΑΝΙΟΥΣ] caelestes *R L*^{II}; cfr L^I ad 8, 1

6

Emicat ex Erebo lux mundi magna triumphans:
Primitias uitae ⟨mors⟩ moribunda stupet.
Prosiliunt Furiae, concurrunt undique Parcae:
Mirantur tristem congemuisse Stygem.
5 Ille dein princeps baratri petit arma sueta,
Quis genus humanum subdidit ipse sibi:
Sed mox ut uidit ruitantia limina fracta,
Territus, attonitus, fugit ad ima domus.
Non tamen euasit tenebrosa per antra tyrannus:
10 Fortior intrauit, qui sua uasa tulit.
Attractus, captus, uinctus, strictusque catenis,
Detentus, domitus, pulsus ab arce, prius
Qua mundi princeps elatus sederat, olim
Bestia saeua, uorax indomitaque diu.
15 Sed uictor mundi praestantior omnibus unus
Totam collisit comminuitque caput.
Aestus aeterni comburunt turpe cadauer,
Pyrflegetontis ⟨enim⟩ feruida flamma furit.
Laetantur miseri, quos laesit dira potestas;
20 Captiui redeunt, uincula laxa uacant.
Iam regnat Verbum patris, iam cuncta gubernat
Virtus, uita, salus; mors fera uicta silet.
Surrexit uiuus rumpens retinacula loeti:
Nulla ualet summum uis retinere Deum.

---

10 cfr Ex. 3, 22: uasa argentea et aurea ac uestes ponetisque eas super filios et filias uestras et spoliabitis Aegyptum   23 rumpens retinacula loeti] cfr Ps. 106, 14: et uincula eorum disrupit

---

1 emicat ex Erebo] cfr adnot. 3, 48   2 primitias] cfr 3, 59   15 cfr 5, 5   18 cfr *Anth. Lat.* 678, 7: In medio mundi fertur Phaëthontia flamma   19 dira potestas] cfr STAT., *Theb.* 5, 324

Trad. text.: *R*

---

2 mors] *suppl. Traube*   11 strictusque *Traube*] strictisque *R*   14 indomitaque diu *R Traube*] diu indomitaque *Mai Floss*   16 totam *R Traube*] totum *Mai*   18 Pyrflegetontis enim *Mai*] Pyrflegetontis *R Traube*; *de scansione cfr 9, 7*: Flĕgĕtontis

CARMEN 6

25 Ipse libens animam posuit propriamque resumpsit:
  Ponere quam potuit, non remanere sinit.
 Quam dat pro mundi uita, reuocauit eandem:
  Quae datur accipitur; tradita salua manet.
 Tale datur pretium mundi, mirabile fatu:
30 Totum seruatur, redditur atque datur.
 Quis fari ualeat quid fecerit ipse redemptor?
  Empto potitur, possidet et pretium.
 O lux perpetuo fulgens mundumque reuelans,
  Victrix umbrarum, quas pia corda timent,
35 Custos sis Karoli, ⟨sis⟩ tutus et undique murus,
  Protege sceptra tui, qui regitat, famuli.

 Sat sat perpaucos ingratos ponere uersus:
  Molestos regi quid ualet astruere?
 Quod plane perhibet iam nuper dedita Musa:
40 Expers mercedis, tristis, inanis erat.

---

29 mirabile fatu] cfr ALDH., *Aenig.* c. 62; *De laud. uirg.* 658; 1593 38 cfr 1, 77

Trad. text.: *R*

31 quid *Mai*] quod *R Traube* 35 sis²] *suppl. Traube* 39 dedita *Mai Traube*] aedita (ēdita) *R, forte recte*

7

ΣΤΙΧΟΙ ΤΟΥ ΙΩΑΝΝΟΥ
ΤΩ ΒΑΣΙΛΕΙ ΚΑΡΟΛΩ

Lux superans animas hominum superumque deorum
    Agmina terrenis constabilita tonis,
In sinibus genitoris erat longeque remota
    Sensibili mundo empyrioque polo.
5 Lustrauit miseros tenebrarum sedibus imis
    Vinctos captiuos Tartareosque reos.
Incarnatus erat Christus de uirgine nascens,
    Confixus ligno, conditus atque tapho;
Corpore sed moriens, uiuens animoque deoque,
10   Est Deus et moritur, uiuat ut ipsa caro.
Mens Erebum, corpus petram, tenet omnia numen;
    In tribus est unus: corpore, mente, Deo.
Postquam per triduum totum destruxerat ΑΔΗΝ,
    Totus surrexit, nil remanente minus.
15 Ascendit totus, totum regit – aspice – mundum,
    Pro quo passus erat, conditor atque Deus.
Humanumque genus totum reuocauit ab antro
    Aeternae mortis, quo cadit omnis homo,
Muneris ingratus uitae spretorque salutis,
20   Quam largitus erat maximus archiater.

3/4 cfr Ioh. 1, 18

1/2 cfr Mart. Cap., 8, 810   3/6 cfr 8, 49-53   5 cfr Verg., *Georg.* 4, 471: at cantu commotae Erebi de sedibus imis; *Aen.* 1, 84   7 Theodvlf., *Carm.* 41, 1, 23: hinc sedet Esaias, Christum de uirgine nasci   12 corpore, mente, deo] cfr Ioh. Scot., *Periphys.* 2, 13 (542A-542B)

Trad. text.: *R L^{II}*

Tit. ΣΤΙΧΟΙ ΤΟΥ *Traube*] ΤΟΥ ΣΤΙΧΟΙ *R L^{II}*   ΚΑΡΟΛΟ add. *L^{II}*
5-6 *hos uersus om. Mai*   10 Est *Traube*] ast *R*   13 ΑΔΗΝ *L^{II} edd.*] achan *R*; cfr 9, 4
18 Aeternae *Mai*] aeternaeque *R*

CARMEN 7

O rex, praeclaro qui lustras lumine mundum,
    Largito Karolo prospera cuncta tuo.
Indulge famulo fragilis contamina uitae,
    Vt ualeat purus cernere regna tua.

21] *Anth. Lat.* 678, 9: Lustrando totum praeclaro lumine mundum

---

Trad. text.: *R L^{II}*

8

ΟΙ ΣΤΙΧΟΙ ΤΟΙ ΙΩΑΝΝΟΥ ΤΩ ΚΥΡΡΙΩ ΑΙΤΟΥ
ΤΟ ΑΝΑΚΤΟ ΚΑΡΟΛΩ

Si uis ΟΥΡΑΝΙΑΣ sursum uolitare per auras
ΕΜΠΥΡΙΟΣque polos mentis sulcare meatu,
ΟΜΜΑΤΕ glauciuido lustrabis templa sophiae,
Quorum summa tegit condensa nube caligo,
5 Omnes quae superat sensus ΝΟΕΡΟΣque ΛΟΓΟΣque.
Inde ΓΝΟΦΟΣ quondam uelabat Sina ΚΟΡΥΦΕΝ,
Dum Deus antiquum ΘΕΣΜΟΝ ΜΟΥΣΕΑ doceret
Vmbrarum medio linquens uestigia ΘΑΡΣΟΝ.
Illic aspicies Seraphin oculosa uolare
10 Et senas ΠΤΕΡΥΓΑΣ terno de cardine pansas

---

cfr HERREN, 'Johannes Scottus Poeta'; PIEMONTE, 'Acotaciónes sobre algunos poemas de Eriúgena', II, p. 28-41
1 uolitare per auras] LVCR., 4, 221 (219): nec uariae cessant uoces uolitare per auras; cfr 9, 51   2/3 cit. HERIC., *Vita Germ. metr.,* inuoc. 69-70: lumen glauciuidas agens in umbras / Caecis ΕΜΠΥΡΙΟC reclude caelos   5 cit. HERIC., *Vita Germ. metr.* inuoc. 44 indidisti: naturae superans ΝΟΕΡΟC ΛΟΓΟCΤΕ   6 cit. HERIC., *Vita Germ. metr.* inuoc. 72: ΕΙC ΓΝΟΦΟΝ Sinay sic indidisti   9 cfr 21, 17; IOH. SCOT., *Ier. Dion. interp.* 7, 83-84: deinde oculosos et pennosos Cherubim, et post eos Seraphim; cfr [Ioh. Scot.,] *Gloss. Mart. Cap.* 428, 23: OCULEA: oculosa

---

Trad. text.: $R\,L^{I\text{-}II}\,P_{I\text{-}2}$

Tit. ΤΩ L^{II}] ΤΟ R ΑΙΤΟΥ R] *om.* L^{II} ΤΟ ΑΝΑΚΤΟ R] ΚΑΙ ΤΟΥΤΟ ΑΝΑΚΤΟ L^{II}
1 ΟΥΡΑΝΙΑΣ $R\,L^I\,P_I$] uranias P_2 2 ΕΜΠΥΡΙΟΣque $L^I\,P_I$] Empyriosque R
3 ΟΜΜΑΤΕ $L^I\,P_I$] Ommate $R\,P_2$ glauciuido $R\,P_I\,P_2$] ΓΛΑΥΚΙΥΙΔΟ L^I 5 ΝΟΕΡΟΣ L^I] noeros(que) R ΛΟΓΟΣ L^I] logos(que) R 6 ΓΝΟΦΟΣ L^I] gnofos R ΚΟΡΥΦΕΝ L^I] κορυphεν R 7 ΘΕΣΜΟΝ] $R\,L^I$ ΜΟΥΣΕΑ] L^I, moysea R 8 ΘΑΡΣΟΝ L^I] ΘΑΡΣΩΝ R 9 uolare] uide uolare $R^{a.c.}$ 10 ΠΤΕΡΥΓΑΣ L^I] pterygas R

Gloss.: Tit. ΟΙ ΣΤΙΧΟΙ] uersus $R\,L^{II}$ ΚΥΡΡΙΩ] domino R ΑΙΤΟΥ] suo R ΑΝΑΚΤΟ] regi R
1 ΟΥΡΑΝΙΑΣ] caelestes $R\,L^I$; cfr 5, 50   2 ΕΜΠΥΡΙΟΣ] igneos $R\,L^I$ 3 ΟΜΜΑΤΕ] oculo $R\,L^I$ glauciuido] noctiuido $R\,L^I$ 5 ΝΟΕΡΟΣ] intellectus $R\,L^I$ ΛΟΓΟΣ] rationes $R\,L^I$ 6 ΓΝΟΦΟΣ] caligo $R\,L^I$ ΚΟΡΥΦΕΝ] uerticem $R\,L^I$ 7 ΘΕΣΜΟΝ] legem $R\,L^I$ ΜΟΥΣΕΑ] .i. moysaica L^I 8 ΘΑΡΣΟΝ] pedum   ΘΑΡΣΟΣ (*add.* enim L^I)] planta pedis $R\,L^I$ 10 ΠΤΕΡΥΓΑΣ] alas $R\,L^I$

CARMEN 8   23

Circa postque deum ΠΟΛΙΜΟΡΦΟΤΑ plurima ΖΩΑ
Claro cunctorum speculantia lumine causam.
Vnum principium, quo rerum uoluitur ordo
In genus in species rithmosque ΚΡΟΝΟΣque ΤΟΠΟΣque,
15   Quae sunt, quae non sunt, sensu seu mente uidentur,
Quae stant, quae uario uoluuntur praedita motu,
ΠΝΕΥΜΑΤΑ uentorum, uis ignea, lucidus aether,
Chorus et astrigerae perpuri luminis ΑΙΓΛΕ
Palladis, hinc gemmis septem redimita corona,
20   ΦΟΕΒΗ ΚΑΙ ΣΤΙΛΒΟΝ ΚΑΙ ΦΟΣ⟨ΦΟΡΟΣ⟩, ΗΛΙΟΣ, ΑΡΗΣ,
ΦΟΕΤΟΝ ΚΑΙ ΦΑΙΝΟΝΟΣ, ΑΚΡΟΙ ΠΕΡΙ ΚΛΙΜΑΤΑ ΠΑΧΝΗΣ,
ΕΞΗΣ ΤΟΥ ΚΟΣΜΟΥ ΚΕΝΤΡΟΝ, ΤΕΘΙΣ ΑΣΧΕΤΟΣ, ΑΛΑΣ.
(Caelestis motus modulaminis ΕΝΝΕΑΠΤΟΝΓΟΣ,
Summa ΧΕΛΙΣ uocum mortales effugit ΩΤΑΣ.)

---

14 cfr Ioh. Scot., *Periphys.* 1, 14 (col. 463A): Haec autem a graecis uocantur ΟΥΣΙΑ, ΠΟΣΟΤΗΤΑ, ΠΟΙΟΤΗΤΑ, ΠΡΟΣ ΤΙ, ΚΕΙΣΘΑΙ, ΕΞΙΣ, ΤΟΠΟΣ, ΧΡΟΝΟΣ, ΠΡΑΤΤΕΙΝ, ΠΑΘΕΙΝ   15 mente uide-] cfr Ov., *Trist.* 4, 2, 57; *Ex Pont.* 4, 4, 5   19 cfr Macr., *Somn.* 1, 6, 11-13; Mart. Cap., 7, 738; cfr Ioh. Scot., *Gloss. Mart. Cap.* 285, 14 (p. 131): ΕΠΤΑΣ ΙΝ ΝΥΜΕΡΙΣ Septenarius numerus tribuitur Palladi multis modis   redimita corona] cfr Ov., *Am.* 3, 11, 29; *Her.* 6, 115; *Fast.* 3, 269; 6, 321   21 cfr Ioh. Scot., *Gloss. Mart. Cap.* 486, 3 (p. 198): ΡΗΟΕΤΟΝΤΟΣ id est φοιτῶντος, φοιτῶν id est ueniens, inde φοιτῶντος genitiuus. Φοιτῶν autem dicitur sol qui cotidie uenit in ortum et occasum   23/24 cfr Mart. Cap., 1, 66: laeua enneaphthongon chelyn innitenti similis imprimebat

---

Trad. text.: $R\,L^{I\text{-}II}\,P_{1\text{-}2}$

---

11 ΠΟΛΙΜΟΡΦΟΤΑ L^I] polymorfota R 14 ΚΡΟΝΟΣ(que) L^I] cronosque R ΤΟΠΟΣ(que) L^I] toposque R 17 ΠΝΕΥΜΑΤΑ L^I] Pneumata R 18 ΑΙΓΛΕ L^I] aigle R 20 ΚΑΙ (*bis*) $R\,L^{II}$] om. L^I ΣΤΙΛΒΟΝ *Mai*] ΙΣΤΙΛΒΟΝ $R\,L^{I\text{-}II}$; cfr 12a, 5; 12b, 1; 17, 11   ΦΟΣ⟨ΦΟΡΟΣ⟩] *suggerit Traube in app. crit.*   21 ΚΑΙ] L^{II}, om. $R\,L^I$ ΑΚΡΟΙ $R\,L^{II}$] ΑΚΡΟΣ L^I ΠΑΧΝΗΣ *scripsi*] ΠΑΧΝΗ $R\,L^I$, ΠΑΧΝΗΝ L^{II} 22 ΕΞΗΣ $R\,L^{II}$] ΕΞΙΣ L^I 23 ΕΝΝΕΑΠΤΟΝΓΟΣ L^I] enneaptongos R 24 ΧΕΛΙΣ L^I] chelis R

Gloss.: 11 ΠΟΛΙΜΟΡΦΟΤΑ] multiformia $R\,L^I$ ΖΩΑ] animalia $R\,L^I$ 14 ΚΡΟΝΟΣ] tempora $R\,L^I$ ΤΟΠΟΣ] locos R, locus L^I 17 ΠΝΕΥΜΑΤΑ] spiritus $R\,L^I$ 18 ΑΙΓΛΕ] claritas $R\,L^I$ 20 ΦΟΕΒΗ] luna $R\,L^{I\text{-}II}$ ΚΑΙ] et $R\,L^{II}$ ΣΤΙΛΒΩΝ] mercurius $R\,L^{I\text{-}II}$ ΚΑΙ] et $R\,L^{II}$ ΦΟΣΦΟΡΟΣ (*ex emend.*)] lucifer $R\,L^{I\text{-}II}$ ΗΛΙΟΣ] sol $R\,L^{I\text{-}II}$ ΑΡΗΣ] mars $R\,L^{I\text{-}II}$ 21 ΦΟΕΤΟΝ] iouis $R\,L^{I\text{-}II}$ ΚΑΙ] et $R\,L^{II}$ ΦΑΙΝΟΜΟΣ] saturnus L^I, saturni R ΑΚΡΟΙ (ΑΚΡΟΣ L^I)] summi $R\,L^{II}$, summus L^I ΠΕΡΙ] circum $R\,L^{I\text{-}II}$ ΚΛΙΜΑΤΑ] plagas $R\,L^{I\text{-}II}$ ΠΑΧΝΗΣ (*ex emend.*)] pruina $R\,L^{I\text{-}II}$ 22 ΕΞΗΣ (ΕΞΙΣΤΟΥ L^I)] deinde $R\,L^{I\text{-}II}$ ΚΟΣΜΟΥ] mundi $R\,L^{I\text{-}II}$ ΚΕΝΤΡΟΝ] medium $R\,L^{I\text{-}II}$ ΤΕΘΙΣ] oceanus $R\,L^{I\text{-}II}$ ΑΣΧΕΤΟΣ] inmensurabilis $R\,L^{I\text{-}II}$ ΑΛΑΣ] salum $R\,L^{I\text{-}II}$ 23 ΕΝΝΕΑΠΤΟΝΓΟΣ] nouenus sonus $R\,L^I$ 24 ΧΕΛΙΣ] cithara (cyth-L^I) $R\,L^I$ ΩΤΑΣ] aures $R\,L^I$

CARMEN 8

25 Rerum principium primum cognoscite Christum:
Verbum cuncta creans natum de pectore patris,
Ars, lex, consilium, ΖΩΗ, sapientia, uirtus,
Fons medium finis, genitum de lumine lumen,
Est, non est, super est, qui praestitit omnibus esse,
30 Qui regit atque tenet totum, quod condidit ipse,
Totus per totum qui nullis partibus haeret,
Cuius summa procul cunctis natura remota,
Cum sit cunctorum substans essentia simplex.
ΩΝ ΤΕΛΟΣ, ΩΝ ΑΡΧΗ ΠΑΝΤΟΝ, ΩΝ ΟΝΤΑ ΤΑ ΕΙΣΙΝ,
35 ΩΝ ΑΓΑΘΟΣ ΚΑΙ ΚΑΛΟΣ, ΚΑΛΛΟΣ ΜΟΡΦΩΝ ΤΕ ΧΑΡΑΚΤΗΡ,
Qui miseros homines reuocans de morte perenni,
ΑΝΤΡΩΠΟΣ factus sumens de uirgine carnem,
Promissus uenit complens oracula uatum.

25/26 cfr Ioh. 1, 1-3   28 cfr Ps. 35, 10: fons uitae in lumine tuo uidebimus lumen

27 cfr CORIPP., *Ioh.* 4, 592: castus amor, pietas, bonitas, sapientia uirtus   28 fons medium finis] cfr IOH. SCOT., *Periphys.* 3, 32 (col. 688B); 4, 1 (col. 741C); *Hymn. Nynie* 2, 1: blandus in arce poli genuit de lumine lumen   genitum de lumine lumen] cit. ex quadam uersione Symboli Nicaenei: lumen de lumine, natum non factum, φῶς ἐκ φωτός ... γεννθέντα οὐ ποιηθέντα   29 cfr IOH. SCOT., *Periphys.* 1, 14 (col. 459D): Essentia igitur dicitur deus. Sed proprie essentia non est. Esse enim opponitur non esse. ΥΠΕΡΟΥΣΙΟΣ igitur est, id est superessentialis   30/34 cfr PIEMONTE, 'Acotaciónes sobre algunos poemas de Eriúgena', II, p. 34   34 cfr IOH. SCOT., *Periphys.* 2, 2 (col. 526C): (Deus) est enim principium omnium quae a se condita sunt et finis omnium quae eum appetunt ut in eo aeternaliter immutabiliterque quiescant; 5, 6 (col. 871A); cfr PIEMONTE, 'Acotaciónes sobre algunos poemas de Eriúgena', II, p. 32-33   35 ΑΓΑΘΟΣ ΚΑΙ ΚΑΛΟΣ ΚΑΛΛΟΣ] cfr IOH. SCOT., *Periphys.* 5, 35 (col. 954C): qui summa honestas est, summa pulchritudo   ΜΟΡΦΩΝ] cfr IOH. SCOT., *Periphys.* 2, 47 (col. 541B-541C); cfr BEIERWALTES, *Denken des Einen*, p. 349-351   36 cfr VERG., *Aen.* 5, 476: reuocatum a morte Dareta   38 complens oracula uatum] cfr ALDH., *Laud. uirg.* 309; 403: promens oracula uatis

---

Trad. text.: $R\ L^{I\text{-}II}\ P_{I\text{-}2}$

---

25 primum *Mai*] primus R 27 ΖΩΗ] $R\ L^I$; *cfr infra notulam ad uersus 85-86*   32 Cuius – remota] *hunc uersum omittunt Mai et Floss*   34 ΩΝ] L^{II}, om. L^I 35 ΩΝ] L^{II}, om. L^I ΚΑΙ] L^{II}, om. L^I ΜΟΡΦΩΝ R^{II}] ΜΟΡΦΩ L^{II}, ΜΟΡΦΩ $L^{a.c.}$ ΧΑΡΑΚΤΗΡ $L^{I\text{-}II}$] ΚΑΡΑΚΤΗΡ R 37 ΑΝΤΡΩΠΟΣ L^I] antropos R

Gloss.: 27 ΖΩΗ] $R\ L^I$ 34 ΩΝ¹] ens $R\ L^{II}$ ΤΕΛΟΣ] finis $R\ L^{I\text{-}II}$ ΩΝ²] *glossa deest*   ΑΡΧΗ] principium $R\ L^{I\text{-}II}$ ΠΑΝΤΟΝ] omnium $R\ L^{I\text{-}II}$ ΩΝ³] *glossa deest*   ΟΝΤΑ] quae sunt L^I, qui est, quae sunt $R\ L^{II}$ ΤΑ ΕΙΣΙΝ] quae subsistunt $R\ L^{I\text{-}II}$ 35 ΩΝ] ens $R\ L^{II}$ ΑΓΑΘΟΣ] optimus $R\ L^{I\text{-}II}$ ΚΑΙ] et $R\ L^{II}$ ΚΑΛΟΣ] bonus $R\ L^{I\text{-}II}$ ΚΑΛΛΟΣ] pulchritudo $R\ L^{I\text{-}II}$ ΜΟΡΦΩΝ] formarum $R\ L^{I\text{-}II}$ ΤΕ] que (quae L^I) $R\ L^{I\text{-}II}$ ΧΑΡΑΚΤΗΡ] exemplar $R\ L^{I\text{-}II}$ 37 ΑΝΤΡΩΠΟΣ] homo $R\ L^I$

CARMEN 8 25

At ΠΡΟΓΟΝΟΣ Dauid proprio de ΣΠΕΡΜΑΤΕ natum
40   Viderat et mundi deuicta morte ΛΥΤΡΩΤΗΝ.
     Nec minus in caelis prosunt mysteria Christi
     Quam terris: merito, cum sit Deus omnibus unus:
     Illic angelicas patefecit lumine mentes
     Ac tenebrosa suae uirtutis prodidit ipsis.
45   Nulla quidem uirtus potuit dinoscere pure
     Quem Pater occultum gremio uelabat opaco;
     Sed caro nunc uerbum factum – mirabile dictu –
     Clare se cunctis hominemque deumque reuoluit.
     ΝΟΥΣ ΤΕ ΛΟΓΟΣ ΤΕ capit quem nullus uiderat ante:
50   ΣΑΡΚΙΚΑ nam ΦΙΣΙΣ diuinas temperat ΑΥΓΑΣ.
     Hic uitam cunctis nascendo contulit atque
     Destruxit mortem, quae totum sorbserat orbem.
     O qualis uirtus potuit superare superbum,
     Qui genus humanum crudeli lege subegit,
55   Restaurare uolens, primus quod perdidit ille
     Formatus limo male usus munere uitae;
     Virgine sed factus dum sumpserat, unde periret,
     Sponte sua propriae bene usus funere carnis.
     Quis modus est animo, dum talia cernere temptat,
60   Quiue ualent sensus meditari famine uocum?

---

39 cfr Matth. 1, 1: Liber generationis Iesu Christi filii Dauid filii Abraham   46 cfr Ioh 1, 18: qui est in sinu patris   47 cfr Ioh 1, 14: Et Verbum caro factum est et habitauit in nobis

---

42 omnibus unus] cfr 5, 5; PROSP., *Epigr.* 41, 3: utque locis praesens simul est Deus omnibus unus   43 cfr PAVL. NOL., *Carm.* 22, 83: diuinoque tuam perfundit lumine mentes   45/46 cfr 7, 3-6   47 mirabile dictu] cfr 6, 29; VERG., *Georg.* 2, 30; 3, 275; *Aen.* 1, 439; 2, 174; 4, 182; 7, 64; 8, 252 (etc.)   47/51 cfr PIEMONTE, 'Acotaciónes sobre algunos poemas de Eriúgena', II, p. 34-35   48 cfr VERG., *Aen.* 1, 229: o qui res hominumque deumque

---

Trad. text.: $R\ L^{I\text{-}II}\ P_{1\text{-}2}$

---

39 at R] ut *coniecit Traube in app.*   ΠΡΟΓΟΝΟΣ L^I] progonos R   ΣΠΕΡΜΑΤΕ L^I] spermate R   40 ΛΥΤΡΩΤΗΝ $L^I R^{p.c.}$] ΛΥΤΡΟΤΗΝ $R^{a.c.}$ 42 unus $R^{a.c.}$] idem $R^{p.c.}$; *suspicor librarium glossam idem, quod forte existebat in* Ω, *pro* unus *substituit*   46 occultum *Mai Floss*] occultus R, occultans *Traube*   49 ΤΕ²] *om.* L^I 50 ΦΙΣΙΣ] $R\ L^I$; *de orthographia cfr 72-73*

Gloss.:   39 ΠΡΟΓΟΝΟΣ] auus $R\ L^I$ ΣΠΕΡΜΑΤΕ] semine $R\ L^I$ 40 ΛΥΤΡΩΤΗΝ] redemptorem $R\ L^I$ 49 ΝΟΥΣ] animus $R\ L^I$ ΤΕ¹] que R   ΛΟΓΟΣ] ratio $R\ L^I$ ΤΕ²] que R   50 ΣΑΡΚΙΚΑ] carnales $R\ L^I$ ΦΙΣΙΣ] natura $R\ L^I$ ΑΥΓΑΣ] claritudines $R\ L^I$

ΠΑΡΘΕΝΟΣ angelico commouit uiscera fatu
Ac comitante fide suscepit ΠΝΕΥΜΑΤΕ partum.
O felix ΓΑΣΤΕΡ! diuinum sustinet ignem,
Virtutis radius solidatur ΣΩΜΑΤΕ sacro.
65 Vnam personam duplex substantia prodit:
Nam Deus aeternus rationem tempore sumens
Corpore compacto sese perfecerat ΑΝΔΡΑ.
Iesum Christum regnantem saecula semper
Te lumen mundi colimus; tu, Christe, redemptor,
70 Fonte tui lateris credentum uulnera tergis
Nilque perire uolens hominis tua prouida uirtus
Ambitur nostram nullo cum crimine ΦΙΣΙΝ.
ΦΙΣΙΣ nostra dehinc plene renouatur in illa,
Antidothumque potens cunctis prodesse paratum
75 Potantum uarias pellit compagine plagas,
Nolentes merito permittens iure perire.
Nullum namque Deus nolentem uiuere cogit,
Nullum uelle boni depellit limine lucis.
Omnes inuitans hos deserit, adiuuat illos;
80 Omnia componens laudatur in omnibus ipse.
Christe, tuos pauidos digneris uisere seruos,
Qui tua festa colunt uenerantes dona salutis.
Parce tuo famulo, cui regia sceptra dedisti;
Diuino radio perfusum perfice, purga.

61/62 cfr Luc. 1, 38   69 lumen mundi] cfr Ioh. 8, 12: ego sum lux mundi (lumen *var.*)   74/76 cfr Ioh. 6, 37-40

69 cfr Theodvlf., *Carm.* 69, 1: gloria laus et honor tibi sit, rex Christe redemptor   70 cfr Verg., *Aen.* 3, 242: sed neque uim plumis ullam nec uulnera tergo   78 limine lucis] cfr Ivvenc., 3, 314; Aldh., *Laud. uirg.* 2663   83 sceptra dedisti] cfr adnot. 2, 61

Trad. text.: *R L*$^{I-II}$ *P1-2*

64 ΣΩΜΑΤΕ *L*^{I}] somate *R*   67 ΑΝΔΡΑ *L*^{I}] ΑΝdra *R*   72 Ambitur] *corr. R ex* abbitur   ΦΙΣΙΝ *L*^{I}] ΦΥΣΙΝ *R*   73 ΦΙΣΙΣ *scripsi*] *om. L*^{I}, ΦΥΣΙΣ *R*

Gloss.: 61 ΠΑΡΘΕΝΟΣ] uirgo *R L*^{I} 62 ΠΝΕΥΜΑΤΕ] spiritu *R L*^{I} 63 ΓΑΣΤΕΡ] uenter *R L*^{I} 64 ΣΩΜΑΤΕ] corpore *R L*^{I} 67 ΑΝΔΡΑ] uirum *R L*^{I} 72 ΦΙΣΙΝ] naturam *R L*^{I} 73 ΦΙΣΙΣ] *glossa deest, certe quod eadem uox in uersu superiore adsit*

85 ⟨ΖΩΗΝ ΑΟΙΝΙΟΝ ΔΩΣΕΙ ΣΟΙ ΠΑΝΤΟΤΕ ΧΡΙΣΤΟΣ.
    ΚΥΡΡΙΕ, ΖΗΣ ΠΟΛΛΟΥΣ ΕΝΙΑΥΤΟΥΣ ΩΔΕ ΣΕΒΑΣΤΕΙΣ.⟩

Trad. text.: $R\,L^{I\text{-}II}\,P_{I\text{-}2}$

85/86 *Hos uersus interpolaui ex codice Laudunensi* ($L^{I\text{-}II}$). *Martinus Laudunensis apud* L^I *perscribit uoces cum glossis quae ad hos uersus pertinent, sed eas perperam posuit. In editione Dublinensi hos duos uersus post uersum 27 posui, sequens ordinem uocum Martini apud* L^I. *Ordo lemmatum (fol. 295r) est:* ΖΩΗΝ, ΑΟΙΝΙΟΝ, ΔΩΣΕΙ ΣΟΙ, ΠΑΝΤΟΤΕ, ΖΗΣ, ΠΟΛΛΟΥΣ, ΕΝΙΑΥΤΟΥΣ, ΩΔΕ, ΣΕΒΑΣΤΕΙΣ. *Mos autem erat Iohannis Scotti uersus Graecos qui preces pro uita et salute Karolis regis continent ad finem carminis ponere; cfr 2, 67-68; 5, 49-50. Textus horum lemmatum* (L^I) *cum uersibus apud* L^{II} *(f. 297r) concordat, ubi uoces* ΚΥΡΡΙΕ ΚΑΡΟΛΕ *praepositae inueniuntur*   **85** ΧΡΙΣΤΟΣ] *om.* L^I **86** ΚΥΡΡΙΕ] *om.* L^I

Gloss.: **85** ΖΩΗΝ] uitam $L^{I\text{-}II}$ ΑΟΙΝΙΟΝ] aeternam $L^{I\text{-}II}$ ΔΩΣΕΙ ΣΟΙ] det tibi $L^{I\text{-}II}$ ΠΑΝΤΟΤΕ] semper $L^{I\text{-}II}$ **86** ΚΥΡΡΙΕ] domine L^{II} ΖΗΣ] uiuas $L^{I\text{-}II}$ ΠΟΛΛΟΥΣ] multos $L^{I\text{-}II}$ ΕΝΙΑΥΤΟΥΣ] annos $L^{I\text{-}II}$ ΩΔΕ] hic $L^{I\text{-}II}$ ΣΕΒΑΣΤΕΙΣ] caesar $L^{I\text{-}II}$

9

VERSVS IΩHANNIΣ ΣKΩΘΟΙ

Postquam nostra salus mundum renouauerat omnem
Quosque Pater uoluit cunctos perfecerat actus,
Fessa labore graui requieuit in arbore pendens,
Tergeminae lucis spatio destruxerat ΑΔΗΝ,
5   Dormitans gelidi duro sub culmine saxi,
Implens uatiuomi prognostica symbola ceti.
Vmbrae tunc pauidae sparsim Flegetontis ab imo
Exiliunt subito mirantes surgere lucem
Tetras atque truces abigentem carcere laruas.
10 O mors, mors uitae, si mors, non uita uocanda
(Quod praestat uitam, non ausim dicere mortem),
Num tenebras recipit clarae substantia lucis?
Feruida uis ignis suescit sibi surpere frigus?
Nemo tamen uitam mortem gustasse negarit:
15 Mors carnis uitae uitae mors iure uocatur;
Nam compassa fuit carni, quae sola pependit.
Altius ingreditur purae rationis acumen
Et carnem uitae uitam sic colligit esse;
Si uita est Verbum, Verbum quoque si caro factum,
20 Profecto sequitur uitam concedere carnem;

---

3 requieuit] cfr Gen. 2, 2: et requieuit die septimo ab uniuerso opere quod patrarat   5/6 cfr Ion. 2, 1-11   12 cfr Ioh 1, 5: et tenebrae eam non conprehenderunt   19 cfr Ioh 1, 14

3/5 cfr JEAUNEAU, 'Jean Scot et l'ironie'   13 surpere] cfr LVCR., 2, 314   15 mors carnis uitae, etc.] cfr AVG., *Ciu.* 13, 12   iure uocatur] cfr ARATOR, *Act.* 1, 287; SEDVL. SCOT., *Carm.* 1, 4, 1

Trad. text.: *R*

Tit. VERSVS IΩHANNIΣ ΣKΩΘΟΙ] *R*
1 renouauerat *R*^{p.c.}] renouerat *R*^{a.c.}   5 sub *Mai*] sul *R*   6 simbola coeti *R*   9 laruas *scripsi*] larbas *R Traube*   13 suescit *Mai*] cescit *R*   surpere *scripsi*] serpere *R*

Gloss.: 4 ΑΔΗΝ] infernus *L¹*

Si caro sit Verbum conuerso tramite facta,
Carnem continuo uitam dare cogere factam.
ΣΑΡΞ igitur Christi substat uerissima uita,
Viuens ac moriens mortem consumpserat omnem.
25 Desursum uenit terrenam sumere uestem;
Indutus uestem sursum cum ueste uolauit
Inque deum uertit uestem de uirgine sumptam,
Vnum conficiens animam carnemque Deumque.
Mors mortis Dominus surrexit uiuus in altum
30 Ac nostram secum naturam uexit eodem.
In tota factus totam conformat in unum.
Mundum calcauit fragilem mundique potentem
Expulsumque foras superauit Marte secundo.
Captiuam reuocans praedam raptoris ab ore
35 Abstulit: ille gemit confossus membra superbus
Vulneribus duris ac secum talia tractans:
'Me uictum uideo, fugitiuum sedibus atris.
Quae noua lux oritur, quam numquam ferre ualebo?
Nunc mea regna ruunt passim: loca nulla tenebris.
40 Sentio me captum, pauidum uinclisque ligatum:
Eheu, quis mihi congreditur, quis fortis in armis
Audax committit mundi cum principe bellum?
Illene confixus ligno septusque sepulchro,
Quem rex Herodes spreuit summusque sacerdos
45 Ruptus non timuit uestem dampnare Caiphas,
Addictus morti, Romano principe caesus?

---

29 Dominus surrexit] Luc 24, 34   44/45 summusque sacerdos – Caiphas] cfr Matth 26, 57: Caiphan principem sacerdotum   45 ruptus – uestem] cfr Matth 26, 65: princeps sacerdotum scidit uestimenta sua

27 de uirgine sumptam] CORIPP., *Iust*. 1, 341: se uoluit formamque deus de uirgine sumpsit   29 mors mortis] cfr IOH. SCOT., *Periphys*. 5, 7 (col. 875C); cfr BEIERWALTES, 'Sprache und Sache', p. 534ff.   30/31 cfr IOH. SCOT., *Periphys*. 5, 8 (col. 994B): totus enim deus est totus ubique, totus super omne, quod dicitur et intelligitur, exaltatus, totus in patre et cum patre unum effectus, totus deus in toto homine, et totus homo in toto deo   33 marte secundo] VERG., *Aen*. 11, 899; 12, 497   41 fortis in armis] cfr *Ilias latina* 184 et 233; CORIPP., *Ioh*. 2, 90; 6 (5), 518; ALCVIN., *Carm*. 9, 159; 62, 117

Trad. text.: *R L¹*

23 ΣΑΡΞ *edd*.] Sarx *R, om. L¹*   32 fragilem] sic *R*; uide commentum uiri eruditi F. Colnago, qui in editione sua, *p. 120*, hanc lectionem bona ratione defendit. In editione Dublinensi ΦΡΑΚΤΟΝ (*i. e.* armatum) *conieci, sed mihi non diutius persuadeo*   36 duris *R*] diris *coniecit Traube in app.*   39 regna ruunt *Mai*] regnarunt *R*

CARMEN 9

  Hoc egomet feci, fateor, totumque peregi:
  Me stultum latuit uirtus humilisque potestas.
  Hunc si cognossem, ΣΤΑΥΡΩ non penderet umquam;
50 Corporis humani seruilis forma fefellit'.
  Interea laetas animas uolitare per auras
  Tartareosque sinus uacuos laxasque catenas
  Suspicit et nutrit tristi sub pectore uulnus.
  'Quod mage me miserum torquet, iam conspicor', inquit.
55 'Clausa diu terris paradisi limina pandi
  Mortaleque genus, quod fluxerat inde per unum,
  Vnius ob mortem rursus super astra redire.
  Illic felices sedes, quas sponte reliqui,
  Terrigenum proles habitabit iure perhenni.
60 Meme torquebit semper mea praua uoluntas:
  Languidus inuidia morior meritoque peruror.
  Vnum confugium superest, solamen et unum:
  Est antiqua domus mortis noctisque profundae,
  Iudaicum pectus, uitiorum plena uorago,
65 Fraudis et inuidiae semper possessio larga,
  Luminis exosi radios irata repellens.
  Illic sola potens ypocrisis perfida regnat;
  Illa putet nimium nimiaque putredine corda
  Carnalis populi corrumpit nescia ueri:
70 Illuc confugiam gentilia pectora linquens,
  Odibilis Christo dominabor gentis auarae,
  Omne meum uirus fundam blasphema per ora
  Ligno suspensum dominum regnare negando'.

---

  49 I Cor. 2, 8: si enim cognouissent, numquam Dominum gloriae crucifixissent 50 seruilis forma] Phil. 2, 7: formam serui accipiens 57 Vnius ob mortem] Rom. 5, 12

---

  51 cfr adnot. 8, 1 53 VERG., *Aen.* 1, 36: cum Iuno aeternum seruans sub pectore uulnus 55 cfr PAUL. NOL., *Carm.* 32, 163: Hic meliore via paradisi limina pandit 59 iure perenni] cfr SEDVL., *Carm. pasch.* 1, 30 60 cfr PROSP., *Epig.* 42, 3: Dumque capit miseros effectus praua uoluntas 63 est antiqua domus] cfr. VERG., *Aen.* 11, 316: est antiquus ager

---

  Trad. text.: *R L¹*

---

  49 ΣΤΑΥΡΩ *Mai*] stauro *R*, ΣΤΑΥΡΟΣ *L¹* 56 mortaleque *Traube*] mortalemque *R*, et mortale *Mai Floss; cfr indicem metricum* 68 putet] sic *R*; an legendum putret? *cfr indicem metricum* 71 dominabor *R^{p.c.}*] dominator *R^{a.c.} Traube*

  Gloss.: 49 ΣΤΑΥΡΩ (-ΟΣ *L¹*)] crux *L¹*

Talia contrectans crudelis bestia fallax
75 Retro lapsa ruit gelidas fugitiua sub umbras.
Imperium Patris quaesitum sanguine Nati
Telluris superat fines Erebumque polumque.
Orthodoxa fides diuersa uoce per orbem
'Abba Pater' clamat laudans mysteria summa:
80 Vnius ac trinae bonitatis fertile germen,
Ingenitum genitumque deum munusque perhenne
Fontis inexhausti, quo manant flumina uitae.

---

79 abba pater] Marc. 14, 36; Rom. 8, 15; Gal. 4, 6   82 cfr Gen. 2, 10

82 flumina uitae] cfr FLOR. LVGD., *Carm.* 3, 116

Trad. text.: *R L¹*

77 superat *Mai*] superis *R*   78 Ortodoxa *R*

10

ITEM STICHOS EIVSDEM

Graculus Iudaeus, iam nunc Agarenus et auster
Paganusque ferus surgens aquilonis ab axe
Subdita colla dabunt: Christus regnabit ubique;
Ipsi succumbunt omnes regique Deoque.
5 Summe Pater Nati, largitor muneris almi,
Festa tui semper celebrantem protege plebem,
Cui tua disponens sapientia regna per orbem
Praefecit Karolum regemque piumque ministrum,
Cui lux interior donauit mentis acumen,
10 Quo diuina simul tractans humana gubernet,
Vere subsistens rex atque theologus idem.
Praesul ab Athenis Dionysi, ΣΥΜΜΑΧΕ Pauli,
Inclyte martyrio, cui seruit Gallia tota,
Prospice caelestis uitae de sedibus altis
15 Vota tui ΤΕΚΝΙ Karoli ⟨tua⟩ ΛΕΙΨΑΝΑ sancta
Ornantis gratamque tuam magnalibus aedem,
Instar flammarum gemmis flagrantibus auro.
Vndique turicremis redolent altaria fumis;
Armonici cantus ΘΙΑΣΟΤΟΝ sidera pulsant;
20 Officio uatum sanctissima cena paratur ...
. . . .

---

4 cfr Ps. 71, 11   12 Act. 17, 34

cfr Dutton, 'Eriugena, the royal poet', p. 65-66
5 Beda, *Cuth.* 47, 1: ergo age, Felgeldus largitor muneris almi   9 mentis acumen] cfr 22, 24; 24, 13; 25, 65; App. 16, 2   14 sedibus altis] cfr Ov., *Met.* 6, 72; Aldh., *Laud. uirg.* praef. 4   19 sidera pulsant] cfr Paul Nol., *carm.* 17, 92; Coripp., *Iust.* 3, 176

Trad. text.: *R L¹*

1 Graculus] *sic R; cf. indicem metricum*   iudeus *R*   12 ΣΥΜΜΑΧΕ] symmache *R*, ΣΥΜΜΑΚΟΣ *L¹*   15 ΤΕΚΝΙ *L¹*] tekni *R*   tua] *suppl. Mai*   ΛΕΙΨΑΝΑ *L¹*] aeiψana *R*   19 ΘΙΑΣΟΤΟΝ *L¹*] thiasotum *R*   sidera] *sic R, ut liquet, non sidere, quod falso positum est ab editoribus*   *Subscriptio manu saeculi XIII, ut uidetur:* Sedulius donatus commentum super imperium armenie ('In perihermeneias') et super porfilium (Porphyrium)

Gloss.: 12 ΣΥΜΜΑΧΕ (ΣΥΜΜΑΚΟΣ *L¹*)] adiutor *L¹*   15 ΤΕΚΝΙ] filii *R L¹*   ΛΕΙΨΑΝΑ] reliquias *R L¹*   19 ΘΙΑΣΟΤΟΝ] deum laudantium *R L¹*

II

ΤΟΙ ΙΩΑΝΝΟΙ ΤΩ ΚΙΡΡΙΩ ΚΑΡΟΛΩ

Versus

ΖΕΣ ΝΥΝ ΖΗΣ, ΒΑΣΙΛΗΣ, ΠΛΙΣΤΟΥΣ ΕΙΣ ΤΟΙΣ ΕΝΙΑΥΤΟΥΣ,
ΜΕΛΛΟΜΕΝΟΣ ΧΡΙΣΤΩ ΣΥΝΖΗΝ ΕΙΣ ΠΟΛΛΑΣ ΑΙΩΝΑΣ.
ΧΡΙΣΤΕ, ΣΟΣΟΝ ΚΑΡΟΛΟΝ ΤΟ ΤΗΝ ΒΑΣΙΛΕΙΑΝ ΕΔΟΚΑΣ.

---

3 ΤΟ ΤΗΝ ΒΑϹΙΛΕΙΑΝ ΕΔΟΚΑϹ] cfr adnot. 2, 6

Trad. text.: L^{II}

Tit. ΤΟΙ ΙΩΑΝΝΟΙ ΤΩ ΚΙΡΡΙΩ ΚΑΡΩΛΩ L^{II}
1 ΠΛΙϹΤΟΥϹ *Traube*] ΠΑΙϹ ΤΟΥϹ L^{II} 2 ΜΕΛΛΟΜΕΝΟϹ] Ο ΜΕΛΛΟΜΕΝΟϹ L^{II}

Gloss.: 1 ΖΕΣ uiuas L^{II} ΝΥΝ] nunc L^{II} ΖΗϹ] uiuas L^{II} ΒΑΣΙΛΗΣ] rex L^{II} ΠΛΙϹΤΟΥϹ (*ex emend.*)] plures L^{II} ΕΙϹ] in L^{II} ΕΝΙΑΥΤΟΥϹ] annos L_2 Ο] articulus L^{II} 2 ΜΕΛΛΟΜΕΝΟϹ] futurus L^{II} ΧΡΙϹΤΩ] x̄p̄o L^{II} ΣΥΝΖΗΝ] congregare L^{II} ΕΙϹ] in L^{II} ΠΟΛΛΑϹ] multa L^{II} ΑΙΩΝΑϹ] saecula L^{II} 3 ΣΟϹΟΝ] salua L^{II} ΤΟ] cui L^{II} ΤΗΝ] articulus L^{II} ΒΑϹΙΛΕΙΑΝ] regnum L^{II} ΕΔΟΚΑϹ] dedisti L^{II}

12a

Versus

Nam ΚΑΚΟΣ atque ΑΓΑΤΟΣ, prorsus ΜΕΓΑΛΟΣΤΕ ΜΙΚΡΟΣΤΕ:
ΛΙΤΟΥΡΓΟΥ ΒΕΒΑΙΟΣ ΓΑΥΡΩΣ ΤΑΥΜΑΣΤΟΣ ΥΨΗΛΟΣ,
ΛΑΜΠΡΟΤΑΤΟΣ doctor, ΣΤΙΛΒΩΝ ΚΗΡΥΓΜΑΤΟΣ ΑΚΡΟΥ,
ΡΗΜΑΤΟΣ ΟΠΛΑ ΘΕΟΥ ΖΩΝΤΟΣ ΤΟΥ ΣΤΟΜΑΤΟΣ ΕΧΩΝ,
5 . . . . ΣΟΦΩΣ ΚΑΤΑ ΤΑΞΙΝ,
ΚΡΥΣΜΑΤΑ non noscens nec ΣΥΜΠΛΕΡΑΣΜΑ requirens.

(Nam malus atque bonus prorsus magnusque paruusque
... ...
Praelucens doctor, splendens praefamine summo,
10 Verbi tela dei uiuentis in ore tenendo.
....
....)

10 tela – in ore tenendo] cfr Apoc. 1, 16: et de ore eius gladius utraque parte acutus exiebat

Trad. text.: $L^{I\text{-}II}$

Ordo vocum graecarum L^I *f. 296r-v*: ΚΑΚΟΣ, ΑΓΑΤΟΣ, ΜΕΓΑΛΟΣΤΕ, ΜΙΚΡΟΣΤΕ, ΛΙΤΟΥΡΓΟΥ, ΒΕΒΑΙΩΣ, ΓΑΥΡΩΣ, ΥΨΗΛΟΣ, ΤΑΥΜΑΣΤΟΣ, ΛΑΜΠΡΟΤΑΤΟΣ, ΣΤΙΛΒΟΝ, ΚΗΡΥΓΜΑ, ΑΚΡΟΥ, ΡΗΜΑΤΟΣ, ΟΠΛΑ, ΘΕΟΥ, ΖΟΗΤΟΣ (*sic*), ΣΤΟΜΑΤΟΣ, ΕΧΩΝ, ΚΑΤΑΤΑΞΙΝ, ΣΟΦΩΣ, ΚΡΥΣΜΑΤΑ, ΣΥΜΠΛΕΡΑΣΜΑ

Traube monstrauit p. 542 quod interpretatio latina carminum 12a, 12b, 14, et 15 tali modo disposita erat ut uersus hexametros latine formaret.
2 *Hunc uersum restauraui ex uocabulis dispositis a Martino librario* L^I ΛΙΤΟΥΡΓΟΥ] *sc.* λειτουργός   3 ΚΗΡΥΓΜΑΤΟΣ L^{II}] ΚΗΡΥΓΜΑ L^I 4 ΖΩΝΤΟΣ L^{IIpc}] ΖΩΝΤΟΣ L^{IIac}
5 *Finem huius uersus restauraui ex uocabulis* L^I.   6 ΚΡΥΣΜΑΤΑ] *i. q.* κρούσις (*fraus*)? ΣΥΜΠΛΕΡΑΣΜΑ] *i. q.* συμπληρώμα.

Gloss.: 1 ΚΑΚΟΣ] malus $L^{I\text{-}II}$ ΑΓΑΤΟΣ] bonus $L^{I\text{-}II}$ ΜΕΓΑΛΟΣ ΤΕ] magnusque $L^{I\text{-}II}$ ΜΙΚΡΟΣ ΤΕ] paruusque $L^{I\text{-}II}$ 2 ΛΙΤΟΥΡΓΟΥ] ministro L^I ΒΕΒΑΙΩΣ] firmiter L^I ΓΑΥΡΩΣ] alacriter L^I ΥΨΗΛΟΣ] excelsus L^I ΤΑΥΜΑΣΤΟΣ] mirabilis L^I 3 ΛΑΜΠΡΟΤΑΤΟΣ] praelucens $L^{I\text{-}II}$ ΣΤΙΛΒΩΝ] splendens $L^{I\text{-}II}$ ΚΗΡΥΓΜΑΤΟΣ (ΚΗΡΥΓΜΑ L^I)] praefamine $L^{I\text{-}II}$ ΑΚΡΟΥ] summo L^I 4 ΡΗΜΑΤΟΣ] uerbi $L^{I\text{-}II}$ ΟΠΛΑ] tela $L^{I\text{-}II}$ ΘΕΟΥ] dei $L^{I\text{-}II}$ ΖΩΝΤΟΣ] uiuentis $L^{I\text{-}II}$ ΤΟΥ] in L^{II} ΣΤΟΜΑΤΟΣ] ore $L^{I\text{-}II}$ ΕΧΩΝ] tenendo $L^{I\text{-}II}$ 5 ΣΟΦΩΣ] sapienter L^I ΚΑΤΑΤΑΞΙΝ] ordinate L^I 6 ΚΡΥΣΜΑΤΑ] i. tria genera musicae artis $L^{I\text{-}II}$ ΣΥΜΠΛΕΡΑΣΜΑ] .i. conclusio, confinis $L^{I\text{-}II}$: *cfr Paris, Bibliothèque Mazarine, cod. 561, f. 125 (Iohannis Scotti translatio Maximi confessoris Ambiguorum)*: ΣΥΜΠΛΕΡΑΣΜΑ est confinis conclusio cum non id quod propositio proponitur in conclusion colligitur: sed aliud quodsi naturaliter confine est, ut omne iustum honestum. Omne honestum bonum. Omne igitur iustum utile.'

12b

Versus

ΛΑΜΠΡΟΤΑΤΟΣ ΚΗΡΥΞ, ΣΤΙΛΒΩΝ ΚΗΡΥΓΜΑΤΟΣ ΑΚΡΟΥ,
ͰΙΝΚΜΑΡΟΣ ΖΗΤΟ ΦΡΟΝΙΜΟΣ ΚΑΙ ΑΞΙΑΓΑΣΤΟΣ,
ΡΗΜΑΤΟΣ ΟΠΛΑ ΘΕΟΥ ΖΩΝΤΟΣ ΤΟΥ ΣΤΟΜΑΤΟΣ ΕΧΩΝ.

(Praelucens praeco splendens praefamine summo,
5 Hincmarus uiuat sapiens et commemorandus,
Verbi tela dei uiuentis in ore tenendo.)

Trad. text.: L^{II}

Gloss.: 1 ΛΑΜΠΡΟΤΑΤΟΣ] praelucens L^{II} ΚΗΡΥΞ] praeco L^{II} ΣΤΙΛΒΩΝ] splendens L^{II} ΚΗΡΥΓΜΑΤΟΣ] praefamine L^{II} ΑΚΡΟΥ] summo L^{II} 2 ͰΙΝΚΜΑΡΟΣ] Hincmarus L^{II} ΖΗΤΟ] uiuat L^{II} ΦΡΟΝΙΜΟΣ] sapiens L^{II} ΚΑΙ] et L^{II} ΑΞΙΑΓΑΣΤΟΣ] commemorandus L^{II} 3 ΡΗΜΑΤΟΣ] uerbi L^{II} ΟΠΛΑ] tela L^{II} ΘΕΟΥ] dei L^{II} ΖΩΗΤΟΣ (sic L2) uiuentis L^{II} ΤΟΥ] in L^{II} ΣΤΟΜΑΤΟΣ] ore L^{II} ΕΧΩΝ] tenendo L^{II}

13

Versus

ΙΔΕ ΒΑΘΟΥ ΤΑΝΑΘΟΥ ΤΗΝ ΤΑΥ ΤΑΠΤΕΝΤΟΣ ΕΓΕΡΣΙΝ
ΚΑΙ ΣΩΝΤΙ ΧΡΙΣΤΩ, ΠΝΥΞ, ΜΕΛΟΔΗΜΑ ΒΟΑ.

cfr BERNT, Das lateinische Epigramm, p. 281

Trad. text.: L^{I-II}

1 ΒΑΘΟΥ] i. q. βαθέος   2 ΠΝΥΞ ΜΕΛΟΔΗΜΑ ΒΟΑ] L^{I-II}; reliqua omittit L^{I}

Gloss.: 1 ΙΔΕ] uide L^{II} ΒΑΘΟΥ] profunda L^{II} ΤΑΝΑΘΟΥ] morte L^{II} ΤΗΝ] articulus L^{II} ΤΑΠΤΕΝΤΟΣ] sepulti L^{II} ΕΓΕΡΣΙΝ] resurrectionem L^{II} 2 ΚΑΙ] et L^{II} ΣΩΝΤΙ] uiuenti L^{II} ΧΡΙΣΤΩ] $\overline{\text{xpo}}$ L^{II} ΠΝΥΞ] ecclesia L^{I-II} ΜΕΛΟΔΗΜΑ] modulatione L^{I}, alleluia L^{II} ΒΟΑ] clama L^{I}, sona L^{II}

14

Versus

ΕΡΗΝΗ ΠΙΣΤΩ ΔΗΜΩ ΒΑΣΙΛΕΙ Η ΚΛΕΟΡ ΑΚΡΩ,
ΟΝ ΘΕΟΣ ΕΚΛΕΚΤΟΝ ΠΑΡΑ ΕΙΣ ΒΑΣΙΛΕΥΣΙΝ ΕΧΕΙ ΝΥΝ.
ΟΠΛΟΥ ΚΑΙ ΕΠΙΛΑΒΩΝ ΑΥΤΩ ΕΙΗΣ, ΧΡΙΣΤΕ, ΒΟΗΘΟΣ.
ΔΕΣΠΟΤΑ ΤΑ ΑΥΤΩ ΥΠΟΤΑΞΟΝ ΒΑΡΒΑΡΑ ΦΥΛΑ.

5 (Pax fido populo, regi sit gloria summo,
Quem Deus electum prae regibus unus habet nunc.
Armaque cum scuto prendens hunc, Christe, iuuato;
Huic quoque barbaricas, Dominator, subice gentes.)

---

3 ΟΠΛΟΥ ΚΑΙ ΕΠΙΛΑΒΩΝ] cfr Ps. 34, 2 (LXX): Ἐπιλαβοῦ ὅπλοῦ

Trad. text.: L^{II}

---

1 ΚΛΕΟΡ] i. q. κλέος   2 ΕΚΛΕΚΤΟΝ *scripsi*] ΕΚΛΕΣΤΟΝ L^{II} 8 Huic quoque – gentes *constituit Traube*] Huic quoque *articulum* subice dominator barbaricas gentes L^{II}

Gloss.: 1 ΕΡΗΝΗ] pax L^{II} ΠΙΣΤΩ] fido L^{II} ΔΗΜΩ] populo L^{II} ΒΑΣΙΛΕΙ] regi L^{II} Η] sit L^{II} ΚΛΕΟΡ] gloria L^{II} ΑΚΡΩ] summo L^{II} 2 ΟΝ] quem L^{II} ΘΕΟΣ] deus L^{II} ΕΚΛΕΣΤΟΝ (*sic*)] electum L^{II} ΠΑΡΑ] prae L^{II} ΕΙΣ] *deest* ΙΝ] unus L^{II} ΒΑΣΙΛΕΥΣΙΝ] regibus L^{II} ΕΧΕΙ] habet L^{II} ΝΥΝ] nunc   3 ΟΠΛΟΥ] arma L^{II} ΚΑΙ] et L^{II} ΕΠΙ] cum L^{II} ΛΑΒΩΝ] scuto L^{II} ΑΥΤΩ] prendens L^{II} ΕΙΗΣ] hunc ΧΡΙΣΤΕ] $\overline{xpe}$ L^{II} ΒΟΗΘΟΣ] iuuato L^{II} 4 ΔΕΣΠΟΤΑ] huic quoque L^{II} ΤΑ] articulus L^{II} ΑΥΤΩ] subice L^{II} ΥΠΟΤΑΞΟΝ] dominator L^{II} ΒΑΡΒΑΡΑ] barbaricas L^{II} ΦΥΛΑ] gentes L^{II}

15

Versus

ΡΩΜΑΙΟΥ ΔΗΜΟΥ ΙΩͰΑΝΝΗΣ Η ΚΛΕΟΡ ΕΣΤΙΝ.
ΕΛΛΗΝΩΝ ΕΛΛΗΝ ΛΑΜΠΕΙ ΝΥΝ ΛΙΥΔΔΟ ΣΕΒΑΣΤΟΣ.

(Romani populi Iohannes gloria constat:
Graecorum Graecus fulget nunc Liuddo colendus.)

---

cfr CONTRENI, *The Cathedral School of Laon from 850 to 930*, p. 136-137

Trad. text.: L^{I-II}
Hoc carmen inter 'Carmina Scottorum' edidit L. Traube, qui cuidam discipulo Martini opusculum sine explanatione adscripsit; uide praefationem, p. XLIII–XLV.

---

1 ΚΛΕΟΡ] i. q. κλέος

Gloss.: 1 ΡΩΜΑΙΟΥ] Romani L^{II} ΔΗΜΟΥ] populi L^{II} ΙΩͰΑΝΝΗΣ] Iohannes L^{II} ΚΛΕΟΡ] gloria L^{II} ΕΣΤΙΝ] constat L^{II} 2 ΕΛΛΗΝΩΝ] Graecorum L^{II} ΕΛΛΗΝ] Graecus L^{II} ΛΑΜΠΕΙ] fulget L^{II} ΝΥΝ] nunc L^{II} ΛΙΥΔΔΟ] Liuddo L^{II} ΣΕΒΑΣΤΟΣ L^{II}] colendus L^{II}

15*

Prosa

ΦΙΛΑΞΟΝ Ω ΘΕΟΣ ΤΗΝ ΒΑΣΙΛΙΣΣΑΝ ΗΡΜΙΝΔΡΟΥΔΑ
ΚΑΙ ΔΟΣ ΑΥΤΗ ΣΟΤΗΡΙΑΝ ΚΑΙ ΔΟΞΑΝ ΚΑΙ ΖΩΗΝ
ΕΙΣ ΤΟΥΣ ΑΙΩΝΑΣ ΤΩΝ ΑΙΩΝΟΝ. ΑΜΗΝ.

Prosa

Ω ΚΥΡΡΙΕ ΒΟΗΤΗΣΟΝ ΤΩ ΚΑΡΟΛΩ ΣΟΥ ΚΑΙ ΘΟΥ ΤΟΥΣ
5   ΕΧΤΡΟΥΣ ΑΥΤΟΥ ΚΑΙ ΤΟΥΣ ΜΗΣΟΥΝΤΑΣ ΑΥΤΟΝ
ΥΠΟΠΟΔΙΟΝ ΤΩΝ ΠΟΔΩΝ ΑΥΤΟΥ.

Trad. text.: L^{II}
Librarius Martinus has lineas uoce prosa *indicat, quae inter opera poetica genuina inclusi in eodem ordine quo dantur a Martino, ut hoc paruum corpus operum quae Iohannes graece composuit perfectum esset.*

---

3 ΑΜΗΝ *scripsi*] ΑΧΗΝ L^{II}

Gloss.: 1 ΦΙΛΑΞΟΝ] custodi L^{II} ΘΕΟΣ] deus L^{II} ΒΑΣΙΛΙΣΣΑΝ] reginam L^{II}
2 ΚΑΙ] et L^{II} ΔΟΣ] da L^{II} ΑΥΤΗ] ei L^{II} ΣΟΤΗΡΙΑΝ] salute L^{II} ΚΑΙ] et L^{II}
ΔΟΞΑΝ] gloriam L^{II} ΚΑΙ] et L^{II} ΖΩΗΝ] uitam L^{II} 3 ΕΙΣ] in L^{II} ΑΙΩΝΑΣ] saecula
L^{II} ΤΩΝ ΑΙΩΝΟΝ] saeculorum L^{II} ΑΜΗΝ] amen L^{II} 4 Ω] articulum L^{II}
ΚΥΡΡΙΕ] domine L^{II} ΒΟΗΤΗΣΟΝ] auxiliare L^{II} ΣΟΥ] tu L^{II} ΚΑΙ] et L^{II} ΘΟΥ] pone L^{II} ΕΧΤΡΟΥΣ] inimicos L^{II} 5 ΑΥΤΟΥ] eius L^{II} ΚΑΙ] et L^{II} ΜΗΣΟΥΝΤΑΣ] odientes L^{II} ΑΥΤΟΝ] eum L^{II} ΥΠΟΔΙΟΝ] scabellum L^{II} 6 ΠΟΔΩΝ] pedum L^{II}
ΑΥΤΟΥ] eius L^{II}

16

[ΣΤΙΧΟΣ ΠΡΕΠΟΣ ΔΙΔΑΣΚΑΛΟΥ ΜΑΡΤΙΝΟΥ]

ΕΙΣΧΡΕ ΑΝΑΓΙΝΟΣΤΗΣ, ΕΝΤΕΥΘΕΝ ΥΠΑΓΕ, ΦΕΥΓΕ,
ΜΗΔ᾽ ΕΛΕΛΥΘΑ ΛΟΓΩ ΣΟΥ ΚΑΙ ΤΑΧΑ ΜΗΔΕ ΠΟΡΕΥΩ.
ΑΡΝΕΤΕ ΣΕ ΗΛΙΚΙΑ ΚΡΟΤΑΦΩΝ ΑΠΑΛΩΝ ΤΕ ΝΕΩΝ ΤΕ.
ΙΔΕ ΛΑΛΕΙΝ ΤΙΘΟΜΑΙ, ΝΥΝ ΩΣ ΠΑΡΑΚΑΛΕΤΕ, ΠΕΡΑΝ.
5   ΝΥΝ ΛΗΓΕ, 'ΝΕΑΝΙΣΚΕ', ΛΕΓΕΙΝ 'ΔΟΣ ΔΕΣΜΑΤΑ ΧΙΛΣΙΝ'.

Trad. text.: L^{II}
Hoc carmen inter ea quae dicuntur 'Carminum Scottorum' edidit L. Traube p. 697. De his uersibus Martino falso adscriptis uide praefationem, p. XLIII-XLV.

---

1 ΥΠΑΓΕ L^{II}] Δ᾽ΥΠΑΓΕ Traube

Gloss.: Tit. ΣΤΙΧΟΣ] uersus ΠΡΕΠΟΣ] pulcher L^{II}
1 ΕΙΣΧΡΕ] improbe L^{II} ΑΝΑΓΙΝΟΣΤΗΣ] lector L^{II} ΕΝΤΕΥΘΕΝ] hinc L^{II} ΥΠΑΓΕ] uade L^{II} ΦΕΥΓΕ] fuge L^{II} 2 ΜΗΔ᾽] neque L^{II} ΕΛΕΛΥΘΑ] ueni L^{II} ΛΟΓΩ] uerbo L^{II} ΣΟΥ] tuo L^{II} ΚΑΙ] et L^{II} ΤΑΧΑ] forsan L^{II} ΜΗΔΕ] neque L^{II} ΠΟΡΕΥΩ] uadam L^{II} 3 ΑΡΝΕΤΕ] negat L^{II} ΣΕ] te L^{II} ΗΛΙΚΙΑ] aetas L^{II} ΚΡΟΤΑΦΩΝ] puerorum L^{II} ΑΠΑΛΩΝ] rudium L^{II} ΝΕΩΝ ΤΕ] nouorumque L^{II} 4 ΙΔΕ] ecce L^{II} ΛΑΛΕΙΝ] loquendi L^{II} ΤΙΘΟΜΑΙ] pono L^{II} ΝΥΝ] nunc L^{II} ΩΣ] sicut L^{II} ΠΑΡΑΚΑΛΕΤΕ] iubetis L^{II} ΠΕΡΑΝ] finem L^{II} 5 ΝΥΝ] nunc L^{II} ΛΗΓΕ] desine L^{II} ΝΕΑΝΙΣΚΕ] o iuuenis L^{II} ΛΕΓΕΙΝ] dicere L^{II} ΔΟΣ] da L^{II} ΔΕΣΜΑΤΑ] uincula L^{II} ΧΙΛΣΙΝ] labiis L^{II}

17

ΤΩ ΚΙΡΡΙΩ ΚΑΡΟΛΩ ΙΩΑΝΝΗΣ ΧΑΙΡΕΙΝ

ΘΑΥΜΑΣΤΩ ΒΑΣΙΛΕΙ ΚΑΡΟΛΩ ΖΩΗ ΤΕ ΦΑΟΣ ΤΕ.
ΟΡΤΩΔΟΞΟΣ ΑΝΑΞ ΦΡΑΓΓΟΝ, ΤΩ ΔΟΞΑ ΤΙΜΕ ΤΕ.
ΘΕΣΠΕΣΙΟΣ ΚΑΙ ΑΓΑΘΟΣ, ΠΙΣΤΟΣ ΚΑΙ ΑΚΡΟΣ ΤΕ ΜΟΝΑΡΧΟΣ,
ΕΛΠΙΣ ΤΗΣ ΠΑΤΡΙΔΟΣ, ΤΗΣ ΑΞΙΟΣ ΑΘΑΝΑΣΙΑΣ,
5   ΩΝ ΔΕ ΦΟΡΟΝ ΣΤΕΦΑΝΟΝ ΧΡΙΣΙΟΝ ΤΑ ΔΕ ΣΤΕΜΜΑΤΑ ΠΑΤΡΟΝ,
ΕΝΧΕΥΡΟΣ ΣΚΕΠΤΡΟΝ, ΡΑΒΔΟΣ ΓΑΡ ΤΗΣ ΒΑΣΙΛΙΑΣ.
ΧΡΙΣΤΕ, ΣΟΣΟΝ ΔΟΥΛΟΝ ΣΟΝ, ΤΟΝ ΜΟΙ ΚΥΡΡΙΟΝ ΕΙΠΩ,
ΤΟΝ ΚΑΡΟΛΟΝ ΜΗΓΑΛΗΝ ΕΜΟΝ ΠΟΛΛΟΝ ΤΕ ΚΟΡΥΦΗΝ,
ΟΣ ΣΟΦΟΣ, ΟΣ ΔΥΝΑΤΟΣ, ΠΑΝΥ ΣΟΦΡΩΝ ΤΕ ΚΡΑΤΟΣ ΤΕ,
10 ΕΙΠΡΕΠΗΣ, ΕΥΜΟΡΦΟΣ, ΦΑΥΝΟΝ ΩΣ ΗΝΚΛΥΤΟΣ ΑΡΧΟΣ,
ΩΣ ΤΟΝ ΟΥΡΑΝΙΟΝ ΣΤΙΛΒΟΝ, ΔΙΑΔΕΜΑΤΟΣ ΑΣΤΡΟΝ,
ΗΛΙΟΣ ΟΣ ΛΑΜΠΡΟΣ, ΟΣ ΦΟΣΦΩΡΟΣ, ΟΣ ΘΕΑ ΛΗΙΚΕ.
ΔΩΣΕΙΩ ΚΑΡΩΛΩ ΖΕΙΝ ΕΙΣ ΤΟΙΣ ΠΑΝΤΑΣ ΑΙΩΝΑΣ.
ΕΥΧΕΤΕ ΤΑΙΤΑ, ΛΑΟΙ, ΝΥΝ ΕΥΧΕ ΣΥ, ΦΡΑΓΓΙΑ ΠΑΣΣΑ.

---

7 cfr Ps. 19, 10 (LXX): Domine saluum fac regem

2 ΟΡΤΩΔΟΞΟΣ ΑΝΑΞ] cfr 2, 67   5 cfr DUTTON – JEAUNEAU, 'The Verses of the "Codex Aureus"', p. 113-115   10 ΗΝΚΛΥΤΟΣ ΑΡΧΟΣ] cfr 2, 67

Trad. text.: L^{II}

Tit. ΤΩ ΚΙΡΡΙΩ ΚΑΡΟΛΩ ΙΩΑΝΝΗΣ ΧΑΙΡΕΙΝ] L^{II}
2 ΟΡΤΟΔΟΞΟΣ Traube] ΟΝΤΟΣ ΔΟΞΟΣ L^{II} 10 ΩΣ ΗΝΚΛΥΤΟΣ Traube] Ω ΣΗΝ ΚΑΥΤΟΣ L^{II} 11 ΩΣ ΤΟΝ L^{II}] ΩΘΙΟΝ Traube   12 ΟΣ Traube] ΔΟΣ L^{II} 13 ΖΕΙΝ scripsi] ΖΟΙΝ Traube, ΖΘΙΝ L^{II}

Fr. 1

	ΤΡΙΑΔΙΣ	Trinitas
	ΑΝΑΡΧΟΝ	carentem principio
	ΦΙΣΕΟΣ	naturae
	ΗΟΣΜΙΦΕΡΑΜ	i. odoriferam
5	ΠΥΡΟΔΕΣ	igneas
	ΑΙΔΕΝ	locus deliciarum
	ΛΕΥΚΟΣ	albus
	ΓΑΣΤΡΟ	uentre
	ΠΝΕΥΜΑΤΙΣ	spiritus, genitiuus
10	ΑΥΓΑΙ	tonitrua, fulgura
	ΑΓΑΡ	*deest*
	Sina	prae (*ex* pro) montis
	ΘΕΟΣΙΣ	*deest*
	ΟΥΣΙΑ	essentia
15	ΠΑΡΑΔΟΞΑ	mirabilia
	ΣΑΡΚΑ	carne
	ΛΟΓΟΝ	uerbum
	ΣΑΡΞ	caro
	ΛΟΓΟΣ	uerbum
20	ΧΑΙΡΕ	salue
	ΑΣΘΕΝΕΣ	infirmus
	ΑΝΑΞ	rex
	ΔΙΚΗ	causa

Trad. text.: *L¹*

Fr. 2

ΘΕΟΣ	Deus
ΥΠΕΡΑΛΗΘΗΣ	i. superuerus
ΦΟΜΕΝΟΡ	*deest*
ΧΟΡΔΑΝ	i. chordam

Trad. text.: *L¹*

FRAGMENTA 2-3

5	ΦΛΕΓΟΜΗΝΟΣ	deest
	ΑΚΑΝΤΩΔΗΣ	deest
	ΓΥΝΗΚΑ	uxor
	ΔΑΨΙΣΕΛΗΣ	deest
	ΟΛΥΜΠΟΣ	caelum
10	ΦΩΤΙΣΜΟΥ	lucis
	spiritus ΥΨΙΣΤΟΣ	i. altissimus
	ΔΩΡΑ	i. dona
	ΖΩΗΣ	uitae
	ΔΙΚΑΙΟΣ ΙΗΣΟΥΣ	deest
15	ΠΝΕΥΜΑΤΟΣ	spiritus, genitiuus
	ΦΟΒΟΣ	timor
	ΤΡΟΜΟΣ	tremor
	ΗΧΟΣ	sonus
	ΘΑΥΜΑΣΤΟΣ	mirabilis
20	ΔΟΥΛΟΣ	seruus

Trad. text.: *L¹*

Fr. 3

	ΣΩΜΑ	deest
	ΣΤΑΥΡΩ	deest
	ΒΑΘΟΥ	deest
	ΑΡΜΟΔΙΟΣ	deest
5	ΒΑΛΗΝ	deest
	ΦΡΟΣΚΕΙΟΣ	i. frustra uel frustruosus

Trad. text.: *L¹*

Subscriptio cum glossis] ΕΛΛΗΝΙΣ [Graecus] ΓΡΑΨΕΝ [scripsit] ΜΑΡΤΙΝΟΣ ΓΡΑΜΜΑΤΑ [litteras] ΑΥΤΑ [istas] *L¹, fol. 296r*

18

Quisquis ΧΕΙΡΟΥΡΓΟΣ nostras incidere flebas
Audet, preuideat ne sua dextra tremet.

---

1 cfr Leonardi, 'Nuove voci poetiche'   2 cfr Contreni, 'The Study and Practice of Medicine in Northern France'

Trad. text.: *V*

19

Bacchus abest siccis Scottorum faucibus estu,
Et uentres nostros morbida replet aqua.

Trad. text.: *V*

20

Hanc libam sacro Graecorum nectare fartam
   Aduena Iohannes spondo meo Karolo.
Maxime Francigenum, cui regia stemmata fulgent,
   Munera uotiferi sint tibi grata tui.
5 Vos qui Romuleas nescitis temnere ΤΕΧΝΑΣ,
   Attica ne pigeat sumere gymnasia.
Quorum si quaedam per me scintilla relucet
   Vsibus Ausoniis, si libet, aspicite.
Molestum si non nostrum munire laborem,
10   Firmetur uestri pondere iudicii.
Si quid nodosum durumue notatur in ipso,
   Parcite Cecropidis: Attica tela sequor.
At si mendosus declinat tramite recto,
   Mellifluo uestro famine corrigite.
15 Quod si quorundam mordetur dente feroci,
   Hoc leue: namque meo contigit Hieronimo.
Vt uero stabilis maneat fundamine firmo,
   Regali stathmo figere sufficiet.

16/17 cfr Matth. 7, 24

---

1 ANON. BOBB. 5, 2: hanc libam nitido doctorum nectare fartam   5 Romuleas – ΤΕΧΝΑC] cfr VERG., *Aen.* 6, 851-852: Romane, memento / hae tibi erunt artes   7 cfr BEDA, *Iud.* 109: lucis ubi miseris nulla scintilla relucet   9/10 cfr 2, 69-72; 6, 36-40   15/16 cfr Ov., *Trist.* 4, 10, 124: ullum de nostris dente momordit opus; ALDH., *Carm. eccles.* 4, 2, 26: uipera dira manum letali dente momordit; cfr JEAUNEAU, 'Jean Scot Erigène et le grec', p. 15   16 meo contigit Hieronimo] cfr HIER., *Adu. Rufin.* 2, 25: obtrectatorum latratibus patens

---

Trad. text.: *B F O Ph β*

---

1 fartam *O Ph β*] fertam *F*$^{a.c.}$, factam *B*   4 uotiferi *B F O Ph*] uociferi *β*   5 ΤΕΧΝΑΣ *F β*] ΤΙΧΝΑ *Ph*, technas *O B*   7 sciat illa *Ph*$^{a.c.}$ 8 accipite *β*   10 iudicis *Ph*   12 tela] *i. q.* τέλη   13 declinet *Ph*   16 Hieronimo *codd.*] Heronimo *Traube*

Gloss.: [*O B β*]

1 libam] a libando *O*, oblationem *β*   fartam] plenam *β*   3 stemmata] insignia uel coronae *β*   5 Romuleas] latinas *β*   ΤΕΧΝΑΣ] totas *O*, artes *β*   6 Attica] graeca *β*   8 Ausoniis] occidenti *O*, latinis *β*   9 non] s. est *O*   12 Cecropides] rex athenarum *O*   18 stathmo] pondere uel auctoritate *β*

Crediderim multos tangentum summa sophiae
   Non despecturos donula nostra fore,
Sudorisque grauis temptabunt carpere fructum:
   Forsan uirtutem uilia uerba tenent.
Saepe solent spinis redolentes crescere flores,
   Nodosae uitis sumitur uua ferax.

---

23 cfr Cant. 2, 2: sicut lilium inter spinas

---

21 cit. *Anon. Bobb.* 89, 5, 4 (p. 412): sudoris grauis temptent quo carpere fructum

---

Trad. text.: *B F O Ph β*

21

    Lumine sidereo Dionysius auxit Athenas
      Ariopagites magnificusque sophos,
    Primo commotus Phoebo subeunte Selena,
      Tempore quo stauro fixus erat Dominus.
5   Mox ut conuersus mira stupefactus eclypsi,
      Consequitur gaudens Ierothea ducem.
    Quo mox edoctus praeclarus namque magister
      Pneumatis excelsi fonte renatus erat.
    Nec mora: perfulgens caelestis luce sophiae
10   Atticas edocuit, de quibus ortus et est.
    Namque ferunt Paulum, qui Christum sparsit in orbem,
      Ipsi felices imposuisse manus.
    Ast mox perfectus doctoris symmachus instar
      Rexit Cecropidas peruigil archiereus.

1/2 cfr Act. 17, 34

4/5 cfr App. 8, 4-5   5/6 cfr IOH. SCOT., *Versio Dion. Ar.* (col. 1032D): dionysius ... diuino ... miraculo solaris eclipseos, quae facta est confixo ... Christo crucis patibulo, commotus: ipse siquidem, ut in quadam suarum epistolarum commemorat, dum esset iuxta Heliopolim cum Polycarpo episcopo ceterisque qui tunc aderant, diuina procurante prouidentia mirabilem in modum conspexerat *lunam soli subeuntem* ac per hoc solem defecisse; moxque sanctissimum uirum, apostolorum discipulum, Ierotheum uidelicet episcopum, secutus ... eundemque magistrum suum uenerabilem nominat ceterisque tunc temporis coepiscopis post apostolos in theologia praeferre non dubitat   9 cit. ANON. BOBB. 5, 1: almo quidem fulgens celestis luce sophie   11 sparsit in orbem] cfr BEDA, *Cuth.* 1, 8: multifidos uarium lychnos qui sparsit in orbem   14 cfr IOH. SCOT., *Versio Dion. Ar.* (col. 1032D): fertur namque praefatus Dionysius fuisse discipulus atque adiutor Pauli apostoli, a quo *Atheniensium constitutus est episcopus*

Trad. text.: *B F O Ph β*

---

1 sydereo *O B β*   Dionisius *codd.*   4 stayro *O B*   5 Mox ut *F Ph*] Mox et *O B* elympsi *F Ph*   7 *totum uersum omisit Ph*   10 Atticas *O B β* (*sc.* Athenienses)] Attidas *F Ph* Traube   et est *O B*] adest *Ph F* Traube, erat *β*   13 instar *Ph*] instans *FOB β*

Gloss.: [*O B β*]
3 Selena] luna *β*   10 Attidas] Athenienses *β*   13 symmachus] coadiutor *β*

CARMEN 21

15   Alta dehinc uolitans Paulum super astra secutus
        Empyrii caeli tertia regna uidet.
    Suspicit et Seraphym primos sanctosque Cherubym
        Aethereosque Thronos, quo sedet ipse Deus;
    Post hos Virtutes, Dominatus atque Potentes
20   Agminibus sacris enitet ordo sequens:
    ΑΡΧΩΝ ΑΡΧΑΓΕΛΩΝ ΤΕ ΧΟΡΩΝ ΑΓΕΛΩΝ ΤΕ ΤΕΛΑΥΤΩΝ
        Mentibus oyraniis tertia taxis inest.
    Hos igitur numeros terno ter limite septos
        Praedicti Patris mystica dicta docent.

---

16 cfr II Cor. 12, 2

---

15 cfr VEN. FORT., *Mart.* 4, 240: stratus homo recubans, precibus super astra relatus   21 cfr glossas ad uersum apud *Scholica Graecarum Glossarum* apud LAPIDGE, 'L'influence stylistique de la poésie de Jean Scot', p. 443-444   23/24 cfr IOH. SCOT., *Ier. Dion.* 6, 80: omnes theologia celestes essentias nouem uocauit

---

Trad. text.: *B F O Ph β*

15 super] sub *Ph*   17 suspicit *O B*] suscipit *Ph β*ᵃ·ᶜ·   et *scripsi*] at *Ph F β,* ac *O B*   18 aetheriosque *O B*   21 ΤΕΛΑΥΤΩΝ *O Ph*] *F B β*   22 ouranis *O B*

Gloss.: 21 ΑΡΧΩΝ] principatuum *β*   ΑΡΧΑΓΕΛΩΝ] archangelorum *β*   ΑΓΕΛΩΝ] angelorum *β*   ΤΕΛΑΥΤΩΝ *sic β*] ipsorum *β*   22 taxis] ordo *O B β*

22

    Kyrrie, caeligenae cui pollet gratia formae,
    Astrea Caesareos cui cingunt stemmata uultus,
    Regum progenies, quos auxit Francia felix,
    Orbis terrarum quos alta uoce salutat,
5   Laudibus amplificat ueneratur ditat honorat,
    Vndique concurrens pontum secat, emetit arua.
    Salue, Christicolum uertex, gratissime regum.
    Rex pie, deuoti ne spernas donula serui:
    Exiguum munus, largo sed fonte receptum,
10 Xristiferum patrum mysteria plurima tractans.
    Hoc opus in Graeco construxit Maximus abba,
    Egregius pastor, scripturis inclitus auctor,
    Magni Gregorii perplanans dicta remota,
    Sensibus humanis theoremeta mente reuoluens.
15 Nec non in multis Dionysius additur ipse
    Ariopagites, ornat quem laudibus amplis,
    Explanat testemque uocat patremque beatum,
    Tangens symbolicas praeclaro lumine byblos,
    Quas nos edidimus uobis poscentibus olim.
20 Hac quoque de causa praefatus Maximus abba
    Editus est nuper nostro sudante labore,
    Effectuque pio uestrum pia iussa sequentes
    Cursim transtulimus, quae multo tempore quaerunt
    Et doctos sensus et purae mentis acumen.

---

   10 mysteria – tractans] cfr VEN. FORT., *Carm.* 10, 6, 5: sacra dum mysteria tractat; 10, 6, 81; ALC. AVIT., *Carm.* 6, 406: plurima tractatores   **12** cfr *Epitaphia ciuitatis Papiae* 1, 1, 2 (p. 102): et pater et pastor, patriae decus, inclitus auctor   **15/16** cfr IOH. SCOT., *Versio Max.,* proem.: fortasis autem ... non tam densas subierim caligines, nisi uiderem ... Maximum saepissime in processu sui operis obscurissimas ... Dionysii Ariopagitae sententias, cuius symbolicos theologicosque [sensus, *supp. Gale*], nuper Vobis similiter iubentibus transtuli, introduxisse mirabilique modo delucidasse   **24** mentis acumen] cfr adnot. 10, 9

   Trad. text.: *ArM*

---

   6 potum $M^{a.c.}$ emetit *scripsi*] eminet *Ar M*   **22** pio] *om. $M^{a.c.}$

23

Quisquis rhetorico uerborum syrmate gaudet
   Quaerat grandiloquos Tullia castra petens;
Ast mihi sat fuerit, si planos carpere sensus
   Possem tardilocus pragmata sola sequens.
Interior uirtus sermonum rite tenenda:
   uerborum bombi fallere saepe solent.
Si quis in ambobus diuino munere pollet,
   Hic primum debet iure tenere modum.
Sed si perspicuos sensus uix uoce loquaris,
   Sis quoque contentus; nam meliora tenes.
Si meliora tenes, quaenam tibi cura tenere
   Quae sunt inferius? semper in alta pete.

---

12 meliora tenes] cfr Luc. 10, 42

---

2 cfr VERG., *Aen.* 10, 635: iliacemque aciem et Laurentia castra petiuit

---

Trad. text.: *ArM*

---

7 pollet] pellet *M*[a.c.]

24

    Quisquis amat formam pulchrae laudare sophiae,
        Te legat assidue, Maxime Graiugena.
    Ac primo motus rerum rationibus altis
        Mundum sensibilem deserat atque neget,
5   Nec non et sensus ipsos, qui saepe retardant,
        Gnostica dum scandit bemata mentis iter.
    Deliciis fragilis uitae mundoque fugaci
        Et carnis cura qui uacat, ista legat;
    Mundanisque datus studiis tardusque pigerque
10   Huc non accedat: nullus adest aditus.
    Sensibus inflatus propriis tumidusque superbus
        Stet procul ipse negans hic reperire locum.
    Artibus imbutus, quas nouit mentis acumen,
        Fidus procedat: nam sua stat patria.
15 Practica hic lucet morum praeclara magistra,
        Custos uirtutum peruigil, idonea.
    Hic Physice causas rerum uestigat opacas
        Inuentasque simul segregat, unificat.
    Hic theo – fert palmam cunctis perpulchra – logia:
20   ON quod, quod non ON, denegat omne simul.

---

6 gnostica] cfr schol. in Ioh Scot., *Periphys.* 2, 28 (col. 535C): Non enim aliter adunationem creatarum substantiarum in angelis esse intelligimus nisi sola gnostica scientia, non autem ipsarum rerum collectione in unum   20 denegat omne simul] cfr Ioh Scot., *Periphys.* 1, 20 (col. 461B-D)

Trad. text.: *ArM*

---

4 negat *M*   20 ON²] *om. M*

Gloss.: [Ar M]
6 bemata] gradus ascensionis *Ar M*

25

VERSVS IOHANNIS SCOTTI
AD KAROLVM REGEM

    Aulae sidereae paralelos undique circos
    Crinibus auratis nectit Titania lampas.
    Vmbram bis luci parilem bis lance staterans
    Sese bis tropicos ambarum uertit in auctus,
5   Ac sic distingens binis bis motibus annum
    Regnat tetragonum pulcro discrimine mundum
    Signis ambitum bis senis limite curuo,
    Quae totidem menses terrenis usibus aptant.
    Talibus articulis, quos circum tempora currunt,
10 Partibus octauis dico Libraeque Criuque
    Nec non Aegoceri, Cancri praefixa tropea.
    Tu Crie, concepti Christi tibi plaude triumphum,
    Vendicet Aegoceros nascentis gaudia uerbi;
    Lucis praecursor nascens in uertice Cancri,
15 Libra conceptus, cernis praefata tropea.
    Si quis corde pio mentis leuauerit alas
    Ac sensim tranet tenero theoremeta lapsu
    Intrans armoniam rerum, ducente sophia,
    Omnia perspiciet rationis acumine claro
20 Intus farta Deo uerbo loca tempora, totum
    Mundum gestantem nascentis symbola Christi.

---

14 cfr Luc. 1, 26

---

cfr Piemonte, 'Acotaciónes sobre algunos poemas de Eriúgena', II, p. 47-53; Herren, 'Eriugena's *Aulae sidereae,* the 'Codex aureus', and the Palatine Church of St. Mary's at Compiègne', p. 593-608
  1 cfr Sedvl. Scot., *Carm.* 1, 1, 24: donec sideream uos ascendatis in aulam   9 cfr Heric., *Vita Germ. metr.* 6, 338: quo sine nocte dies, sine tempore tempora currunt   13 gaudia uerbi] cfr App. 14, 2

Trad. text.: C

---

3 staterans $C^{in\ ras.}$ 5 distingens *sic* C   17 sensum C

Verbum nanque Deus processit uirginis aluo
Lucis in augmento, quam noctis uicerat umbra,
Nos homines miseros paradisi luce remotos,
25 Olim commissae septos umbramine culpae
Sponte relinquentes praeclara sedilia uitae,
Mortis perpetuae deuinctos iure catenis,
Quo mortale genus lueret sua debita soluens,
Sentiret meritas inflata superbia poenas,
30 Restaurare uolens priscasque reducere sedes.
Haec octaua tibi bifrontis rite Kalendas
Insinuat typicas, dum uincit luce tenebras.
Octonus numerus diuinos symfonat actus;
Nam Dominus noster, quem tempus formulat omne,
35 Octauis natus, conceptus, morte reuersus,
Octauis ueteris subiit signacula legis,
Mundus in octaua finem dabit omnibus unum
Cursibus annorum uariis rebusque caducis
Sumpturus stabilem mutato schemate formam,
40 Dum genus humanum generali matre renatum
Pro limo terrae caelestis corpora sumet,
Densa seges uirides miro teget ordine sulcos
Tellurisque nouae facies reuocabitur actu
Et rerum propriae consument omnia causae.
45 Haec sunt, quae tacite nostris in cordibus intus
Octoni numeri modulatur nabla sonorum,
Spiritus interior clamat nec desinit unquam
Semper concrepitans, quidquid semel intonat annus;
Haec scriptura docet, cui rerum concinit ordo.
50 Quae sibi nascendi tempus prudentia fecit,
Ipsa locum statuit, quo primum nata pateret.

---

41 cfr I Cor. 15, 52-53

28 debita soluens] cfr adnot. 1, 81   43/44 cfr IOH. SCOT., *Periphys.* 5, 34 (col. 952B-952C): cur autem mundus iste soluetur inque suas causas reuertetur?   46 cfr MÜNXELHAUS, 'Aspekte der Musica Disciplina bei Eriugena', p. 259-262

CARMEN 25

Bethleem fertur quondam possessio Dauid,
Regis psalmidici, genitoris origine Christi.
Salue, sancta domus, panis ditissima patrum,
Area caelestis diuina fruge referta,
In qua natus erat, qui sustinet omnia, panis,
Panis perpetuus, quo uescitur aula superna:
In te manna pluit summis uirtutibus aptum.
Felix illa domus, quae fraglat aromata uitae
Arcanisque suis paradisi prodidit escam.
Angelicus panis, quem primus perdidit Adam,
Vilibus in stabulis prono reperitur in antro.
Lucis praeclarae qui uestit sidera peplo,
Pannos induitur furuo sub culmine cruptae.
Quem nullus nouit sensus nec mentis acumen,
Mandra boum uidit tenero uelamine carnis.
Quae mens, quae uirtus, superum quae facta sophia
In carnem poterit descensum dicere Verbi,
Carnis et in Verbum sublimia bimata nosse?
Vt Deus aeternus factus caro lapsus ad ima,
Sic caro facta Deus uere leuis euolat alta.
Nate Dei Patris, cui mater Virgo beata,
Cui genus egregium Dauid rex atque sacerdos
Cuique remota domus septenis fulta columnis,
Sanctae scripturae cui fulget candida uestis,
Sanguine quem redimis cui mundus subditur omnis,
Vita, salus hominum, caelorum gloria summa:
Da nostro regi Karolo, cui sciptra dedisti,
Vt semper famulus tibi uiuat mente benigna.

52/53 cfr Luc. 2, 4; Ioh. 7, 42   57 cfr Ioh 6, 55   74 domus – columnis] cfr Prou. 9, 1

57/60 cfr HILDVIN., *Dion. metr.* 1, 579-580: angelici panis uerbo se namque refertum, / ostendens superae quo uiuunt nempe cohortes   63 MART. CAP., 2, 116 (uers.): et iam tunc roseo subtexere sidera peplo   65 mentis acumen] cfr adnot. 10, 9   66 uelamine carnis] cfr PAVL. PETRIC., *Mart.* 3, 202; CORIPP., *Iust.* 2, 59   69 bimata *i. q.* βήματα   70/71 cfr adnot. 1, 28   74 ALCVIN., *Carm.* 1, 1508: haec nimis alta domus solidis suffulta columnis; cfr 25, 87; 2, 57; App. 2, 11   78 cui sciptra dedisti] cfr adnot. 2, 61

78 sciptra (*i.q.* σκῆπτρα *cum itacismo*) sic C hic et ad 99, alibi sceptra

80 Prospera labentis uitae reuolumina praesta
Atque simul tecum caelestis gaudia regni.
Magna Dei genitrix, ter felix, sancta Maria –
Te laudant caeli, te uotis inclytat orbis –:
Proxima sis Karolo tutrix, munimen et altum,
85 Qui tibi mirifice praeclaram fabricat aedem.
Aedes marmoreis uarie constructa columnis,
Alta domus pulcre centeno normate facta.
Aspice polygonos flexus arcusque uolutos,
Compages laterum similes, capitella basesque,
90 Turres, luriculas, laquearia, daedala tecta,
Obliquas tyridas, ialini luminis haustus,
Intus picturas, lapidum pauimenta gradusque,
Circum quaque stoas, armaria, pastaforia,
Sursum deorsum populos altaria circum,
95 Lampadibus plenas pharos altasque coronas.
Omnia collucent gemmis auroque coruscant;
Pallia, cortinae circumdant undique templum.
Ipse throno celso fultus rex prospicit omnes
Vertice sublimi gestans diadema paternum,
100 Plena manus sciptris enchiridon aurea bactra;
Heros magnanimus longaeuus uiuat in annos.

---

86 marmoreis – columnis] cfr Esth. 1, 6: et columnis marmoreis fulciebantur 87 centeno normate] cfr Ez. 40, 19 93 pastaforia] cfr Ier. 42, 4 (LXX)

85ff. cfr Piemonte, 'Acotaciónes sobre algunos poemas de Eriúgena', II, p. 44 87 Greg. M., *In Ezech.* 2, 6, (col. 1007B, col. 1067D): denarius autem numerus per semetipsum multiplicatus in centenarium surgit, unde recte per centenarium magna perfectio designatur; cfr Christe, 'Sainte-Marie de Compiègne et le temple d'Hézéchiel', p. 480 90 Verg., *Georg.* 4, 179: et munire fauos et daedala fingere tecta 91 obliquas tyridas] cfr Christe, 'Sainte-Marie de Compiègne et le temple d'Hézéchiel', p. 478-479 94 altaria circum] cfr Verg., *Ecl.* 8, 74; *Aen.* 2, 515; 4, 145; 8, 285

---

90 luricolas *scripsi*] luriculos C 100 sciptris] cf. adnot. 78 enchiridon (*i. q.* ἐγκειριδίων) C

App. 1

Caesare sub Karolo Francorum gloria pollet,
 Litora ceu pelagi piscibus atque salo:
Secta diabolici damnatur dogmatis atque
 Pastorum cura splendet amoena fides.

Trad. text.: *P3*

App. 2

ΓΡΑΜΜΑΤΑ ΓΡΑΙΥΓΕΝΩΝ ΚΑΤΑ ΣΚΗΜΑΤΑ, ΣΟΦΕ, ΓΥΝΟΣΚΕΙΣ.
 Cerne: labore meo lingua Pelasga patet.
Quisque uelit sapiens sapientes gnoscere causas,
 Sensibus in sacris sentiat artis opes.
5 Has euangelicas doctrinas doctor ab astris
 Nobis praecipiens contulit ore Deus.
Qui regit omne quod est, qui condidit omne creatum,
 Qui factor mundi uirgine factus homo est;
Principium sine principio, finis sine fine est,
10 Omnipotens Dominus, lucis origo, Deus.
Lux aeterna, Dei Verbum, sapientia Patris,
 Caelestis patriae uerba superna dare
Venit in hunc mundum, rex regum rexque Sabaoth,
 Ipse Deus hominum, qui dedit omne bonum.

11 cfr 1 Cor. 1, 24

1/2 SEDVL. SCOT., *Carm.* 2, 7, 153: graiugenae Musae nomen hoc esse Pelasgum   1 ΓΡΑΙΥΓΕΝΩΝ] cfr VERG., *Aen.* 3, 550: graiugenumque domos suspectaque linquimus arua; cfr 24, 2: te legat assidue, Maxime Graiugena   2 cfr ALDH., *Aenig.* 60, 10: indidit ex cornu nomen mihi lingua Pelasga   3 VERG., *Georg.* 2, 490: felix qui potuit rerum cognoscere causas   7 cfr 8, 30: qui regit atque tenet totum, quod condidit ipse   9 cfr IOH. SCOT., *Periphys.* 4, 20 (col. 741C): unum principium ... sine principio, principium et finis   10 cfr VEN. FORT., *Carm.* 6, 5, 34: ex quibus ante sibi lucis origo fuit; 2, 16, 70: et tua mors illi lucis origo fuit   11 cfr 2, 57: Christe, dei uerbum, uirtus, sapientia patris, 12 cfr 4, 36: caelestis patriae symbola sacra uidet   14 cfr ERMOLD. NIGEL., *Ludow.* 2, 586 et 4, 174: qui dedit omne bonum

Trad. text.: *S*

1 ΓΥΝΟΣΚΙΣ *S*^{a.c.}

15 Fons bonitate potens, fons uitae fonsque sophiae,
    Cor mundum famulis da, bone Christe, tuis.
    Saluator mundi, qui saecula sordida mundas,
    Cum uirtute crucis crimina cuncta lauans,
    Omnipotens, miserere mei, miserere dolentis:
20 Sum mihi namque mei causa doloris ego.
    Da dolor absistat, da uitam daque sophiam:
    Des mihi perpetui, te rogo, regna poli.

---

15 cfr App. 13, 3: hic deitate potens   **17** cfr HRABAN., *Carm.* 16, 25; 83, 1   **18** cfr *Inscriptiones locorum sacrorum* 15, 8 (p. 315): sanguine qui mundi crimina cuncta tulit   **19** cfr Ov., *Her.* 12, 81: O uirgo, miserere mei, miserere meorum

---

Trad. text.: *S*

---

16 dā *S*

App. 3

Nunc inuise bonis, uocitaris nomine prisco;
Vt tua praeualeant munera, Bache, ueni.

---

1 cfr BERNT, *Das lateinische Epigramm*, p. 277-278

Trad. text.: *So*

---

1 Nunc inuise bonis *scripsi*] Nunc inuisa bonis *So*, Hinc ceruisa abeas *Traube* (*Carm. Scot. VII.1*, p. 690) *magna cum audacia*   uocitaris *So*] uocitatus *Traube*; cfr G. BERNT, *Das lateinische Epigramm im Übergang von der Spätantike zum frühen Mittelalter*, p. 277-278

App. 4

Sume, precor, Bacchum; ne spernas munera Bacchi;
Quae tragos reperit flumina nota ⟨pete⟩.

---

1 munera Bacchi] cfr SCHUMANN, *Lateinisches Hexameter-Lexikon*, I, 454-455   **2** flumina nota] cfr VERG., *Ecl.* 1, 51: hic inter flumina nota

---

Trad. text.: *So*

---

1 spernas *Traube*] spernis *So*   **2** reperit *scripsi*] repperit *So, forte legatur* repetit nota *So*] nosce *Traube*   pete *scripsi*] petens *Traube, lectio codicis So obscuratur*

App. 5

Hic duo sunt soniui, ardens ast angulus unuS:
  Non satis expellit frigora lusqua domuS.
Karlomanne, tuis arridet partibus igniS,
  Nos uero gelidos urit iniqua hiemS.
Vulfadus praeses nostrum flagrare caminum
  Diues lignorum, prouidus ipse roget.

Trad. text.: *So*

---

1 soniui *scripsi*] fonsiui *So*, fratres *sic Traube*   ardens] *Traube*, omdens *So*   2 lusqua] *i. q.* lusca   domus *sc.* domūs   4 hurit *So*   5 praeses] *scripsi*, praesens *So*, praestet *Traube*   6 roget *So*] rogi *Traube*

App. 6

Hoc nemus umbriferum crebris de flatibus austri
  Componit leni murmure dulce melos.
Iam canit allector praedicens luminis ortum,
  Horam, qua Christus prosilit ex Erebo.

---

3 cfr Matth. 26, 34; 26, 74-75; Marc. 14, 30; 14, 68; 14, 72; Luc. 22, 34; 22, 60-61; Ioh. 13, 38; 18, 27

---

1 hoc nemus umbriferum] cfr VERG., *Aen.* 6, 473 in nemus umbriferum   flatibus austri] cfr 4, 49: in Syrtes uarias spargantur flatibus austri   4 prosilit ex Erebo: cfr 6, 1: emicat ex Erebo, lux mundi magna triumphans; 6, 3: prosiliunt Furiae

---

Trad. text.: *So*

---

3 allector *i. q.* ἀλέκτωρ

App. 7

Sidera, si sparsim speciali lumine fulgent,
  O quam collectim ΦΩΣ animosa foret!

Trad. text.: *La* (flyleaf); cfr DUTTON, 'Eriugena, the Royal Poet', p. 55

App. 8

Semeron, autokrator fronimos kai timie Karle,
Martyros ypelos lampei Dyonisios, idoy,
On Theos oyranonen, epiges kai soy, megalinay.
Idon tos skotois ως kyrrios alfeiletoy
5   Stayron toy kysmoy tas amartias alale sente:
'Ouk fysis fetoy litirgin kai poiesin.
Estin nyn ellinsin kai mato poietin
Toy kosmoy gnorizo kai nun oila ratinta'.

5/8 cfr *Passio Dionysii (prosa)* cap. 5, ed. Lapidge, *Hilduin of Saint-Denis,* The Passio S. Dionysii *in Prose and Verse* (2017), p. 238-40

Trad. text.: G

Textus graecus constitutus a Ludovico Traube: Σήμερον, αὐτοκράτωρ φρόνιμος καὶ τίμιε Κάρλε, / Μάρτυρος ὑψηλὸς λάμπει Διονύσιος ἰδού, / ὃν θεὸς οὐρανόθεν, ἐπὶ γῆς καὶ σύ, μεγαλίνει, / εἶδεν τοὺς σκότους, ὡς κύριος ἀφεῖλεν τῷ / σταυρῷ τοῦ κόσμου τὰς ἁμαρτίας ἐλάλησέν τε / 'ὀυ φύσις εἰώθει λιτουργεῖν καὶ ποιῆσαι / ἐς τὴν νῦν ἔκλειψν καὶ διὰ τοῦτο ποιήτην / τοῦ κόσμου γνωρίζω καὶ νῦν οἶδα παθόντα.'

Gloss.: [G]
1 Semeron] hodie   autokrator] imperator   fronimos] sapiens   kai] et   timie] preciose   Karle] Carle   2 Marytros] martyr   ypelos] excelsus   lampei] fulget   dyonisios] Dionisius   idoy] ecce   3 On] quem   theos] deus   oyranonen] caelitus   epiges] in terris   kai] et   soy] tu   megalinay] magnificauit   4 Idon (*subaudens* ἰδών)] uidens   tos] hic   skotosis] tenebras   ως] dum   kyrrios] dominus   alfeile (toy)] abstulit   5 stayron] cruce   toy] articulus   kysmoy] mundi   tas] articulus   amartias] peccata   alale sente] dixitque   6 Ouk] non   fysis] natura   fetoy] solet   litirgin] ministrare   kai] et   poiesin] facere   7 estin] est   nyn] nunc   ellinsin] defectum   kai] et   mato] ideo (*i.q.* uideo?)   poietin] factorem   8 toy] articulus   kosmoy] mundi   gnorizo] cognosco   kai] et   nun] nunc   oila] scio   ratinta] passum

App. 9

a

Hic iacet Hincmarus clepthes uehementer auarus:
hoc solum gessit nobile quod periit.

---

cfr Dutton, 'Eriugena, the royal poet', p. 57-59; Bernt, *Das lateinische Epigramm*, p. 282-286

Trad. text.: *At Mo*

---

1 igma ... *At*   2 solum *Mo*] tantum *At*   Gessit *Mo*] gestit *At*

Gloss.: [*At*]
1 Igmarus] GOTISCALT   cleptes] clepit, foromat dicitur cleptes (*i. q.* φώρ κλέπτης ὀνόμαται); *super* cleptes *scribitur* fur et clepus

b

HOC EPITAPHIVM COMPOSVIT IOHANNES LICET
HERETICVS

Hic iacet Igcmarus cleptes et semper auarus:
hoc solum fecit nobile quod periit.

---

cfr Dutton, 'Eriugena, the royal poet', p. 57-59; Bernt, *Das lateinische Epigramm*, p. 282-286
2 Avson., 21, 2, 33-36: hoc solum fecit nobile, quod periit; cfr Bernt, *Das lateinische Epigramm*, p. 282

Trad. text.: *Va*

c

Hic iacet Incmarus cleptes uehementer auarus:
Sordidus, instabilis, madescit rore pericli;
hoc solum fecit nobile quod periit.

---

cfr Dutton, 'Eriugena, the royal poet', p. 57-59; Bernt, *Das lateinische Epigramm*, p. 282-286

Trad. text.: *H*

App. 10

Francia grata tibi, rex inclite, munera defert.
Gotia te pariter cum regnis inchoat altis.

Hic residet Karolus diuino munere fultus,
   Ornat quem pietas et bonitatis amor.
Hludouuic iustus erat, quo rex non iustior alter,
   Qui genuit prolem hanc tribuente deo.
Alma uiro peperit Iudith de sanguine claro,
   Cum genitor regnis iura dabat propriis.
Hic nomen magni Karoli de nomine sumpsit,
   Numen et indicium sceptra tenendo sua.
Hic Dauid uario fulgescit stemmate regis
   Atque Salomonica iura docentis habet.
Istius imperio hic codex resplendet et auro,
   Qui bona construxit multa fauente Deo.
Arma tibi faueant Christi stabilita per aeuum
   Muniat et clipeus semper ab hoste suus.

---

cfr Dutton – Jeauneau, 'The Verses of the "Codex Aureus" of Saint-Emmeram'
   1 cfr Beda, *Cuth.* II, 16   3 cfr Pavl. Nol., *Carm.* 22, 64: huius diuino mortales munere fulti; Aldh., *Laud. uirg.* 2903: ultimus in requie diuino munere fretus   5 Verg., *Aen.* 1, 544-545: rex erat Aeneas nobis, quo iustior alter / Nec pietate fuit   7 cfr Stat., *Theb.* 9, 777: primusque Iouis de sanguine claro   11 cfr 25, 73-76 uario – stemmate] cfr 17, 5   stemmate regis] cfr Aldh., *Laud. uirg.* 154; 1044; Sedvl. Scot., *Carm.* 2, 15, 17   14 Theodvlf., *Carm.* 1, 40: haec qui construxit tecta fauente deo

---

Trad. text.: *E*

---

10 Numen *scripsi*] Nomen *E*

App. 11

Suscipit, agne, tuum populus, uenerande, cruorem
Et synagoga suo fuscata colore recessit.
Omnia quae praesens tellus producit alendo
Et maris haec facies limbo circumuenit amplo,
5   Agne, Deum solio temet uenerantur in alto.
Cana caterua cluens, uatum et uenerabilis ordo,
Coetus apostolicus sertis caelestibus instans
Laudat, adorat, amat deuoto pectore temet.
Et princeps Karolus uultu speculatur aperto
10 Orans, ut tecum uiuat longeuus in aeuum.

---

cfr Dutton – Jeauneau, 'The Verses of the "Codex Aureus" of Saint-Emmeram'; cfr Herren, 'Eriugena's *Aulae Sidereae*', p. 607-608

2 Sedvl., *Carm. pasch.* 5, 357: discedat synagoga suo fuscata colore   9 cfr 25, 98: Ipse throno celso fultus rex prospicit omnes

---

Trad. text.: *E*

App. 12

    Ordine quadrato uariis depicta figuris
        Agmina sanctorum gaudia magna uident.
    Pagina nunc praesens retinet splendore uenusto,
        Quae proceres octo ore pio reboant.
5   Ex quibus Isaias diuino munere fartus,
    Hieremias pariter Domini miracula psallunt,
    Hiezechihel sedemque Dei describit et ista,
    Et Danihel Christum narrat de monte recisum.
    Humanum Christi describit Mattheus ortum,
10 More boat Marcus frendentis uoce leonis,
    Mugit amore pio Lucas in carmine Christi,
    Scribendo penitras caelum tu mente, Iohannes.
    Christus, uita hominum, caelorum gloria summa,
    Librat tetragonum miro discrimine mundum.

---

7 sedemque Dei] cfr Ez. 40-48   8 cfr Dan. 9, 20-26

---

1 cfr Dutton – Jeauneau, 'The Verses of the "Codex Aureus" of Saint-Emmeram', p. 93ff.   5 diuino munere] cfr Aldh., *Aenig.* 55, 1: diuino munere plena; Hraban., *Carm.* 44, 1, 1: diuino munere pollet   fartus] cfr 20, 1: sacro ... nectare fartam   7 sedemque Dei] cfr Dutton – Jeauneau, 'The Verses of the "Codex Aureus" of Saint-Emmeram', p. 99-102   8 cfr Amarc., *Serm.* 2, 25, 251: scilicet absque manu lapidem de monte recisum   11 cfr Aldh., *Laud. uirg.* 2232; 2896; *Carm. eccles.* 3, 43   12 cfr App. 16, 1. 3   13 cfr 25, 77: Vita, salus hominum, caelorum gloria summa   14 25, 6: regnat tetragonum pulcro discrimine mundum; cfr Dutton – Jeauneau, 'The Verses of the "Codex Aureus" of Saint-Emmeram', p. 99

Trad. text.: *E*

---

12 penitras *E*

App. 13

Christus ut humanam traxit de uirgine uestem,
Mattheus ter iuncto componit in ordine patrum.
Hic Deitate potens actus quos gessit Iesus
Pandit, et in hominis speciem depingitur idem.
5 Multa legenda sibi genti descripsit Hebreae,
Quo numquam legis sese succumbat in umbris.
Hic leo surgendo portas confregit Auerni,
Qui numquam dormit, nusquam dormitat in aeuum.

   1 cfr 9, 27: inque deum uertit uestem de uirgine sumptam   3 hic deitate potens] cfr App. 2, 15: Fons bonitate potens   7 hic leo] cfr DUTTON – JEAUNEAU, 'The Verses of the "Codex Aureus" of Saint-Emmeram', p. 94

Trad. text.: *E*

App. 14

Filius hic Petri Marcus quia fonte renatus,
Famine praepulchro perstringit gaudia uerbi.
Quae didicit sollers ipso monstrante magistro
Peruigil Italicam fecit cognoscere plebem.
5 Terribili specie formaris rite leonis
Tu, quia terribilem fingis rugire leonem.

   1 cfr I Petr. 5, 13

cfr DUTTON – JEAUNEAU, 'The Verses of the "Codex Aureus" of Saint-Emmeram'
   1 fonte renatus] cfr 21, 7-8: pneumatis excelsi fonte renatus erat

Trad. text.: *E*

App. 15

Lucas Achaicis calamo describit honesto
Quae tanti sedulus Pauli per uerba secutus
Audierat docilis, peregrina ueste decorus.
Nec pelagi fluctus potuit compescere uerbis,
₅ Iura sacerdotis quin scriberet themate primo.
Haec ideo facies uituli depingitur illi.
Hunc Moyses agnum monstrauit lege futurum
Cunctis pro populis sufferri uulnera mortis.

---

2 sedulus] cfr II Tim. 4, 11: Lucas est mecum solus 5 Luc. 1, 8-20

---

7 cfr Dutton – Jeauneau, 'The Verses of the "Codex Aureus" of Saint-Emmeram', p. 95

Trad. text.: *E*

App. 16

Cum sancto penitras arcana labore, Iohannes,
Quae nullus potuit hominum nec mentis acumen
Alta sophya nitens unquam penitrare legendo:
Vt Deus aeternus factus caro uirgine natus;
₅ Et quia uerborum pennis super astra petisti,
Te species aquilae sequitur, quae peruolat ethra.

Dextera haec Patris mundum dicione gubernans
   Protegat et Karolum semper ab hoste suum.

---

cfr Dutton – Jeauneau, 'The Verses of the "Codex Aureus" of Saint-Emmeram'
2 mentis acumen[cfr 10, 9; 22, 24; 24, 13; 25, 65

Trad. text.: *E*

App. 17, Fr. 1

GRAECA AD VERSVS

	ΣΠΕΡΜΑ	i. semen
	ΥΨΙΣΤΟΣ	altissimus
	ΕΞΑΡΧΩΝ	procerum
	ΘΑΥΜΑΣΤΟΣ	mirabilis
5	ΕΞ ΑΡΧΗΣ	a principio
	ΕΠΙΛΕΚΤΟΣ	electus
	ΔΙΚΑΙΟΣ	iustus
	ΑΓΑΘΟΣ	bonus
	ΜΕΓΑΛΟΣ	magnus
10	ΤΙΜΙΟΣ	pretiosus
	ΦΡΟΝΙΜΟΣ	sapiens
	ΑΚΡΟΣ	summus
	ΒΑΣΙΛΕΥΣ	rex
	ΣΕΒΑΣΤΟΣ	colendus. augustus
15	ΕΓΓΕΟΝ	terrestre
	ΕΥΦΡΟΣΥΝΙ	laetitia
	ΕΟΥΣ	oriens
	ΔΥΣΙΣ	occasus
	ΧΡΥΣΩ	auro
20	ΜΑΓΑΛΥΝΙ	magnificauit
	ΔΟΞΟΛΟΓΟΥΜΕΝ	glorificamus
	ΥΣΧΥΡΟΣ	fortis
	ΑΘΑΝΑΤΟΣ	immortalis
	ΚΑΤΙΣΤΩΝ	ordinans
25	ΔΥΝΑΣΤΑΣ	potentes
	ΠΙΝΟΥΝΤΕΣ	esurientes
	ΠΝΕΥΜΑΤΕ	spiritu
	ΥΔΡΟΣ	serpens
	ΦΡΟΣΚΕΙΟΣ	frustra uel frustruosus

Trad. text.: L^1, f. 294r: GRAECA AD VERSVS, *glossarium cuius lemmata consistunt ex uocibus Graecis quae saepe in uersibus authenticis Iohannis Scotti inueniuntur. Quippe ultima tria lemmata glossarii* 'Graeca ad uersus' *eadem sunt quae lemmata occurruntia apud* 'Graeca quae sunt in uersibus Iohannis Scotti'

30	ΛΙΚΝΟΣ	lucerna
	ΦΩΣ	lux
	ΠΕΠΛΙ	uestis
	ΚΛΕΟΡ	gloria
	ΑΡΜΟΔΙΟΣ	aptus
35	ΒΑΛΗΝ	*deest*
	ΦΟΜΕΝΟΡ	*deest*

IOHANNIS SCOTTI ERIVGENAE

DE IMAGINE

cura et studio
Giovanni Mandolino

CONSPECTVS SIGLORVM

Codices Latini

B   BAMBERG, Staatsbibliothek, Patr. 78 (*olim* B.IV.13), f. 88^r-114^r
C   PARIS, Bibliothèque nationale de France, n.a. lat. 2664, f. 122^r-139^v (I, 10 - XXIII, 34)
F   PARIS, Bibliothèque nationale de France, lat. 18095, f. 40^v-41^r (fragm. XXII, § 5-6)
Q   BERLIN, Lat. Qu. 690 (Görres 87), f. 186^r-186^v (fragm. XXII, § 5-6)
R   REIMS, Bibliothèque Municipale 875, continens Eriugenae *Periphyseon* (libros I-IV) iuxta uersiones I (*R**) et II (cum notis et correctionibus manus *i^1*, hoc est manus Eriugenae, et *i^2*)
V   CITTÀ DEL VATICANO, Vat. Reg. lat. 195, f. 61^v-62^r (fragm. XXII, § 5-6)

Codex Graecus

q   PARIS, Bibliothèque nationale de France, Coisl. gr. 235

Editiones

Capp.   M. CAPPUYNS, 'Le *De imagine* de Grégoire de Nysse traduit par Jean Scot Érigène', *Recherches de Théologie Ancienne et Médiévale*, 32 (1965), p. 205-262
Forb.   *Sancti Patris Nostri Gregorii Nysseni Basili Magni fratris opera quae supersunt omnia*.ed. G. H. Forbes, 2 vol., Burntisland, 1855-1861
Periphys.   *Iohannes Scottus Eriugena, Periphyseon* – ed. É. Jeauneau (*CC CM*, 161-165), Turnhout, 1996-2003
PG   *S. Gregorii Nysseni De Hominis Opificio, J. Lewenclaio Interprete* (*PG*, 44), Paris, 1863, col. 124C-256C

SERMO GREGORII EPISCOPI NYSAE DE ⟨IMAGINE⟩ IN EA QVAE RELICTA SVNT IN EXAMERO A BEATO BASILIO SVO FRATRE

1. Si proprietates rerum honoras – oportet enim dicere eos qui in uirtute differunt – breuis erit, ut ait Salomon, sermo, sicut ex rebus manifestabitur tuae uirtuti comparatus, quoniam melioribus diuitiis merito honorificanda est tuae sanctitatis gratia. Expetit uero bonum pascha solitam caritatis munerum oblationem, quam tuae magnae sapientiae offerimus munus, uidelicet homo Dei, minus quidem quam ut sit dignum tibi offerri, sed non minus quam nostra est uirtus. Hoc autem munus sermo est, ueluti quoddam uestimentum exiguum ex paupertate nostrae intelligentiae non sine sudore contextum. Sermonis uero materies audax quidem multis merito esse uidebitur, uerumtamen non inconsequens est arbitranda. Solus siquidem digne creatura⟨m⟩ Dei intellexit qui secundum Deum uere creatus est, et in imagine creatoris animam formatus, communis noster pater atque magister, qui sublimem uniuersitatis ornatum multis uenerabilem ex sua fecit theoria, ipsum in uera sapientia ex Deo constitutum mundum per suam intelligentiae intelligentiam introductis in theoriam notum faciens. Nos uero etiam admirando ipsum deficimus; tamen quod in contemplationibus ab ipso magno relictum est addere procurauimus: non ut curiosi simus illius laborem supplere (iniustum siquidem esset illud os excelsissimum iniuriam pati nostris sermonibus infamatum), sed ne uideretur magistri gloria in discipulis defecisse.

Praef., 2 cfr Prou. 17, 6a (LXX)

Tit., 1 imagine] *om. spatium relinquens* B

Praef., 1 si proprietates – dicere] Εἰ ταῖς διὰ τῶν χρημάτων τιμαῖς ἔδει γεραίρειν *PG Forb.* (Εἰ τὰ ἴδια τῶν χρημάτων τιμᾷς ἔδει γὰρ εἴρειν *E. uidetur legisse*) (*cfr* P. LEVINE, 'Two Early Latin Versions', *p. 491*)   2/3 sermo sicut ex rebus] ὅλος ὁ κόσμος τῶν χρημάτων *PG Forb.* (ὁ λόγος ὡς ὑπὸ τῶν χρημάτων *uel similiter E. legisse uidetur*)   3/4 comparatus – diuitiis] *bis scr.* B   5 quam] ἢν *PG, non praeb. Forb.* q   6 uidelicet homo Dei] ὦ ἄνθρωπε τοῦ Θεοῦ *PG Forb.*   9 intelligentiae] intelle- B   12 creaturam] *correxi* (*cfr* τὴν κτίσιν *PG Forb.*), creatura B, creaturas *Capp.*   14 formatus communis] μεμορφωμένος Βασίλειος ὁ κοινὸς *PG Forb.* (Βασίλειος] *om. Forb.*^{u.l.})   15 uenerabilem] εὔληπτον *PG Forb.* (εὔσεπτον *E. legisse uel intellexisse uidetur*)   16/17 intelligentiam] intelle- B   18 in contemplationibus] τοῖς τεθεωρημένοις *PG Forb.*

2. Si enim, dum in Examero ipsius theoria hominis desit, nemo eruditorum ab eo sollicitudinem quandam ad supplementum eorum quae relicta sunt inferret, fortassis non immerito magnae ipsius gloriae aestimatio suspicionem acciperet, tamquam nolentis habitum quendam intellectualem auditoribus perficere. Nunc autem secundum nostras uires expositionis ipsius residuum audentes tractare, si quid tale in nostris inuentum fuerit quod doctrina illius non indignum uideatur esse, per omnia magistro deputabitur; si uero noster sermo magnitudinem theoriae inuestigare non ualuerit, ille solus extra talem accusationem erit, qui quaerelam effugiens uideri aliquid boni in discipulis esse non consulit, nos autem merito fortassis obnoxii reprehensionibus aestimabimur, tamquam non ualentes capere nostri cordis paruitate magistri sapientiam.

3. Est autem nobis non parua intentio in contemplatione proposita nullique miraculorum mundi posterius prolata, atqui maior omnibus quae cognosci possunt, eo quod nihil aliud existentium Deo simile dicitur ultra humanam creaturam. A fidelibus itaque auditoribus facile nobis erit de his quae dicenda sunt ueniam adipisci, etsi prolixus sermo in conspectu suae dignitatis processerit. Oportet enim, ut arbitror, ex his quae circa hominem sunt – hoc est quae antequam fieret fuisse creduntur, et quae postmodum euentura fore spectantur, et quae nunc in contemplationem ueniunt – nihil praetermittere inexquisitum: minor siquidem sollicitudo quam est promissio reprehendetur, si hominis in contemplatione propositi quippiam ad causam pertinentium desit. Sed et quae uidentur circa se contraria habere, eo quod non eadem quae ab initio facta sunt, et quae nunc circa naturam aspiciuntur ex quadam necessaria consequentia, et quae Scripturae historia et excogitationum inuentione pulchre omnem sibimet materiam conuenit adunare ordine ac serie eorum quae uidentur e contrario haberi, ad unum tamen eundemque finem conuenientium: sic diuina potentia spem his quae sunt supra spem uiamque

---
30 non indignum] μὴ ἀνάξιον *PG Forb.*, ἄξιον *q Forb.*ᵘ·ˡ·   34 reprehensionibus] *fort.* reprehensoribus *legendum* (*cfr* μωμοσκοποῦσιν *PG Forb.*)   37 in contemplatione] εἰς θεωρίαν *PG Forb.*   42 prolixus] *fort.* prolixius *legendum* (*cfr* πολὺ κατόπιν τῆς ἀξίας ὁ λόγος ἔλθοι *PG Forb.*)   44/46 et quae postmodum – ueniunt] *eodem ordine PG q* (*sed καὶ τῶν νῦν θεωρουμένων καὶ τῶν εἰς ὕστερον ἐκβήσεσθαι προσδοκωμένων non praeb. q*)   49 contraria] e contrario *B*ᵃ·ᶜ·   51 et] ex *B*ᵃ·ᶜ·   52/53 pulchre – adunare] συναρτῆσαι προσήκει, ὡς ἂν συμβαίνοι πᾶσα πρὸς ἑαυτὴν ἡ ὑπόθεσις *PG Forb.* (*fortasse* προσηκόντως *pro* προσήκει, ὡς ἂν *E. intellexit et per* pulchre *interpretatus est*)

his quae impossibilia uidentur esse inuenit. Declarationis autem gratia bene esse aestimauimus in capitulis tibi sermonem proponere, ut actionem totam in paucis contineas, hoc est singularum mentis conceptionum uirtutem.

Capvt I
In quo particularis est de mundo ΦΥΣΙΟΛΟΓΙΑ quaedamque clarior de his quae facta sunt ante hominis generationem narratio

128C

5 1. *Hic est liber generationis caeli et terrae*, inquit Scriptura, quando consumatum est omne uisibile et ad propriam positionem unumquodque existentium discretum reuersum est, quando caeleste corpus omnia in giro ambiuit: medium uero uniuersitatis grauia corpora quae deorsum feruntur accipiebant, terra quoque et aqua
10 a se inuicem discreta sunt. Coniunctio autem quaedam ac firmitas naturae existentium diuina arte atque uirtute adiecta est, duplis operationibus uniuersa gubernans. In statu siquidem et motu generationem non existentibus et perseuerantiam existentibus machinata est; circa graue ac stabile immutabilis naturae, ueluti circa
15 quempiam fixum axem, uelocissimum poli motum in modum rotae circulariter circumagens, et utrisque a se inuicem inseparabile conseruans, dum circulariter means essentia acuto motu stabilitatem terrae in giro circumstringat, solidum uero atque intimum per immobilem fixuram indesinenter eorum, quae circulariter
20 circa ipsam sunt motum extendat. Aequalis autem utrique operationibus distantibus supereminentia perfecta est, stabilis uidelicet naturae et instabilis ambitus: neque enim terra sua statione transmutatur, neque caelum umquam motionis nimietate indignationeque prohibetur.

C 122ʳ

128D

Capp. 211

I, 5   Gen. 2, 4

I, 5/41   hic est liber – congregans] uide etiam Ioh. Scot., *Periphys.* 3 (p. 135, 3925-3929) (= col. 714A)

I, 3 clarior] ἁβροτέρα *PG Forb.*   10 a se inuicem discreta sunt] ἐν ἀλλήλοις διακρατούμενα *PG Forb.* (διακρινόμενα *E. legisse uel intellexisse uidetur*)   10/11 ac firmitas] *hic inc.* C (*f. 122r*) *et* Liber est de creatione uel opificio hominis re uera est Gregorii Nisseni antiqua translatio *in marg. not.* Anselme Le Michel (*1645*)   16 circumagens] circuagens *B*

2. Haec autem prima existentium iuxta conditoris sapientiam, ueluti quoddam uniuersitatis principium machinantis, constituta sunt; et hoc tibi magnus Moyses ostendit in principio caelum ac terram a Deo facta fuisse, dicendo quia in motu ac statu edita sunt omnia quae apparent in creatura secundum diuinum consilium in generationem adducta. Dum igitur caelum et terra ex diametro a se inuicem contrarietate operationum distent, ipsa creatura quae inter contraria est, partem oppositorum participans, per se ipsam extremitatibus medietatem facit, ut praeclara fieret ad se inuicem contrariorum per medietatem societas. Quod enim semper mouetur et subtile est igneam imitatur essentiam, ut est aer in concauitate naturae deorsum uersus ad motum oportunitatem habens. Non tamen talis est ut ad ea quae fixa sunt cognatione alienetur, neque semper manet immobilis, neque semper fluens et sparsus, sed societate ad quoddam confinium operationum contrarietate fit, mixtus simul etiam in se ipso quae natura distant congregans.

⟨deest par. 3⟩

4. Magis autem subtili ratione, neque ipsa oppositorum natura proprietatibus alterius omnino pura est. Omnia, ut arbitror, quae in mundo apparent ad se inuicem respiciunt, et ad se ipsam creatura conspirat in oppositorum proprietatibus inuenta. Nam dum motus non solum iuxta typicam transmutationem intelligitur, sed etiam in conuersione et mutatione consideratur, iterumque ipsa natura dum mouetur non immensurabiliter motum producit. Ipsa Dei sapientia rerum proprietates concatenatas fecit: mobili quidem semper inconuersibile, immobili uero conuersionem adunauit, prouidentia quadam fortassis hoc administrans ne, si di-

---

27/28 caelum – dicendo] cfr Gen. 1, 1

30/41 dum igitur – congregans] uide etiam IOH. SCOT., *Periphys.* 1 (p. 50, 1488-1516) (= col. 477B)

---

26 machinantis] μηχανήματος *PG Forb.* (μηχανήσαντος *E. legisse uel intellexisse uidetur*)   27 Moyses] Moses *B*   31 operationum] -nem *C*   32 participans] paricipans *B*   35 subtile] -lem *B*$^{a.c.}$ 36 deorsum uersus] *non praeb. PG Forb.*   37/38 cognatione] cogitatione *B Capp.*, cognacione *C*   40 mixtus simul etiam in se ipso] μιγνὺς ἅμα καὶ διαιρῶν ἐν ἑαυτῷ *PG Forb.* (διαιρῶν *om. E. ut uid.*)   47 typicam] τοπικὴν *PG Forb.* (τυπικὴν *E. legisse uel intellexisse uidetur*)   48/49 iterumque ipsa natura – motum producit] πάλιν δ' αὖ τῆς (δ' αὖ τῆς) δι' αὐτῆς *q Forb.*$^{u.l.}$) ἀμεταθέτου φύσεως τὴν κατὰ τὸ ἀλλοιοῦσθαι κίνησιν οὐ προσιεμένης *PG Forb.* q (*cfr P. LEVINE, 'Two Early Latin Versions', p. 491*)   52/53 diuinae naturae] φύσεως *PG*, θείας φύσεως *q Forb.*$^{u.l.}$

uinae naturae proprietas – quae est inconuersibilitas et immutabilitas – in aliqua creatura uideretur, Deum faceret creaturam
55 aestimari. Nondum enim diuinitatis susceptionem habere potuerit quodcumque mobile ac uarium secutum sit. Propterea terra quidem stabilis est, sed non inconuersibilis; caelum uero e contrario conuersibile non habens, stabile non est (eodem enim motu semper uoluitur), ut in natura stabili conuersionem, in uero inconuersibili motum diuina uirtus complicans, et utrasque sibimet inuicem proprietatum societate alligaret, et ab ipsa susceptione quae de deo est alienas faceret. Neutrum enim horum, sicut dictum est, 132A in diuina natura arbitrandum, neque instabile neque uarium.

5. Omnia itaque iam ad proprium aspexerunt finem. *Consu-*
65 *mata enim sunt*, sicut ait Moyses, *caelum et terra* et omnia quae in medio sunt, et singula consequenti pulchritudine: caelum quidem ornatum est luminarium splendoribus, mare natatilibus aerque animalibus, terra uniuersalibus germinum pecorumque differentiis ornata, omnia cumulatim diuina uoluntate corroborata simul
70 peperit. Et impleta est montibus terra, flores simul fructusque germinans; plena etiam prata his quaecumque prata occupant; omnia aspera montium iuga, et omne quodcumque est procliuum et supinum, et omne quodcumque in conuallibus uirescit in pabulum, uaria quoque arborum speciositate coronata est, tunc quidem 132B
75 terra surgentium continuoque ad perfectam pulchritudinem currentium. Humi autem omnia consequenter exultantia iussu Dei fecunda pecora rident, genera quoque consitis indigentia locis

---

64/65 Gen. 2, 1

---

53 proprietas] -tates *C*   53/54 et immutabilitas – faceret] inconuersibilitas in aliqua creatura uideretur et immutabilitas faceret *C*   53 et immutabilitas] *suppl. in marg.* *B*   57 sed non inconuersibilis] sed inconuersibilis *B*, καὶ οὐκ ἄτρεπτος *PG Forb.*   58/59 eodem enim motu semper uoluitur] *non praeb. PG Forb.*   59 in uero] *om. spatium relinquens B*   65 sicut – terra] ὅ, τε οὐρανὸς καὶ ἡ γῆ, καθώς φησι Μωυσῆς *q Forb.*[u.l.] Moyses] Moses *B*   67/68 aerque animalibus] καὶ ἀὴρ τοῖς νηκτοῖς τε καὶ ἐναερίοις τῶν ζώων *PG Forb.*   67 aerque] aerisque *B*   70 montibus terra] *tr. B*[d.c.] *Capp.*, τῶν ὡραίων *PG Forb.* (ὅρων *E. intellexisse uidetur*)   70/71 simul ... germinans] συμβλαστήσασα *q Forb.*[u.l.], ἐκβλαστήσασα *PG Forb.*   71 his quaecumque prata] *om. C*   72/73 est procliuum – quodcumque] *om. B*   supinum] sopinum *C*   76/77 humi autem – pecora rident] ἐγεγήθει δὲ πάντα κατὰ τὸ εἰκὸς καὶ διεσκίρτα τὰ τῷ προστάγματι τοῦ Θεοῦ ζῳογονηθέντα βοτὰ *PG Forb.* (*fort.* ἐκ γῆς γηθεῖ *E. intellexit et per* humi – rident *interpretatus est*)

currunt. Cantus item musicorum petasum ubique circumsonant omne quodcumque erat opertum et obumbratum prosilit. Species item maris praesertim alia quaedam erat, tunc talis ad silentium et serenitatem in congregationibus conuallium constituta, propter quam portus et portitores diuino consilio in litoribus sedato mari ultro terrae insinuantur. Quieti quoque fluctuum motus pratorum pulchritudini comparantur, lenibus sollemniter sonantes et omnes per creaturam in terra et in mari diuitiae praeparatae.

Capvt II
Quare postremus post creaturam homo

1. Sed qui participaret non erat. Nondum enim magna haec et pretiosa res, homo, inter ea quae sunt in mundo locata est. Non enim consequens erat principem ante ea quibus dominaretur apparere, sed prius praeparato imperio conuenerat regem ostendere, quoniam itaque ueluti quandam regalem receptionem futuro regnare uniuersitatis conditor praeparauit. Haec autem erat receptio terra insulaeque ac mare, caelumque super haec culminis instar superexpansum. Variae diuitiae in regalibus his sedibus adiectae sunt. Diuitias autem dico omnem creaturam, quodcumque in plantis est atque germinibus et quodcumque sensibile est et inspiratum et animatum, et – si opus est etiam materias inter diuitias connumerari, quaecumque quadam coloris pulchritudine humanis obtutibus pretiosa aestimata sunt, ut est aurum, argentum ac tales lapides quos homines diligunt – omnium copia ueluti in regalibus thesauris in sinibus terrae abscondita est; sic in mundo ostenditur

---

78 musicorum petasum] = τῶν μουσικῶν ὀρνίθων (PG, 44, 132B7); uide etiam Ioh. Scot., Hom. Ioh. 4, 1 (p. 8, 35)

II, 3/38 sed qui – perfruens] uide etiam Ioh. Scot., Periphys. 4 (p. 60, 1660-1662) (= col. 782B)

---

78 circumsonant] circumssonant $B^{a.c.}$ 79 obumbratum] umbratum C, σύσκιον PG Forb.   prosilit] non praeb. PG Forb.   84 lenibus sollemniter sonantes] ὑπὸ λεπταῖς τε καὶ ἀπήμοσιν αὔραις κατ' ἄκραν τὴν ἐπιφάνειαν γλαφυρῶς ἐπιφρίσσουσαι PG Forb.   85 praeparatae] correxi (sc. diuitiae), -tam B Capp., -ta C

II, 2 quare – homo] διὰ τί τελευταῖος μετὰ τὴν κτίσιν ὁ ἄνθρωπος q Forb., διὰ τί μετὰ τὴν κτίσιν τελευταῖος ὁ ἄνθρωπος PG   3 sed qui participaret non erat] haec uerba ad cap. praec. pertinent   3/4 pretiosa] prec- B C   4 res] κτῆμα q Forb.$^{u.l.}$, χρῆμα PG Forb.   9 insulaeque] correxi, insoleque B, insolęque C, in soleque Capp.   9/10 superexpansum] correxi, superexparsus B, superexpassum C, ἐπικυρτούμενος PG   15 pretiosa] prec- B C

homo, mirabilium quae in ipso sunt quorundam quidem contemplator futurus, quorundam uero dominus, ut talibus utendo cognitionem largitoris haberet, pulchritudine magnitudineque uisibilium ineffabilem et super rationem conditoris uirtutem inuestigando.

2. Propterea postremo post creaturam introducitur homo, non ut expulsus in ea quae nouissima sunt atque abiecta, sed ut simul cum generatione rex fieret subiectorum sibi atque conuenientium. Ac ueluti quidam bonus caenam praeparans non antea praeparationem delectabilium caenaturum introducit, sed omnia honesta praeparans decentibusque splendificans ornamentis domum, recubitum, mensam, paratis iam ad escam commodis facit ipsum caenare: in hunc modum diues atque perfectus naturae nostrae satiator omnigenis formis habitationem ornauit, magnamque talem ac uariam refectionem praeparauit, ac sic hominem introduxit, opus ei dans non ut ea quae non erant crearet, sed ut his quae aderant frueretur, ac per hoc duplicis ei formationis occasiones constituit, terreno diuinum commiscens, ut ambobus per cognationem et societatem quae ad utrumque est potiretur, Deo quidem per diuiniorem naturam, terrenis uero bonis per cognatum sensum perfruens.

Capvt III
Quia pretiosior omni uisibili creatura hominis natura

1. Hoc quoque indignum est inconsideratum despicere, quia tanto mundo partibusque eius ordinate ad uniuersitatis ⟨constitutio-

---

23/24 non ut expulsus – abiecta] = οὐχ ὡς ἀπόβλητος ἐν ἐσχάτοις ἀπορριφεὶς (*PG*, 44, 133A14); cfr fort. Plat., *Phaedr.* 246d: τὴν δὲ αἰτίαν τῆς τῶν πτερῶν ἀποβολῆς, δι' ἣν ψυχῆς ἀπορρεῖ, λάβωμεν   34/38 ac per hoc – perfruens] uide Gvill. S. Theod., *Nat. corp.* 77 (p. 130, 935-939)

III, 3/27 hoc quoque – haberet] cfr Bas., *Struct. hom.* 1, 3 (p. 170-172). Vide etiam Ioh. Scot., *Periphys.* 4 (p. 63, 1761-1763) (= col. 784C)

23 post creaturam introducitur homo] ὁ ἄνθρωπος μετὰ τὴν κτίσιν εἰσήχθη *q Forb.*^{u.l.}, μετὰ τὴν κτίσιν εἰσήχθη ὁ ἄνθρωπος *PG Forb.*   25 rex fieret] βασιλεύειν *q Forb.*^{u.l.}, βασιλεὺς εἶναι *PG Forb.*   27 delectabilium] τῶν ἐδωδίμων *PG Forb.* (*fort.* ἡδονῶν *E. legit uel intellexit*)   33 non ut ea quae non erant crearet] οὐ τὴν κτῆσιν (κτίσιν *Forb.*^{u.l.}) τῶν μὴ προσόντων *PG Forb.*

III, 2 pretiosior] preciosior *B*   4/5 constitutionem ...] *suppleui* (*cfr* σύστασιν ὑποβληθέντων ἀποσχεδιάζεταί *et ll. seqq. PG Forb.; praeterea E. saepe* σύστασις *per* constitutio *interpretatus est*), *sed nonnulla desunt*

nem ...⟩, ⟨quomodo creatura diuina uirtute simul cum praecepto constituta sit; hominis uero⟩ constitutionem consilium praecedit, et praeformatur ab artifice per uerbum Scripturae quid futurum esset, et quale esse conueniret, et ad quale principale exemplar similitudinem ferret, et in quo fieret, et quid operaretur factum, et quibus dominaretur. Omnia prius sermo circumspicit, ut uenerabiliorem generationis dignitatem, priusquam in essentiam ueniret, ipse sortiretur qui principatum eorum quae sunt possessurus foret. *Dixit* – enim inquit – *Deus: "Faciamus hominem ad imaginem nostram et similitudinem, et dominetur piscium maris et bestiarum terrae et uolatilium caeli et pecorum et omnis terrae"*.

2. O miraculum! Sol formatur et nullum praecedit consilium; caelum similiter in conditione aequale est, solo uerbo tantum miraculum constituitur, neque unde, neque quomodo, neque aliud quid praeter significatiuum uerbum; sic et per singula omnia, aether, stellae, aer in medio, mare, terra, animalia, germina: omnia uerbo ad generationem ducuntur. Solam uero hominis formationem circumspecte uniuersitatis conditor praecedit, ut et materiam constitutionis sibi praepararet pulchrique cuiusdam principalis exempli formae similis fieret, et ad propositam speculationem, cuius gratia futurus esset, consequentem sibi propriamque naturam conderet quae congruentiam ad propositum haberet.

Capvt IIII
Quia per omnia principalem potentiam formatio hominis indicat

Vt enim in hac uita consequenter ab artificibus organum utilitati figuratur sic, tale quoddam uas, in operationem regni commodum

---

III, 13/15 Gen. 1, 26

5/15 quomodo – terrae] uide etiam Ioh. Scot., *Periphys.* 4 (p. 25-26, nota ⟨8⟩ = p. 242, 1199-1219) (= col. 758C) uerbatim

IV, 5/12 in operationem – regis] uide Gvill. S. Theod., *Nat. corp.* 77-78 (p. 130, 939-950) quasi uerbatim

5/6 quomodo creatura – hominis uero] *suppleui ex Periphys.*   14 piscium] piscibus *C*   15 et uolatilium – et omnis terrae] *om. C*   17 caelum – aequale est] ὧν οὐδέν (*om. q Forb.*$^{u.l.}$) τι τῶν κατὰ τὴν κτίσιν ἰσόν ἐστι *PG Forb. q*   19 praeter significatiuum uerbum] παρασημηναμένου τοῦ λόγου *PG Forb.*

IV, 1 *om. C, post* indicat (*l.* 3) *pos. B*   2/3 *om. C*   4 ut] t *pro prima littera spatium relinquens C*

nostram naturam optimus artifex condidit, et in obseruationibus animae in ipsaque corporis figura tale esse praeparauit, quale oportunitatem ad regnum haberet. Anima siquidem regale quiddam est atque excelsum, hinc ostendens rustica humilitate longe esse segregatam, dum ipsa sit libera et per se potens, suis uoluntatibus suisque potentiis administrata. Cuius enim alius est hoc et non regis? Et adhuc cum his, potentis omnium naturae imaginem fieri nihil aliud est quam continuo regalem conditam fuisse naturam. Vt enim iuxta humanam consuetudinem qui imagines potentum componunt figuram formae purificant amictuque purpureo regalem dignitatem depingunt, diciturque iuxta consuetudinem etiam imago "rex", sic humana natura, quoniam ad imperium aliorum constituta est, per similitudinem ad uniuersitatis regem ueluti quaedam animata imago erecta est, principali exemplo et dignitate et nomine communicans, non amicta purpuram, neque sceptro ac diademate dignitatem indicans (neque enim principale exemplum in talibus est), sed pro purpura uirtutem induitur – quod omnium uestimentorum regalissimum est –, pro sceptro autem beatitudine immortalitatis contenta, pro uero regali diademate corona iustitiae ornata, ita ut per omnia in regni dignitate ostendatur diligenter principalis exempli formam assimulans.

Capvt V
Quia similitudo diuini regni homo

1. Diuina autem forma non in quadam figura seu formae pulchritudine ex quodam colore clarificatur, sed in beatitudine ineffabili secundum uirtutem conspicitur. Itaque, sicut humanas formas quibusdam coloribus pictores in tabulas transferunt propriasque et conuenientes picturas imitationi illinunt, ut diligenter principalis exempli forma transferatur ad similitudinem, sic mihi uidetur noster formator ueluti quibusdam tincturis uirtutum

---

14/26 ut enim – assimulans] uide GVILL. S. THEOD., *Nat. corp.* 85 (p. 133, 1029-1042) quasi uerbatim

---

6 obseruationibus] προτερήμασι PG Forb.   7 esse] esset C   11 alius] ἄλλου PG Forb.   17 imago rex] tr. C$^{a.c.}$ 24 contenta] conten C   uero regali] tr. B

V, 3 forma] forme B   7 picturas] *fort.* tincturas *legendum* (*cfr* βαφάς PG Forb.; *uide etiam l. 9*)

adiectione ad formam suam floridam faciens imaginem, proprium suum principatum in nobis ostendisse. Multiformes autem uariique sunt tales imaginis colores, ex quibus uera depingitur forma, non rubeus, non splendidus, non qualiscumque talium ad se inuicem mixtura, neque cuiuspiam nigredinis subscriptio supercilium oculumque subscribit ⟨...⟩, et quaecumque huiusmodi pictorum manus machinatae sunt. Sed pro his mundicia, impassibilitas, beatitudo, ab omni malitia alienatio, et quaecumque id genus sunt, ex quibus in hominibus similitudo ad Deum formatur: his floribus conditor suae imaginis nostram depinxit naturam.

2. Si autem et alia inquiris per quae diuina forma figuratur, inuenies subtiliter in ipsa imagine quae nos sumus saluam ad illam quae Deus est similitudinem. Animus et uerbum diuinitas est: *in principio* enim *est uerbum*; et quidam secundum Paulum *animum Christi* habent in se loquentem. Non longe ab his etiam humanitas. Vides in teipso et rationem et intellectum, imitationem ueri animi ac ueri uerbi. Iterum caritas est Deus, et caritatis fons: hoc enim dicit magnus Iohannes, quia *caritas est Dei*, et *Deus est caritas*. In hoc etiam nostram personam fecit naturae formator: *In hoc* – enim inquit – *cognoscent omnes quia discipuli mei estis, si diligitis uos inuicem*. Nempe igitur dum haec praesens sit, omnis character imaginis perficitur. Omnia inspicit et omnia audit Deus, et omnia scrutatur: habes et tu uisum et auditum ad eorum quae sunt receptionem, uitalemque et scrutantem ea quae sunt intellectum.

V, 22/23 Ioh. 1, 1   23/24 cfr I Cor. 2, 16; II Cor. 13, 3   27/28 I Ioh. 4, 7-8   29/30 Ioh. 13, 35

V, 22/23 in principio – uerbum] ἐν ἀρχῇ τε γὰρ ἦν ὁ λόγος; de hac interpretatione (est *pro* erat) uide etiam Ioh. Scot., *Hom. Ioh.* 6 (p. 11-13), et *Comm. Ioh.* 1, 23 (p. 49-50)

12 tales] talis *C, cfr PG Forb.* (τὰ οἱονεὶ χρώματα τῆς εἰκόνος)   depingitur] depingetur $C^{a.c.}$ 15 oculumque subscribit] ὀφθαλμὸν (-οὺς *PG*) ὑπαλείφουσα καὶ κατά τινα κρᾶσιν τὰ κοῖλα τοῦ χαρακτῆρος ὑποσκιάζουσα *PG Forb.*; *fortasse iam in Graeco textu haec omissio orta est*   24 habent] habentem *C*   26 caritatis] caritas *C*   28/29 in hoc – formator] *om. C*   30/31 nempe igitur – perficitur] οὐκοῦν μὴ παρούσης ταύτης, ἅπας ὁ χαρακτὴρ τῆς εἰκόνος μεταπεποίηται *PG Forb.*   31 character] car- *B C*

⟨Capvt⟩ VI
Exquisitio cognationis animi ad naturam,
in quo etiam consequenter Anomiorum redarguitur doctrina

1. Et nemo me aestimet dicere iuxta similitudinem humanae operationis differentibus potentiis Deum ea quae sunt tangere. Non enim est possibile in simplicitate deitatis receptionem et multiformitatem receptoriae operationis intelligere, neque enim et apud nos multae quaedam sunt receptiuae rerum potentiae, etsi multiformiter per sensus ea quae in hac uita sunt tangamus. Vna siquidem quaedam est potentia, ipse qui insitus est animus, qui per singula sensuum instrumenta exiens ea quae sunt transcurrit: ipse aspicit per oculos quod uidetur, ipse intelligit per aures quod dicitur, diligit quod est concupiscibile; item nolit post uoluptatem uerti, et manibus utitur ad quodcumque uelit, per eas quippiam tenens seu repellens, prout expedire iudicauerit cooperationem organi ad id quo utitur.

2. Si igitur in homine, etsi ex natura constructa differentia ad sensum consequatur organa, qui per omnes operationes mouetur, et consequenter singulis ad propositum utitur, unus est atque idem et in diuersis operationibus non compartitur naturam, quomodo quis in Deo propter uarias uirtutes partitam multipliciter essentiam suspicatus fuerit? *Qui enim finxit oculum*, ut ait propheta, *et plantauit aurem*, ad paradigmata quae in seipso sunt has operationes ueluti quosdam cognoscibiles characteres in natura hominum signauit: *Faciamus* – enim inquit – *hominem ad imaginem nostram*.

3. Sed ubi mihi Anomiorum heresis? Quid aduersus hanc uocem dicent? Quomodo in his uerbis dogmatis sui nouitatem saluabunt? Dicuntne unam imaginem possibile esse diuersis formis

---

VI, 22/23 Ps. 93, 9   25/26 Gen. 1, 26

VI, 5/13 non enim – concupiscibile] uide Gvill. S. Theod., *Nat. corp.* 72 (p. 128, 869-876)   27/44 sed ubi – nostram] cfr Bas., *Hex.* 9, 6 (p. 294) (contra Philonem, *Opif.* 72-75); Bas., *Struct. hom.* 1, 4 (p. 172-176)

VI, 1 om. C   caput] om. B   6 receptionem] τὸ ποικίλον PG Forb.   7 intelligere] intellegere B   7/8 apud nos] παρ'ἡμῖν q Forb., ἡμῖν PG Forb.$^{u.l.}$ 8 etsi] et etsi C   11 transcurrit] ἐπιδρασσόμενος PG Forb. (*quod quasi ab* ἔδραμον *E. intellexisse uidetur*)   12 intelligit] intellit B, intell(eg)it Capp.   13 diligit] diligite $B^{a.c.}$ C   nolit] nolite $B^{a.c.}$ C   20 compartitur] conpatitur *sed corr. s.l.* C   24 characteres] car- B C   25/26 ad imaginem nostram] καὶ καθ'ὁμοίωσιν *add.* q Forb.$^{u.l.}$ 27 aduersus] auersis $C^{a.c.}$ 28 nouitatem] κενότητα PG Forb. (καινότητα E. *legisse uel intellexisse uidetur*)

similem fieri? Si dissimilis secundum naturam Patri Filius, quomodo unam imaginem differentium naturarum perficiunt? Qui enim *Faciamus ad imaginem nostram* dixit, per pluralem significationem sanctam Trinitatem declarans, non etiam imaginem singulariter significaret, si dissimiliter ad se ipsa principalia haberent exempla. Non enim possibile erat sibi inuicem non conuenientium unam manifestari similitudinem; sed si differentes essent naturae, differenter omnino etiam imagines earum stetissent, ad conuenientiam unicuique creatae. Sed quoniam una quidem imago, non autem unum principale imaginis exemplum; quis sic est extra intelligentiam, ut ignoret quia quae sunt uni similia etiam ad se ipsa omnino habent similitudinem? Propterea inquit, fortassis hanc malitiam in constitutione humanae uitae sermo succidens: *"Faciamus hominem ad imaginem et similitudinem nostram"*.

⟨CAPVT⟩ VII
Quare nudus naturalibus armis uelaminibusque homo creatur

1. Sed quid uult figurae rectitudo? Quare conuenientes huic uitae non sunt corpori uirtutes? Sed nudus quidem naturalibus protectionibus inermisque atque pauper homo et omnium quae ad usum sunt egenus ad hanc uitam ducitur, miser uideri magis quam beatificari quantum apparet dignus. Non acie cornuum armatus, non unguium acuminibus, non ungulis seu dentibus seu quodam aculeo mortifero uenenum ex natura habente, qualiter multa animalium in se ipsis ad offendentium repulsionem possident, non

---

32 Gen. 1, 26   43/44 Gen. 1, 26

31/44 qui enim – nostram] uide etiam IOH. SCOT., *Periphys.* 4 (p. 65, 1839-1840) (= col. 786B)

VII, 4/5 nudus – inermisque] uide GVILL. S. THEOD., *Nat. corp.* 78 (p. 131, 951-952) uerbatim   5/11 pauper – tegitur] uide GVILL. S. THEOD., *Nat. corp.* 81-82 (p. 132, 990-995) quasi uerbatim

31 differentium] -iam *B*   qui] quid *C*   37/38 imagines ... stetissent ... creatae] imagines ... stetissent ... creaturae *C* (τὰς εἰκόνας ... ἐνεστήσατο ... δημιουργήσας *PG Forb.*)   40 intelligentiam] intelle- *B*   41 ipsa] ipse *C*   propterea] -era *C*[a.c.]

VII, 1 *om. C*   caput] *om. B*   4 quidem] quisquedem *C*[a.c.]   7 quantum apparet] κατὰ τὸ φαινόμενον *PG Forb.*, *non praeb. q*   8 non ungulis] οὐχ ὁπλαῖς *PG Forb.*   9 mortifero] θανατηφόρον *PG Forb.*, θανατηφόρῳ *Forb.*[u.l.]

pilorum amictu corpus tegitur. Recte siquidem oportebat praeordinatum ad aliorum imperium suis armis a natura perfici, ne aliorum auxilii ad suum praesidium indigeret. Nunc uero leo quidem et sus et tigris et pardalis et quodcumque aliud huiusmodi sufficientem habet ad salutem ex natura potentiam; et tauro cornu, et lepori uelocitas, et capreolae saltus et oculorum tutela, aliisque quibusdam animalibus magnitudo, aliis catulorum rapina, uolatilibus penna, apibus aculeus, et omnibus omnino unum aliquod ex natura in salutem subsistit. Solus autem omnium homo uelociter quidem currentium tardior, inormium breuior, naturalibus armis munitorum expugnabilior. "Et quomodo – dicet quis – qui talis est imperium per omnia possedit?".

2. Sed, ut arbitror, nil difficultatis est ostendere quia quod uidetur nostrae naturae egenum occasio est ad eorum quae sibi subiecta sunt dominatum. Si enim sic uirtutem homo haberet, ut uelocitate equum praecurreret, durum soliditate pedem habere, ungulis quibusdam seu labiis contendere, cornua quoque aculeosque et ungues in se ipso ferre, primum quidem bestialitas quaedam esset pugnaxque ferocitas, talia ipsi corpori connaturaliter subsistere; deinde forsitan per alia imperium despiceret, dum nullius subditorum cooperationis indigeret. Nunc uero huius rei gratia per singula subiugatorum nobis huius uitae utilitates dispertitae sunt, ut necessarium per illa faceret imperium.

3. Tarditas namque nostri corporis et ad mouendum difficultas usui aequum adduxit atque edomuit; carnis autem nuditas necessarium fecit ouium dominatum, ex anniuersario lanarum ambitu nostrae naturae indigentia suppleta est; occasiones nobis ad hanc uitam etiam ex aliis cognoscuntur, animalia onera baiolantia tali-

---

19/22 solus – possedit] uide GVILL. S. THEOD., *Nat. corp.* 82 (p. 132, 995-999) quasi uerbatim   23/25 quod uidetur – dominatum] uide GVILL. S. THEOD., *Nat. corp.* 82 (p. 132, 1002-1003) uerbatim   30/50 forsitan – circumpositum] uide GVILL. S. THEOD., *Nat. corp.* 82-83 (p. 132-133, 1003-1021) quasi uerbatim

---

11/12 praeordinatum] per ordinatum *Capp.*   12 perfici] περιπεφράχθαι *PG Forb.*, πεφράχθαι *q Forb.*[u.l.] (πεπρᾶχθαι *E. legisse uel intellexisse uidetur*)   16 capreolae] capreole *B C*   17 catulorum rapina] προνομαία *PG* (προνομή *E. legisse uel intellexisse uidetur, quod* rapina *interpretatus est; incertum unde* catulorum) (*cfr* P. LEVINE, 'Two Early Latin Versions', p. 492)   18 aculeus] aculeis *B*, τῇ μελίσσῃ (ταῖς μελίσσαις *Forb.*[u.l.]) τὸ κέντρον *PG Forb., non praeb. q*   aliquod] aliquot *B*   20 currentium] currentior *C*   23 difficultatis] diffilcutatis *sed corr. ut uid. C*   26 uelocitate] ὠκύτητι *PG Forb.*, ὀξύτητι *q Forb.*[u.l.]   soliditate] solitate *C*[a.c.]   34 difficultas] difficillitas *B*[a.c.]   36 ex anniuersario lanarum ambitu] ἐκ τῆς ἐτησίου τῶν ἐρίων φορᾶς *PG Forb.*

bus administrationibus subiugata sunt; sed et impossibilitas iuxta
similitudinem armentorum pabula comedendi subditum huic
uitae bouem operata est, qui suis laboribus uitam nobis copulat.
Quoniam aduersus quaedam aliorum animalium ad confligendum dentibus ac morsu nobis opus erat per occasionem dentium, 141D
canis cum uelocitate suas maxillas nostrae indigentiae praestitit,
ueluti quaedam uitalis machera homini factus. Cornuum uero
acie unguiumque acumine fortius atque robustius distribuitur hominibus ferrum, non semper connaturaliter nobis quemadmodum bestiis illa, sed in tempore adiuuans, ceterum in se ipso
manet; et pro crocodili squamis, est quidem et illud ipsum arma
facere, secundum tempus aduersus tela circumpositum. Vide
nempe ad hoc formatur ab arte ferrum, ut in tempore ad bellum
ministrans, iterum liberum pondere armatum in pace relinquat.
Ministrat quoque huic uitae etiam ala uolatilium, ut uolucris uelocitas per intelligentiam nos non deserat: quaedam enim ex ipsis 144A
mansueta fiunt, et cooperantur uenatoribus, quaedam ex illis usibus nostris per intelligentiam rediguntur; sed et uolatiles nobis sagittas ars per intelligentiam faciens, uelocem uolucrem nostris
usibus per arcum donat. Quod autem passibiles mollesque nobis
ad iter agendum sint plantae, necessariam ex subiectis facit cooperationem: inde enim sunt pedibus calciamenta circumpacta.

Capvt VIII

Quare hominis figura recta est, et quia propter rationem manus
sunt; in quo quaedam etiam de differentia animarum
philosophia

1. Erecta uero hominum figura et ad caelum extenditur et sursum
aspicit: imperialia haec regalemque dignitatem significant. Nam 144B

VIII, 5/9 erecta – declarat] uide Gvill. S. Theod., *Nat. corp.* 73 (p. 129, 887-890)
5 erecta ... figura] uide etiam Ioh. Scot., *Periphys.* 1 (p. 73, 2243-2245) (= col. 494CD)
5/10 erecta – potentiae] cfr Ov., *Met.* 1, 76-88; Bas., *Hex.* 9, 2 (p. 273-274); Bas., *Struct. hom.* 2, 15 (p. 268-270)

---

39 administrationibus] ammin- *B*   41 copulat] ἐξευμαρίζοντα *PG Forb.* (ζεύγνυμι *uel similiter E. legisse uel intellexisse uidetur*)   44 praestitit] praestetit *C*   45 machera] macera *B*, μάχαιρα *PG Forb.*   46 robustius] τομώτερος *PG* distribuitur] ἐπινενόηται *PG Forb.* (*fort.* νέμω *uel similiter E. intellexit*)   49 pro crocodili squamis] procor quod illis quam is *B Capp.*   51/52 uide nempe] εἰ δὲ μὴ *PG Forb.*   51 ut] ὅς *PG Forb.*   53 uolucris] uolueris *Capp.*   54, 56, 57 intelligentiam[1, 2, 3]] intelle- *B*
59 plantae] plante *B C*
VIII, 1 caput] om. *B*

quod solus in his quae sunt talis sit homo, dum aliorum omnium corpora deorsum aspiciant, dignitatis differentiam aperte declarat, eorum uidelicet quae prona sunt et uirtutis et supereminentis ea potentiae. Siquidem in aliis omnibus anteriora corporis membra pedes sunt, eo quod pronum oportebat esse quod omnino est deorsum aspiciens. At uero in humana constitutione anteriora membra manus factae sunt: nam formae rectitudini sufficiens erat ad usum una basis, in duobus pedibus statum firmiter continens.

2. Est quoque quaedam rationis usui cooperatrix manuum subministratio; et si quis proprium rationabilis naturae manuum subministrationem esse dixerit, non omnino ab uniuersitate aberrabit, non solum ad commune hoc promptumque intellectui recurrens, quia litteris rationem per manum ingenia notamus (non enim est rationabilis gratiae expers, quod nos per litteras loquimur et quodammodo per manus, elementorum characteribus uoces compactas pronuntiamus), sed et aliud aspiciens cooperari manus dico rationis enuntiationi.

3. Magis autem priusquam de hoc additus sermo disserat aliud considerabimus. Illud enim paulisper in ordine eorum quae facta sunt nos latuit, ob quam causam germinatio uirgultorum ex terra praecedit, irrationabilia uero animalia inferuntur, ac sic post horum constitutionem homo: forsitan enim non solum illud quod facile est ad intelligendum per haec docemur, quia propter animalia pabulorum utilitas a conditore manifestata est, propter uero hominem pecora; quamobrem ante pecora quidem illorum cibus, ante uero hominem quod humanae uitae administraturum foret.

4. Sed mihi uidetur occultorum doctrinam per haec Moyses declarasse, ac de anima arcanam philosophiam tradidisse, quam etiam extrinsecus disciplina manifestauit, non tamen praeclare notam fecit. Docet enim ut arbitror per haec ratio in tribus diffe-

---

33/105 sed mihi uidetur – ascensum] GREG. NYSS., *Anim. et res.* (p. 40, 11 – p. 42, 4)
36/49 docet – animo ministrat] uide etiam IOH. SCOT., *Periphys.* 3 (p. 167, 4910-4924)
(= col. 735D-736A) uerbatim

---

19 ingenia] εὐφυίας *PG Forb.*   21 per manus] *post* per manus *E. uerbum om. ut uid.* (*cfr* τὸ φθέγγεσθαι διὰ γραμμάτων ἡμᾶς, καὶ τρόπον τινὰ διὰ χειρὸς διαλέγεσθαι *PG Forb.*) elementorum characteribus] elim- car- *B C*   23 enuntiationi] enunci- *B*   27 praecedit] procedit *B*, προηγεῖται *PG Forb.*   29 intelligendum] intelle- *B*   30/31 propter uero hominem] propter hominem uero *B*, διὰ δὲ τὸν ἄνθρωπον *PG Forb.*   31 pecora[1,2]] peccora *C*   cibus] cybus *C*   32 ante uero hominem] ante hominem uero *B*, πρὸ δὲ τοῦ ἀνθρώπου *PG Forb.*   34 arcanam] arcana *C*   35 extrinsecus disciplina] ἡ ἔξωθεν παίδευσις *PG Forb.*   36 ut arbitror] ἡμᾶς *PG Forb.*, οἴμαι *q Forb.*[u.l.]

rentiis uitalem animalemque uirtutem considerari. Vna enim quaedam est quae solummodo incrementum dat et nutrit, et uocatur auctiua et nutritoria, quia in augmentum eius quod nutritur
40 quicquid conueniens est affert. Ipsa etiam germinalis dicitur et circa germina consideratur: necesse est enim etiam in germinibus uitalem quandam uirtutem sensus expertem intelligi. Altera uero praeter hanc species uitae est, quae et hoc habet quod praedicta possidet, insuper etiam per sensum administrare accepit; quae
45 species in natura irrationabilium est. Nam non solum nutrit et auget, sed etiam sensualem operationem perceptionemque habet. Perfecta uero in corpore, uita in rationabili (humana dico) formatur natura, et nutritiua est et sensualis et rationem participat et animo ministrat.
50 5. Fiat autem nobis talis rationis diuisio: eorum quae sunt, hoc quidem intellectuale est, hoc autem omnino corporale. Sed intellectualis sectio nunc cum suis stet: non enim de his sermo est. Corporalium uero, hoc quidem uniuersaliter expers est uitae, hoc autem uitalem participat operationem; iterum uitalium corpo-
55 rum, hoc quidem sensui coniungitur, hoc autem expers est sensus. Deinde sensuale iterum secatur in rationale et in irrationale. Propterea primum post carentem anima materiam ueluti fundamentum quoddam speciei animatarum naturalem hanc uitam consistere, quae in pullulatione germinum praesubstituta est, Le-
60 gislator dicit. Deinde eorum quae per sensum administrantur generationem infert. Et quia, per eandem consequentiam, eorum quae per carnem acceperunt uitam, quaedam quidem sensualia ac sine intellectuali natura in se ipsis esse possunt, quod uero rationale est non aliter corpori inhereret, nisi sensuali concretum fieret,
65 propterea nouissimus post germina pecoraque constitutus est homo, uia quadam ad id quod perfectum est consequenter progre-

---

50/55 fiat – sensus] uide etiam IOH. SCOT., *Periphys.* 2 (p. 75, 1745-1752) (= col. 580D); 4 (p. 21, 551-553) (= col. 755B)   50/51 fiat – corporale] uide etiam IOH. SCOT., *Periphys.* 4 (p. 118, 3542-3545) (= col. 824D)

38/39 quae solummodo – et nutritoria] ἡ μὲν γάρ τις ἐστὶν αὐξητική τε μόνον καὶ θρεπτικὴ *PG Forb.* (*quod E. apertius interpretari uoluisse uidetur*)   39 auctiua] actiua $B^{a.c.}$ C   47 in rationabili] *correxi ex Periphys.* (*cfr* ἐν τῇ λογικῇ *PG Forb.*), irrationabili B C   52 nunc] *om.* B   55 coniungitur] συζῇ *PG Forb.* (*quod a* συζυγέω *uel* συζεύγνυμι *E. legisse uel intellexisse uidetur*)   58 naturalem] φυτικήν q *Forb.*$^{u.l.}$, ψυχικήν *Forb.*$^{u.l.}$, φυσικήν *PG Forb.*   60 administrantur] ammin- B   62 acceperunt] εἰληφότων q *Forb.*$^{u.l.}$, ἀνειληφότων *Forb.*$^{u.l.}$, εἰληχότων *PG Forb. Forb.*$^{u.l.}$

diente natura. Ac per omnem animarum speciem rationabile hoc animal commiscetur. Nutrit enim secundum germinalem animae speciem; auctiuae uero uirtuti sensualis cognata est, mediatatem habens secundum propriam naturam intellectualis et materialioris essentiae, tantum crassior hac quantum purior illa. Deinde quaedam fit societas atque concretio sensualis naturae ad subtile ac lucidum intellectualis essentiae; ita ut in his tribus homo habeat constitutionem, sicut etiam ab Apostolo idipsum didicimus in his quae ait ad Ephesios, optans eos *perfectissimam gratiam corporis et animae et spiritus in aduentum Domini custodire*, pro nutritoria parte corporis dicens, sensualem uero anima significans, intellectualem spiritu. Similiter etiam in Euangelio Dominus scribam erudit, caritatem quae in Deum est omni mandato praeferre, quae *ex toto corde et anima et intellectu* operatur: etenim hic eandem differentiam uidetur mihi uerbum interpretatum fuisse, corporaliorem quidem constitutionem cor dicens, animam uero mediam, intellectum excelsiorem naturam, spiritualemque et intellectualem uirtutem.

6. Vnde etiam tres differentias uoluntatum Apostolus nouit, carnalem quidem nominans eam quae circa uentrem passibilesque eius uoluptates sollicita est, animalem uero eam quae mediatatem ad uirtutem habet atque malitiam (unam quidem superat, alteram uero pure non participat), spiritualem uero eam quae perfectionem conuersationis secundum Deum intuetur. Ideo ait ad Corinthios passibilem eorum usum increpans quia *carnales estis* et perfectiorum dogmatum incapaces. Alibi comparationem quandam medii ad perfectum faciens dicit *animalis autem homo non recipit ea quae sunt spiritus, stultitia enim est ei; spiritualis uero diiudicat omnia, ipse autem a nemine diiudicatur*: ut enim superat animalis carnalem, eadem analogia spiritualis animalem superascendit.

VIII, 75/76   I Thess. 5, 23, cfr Eph. 4, 23; 5, 18   79/80   ex toto corde – intellectu] cfr Matth. 22, 37; Marc. 12, 30; Luc. 10, 27   91/92   I Cor. 3, 2-3   93/95   I Cor. 2, 14-15

67/68 hoc animal] τοῦτο ζῷον, ὁ ἄνθρωπος *PG Forb.*   69 auctiuae] actiuae $B^{a.c}$ 71/73 deinde quaedam fit – intellectualis essentiae] εἶτά τις γίνεται πρὸς τὸ λεπτὸν καὶ φωτοειδὲς τῆς αἰσθητικῆς φύσεως ἢ τῆς νοερᾶς οὐσίας οἰκείωσίς τε καὶ ἀνάκρασις *PG Forb.*   73 habeat] habet $C^{a.c.}$ 75 Ephesios] Effesios *B*   78 spiritu] spiritum *B*   83 naturam] natura *B*   86 eam quae] eamque *B*   91 Corinthios] Chorinthios *C*   passibilem eorum usum] τὸ ἀπολαυστικὸν αὐτῶν καὶ ἐμπαθὲς *PG Forb.*   92 dogmatum] διδαγμάτων *q Forb.*$^{u.l.}$ 94 ea] *om. C*

7. Si igitur postremum post animata factum fuisse hominem dicit Scriptura, nihil aliud quam de anima nobis Legislator philosophatur, necessaria quadam ordinis consequentia perfectum in nouissimis uidens. Nam in rationabili cetera comprehenduntur, in sensuali uero etiam naturalis species omnino est, illa uero circa materiale tantummodo uidetur; non ergo inconsequenter ueluti per gradus proprietates uitae dico, a minoribus ad id quod perfectum est natura facit ascensum.

Capvt VIIII
Quia organica constituta est hominis figura et ad rationis usum accomodata

1a. [VIII, 8] Quoniam igitur rationabile quoddam animal est homo, consequenter oportebat usui rationis organum corporis sui constitui. Sicut in musicis conspicue uidetur, qui ad organorum speciem musicam exercent neque per barbitas tibicinantes neque in tibiis citharizantes, ad hunc modum oportebat rationi conuenientem fieri organorum constitutionem, ut connaturaliter ad eam sonaret in ipsis particulis uerborum uocibus coaptatis formata. Propterea manus corpori copulatae sunt: et si enim multi sint huius uitae usus dum enumerantur ad quos emachinata haec ac multum principalia manuum organa utiliter habentur, ad omnem artem omnemque operationem quae seu in bello seu in pace est tractabiliter transeuntia; attamen ante alios differenter rationis gratia eas corpori adiecit natura. Nam si expers manuum homo fieret, omnino ei iuxta similitudinem quadrupedum conuenienter escae usui oris particulae configurarentur, ita ut forma prolongaretur et in nares extenuaretur, labia quoque ori praemitterentur callosa, ponderosa, crassa, ad sectionem pabuli oportunitatem ha-

---

IX, 11 manus corpori copulatae sunt] uide Gvill. S. Theod., *Nat. corp.* 66 (p. 126, 810) quasi uerbatim   11/31 et si enim – uacat] uide Gvill. S. Theod., *Nat. corp.* 67-68 (p. 126-127, 814-828)

IX, 1 caput] *om.* B. Sic diuidit et Dionysius Exiguus in interpretatione sua; sed §1a ad cap. praec. pertinet (*VIII, §8 iuxta ed. Forb.*)   6 conspicue] conspicuae B, ἔστιν ἰδεῖν PG Forb.   9/11 ad eam sonaret – coaptatis formata] πρὸς τὴν τῶν ῥημάτων χρείαν ὑπὸ τῶν φωνητικῶν μορίων τυπούμενος PG Forb.   13 principalia] πολυαρκῆ PG (πολυαρχῇ E. *legisse uel intellexisse uidetur*)   19 praemitterentur] pro- C, προβεβλῆσθαι PG   20 pabuli] pubuli C

bentia. Illud etiam quod sub dentibus fieret, tali cuipiam parti, carnosae uidelicet ac solidae asperaeque, dentibus quoque cooperanti, incumberet, uel umidae perque obliqua diffusae, qualis est ipsa pars canum ceterorumque carnes deuorantium, densitati
25 dentium inter spatia intus defluens. Si ergo manus corpori non adessent, quomodo articulata uox formata in eo fieret, dum particularium oris constitutio ad usum soni non conformaretur? Ita ut necesse esset omnino aut balare, aut milcire, aut latrare, aut hinnire hominem, aut bubus seu asinis similem boare, seu quendam
30 bestialem fremitum emittere. Nunc uero, dum sit manus ori adiecta, administrationi rationis os uacat. Non ergo proprium rationabilis naturae manus apparuerunt, ac per hoc ita conditor rationi facultatem excogitauit.

1b. [IX, 1] Quoniam itaque diuinam quandam gratiam formationi nostrae conditor donauit, suorum bonorum similitudines
35 suae imagini inserens, propterea cetera quidem bona honoris gratia humanae dedit naturae. Intellectum uero atque sapientiam non est proprie dicendum quia dedit, sed quia tradidit, proprium suae naturae ornatum imagini addens. Quoniam igitur spiritualis
40 quaedam res et incorporalis est animus, incommunicabilem haberet gratiam ac per se incommixtam, dum per nullum organum intelligentiae suae motus manifestaretur. Huius rei gratia talis organica constitutio adiecta est ut, plectri instar particulas uoci coaptatas tangens, per talem sonorum formationem interiorem
45 suum interpretaretur motum.

2. Ac ueluti si quis, musicae peritus existens, propriam ex passione quadam non haberet uocem, uolens autem manifestam facere musicam alienis uocibus modularetur, per tibias seu lyras

---

39/54 quoniam igitur – impetus ostendere] uide Gvill. S. Theod., *Nat. corp.* 68-69 (p. 127, 828-838)

21/23 illud etiam quod – incumberet] ἐγκεῖσθαι δὲ τοῖς ὀδοῦσι τὴν γλῶτταν (-σσαν *PG*) ἄλλην τινὰ τοιαύτην πολύσαρκον καὶ ἀντιτυπῆ καὶ τραχεῖαν καὶ συγκατεργαζομένην τοῖς ὀδοῦσι τὸ ὑπ'ὀδόντα γινόμενον *PG Forb.* (τὴν γλῶτταν *E.* om. *ut uid.*) 22 asperaeque] aspereque *B*, τραχεῖαν *PG Forb.* 23 umidae] humidae *B*[p.c.] 26 formata in eo fieret] τούτῳ ἐνετυπώθη *PG Forb.*, ἐνετυπώθη τούτῳ *q Forb.*[u.l.] 27 ita ut] ut *B* 28/29 hinnire] innire *B* non ergo] οὐκοῦν *PG Forb.* (*quod E. saepe quasi* οὐκ οὖν *interpretatur*) 34 *hic inc. cap.* IX (IX, §1 *iuxta ed. Forb.*) 34/35 formationi] -nis *B* 35 similitudines] similituditunes *C*[a.c. ut uid.] 36 imagini] imigini *B* 41/42 dum per nullum – manifestaretur] μὴ διά τινος ἐπινοίας φανερουμένης αὐτοῦ τῆς κινήσεως *PG Forb.* intelligentiae] intelle- *B* 43 adiecta est] προσεδεήθη *PG Forb.* (προσετέθη *E. legisse uel intellexisse uidetur*) 48 musicam] ἐπιστήμην *PG Forb.*

artem publicans, sic et animus humanus, diuersorum intellectuum
50 dum sit inuentor, non ualendo per nudam dictionibus animam
(dicit quia anima per se ipsam dum sit incorporea sine corpore
dictiones habere sensibiles non potest), [nudam dictionibus animam] quae sunt per corporales sensus intelligentiae impetus ostendere, ueluti quidam coaptatus in arte, animata talia organa
55 tangens, per sonum qui in eis est occultos intellectus manifestos
facit.

3a. Mixta autem quaedam musica est circa humanum organum
ex tibia ac lyra, ueluti in concentu in idipsum sibi inuicem consonantibus. Spiritus enim per arteriam ex follibus spiritum reci-
60 pientibus repulsus, cum impetus sonantis arteriam ad uocem
roborauerit, interiores ordines eleuans, circulariter tibialem hanc
pertranat uiam, imitaturque omnino factam ex tibia uocem, membranalibus uehiculis in giro circummodulans; superiora autem sonum qui deorsum est arteriae in concauitate ipsius recipiunt,
65 geminis tibiis in nares peruenientibus, ac ueluti squamarum quibusdam uehiculis circa colatorium iliis uocem descisam, in maiorem sonum perficiunt. Maxillae uero et lingua ipsaque circa guttur
conformatio, iuxta quam mentorum subfoditur uallis, acutae extendunt, haec omnia in neruis plectri motum subsimulant uarie
70 multiformiterque, oportuna multaque uelocitate sonos ad usum
coaptantia. Labiorum uero distinctio atque impressio idipsum facit his qui spiritum tibiae per digitos accipiunt iuxta adunationem
melodiae.

59/79 spiritus − demisserunt] uide GVILL. S. THEOD., *Nat. corp.* 70-71 (p. 127-128, 845-862)

---

49 publicans] puplicans C   51/52 dicit quia anima − non potest] *non praeb.* PG Forb.   52/53 nudam dictionibus animam] *seclusi* (*repet.* B C *cfr l. 50*)   53 intelligentiae] intelle- B   54 in arte] ἔντεχνος PG Forb., ἐν τέχνῃ q Forb.$^{u.l.}$, ἐντέχνῃ Forb.$^{u.l.}$ 60 arteriam] *non praeb.* PG Forb. (*fort. bis* E. *uel Graecum exemplar scripsit: cfr l. 59*)   61 interiores ordines eleuans] ταῖς ἔνδωθεν προσαρασσόμενον προσβολαῖς PG Forb. (*quod obscure* E. *interpretatus est*)   62 pertranat] διειλήφασι PG Forb.   omnino] πως PG Forb. (πάντως E. *legisse uel intellexisse uidetur*)   63 giro] gyro B   65 peruenientibus] *per praem.* C   66 descisam] *i.e.* descissam (*cfr* περισχίζουσα PG Forb.)   67/68 maxillae − extendunt] παρειὰ δέ, καὶ ἡ γλῶσσα, καὶ ἡ περὶ τὸν φάρυγγα διασκευή, καθ' ἣν ὁ ἀνθερεὼν ὑποκαλᾶται κοιλανόμενος, καὶ ὀξυτονῶν ἐπιτείνεται PG Forb. (*quod obscure* E. *interpretatus est*)   68 mentorum] meritorum C   acutae] acute C   69 uarie] uariae B, ποικίλως PG Forb.   71 distinctio] distinc C   72/73 iuxta adunationem melodiae] *hic in* PG Forb. q *terminatur cap.* IX

3b. [X, 1] Sic itaque, animo per organicam talem in nobis constitutionem modulante rationem, rationabiles facti sumus, non habituri, ut arbitror, rationis gratiam, si graue ac laboriosum seruitutis quae est erga cibum usui corporis labiis distribueretur. Nunc autem talem administrationem manus in se ipsas transferentes rectum administrationi rationis os demisserunt.

Capvt X
Quia per sensus operatur intellectus

1. [2] Duplex autem circa organum operatio est: una quidem ad officium soni, altera uero ad susceptionem extrinsecus intellectuum; et non altera alteri miscetur, sed in ipso officio in quod ordinata est ex natura permanet, neque ex uicina perturbatur – non enim auditus loquitur, neque uox audit – uox enim semper et omnino auditui procedit, auditus uero semper accipit neque impletur, sicut ait alibi Salomon.

2. [3] Hoc ut mihi uidetur maxime ex his quae in nobis sunt mirandum, quae sit latitudo illa internae capacitatis in quam omnia confluunt quae per auditum infunduntur. Qui sunt stili a memoria introductorum in ipso uerborum, qualisque impositorum in auditu intellectu⟨u⟩m susceptio? Et quoniam, multorum diuersorumque sibi inuicem adiectorum, confusio et error per consequentem impositorum positionem non efficitur? Aequaliter quis etiam in uisuum operatione miraretur: similiter enim per eos animus in his quae extra corpus sunt peragit et ad se uisi-

---

X, 8/9 auditus uero – Salomon] cfr Eccle. 1, 8

X, 3/62 duplex – imponunt] uide etiam Ioh. Scot., Periphys. 2 (p. 60, 1375-1383) (= col. 569 CD); 3 (p. 162, 4732-4735) (= col. 732A) 10/34 hoc ut mihi – habeant] uide etiam Ioh. Scot., Periphys. 5 (p. 164, 5340-5343) (= col. 977C)

74/79 sic diuid. et Dionysius Exiguus in interpretatione sua et Forb.*u.l.* (*inter quos non est q*) 76 habituri] habitum B

X, 1 caput] *om.* B 2 operatur] ἐνεργεῖ *PG Forb.*, ἐνεργεῖται *q Forb.*^{u.l.} 7/8 uox enim – procedit] ἡ μὲν γὰρ (φωνὴ *add. Forb.*^{u.l.}) ἀεί τι πάντως προίεται *PG Forb.* 11 mirandum] ἄξιον εἶναι καὶ θαυμάζεσθαι *PG Forb.* illa] ἐκείνου *PG Forb.*, ἐκεῖνο *q Forb.*^{u.l.} 12 quae] *suppl. s.l.* C 14 intellectuum] *correxi* (*cfr* τῶν ἐντιθεμένων … νοημάτων *PG*), intellectum B C quoniam] *fort.* quomodo *legendum* (*cfr* πῶς *PG*) 18 peragit] ἐπιδράσσεται *PG Forb.* (*quod quasi ab* ἐπιδράω *uel quasi* ἐπιπράσσεται *E. legisse uel intellexisse uidetur*)

bilium imagines trahit, characteres eorum quae uidentur in se ipso describens.

3. [4] Ac ueluti quaedam amplissima sit ciuitas in differentiis conuentuum concurrentes ad eam suscipiens, non ad eundem locum in ciuitate omnes concurrunt, alii quidem ad forum, quidam uero ad possessiones, alii per ecclesias seu plateas seu angustos uicos seu theatra, unusquisque secundum suam uoluntatem transeunt, talem quandam uideo etiam animi ciuitatem intra nos cohabitatam, quam differentes quidam introitus implent per sensus. Vnumquemque uero introeuntium animus inquirens perque gentes discernens conuenientibus scientiae locis imponit.

4. [5] Ac sicut in exemplo ciuitatis, est uidendum saepe quidam dum sint ex uno genere et cognatione per eandem ciuitatem non simul, sed alius quidem per alium introitum prout accidit incurrunt; nihil uero minus intra ambitum muri uenientes, iterum apud se inuicem sunt, dum ad se inuicem proprietates habeant. E contrario etiam est inueniendum quid efficitur. Peregrini enim et se inuicem non cognoscentes uno in ciuitatem introitu saepe utuntur, sed eosdem sibi inuicem non copulat ipsa per introitum societas: possunt enim etiam intus dum sint discerni ad suas cognationes. Tale aliquid uideo etiam in amplitudine quae in animo est: saepe siquidem ex differentibus sensuum instrumentis una nobis notitia eiusdem rei congeritur, multiformiter ad sensus dispertitae. Iterum illud est e contrario ex uno aliquo sensu multa uariaque discere, in nullo sibi inuicem secundum naturam accedentia.

5. [6] Verbi gratia (melius enim per exemplum declarare sermonem), proponatur ad inquirendum aliqua proprietas circa liquida. Quaedam quidem delectabilis ad sensum, quaedam uero fugienda gustantibus. Nonne ergo inuentum est ab experimento fellis amaritudo et commoditas qualitatis quae in melle est? His autem manifestis existentibus, eiusdem rei unam introducunt notitiam multiformiter intellectum intrantis gustus, uisus, auditus, saepe

---

26/33 talem – incurrunt] uide Gvill. S. Theod., *Nat. corp.* 62 (p. 125, 752-759)

31 per eandem ciuitatem] διὰ τῆς αὐτῆς πύλης *PG Forb.* (διὰ τῆς αὐτῆς πόλεως *E. legisse uel intellexisse uidetur*)   41/42 rei – despertitae] τοῦ αὐτοῦ πράγματος πολυμερῶς πρὸς τὰς αἰσθήσεις μεριζομένου *PG Forb.*   42 dispertitae] despertite *B*, dispertite *C*   44 accedentia] *i.e.* accidentia (συμβαίνοντα *PG Forb.*)   48 nonne] οὐκοῦν *PG*   51 uisus] ἢ ὀσφρήσει *PG*, ἡ ὄσφρησις *Forb.*, ἡ ὄψις *q Forb.*[u.l.]

etiam et tactus et olfactus; etenim uidens quis mel et nomen audiens et gustui accipiens, uaporemque per olfactum cognoscens, tactu quoque approbans, eandem rem per singulas sensuum sedes cognoscit.

6. [7] Iterum autem uaria et multiformia per unum quendam sensum discimus; dum auditus omnigenas recipit uoces, oculorum uero receptio indiscretam habeat in diuersorum generum contemplatione operationem; similiter albo accidit et nigro omnibusque e contrario distantibus colore. Sic gustus, sic olfactus diuersarum rerum unusquisque per propriam susceptionem notitiam imponunt.

⟨Capvt⟩ XI
Quia inuisibilis est animi natura

1. Quid igitur est animus secundum sui naturam, qui sensuum uirtutibus se ipsum impartitur et per singulas conuenienter eorum quae sunt scientiam recipit? Nam quia aliud quid praeter sensus est, non arbitror quempiam sapientum dubitare. Si enim id ipsum esset sensui, ad unum omnino haberet secundum sensum operum societatem, eo quod simplex quidem ipse est, nihil autem uarium in simplo consideratur. Nunc uero, omnibus comparatis, aliud quidem tactum esse, aliud olfactum, aliis similiter absque communione ad se inuicem dispositis, quoniam aequaliter unicuique et conuenienter adest, alterum quid oportet omnino ipsum animum praeter sensum substituere naturam, ne quis uaria intellectuali commisceat.

XI, 3/39 quid igitur – characterizans] uide etiam Ioh. Scot., *Periphys.* 4 (p. 68-69, 1918-1954) (= col. 788B-789A) uerbatim; 2 (p. 81, 1894-1899) (= col. 584D-585A); (p. 82, 1941-1944) (= col. 586A)   3/8 quid igitur – societatem] uide Gvill. S. Theod., *Nat. corp.* 62 (p. 125, 759-764) quasi uerbatim   8/11 nihil autem – dispositis] uide Gvill. S. Theod., *Nat. corp.* 63 (p. 125, 767-769)

52 olfactus] τῇ ὄψει *PG*, ἡ ὄψις *Forb.*, ἡ ὄσφρησις *q Forb.*^{u.l.}   58 indiscretam] in indiscretam *B*   59 operationem] et *praem. B*   60 sic gustus, sic olfactus] οὕτως ἡ γεῦσις, οὕτως ἡ ὄσφρησις, οὗτος ἡ διὰ τῆς ἀφῆς κατανόησις *PG Forb.*   61 per] *om. B*

XI, 1 *om. C*   caput] *om. B*   4 impartitur] impertitur *Periphys.*   10 esse] *correxi ex Periphys.* (cfr εἶναι *PG Forb.*), esset *B C Capp.*   10/11 absque communione] ἀκοινωνήτως τε καὶ ἀμίκτως *PG Forb.*   13 praeter sensum substituere naturam] παρὰ τὴν αἰσθητικὴν ὑποτίθεσθαι φύσιν *PG Forb.*, substituere per naturam *Periphys.*   uaria] ποικιλία *PG Forb.*, ποικίλα *Forb.*^{u.l.}

2. *Quis cognouit animum Domini?* ait Apostolus. Ego autem praeter hoc dico: quis suum animum intellexit? Dicant qui Dei naturam inter ea quae in eorum comprehensione sunt faciunt, si se ipsos intellexerunt, sui animi naturam cognouere. Multum partibilis quidam est multumque compositus? Et quomodo intellectuale in compositione est? Aut quis modus est diuersorum generum concretionis? Sed simplex et incompositus. Quomodo in multipliciter partitam sensualitatem diuiditur? Quomodo in singularitate uarium? Quomodo in uarietate unum?

3. Sed cognoscens eorum de quibus dubitatur solutionem, in ipsam Dei uocem recurro. *Faciamus* – enim inquit – *hominem ad imaginem nostram et similitudinem.* Imago enim, donec in nullo eorum quae in principali intelliguntur exemplo deficiat, proprie est imago. Si uero in aliquo ex similitudine principalis exempli excesserit, in illa parte imago non est. Non ergo, quoniam in his quae circa diuinam considerantur naturam incomprehensibilitas essentiae est, necessarium est eum qui sortitur imaginem omnem ad principale exemplum imitationem habere.

4. Si enim imaginis natura principale exemplum comprehenderet, super comprehensionem esset, si contrarietas eorum quae considerantur quod oportet peccatum imaginis reprehenditur. Quoniam uero scientiam fugit ipsa nostri animi natura, quae est secundum imaginem conditoris, diligentem ad id quod ei superponitur habet similitudinem, eo quod secundum se ipsum est incognitus incomprehensibilem naturam characterizans.

XI, 15 Rom. 11, 34   25/26 Gen. 1, 26

21/23 sed simplex – in uarietate unum] uide GVILL. S. THEOD., *Nat. corp.* 63 (p. 125, 765-767)   26/39 imago – characterizans] uide GVILL. S. THEOD., *Nat. corp.* 72-73 (p. 128-129, 877-886)   33/39 si enim imaginis – characterizans] uide etiam IOH. SCOT., *Periphys.* 2 (p. 81, 1914-1920) (= col. 585B)   36/39 quoniam uero – characterizans] uide etiam IOH. SCOT., *Periphys.* 4 (p. 45, 1211-1214) (= col. 771C)

18 multum] fortassis *add. Periphys.*   23 unum] unium $C^{a.c.}$ 25/26 ad imaginem nostram et similitudinem] ad imaginem et similitudinem nostram *B*, ad imaginem et similitudinem R^* (*Periphys.*), κατ' εἰκόνα καὶ καθ' ὁμοίωσιν ἡμετέραν PG Forb., κατ' εἰκόνα ἡμετέραν καὶ καθ' ὁμοίωσιν Forb.$^{a.l.}$ 26 enim] *om. Periphys.*   27 intelliguntur] intelle- *B*   29 non ergo] οὐκοῦν PG Forb.   29 in] ἐν PG Forb.   31 est^2] erit *Periphys.*   34 esset] est et *Capp.*, erit *Periphys.*   si] *non praeb.* PG (εἰ ἐναντιότης *E. legisse uel intellexisse uidetur*)   35 considerantur] inuenitur quod *add. Periphys.*   quod oportet peccatum] τὸ διημαρτημένον PG Forb. (δεῖ ἡμαρτημένον *E. legisse uel intellexisse uidetur*)   39 characterizans] car- *B*

Capvt XII
Exquisitio in qua parte corporis principale animi esse aestimandum; in quo etiam de lacrimis ac risu fysiologia

1. Sileat igitur omnis coniecturalis ac uana ratiocinatio eorum qui in particulis quibusdam corporis intellectualem includunt operationem. Quorum alii quidem in corde principatum esse constituunt, alii uero in cerebro animum ordinari dicunt, in quibusdam ciuitatibus suasione tales opiniones tenentes. Nam qui in corde ponit principatum, ipsius secundum locum positionem suae rationis facit argumentum, eo quod uidetur quodammodo illud mediam uniuersi corporis obtinere regionem, quasi uoluntario motu facile ex medio ad omne corpus diuisio, ac sic in operationem proueniente; testemque facit suae rationis tristem irascibilemque hominis affectum, quia uidentur quodammodo tales passiones illam particulam ad compassionem commouere. Qui uero cerebrum ratiocinationi offerunt, ueluti arcem quandam totius corporis caput ab ipsa natura possideri dicunt in ipsoque ueluti quendam regem animum possidere, quasi quibusdam nuntiis seu protectoribus, sensuum instrumentis in giro armigeris. Insignem ipsi etiam tali opinione hesitantis cogitationem adtrahi faciunt eos quidem quorum membranula cerebri uitiatur, etiam in ignorantia honestatis fieri inebriatosque capite grauari.

2. Addunt quoque quasdam naturaliores causas talis circa principatum opinionis utrique huiusmodi aestimationes demonstrantium. Vnus enim dicit motum qui est ex intelligentia cognationem habere ad igneum, eo quod incommunicabilis est etiam ignis sicut

---

XII, 4/7 sileat – dicunt] uide Gvill. S. Theod., *Nat. corp.* 63 (p. 125, 772-776) uerbatim *sed* dicunt] contendunt   7 alii uero – dicunt] cfr Plat., *Tim.* 45a-b et 70a   8/15 nam qui in corde – commouere] cfr Alex. Aphr., *De An.* p. 94, 7-11; Chalc., *Comm.* 2, 220 (p. 232-234) et 2, 224 (p. 238-239)   15/22 qui uero cerebrum – grauari] cfr Gal., *Plac.* 2, 4, 17 (p. 230); Chalc., *Comm.* 2, 213 (p. 228) et 2, 231 (p. 245)   16 arcem] = ἀκρόπολιν (*PG*, 44, 156d7); cfr Plat., *Tim.* 70a, *R.* 8, 560b

XII, 1 *om.* B   XII] XI $C^{a.c.}$ 2 corporis] *non praeb.* PG Forb.   3 fysiologia] *in Graeco textu sequitur* καὶ θεώρημά τι φυσικὸν περὶ τῆς κατὰ τὴν ὕλην, καὶ τὴν φύσιν, καὶ τὸν νοῦν κοινωνίας. *Vide XIII, 2*   4 ratiocinatio] racionatio $C^{a.c.}$ 7/8 in quibusdam ciuitatibus suasione] ἐπιπολαίοις τισὶ πιθανότησι PG Forb.   8 opiniones] ἐπινοίας PG Forb., ὑπονοίας q Forb.$^{u.l.}$ 18 nuntiis] nunciis B   19/21 insignem ipsi – cerebri uitiantur] σημεῖον δὲ καὶ οὗτοι τῆς τοιαύτης ὑπονοίας ποιοῦνται, τὸ παράγεσθαι τοῦ καθεστηκότος τὸν λογισμὸν τῶν κεκακωμένων τὰς μήνιγγας PG Forb.   25 intelligentia] intelle- B   26 incommunicabilis] ἀεικίνητον PG Forb. (ἀκοινώτητον E. *legisse uel intellexisse uidetur*)

intelligentia; et quoniam manare in particula cordis confitentur, propterea mobilitati caliditatis motum animi misceri dicit, receptionemque intellectualis naturae cor esse affirmat, in quo calidum comprehenditur. Alter uero omnibus sensuum instrumentis ueluti quoddam fundamentum radicemque esse dicit ΜΕΝΗΓΓΑ (sic enim nominant membranulam quae cerebrum continet) ac sic suam rationem credibilem facit: quasi non aliter intellectualis operatio collocaretur, nisi in illa parte cui etiam auris adiuncta incidentes in eam uoces profundit. Visus etiam, iuxta membranulam oculorum aedificii constitutus, incidentium in pupillas imaginum formationem aequaliter permittit. Vaporum quoque qualitates per olfactuum pondus in eadem parte discernuntur, sensus item gustandi discretione membranulae approbatur, e uicino quasdam effusiones neruales ex se ipso sensiuas per ceruices collorum in colatoriam uiam et inde in medullas permiscens.

3. Ego autem perturbari quidem saepe ad passionum intentiones intellectuale animae et obscurari naturalis operationis cogitationem ex quadam corporali compressione uerum esse dico; et fontem quendam ignei quod in corpore est cor esse ad furibundos impetus commotum; et cum his adhuc meniggam sensuum instrumentis subornari quae, iuxta rationem talia philosophantium de natura, amplectitur in se cerebrum uaporibusque inde resusci-

---

27/30 quoniam manare – comprehenditur] cfr GAL., *UP* 6, 7 (vol. 3, p. 436); ALEX. APHR., *De An.* p. 96, 5-6; CHALC., *Comm.* 2, 224 (p. 239)   30/56 alter uero – nomen est] uide etiam IOH. SCOT., *Periphys.* I (p. 54, 1635-1639) (= col. 480C); 3 (p. 160, 4666-4671) (= col. 730C); *Gloss. Mart. Cap. ex ms. Ox.* (p. 102-103): "Hymeneus: Isidorus dicit membranulam in lumbis possitam. Qui autem de natura rerum disputant aiunt duas membranulas esse, una quae est circa cerebrum quae grece uocatur ΜΗΝΙΚΑ, altera uero quae est in lateribus, quae gr(ece) dicitur ΦΡΕΝ, inde frenetica passio"; *Gloss. Mart. Cap.* 208, 11 (p. 105, 23-28): "ΥΜΕΝ ipse est deus nuptiarum, filius Veneris, qui etiam Menica vocatur. Re vera μήνιγγα dicitur membranula circa cerebrum ex quo cerebro omnes voluptates et semina per poros, id est venas, descendunt per totum corpus. Nam due sunt membranule, id est φρήν et ὑμήν. Diximus quid sit ὑμήν; φρήν vero membranula quae adheret costis intrinsecus, inde frenetica passio dicitur."   30/32 alter uero – continet] cfr GAL., *Plac.* 6, 3, 4 (p. 520); *UP* 8, 4 (vol. 3, p. 625)

27 intelligentia] intelle- *B*   in particula] imparticula *B*   confitentur] ἡ θερμότης (ἡ θερμότης] *om. Forb.*$^{u.l.}$) ὁμολογεῖται *PG Forb.*   36 aedificii] ed- *C*   37 aequaliter] τὸ ἔσω *PG Forb.*, τὸ εἴσω *Forb.*$^{u.l.}$ (τὸ ἴσον *E. legisse uel intellexisse uidetur*)   40 sensiuas per] *correxi* (*cfr* αἰσθητικὰς διὰ *PG Forb.*), sensui asper *B C Capp.*   41 et inde] καὶ αὐτόθεν *q*, αὐτοθί *PG Forb.*   47/48 philosophantium de natura] φυσιολογούντων *PG Forb.*, φιλοσοφούντων *Forb.*$^{u.l.}$ 47 philosophantium] philophantium *C*$^{a.c.}$ 48 cerebrum] celebrum *B*$^{a.c.}$ inde] *om. B*

DE IMAGINE, XII 95

tatur, ex his qui incisoriis contemplationibus uacant hoc audiens
50 quod dictum est, non sperno. Non tamen approbationem talem   *B* 95ʳ 157D
facio localibus puniri circumscriptionibus incomprehensibilem
incorporalemque naturam.

4. Nam insanias non ex solo corde fieri didicimus, ex subeuntibus etiam latera pelliculis passibiliter dispositis similiter infirmari
55 intellectuale diffiniunt periti medicinae, frenecin uocantes passionem, quoniam frenes talibus pelliculis nomen est. Ipsam quoque
ex tristitia in cor uenientem combustionem ambigue opinantur:
non enim ex corde, sed ex ore uentris exasperati, in cor passionem
per imperitiam reducunt. Tale uero aliquid dicunt qui diligenter
60 passiones inspiciunt, quia cum casu uiarum quas poros dicunt et
coartatione in tristitiae affectibus naturaliter circa totum corpus
facto, ad ipsas concauitates quae in profundo sunt omne quod in-   *Capp.* 223 160A
spirationem prohibet compellitur. Vnde respiratoriis uisceribus
coangustatis ab eo quod ea coartat, fortius saepe pondus spiritus
65 ex natura efficitur, ad eorum quae concadunt distinctionem quod
coangustatum est latificans. Talem anhelitum in concasu tristitiae
facimus, hanc coangustationem suspirium nominantes. Sed aestimantibus contritionem quae circa cor est, non ex corde sed ex ore
uentris affligi, fortassis ex eadem causa opinio est: dico autem po-
70 rorum concasu dum follis fellifer asperum illum mordacemque
fluctum prae tristitia in os uentris infundit. Approbatio autem
huius est grauem umidamque contristatis fieri superficiem ex as-   160B
siduo ualde felle undam suam in uenas infundente.

5. Sed et ipsam quae e contrario efficitur passionem, eam dico
75 quae est in laetitia magis autem risus rationem constituunt. Diffunduntur enim quodammodo atque soluuntur per delectationem pori corporis eorum qui contristantur ex quodam delectabili
auditu: ut enim illic per tristitiam cohibentur subtiles occultaeque pororum inspirationes constipantesque intrinsecus uiscerum   160C
80 affectum, in caput ac meniggas (hoc est membranulas cerebri)

---

50 talem] ταύτην *PG Forb.* (τοιαύτην *E. legisse uel intellexisse uidetur*)   51/52 localibus puniri – incorporalemque naturam] τοπικαῖς τισι περιγραφαῖς ἐμπεριειλῆφθαι τὴν ἀσώματον φύσιν *PG Forb.*   51 localibus] locabus C^{a.c.}   53 ex solo corde] ἐκ μόνης καρηβαρίας *PG Forb.*   didicimus] dedic- *C*   55 frenecin] φρενῖτιν *PG*, φρενίτιν *Forb.*   57 combustionem] συναίσθησις *PG Forb.*   72 umidamque] hum- *B C*   74/75 eam dico quae – constituunt] τὸ κατὰ τὴν εὐφροσύνην φημὶ καὶ τὸν γέλωτα, μᾶλλον τὸν λόγον συνίστησι *PG Forb.*   79 pororum] porrorum *C*   uiscerum] *correxi*, -orum *B C Capp.*   80 hoc est membranulas cerebri] *non praeb. PG Forb.*, *glossa E. uidetur*

austeriorem (id est umidiorem) uaporem repellunt, qui multus quibusdam cerebri concauitatibus introreceptus, per naturales poros in oculos expellitur, superciliorum concasu attrahente per stillicidium umiditatem. Stilla autem lacrima dicitur: sic mihi uidetur, ex contrario affectu plus consuetudine amplificatis poris, spiritus attrahi per eos in profundum, et inde iterum expelli a natura per porum in ora, omnium uiscerum (et maxime iecoris, ut aiunt) per quandam perturbationem instabilemque motum talem spiritum compellentium; unde facilitatem quandam egressioni spiritus natura machinans, porum qui est in ore amplificat, ex utraque parte circa anhelitum maxillas discernens: nomen autem facto risus est.

6. Neque igitur in iecore principale cogitandum est, neque per calorem sanguinis circa cor irascibilibus affectibus in corde arbitrandum est esse animi collocationem. Sed haec quidem in qualescumque corporum constitutiones referenda sunt, animum uero singulas quasque particularum per ineffabilem commixturae rationem tangere aestimandum est.

7. Etsi quidam nobis aduersus hoc Scripturam praetendant, quae principale in corde esse perhibet, non sine inquisitione sermonem accipiemus. Nam qui cordis meminit, renium etiam recordatus est dicens: *scrutans corda et renes Deus*; ita ut aut in utrisque aut in neutro intellectualem concludat.

8. Obscurari autem intellectuales operationes seu per omnia in omnibus inactuales fieri in qualicumque corporis affectu docens, non magnopere facio argumentum loco quodam uirtutem animi prohiberi, ac si superuenientibus particulis flagrantibus sua amplitudine uetitam. Corporalis enim est talis opinio, non posse praeoccupato organi folle per quoddam eorum quae in eo inspici-

---

XII, 102 Ps. 7, 10

96/103 animum uero – concludat] uide Gvill. S. Theod., *Nat. corp.* 64 (p. 125-126, 778-784)

81 austeriorem id est umidiorem] νοτερὸν PG Forb. (*fort. E.* σεμνότερον *intellexit, sed bene* νοτερὸν *per* id est umidiorem *exposuit*)   umidiorem] hum- B   multus] multis C   82 cerebri] celebri B^{a.c.}   82/83 per naturales poros] διὰ τῶν κατὰ τὴν βάσιν πόρων PG Forb. (διὰ τῶν κατὰ τὴν φύσιν πόρων E. *legisse uel intellexisse uidetur*)   84 stillicidium] stili- C   umiditatem] hum- B   86 attrahi] attrai C   87 iecoris] *correxi*, iacoris B C Capp.   93 iecore] *correxi*, iacore B C Capp.   96 animum uero] τὸν δὲ νοῦν ὁμοτίμως PG Forb.   105 docens] διδαχθεὶς PG Forb.   109/110 inspiciuntur] conspiciuntur C, ἐμβεβλημένων PG Forb. (ἐμβεβλεμμένων E. *legisse uel intellexisse uidetur*)

110 untur, alterum quendam locum inuenire: intellectualis enim natura neque concauitatibus corporum interius locatur, neque abundantia carnis expellitur. Sed quoniam ueluti organum musicum omne corporis creat, quaedam quidem accidunt modulari scientibus, non ualentibus autem notitiam organorum inusitatio-
115 nis ostendere quae artem non recipit. Aut enim tempore corruptum aut ex laxitate tardum aut a quodam ueneno cariosum aut atritum absonum manet et inactuosum, et ab eo qui habere uidetur contra artem tibicinalem inspiratur. Sic et animus per totum organum ueniens et conuenienter intellectualibus operationibus
120 singulas partium per quas consueuit tangens, in his quidem quae secundum naturam disponuntur quod suum est operatur, in his uero quae infirmantur artificalem sui motum inactuosus et piger manet accipere. Consueuit enim animus quodammodo ad id quidem quod secundum naturam disponitur societatem habere, ab
125 eo uero quod ab ea distat alienari.

161B
Capp. 224

⟨Capvt⟩ XIII
Speculatio quaedam de materiae et naturae et animi theoria

1. [XII, 9] Et mihi uidetur etiam naturaliorem quandam in hac parte speculationem esse, per quam quiddam ciuiliorum dogma-
5 tum est discendum. Quoniam enim pulcherrimum omnium et ex-

161C

110/123 intellectualis – accipere] uide Gvll. S. Theod., *Nat. corp.* 65-66 (p. 126, 796-808)

XIII, 5/48 quoniam enim – conformari] uide etiam Ioh. Scot., *Periphys.* 4 (p. 69-70, 1955-1997) (= col. 789A-790B) uerbatim   5/21 quoniam enim – formificat] cfr Greg. Naz., *Or.* 2, 17 (p. 112)

112 abundantia] hab- C   112/113 sed quoniam – omne corporis creat] Ἀλλ' ἐπειδὴ καθάπερ τι μουσικὸν ὄργανον ἅπαν τὸ σῶμα δεδημιούργηται *PG Forb.*   113/115 quaedam quidem accidunt – non recipit] ὥσπερ συμβαίνει πολλάκις ἐπὶ τῶν μελῳδεῖν μὲν ἐπισταμένων, ἀδυνατούντων δὲ δεῖξαι τὴν ἐπιστήμην, τῆς τῶν ὀργάνων ἀχρηστίας οὐ παραδεχομένης τὴν τέχνην *PG Forb.*   113 quaedam] ὥσπερ *PG Forb.*, ἅπερ *Forb.*[u.l.]   117 atritum] ἠχρειωμένον *PG Forb.*   118 per totum] ter totum *Capp.*   120/123 in his – manet accipere] ἐπὶ δὲ τῶν ἀσθενούντων δέξασθαι τὴν τεχνικὴν αὐτοῦ κίνησιν, ἄπρακτός τε καὶ ἀνενέργητος ἔμεινε *PG Forb.*   124/125 ab eo] habeo C

XIII, 1 *om.* C. Hoc cap. a praec. cap. XII diuidunt E., Dionysius Exiguus, q et Forb.[u.l.]; quamobrem abhinc discrepat apud istos numeratio capp. a numeratione iuxta PG Forb. caput] *om.* B   2 speculatio quaedam – theoria] θεώρημά τι φυσικὸν περὶ τῆς κατὰ τὴν ὕλην καὶ τὴν φύσιν καὶ τὸν νοῦν κοινωνίας (*cfr PG Forb. et XII, 2*)   5 enim] *om. Periphys.*

cellentissimum bonum ipse Deus est, ad quem omnia respiciunt
quaecumque boni habent desiderium, propterea dicimus etiam
animum sic ad imaginem formosissimi factum, quatenus ad principale exemplum similitudinem participarit, quantum quidem ipsum in bono licet permanere. Si uero quodammodo extra hoc
fuerit, pulchritudine illius in quo erat denudatur: siquidem dicimus similitudine principalis exempli pulchritudinis animum ornari, ueluti quoddam speculum charactere apparentis formatum,
iuxta eandem analogiam etiam administratam a se naturam habere animum arbitramur, pulcritudineque quae ab illo est ipsam
ornari, ueluti quoddam speculi speculum factam, tenerique ab
ipsa et comprehendi materiale substantiae, circa quam consideratur natura.

2. [XII, 10] Si ergo habetur ab altero alterum, per omnia corrationabiliter ipsa ueri boni societas deducendo, per id quod superponitur id quod consequens formificat; cum uero efficitur huius
optimae connaturalitatis dispersio et ad contrarium consequens
fuerit supereminenti supereminens, tunc ipsius materiae, cum de-
solata fuerit ex natura, redarguitur deformitas. Informis enim res
quaedam est per se ipsam materia et imperfecta, et ipsius informitati concorrumpitur pulchritudo naturae in qua per animum formatur; ac sic in ipsum animum turpitudinis materiae per naturam
distributio efficitur, ut non iam Dei imaginem in charactere fig-
menti consideres. Nam ueluti quoddam speculum retro bonorum
formam animus factus, proicit quidem fulgoris boni notitias, materiae uero informitatem in se ipsum absorbet.

3. [XII, 11] Et hoc modo fit mali generatio, per priuationem
boni subtexta. Bonum uero est omne quodcumque consequitur
quod primum bonum proprie habet. Quodcumque uero extra illam copulam et similitudinem quae ad illud est efficitur, expers
boni omnino est. Si ergo unum quidem iuxta consideratam rationem bonum quod uere est, animus autem ad imaginem boni effi-
ciendo etiam ipse habet bonus esse. Natura uero quae ab animo

---

8 quatenus] quatinus *B*   8/10 ad principale exemplum – licet permanere] ἕως ἂν μετέχῃ τῆς πρὸς τὸ ἀρχέτυπον ὁμοιότητος καθόσον ἐνδέχεται, καὶ αὐτὸν ἐν τῷ καλῷ διαμένειν *PG Forb.*   11 pulchritudine] pulcr- *C*   13 charactere] car- *B*   20 ueri boni] ὄντως κάλλους *PG Forb.*, ὄντος καλοῦ *Forb.*ᵘˑˡ·   23 supereminenti supereminens] τῷ ὑποβεβηκότι τὸ ὑπερέχον *PG* ὄντως κάλλους *PG Forb.*, transgredienti supereminens *R** (*Periphys.*)   24 redarguitur] διηνέχθη *PG*, διηλέγχθη *q Forb.*   24/25 res quaedam] τι *PG Forb.*, τι χρῆμα *q Forb.*ᵘˑˡ·   26 pulchritudo] pulcri- *C*   in qua] ᾖ *PG*, ᾧ *q Forb.*ᵘˑˡ·   28 charactere] car- *B*   32 hoc] *suppl. s.l. C*   37/38 efficiendo] fficiendo *sed corr. s.l. C*

DE IMAGINE, XIII

continetur, ueluti quaedam imago imaginis est. Ex his ostenditur
quia materiale nostrum constituitur quidem et comprehenditur
cum ex natura administratur. Soluitur uero iterum et decidit cum
a continente animo et comprehendente separatur et ab ipsa ad bonum connaturalitate dispergitur.

4. [XII, 12] Hoc autem non aliter efficitur quam cum naturae
ad contrarium fit conuersio, dum desiderium non ad bonum, sed
ad id quod formantis indiget intuetur. Necesse est enim omnem
materiam per egestatem propriae formae ad aliquod inhonestum
ac deforme simulandum conformari.

5. [XII, 13] Sed haec quidem a nobis ex quadam consequentia
exquisita sunt propter theoriam propositi superintrantia. Hoc
enim quaesitum erat, si in quadam parte eorum quae in nobis sunt
intellectualis uirtus collocatur, an per omnia aequaliter peruenit.
Eos namque qui localibus partibus animum circumcludunt et in
constitutionem talis suae susceptionis proferunt intelligentiam in
eorum qui contra naturam disponuntur membranulas non prospere prouenire ratio demonstrauit, quia per omnem partem humanae concretionis, iuxta quod consueuit singulas operari,
aequaliter animae uirtus efficax manet, dum in naturae parte non
permaneat; ac per haec ex consequentia ipsa contemplatio quae
adiecta est rationi occurrit, per quam discimus in humana concretione a Deo quidem animum administrari, ab illo autem materialem nostram uitam, cum in natura manet. Si autem auersa fuerit a
natura, etiam ab ipsa quae est per animum operatione alienari.

6. [XII, 14] Sed redeamus iterum unde egressi sumus: quia in
his quae ex passione quadam naturali constitutione non subuertuntur propriam uirtutem animus operatur, et in his qui naturaliter consistunt fortis efficitur, infirmatur uero iterum in his qui sui
operationem non capiunt. Est etiam per aliam doctrinam quae de

---

39 imago imaginis] uide etiam Ioh. Scot., *Periphys.* 1 (p. 10, 198) (= col. 447A); 2 (p. 100, 2404-2405) (= col. 598C); 4 (p. 71, 2016) (= col. 790C)   59/63 contemplatio – operatione alienari] uide etiam Ioh. Scot., *Periphys.* 4 (p. 70, 1998-2003) (= col. 790B) uerbatim

41 administratur] ammin- *B*   47 aliquod] aliquot *B*   50 superintrantia] super intrantia *Capp.*   54 intelligentiam] intelle- *B*   58 efficax] ἀνενέργητος *PG Forb*.
59/60 haec – adiecta est] hoc consequens contemplatio rationi *R** (*Periphys.*)
62 cum in natura] dum in natura (hoc est in imagine animi) *Periphys.*   68/70 est etiam – de talibus] ἔστι γὰρ καὶ δι' ἑτέρων τὸ περὶ τούτων δόγμα *PG* (δι' ἕτερον *E. legisse uel intellexisse uidetur*)

talibus est suadere et, si non graue proposito iam sermoni, etiam
de talibus per pauca, ut arbitramur, excipiemus.

Capvt XIIII [XIII]
De somniis et oscitatione et uisione ΑΕΤΙΟΛΟΓΙΑ, hoc est causalis ratio

1. Materialis et fluxilis haec corporum uita, semper per motum proueniens, in hoc habet essendi uirtutem, in non stanti umquam motu. Vt enim quidam fluuius, iuxta suum ruens impetum, implere quidem uallem ostenditur per quamcumque consequitur ferri, non tamen in eadem aqua circa eundem semper locum cernitur, sed illa quidem subter lapsa cucurrit, illa uero desuper fluxit, sic et materiale huius uitae per quendam motum fluxumque uicissitudinum successionis continuitate permutatur, ut numquam mutabilitate stare possit, sed in potentia quiescendi incessabilem habet alternum per similia motum. Si autem aliquando motus cessauerit, omnino etiam essendi quietem habebit (hoc est omnino etiam esse cessabit).

2. Veluti, acceperit plenitudinem uanitas, et iterum quaedam uenerit uanitati plenitudo. Somnus uigorem uigiliae sublaxauit, deinde uigilia quod laxatum est extendit: et neutrum horum in perennitate commanet, sed recedunt inuicem aduenientibus utraque. Sic natura se ipsam uicissitudinibus renouante, ueluti utrumque in parte ponderantem, indesinenter ab altero transeundo in alterum. Nam semper in operationibus animal consistere rigiditatem quandam atque attractum superextentarum partium facit.

XIV, 4/15 materialis – cessabit] uide etiam Ioh. Scot., *Periphys.* 4 (p. 72, 2057-2069) (= col. 791C-792A) uerbatim

69 et si non graue – sermoni] καὶ εἰ μὴ βαρὺ τῇ ἀκοῇ (τῇ ἀκοῇ *om. q Forb.*^{u.l.}) τῶν προκεκμηκότων (τῶν προκεκμηκότων] τῷ προκεκμηκότι *q*) ἤδη τῷ λόγῳ *PG Forb. q* 70 ut arbitramur] ὡς ἂν οἷοί τε ὦμεν *PG Forb.* (οἷοί τε ὦμεν *quasi ab* οἴω *E. legisse uel intellexisse uidetur*)

XIV, 1 *om. C. In PG et Forb. inc. cap. XIII* 4 materialis] aterialis *pro prima littera spatium relinquens C* per motum] διὰ κινήσεως *PG Forb.*, motu *R** (*Periphys.*) 5 stanti] stante *R** (*Periphys.*) 12 mutabilitate] *post* mutabilitatem *R** (*Periphys.*) in potentia] τῇ δυνάμει *PG q Forb.*^{u.l.}, τῇ ἀδυναμίᾳ *Forb.*, impotentia *R** (*Periphys.*) 14/15 hoc est – cessabit] *non praeb. PG Forb.*, praeb. *R** (*Periphys.*) 16 veluti] οἶον *PG Forb.* 19 perennitate] perhenn- *B*

DE IMAGINE, XIV   101

Ipsa quoque diuturna corporis quies casum quendam atque solutionem consistentis operatur; mensurate autem utrumque secundum tempus consequi ad permanentiam uirtus est naturae, per
assiduum ad opposita transitum qui in utrisque ipsam ab utrisque   165C
quietam facit. Sic itaque uegetatum corpus per uigilias [natura]
accipiens, solutionem per somnum uigori cogitat, sensiuas uirtutes ad tempus ex operationibus quiescere faciens, ac ueluti quosdam pullos post curruum certamina soluens.

3. Necessaria autem constitutioni corporis oportuna quies, ut
consequenter in omne corpus per poros qui in eo sunt esca diffun-
deretur, nullo uigore meatui impediente. Quemadmodum ex
umida terra, cum calidioribus radiis sol fouerit, uapores quidam
caliginosi ex profundo trahuntur, similiter fit etiam in terra nostra
dum cibus ex naturali caliditate intus calificatur: uapores, aerei qui   165D
sunt, secundum naturam sursum feruntur et ad superpositum res-
pirantes in regionibus capitis fiunt, ueluti quidam fumus in adunationem parietis solutus; inde post in poros instrumentorum
sensus uapores discernuntur, per quos necessario sensus cessat,
transitu illorum uaporum subtractus. Nam ipse uisus palpebris
comprehenditur, ueluti quodam artificali plumbeo, huiusmodi
dico grauitate palpebram in oculos obruente. Incrassatus autem
talibus uaporibus auditus, ueluti ostio quodam auditoriis particulis superposito, silentium naturali operationi adducit: ast talis passio somnus est, dum sensus in corpore quiescit, et omnino ex
naturali motu otiosus, ut distributiones escae peruiae sint, per sin-
gulos poros uaporibus coeuntes.

4. Huiusque rei gratia sciendi sunt loci, quod quidem intus sub   C 131ʳ *Capp.* 227
ipsa uaporatione est circa sensus officinas dispositio est, prohibe-   168A
tur autem hoc iuxta quandam utilitatem somnus; neruosum illud,
plenum uaporibus factum, a se ipso naturaliter distendit, ut per

---

40/49 inde post – uaporibus coeuntes] uide etiam Ioh. Scot., *Periphys.* 2 (p. 76,
1778-1779) (= col. 581C)

24/25 casum quendam atque solutionem consistentis] διάπτωσίν τινα τοῦ συνεστῶτος
καὶ λύσιν *PG Forb.*, διάπτωσίν τινα καὶ λύσιν τοῦ συνεστῶτος *Forb.*ᵘˡ   25 mensurate]
mensuratae *B*, μετρίως *PG Forb.*   28 uegetatum] τετονωμένον *PG Forb.*   natura]
seclusi (*non praeb. PG Forb.*, *glossa E. uidetur*)   30 quiescere faciens] quiescere et faciens
C, ἀναπαύσασα *PG Forb.*, ἀναπαύουσα *Forb.*ᵘˡ   31 pullos] ἵππους *PG Forb.*, πόλους *q*
35 umida] hum- *B*   37 caliditate] calliditate *B*   40 solutus] διαδυόμενος *PG Forb.*,
διαλυόμενος *Forb.*ᵘˡ   45 ostio] hostio *C*   46 adducit] ἄγει *PG Forb.*, εἰσάγει *q*
50 huiusque] huius *B*   sciendi sunt loci] εἰ στενοχωροῖτο *PG Forb.* (ἐπιστητέοι χῶροι *uel
similiter E. legisse uel intellexisse uidetur*)

mentis raptum pars illa ex uaporibus incrassata extenuatur, quale
faciunt qui ualidiore pressura ex uestimentis aquam exprimunt.
Et quia rotundiores circa guttur partes sunt – abundat autem in
talibus neruosum – cum etiam ex his uaporum crassitudinem
oporteat expelli, quoniam impossibile est circularem partem per
rectitudinem extendi, nonnisi per rotundam figuram deponere-
tur, hac de causa recepto in oscitatione spiritu, quando infra
mentum (in eo enim subsistit) subcollocatur, dum intus omnis
figura omnium ordinatorum in circulo sit, illa fumida crassitu-
do quae in partibus relinquitur cum transitu spiritus expiratur.
Saepe autem post somnum hoc euenire nouit, cum aliquid illorum uaporum comprehensum fuerit in illis locis non degestum et
non expiratum.

5. Ex his igitur humanus animus euidenter ostenditur quia a natura possidetur: consistente quidem illa et uigilante, ipse etiam
operatur et mouetur, illa uero prostrata somno ipse manet immobilis. Nisi forte quis somnialem phantasiam motum animi susceperit in somno operantem: nos autem dicimus solam sapientem et
consistentem operationem oportere in animum referri, phantasias
uero per somnum in superfluitates imaginesque quasdam operationis animi aestimamus, in irrationabiliori animae specie secundum quod accidit effingi. Nam absolutam sensibus animam per
somnum, etiam extra animi operationes esse iuxta necessitatem
accidit. Per hos enim ad hominem ipsa animi commixtura efficitur: quiescentibus itaque sensibus necessarium est etiam intelligentiam uacare. Argumentum est autem in incongruis et
impossibilibus saepe uideri esse imaginantem; quod non fieret, si
in cogitatione et intelligentia anima tunc administraret.

6. Sed mihi uidetur ex uenerabilioribus uirtutibus anima silente – dico autem operationibus quae secundum animum sunt et
sensum – solam threpticam (hoc est nutritiuam) eius partem ope-
ratricem per somnum esse. In hac uero dum anima extra somnum
fit, imagines quasdam resultationesque et eorum quae secundum

---

56 abundat] hab- C   60 quando] ὅτε PG, ὅ, τε Forb.   60/61 infra mentum – sub-
collocatur] ἀνθερεὼν ἐπὶ τὸ κάτω τοῖς γαργαρεῶσιν ὑποκοιλαίνεται PG Forb. (quod E.
obscure interpretatus est ut uid.; fort. in eo enim subsistit glossa est)   72 phantasias]
fant- B   73 in superfluitates] φαντασιώδεις φλυαρίας PG Forb. (φαντασιώδεις εἰς
φλυαρίας uel similiter E. legisse uel intellexisse uidetur)   77 per hos] per os B, διὰ γὰρ
τούτων PG Forb.   78/79 intelligentiam] intelle- B   81 intelligentia] intelle-B   ad-
ministraret] ammin- B   84 nutritiuam] nutriuam C

sensum sunt et eorum quae secundum intelligentiam aguntur fieri, easdemque quas ipsa per recordabilem animae speciem informat, prout consequens est reformari, reboatione quadam recordabili in eadem animae specie permanente.

7. In his homo coimaginatur, non ordine quodam ad apparentium pluralitatem ductus, sed commixtis quibusdam et inconsequentibus seductionibus errans. Quomodo autem per corporales operationes, in unaquaque partium specialiter quid iuxta impositam sibi naturaliter uirtutem operante, fit quaedam etiam silente membro ad id quod ponitur coaffectatio, ita corrationabiliter et in anima, etsi quoddam quidem eius sileat, quoddam uero moueatur, totum parti coaffectari consequitur. Non enim alicubi naturalem unitatem recipit segregari, dum pars quadam suarum uirtutum operatione potiatur; sed quemadmodum et uigilantibus et sollicitantibus imperat quidem animus, ministrat autem sensus, non relinquitur tamen ab his ipsa administratoria corporis uirtus (animus enim cibum usui adquirit, sensus autem adquisitum recipit, nutritiua uero corporis uirtus in se ipsa quod sibi datum est administrat), sic etiam per somnum quodammodo in nobis ipse talium uirtutum principatus participatur ac dominante irrationabiliore quiescit quidem aliarum operatio, non tamen omnino extinguitur. Festinante autem tunc per somnum ad degestionem threptica (id est nutritiua) omnemque naturam ad se ipsam collocante, neque omnino ab ea ipsa quae est secundum sensum uirtus distrahitur (non enim recipit quod semel connaturaliter inest secari), neque eius operatio potest extingui officiorum sensus uacatione per somnum impedita. Iuxta eandem rationem etiam animo ad sensualem animae speciem sociato, consequens est etiam dum ipsa mouetur ipsum commoueri dicere et silentio conquiescere.

8. Tale quid circa ignem fieri consueuit, cum quidem paleis undique suboccultatur, nullo flatu flammam sufflante, neque adapposita distribuitur neque omnino extinguitur, sed pro flamma

---

87 intelligentiam] intelle- B   88 ipsa] αὐτῇ PG Forb., αὐτὴ q Forb.*u.l.*   91 coimaginatur] οὖν φαντασιοῦται PG Forb. (συμφαντασιοῦται E. *legisse uel intellexisse uidetur*) 96 membro] μέρους PG, μέλους Forb.   98 coaffectari consequitur] συνδιατίθεται PG Forb.   99 uirtutum] -tem C   102 administratoria] ammin- B   103 adquirit] acq- B   adquisitum] acq- B   105 administrat] ammin- B   106 participatur] ἀντιμεθίσταται PG Forb.   109 threptica] trep- C   id est nutritiua] *haec glossa E. uidetur, fort.* threptica, id est nutritiua, uirtus *legendum* (*cfr* τῆς θρεπτικῆς δυνάμεως PG Forb.)

fumus quidam per paleas in aera dirigitur; si autem a quodam suf-
flationem acceperit, in flammam fumus efficitur. Eodem modo
etiam animus in otio a sensibus per somnum occultatus neque elu-
cere per eos potenter habet, non tamen omnino extinguitur, sed
ueluti fumiformis mouetur, quoddam quidem operans, quoddam
uero non ualens.

9. Ac ueluti quidam musicus laxatis cordis lyrae plectrum immittens, non secundum numerum melos adducit (non enim inordinatum sonuerit), sed manus quidem artificaliter saepe mouetur,
ad localem tonorum positionem plectrum ducens, quod autem
sonat nil est nisi ignobilem quendam et inordinatum in motu cor-
darum bombum subsonare. Sic per somnum organica officinarum
sensuum laxata constitutione, uniuersaliter artifex silet, siquidem
perfectam solutionem ex umiditate quadam et grauitate organum
patitur; uel infirmiter uel obscure operabitur, dum sensuale organum diligenter artem non susceperit.

10. Ac per hoc ipsa memoria confusa ipsaque praescientia
quibusdam praeuelaminibus ambiguis dubitans, in imaginibus
quibusdam sollicitudinum eorum quae extra somnum sunt imaginatur, atque aliquid euenientium saepe indicauit. Nam in
subtili naturae quiddam plus habet quam corporalem crassitudinem in contemplandi aliquod eorum quae sunt potentiam;
non tamen per quandam rectitudinem potest declarare quod
dicitur, ut praeclara ac lucida sit eorum quae proponuntur doctrina, sed opinio et ambigua futuri declaratio, quod enigma uocant qui talia discernunt.

11. Sic pincerna botrum expressit in calicem pharaonis; sic ca-
nistrum ferre pistor imaginauit: in quibus uigilanter uterque sollicitudinem habuit, in his esse etiam in somniis aestimauit. Nam
consuetarum eis oportunitatum formulae in prognostico animae
formatae, de his quae in tempore euentura erant per talem animi
prophetiam diuinare praestiterunt.

XIV, **145/146** sic pincerna – pistor imaginauit] cfr Gen. 40, 1

119 fumus] ἀτμός *PG Forb.* (*quod E.* uapor *alibi interpretatur*), καπνός *q Forb.*^{u.l.} (*quod E.* fumus *saepe interpretatur*)   121 otio] ocio *B*   129 ignobilem] ἄσημον *PG Forb.* (ἄσεμνον *E. legisse uel intellexisse uidetur*)   130 subsonare] ὑπηχεῖ *PG Forb.*, ὑπηχεῖν *Forb.*^{u.l.}, ὑφηχεῖν *q*   132 umiditate] humiditate *B*, ἐκ πληθώρας *PG Forb.*, ἐκ πληθούρας *q Forb.*^{u.l.}   133 obscure] obscurae *B* ἀμυδρῶς *PG Forb.*   140 aliquod] aliquot *B*   143 enigma] enigmata *C*^{a.c.}   148 oportunitatum] oportunitate *C*^{a.c.}   150 praestiterunt] -rint *C*, παρέσχεν *PG Forb.*

12. Si autem Danihel et Ioseph ipsa quae in illis erat diuina uirtus, nullo in eis superuoluto sensu, futurorum scientiam erudiuit, nil hoc ad propositum sermonem. Non enim quis talia somniorum uirtuti deputauerit, alioquin omnino ex consequentia etiam factas uigilanter theophanias non uisionem sed naturae consequentiam sponte operantem aestimabit. Sicut ergo omnibus hominibus iuxta suum animum administratis pauci quidam sunt diuino colloquio clare digni, sic, communiter omnibus et sociabiliter ipsam in somnis phantasiam naturaliter ingenitam participantibus, quidam, non omnes, per somnos diuiniorem manifestationem communicant; aliis autem omnibus, si inest quaedam ex somniis circa aliquod praescientia, secundum praedictum fit modum.

13. Si uero et Aegyptius et Assirius tyrannus diuinitus ad futurorum ducuntur scientiam, aliud est quod per tales administratur. Oportebat enim occultam sanctorum sapientiam manifestari, ne inutilis communioni hanc uitam transcurreret. Quomodo enim cognosceretur qualis erat Danihel, nisi in cantantibus ac magis ad inuentionem phantasiae infirmatis? Aut quomodo saluaretur Aegyptus prohibito Ioseph in carcere, si non adduceretur in medio eorum iudicium somnii? Non ergo aliud quid haec et non secundum communes phantasias duci oportet.

14. Consueta autem haec in somnis uisio communis est omnium, multipliciter et multiformiter phantasiis ingenita: aut enim, ut dictum est, in recordabili animae diurnalium oportun⟨it⟩atum reboationes permanent, aut saepe etiam ad qualescumque corporis affectus ipsa in somnis constitutio reformatur. Sic enim qui sitit in fontibus esse uidet, et in aepulis qui escae indiget, et iuuenis adulta sibi aetate conuenienter passioni imaginat.

151/172 si autem – oportet] cfr Gen. 41, 1-36; Dan. 2, 19-46

151 Danihel] Daniel C   151/152 ipsa quae – diuina uirtus] καὶ οἱ κατ᾽ ἐκείνους θείᾳ δυνάμει *PG Forb.*   154 deputauerit] -arit *B*   155 theophanias] teo- *B*   159 phantasiam] fant- *B*   162 aliquod] aliquot *B*   164 Aegyptius] egyptiis $C^{a.c.}$, egyptius $C^{p.c.}$ 168 Danihel] Daniel *C*   169 phantasiae] fant- *B*   169/170 Aegyptus] aegiptus *C*, τὸ Αἰγύπτιον *PG Forb.* (τὸν Αἴγυπτον *E. legisse uel intellexisse uidetur, uel* Aegyptius *legendum*)   172 phantasias] fant- *B*   duci] λογίζεσθαι *PG Forb.*, ἡγεῖσθαι *q Forb.*$^{u.l.}$ 174 phantasiis] fant- *B*   175/176 oportunitatum] *correxi (cfr* ἐπιτηδευμάτων *PG Forb.*), oportunatum *B C Capp.*   177 in somnis] *i.e.* in somniis (*cfr* τῶν ἐνυπνίων *PG Forb., quod uocabulum in hoc cap. E. per* somnium *interpretatur*)

15. Cognoscebam autem ego et aliam enigmatum somni causam, curans quendam captum frenesi his quibus oportebat curari qui, grauatus esca plus quam uirtus sibi suppetebat, clamabat, circumstantes querens quia erant qui interiora fimo implebant ac sibi superponebant; etiam corpus ei ad sudorem festinabat, causabat praesentes aquam habere paratam in eaque mergere iacentem; et non differebat clamans donec euentus talium quaerelarum causas interpretatus est. Cumulatim enim sudor multus influebat corpore, et uenter corruptus in interioribus grauitatem significauit. Quod igitur ex obscuro lauacro quod passioni congruit corporis quidem perturbati natura passa est, non etiam sensibiliter habuit, manifestauit autem euidenter tristitia, per ipsam ex infirmitate inaniam non ualens. Hoc iuxta quod consequens est, nisi ex infirmitate sed in somno naturaliter, dum intellectuale animae soporaretur, somnium fortassis ipso sic disposito factum est, aqua quidem sudoris influente, interiorum uero grauitatem per escam tristitia significante.

16. Hoc quoque in multis medicinam eruditorum uidetur, praeter passionum differentias etiam somniorum uisiones laborantibus fieri: alias quidem irascentium, alias autem membranulas cerebri uitiatorum, et eorum qui in febribus sunt iterum alias, et eorum qui felle et eorum qui in flegmate uitiantur non easdem, etiam publicorum et priuatorum iterum alias. Ex quibus est scire quia nutritiua et auctiua animae uirtus habet quid etiam intellectualis conspersum sibi per concretionem quia, qualicumque affectu corpori utens, quoddam iuxta dominantem passionem phantasiis coaptatum conformat.

17. Adhuc autem etiam ad morum constitutiones in multis somnia formantur: alia fortis, alia timidi phantasmata, aliae incontinentis uisiones, aliae temperati, in aliis largus et in aliis imaginatur auarus. Nullo modo intelligentia, sed altero in ani-

---

181/182 curans quendam – oportebat curari] θεραπεύων τινὰ τῶν ἐπιτηδείων ἑαλωκότα φρενίτιδι *PG Forb.*   181 frenesi] *cfr* φρενίτιδι *PG Forb.*   183 querens] quęrens *B*   184/185 causabat] ἠτιᾶτο *PG Forb.*   189/190 corporis quidem perturbati] τοῦ σώματος, τοῦ μὲν ὀχλοῦντος (ἐνοχλοῦντος *q Forb.*[u.l.]) *PG Forb. q*   190 natura] -re *C*[a.c.] non etiam sensibiliter] οὐκ ἀναισθήτως *PG*   195 sudoris influente] *om. C sed hic iterum fortassis ipso* (*l. 194*) *scr. C*   199/200 membranulas cerebri] τὰς μήνιγγας *PG*   203 animae uirtus] δύναμις τῆς ψυχῆς *PG Forb.*, τῆς ψυχῆς δύναμις *q Forb.*[u.l.]   206 phantasiis] fant- *B*   208 phantasmata] fant- *B*   209 temperati] temperanti *C*, τοῦ σώφρονος *PG Forb.*   210 intelligentia] intelle- *B*   altero] ἀλογωτέρας *PG Forb.* (ἀλλοιοτέρας *E. legisse uel intellexisse uidetur*)

ma affectu, has phantasias reformante, qui eorum quibus assuetus est per meditationem extra somnium imagines, etiam in somniis figurat.

⟨Capvt⟩ XV [XIV]
Quia non in parte corporis animus;
in quo etiam discretio corporalium et animae motuum

1. Sed multum ab his quae proposita sunt declinauimus. Nam nobis sermo erat propositus ostendere non in parte corporis animum detineri, sed totum aequaliter attingere, consequenter naturae subiectae partis motum operans. Est autem ubi etiam naturales affectus animus subsequitur, ueluti minister factus. Nam saepe praecipit corporis natura, et contristati sensum et laetantis concupiscentiam animo imponit, ita ut ipsa quidem prima praestet principia, uel ciborum appetitum, uel cuiusdam omnino eorum quae secundum delectationem sunt desiderium ingerens. Animus uero tales impetus accipiens suis cogitationibus occasiones ad id quod desideratur cum corpore exquirit: hoc autem non in omnibus est, sed solummodo in his qui plus captiui disponuntur, qui, rationem seruire facientes desideriis naturae per auxilium mentis libidini, quae per sensus est, seruiliter blandiuntur. In perfectioribus uero non sic efficitur: imperat enim animus rationi et non patitur quod utile est eligens, natura autem e uestigio sequitur praecipientem.

2. Quoniam uero tres secundum uitalem uirtutem differentias ratio inuenit, primam quidem nutritiuam sine sensu, secundam uero nutritiuam quidem et sensiuam, expertem uero rationabilis

---

XV, 4/35 nobis sermo – fit operatio] uide etiam Ioh. Scot., *Periphys.* 4 (p. 72-73, 2073-2106) (= col. 792AD) uerbatim; 2 (p. 59, 1353-1354) (= col. 569A); 4 (p. 19, 498-502) (= col. 754A), (p. 67, 1903-1904) (= col. 788A), (p. 118, p. 3542-3545) (= col. 824D) 7/10 naturales – imponit] uide Gvill. S. Theod., *Nat. corp.* 74 (p. 129, 896-899) quasi uerbatim 15/19 qui rationem – eligens] uide Gvill. S. Theod., *Nat. corp.* 73 (p. 129, 892-895) 20/24 tres secundum – penetrans] uide etiam Ioh. Scot., *Periphys.* 3 (p. 167-168, 4925-4930) (= col. 736AB)

---

211 phantasias] fant- *B*

XV, 1 *om. C. In PG et Forb. inc. cap. XIV* caput] *om. B* 4 sed] ed *pro prima littera spatium relinquens C* 9 laetantis] laetattis *B*[a.c.] 17 in perfectioribus] imperfe- *B* 18/19 imperat enim – eligens] καθηγεῖται γὰρ ὁ νοῦς, λόγῳ καὶ οὐχὶ πάθει τὸ λυσιτελὲς προαιρούμενος *PG* (πάσχει *pro* πάθει *E. legisse uel intellexisse uidetur*) 21 primam] prima *C*

operationis, item tertiam rationabilem et perfectam, perque omnem uirtutem penetrans, ut et in illis sit etsi intellectuali plus possideat; nemo ex his opinetur tres animas commixtas esse in humana concretione, in propriis circumscriptionibus consideratas, ita ut conformatione multarum animarum humanam ⟨naturam⟩ esse arbitretur. Sed uera quidem perfectaque anima una in natura est, intellectualis et immaterialis, quae per sensus materiali copulatur naturae; materiale autem omne in conuersione et mutabilitate positum est: siquidem animantem uirtutem participauerit, iuxta incrementum mouebitur; si uero uitali operatione deciderit, motum in corruptionem resoluet.

3. Neque igitur sensus absque materiali essentia, neque intellectualis uirtutis sine sensu fit operatio.

⟨Capvt⟩ XVI [XV]
Quia proprie anima rationalis et est et dicitur, ceterae uero aequiuoce nominantur; in quo etiam quod animi uirtus per corpus uenit consequenter singulas partes attingens

1. Si autem quaedam in creatura nutritoriam operationem habeant, seu iterum quaedam sensiua administrentur potentia, neque illa sensum, neque haec intellectum participat, ac per hoc, qui animarum multitudinem suspicatur, non secundum excelsam rationem animarum differentiam talis docebit: eo quod omne quod in his quae sunt intelligitur, siquidem perfecte sit hoc quod est, proprie nominantur quod dicitur; quod uero non per omnia est illud quod nominatur, uanam appellationem habet: ut puta, si

---

XVI, 5/53 si autem – titubat] cfr Greg. Nyss., *Anim. et res.* (p. 26-27). Vide etiam Ioh. Scot., *Periphys.* 4 (p. 67, 1903-1904) (= col. 788A)   5/34 si autem – habetur] uide Gvill. S. Theod., *Nat. corp.* 61 (p. 124-125, 738-751) ad sensum   5/7 si autem – participat] uide etiam Ioh. Scot., *Periphys.* 3 (p. 169, 4964-4967) (= col. 737A) uerbatim

23 tertiam] *correxi*, terciam *B C*   23/24 perque omnem uirtutem penetrans] *sic et R* (Periphys. 4), in* omnemque uirtutem penetrantem *corr. R* (Periphys. 3 [p. 168, 4930 = col. 736B]) (cfr* δι' ἁπάσης [διὰ πάσης *Forb.*] διήκουσαν τῆς δυνάμεως *PG Forb.*)   26 humana] huma *C*   27 conformatione] συγκρότημά τι *PG Forb.*, συγκροτήματι *q*   27/28 humanam naturam esse] naturam *suppleui (cfr* τὴν ἀνθρωπίνην φύσιν *PG Forb. q sed* φύσιν] *om. q*), humanam esse *Periphys.*

XVI, 1 *om. C. In PG et Forb. inc. cap. XV*   caput] *om. B*   2 ceterae] -e *B C*   5 si] i *pro prima littera spatium relinquens C*   6 administrentur] administrantur *R* (Periphys.)*   8 excelsam] διαιροῦντα *PG Forb.* (διαίροντα *E. legisse uel intellexisse uidetur*)   10 hoc quod est] *correxi (cfr* εἰ μὲν τελείως εἴη ὅπερ ἐστὶ *PG Forb.*), hoc est quod *B C Capp.*

quis uerum ostenderit panem, dicimus talem proprie subiecto nomen dicere. Si uero quis machinatum de lapide pro eo qui naturaliter est ostenderit, cui figura quidem eadem et magnitudo aequalis, coloris quoque similitudo, ita ut in pluribus idem esse principali exemplo uideatur, deficit autem ab eo quod et cibus esse non ualeat, propterea non propriam, sed in abusione nominationem panis adeptum fuisse lapidem dicimus, et omnia eadem ratione quae non per totum sunt quae dicuntur, sed abusione uocationem habent.

2. Sic igitur anima est dum intellectuali et rationali perfectionem habet, omne quod non ita est aequiuocum quidem animae esse potest, non tamen uere anima, sed quaedam operatio uitalis uocatione animae coutens. Ac per hoc irrationabilium naturam, ut non longe a uita positam, similiter dedit usui hominis qui per singula legem distribuit, ut pro herba participantibus esset: *Omnes* – enim inquit – *carnes comedite, sicut herbam faeni*. Paruum namque aliquid superabundare uidetur in sensuali operatione, ab eo quod per eandem et nutritur et augetur. Discant amatores carnis non ualde uisibilibus secundum sensum alligare intelligentiam, sed in animarum obseruationibus uacare. Vera quippe anima in talibus consideratur, sensus uero etiam in irrationabilibus aequaliter habetur.

3. Sed ad aliud consequentia sermonis adducta est. Non enim hoc contemplationi propositum est, quid praehonorabilius quantum in homine est intelligitur, utrum operatio quae est iuxta animum an materiale substantiae; sed quia non in parte quadam eorum quae in nobis sunt animus comprehenditur, sed aequaliter

---

XVI, 27/28 Gen. 9, 3

22/25 anima – animae coutens] uide etiam Ioh. Scot., *Periphys.* 3 (p. 169, 4967-4970) (= col. 737A) uerbatim   30/34 discant amatores – habetur] uide etiam Ioh. Scot., *Periphys.* 3 (p. 172, 235-239, nota ⟨38⟩ = p. 682, 8878-8886 / 8986-8993) (= col. 739C) uerbatim   38/53 non in parte – titubat] uide etiam Ioh. Scot., *Periphys.* 4 (p. 73-74, 2108-2125) (= col. 792D-793A) uerbatim

17 cibus] cybus C   21 uocationem] uaca- *sed corr. s.l.* C   25 coutens] συγκεκριμένη PG Forb., συγκεχρημένη q Forb.$^{u.l.}$; utens R* (*Periphys.*)   28 carnes comedite] *tr.* B, τὰ κρέα φάγεσθε PG Forb.   faeni] foeni C   29 superabundare] superhab- C   30 per eandem] δίχα ταύτης PG Forb. (διὰ ταύτης E. *legisse uel intellexisse uidetur*)   30 et nutritur] enutritur B   discant] παιδευοῦσα τὸ q, παιδευσάτω PG Forb.   31/32 intelligentiam] intelle- B   32 obseruationibus] -ebus B   uacare] care *sed corr. s.l.* C   33 in talibus] in hominibus i^1 (*Periphys.*)   36 praehonorabilius] perręhono- B   38/39 non in parte quadam ... comprehenditur] in parte quadam ... non comprehenditur R* (*Periphys.*)

40 in omnibus et per omnia est, neque extrinsecus comprehendens, neque intrinsecus comprehensus: haec enim in cadis, seu aliis quibusdam corporibus sibi inuicem impositis proprie dicuntur. Ipsa autem intellectualis ad corporale societas ineffabilem et inintelligibilem habet contactum, neque intus existens (non enim in cor-
45 pore incorporale tenetur) neque extra comprehendens (non enim circumprehenditur incorporale), sed secundum quendam modum superrationabilem et ⟨in⟩intelligibilem appropinquat animus naturae et coaptatus in ipsa et circa ipsam consideratur, neque intus positus, neque circumplexus; sed quomodo non est dicen-
50 dum neque intelligendum, praeter hoc quod iuxta proprium ordinem ipsius permeabilis naturae etiam animus efficax fit; si autem aliquod delictum circa ipsam contigerit, secundum illud motus intelligentiae titubat.

C 133ᵛ
177C

Capp. 232

⟨CAPVT⟩ XVII [XVI]
Theoria diuini uerbi dicentis *faciamus hominem ad imaginem nostram*; in quo exquiritur quae sit imaginis ratio; et si assimulatur beato et impassibili passibile et mortale; et
5 quomodo in imagine masculus et femina, dum in principali exemplo talia non existant

177D

1. Sed recipiamus iterum diuinam uocem: *Faciamus hominem ad imaginem et similitudinem nostram.* Quomodo parua et indigna

---

XVII, 2/3 Gen. 1, 26   7/8 Gen. 1, 26

42/51 ipsa autem – efficax fit] uide GVILL. S. THEOD., *Nat. corp.* 64-65 (p. 126, 784-795) quasi uerbatim

XVII, 7/191 recipiamus – adiecta est] uide etiam IOH. SCOT., *Periphys.* 4 (p. 74-79, 2141-2332) (= col. 793C-797C) uerbatim   7/137 recipiamus – transmutati] uide etiam IOH. SCOT., *Periphys.* 2 (p. 11, 193-199) (= col. 531AB), (p. 19, 393-396) (= col. 538A), (p. 81, 1900-1902) (= col. 585A)   8/26 quomodo parua – factus est] uide etiam IOH. SCOT., *Comm. Ioh.* 3, 6 (p. 89, 15-20)   8/23 quomodo parua – praetereuntibus] cfr BAS., *Struct. hom.* 2, 14 (p. 266-268); GREG. NAZ., *Or.* 38, 11 (p. 124)

43/44 inintelligibilem] intelligibilem *B*, ἀνεπινόητον *PG Forb.*   46 circumprehenditur] circumprenditur *B*, circum prenditur *Capp.*   46/47 quendam modum] quemadmodum *C*   47 superrationabilem] ἀμήχανον *PG Forb.*   inintelligibilem] correxi ex Periphys. (cfr ἀκατανόητον *PG Forb.*), intelligibilem *B C Capp.*   50 intelligendum] intelle- *B*   53 intelligentiae] intelle- *B*

XVII, 1 *om. C. In PG et Forb. inc. cap. XVI* caput] *om. B*   2/3 ad imaginem nostram] κατ' εἰκόνα καὶ ὁμοίωσιν ἡμετέραν *PG Forb.*ᵘ·ˡ·, κατ' εἰκόνα ἡμετέραν καὶ ὁμοίωσιν *Forb.*, κατ' εἰκόνα ἡμετέραν *q Forb.*ᵘ·ˡ·   7 sed] *ed pro prima littera spatium relinquens C*

DE IMAGINE, XVII

magnanimitate hominis ex his quae extra sunt quidam imaginauerunt, comparatione ad hunc mundum, quasi in ipso existeret, hominem magnificantes! Dicunt enim hominem paruum mundum esse, ex isdem quibus uniuersum elementis consistens. Nam qui ornamento nominis talem laudem humanae donant naturae, obliti sunt semet ipsos in proprietatibus quae circa culicem et murem sunt uenerabilem hominem facientes: etenim et in illis ex his quatuor concretio est, eo quod omnino in unoquoque existentium aut ex pluribus aut minoribus quaedam portio circa animatum consideratur, eorum sine quibus consistendi aliquid ex his quae sensum participant naturam non habet. Quid igitur post mundi charactera et similitudinem arbitrandum est esse hominem, caelo praetereunte, terra mutata, omnibusque quae in his comprehenduntur cum transitu comprehendentis praetereuntibus?

2. Sed in quo iuxta ecclesiasticam rationem humana magnitudo est? Non in ipsa ad creatum mundum similitudine, sed in ipso, quod secundum imaginem naturae creatoris factus est.

3. Quae igitur est imaginis ratio? – merito dices. Quomodo assimulatur incorporeo corporale, quomodo sempiterno temporale, immutabili quod per conuersionem mutabile est, impassibili et incorruptibili passibile et corruptibile, puro ab omni malitia quod semper ei cohabitat et ad eam conuertitur? Multa enim medietas est illius animi qui est principale exemplum et illius qui secundum imaginem factus est: imago siquidem si habuerit ad principale exemplar similitudinem, proprie illud etiam nominatur; si uero

---

11/12 dicunt – consistens] cfr PLAT., *Tim.* 30a-31a; ARIST., *Phys.* 8, 2, 252b26-7; METH., *Res.* 2, 10 (p. 349, 10)   27/31 quae igitur – conuertitur] cfr BAS., *Struct. hom.* 1, 6 (p. 178-180)

---

9 ex his quae extra sunt] τῶν ἔξωθέν τινες *PG Forb.*   10 quasi in ipso existeret] ὡς ᾤοντο *PG Forb.* (ὡς ἐν αὐτῷ ὂν *uel similiter E. legisse uel intellexisse uidetur*)   12 isdem] *correxi*, hisdem *B C Capp.*, eisdem *Periphys.* 4 (*p. 75, 2147 = 793C*)   13 ornamento] κόμπῳ *PG Forb.* (κόσμῳ *E. legisse uel intellexisse uidetur*)   16 quatuor] IIIIor *C*   19/20 quid igitur post – esse hominem] τί οὖν μέγα, κόσμου χαρακτῆρα καὶ ὁμοίωμα νομισθῆναι τὸν ἄνθρωπον *PG Forb.* (μετὰ *pro* μέγα *E. legisse uel intellexisse uidetur*)   24 in quo] in *sed corr. s.l. C*   28 incorporeo corporale] τῷ σώματι τὸ ἀσώματον *PG*, τῷ ἀσωμάτῳ τὸ ἐνσώματον *Forb.*^{u.l.}   30/31 puro ab omni malitia – ad eam conuertitur] τῷ ἀμιγεῖ πάσης κακίας τὸ πάντοτε συνοικοῦν ταύτῃ καὶ συντρεφόμενον *PG Forb.* (συντρεπόμενον *E. legisse uel intellexisse uidetur*)   33 siquidem si habuerit] εἰ μὲν ἔχει *PG Forb.*, εἰ μὲν ἔχοι *q Forb.*^{u.l.}   34 etiam nominatur] κατονομάζεται *PG Forb.*, καὶ ὀνομάζεται *q*

imitatio ab eo quod praeponitur distauerit, aliud aliquid et non imago illius illud est.

4. Quomodo ergo homo, mortale hoc et passibile citoque deficiens, immortalis ac purae semperque existentis naturae est imago? Sed ueram de hoc rationem sola nouerit aperte quae uere est ueritas. Nos uero, quantum capimus, speculationibus quibusdam et opinionibus quod uerum est inuestigantes, haec de questionibus susceptis dicimus. Neque diuinus mentitur sermo secundum imaginem Dei fieri hominem dicens, neque miseria humanae naturae usque ad infelicitatem beatitudini impassibilis uitae assimilatur. Necesse enim est e duobus alterum fateri, si quis comparat Deo quod nostrum est: aut passibile esse diuinum, aut impassibile humanum, ut ex aequalibus similitudinis ratio in utrisque comprehendatur. Si autem neque diuinum passibile neque nostrum extra est passionem, igitur quae alia relinquitur ratio per quam ueridicam dicimus diuinam uocem quae in imagine Dei factum fuisse hominem dicit?

5. Non ergo ipsa recipienda nobis est sancta Scriptura? Fiat igitur quaedam ex his quae scripta sunt ad id quod quaeritur a nobis manuductio. Postquam dixit *faciamus hominem*, et in talibus faciamus, infert hunc sermonem quia *fecit Deus hominem, secundum imaginem Dei fecit eum, masculum et feminam fecit eos*. Dictum est igitur iam et in his quae coram sunt quia ad solutionem hereticae impietatis talis sermo praenunciatus est ut, discentes quia fecit hominem unigenitus Deus secundum imaginem Dei, nulla ratione diuinitatem Filii et Patris segregemus, fideli diuina Scriptura Deum utrumque nominante, eum uidelicet qui fecit hominem, et eum ad cuius imaginem factus est.

6. Sed de hoc quidem sermo demittatur. Ad uero propositum conuertenda est quaestio: quomodo diuinum et beatum et miserum et simile illi hoc a sancta Scriptura nominatur?

---

54 Gen. 1, 26   55/56 Gen. 1, 27

52 non ergo] οὐκοῦν *PG Forb.*   53 nobis] ἡμῖν *PG Forb., non praeb. q*   54 faciamus hominem] ποιήσωμεν ἄνθρωπον κατ'εἰκόνα (κατ'εἰκόνα] *om. q Forb.*ᵘ·ˡ·) *PG Forb. q*   57 quae coram sunt] ἐν τοῖς ἔμπροσθεν *PG Forb.*   solutionem] καθαίρεσιν *PG Forb.*, κατάλυσιν *q*   hereticae] heretice *B C*   60 fideli] ἐπίσης *PG* (πιστῆς *E. legisse uel intellexisse uidetur*)   64/65 quomodo diuinum – scriptura nominatur] πῶς καὶ τὸ Θεῖον μακάριον καὶ ἐλεεινὸν τὸ ἀνθρώπινον, καὶ ὅμοιον ἐκείνῳ τοῦτο παρὰ τῆς γραφῆς ὀνομάζεται *PG Forb.* (τὸ ἀνθρώπινον *om. E. ut uid.*)

DE IMAGINE, XVII
113

7. Non itaque diligenter ordinanda sunt uerba? Inuenimus enim quia alterum quid quod secundum imaginem factum est, alterum quod nunc in infelicitate ostenditur. *Fecit Deus* – inquit – *hominem, ad imaginem Dei fecit eum*: finem habet ipsa ad imaginem facti creatio. Deinde ΕΠΑΝΑΛΗΜΨΙΝ (id est adiectionem) facit secundum constitutionem sermonis, et ait: *masculum et feminam fecit eos*. Omnibus enim arbitror notum esse quia hoc extra principale exemplum intelligitur. *In Christo* enim *Ihesu* – sicut ait Apostolus – *neque masculus neque femina est*; sed in haec hominem diuidi sermo dicit.

8. Nonne itaque duplex quaedam est nostrae naturae constitutio, una ad Deum assimulata, altera ad talem differentiam diuisa? Tale enim aliquid ex constructione eorum quae scripta sunt ratio insinuat, primum quidem dicens quia *fecit Deus hominem, secundum imaginem Dei fecit eum*, iterum uero his quae dicta sunt addens quia *masculum et feminam fecit eos*, quod alienum est ab his quae de Deo intelliguntur.

9. Ego enim arbitror magnam quandam excelsamque doctrinam ex his quae dicta sunt a sancta Scriptura tradi. Talis autem doctrina est. Duorum quorundam per extremitatem a se inuicem distantium medium est humanitas, diuinae uidelicet incorporalisque naturae et irrationabilis pecudalisque uitae. Licet enim utrumque praedictorum in humana comparatione considerari: portionem quidem Dei quod rationabile est atque intellectuale, quod iuxta masculum et feminam differentiam non admittit; irrationabilis uero corporalem constitutionem et duplicationem in masculum et feminam partitam. Vtrumque horum est omnino in omnibus humanam uitam participantibus; sed prius esse intel-

---

68/69 Gen. 1, 27   71/72 Gen. 1, 27   73/74 Gal. 3, 28   79/80 Gen. 1, 27
81 Gen. 1, 27

66/82 non itaque – intelliguntur] uide etiam Ioh. Scot., *Periphys.* 4 (p. 118, p. 3542-3545) (= col. 824D)   76/77 nonne – diuisa] uide etiam Ioh. Scot., *Periphys.* 4 (p. 131, 3973-3980) (= col. 833D)   84/87 talis autem – pecudalis uitae] uide etiam Ioh. Scot., *Hom. Ioh.* 19 (p. 35, 12-15)

---

66 non itaque] οὐκοῦν *PG Forb*.   ordinanda sunt] ἐξεταστέον *PG Forb*. (*quod E. quasi a* τάσσω *interpretatus est*)   69 imaginem] imanem B   70 id est adiectionem] glossa E. uidetur   70/71 facit] fecit *sed corr. s.l.* C   76 nonne itaque] οὐκοῦν *PG Forb*.   77 assimulata] assimula C   82 intelliguntur] intelle- B   88 in humana comparatione] ἐν τῷ ἀνθρωπίνῳ συγκρίματι *PG Forb*.   91 duplicationem] διάπλασιν *PG Forb*. (δίπλωσιν *E. legisse uel intellexisse uidetur*)   93/94 intellectuale] τὸ νοερὸν καθὼς (*om. q Forb.*ᵘ·ˡ·) *PG Forb. q*

lectuale ab eo qui humanam generationem in ordine percurrit
didicimus, supergenitiuam uero esse homini ad irrationabile so- C 134ᵛ
cietatem et cognationem. Primum namque ait quia *fecit Deus ad
imaginem Dei hominem*, ostendens ex his quae dicta sunt, sicut ait
Apostolus, quia in eo qui talis est, masculus et femina non est.
Deinde infert humanae naturae proprietates, quia *masculum et fe-* 181D
minam fecit eos.
10. Quid ergo ex hoc discemus? Et mihi nemo imputet longius
sermonem producenti proposito intellectu. Deus in sua natura 184A
omne quodcumque est per notitiam accipiendum bonum, illud
est; magis autem, omnis boni intellecti et comprehensi summitas
existens, non ob aliud aliquid humanam uitam creat quam quod
bene esse talem oportet. Ac per hoc ad conditionem nostrae naturae motus non nisi imperfectam bonitatis ostenderet uirtutem,
aliquod quidem dans ex his quae sibi insunt, in aliquo autem inuidens participationi. Ast perfecta bonitatis species in hoc est, et
adducere hominem ex non existente in generationem et non indi-
gentem bonorum perficere. Quoniam uero multus singulorum
bonorum catalogus est, neque facile est eum numero percipere,
propterea comprehensiua quadam uoce omnia comprehendens 184B
sermo significauit dicendo ad imaginem Dei hominem factum
fuisse. Tale enim est hoc ac si diceret quia omnis boni humanam
naturam participem fecit: si enim plenitudo bonorum Deus, illius
autem hoc (id est homo) imago, igitur in eo quod sit plenitudo
omnis boni ad principale exemplum imago habet similitudinem.

96/97 Gen. 1, 27   98 cfr Gal. 3, 28   99/100 Gen. 1, 27

102/118 Deus – similitudinem] cfr GREG. NYSS., *Or. catech.* (p. 16, 16 – p. 18, 7)
102/109 Deus – inuidens participationi] cfr PLAT., *Tim.* 29d-30a   105/111 non ob
aliud – perficere] uide etiam IOH. SCOT., *Periphys.* 5 (p. 128, 4148-4150) (= col. 952B)
113/125 propterea – potest] uide etiam IOH. SCOT., *Praed.* 4, 5 (p. 44, 24 – p. 46, 8)
(= col. 373AB)   114/125 dicendo – potest] uide GVILL. S. THEOD., *Nat. corp.* 86
(p. 133, 1043-1054) quasi uerbatim   115/125 tale enim – potest] uide etiam IOH. SCOT.,
Periphys. 5 (p. 149, 4837-4838) (= col. 966D)

---

95 supergenitiuam] ἐπιγεννηματικὴν PG Forb.   104 summitas] ἐπέκεινα PG Forb.
106 bene] ἀγαθὸς PG Forb., ἀγαθὸν Forb.ᵘˡ (ἀγαθῶς E. *legisse uel intellexisse uidetur*)
ac per hoc] τοιοῦτος δὲ ὢν καὶ διὰ τοῦτο PG Forb.   110 ex non existente] *correxi ex R**
(*Periphys. 4 [p. 77, 2247= col. 796A]*) (cfr ἐκ τοῦ μὴ ὄντος PG Forb.), et non existere B, et
non existe C   112 percipere] διαλαβεῖν PG Forb., perficere R* (*Periphys. 4 [p. 77, 2250 =
col. 796A]*)   116 participem] μετέχουσαν q, μέτοχον PG Forb.   117 id est homo] *non
praeb. PG Forb.*

11. Non igitur est in nobis omnis boni forma, omnis uirtus et sapientia et omne quodcumque est in melius intelligendum? In eo item quod sit omnium necessitate liberum nullique naturali (hoc est materiali) potentiae subiugatur, sed per se potentem ad id quod desiderat habet uoluntatem. Res enim est dominatu carens ac uoluntaria uirtus, quod autem cogitur uiolentiamque patitur uirtus esse non potest.

12. Itaque in omnibus imagine principalis exempli charactera pulchritudinis gestante, siquidem in aliquo differentiam habuerit, non iam erit omnino similitudo, sed hoc in illo per omnia ostendetur quod in uniuerso non distat. Igitur qualem ipsius Dei et Deo similis differentiam contemplabimur? In hoc, illud quidem non creatum, hoc autem per creationem subsistit. Talis autem proprietatis differentia aliarum iterum proprietatum consequentiam fecit: conceditur enim omnino increatam naturam inconuersibilem esse semperque similiter habere, creaturam uero non sine mutabilitate consistere. Nam ipse ex non existente in esse transitus motus quidam est et mutatio non existentis in esse secundum diuinam uoluntatem transmutati.

13. Ac sicut in aere charactera Caesaris imaginem Euangelium dicit, per quod discimus iuxta quidem figuram similitudinem esse formati ad Caesarem, in subiecto uero differentiam habere; sic etiam secundum praesentem rationem, imaginationum quae con-

---

138/139 cfr Marc. 12, 16

119/125 non igitur est – potest] cfr GREG. NYSS., *Or. catech.* (p. 19, 15 – p. 20, 5)   123/124 res enim – uoluntaria uirtus] = ἀδέσποτον γάρ τι χρῆμα ἡ ἀρετὴ καὶ ἑκούσιον (*PG* 44, col. 184b13-14), cfr PLAT., *R.* 10, 617e (ἀρετὴ δὲ ἀδέσποτον)   126/154 itaque in omnibus – natura] cfr ORIG., *Princ.* 4, 4, 8 (vol. 268, p. 422); 2, 9, 2 (vol. 253, p. 354)   126/144 itaque in omnibus – consideratur] cfr GREG. NYSS., *Anim. et res.* (p. 26, 12-16)   126/138 itaque in omnibus – transformati] uide etiam IOH. SCOT., *Periphys.* 1 (p. 41, 1188-1190) (= col. 470A); 2 (p. 100, 2399-2402) (= col. 598BC)   129/137 igitur qualem – transmutati] cfr GREG. NYSS., *Or. catech.* (p. 24, 1-6; 55, 4-21)   138/140 ac sicut in aere – differentiam habere] cfr METH., *Res.* 2, 24 (p. 240-241)

---

119 non igitur est] non est igitur *B*, οὐκοῦν ἐστιν *PG Forb.*   120 intelligendum] intelle- *B*   120/121 in eo item quod sit omnium] ἓν δὲ τῶν πάντων *PG Forb.*   121/122 hoc est materiali] *non praeb. PG Forb.*   126 charactera] car- *B*   128 hoc] ταὐτὸν *PG Forb.*   130/131 non creatum] ἄκτιστον *q*, ἀκτίστως *PG Forb.*   138/139 ac sicut – dicit] καὶ ὥσπερ τὸν ἐπὶ τοῦ χαλκοῦ χαρακτῆρα Καίσαρος εἰκόνα λέγει τὸ εὐαγγέλιον *PG Forb.*   138 charactera] *correxi ex R** (*Periphys.* 4 [p. 77, 2264 = col. 796B]), charactere *C*, caractere *B Capp.*   141 imaginationum quae] imaginationumque *C*, ἀντὶ χαρακτήρων τὰ ἐπιθεωρούμενα *PG Forb.*

siderantur in diuina natura in humana etiam cogitantes, in his in quibus similitudo est; in subiecto differentiam inuenimus quae in non creato et creato consideratur.

14. Quoniam igitur illud quidem semper similiter habet, hoc autem per creationem factum ex mutabilitate esse inchoauit et cognatim ad talem mutabilitatem habet conuersionem, propterea *qui nouit omnia ante generationem eorum*, sicut ait prophetia, consecutus – magis autem praeintelligens prognostica uirtute – ad quid destillaret per suam uirtutem suamque potentiam humanae uoluntatis motus, quoniam quod futurum erat uidit, supermachinatus est imagini secundum masculum et feminam differentiam, quae non iam ad diuinum principale exemplum aspicit sed, sicut dictum est, in mutabiliori possidet natura.

15. Causam uero talis supermachinationis soli quidem nouerint qui ueritatem *per se uident et ministri sunt uerbi*. Nos autem, quantum possibile est, ex quibusdam coniecturis atque consequentiis ueritatem silentes, quod in animum uenit non pronunciatiue exponemus, sed ueluti in gymnasia, si oportet, fidelibus audienda proponemus.

16. Quid ergo est quod de his cogitamus? Sermo qui dicit *fecit Deus hominem* infinita significatione omnem humanitatem ostendit; non enim nunc connominatur creaturae Adam, sicut in sequentibus historia dicit, sed nomen creato homini non aliud

---

148 Dan. 13, 42   156 Luc. 1, 2   161/162 Gen. 1, 27

159 gymnasia] Prisc., *Inst. gramm.* 6, 72 (vol. II, p. 256): "'hic exercitus' ἡ γυμνασία καὶ ὁ στρατός"; cfr Martin. Lavd., *Prisc.* (p. 135): "ΓΥΜΝΑϚΙΑ (γυμνασία), i. cura, exercitatio. ΚΑΙ ΟϚΤΡΑΤΩϚ (καὶ ὁ στρατός), i. exercitus". Vide etiam Ioh. Scot., *Periphys.* 4 (p. 78, 2296) (= col. 797A); *Gloss. Mart. Cap.* 152, 3 (p. 82, 10): "Γυμνόω exerceo, inde gymnasium exercitatio". Ioh. Scot., *Epist.* = *Epist. uar. III* 14 (p. 159, 3-4): "Elladicarum gymnasiarum"   161/191 quid ergo – constitutioni formationis adiecta est] uide etiam Ioh. Scot., *Periphys.* 5 (p. 88-89, 2821-2852) (= col. 922D-923C) uerbatim

---

149 praeintelligens] praeintelle- B   149/150 ad quid] *correxi ex R** (*Periphys. 4* [p. 78, 2289 = 796D]) (*cfr* πρὸς ὅ τι *PG Forb.*), aliquid B C Capp.   150 destillaret] ῥέπει PG Forb.   suam uirtutem suamque potentiam] τὸ αὐτοκρατές τε καὶ αὐτεξούσιον PG Forb.   151 erat] est R* (*Periphys. 4, p. 78, 2291 = col. 496D*)   154 in mutabiliori] *correxi ex Periphys.* 4 (*p. 78, 2294* = *col. 797A*), immutabiliori B C Capp., τῇ ἀλογωτέρᾳ PG Forb.   possidet] προσῳκείωται PG Forb. q, προσοικείωται Forb.^{u.l.}   157 consequentiis] εἰκόνων PG Forb. (εἱρμῶν *uel similiter E. legisse uel intellexisse uidetur*)   158 silentes] φαντασθέντες PG Forb., φράσαντες q, φθάσαντες Forb.^{u.l.}   159 in gymnasia si oportet] ἐν γυμνασίας εἴδει PG Forb. (εἰ δεῖ *E. legisse uel intellexisse uidetur*)   gymnasia] gimnasia C   163 connominatur] cogn- B, συνωνομάσθη PG Forb.   164 historia] istoria B

165 quoddam uniuersaliter est. Non igitur uniuersali naturae uocatione tale aliquid suspicari introducimur, quia in diuina praescientia et uirtute omnis humanitas in prima constitutione comprehensa est? Oportet enim nil Deo infinitum in his quae ab eo facta sunt aestimare, sed uniuscuiusque eorum quae sunt finis et mensura circumponderans factoris sapientia est.

17. Quemadmodum igitur aliquis homo corporis quantitate coartatur, et mensura sibi substantiae magnitudo est quae in superficie corporis perficitur, sic arbitror ueluti in uno corpore totam humanitatis plenitudinem prognostica uirtute a Deo omnium comprehensam fuisse: et hoc docet sermo qui dicit quia *fecit Deus hominem, secundum imaginem Dei fecit eum.* Non enim in parte naturae imago, neque in quodam eorum quae secundum ipsam considerantur gratia est, sed in totum genus aequaliter talis peruenit uirtus. Signum uero est: omnibus similiter animus collocatur, dum omnes intelligendi et consiliandi uirtutem habeant et alia omnia ex quibus diuina natura in eo quod secundum ipsam factum est imaginatur. Similiter habet et ipse in prima mundi constitutione ostensus homo et post uniuersitatis consumationem futurus: aequaliter in se ipsis diuinam ferunt imaginem.

18. Propterea unus homo nominatum est omne, quia in uirtute Dei nihil praeterit, nihil instat, sed et quod spectatur aequaliter praesenti comprehensiua uniuersitatis operatione continetur. Omnis itaque natura quae a primis usque nouissima peruenit, una quaedam uere existentis imago est. Ipsa uero in masculum et feminam generis differentia nouissime constitutioni formationis adiecta est, ob hanc causam, ut arbitror.

B 101ʳ
185C

Capp. 236

185D

---

176 Gen. 1, 27

185/191 propterea – arbitror] uide etiam Ioh. Scot., *Hom. Ioh.* 19 (p. 35, 21-22)

165 non igitur] οὐκοῦν *PG Forb.* 180 intelligendi] intelle- *B* uirtutem] -te *B* 182 habet] habent *R** (*Periphys. 4 [p. 79, 2323 = col. 797C]*) 183 post] κατά *PG*, μετά *q Forb.* 189 uere existentis] τοῦ ὄντος *PG Forb.* (τοῦ ὄντως ὄντος *E. legisse uel intellexisse uidetur*)

Capvt XVIII [XVII]

Quid oportet dicere aduersus eos qui deliberant si post peccatum propagatio, quomodo fierent anime si sine peccato homines qui erant ab initio perseuerarent

1. Magis autem priusquam propositum perscrutemur et melius iure illius quod a repugnantibus nobis profertur solutionem inquirere. Dicunt enim: ante peccatum neque parens narratur neque partus neque ad propagationem filiorum impetus; migrantibus uero ex paradiso post peccatum muliereque ultione partuum condemnata, sic uenisse Adam in nuptialem coniugis cognitionem, et tunc propagationis initium fuisse. Si ergo nuptiae in paradiso non essent neque parturiens neque parens, necessarium esse dicunt ex consequentia aestimari non in multitudine animas hominum futuras esse, si non ad mortale immortalitatis gratia caderet et nuptiae per superuenientes et pro oboedientibus reductos naturam conseruarent, ita ut quodammodo utile sit peccatum hominum uitae superueniens. Maneret enim in dualitate primo formatorum humanum genus, dum mortis timor ad successionem naturam non cogeret.

2. Sed in his iterum uera ratio est quae, dum adsit, constituenda est solummodo si clara sit, ut his qui iuxta Paulum paradisi secreta eruditi sunt. Nostra uero talis est: contradicentibus quondam Sadduceis resurrectionis sermoni illamque multinubam feminam, quae septem fratribus nupsit, in constitutionem sui dogmatis proferentibus, deinde cuius post resurrectionem erit interrogantibus, Dominus aduersus sermonem respondit non solum Sadduceos corripiens, sed etiam omnibus uitae post resurrectionem myste-

---

XVIII, 21/22 iuxta Paulum – sunt] cfr II Cor. 12, 4

XVIII, 5/78 magis autem – inclinationem] uide etiam Ioh. Scot., *Periphys.* 4 (p. 32, 840-842) (= col. 763A); 5 (p. 150, 4862-4864) (= col. 967B), (p. 167, 5439-5441) (= col. 979D)

XVIII, 1 *om. C. In PG et Forb. inc. cap. XVII* 5/6 magis autem priusquam – et melius iure] *capitalibus litteris scr.* (*sed* magis] agis, *pro prima littera spatium relinquens*) C 9 paradiso] -dyso B 15/16 et nuptiae – naturam conseruarent] καὶ ὁ γάμος διὰ τῶν ἐπιγινομένων συνετήρει τὴν φύσιν, ἀντὶ τῶν ὑπεξιόντων τοὺς ἐξ αὐτῶν ἀντεισάγων *PG Forb.* 15 oboedientibus] obęd- B 20/22 quae dum adsit – eruditi sunt] ὅστις ποτὲ ὢν τυγχάνει, μόνοις ἂν εἴη δῆλος τοῖς κατὰ Παῦλον τὰ τοῦ παραδείσου μυηθεῖσιν ἀπόρρητα *PG Forb.* 21 paradisi] -dysi B 23 Sadduceis] Sadu- C 26 Sadduceos] Sadu- C 27/28 mysterium] mist- C

rium manifestans. *In resurrectione* – enim inquit – *neque nubunt neque nubuntur, neque enim mori adhuc possunt: aequales enim angelis sunt, et filii sunt Dei filii resurrectionis qui sunt*. Resurrectionis autem gratia nihil aliud nobis promittit quam in antiquitatem cadentium restitutionem. Est enim reditus quidam in primam uitam ipsa spectanda gratia, expulsum paradiso iterum in ipsum reducens. Ipsa igitur restitutorum uita ad eam quae proprie angelorum habetur. Profecto ante ruinam angelus quidam erat: propterea etiam ipse ad antiquitatem uitae nostrae reditus angelis assimulatur. Attamen, sicut dictum est, nuptiis apud eos non existentibus, in myriadibus infinitis militiae angelorum sunt: sic in uisionibus Danihel narrauit. Non igitur per eundem hominem, si nulla conuersio et recessus ab angelica societate ex peccato nobis fieret, fortassis nos nuptiis ad multiplicationem alligaremur. Alius quidam est in natura angelorum multiplicationis modus, ineffabilis quidem et inintelligibilis humanis argumentationibus, uerumtamen quia omnino est, ipse etiam in his qui *paulo minus ab angelis minorati sunt* operaretur, in ipsam diffinitam factoris consilio mensuram humanitatem augens.

3. Si uero coartat quis, generationis animarum modum inquirens nisi alligaretur nuptiarum cooperationi homo, respondebimus et nos angelicae substantiae modum, quomodo in infinitis myriadibus illi et una essentia existunt et in multis numerantur. Hoc enim apte respondemus proponenti quomodo esset sine nuptiis homo, dicentes: sicut sunt angeli sine nuptiis; hominem

---

28/30 Matth. 22, 30; Luc. 20, 35-36   38/39 sic in uisionibus Danihel narrauit] cfr Dan. 7, 10   44/45 Ps. 8, 6; Hebr. 2, 7

30/78 resurrectionis autem – inclinationem] uide etiam IOH. SCOT., *Periphys.* 4 (p. 80-81, 2333-2384) (= col. 797D-799A) uerbatim   47/54 si uero coartat – restitutio] uide etiam IOH. SCOT., *Periphys.* 3 (p. 149, 197-199, nota ⟨34⟩) (col. 723C)

---

28 inquit] inquid $C^{a.c.}$ 29 nubuntur] nubentur C, γαμίσκονται PG Forb.   33 paradiso] -dyso B   35 ante ruinam] sic et Dionysius Exiguus, πρὸ τῆς καταπτώσεως q Forb.$^{u.l.}$, πρὸ τῆς παραβάσεως PG Forb.   angelus] βίος ἀγγελικός PG Forb., ἄγγελός τις q   36 etiam] *om. Periphys.*   39 non igitur] οὐκοῦν PG Forb.   per eundem hominem] κατὰ τὸν αὐτὸν τρόπον PG Forb. (κατὰ τὸν αὐτὸν ἄνθρωπον E. legisse uel intellexisse uidetur)   41 alligaremur] ἐδεήθημεν PG Forb. (ἐδεήθημεν E. legisse uel intellexisse uidetur)   41/42 alius quidam] ἀλλ' ὅστις PG (ἄλλος τις E. legisse uel intellexisse uidetur) (cfr P. LEVINE, 'Two Early Latin Versions', p. *491*)   44 in his] *om.* C   45 minorati sunt] ἠλαττωμένων ἀνθρώπων (*om.* q Forb.$^{u.l.}$) PG Forb. q   47 coartat] στενοχωρεῖται PG Forb., στενοχωρεῖ Forb.$^{u.l.}$ 48 alligaretur] προσεδεήθη PG Forb. (προσεδέθη E. legisse uel intellexisse uidetur)   50 myriadibus] mir- B

enim similiter illis fuisse ante praeuaricationem ostendit ipsa in illum iterum restitutio.

4. His igitur a nobis sic iam bene discretis, in priorem rationem redeundum est: quomodo, post constitutionem imaginis, ipsam secundum masculum et feminam differentiam supermachinatus est Deus formationi. Ad hoc enim dico utilem esse prius perfectam a nobis theoriam. Qui enim omnia adduxit in esse totumque in sua uoluntate hominem ad diuinam imaginem formauit, non paulatim adiectionibus futurorum moras fecit, sciendo in suam plenitudinem animarum numerum perficiendum; sed cumulatim in ipsa plenitudine omnem humanam naturam per prognosticam operationem intellexit et in excelsitudine et in coaequali angelis quiete honorificauit. Quoniam uero praeuidit contemplatoria uirtute non recte euntem ad bonum uoluntatem, atque ideo ex angelica uita recedentem, ne animarum humanarum multitudo minueretur cadens ex illo modo per quem angeli ad multitudinem aucti sunt, propterea conuenientem in peccatum anullatis incrementi excogitationem in natura conformauit, pro angelica magnificentia pecudalem et irrationalem ex se inuicem successionis modum humanitati inserens.

5. Hinc mihi uidetur etiam magnus Dauid, dolens hominis miseriam, talibus uerbis planxisse naturam, quia *homo, in honore dum esset, non intellexit,* honorem dicens aequalem angelis reuerentiam; propterea *comparatus est iumentis insipientibus.* Vere enim pecorinus factus est, qui animalem hanc generationem accepit propter ad materiale inclinationem.

74/76 Ps. 48, 13. 21

59/65 qui enim – honorificauit] uide etiam Ioh. Scot., *Periphys.* 4 (p. 100, 2969-2975) (= col. 812A) uerbatim   60/64 non paulatim – intellexit] uide etiam Ioh. Scot., *Praed.* 18, 8 (p. 198, 15-18) (= col. 434D)   65/72 quoniam uero – inserens] uide etiam Ioh. Scot., *Periphys.* 4 (p. 100-101, 2982-2989) (= col. 812B) uerbatim   65/78 quoniam uero – inclinationem] uide etiam Ioh. Scot., *Periphys.* 2 (p. 21-22, 434-437) (= col. 539D)

54 iterum] *om.* C   65 quoniam uero] ἐπειδὴ *PG Forb.* (ἐπεὶ δὲ *E. legisse uel intellexisse uidetur*)   66 non recte – uoluntatem] *sic et Periphys.* 4 (*p. 81, 2372 = col. 798C; et p. 100, 2983 = col. 812B*) (*cfr* μὴ εὐθυπορούσαν πρὸς τὸ καλὸν τὴν προαίρεσιν *PG Forb.*), non recte ad bonam uoluntatem euntem C   74 planxisse] plancxisse C   76 comparatus est iumentis insipientibus] παρασυνεβλήθη τοῖς κτήνεσι τοῖς ἀνοήτοις καὶ ὡμοιώθη αὐτοῖς *PG Forb.*   77 animalem] *sic et Dionysius Exiguus,* ῥοώδη *PG Forb.,* ζῳώδη *Forb.*[u.l.]

Capvt XVIIII [XVIII]
Quia irrationabiles in nobis passiones ex cognatione ad irrationabilem naturam occasiones habent

1. Arbitror enim ex hoc principio etiam singulas passiones ueluti ex fonte quodam inundationem in humana uita conditas. Confirmat autem rationem ipsa passionum cognatio, aequaliter et in nobis et in irrationabilibus manifestata. Non enim iustum est in humana natura, ad diuinam speciem formata, passibilis affectus perhibere principia; sed quoniam praecessit in hunc mundum irrationabilium uita, habebat autem aliquid propter causam praedictam ex uita quae ibi est etiam homo (quod secundum generationem dico), propterea etiam reliqua quae ibi considerantur naturae comparticipauit. Non enim secundum furorem est ipsa hominis ad Deum similitudo, neque ex uoluptate ipsa supereminens natura characterizatur; formido quoque et ferocitas, et ad id quod plus est desiderium, et ad id quod minus est odium, et omnia huiusmodi longe diuinae pulchritudinis charactere sunt.

2. Haec itaque ex irrationabili parte humana natura ad se ipsam attraxit. In his enim irrationabilis uita ad conseruationem suam munita est; haec, ad humanam uitam transducta, passiones factae sunt. Furore enim conseruantur carne uescentia, uoluptatis uero amor foecunda animalia: saluat infirmum formido, expugnabilem ex fortioribus timor, corpulentum edacitas et reiectio; a nullo itaque eorum quae secundum libidinem sunt tristitiae materies in

---

XIX, 4/9 arbitror – perhibere principia] uide etiam Ioh. Scot., *Periphys.* 5 (uersio II iuxta codd. *HM*, p. 23, 641-648) (= col. 875A) uerbatim   13/21 non enim – factae sunt] uide etiam Ioh. Scot., *Periphys.* 5 (uersio II iuxta codd. *HM*, p. 23, 648-656) (= col. 875AB) uerbatim; Gvill. S. Theod., *Nat. corp.* 74 (p. 129, 901-908) quasi uerbatim   21/25 furore enim – in irrationabilibus est] uide Gvill. S. Theod., *Nat. corp.* 75 (p. 129-130, 914-918) quasi uerbatim

XIX, 1 *In PG et Forb. inc. cap. XVIII*   4 arbitror] rbitror *pro prima littera spatium relinquens* C   6 confirmat autem rationem] τεκμήριον δὲ τῶν λόγων *PG Forb.*, τεκμηριοῖ δὲ τὸν λόγον *q Forb.*$^{u.l.}$, hanc autem rationem confirmat ipsa *Periphys.*   7 irrationabilibus] inraci- C   9 principia] πρώτας ἀρχάς *PG Forb.*, ἀρχάς *q*   11 ex uita quae ibi est] τῆς ἐκεῖθεν φύσεως *PG*   12 propterea etiam reliqua – comparticipauit] συμμετέσχε διὰ τούτου καὶ τῶν λοιπῶν τῶν ἐν ἐκείνῃ (ἐν ἐκείνῃ ἐκεῖθεν *q*) θεωρουμένων τῇ φύσει *PG Forb. q*   14 uoluptate] *correxi (cfr* ἡδονῆς *PG Forb.)*, uoluntate B C Capp. *Periphys.*   15 characterizatur] formatur *Periphys.*   16 odium] hod- C   17 pulchritudinis] pulcritudini C charactere] car- B   20 ad humanam] ad diuinam C$^{a.c.}$ 22 foecunda] fęcunda B   24 materies] matheries C

irrationabilibus est. Haec omnia et his similia ex pecudali generatione in constitutionem hominis cointrauerunt.

3. Et mihi concedatur iuxta aliquam fictilem miraculorum facturam humanam imaginem sermone describere, sicut enim noscendum in figmentis. Nam sculptas formas machinantur et, ad stuporem consistentium, in uno capite duarum personarum formas perfigurant qui talibus student; sic mihi uidetur homo duplicem ad contraria ferre similitudinem: in deiformitate quidem intelligentiae ad diuinam pulchritudinem formatus; ingenitis uero per passionem affectionibus ad pecudalem fert societatem. Saepe autem ratio perimitur ab ipsa inclinatione et affectione ad irrationabile, quod id quod melius est in deteriori abscondit. Nam cum quis ad haec intellectualem operationem adtraxerit ministramque fieri passionum cogitationem coegerit, conuersio quaedam fit boni characteris ad irrationabilem imaginem, omni intellectuali operatione ad hoc transfigurata, dumque, ueluti agricola, cogitatio passionum principia et deliberationum cooperationem apud se ipsam in multitudinem coauget, accommodata passioni, turbulentissimam ambiguamque in consequentium generationem operatur.

4. Sic uoluptatis amor principium quidem habuit ex ipsa similitudine ad ipsum irrationabile, sed in humanis delictis coaugmentata est, tantas differentias per libidinem peccantium gignens, quantas in irrationabilibus non est inuenire. Sic ipsa in furorem insurrectio cognata quidem est irrationabilium affectui, augetur uero cogitationum auxilio; inde enim insania, inuidia mendacium, insidiae, ypocrisis. Haec omnia malignae operationis animi sunt. Nam si denudata fuerit passio ex cogitationum auxilio, cito deficiens quidam et imbecillis furor relinquitur, bullae instar, simul factus et continuo perditus. Sic suium edacitas auaritiam in-

---

25/26 haec omnia – cointrauerunt] uide GVILL. S. THEOD., *Nat. corp.* 77 (p. 130, 932-933) uerbatim   35/67 saepe autem ratio – conformat] cfr GREG. NYSS., *Anim. et res.* (p. 42-43)   40/54 dumque ueluti agricola – perditus] uide GVILL. S. THEOD., *Nat. corp.* 76-77 (p. 130, 919-932) quasi uerbatim   54/57 sic suium – facta est] uide etiam IOH. SCOT., *Periphys.* 5 (p. 81-82, 2579-2620) (= col. 917A-918A)

25 pecudali] pecudiali $C^{a.c.}$ 28 sermone] -nem $B^{a.c.}$ $C^{a.c.\ ut\ uid.}$ 29 sculptas] scultas $B^{a.c.}$ C 33 intelligentiae] intelle- B pulchritudinem] pulcri- C 39 characteris] car- B 50/51 mendacium] -tium B 51/52 haec omnia – animi sunt] ταῦτα πάντα τῆς πονηρᾶς τοῦ νοῦ γεωργίας (ἐνεργείας Forb.$^{u.l.}$) ἐστίν PG Forb.   54 suium] *om. spatium relinquens* C

55 troduxit, equi quoque elatio facta est superbiae principium; per singula omnia pecudalis irrationabilitatis occasione per malignum animi usum malitia facta est.

5. Similiter igitur et hoc iterum, si cogitatio talium motuum potentiam in contrarium receperit, in uirtutis speciem unumquod-
60 que talium transmutabitur. Facit enim furor fortitudinem, formido tutelam, timor credulitatem, odium ex malitia reditum, amatoria uirtus ueri boni concupiscentiam, elatio morum superat *C* 137ʳ 193C passiones, ac liberam a malo custodit sapientiam. Hanc autem elationis speciem magnus Apostolus laudat, assidue imperans *quae*
65 *sursum sunt sapere*. Ac sic est inueniendum quia semper altitudo intelligentiae per se ipsam mota confinitatem, pulchritudini quae est secundum diuinam imaginem conformat.

6. Sed quoniam grauitas quaedam est ac deorsum ferens ipsa peccati inflexio, plus alterum fit: magis enim grauitati irrationabi-
70 lis naturae principale animae condeflectitur quam altitudini mentis graue quoque ac terrenum non exaltatur ac per hoc saepe diuinum donum ignorari facit ipsa quae circa nos est miseria, ueluti foedum uultum pulchritudini, quae est secundum imaginem passiones carnis superfingens.

75 7. Non ergo cogniti quomodo sunt qui ad talia aspiciunt, de- 193D
hinc diuinam formam in se ipsis esse non facile constituunt; sed per eos qui uitam corrigunt licet diuinam in hominibus imaginem aspicere. Nam, si passibilis quis atque carnalis est, facit hominem sic diuina forma ornatum non credi; si excelsus omnino uirtute,
80 firmabit suam ad id quod melius est in hominibus susceptionem.

8. Vtputa (melius enim exemplo rationem ostendere): defecit malitiae contagione naturae forma, quidam eorum qui in malitia notantur, Iechonias fortassis seu si quis alter in malo habet memo-

---

XIX, 64/65 Col. 3, 1   83 cfr Matth. 1, 11; Ier. 36, 23-31

61 reditum] ἀποστροφήν *PG Forb.*, ἀποτροπήν *q*   64 assidue] συνεχῶς *PG Forb.*, *non praeb. q*   65 sunt] *suppl. sup. l. C*   65/66 semper altitudo – confinitatem] πᾶν τὸ τοιοῦτον κίνημα τῷ ὑψηλῷ τῆς διανοίας συνεπαιρόμενον *PG Forb.* (*fort. E.* πάντως *pro* πᾶν τὸ *et* συμπεραινόμενον *pro* συνεπαιρόμενον *legit uel intellexit; fort. et* δι᾽ ἑαυτοῦ *uel similiter pro* τοιοῦτον *legit uel intellexit*)   66 intelligentiae] intelle- *B*   pulchritudini] pulcri- *C*   72 ipsa quae] ipsaque *C*   73 foedum] fędum *B*   pulchritudini] pulcri- *C*   75 non ergo] οὐκοῦν *PG Forb.*   79/80 si excelsus – firmabit] ὁ ὑψηλὸς πάντως τὴν ἀρετὴν καὶ καθαρεύων ἐκ μολυσμάτων βεβαιώσει κτλ. *PG Forb.* (καθαρεύων ἐκ μολυσμάτων *om. E. ut uid.*)

riam; sed in Moysi et his qui secundum illum sunt pura custodita
est imaginis forma. In quibus itaque non est obscurata pulchritudo, in eis euidens eorum quae dicta sunt fides est, quia homo
Dei imitatio factus est.

9. Sed forsitan erubescit quis, eo quod per cibum nobis iuxta
similitudinem irrationabilium uita constituta est, ac per hoc indignum ducit hominem secundum imaginem Dei formari putare.
Sed speret ab hac administratione immunitatem naturae quando-
que dandum fore in futura uita: *non enim est* – ut ait Apostolus –
regnum Dei esca et potus; neque *in pane solo uiuet homo* Dominus
respondit, *sed in omni uerbo procedenti ex ore Dei*. Sed et resurrectione nobis in angelicam uitam subostensa, ciboque apud angelos
non existente, sufficiens fides hominem ab hac administratione
mutandum fore, secundum similitudinem angelorum futurus.

Capvt XX [XIX]
Aduersus eos qui dicunt iterum in cibo et potu sperandorum
bonorum usum futurum esse, eo quod ex principio in paradiso
scriptum est per haec hominem uixisse

1. Recteque quis non in eandem iterum uitae speciem reuersurum
esse hominem dicit; et si prius in comedendo nobis species uitae
erat, posthac tali administratione liberabimur. Sed et ego, sanctae
auscultans Scripturae, non solum corporalem cognosco cibum neque solam carnis laetitiam, sed etiam alteram quandam escam,
analogiam quandam ad corporis alimenta habentem, cuius

92/93 Rom. 14, 17   93/94 Matth. 4, 4   94/95 et resurrectione – subostensa] cfr
Matth. 22, 30; Luc. 20, 36

84/85 sed in Moysi – imaginis forma] cfr Greg. Nyss., *Anim. et res.* (p. 36, 9-17); *Vit. Moys.* 2, 319 (p. 143, 19)

XX, 5/51 recteque – superponeretur] uide etiam Ioh. Scot., *Periphys.* 4 (p. 110-111, 3291-3339) (= col. 819A-820A) uerbatim

---

84 Moysi] Mosi *B*   85/86 pulchritudo] pulcri- *C*   88 forsitan] forsan *B*
93 uiuet] uiuit *C*, ζήσεσθαι *PG Forb.*

XX, 1 *om. C. In PG et Forb. inc. cap. XIX*   2 cibo] cybo *C*   2/3 sperandorum – futurum esse] εἶναι τῶν ἐλπιζομένων ἀγαθῶν τὴν ἀπόλαυσιν *PG Forb.*, τῶν ἐλπιζομένων ἀγαθῶν τὴν ἀπόλαυσιν εἶναι *q Forb.*[u.l.] (sic et Dionysius Exiguus)   3 paradiso] -dyso *B*
5 recteque] ecteque *pro prima littera spatium relinquens C*   quis] quisque *Periphys.*
7 sed et ego] sed ego *Periphys.*   8, 12 cibum[1, 2]] cybum *C*

DE IMAGINE, XX   125

perfructio in animam solam pertransit. *Comedite ex meis panibus sapientia* esurientibus iubet, et eos qui talem cibum esuriunt Dominus beatificat et *si quis sitit* – inquit – *ueniat ad me et bibat*. Magnus item Esaias *bibite laetitiam* ualentibus magnificentiam
15 eius laudare praecipit. Est autem quaedam comminatio prophe- 196D
tica aduersus eos qui ultione digni sunt ueluti fame torquendos; fames uero non panis est quaedam egestas et aquae, sed uerbi defectus: *non enim famem panis* inquit *uel sitim aquae, sed famem audiendi uerbum Domini*.
20 2. Numquid ergo plantationis Dei in ΕΔΕΜ (deliciae autem ipsa ΕΔΕΜ interpretatur), dignum quendam conuenit fructum intelligere, ac per hoc comedisse hominem non dubitare; et non omnino transitoriam fluxilemque hanc escam in paradisi conuersatione intelligere hoc: *ab omni ligno quod est in paradiso cibum*
25 *comedere.*
3. Quis dabit sanando sic esurienti lignum illud quod est in paradiso, quod omne bonum comprehendit, cui nomen est "omne", cuius participationem homini lex donat? Generali enim et supe- 197A
reminenti ratione omnis bonorum forma apud se ipsam connatu-
30 raliter habet, totum et unum est. Quis me commixto et utroque ligni gusto segregabit? Omnino enim non est perspicat(i)oribus obscurum quid "omne" illud cuius fructus uita, et iterum quid hoc mixtum. Nam qui ab omni usum copiose proponit, ratione quadam omnino et prouidentia promiscuorum participatione ho-
35 minem prohibet.
4. Et mihi uidetur magnus Dauid et sapiens Salomon magister huius legis expositionem suscepisse: uterque enim concessae escae unam intelligunt gratiam, ipsum bonum quod uere est, quod

---

XX, 11 Prou. 9, 5   13 Ioh. 7, 37   14/15 magnus item Esaias – praecipit] cfr Is. 12, 3; 25, 6   18/19 Am. 8, 11   24/25 Gen. 2, 16

---

15 praecipit] praecepit *B*, ἐγκελεύεται *PG Forb*.   20 numquid] οὐκοῦν *PG Forb*. 21 dignum] ἄξιον *PG Forb*., lignum *R* (Periphys.)*   21/22, 24 intelligere[1, 2]] intelle- *B* 24 paradiso] -dyso *B*   cibum] cybum *B*   25 comedere] comedite *R* (Periphys.)* 26/27 paradiso] -dyso *B*   27 omne] pan (id est omne) *R*(Periphys.)*   28 participationem] -cionem *C*   lex] λόγος *PG Forb*., νόμος *q Forb.*[u.l.] (*sic et Dionysius Exiguus*) 30 et unum] e unum *sed corr. s.l. B*   31 perspicatioribus] correxi ex *Periphys*. (*cfr* διορατικωτέροις *PG Forb.*), perspicatoribus *B C Capp*.   32/33 quid hoc mixtum] τί τὸ ἐπίμικτον τοῦτο οὐ πέρας ὁ θάνατος (οὐ πέρας ὁ θάνατος) om. *Forb.*[u.l.]) *PG Forb*. 33 usum] usu *C*   36 magister] διδασκάλους *PG Forb.*, διδάσκαλον *Forb.*[u.l.]   37 huius legis] τοῦ λόγου τούτου *PG Forb*., τοῦ νόμου τούτου *q Forb.*[u.l.] (*sic et Dionysius Exiguus*) concessae] concese *C*   38 intelligunt] intelle- *B*

etiam omne est bonum, Dauid quidem dicens *delectare in Do-*
40 *mino,* Salomon autem ipsam sapientiam quae est Dominus *lig-*   197B
num uitae nominans.

    5. Non ergo idipsum est uitae ligno omne lignum, cuius cibum   *Capp.* 241
secundum Deum formato lex dat? E contrario autem separatur ab
hoc ligno alterum lignum, cuius cibus boni et mali scientia est,
45 dum non specialiter alterutrum e contrario significatorum in
parte fructificet, sed quendam confusum mixtumque fructum
pullulat contrariis qualitatibus concretum; cuius escam prohibet
dux uitae, consilium uero dat serpens, ut morti praepararet introitum. Et suasor factus est consilium dans, bona quadam pulchritu-
50 dine ac delectatione fructum circumcolorans, ut delectabiliter   *C* 138ʳ
uideretur ac desiderium ad gustum superponeretur.

CAPVT XXI [XX]   197C
Qualis in paradiso uita et quid uetitum illud lignum

1. Quid ergo est illud quod bono ac malo commixtam habet scientiam, delectationibus quae secundum sensum sunt insitum? Non   *B* 103ᵛ
5 longe itaque a ueritate intueor (lignum scientiae boni et mali
"gnoston" Greci uocant, lignum uero uitae "pan") "gnosti" ligni
intellectu in occasionem theoriae utens. Arbitror enim non disciplinam hic a Scriptura intelligi scientiam, sed quandam differentiam ex Scripturae consuetudine inuenio scientiae et

---

39/40 Ps. 36, 4   40/41 Prou. 3, 18

    XXI, 3/68 quid ergo – non sunt] cfr GREG. NYSS., *Or. catech.* (p. 56, 6 – p. 57, 3). Vide
etiam IOH. SCOT., *Periphys.* 4 (p. 111-114, 3340-3417) (= col. 820A-821D) uerbatim
5/6 lignum – pan] uide etiam IOH. SCOT., *Periphys.* 4 (p. 118, 3531-3538) (= col. 824C),
p. 125, 3800-3801) (= col. 830A)

    42 non ergo] οὐκοῦν *PG*   uitae ligno omne] lignum uitae et omne *Periphys.*
43 lex] ὁ λόγος *PG*, ὁ νόμος *q Forb.*ᵘˑˡ· (*sic et Dionysius Exiguus*)   49 factus est] γίνεται
PG, γέγονε *n q Forb.*ᵘˑˡ· (*sic et Dionysius Exiguus*)   49/50 pulchritudine] pulcritudine *C*
50 circumcolorans] circunco- *C*

    XXI, 1 *om. C. In PG et Forb. inc. cap. XX*   2 paradiso] -dyso *B*   3 quid] uid *pro
prima littera spatium relinquens C*   illud] illud (lignum uidelicet) *R** (*Periphys.*)
4 insitum] ἐπηνθισμένον *PG Forb.* (ἐπενθέμενον *uel similiter E. legisse uel intellexisse
uidetur*)   5/6 lignum scientiae – pan] *glossa E. uidetur*   7 utens] utor *R** (*Periphys.*)
8 scientiam] per scientiam *R** (*Periphys.*)

DE IMAGINE, XXI   127

10 diiudicationis. Nam *discernere* disciplinaliter *bonum ex malo perfectioris* habitudinis esse Apostolus dicit, *et exercitatorum officiorum sensuum*: propter hoc etiam praeceptum facit omnia probandi, et *spiritualis diiudicare* proprium esse dicit. Scientia   197D
    uero non ubique disciplinam et peritiam illius quod significatur
15 ⟨indicat⟩, sed ad id quod gratia donatum est affectum, ut: *cognouit Dominus qui sunt eius*; et ad Moysen ait quia *cognoscebam te super omnes*; de his autem qui in malitia redarguuntur, dicit qui omnia nouit quia *numquam cognoscebam uos*.
    2. Non ergo lignum ex quo mixta scientia fructificatur prohibi- 200A
20 tum est? Miscetur autem ex contrariis fructus ille qui causidicum suum habet serpentem, iuxta hanc forsitan rationem, quia non nudum proponitur malum, ipsum in se ipso secundum propriam naturam manifestum. Ipsa enim malitia otiosa esset, nullo accolorata bono quo ad concupiscentiam suam seductum attraheret. Nunc
25 autem commixta quodammodo mali natura est, in profundo si-   *Capp.* 242
    quidem perniciem ueluti quasdam insidias occultas habens, aperte uero in seductione quandam boni phantasiam ostendens. Bonum uidetur auaris materiae pulchritudo, sed *radix omnium malorum philargiria* fit. Quis forsitan in fetidam paludem intemperantiae

---

XXI, 10/12 Hebr. 5, 14   13 I Cor. 2, 15   15/16 Num. 16, 5; II Tim. 2, 19   16/17 Ex. 33, 17   18 Matth. 7, 23   28/29 I Tim. 6, 10

13/18 scientia uero – cognoscebam uos] uide etiam Ioh. Scot., *Periphys.* 2 (p. 94, 2224-2231) (= col. 594B)   20/22 miscetur autem – malum] uide etiam Ioh. Scot., *Periphys.* 4 (p. 123-124, 3736-3742) (= col. 828C)

10 diiudicationis] deiudicationis $B^{p.c.}C$, diiudicationis (hoc est discretionis) R^* (*Periphys.*)   10/11 perfectioris] perfectae *Periphys.*   11/12 officiorum] officii R^* (*Periphys.*)   12 propter hoc] propterea enim R^* (*Periphys.*)   13 spiritualis] hominis add. R^* (*Periphys.*)   diiudicare] deiud- B   14/15 quod significatur indicat] ὑφηγεῖται κατὰ τὸ σημαινόμενον PG Forb., κατὰ τὸ σημαινόμενον ὑφηγεῖται q Forb.$^{u.l.}$ 15 indicat] suppleui ex *Periphys.*, om. B C   quod ... donatum] cui ... donata R^* (*Periphys.*)   ut] om. *Periphys.*   16 sunt eius] (hoc est suam gratiam eis donauit) add. R^* (*Periphys.*)   17 de his] his R^* (*Periphys.*)   18 cognoscebam uos] noui uos B, cognoscebam uos (hoc est meam gratiam numquam uobis largiebar) R^* (*Periphys.* 4 [p. 112, 3358-3359 = col. 820C])   19 non ergo] οὐκοῦν PG   20 ex contrariis] (bono uidelicet et malo) add. R^* (*Periphys.*)   causidicum] (hoc est aduocatum) add. R^* (*Periphys.*)   21 iuxta] iusta C   22 proponitur] (id est ostenditur) add. R^* (*Periphys.*)   23 accolorata] colorato R^* (*Periphys.*)   24 seductum] (hominem scilicet) add. R^* (*Periphys.*)   25 mali natura est] ἐστὶν ἡ τοῦ κακοῦ φύσις PG Forb., τοῦ κακοῦ φύσις ἐστί q Forb.$^{u.l.}$ mali natura] malitia R^* (*Periphys.*)   27 seductione] -nem R^* (*Periphys.*)   phantasiam] fant- B C   28 materiae] materię C   pulchritudo] pulcri- C   29 philargiria] philargia R^* (*Periphys.*)   fetidam] fętidam C

perderetur, nisi delectationem bonum atque eximium quodammodo aestimaret, qui tali illecebra ad passionem attrahitur? Sic habent et cetera peccata occultam differentiam habentia, per primam delectationem ex quadam seductione eximia uidentur minus considerantibus pro bono sollicitanda.

3. Quoniam igitur multi illud in quo sensus delectantur bonum iudicant, et quia est cognominatio existentis boni et ipsius boni quod uidetur esse, huius rei gratia ipsa ad malum ueluti ad bonum facta concupiscentia *boni et mali scientia* a Scriptura nominata est, dum coaffectationem quandam et concretionem interpretetur scientia. Neque absolute malum, eo quod ambitur bono, neque pure bonum, eo quod suboccultatur malum; sed commixtum ex utrisque interdicti ligni fructum esse inquit, cuius gustum dixit in mortem tangentes ducere, solummodo non aperte doctrinam clamans quia bonum quod uere est simplum et uniforme natura est, omnique duplicitate et ad contrarium coniugatione alienum. Malum uero uarium et configuratum est, alicui commixtum et alterum per experimentum apparens, cuius scientia, hoc est per experimentum assumptio, mortis et corruptionis principium causaque fit.

4. Propterea serpens praemonstrat malignum peccati fructum, sic ex propatulo malum non habere naturam ostendens. Non enim forsitan seduceretur homo aperto malo, sed per quandam speciositatem apertum declarauit, quandamque delectationem se-

---

38 Gen. 2, 9   42/43 cfr Gen. 2, 17

30 delectationem] -ne *R**(*Periphys.*)   31 aestimaret] eam *add. R**(*Periphys.*)   passionem] -nes *C*   sic] similiter *R**(*Periphys.*)   32 occultam] -ta *R**(*Periphys.*)   differentiam] διαφθορὰν *PG Forb.*, διαφορὰν *q Forb.*^{u.l.} (*sic et Dionysius Exiguus*)   32/33 per primam delectationem] παρὰ τὴν πρώτην *PG Forb.*, παρὰ τὴν πρώτην γνῶσιν *Forb.*^{u.l.}   36 est] *om. B*   existentis] (hoc est ueri) *add. R**(*Periphys.*)   37 quod uidetur esse] (dum non sit bonum) *add. R**(*Periphys.*)   39 interpretetur] interpretatur (hoc est significat) *R**(*Periphys.*)   42 esse inquit] scriptura *add. R**(*Periphys.*)   43 solummodo non] μονονουχί *PG Forb.*   44 uniforme] -mae *B*   45 duplicitate] διπλόης *PG Forb.*   coniugatione] copulatione *R**(*Periphys.*)   46 alicui commixtum] ἄλλο τι νομιζόμενον *PG Forb.*, alicui bono commixtum *Periphys.*   47 apparens] ἀνακρινόμενον *PG*, ἀναφαινόμενον *Forb.*   47/48 apparens – per experimentum] *om. C*   48 per experimentum] non enim ita inuenitur sicut aestimatur esse *add R**(*Periphys.*); *cfr E. Jeauneau, Introduction, p. xlv*: «*les mots* non enim ita inuenitur sicut aestimatur esse *sont une glose qui a été introduite dans le texte, peut etre pas au bon endroit: elle serait mieux placée après* apparens»   49 fit] efficitur *Periphys.*   51 sic ex propatulo – naturam ostendens] οὐχ ὡς εἴχε φύσεως τὸ κακὸν ἐκ τοῦ προφανοῦς ἐπιδείξας *PG Forb.*   52 aperto] perto *sed corr. s.l. C*   53 declarauit] malum *add. R**(*Periphys.*)

cundum sensum seducens gustuique suadens mulieri manifestauit, sicut ait Scriptura: *et uidit femina quia bonum lignum in
escam, et quia placabile oculis uidere, et speciosum cognoscere; et accipiens fructum eius comedit.* Esca illa mater mortis hominibus
facta est. Ipsa igitur mixtura[e] est fructifera, aperte intellectum
ratione interpretante, per quem "boni et mali cognitio" lignum illud nominatum est, quia iuxta mortiferorum malitiam quae in
melle fiunt, in quantum quidem dulcorat in sensu, bonum esse
uidetur, in quantum uero tangentem corrumpit, omnis mali no-
uissimum efficitur. Cum itaque operatum est in hominis uita malum mortiferum, tunc homo, magna res et nomen, diuinae
naturae imago, *uanitati*, sicut ait propheta, *assimulatus est.*
5. Ergo siquidem imago ad id quod melius in nobis intelligitur
sociatur; quaecumque circa hanc uitam tristia miseraque sunt, similitudinis quae ad Deum est non sunt.

⟨Capvt⟩ XXII [XXI]
Quia resurrectio non tantum ex praedicatione Scripturae
quantum ex ipsa rerum necessitate speratur

1. Sed non sic est fortis malitia ut bonitatis uincat uirtutem: neque
melius neque singularius est naturae nostrae inconsultum quam
Dei sapientia. Non enim possibile est conuersibile atque mutabile
potentius esse atque singularius quam quod semper similiter habet in bono faciens; sed diuinum quidem consilium semper et ubi-

---

55/57 Gen. 3, 6   65 Ps. 143, 4

60/63 quia iuxta mortiferorum – efficitur] cfr Greg. Nyss., *Or. catech.* (p. 29, 13 – p. 30, 9)

XXII, 4/43 sed non sic – dignitas] uide etiam Ioh. Scot., *Periphys.* 5 (p. 81-82, 2580-2620) (= col. 917A-918A) uerbatim   4/22 sed non sic – excipiet] uide etiam Ioh. Scot., *Praed.* 18, 7 (p. 196, 10 – p. 198, 5) (= col. 434AC)

57 esca] aesca *B*   58 mixtura] *correxi* (*cfr* αὕτη τοίνυν ἡ σύμμικτός ἐστι καρποφορία *PG Forb.*), mixturae *B C Capp. R** (*Periphys.*)   60 iuxta] iusta *C*   60/61 quae in melle fiunt] τῶν παραρτυθέντων τῷ μέλετι *PG Forb.*, τῶν τῷ μέλι κεκραμμένων *q*   62/63 nouissimum] (pessimum) *add. R** (*Periphys.*)   65 assimulatus] assimilatus *B*   66 ergo] οὐκοῦν *PG Forb.*

XXII, 1 *om. C. In PG et Forb. inc. cap.* XXI   3 ex ipsa – speratur] ἐξ αὐτῆς τῆς τῶν πραγμάτων ἀνάγκης ἀκολούθως (*om.* Forb.*u.l.*) ἐλπίζεται *PG Forb.*   4 sed] *ed pro prima littera spatium relinquens C*   4/5 neque melius] neque enim melius *Periphys.*

que immutabile habet, conuersibile autem nostrae naturae non in
malo fixum manet.

2. Quod enim semper omnino mouetur, siquidem ad bonum processionem habuerit, propter eximietatem rei perquirendae, numquam desinet ab ipso qui sursum est meatu. Non enim inueniet terminum quaesiti nihil non nanciscentis stabilitabit umquam motum, ⟨neque ad id quod contrarium est momentum⟩ susceperit. Cum uero cursum malitiae peregerit et in sublimissimam mali mensuram peruenerit, tunc quod semper impetu mouetur, nullum ex natura statum inueniens, dum spatium quod in malitia est transcursum fuerit, secundum necessitatem in bonum conuertit motum. Nam dum malitia in infinitum non progrediatur, sed necessariis finibus comprehenditur, consequenter boni successio finem malitiae excipiet. Ac, sicut dictum est, semper mobile nostrae naturae iterum firmiter in bonam recurret uiam, dum ex memoria priorum calamitatum ad essendum iterum in his quae recta sunt compescitur.

3. Non ergo iterum erit nobis cursus in bonis, eo quod finibus necessariis malitiae natura circumterminatur? Vt enim qui aetheria sapiunt spatia luminis quidem omnem mundum plenum esse dicunt, tenebras uero oppositione terreni corporis obumbrationem fieri (sed hoc quidem per figuram spheriformis corporis considero, solari radio coni figuram concludente, solem uero multipliciter magnitudine terram superare, undique ipsam radiis in giro comprehendens, in summitate coni commissuras luminis copulando; ita ut, secundum materiem, si fieret cuipiam uirtus transgrediendi mensuram in quam umbra extenditur, omnino in lumine fieret a tenebris illesus). Sic arbitror oportere etiam de no-

---

11/16 quod enim – susceperit] cfr GREG. NYSS., *Or. catech.* (p. 55, 21 – p. 56, 2)
13/15 non enim – motum] uide etiam IOH. SCOT., *Hier. Dion.* 6, 1 (p. 87-88, 35-42)
26/34 non ergo – copulando] uide etiam IOH. SCOT., *Periphys.* 1 (p. 81-82, 1562-1564)
(= col. 501C)

---

12 eximietatem] ἀόριστον *PG Forb.* (ἄριστον *E. legisse uel intellexisse uidetur*) 13/
15 non enim inueniet – umquam motum] οὐδὲ γὰρ εὑρήσει τοῦ ζητουμένου πέρας οὐδὲν, οὐ δραξάμενον στήσεταί ποτε τῆς κινήσεως *PG Forb.* 15 neque ad id – momentum] *suppleui ex Periphys.* (*cfr* εἰ δὲ πρὸς τὸ ἐναντίον τὴν ῥοπὴν σχοίη κτλ. *PG; in Periphys.* monimentum *legitur iuxta uersionem II, sed* ῥοπή *per* momentum *saepe E. interpretatur*) 20/
21 progrediatur] -diar *B* 23 firmiter] ὕστατον *PG Forb.*, συντόνως *Forb.*$^{u.l.}$ 26 non ergo] οὐκοῦν *PG Forb.* 30 spheriformis] spheri formis *Capp.* 31 considero] κατὰ νώτου *PG Forb.* (κατανοῶ *E. legisse uel intellexisse uidetur*) 34 secundum materiem] καθ᾽ ὑπόθεσιν *PG Forb.*

bis intelligere, quia transeuntes malitiae terminum cum in summitate umbrae peccati fuerimus, iterum in lumine conuersabimur, secundum infinitam multiplicationem quantum ad malitiae mensuram bonorum natura abundante.

4. Iterum ergo paradisus, iterum ergo "omne" illud lignum, quod etiam uitae est lignum; iterum imaginis gratia et principii dignitas. Non mihi uidetur horum quaecumque ad huius uitae usum hominibus a Deo subiugantur spes irrationabilis sed in alterius cuiusdam uitae ineffabilibus manere. Sed consequentiam inquisitionum habeamus.

⟨...⟩

[XXII, 5] ... Peracta quidem hominum genitura, eiusque termino conterminari tempus, et sic omnium reparationem fieri commutationique omnium adunari et humanum, a corruptibili ac terreno ad inpassibile et sempiternum.

[XXII, 6] Hoc mihi uidetur beatus Apostolus considerans praedicere per epistolam ad Corinthios propter repentinum temporis statum et iterum in unum futuram mouentium resolutionem, in quibus dicit: *Ecce mysterium uobis dico: non omnes quidem dormiemus, omnes autem immutabimur, in momento, in ictu oculi, in nouissima tuba.* Plenitudinis quidem, ut mihi uidetur, humanae naturae secundum praecognitam mensuram ad finem uenien-

---

XXII, 55/57 I Cor. 15, 51-52

---

37 intelligere] intelle- *B*   41 paradisus] -dysus *B*   44/45 spes irrationabilis – ineffabilibus manere] ἀλλ᾽ ἑτέρας τινὸς βασιλείας ἐστὶν (βασιλείας ἐστὶν *om. q*) ἡ ἐλπὶς, ἧς ὁ λόγος ἐν ἀπορρήτοις μένει *PG Forb. q* (ἀλογωτέρας *E*. *pro* ἀλλ᾽ ἑτέρας *legisse uel intellexisse uidetur*)   45 sed] *hic inc. cap. XXII PG Forb.*   46 habeamus] *hic des. cap. XXII q et Dionysius Exiguus in uersione sua*   47 ⟨...⟩] *deest in B C Capp.*   48/71 *deest in B C Capp. sed fragmentum* (*Graece cap. XXII, §5-6 iuxta ed. Forb.*) *praeb. V Q F in quibus quasi titulus* Sancti Gregorii episcopi Niseni *praeponitur*   48 peracta quidem hominum genitura] perctam quidem hominum genituram *F*   eiusque] eius quae *V*   49/50 omnium reparationem fieri commutationique] *om. sed suppl.* omnium *s.l. F*   reparationem fieri commutationique omnium] *om. V*   50 a corruptibili] a corruptibile *sed* -o- *expunx. et -e in -i corr. ut uid. Q* (*ac ruptibili fort. corrector putauit legendum*)   50/51 ac terreno] aeternum *sed in* ad aeternum *corr. s.l. F*   53 praedicare] pred- *F V*, προειπεῖν *PG Forb.*   Corinthios] -eos *Q V*   54 mouentium] morientium *F*, τῶν κινουμένων *PG Forb.*   55/56 non omnes – immutabimur] omnes quidem dormiemus, non omnes autem immutabimur *V* (*cfr Vulg.*: omnes quidem resurgemus, sed non omnes immutabimur), πάντες μὲν οὐ κοιμηθησόμεθα πάντες δὲ ἀλλαγησόμεθα *PG Forb.*   56 ictu] hictu *V*   57 plenitudinis quidem] plenitudini siquidem *Q*, τοῦ γὰρ πληρώματος *PG Forb.*   plenitudinis] *F*[a.c.], plenitudine *F*[p.c.] *ut] suppl. in mg. F*   58 praecognitatem] precogn- *V*   58/59 uenientis] *correxi* (*cfr* τοῦ γὰρ πληρώματος – εἰς πέρας ἐλθόντος *PG Forb.*), uenienti *V Q F*

ti⟨s⟩, pro eo quod non iam deest animarum numero aliquid ad augmentum, in celeritate temporis fieri immutationem eorum quae sunt ostendit, momentum nominans et ictum oculi inpartilem illius temporis et indiuiduum finem; nec iam possibile esse ad extremum et summum maturitatis aliquid accedere temporis, propterea quia non deest summitati pars, circatoriam hanc commutationem per mortem habenti; sed tantum canet resurrectionis tuba, quae hoc quod mortuum est suscitat et eos qui in uita relicti sunt ad similitudinem eorum qui ex resurrectione immutantur ad incorruptionem repente transfert, ut non ultra pondus corporis deorsum premat et terrae grauitudine teneatur, sed sublime possit in aerem permeare. *Rapiemur – enim inquit – in nubibus obuiam Domino, et sic semper cum Domino erimus.*

⟨...⟩

⟨Capvt⟩ XXIII
Quia principium constitutionis mundi qui confitetur, necessario etiam de fine consentiet

1. Si autem quis, nunc mundi meatum serie quadam deductum aspiciens, per quam temporale consideratur spatium, non esse recipiendum dixerit promissum eorum quae mouentur futurum fore statum, clarum quia qui talis est neque in principio a Deo caelum et terram credidit facta fuisse. Nam qui principium motui dat, omnino de fine non ambigit; et qui finem non accipit, neque prin-

---

70/71 I Thess. 4, 17

XXIII, 4/XXIV, 42 si autem – dubitamus] cfr Bas., *Hex.* 1, 3 (p. 12-14) et 2, 2 (p. 42-44); Orig., *Princ.* 4, 4, 7 (vol. 268, p. 416-418)

60 celeritate] cael- *F*   61 ictum] ictu *V*   non deest] non est *V F*, διὰ τὸ μηδὲν ὑπολείπεσθαι *PG Forb.*   circatoriam] circatotam *sed corr. in mg. F*   68 repente] ἀθρόως *PG Forb.* (θοῶς *E. legisse uel intellexisse uidetur*)   ut] et *F*   69 teneatur] *F*$^{a.c.}$, teneantur *F*$^{p.c. s.l.}$ sublime] *F*$^{a.c.}$, sublimes *F*$^{p.c. s.l.}$ 69/70 possit] *F*$^{a.c.}$, possint *F*$^{p.c. s.l.}$ 70 permeare] permanere *F*   enim] *om. F*   inquit] inquid *V*   70/71 obuiam Domino] εἰς ἀπάντησιν τοῦ Κυρίου εἰς ἀέρα *PG Forb.* (εἰς ἀέρα *E. om. ut uid.*)   71 Domino²] Deo *V*, Κυρίῳ *PG Forb.*

XXIII, 1 *Abhinc iterum eodem modo numerant capp. Graecae edd. et interpretatio Eriugenae*   caput] *suppleui cum Capp., om. B C*   XXIII] *om. C*   4 si] i *C pro prima littera spatium relinquens C*

DE IMAGINE, XXIII 133

cipium accepit; sed sicut *perfecta esse saecula intelligimus uerbo Dei credentes*, sicut ait Apostolus, *in id quod non uidetur id quod apparet factum fuisse*, eadem fide utimur de uerbo dei, hunc necessa- 209C
rium eorum quae sunt statum praedicantis.

2. Hoc autem quantum eximium est dum sciscitatur: et enim illic *quod uidetur ex his quae non apparent fide accepimus factum esse*, praetereuntes eorum quae impossibilia sunt inquisitionem: etenim de multis ignorare sermo nobis constituit, non paruas praestans occasiones ad eorum quae credita sunt amphiboliam.

3. Licet enim etiam illic contentiosis, ex his quae benedicuntur per consequentiam fidem subuertere, ad aestimandum de creatione materiae sermonem ueracem non esse, quem sancta legauit Scriptura omnium existentium generationem ex Deo esse confirmans. Nam qui contrariam praestant rationem, coaeternam esse Deo materiam conformant, talibus rethoricis conclusionibus ad doctrinam utentes: si simplex Deus natura et immaterialis, ac sine 209D
quantitate et sine magnitudine et incompositus et ab ea quae est secundum figuram circumscriptione alienus existit, omnis uero materies in spatiosa extensione comprehenditur et comprehensiones quae per officia sensuum sunt non effugit, in re atque tumore et quantitate et soliditate ceterisque circa eam consideratis cognita, quorum nihil in diuina natura possibile est intelligi; quae 212A
machina ex immateriali materiem creatam fuisse, ex non distante spatiabilem naturam? Si enim inde haec subsistere creduntur, profecto in ipso existunt quae iuxta ineffabilem rationem ab ipso in C 139ᵛ
generationem processerunt. Si autem in illo materiale erat, quomodo immaterialis in se ipso materiem habet? Similiter etiam alia omnia ex quibus materialis natura configuratur: si in Deo quantitas, quomodo quantitate caret Deus? Si in illo compositum, quomodo simplex ac sine partibus et incompositus est? Itaque aut materialem ipsum esse secundum necessitatem eo quod inde materia subsistit ratio cogetur; aut, si tale aliquid fugit, extrinsecus

---

XXIII, 10/12 Hebr. 11, 3   15/16 Hebr. 11, 3

---

14 hoc autem – sciscitatur] Τὸ δὲ "πῶς" ἐξαιρετέον (ἐξαίρετον] Forb.*u.l.*) τῆς πολυπραγμοσύνης PG Forb.   23 praestant] περιστάμενοι q, παριστάμενοι PG Forb.   24 conformant] *om.* B   rethoricis conclusionibus] ἐπιχειρήμασι PG Forb.   25 immaterialis] inm- C   25/26 sine quantitate] ἄποιος PG Forb., ἄποσος q Forb.*u.l.* (sic et Dionysius Exiguus)   29/30 in re atque – et soliditate] ἐν χρώματι καὶ σχήματι καὶ ὄγκῳ καὶ πηλικότητι καὶ ἀντιτυπίᾳ PG Forb.   32 immateriali] inm- B C   35 processerunt] processerunt C   36 immaterialis] inm- C

materiam introductam fuisse ipsi ad constitutionem uniuersitatis
ex necessitatibus sumere.

4. Si ergo extra Deum erat, aliud quiddam praeter Deum omnino erat, iuxta rationem aeternitatis ingenito existenti cointellectum, ita ut duo anarcha (hoc est principio carentia) et ingenita in idipsum sibi inuicem comprehendantur, uno quidem artificaliter operante, altero uero disciplinabilem hanc operationem recipiente; et si quis ex necessitate hac aeternam obligauerit conditori omnium succumbere materiem, is inueniet propriorum dogmatum quod etiam Manicheus causae auxilium, qui materialem causam secundum ingenitum e contrario bonae naturae adducit! Sed et ex Deo omnia Scriptura dicente audientes credidimus. Et quomodo erat in Deo, quod est super nostram rationem indignum ducimus curiose quaerere, omnia diuina uirtute plena credentes: quod non est substituisse et existenti ut uideatur qualitates addere.

5. Non ergo consequenter sufficere diximus in his quae sunt ad non existentis substantiam diuinae uoluntatis uirtutem. Sic, etiam reformationem consistentium in eandem reducentes uirtutem, in nihil extra quod consequens est disciplinam accipiemus. Et fortassis quidem possibile erat inuentione quadam rationis his qui de materia contendunt credere, nisi uiderentur desolatam ratione transcurrere.

⟨Capvt XXIIII⟩
Controuersia aduersus eos qui dicunt
coaeternam esse Deo materiem

1. Neque enim extra ea quae consequenter inuenta sunt de materia susceptio illa fertur, quae ex intellectuali et immateriali eam subsistere profert. Omnem siquidem materiam ex quibusdam quali-

---

XXIV, 4/37 neque enim – adducente] uide etiam Ioh. Scot., *Periphys.* 1 (p. 83-84, 2570-2603) (= col. 502B-503A) uerbatim; 1 (p. 52, 1562-1564) (= col. 479A), (p. 53, 1583-1586) (= col. 479B), (p. 76, 1345-2349) (= col. 497A), 2 (p. 111, 2720-2723) (= col. 605D)

45 existenti] -tia *ut uid.* C 46 hoc est principio carentia] *non praeb.* PG Forb., *glossa* E. *uidetur* 50 materiem] -rie C. Hic *expl.* C 55 curiose] -sae B plena] χωρητὰ PG Forb. 58 non ergo] οὐκοῦν PG Forb. 61 disciplinam] τὴν ἐπιστείμην q, τὴν πίστιν PG Forb.

XXIV, 1 suppleui cum Capp., *om.* B

DE IMAGINE, XXIV

tatibus consistere inuenimus, quibus si nudata fuerit per se ipsam nulla ratione comprehendetur atqui unaquaeque qualitatis species ratione subiecto separatur. Ratio autem intellectualis est quaedam et incorporalis theoria; ut puta: proposito quopiam animali seu ligno in theoria, seu aliquo alio materialium constitutionem habentium, multa circa subiectum secundum intelligentiam diuisione intelligimus, quorum uniuscuiusque ad id quod consideratur inconfuse habetur ratio: alia siquidem coloris et alia grauitatis ratio, alia iterum quantitatis et alia intelligentiae quae est secundum tactum proprietatis; mollities enim et bicubitale, cetera etiam eorum quae dicta sunt, neque sibi inuicem neque corpori secundum rationem commiscentur. Nam in unoquoque horum specialis iuxta quam est interpretata intelligitur causa, nullaque eorum quae circa subiectum theorizantur alteri qualitati promiscetur.

2. Si ergo intelligibilis color, intelligibilis etiam soliditas et quantitas et cetera talium specialitatum, horum autem unumquodque, si sublatum fuerit subiecto, omnis ratio corporis simul soluitur, consequens erit, quorum absentiam solutionis corporis causam inuenimus, horum concursum materialem naturam creare assumere. Vt enim non est corpus cui res (ΟΥϹΙΑ) et figura et soliditas et distantia et grauitas ceteraque specialitatum non adsunt, horum autem unumquodque corpus non est, sed alterum quid praeter corpus seorsum inuenitur; sic conuersim ubicumque quae dicta sunt concurrerint, corporalem substantiam perficiunt. At si intelligibilis ⟨est specialitatum intelligentia, intelligibilis⟩ quoque natura Deus, nihil inconsequens ex incorporali natura has intellectuales occasiones ad corporum generationem substitutas esse ab intellectuali quidem natura intelligibiles substituente uirtutes, harum uero ad se inuicem concursu materialem naturam in generationem adducente.

3. Sed haec quidem a nobis iuxta quod promptum est discussa sunt. Iterum uero nobis in fidem sermo reducendus, per quam ex non existente uniuersitatem substitutam esse accepimus, et ite-

---

10 quopiam] *correxi ex Periphys.*, copiam *B Capp.*   12 intelligentiam] intelle- *B*   14 inconfuse] -sae *B*   15 intelligentiae] intell- *B*   19 causa] ὅρος *PG Forb.*, λόγος *q Forb.*ᵘˑˡ·   21 promiscetur] permiscetur *Periphys.*   25 soluitur] solueutur *Periphys.*   27 res (ΟΥϹΙΑ)] τὸ χρῶμα *PG Forb.* (χρῆμα *E. legisse uel intellexisse uidetur, quod per glossam* ΟΥϹΙΑ *exposuit*)   28 specialitatum] τῶν ἰδιωμάτων τούτων (*om. q*) *PG Forb. q*   32 est specialitatum – intelligibilis] *suppleui ex Periphys., om. B Capp.*

rum in alium quendam statum ex Scriptura discentes transformandam non dubitamus.

⟨Capvt XXV⟩
Quomodo quis, ex his quae extrinsecus sunt adiutus, crediderit Scripturae de resurrectionis doctrina

1. Sed forsitan quis ad ea quae soluuntur aspiciens corpora, et ad mensuram suae uirtutis Deum comparans, resurrectionis sermonem impossibilem esse dixerit, et statura fore quae nunc mouentur et resurrectura esse quae nunc non mouentur non recipiendum dicens.

2. Sed qui talis est primum quidem maximumque intellegat argumentum de resurrectionis ueritate, quod est praedicationis eius dignum fide; eorum quae dicta sunt fides ex ceterorum quae praedicta sunt exitu firmitatem habet; quoniam quidem multos ac uarios diuina Scriptura addidit sermones, possibile est ut ueritas sustineat mendaces ut, cetera quae dicta sunt contemplantes, per illa etiam de resurrectione doctrinam intelligant. Nam si in aliis mendaces sermones ueritatis et deceptores inueniuntur, neque hoc omnino extra mendacium est. Si uero alia omnia testimonium perhibent experimentum habentia ueritatis, consequens erit per illa etiam de resurrectione praedicationem ueram aestimare. Non igitur recordabimur unius uel duorum ex his quae prius promissa sunt et referemus praedictis exitum, ita ut cognoscant si eorum ratio ad ueritatem aspiciat?

3. Quis nesciat quomodo interponebatur antiquitus Israheliticus populus, aduersus omnes per orbem terrarum potentias insurgens? Quale erat regnum in ciuitate Hierosolimitarum, quales

---

XXV, 1 *suppleui cum Capp.*, *om.* B   2/3 quomodo quis – de resurrectionis doctrina] πῶς ἄν τις καὶ τῶν ἔξωθεν προσαχθείη πιστεῦσαι τῇ γραφῇ περὶ τῆς ἀναστάσεως διδασκούσῃ *PG Forb.*   2 ex his quae extrinsecus sunt] τῶν ἔξωθεν *PG Forb.*, ἐξ τῶν ἔξωθεν *Forb.*^{*u.l.*}
9 intelligat] intelleg- B   10 praedicationis] τοῦ κηρύγματος *PG*, τοῦ κήρυκος *Forb.*
13 addidit] παρέχεται *q*, παρέθετο *PG Forb.*   13/14 ut ueritas sustineat mendaces] ὅπως ἂν ἔχῃ ψεύδους ἢ ἀληθείας *PG Forb.* (ὅπως ἀνέχῃ ψεύδους ἢ ἀλήθεια *uel similiter E. legisse uel intellexisse uidetur*)   15 intelligant] intelleg- B   16 mendaces sermones ueritatis et deceptores] ψευδεῖς οἱ λόγοι καὶ διεσφαλμένοι τῆς ἀληθείας *PG Forb.*   19/20 non igitur] οὐκοῦν *PG Forb.*   21 eorum] δι᾿ αὐτῶν *PG Forb.*   23 interponebatur] ἤνθει *PG Forb.* (ἐνετίθει *uel similiter E. legisse uel intellexisse uidetur*)   25 in ciuitate Hierosolimitarum] κατὰ τὴν τῶν Ἱεροσολύμων (Ἱεροσολυμιτῶν *q Forb.*^{*u.l.*}) πόλιν *PG Forb. q*

muri, quae turres, quae templi magnificentia? Quae quidem etiam discipulis Domini digna miraculo aestimata sunt, et Dominum cognoscere dignum ducunt, mirabiliter de his quae apparebant disputantes, sicut Euangelii historia declarat, dicentes *qualia opera et qualia aedificia*. Ipse uero futuram circa locum desolationem et abolitionem pulchritudinis illius his qui quod praesens erat admirabantur ostendit, dicens nil eorum quae apparebant paulo post relinquendum. Sed et circa passionis tempus mulieres quidem sequebantur plorantes iniustum de ipso iudicium (nondum enim in eorum quae futura erant administrationem respiciebant); ipse autem consilium dabat ea quidem quae de eo facta erant silere – neque enim erant lacrimis digna –, procrastinare uero fletum luctumque in uerum lacrimarum tempus, cum circumdata fieret ab obsidentibus ciuitas, et in quod pressurae uenirent passiones, ut beatum duceretur si futurum non foret; in quibus etiam de filiorum comestione doloris commemorat, dicens in illis diebus sterilem uentrem beatum esse futurum. Vbi nunc illa regalia? Vbi templum, ubi muri, ubi turrium propugnacula, ubi Israhelitarum potentia? Numquid paulo minus per uniuersum orbem terrarum alius alibi dispersi sunt, horum uero subuersione etiam regna sunt concisa?

4. Videtur enim mihi haec et similia praeindicasse Dominus non rerum gratia (quid enim tam magnum aut quod audientibus lucrum eorum quae omnino euentura erant praedictio? Experimento enim cognoscerent et si non praediscerent quod futurum erat), sed ut per haec eis etiam de maioribus fides in consequentiam ueniret. In his enim per opera testimonium, in illis ueritatis est approbamentum.

5. Vt enim si quis agricola seminum narraret uirtutem, contingeret autem agriculturae imperitum non credere, sufficeret fortassis ad approbationem ueritatis terrae laboratori in uno semine ex his quae in medimno ponuntur ostendenti uirtutem etiam de ceteris promittere. Nam qui uidens unum tritici semen uel ordei, uel cuiuscumque in pleintudine medimni consecutus fuerit, postquam seminatum sit in culmo spicam futuram, non iam ex uno de aliis dubitarit. Sic mihi uidetur ad testimonium mysterii

---

XXV, 29/30 Marc. 13, 1   32/42 cfr Luc. 23, 27-29

29 dicentes] λέγοντες *q*, λέγοντες πρὸς αὐτὸν *PG Forb.*   31/32 admirabantur] admirabatur *sed corr. s.l. B*   60 in culmo] τῇ βώλῳ *PG Forb.*, τῷ βόλῳ *q Forb.* [u.l.]

resurrectionis sufficere ipsa in reliquis eorum quae dicta sunt confessa ueritas.

6. Magis autem etiam ipsius resurrectionis experimentum, quod non tantum ex uerbis quantum ex operibus ipsis didicimus. Quoniam enim magnum et supra fidem erat resurrectionis miraculum, ex inferioribus operationem miraculorum inchoans quodammodo paulatim fidem nostram in maioribus nutribat.

7. Veluti quaedam mater paruulum conuenienter lactans, interim quidem molli umidoque ori lac per mammam ingerit, dum uero dentes nascuntur iam etiam crescenti panem affert, non asperum et incongruum, ne asperitate escae molle gingularum et inexercitatum circumrubescat, sed suis dentibus comminuens commensuratam conuenientemque oblati (uidelicet panis) fecit uirtutem, deinde secundum adiectionem inditae uirtutis, additum paulatim mollioribus paruulum solidiori escae adducit; sic humanam pusillanimitatem Dominus, ueluti quendam paruulum inperfectum per miracula nutriens lactansque, primum quidem in incognitam resurrectionis paulisper praecedit uirtutem: magnum quidem erat hoc re gesta, non tamen tantum ut incredibile diceretur. Comminatus enim febribus socrum Simonis ualide urentibus, tantam mali transmutationem fecit, ut praesentibus administrare ualeret quae iam moritura fore spectabatur.

8. Deinde pusillum quid uirtuti addidit, reguli filium in confesso periculo positum (sic enim historia dicit, quia futurum erat mori, patre clamante: *"Descende, priusquam moriatur puer!"*) operatur iterum in credito quod moriturus esset, maiori uirtute resurrectionis miraculum perficiens, non appropinquans loco, sed de longe praecepti fortitudine uitam mittens.

75/76 uirtutem – adducit] cfr I Cor. 3, 1-2   81/83 cfr Luc. 4, 38-39   86 Ioh. 4, 49; cfr 4, 46-54

XXV, 64/185 magis autem – non est] cfr Greg. Nyss., *Anim. et res.* (p. 104, 7 – p. 105, 2)

---

68 nutribat] προσεθίζει *PG Forb.* (προσ)ετίτθιζε *uel similiter E. legisse uel intellexisse uidetur; cfr ll. seqq.*)   69 lactans] τιθηνουμένη *PG Forb.*   70 umidoque] hum- B   74 uidelicet panis] *non praeb. PG Forb.*   75/76 additum] προσεθισθέν *PG Forb.* (προστεθέν *E. legisse uel intellexisse uidetur*)   78 lactansque] καὶ τιθηνούμενος *PG Forb.*   78/79 in incognitam – praecedit uirtutem] ἐν ἀπεγνωσμένῃ νόσῳ τὴν τῆς ἀναστάσεως προοιμιάζεται δύναμιν *PG Forb.*   80 re gesta] κατορθώματι *PG Forb.*   86/88 operatur iterum – miraculum perficiens] ἐνεργεῖ πάλιν τοῦ τεθνήξεσθαι πεπιστευμένου τὴν ἀνάστασιν· ἐν μείζονι τῇ δυνάμει τὸ θαῦμα κατεργασάμενος *PG Forb.*

9. Iterum per consequentiam in excelsioribus miraculis ascendit. Nam ad centurionis puellam ipse uolens uenit ociumque dedit itineri, patientis fluxum sanguinis sanitatem latentem publicans, ut in tali mora mors infirmitatem superaret. Modo igitur anima recedente a corpore, turbis flebili clamore in passione prohibentibus, ueluti ex somno imperiali uerbo iterum ad uitam resuscitat puellam, uia quadam consequentiaque ad maiora humanam infirmitatem recipiens.

10. Deinceps miraculum quod in his erat supergreditur, ac per excelsiorem uirtutem hominibus uiam facit fidem uidelicet de resurrectione. Naei quandam ciuitatem in Iudaea narrat Scriptura: puer erat in ea unigenitus cuiusdam uiduae; non iam talis puer qualis in impubibus solet esse, sed ex pueris in uiros tendebat. Adolescentem ipsum nominat sermo. Multa in paucis narrat historia. Luctus est narrationi oppositus: uidua, inquit, erat morientis mater. Vides grauitatem miseriae, quomodo in paucis passionem aspere narrauit? Quid enim est quod dicitur unicus? Quia non erat ei propagationis spes qua de cetero calamitatem curaret. Vidua enim mulier non habebat ad alterum pro decessore respectum. Vnigenitus enim erat ipse; quantum uero in hoc malum, omnibus facile est cognoscere, cum non peregrinaret ex natura: solum inter parturientes illum cognouit, mammillis lactauit, solus ei splendidam faciebat mensam, solus erat per domum claritatis causa, ludens, festinans, studens, lucens in processionibus, in palestris, in colloquiis iuuentutis. Omne quodcumque matris oculis dulce erat ac pretiosum solus ille erat, iam nuptiarum horam ducebat, generis pullulatio, ramus successionis, baculum senectutis. Sed etiam aetatis adiectio alius luctus est: nam qui adolescentem dicebat, florem dixit uiridis pulchritudinis, iam genarum lanugine subcoloratum, nondum barba ex profundo suppletum, in pulchritudine genarum sublucentem. Quid igitur pati credibile in eo

---

95/97 Marc. 5, 22-43   100/129 cfr Luc. 7, 11-17

---

91 centurionis] ἀρχισυναγώγου *PG Forb.* (*cfr Marc. 5, 22; sed in Matth. 9, 23 pro* ἀρχισυνάγωγος *legitur* ἄρχων, *Latine* princeps, *unde fort. E.* centurio *interpretatus est*) ipse] *non praeb. PG Forb.*, αὐτὸς *q*   94/95 prohibentibus] ἐπικωκυόντων *PG Forb.* (ἐπικωλυόντων *E. legisse uel intellexisse uidetur*)   104 luctus est narrationi oppositus] θρῆνος ἀντικρύς ἐστι τὸ διήγημα *PG Forb.*   106 unicus] *non praeb. PG Forb., fort. glossa ad* unigenitus *pertinens* (*cfr ll. seqq.*)   109 ipse] ὁ τόκος *PG Forb.*   109/110 omnibus facile – ex natura] παντὶ ῥᾴδιον (ῥαδίως *q*) συνιδεῖν τῷ μὴ ἀπεξενωμένῳ τῆς φύσεως *PG Forb. q*   115 pretiosum] precios- *B*

matrem, tali igne in uisceribus ardere? Amarissime in ipso luctum protendere circa feretrum proposito cadauere, ut non festinaret mortuo exequias, sed in plus passionis se inferret, sic lamenta extendens: neque hoc praeteriuit sermo. *Videns* enim *eam* inquit
125 *Dominus misertus est, et accedens tetigit loculum, portantes steterunt. Et dicit mortuo: "Adolescens, tibi dico, surge" et tradidit eum matri suae uiuentem.* Nunc non in paruo spatio mortuo facto, et quantum nondum depositus in sepulchro, fit a Domino maius quidem miraculum, aequale uero praeceptum.

130 11. Adhuc ad altiora miraculorum factura procedit, ut magis per uisibilia incredibili miraculo circa resurrectionem adpropinquaret. Infirmatur quidam assuetorum Domino et amicorum, Lazarus nomen aegrotanti, et praeparat Dominus uisitationem amici, longe ab aegrotante factus, ut locum uirtutemque in absen-
135 tia uitae quod suum erat operari per infirmitatem mors inueniret. Dominus discipulis indicat in Galilea passionem Lazari, sed ad eum impetum praeparat, in ipsa dico autem passione resuscitare positum. Vndique uero illi conuenerant propter Iudaeorum crudelitatem, saeuum ac periculosum facientes iterum in Iudaea in
140 medio homicidarum fieri; ac per hoc tempus dilaturi a Galilea reditum faciunt. Superat enim potentia, et discipuli a Domino ducuntur, ueluti praesagia uniuersalis resurrectionis in Bethania discituri. Quatuor erant iam post passionem dies. Omnia quae debebantur decedenti impleta sunt: corpus sepulchro absconditur;
145 exterius quantum consequens erat apparet, iam etiam ad corruptionem solutum est, madefacto sudore terrae, cadenteque sub necessitatem corpore. Fugienda erat res uim patiente natura in fetorem solutum est. Tunc incredibile catholicae resurrectionis opus ex euidentiori miraculo in approbationem ducitur: non
150 enim ex atroci aegritudine aliqua resuscitatur, neque in extremis spiritibus existens in uitam reducitur, neque puella nuper mortua uiuificatur, neque futurus sepulchro adduci adolescens iterum ex

---

125/127 Luc. 7, 13-15   132/158 cfr Ioh. 11, 1-44

138 undique uero illi conuenerant] περιδεεῖς δὲ ἦσαν ἐκεῖνοι *PG Forb.*   141/142 ducuntur] *correxi (cfr* ἤγοντο *PG Forb.*), dicuntur *B*   143 discituri] μυηθησόμενοι *PG Forb.*   145 exterius – apparet] ἐξῳδήκει κατὰ τὸ εἰκὸς *PG Forb.* (δοκεῖ κατὰ τὸ εἰκὸς *uel similiter* E. *legisse uel intellexisse uidetur*)   147/148 fugienda erat res – solutum est] φευκτὸν ἦν τὸ πρᾶγμα, βιαζομένης τῆς φύσεως τὸ διαλυθὲν εἰς δυσωδίαν ἀποδιδόναι πάλιν τῷ ζῆν (ἀποδιδόναι πάλιν τῷ ζῆν] *om.* q *Forb.*ᵘˑˡ·) *PG Forb.* q   149 euidentiori] euedentiori *B*

DE IMAGINE, XXV

capulo resoluitur; sed uir extra quod consequens erat transiens, iam etiam solutus, ut neque familiaribus tolerabile fieret Dominum sepulchro appropinquare propter impositam cadentis in cadauer corporis deformitatem, una iussione uiuificatur, praedicatio resurrectionis creditur: hoc est, quod communiter spectatur, illud in parte experimento didicimus. Vt enim in uniuersitatis reformatione ait Apostolus *ipsum Dominum descensurum esse in iussu, in uoce Arcangeli et tuba dei,* mortuos in incorruptionem exsuscitare, sic etiam nunc ueluti somnum mortem uoce praecepti ipse in sepulchro positus excutit, superueniente morte corruptionem a se ipso repellens, perfectus ac sanus sepulchro exilit, neque uinculo circa manus ac pedes fasciarum prohibetur ad exitum.

12. Parua igitur haec ad fidem resurrectionis mortuorum? Si quaeris etiam ex aliis firmari tibi de talibus iudicium, sed mihi uidetur non in uanum his qui erant in Capharnaum Dominus ex persona hominum sic dixisse hoc ad se ipsum dicens: *"Omnino dicitis mihi parabolam hanc: 'medice, cura teipsum'"*. Oportebat enim in aliis corporibus ad fidem homines propagantem resurrectionis miraculi, in suo quem in se ipso gestabat homine firmare rationem. Vides in aliis euidentem praedicationem, uides morituros, puellam nuper uiuere cessantem, ad sepulchrum adolescentem delatum, mortuum diu, omnes aequaliter uno praecepto ad uitam redeuntes. Quaeris etiam per uulnera seu sanguinem in morte factos, ne quis in his infirmitate uiuificantis uirtutis gratiam prohibeat? Vide in clauis manus expansum, uide latus lancea perforatum, infer digitos per fixuram clauorum, mitte manum tuam in uulnus ex lancea: considera omnino in quantum credibile erat intus acumen subintrasse, per latitudinem cicatricis in id quod interius erat transitum cogitans; introitum namque manus humanae plaga capiens, quantum intus in profundo ferrum fuerat ostendit. Si ergo ipse surrexit, oportunum ne sit illud Apostoli-

---

159/160 I Thess. 4, 16   168/169 Luc. 4, 23

---

153 uir extra quod consequens erat] ἀνὴρ τῶν ἐξώρων *PG*   transiens] νεκρὸς, ἕωλος (νεκρὸς, ἕωλος *om. Forb.*^{u.l.}) ἐξῳδηκὼς (ἐξῳδικὼς *q*) *PG Forb. q* (νεκρὸς, ἕωλος *om. E. ut uid.*; ἐξῳδηκὼς] ἐξοδικὸς *E. legisse ac quasi* transiens *intellexisse uidetur*)   156 uiuificatur] *fort.* uiuificatus *legendum* (*cfr* ζωοποιηθεὶς *PG Forb.*)   158 in parte] *correxi,* imparte *B Capp.* 160 Arcangeli] ἀρχαγγέλου *PG Forb.*, ἀγγέλου *q*   165 si] εἰ *PG,* ἢ *Forb.*   166 quaeris] queris *B*   170 propagantem] προσεθίσαντα *PG Forb.*, προσεθίσαντας *q*   172 euidentem] ἐνεργόν *PG Forb.* (ἐναργές *E. legisse uel intellexisse uidetur*)

cum clamare: *Quomodo dicunt quidam quia resurrectio mortuo-*
rum non est?

13. Quoniam itaque omnis quidem praedicatio Domini per eorum quae facta sunt testimonium uera ostenditur, hoc autem non uerbo didicimus solummodo sed, ex ipsis in uitam ex resurrectione redeuntibus, opere approbationem promissionis accepimus. Qualis occasio incredulis relinquitur? Exponentes non infirmari ab his qui *per philosophiam et inanem seductionem* imperfectam fidem concutiunt, nudam confessionem habebimus, discentes in paucis per prophetam modum gratiae, in quibus ait: *auferes spiritum eorum et deficient, et in puluerem suum reuertentur. Emitte spiritum tuum et creabuntur, et renouabis faciem terrae*; qui etiam *laetari Dominum in operibus suis* dicit, *deficientibus peccatoribus a terra.* Quomodo enim quis ex peccato nominabitur, peccato non existente?

⟨Capvt XXVI⟩
Quia non extra credibile resurrectio est

1. Sed sunt quidam qui per humanarum cogitationum infirmitatem ad ea quae nostra sunt diuinam comparantes uirtutem, quod nobis incaptabile est neque Deo possibile, esse conformant. Ostendunt enim antiquorum mortuorum abolitionem, eorumque qui per ignem in cinerem redacti sunt reliquias, et adhuc cum his animalia carnem comedentia rationi addunt, et piscem suo corpori carnem naufragium patientis recipientem, eumque iterum escam hominum factum, et in comedentis molem per digestionem transeuntem, ac multa huiusmodi minuta magnaque Dei uirtute potentiaque indigna in subuersionem doctrinae degrediuntur, quasi non ualente Deo iterum per easdem uias in reditu quod suum est homini restituere.

184/185 I Cor. 15, 12   191 Col. 2, 8   193/195 Ps. 103, 29-30   196 Ps. 103, 31
196/197 Ps. 103, 35

XXVI, 3/5 sed sunt quidam – conformant] cfr Meth., *Res.* 2, 29 (p. 386, 4-15)

191/192 imperfectam fidem concutiunt, nudam confessionem habebimus] τὴν ἀκατάσκευον πίστιν, (ἀγαπήσωμεν καὶ *add. q*) ψιλῆς ἐξόμεθα *PG Forb. q*

XXVI, 1 *suppleui cum Capp., om.* B

2. Sed nos in paucis longas eorum rationabilis uanitatis discursiones succidemus, confitentes solutionem quidem corporis in ea ex quibus constitutum est fieri, et non solum iuxta diuinum sermonem in terram resolui, sed etiam in aera et ignem et humorem redire in id quod sibi cognatum est, et uniuscuiusque eorum quae in nobis sunt ad id quod sibi congenitum est reditum fieri, et si carnem comedentibus alitibus, et si deuorantibus bestiis humanum corpus commixtum fuerit per cibum, et si sub dentem piscium uenerit, et in uapores et cineres transmutatum sit in igne; et quocumque quis per materiem hominem ratione circumduxerit, in his quae mundi sunt omnino est: *hoc autem manu Dei contineri ex Deo inspirata uox edocet*. Si ergo tu aliquid eorum quae in palma tua sunt non ignoras, arbitrandumne tua uirtute infirmiorem diuinam esse scientiam, ut non inueniat eorum quae diuina palma continentur subtilitatem?

⟨Capvt XXVII⟩
Quia possibile est in uniuersitatis elementa humano corpore soluto iterum ex communione unicuique quod suum est saluari

1. Sed forsitan ad uniuersitatis elementa qui aspicit, difficile arbitratur aere qui in nobis est ad cognatum elementum redeunte, calido quoque et umido atque terreno cognationibus similiter commixtis, iterum ex communione proprium ad proprium recurrere.

2. Deinde non cogitat per humana exempla quod neque hoc diuinae uirtutis supergreditur diffinitiones? Vidisti alicubi omnino [uidisti] in humanis possessionibus communem gregem, ex communi constitutum; sed iterum cum ad possessores ipse diuiditur, ipsa ad possessiones consuetudo signaque imposita proprium unicuique restituit: tale aliquid etiam circa teipsum

---

XXVI, 25/26 hoc autem – edocet] cfr Ps. 94, 4

15/20 sed nos in paucis – reditum fieri] cfr Meth., *Res*. 1, 14 (p. 237, 1). Vide etiam Ioh. Scot., *Praed*. 19, 1 (p. 204, 4-7) (= col. 436D)

XXVII, 4/93 sed forsitan – contemplantur] cfr Greg. Nyss., *Anim. et res*. (p. 53, 13-15; p. 55, 1-5; p. 56, 10-11)

XXVII, 1 *suppleui cum* Capp., *om*. B   2 elementa] elim- B   6 umido] hum- B   10 uidisti] *seclusi, bis praeb*. B Capp. (*cfr l. 9*)   11 communem gregem] κοινὴν ἀγέλην ζῴων τινῶν (ζῴων τινῶν] *om*. Forb.$^{u.l.}$) PG Forb.

intelligens, ab eo quod consequens est non aberrabis. Naturali enim quadam coniunctione ac delectatione cohabitationem ad corpus anima disponente, est quaedam clam in ipsa per concretionem quae nunc est proprii habitudo atque cognitio, ueluti quibusdam signis ex natura impositis, ex quibus inconfusa communio manet in proprietatibus discreta. Anima igitur congenitum suumque in se ipsam iterum trahente, quis labor, dic mihi, diuinae uirtuti non prohibere propriorum concursum, ineffabili quodam naturae pondere ad id quod suum est festinantium? Nam quod quaedam in anima etiam post effusionem nostrae concretionis signa permaneant, ipsa in inferno disputatio ostendit, corporibus quidem sepulchro traditis, notione uero quadam corporali in animabus permanente, per quam etiam Lazarus cognitus est, et non ignoratus est diues.

3. Non igitur extra credibile est credere ex communione ad proprium resolutionem resurgentium corporum fieri, et maxime studiosius naturam inquirenti. Non enim per omnia quod nostrum est in fluxu et transmutatione est – si enim esset reprehensibile uniuersaliter quod nullum statum habet ex natura – sed, iuxta subtiliorem rationem, eorum quae in nobis sunt quoddam quidem stat, quoddam uero ex mutabilitate prouenit. Mutatur enim per auctionem et diminutionem corpus, ueluti uestimenta quaedam consequentes aetates indutum; stat uero per omnem conuersionem intransmutabilis in se ipsa forma, insitis sibi semel ex natura signis non desistens, sed in omnibus secundum corpus transmutationibus cum suis notionibus apparet.

XXVII, 25/28 ipsa in inferno – diues] cfr Luc. 16, 19-31

29/49 non igitur – inseritur] uide etiam IOH. SCOT., *Periphys.* 5 (uersio II iuxta codd. *HM*, p. 19, 514-536) (= col. 872BC) uerbatim *sed* cum suis notionibus] cum suis notis ingenitis   31/58 non enim – characterizata sunt] uide etiam IOH. SCOT., *Periphys.* 4 (p. 84-85, 2472-2500) (= col. 801AC) uerbatim

---

15 intelligens] intelle- B   16 coniunctione] σχέσει *PG Forb.* (*quod in l. 18 E. per* habitudo *interpretatus est*)   18 nunc] *non praeb. PG Forb.*, νῦν *q Forb.*[u.l.]   29 non igitur – credere] non est incredibile *Periphys. 5 (p. 19, 514-515 = col. 872B)*   non igitur] οὐκοῦν *PG Forb.*   32 si] ἤ *PG Forb.*   reprehensibile] ἂν ἄληπτον *PG Forb.* (*E. quasi* ἀνάληπτον *intellexisse uidetur*)   33 uniuersaliter] fieret *add. Periphys. 5 (p. 19, 519 = col. 872B)*   35 prouenit] accidit *R* (Periphys. 4 [p. 84, 2476 = col. 801AJ])*   36 auctionem] augmentum *Periphys. 5 (p. 19, 522 = col. 872B)*   40 cum suis notionibus] suis notis ingenitis *Periphys. 5 (p. 19, 527 = col. 872C)*

4. Subtrahatur autem per uerbum ipsa quae ex passione est mutatio quae forme superaccidit. Nam ueluti facies quaedam aliena, ipsa per infirmitatem deformitas formam deprehendit. Qua informitate per uerbum circumablata, sicut in Neman Syro, seu in his qui in Euangelio narrantur, iterum occultata sub passione species per sanitatem in suis notionibus relucet.

5. Igitur in de⟨i⟩formitate animae non fluxile per mutabilitatem et transmutabile est, sed quod permanet similiterque in nostra concretione habet, hoc inseritur; et quoniam ipsas per speciem differentias ipsae mutabiles concretionis qualitates performant, concretio uero non alia quaedam est praeter elementorum mixturam (elementa autem dicimus uniuersitatis constitutioni subiecta, ex quibus etiam humanum corpus constat), necessario specie ueluti descripti signaculi in anima permanente, neque reformanda in signaculo ad formam ab ea (uidelicet anima) ignorantur, sed in tempore reformationis illa iterum ad se ipsam recipiet quaecumque formae characteri coaptabit, coaptabit autem omnino illa quae ab initio in forma characterizata sunt. Non ergo extra credibile est iterum ex communi ad unumquemque quod suum est redire.

6. Dicitur autem et uiuum argentum, ex continenti uase quodam profusum et in puluerio loco in minuta means, per terram descendi et ad nullum attingentium inmixtum. Si uero quis ite-

---

43/44 qua informitate – in Neman Syro] cfr IV Reg. 5, 10-14   44/45 seu in his – narrantur] cfr Luc. 17, 12

53/56 necessario specie – ignorantur] uide etiam IOH. SCOT., *Periphys.* 4 (p. 86, 2548-2550) (= col. 802C) uerbatim

41 subtrahatur] subtrahitur *Periphys. 4* (*p. 84, 2482 = col. 801A*), subtrahetur *Periphys. 5* (*p. 19, 527-528 = col. 872C*)   43 infirmitatem] *cfr* νόσον *PG*, informitatem *Periphys. 4* (*p. 84, 2484 = col. 801B*)   qua informitate per uerbum] qua (deformitate) per uerbum (dei) *Periphys. 5* (*p. 19, 531 = col. 872C*)   43/45 sicut in Neman Syro] sicut Neman Syrus *R** (*Periphys. 4 [p. 84, 2485-2486 = col. 801B]*)   44 his] illis leprosis *Periphys. 5* (*p. 19, 532 = col. 872C*)   45 occultata ... species] obscurata ... facies *R** (*Periphys. 4 [p. 84, 2487 = col. 801B]*)   46 relucet] -cebit *Periphys. 5* (*p. 19, 534 = col. 872C*)   47 deformitate] *correxi ex R** (*Periphys. 4 [p. 84, 2488 = col. 801B]*) *et Periphys. 5* (*p. 19, 534 = col. 872C*) (*cfr* τῷ ... θεοειδεῖ *PG Forb.*), deformitate *B et Periphys. 5* – *uersio II iuxta codd. HM* (*p. 282, 905*)   49 inseritur] insitum est *Periphys. 5* (*p. 19, 56 = col. 872D*)   50 ipsae] ipse *B*   51 concretio] *scripsi cum Capp.*, -cio *B*   55 uidelicet anima] *non praeb. PG Forb.* (*cfr R* [Periphys. 4, p. 86, 2550 = col. 802C]*), *E. glossam add.* (*cfr R* [Periphys. 4, p. 85, 2497 = col. 801C]*)   57 characteri] τῷ τύπῳ *PG Forb.*   characteri] car- *B*   58 characterizata sunt] ἐνετυπώθη *PG Forb.*   characterizata sunt] car- *B*   58/59 non ergo] οὐκοῦν οὐδὲν (οὐδὲν *om. q*) *PG Forb. q*   62 in minuta] *correxi* (*cfr* εἰς λεπτὰ *PG Forb.*), immin- *B*

rum ubique dispersum in unum collegerit, sponte ad cognatum
refunditur, nullo medio ad propriam mixturam prohibitum. Tale
aliquid oportere arbitror etiam circa humanam concretionem intelligi: si solummodo fieret quod a Deo inditum, sponte conuenientes partes suis proprietatibus reflorerent, nulla operositate
reformanti naturam ex his ingenita.

7. Etenim in germinibus terrae nullum laborem naturae uidemus in tritico seu milio seu alio quodam frumentalium aut orde-
aceorum seminum transmittendo in calamum et aristas et spicas.
Nam inoperose spontaneeque ipsa conueniens esca ex communione ad uniuscuiusque seminum proprietatem transcendit. Si ergo
ex communi omnibus germinibus humore subiecto unumquodque eorum quae ex eo nutriuntur in proprietatis adiectionem
quod conuenit attrahit, quid nouum etiam in resurrectionis ratione, in unoquoque resurgentium, sicut in seminibus, accidit
proprium pondus ei fieri?

8. Ita ut ex omnibus possibile sit discere nil eorum quae exterius
experimento nota sunt praedicationem resurrectionis prohibere.

9. Atqui notissimum eorum quae nostra sunt siluimus, ipsam
dico primam constitutionis nostrae occasionem. Quis enim igno-
rat mirabilem naturae operationem? Quid in utero informe accipit, quid perficit? Vides quomodo in simplum quendam modum
est partibus simile quod in occasionem constitutionis corporis in
uisceribus proicitur? Varietatem uero conformatae concretionis
quis sermo digesserit? Quis, nisi communi natura discens quod
tale potens est quod factum est narrarit quia illud paruum ac
prope nihil tantae rei fit principium? Magnum inquam, non solum eam formationem quae est secundum corpus uisibile, sed et
prius miraculo dignum: ipsam dico animam, et quae circa eam
contemplantur.

---

68 reflorerent] ἐπανακίρνασθαι *PG Forb.*, παρακίρνασθαι *q*   70 nullum laborem] οὐδὲν ἄπονον *q*, οὐδένα πόνον *PG Forb.*   73 inoperose spontaneeque] *correxi (cfr* ἀπραγματεύτως γὰρ κατὰ τὸ αὐτόματον *PG)*, -sae -neaeque *B*   77 etiam] εἰ *(om. q Forb.*^{u.l.}*)* καὶ *PG Forb. q*   84 informe] -mae *B*   84/85 quid in utero – quid perficit] τί λαβοῦσα ἡ μητρῴα (μητρῶα *Forb.)* νηδὺς, τί ἀπεργάζεται *PG Forb. (fort.* ἀφορμὴν *[cfr l. 83 et 86] per* informe *E. interpretatus est – quasi* ἄμορφον)   86 occasionem] ἀφορμήν *PG Forb.*   88/90 quis nisi communi – fit principium] τίς δ᾽ ἄν, μὴ τῇ κοινῇ φύσει τὸ τοιοῦτον μαθών, δυνατὸν ἡγήσαιτο τὸ γινόμενον, ὅτι τὸ βραχύ τε καὶ ἀντ᾽ οὐδενὸς ἐκεῖνο τοῦ τοσούτου πράγματός ἐστιν ἀρχή *PG Forb.*

⟨Capvt⟩ XXVIII
Aduersus eos qui dicunt animas ante corpora substitisse,
aut e contrario ante animas corpora formata fuisse; in quo etiam
quaedam reuersio est aduersus fabulosa figmenta
transanimationis

1. Fortassis enim non extra propositam nobis est actionem illud perquirere quod in ecclesiis ambiguum est de anima et corpore. Nam quibusdam uidetur qui ante nos sunt, in quod etiam de principiis actitatus est sermo, ueluti quendam populum in speciali conuersatione animas dicere prius substitisse; proponi etiam illic malitiae atque uirtutis exempla, et permanentem quidem in bono animam copulationis ad corpus manere inexpertam. Si uero ex participatione boni fluxerit, ad hanc uitam perdi, ac sic in corpore fieri. Alii uero, ordini constitutionis hominis secundum Moysea attendentes, secundam esse corpore animam iuxta tempus dicunt, quoniam prius accipiens Deus limum ex terra hominem formauit, deinde sic per insufflationem animauit. Et hac ratione praehonorabiliorem anima carnem ostendunt, tempore posteriori prius formatam. Dicunt enim propter corpus animam fuisse, ne expers spiritus et immobile fieret figmentum. Omne autem quod propter aliquid factum est, omnino inferius est eo propter quod factum est, sicut ait Euangelium quia *plus est anima quam esca, et corpus plus quam uestimentum*, eo quod ista propter illa: non enim propter escam anima, neque indumenti gratia constituta sunt corpora, sed his existentibus illa propter utilitatem adinuenta sunt.

2. Quoniam igitur in utrisque opinionibus contemptibilis ratio est, eorum uidelicet prius uixisse animas in speciali quadam ordinatione fabulose dicentium, et posteriores corporibus constitutas esse arbitrantium, necessarium fieret nil eorum quae in doctrinis

---

XXVIII, 16/17 quoniam prius – animauit] cfr Gen. 2, 7 22/23 Matth. 6, 25

XXVIII, 6/XXIX, 119 fortassis – pullulationum efficitur] uide etiam Ioh. Scot., *Periphys.* 2 (p. 76, 1787-1795) (= col. 582A); 4 (p. 83, 2460-2466) (= col. 800C); 5 (p. 36, 1085-1089) (= col. 884C) 8/14 nam quibusdam – in corpore fieri] cfr fort. Orig., *Princ.* 4, 3, 8-10 (vol. 268, p. 368-380); Greg. Nyss., *Anim. et res.* (p. 84, 14 – p. 85, 9); Greg. Naz., *Or.* 37, 15 (p. 302) 14/25 alii uero – adinuenta sunt] cfr fort. Porph., *Gaur.* 9, 1 (p. 45, 5-10); Greg. Nyss., *Anim. et res.* (p. 94, 21 – p. 95, 28)

XXVIII, 1 *suppleui cum Capp., om.* B 10 conuersatione] πολιτείᾳ *PG Forb.*
14 Moysea] *correxi,* Mosea *B,* mos ea *Capp.* 28 fabulose] -sae *B*

30 dicta sunt circumspicere inexquisitum. Sed equidem diligenter utriusque partis denudare rationes et omnes insitas inconsequentias opinionibus reuelare prolixi forsitan sermonis temporisque aestimabitur. In paucis ergo quantum possibile est utrumque eorum quae dicta sunt inspicientes, iterum quae dicenda sunt reci- 232A
35 piemus.

3. Qui priori instant rationi et antiquiorem ea quae in carne est uita conuersationem animarum dogmatizant, non mihi uidentur Grecis doctrinis de transincorporatione sibi fabulose ratiocinantibus puri esse. Nam si quis subtiliter inquisierit, ad hoc per om-
40 nem necessitatem rationem eos contrahentem inueniet, quod aiunt quendam apud illos sapientum dixisse, quia uir factus est idem, etiam feminae corpus indutus est, et cum uolatilibus uolauit et cum uepribus germinatus est, et aquatilem sortitus est uitam. Non longe a ueritate recessit nostrum iudicium ranam ferens eum
45 qui de se ipso haec dicebat: uere enim ranarum quarundam, seu gracularum loquacitate, seu irrationabilitate piscium, seu nemorum insensualitate talia dogmata digna sunt, unam animam dicere per tanta uenire.

4. Talis autem inconsequentiae causa est prius substitisse ani- 232B
50 mas aestimari. Nam congruenter talis doctrinae principium attente propositum rationem usque ad hoc monstruosum exitum adduxit. Si enim, per quandam malitiam excelsiori conuersatione attracta, anima homo efficitur, passibilior autem omnino ipsa in carne uita quam aeterna et incorporalis conceditur, necessarium
55 est omnem animam, in tali uita factam in qua plures ad peccan-

---

36/39 qui priori instant – puri esse] GREG. NYSS., *Vit. Moys.* 2, 40 (p. 44, 11-19)   40/48 quod aiunt – uenire] uide etiam IOH. SCOT., *Gloss. Mart. Cap. ex ms. Ox.* (p. 122): "Gregorius Nyseus, germanus Basilii, ait quia iuuenis quidam dicebat se esse aliquando sicut uir, aliquando sicut femina, uel etiam sicut uolatile, uel sicut piscis, uel sicut rana. Ideo dicit hoc propter nimiam miseriam animarum."   41/43 quendam apud illos – uitam] cfr EMP., fr. B117 DK et etiam CHALC., *Comm.* 2, 197 (p. 218); GREG. NYSS., *Anim. et res.* (p. 85, 9 – p. 87, 1)

32 forsitan] *correxi cum Capp.*, fonsitan B   34 quae dicenda sunt] τῶν προκειμένων PG Forb., τῶν εἰρημένων q   38/39 ratiocinantibus] racio- B   44 recessit nostrum iudicium] κατά γε τὴν ἐμὴν κρίσιν PG (κατά γε *quasi* κατάγει *uel similiter* E. *legisse uel intellexisse uidetur*)   ranam] *non praeb.* PG Forb.   46 seu irrationabilitate] se uir racionabilitate *Capp.*   irrationabilitate] *correxi*, irracio- B   53 anima homo efficitur] ἡ ψυχὴ πολιτείας, μετὰ τὸ (καθώς φασιν) ἅπαξ γεύσασθαι τοῦ σωματικοῦ βίου πάλιν (μετὰ τὸ – πάλιν *om.* q Forb.*u.l.*) ἄνθρωπος γίνεται PG Forb. q   54/55 necessarium est omnem animam] ἀνάγκη πᾶσα PG Forb.

dum sunt occasiones, in plurima malitia fieri, et passibiliorem quam primam disposuisse. Humanae autem animae passio est ipsa ad irrationale similitudo; ad familiaritatem quoque huic irrationali uidelicet ipsam in pecudalem naturam transfluere; semel autem per malitiam proficiscens, neque in irrationale ueniens a processione in malum umquam desinet: nam stationis mali principium est ipsius motus qui est in uirtutem. Virtus autem in irrationabilibus non est. Non ergo semper in peius ex necessitate mutabitur, semper ad id quod ignobilius est proueniens ac semper deterius ea natura in qua est inueniens, sicut autem sensualem rationalis supergreditur, sic etiam ex sensuali in eam quae sensu caret casus fit.

5. Sed usque ad eam ratio eorum procedit, etsi extra ueritatem feratur, attamen per quandam consequentiam inordinatum ex inordinato accipit. Quod uero deinceps est iam per incongrua eis doctrinam fabulosam facit. Nam consequentia perfectam animae corruptionem ostendunt: etenim quae semel excelsa conuersatione perdita est, in nulla mensura malitiae stare poterit, sed per copulationem quae est ad passiones ex rationali quidem ad irrationale transiet, ex illo uero ad germinum insensualitatem transmutabitur. Insensuali uero uicinum quodammodo est inanimale; post hoc autem (id est inanimale) illud quod subsistentia caret sequitur: itaque uniuersaliter per consequentiam ad id quod non est, in his anima reuertetur. Non ergo impossibilis ei iterum ex necessitate ad id quod melius est erit reditus? Sed tamen ex dumo in hominem animam reducunt. Non igitur honorabiliorem in dumo uitam incorporali conuersatione ex his ostendunt?

6. Ostensum est enim quia ad id quod deterius est facta animae processio ad inferius per id quod consequens est subingredietur. Subingreditur autem carentem sensu naturam inanimale, in quod per consequentiam principium dogmatis eorum animam adducit. Sed quoniam hoc nolunt, aut in eo quod sensu caret animam includent, aut, si inde eam in humanam uitam reducunt, honorabiliorem (ut dictum est) ligneam uitam priori statione ostendent, si

---

56/57 passibiliorem quam primam] ἐμπαθέστερον ἢ πρότερον (ἢ πρότερον om. q) PG Forb. q   63 non ergo] οὐκοῦν PG Forb.   67 casus] μετάβασις q, μετάπτωσις PG Forb.   68 usque ad eam] μέχρι τούτου PG Forb.   76 inanimale] τὸ ἄψυχον PG Forb.   77 id est inanimale] non praeb. PG Forb., τῷ δὲ ἀψύχῳ Forb.$^{u.l.}$ 79 non ergo] οὐκοῦν PG Forb.   81 non igitur] οὐκοῦν PG Forb.   89 dictum] digtum $B^{a.c.}$

90 inde quidem ad malitiam casus factus est deorsum, hinc uero ad uirtutem fit reditus.

7. Non igitur quaedam inperfecta et sine capite talis reprehenditur ratio, quae animas in se ipsis ante uitam quae in carne est uixisse conformat, ac per malitiam corporibus colligari: eorum 95 uero qui iuniorem esse corpore animam inconsequentia ex his quae ante conspectum sunt constituitur.

8. Non ergo dixeris utrorumque depulsa est ratio? Per medium uero opinionum oportere arbitror nostram doctrinam in ueritate dirigere. Est autem haec: quod neque secundum Grecum errorem 100 in quadam malitia grauatas animas cum uniuerso circumuolutas, per inpotentiam concurrendi cum uelocitate caelestis motus, in terram cadere aestimandum; neque bene iterum ueluti luteam statuam prius formatum a uerbo hominem, propter quem anima fieret, dicendum. Ipsa enim ignobilior luteo plasmate intellectualis 105 natura ostenderetur. 233C

⟨Capvt⟩ XXVIIII
Constitutio unam eandemque anime et corpori [subsistentiae] causam esse subsistentiae

1. Sed dum sit unus homo, ex anima et corpore constitutus, unum 233D
5 ipsius atque commune constitutionis principium substituitur, ne ipse se ipso antiquior iuniorque fiat, corporali quidem prius existente in ipso, altero uero posterius constituto. Sed in prognostica quidem Dei uirtute, iuxta paulo ante redditam rationem, omnem

---

99/102 neque secundum – aestimandum] cfr Plat., *Phaedr.* 246c; Greg. Nyss., *Anim. et res.* (p. 84, 14 – p. 85, 9)

XXIX, 4/119 sed dum – pullulationum efficitur] cfr Greg. Nyss., *Anim. et res.* (p. 80, 8 – 81, 2)   8 iuxta paulo ante redditam rationem] cfr *supra*, cap. XVII, 66-76 (p. 113); XVIII, 55-72 (p. 120)

---

92 non igitur] οὐκοῦν *PG Forb.*   97 non ergo] οὐκοῦν *PG Forb.*   dixeris] ἐπίσης *PG Forb.* (εἴπῃς *E. legisse uel intellexisse uidetur*)   100 circumuolutas] *correxi* (*cfr* συμπεριπολούσας *PG Forb.*, περιπολούσας *Forb.*^{u.l.}), circum uoluptas *B*   101 concurrendi] συμπαρέχειν *q*, συμπαραθέειν *PG Forb.*   102 neque bene] *abhinc cap. diu. Forb..; E. et PG Forb.*^{u.l.} *et Dionysius Exiguus aliter diuidunt*   bene] αὖ *PG Forb.* (εὖ *E. legisse uel intellexisse uidetur*)

XXIX, 1 *suppleui cum Capp., om.* B   2/3 Κατασκευὴ τοῦ μίαν καὶ τὴν αὐτὴν ψυχῇ τε καὶ σώματι τὴν αἰτίαν τῆς ὑπάρξεως εἶναι *PG Forb.*   2 subsistentiae] *seclusi, bis praeb.* B (*cfr l. 3) non praeb. PG Forb.*

DE IMAGINE, XXIX

humanam plenitudinem substitisse dicendum, contestante in hoc prophetia quae dicit *Deum uidisse omnia ante generationem eorum*, in conditione uero per singula alterum altero praeposuisse, neque ante corpus animam, neque iterum ante animam corpus, ne dissideat a se ipso homo temporis differentiam partitus.

2. Nam dum natura nostra duplex intelligitur, iuxta doctrinam apostolicam, uisibilis quidem hominis et occulti, si unum quidem prius subsisteret, alterum uero superueniret, imperfecta conditoris reprehenderetur uirtus, uniuersitati simul cumulatim non sufficiens, sed opus segregans et particulariter circa utrumque separatorum sollicita.

3. Sed sicut in frumento dicimus, uel in altero quodam seminum, totum simul unum comprehendi uirtute spicae speciem, faenum, culmum, per medium zonas, fructum, aristas, et nihil horum in ratione naturae prius subsistere seu post aduenire dicimus naturae seminis, sed ordine quodam naturali insitam semini uirtutem manifestari, non tamen alt(er)am naturam supermisceri; eadem ratione etiam humanam seminationem (hoc est generationem uel creationem) suscepimus in prima constitutionis occasione conseminatam quidem iuxta naturae uirtutem, expandi uero ac manifestari per quandam naturalem consequentiam, ad id quod perfectum est prouenientem, non accipiens aliquid eorum quae extra sunt in occasionem perfectionis, sed se ipsam ad perfectum per consequentiam adducens. Sic neque animam ante corpus, neque sine anima corpus uerum esse dicere, sed unum utriusque principium, iuxta rationem quidem in primo Dei consilio fundatum, iuxta uero alteram rationem in generationis occasionibus constitutum.

4. Vt enim non est unum per membra diuisionem artuum scire et quod ad conceptionem corporis ante formationem inseritur, sic

---

XXIX, 10/11 Dan. 13, 42

35/50 iuxta uero – proueniens] uide etiam Ioh. Scot., *Periphys.* 3 (p. 166, 4876-4881) (= col. 735AB)

---

11 in conditione – praeposuisse] ἐν δὲ τῇ καθ᾽ ἕκαστον δημιουργίᾳ μὴ προτιθέναι τοῦ ἑτέρου τὸ ἕτερον *PG Forb.* 12 neque ante corpus – ante animam corpus] μήτε πρὸ τοῦ σώματος τὴν ψυχήν, μήτε τὸ ἔμπαλιν *PG Forb.* 25 alteram] *correxi (cfr* ἑτέραν *PG Forb.)*, altam *B* 26/27 hoc est – creationem] *non praeb. PG Forb.* 28 quidem iuxta naturae uirtutem] μὲν κατὰ (μὲν κατὰ *om. PG Forb.*) τὴν τῆς φύσεως δύναμιν *PG Forb. q* 37 ut enim – artuum scire] ὡς (ὡς γὰρ *Forb.*) οὐκ ἔστι τὴν κατὰ τὰ μέλη διάρθρωσιν ἐνιδεῖν *PG Forb.* (ἐν ἰδεῖν *E. legisse uel intellexisse uidetur*)

neque animae proprietates in eodem possibile est intelligere priusquam in operationem proueniant. Ac sicut nemo dubitarit ad artuum uiscerumque differentias illud quod intus est figurari, non alia quadam uirtute superueniente, sed insita naturaliter ad hanc operationem sufficiente; sic etiam de anima proportionaliter est aeque intelligi, quia etsi per quasdam operationes manifestas non cognoscatur, nihil minus est in illo. Et enim species futuri hominis constituendi in illo est uirtute, latet uero eo quod impossibile est ante necessariam consequentiam apparere: similiter etiam anima est quidem in illo et non apparet, apparebit autem per propriam in se ipsa naturalem operationem, cum corporali incremento proueniens.

5. Nam quia non ex mortuo corpore ipsa ad conceptionem uirtus segregatur, sed ex animato atque uiuenti, propterea dicimus rationabile esse dicere non mortuum neque inanimatum esse quod ex uiuente in uitae occasionem procedit; quod enim in carne anima caret, omnino est mortuum; mors autem per priuationem animae fit. Nemo autem in hoc antiquiorem habitudine dixerit priuationem, siquidem inanimatum, hoc est mortuum, antiquius esse animo quis constituerit. Si uero quis etiam euidentius quaesierit argumentum uiuendi illam partem quae principium constituendi fit animalis, possibile est etiam ex aliis signis ex quibus animatum ex mortuo discernitur inuenire, ac per hoc intelligere. Argumentum enim uiuendi in hominibus facimus calidum esse quoddam et efficax et mobile; frigidum uero et immobile in corporibus nihil aliud nisi mortuum est.

6. Quoniam igitur calidum et efficax uidemus hoc de quo sermonem facimus, non inanimatum esse ex his argumentamur. Sed sicut secundum corporalem eius partem non carnem dicimus illud et ossa et capillos et quaecumque circa humanum corpus considerantur, sed in uirtute quidem esse horum singula, nondum uero uisibiliter apparere; sic etiam in parte animali nondum quidem totum animosum scilicet et quaecumque circa animam considerantur in illo regionem habere dicimus, proportionaliter uero, cum constitutione corporis ac perfectione, etiam animae operationes in subiecto crescere.

---

30 intelligere] intelleg- *B*   43 proportionaliter] *scripsi cum Capp.*, proporci- *B*   44 aeque] aequae *B*   intelligi] intelleg- *B*   53 esse²] οἴεσθαι *PG Forb.*, οἴεσθαι εἶναι *Forb.*^{*u.l.*}, εἶναι *q*   62 intelligere] intelleg- *B*   70/71 nondum quidem totum animosum scilicet] οὔπω μὲν τὸ λογικὸν καὶ ἐπιθυμητικὸν καὶ θυμοειδὲς *PG Forb.* (τὸ λογικὸν καὶ ἐπιθυμητικὸν *om. E. ut uid.*)

7. Sicut enim perfectus homo in maioribus manifestam animae habet operationem, sic in principio constitutionis conuenientem commensurabilemque praesenti utilitati cooperationem animae in se ipso ostendit, dum ipsa sibi ipsi per impositam materiem conueniens habitaculum conformat: neque enim possibile esse cogitamus alienis aedificiis animam coaptari, quemadmodum non est in cera sigillum ad alienam adunari sculpturam.

Capp. 256

8. Sicut autem corpus ex paruissimo ad perfectum prouenit, sic etiam animae operatio conuenienter ingenita subiecto coinditur et concrescit. Praecedit enim ipsius animae in prima constitutione, ueluti radicis cuiusdam in terra occulti, ipsa sola a⟨u⟩ctiua et nutritiua uirtus: non enim plus capit assumpti in conceptionem paruitas. Deinde, accedente in lucem germine soleque pullulationem ostendente, sensiua gratia superadicitur. Corroborato uero iam et in commensurabilem longitudinem recurrente, rationabilis uirtus ueluti quidam fructus incipit lucere: non tota cumulatim apparet, sed organi perfectioni studiose concrescens, tantum semper fructifera quantum subiecti uirtus capit.

237C

9. Si autem quaeris in formatione corporis animales operationes, *attende tibi ipsi*, ait Moyses, et lege ueluti in libro operationum animae historiam: ipsa enim tibi natura narrat, sermone omni euidentius uarias in corpore animae sollicitudines, et in uniuersalibus et particularibus formationibus.

237D

10. Sed superfluum arbitror ea quae secundum nos ipsos sunt edisserere, ueluti quorundam perspicuorum miracula narrantes. Quis enim, se ipsum aspiciens, sermone indiget suam naturam doceri? Nam possibile est eum, qui uitae modum intelligit ac ueluti ad omnem uitalem operationem oportunum habere corpus discit, cognoscere circa quid germinalis animae uita uacarit, praeter primam nascentis formationem; ita ut per hoc manifestum sit etiam minus intuentibus non mortuum et inanimatum in officina animae fieri quod ad animalis germinationem ex animantis corpore adtractum inseritur.

240A

11. Etenim et fructuum corda et radicum euulsiones non mortua ab insita naturae uitali uirtute terrae committimus, sed conseruantia in se ipsis occultam quidem, uiuentem uero omnino

---

94 Deut. 4, 23

85 auctiua] *correxi* (*cfr* αὐξητική *PG Forb.*), actiua *B*   88 superadicitur] ἐπήνθησεν *PG Forb.* (ἐπενετέθη *uel similiter E. legisse uel intellexisse uidetur*)   95 historiam] ist- *B*   103 germinalis animae uita] τὸ φυσικὸν (φυτικὸν *Forb.*ᵘˑˡ·) τῆς ψυχῆς *PG Forb.*

occulti proprietatem. Talem quoque uirtutem non terra continens ingerit extrinsecus a se ipsa discernens – ipsa enim etiam mortua lignorum in pullulationem producit – sed insitam uirtutem praeclare perficit, per proprium humorem ipsa quidem nutri-
115 tum germen in radicem, in robur, in cor, et ramorum propagines perficit: quod impossibile esset fieri, nisi quadam naturali uirtute imposita, quae dum cognatam et conuenientem ex accu⟨m⟩bentibus humoribus escam in se ipsam attrahit, dumus et arbor uel spica uel quodcumque fotarum pullulationum efficitur.

⟨Capvt XXX⟩
Speculatio quaedam medicinalis
de constitutione corporis nostri per pauca

1. Sed subtilem quidem corporis nostri formationem unusquisque
5 se ipsum docet ex his quibus uidet et uiuit et sentit, suam naturam se ipsam docentem habens. Licet etiam eum qui studiosam in libris talia sapientum de talibus historiam recipit omnia subtiliter discere; alii quidem quomodo habeant singula eorum quae in nobis sunt duce positione docuerunt; alii uero ad quid omnes cor-
10 poris particulae factae sunt cogitauerunt et edisseruerunt, ut sufficiens inde humanae constitutionis scientia studiosis fieret. Si autem quis quaesierit horum omnium ecclesiam magistram fieri (nam ipse spiritualium ouium pastor, sicut ait Dominus, non alienam uocem audit), per pauca etiam de his sermonem accipiemus.
15 2. Tria circa corporis naturam intelleximus, quorum causa singula quae in nobis sunt constituuntur. Nam quaedam propter ui-

---

XXX, 13/14 nam ipse – uocem audit] cfr Ioh. 10, 5

XXX, 15/40 tria circa – principia] uide Gvill. S. Theod., *Nat. corp.* 52-54 (p. 121-122, 630-658)   15/27 tria circa – respicit] cfr Gal., *UP* 6, 7 (vol. 3, p. 435-436) et 14, 1 (vol. 4, p. 142-143)

---

111 occulti] τοῦ πρωτοτύπου *PG Forb.* (τοῦ κρυπτοῦ *uel similiter E. legisse uel intellexisse uidetur*)   112 ingerit] iggerit *B*, ἐντίθησιν *PG Forb.* (*cfr XXV, 70; XXX, 195*)   113 in pullulationem] *correxi* (*cfr l. 87;* εἰς βλάστην *PG Forb.*), pupulationem *B*, inpupulationem *Capp.*   117/118 ex accumbentibus humoribus] ἐκ τῶν παρακειμένων *PG Forb.*   117 accumbentibus] *correxi*, accubentibus *B*   119 fotarum] φρυγανικῶν *PG Forb.*

XXX, 1 *om. B*   8/9 alii – docuerunt] ὧν οἱ μὲν ὅπως ἔχει θέσεως τὰ καθ' ἕκαστον τῶν ἡμῖν, διὰ τῆς ἀνατομῆς ἐδιδάχθησαν *PG Forb.*   12 fieri] ὡς εἰς μηδὲν τῆς ἔξωθεν φωνῆς ἐπιδέεσθαι *add. PG Forb.* (*quod om. E. ut uid.*)

uere, quaedam propter bene uiuere, alia uero ad successionem futurorum oportunitatem habent. Quaecumque igitur in nobis talia sunt sine quibus consistere humana uita non recipitur, in tribus particulis intelleximus: in cerebro, in corde et in epare. Quaecumque uero adiectio quaedam sunt bonorum et honorabilia, bene uiuere per illa donante homini natura, haec circa sensuum sunt organa. Nam talia uitam quidem nobis non constituunt quoniam, deficientibus quibusdam saepe, nihil minus in uiuendo est homo. Sed impossibile est, ex his quae operantur, secundum uitam deliciarum participationem habere. Tertia uero consideratio ad futuram successionem respicit. Sunt autem et alia quaedam praeter haec quae ad permanentiam communia omnibus subiecta sunt, conuenientes adiectiones per se introducentia, ut uenter et pulmo: pulmo quidem spiritu ignem qui in corde est sufflans, uenter uero escam uisceribus introducens.

3. Sic itaque nostra constitutione diuisa, diligenter est intuendum quia non uniformiter nobis ex una ad uiuendum uirtus deducitur, sed plurimis particulis natura ad constitutionem nostram occasiones inspirans necessariam facit ad totum ex singulis collationem. Itaque quae ad munimen uitae pulchritudinemque natura machinata est et plura sunt et ea ad se inuicem differentiam habent.

4. Sed arbitror prius in paucis oportere eorum quae ad constitutionem uitae nobis constituta sunt prima segregare principia. Ipsa igitur uniuersi corporis materia, communis singulis membris subiecta, sileat nunc: nil enim nobis ad speculationem perficiet ipsa uniuersalis naturae ratio cum particulari theoria.

5. Hoc igitur ab omnibus confesso, omnia elementa quae in mundo considerantur in nobis esse particula, calidi et frigidi et alterius symsugiae quae in umido et sicco intelligitur, per singula in nobis accipienda est.

27/31 sunt – introducens] cfr Plat., *Tim.* 70c-d; Gal., *UP* 6, 2 (vol. 3, p. 412); 4, 1 (vol. 3, p. 266-267)   30 pulmo] uide etiam Ioh. Scot., *Periphys.* 5 (p. 121, 3900-3913) (= col. 947AB)   32/38 itaque – habent] cfr Gal., *UP* 9, 8 (vol. 3, p. 714)

19 humana uita] -am -am $B^{a.c.}$ 21 honorabilia] φιλοτιμία *PG Forb.* (φιλότιμα *uel quasi* φιλοτίμια *E. legisse uel intellexisse uidetur*)   25 ex his quae operantur] δίχα τούτων τῶν ἐνεργειῶν *PG Forb.*   26 tertia] -cia *B*   35 inspirans] ἐπινείμασα *PG Forb.* (ἐμπνεύσασα *E. legisse uel intellexisse uidetur*)   necessariam] -ia *Capp.*   43 naturae ratio] φυσιολογία *PG Forb.* (*cfr I, tit.*)   46 symsugiae] συζυγίας *PG Forb.*   umido] hum- *B*

6. Non ergo uidemus tres administratorias uitae uirtutes? Quarum una quidem totum caliditate fouet; altera uero humore calefactum subirrigat, ut aequali potentia contrariorum qualitatis in medio animal conseruaretur, neque umido suffocante superabundantia caliditatem, neque calido extinguente supereminentia humefactum; tertia uero uirtus per se ipsam continet iuxta quandam commissuram et adunationem discretos artus, coniunctionibus a se ipsa copulans omnibusque per se mobilem et uoluntariam uirtutem immittens quae, dum administrationem artuum relinquens, deficit neglectum corpus, uoluntarii spiritus expers facit.

7. Magis autem ante haec dignum est artificale nostrae naturae in conditione corporis intelligere. Quoniam enim durum densumque sensuales operationes non recipit, sicut est nosse in nostris ossibus et in germinibus terrae, in quibus uitae quidem quandam intelligimus speciem in crescendo et nutriendo, non tamen densitas subiecti sensum accipit; huius rei gratia oportebat, ueluti ceream quandam constitutionem operationibus quae in sensu sunt substituere, quae receptis characteribus insigniri ualeret, neque diffusam per excellentiam umiditatis (non enim permaneret in umido quod formaretur), neque densam in immensurabili fixura (non enim expressibile est ad characteres quod formabile non est), sed habentem teneritatis compactaeque soliditatis medietatem, ne pulcherrimae naturalium operationum, sensualis dico motionis, expers animal fieret.

8. Quoniam igitur et molle et formabile, nullam ex solidis habens cooperationem, immobile omnino esset et inerigibile secundum marina spirantia: propterea natura ossuum soliditatem corpori immiscuit, et haec ad se inuicem per connaturalem compaginem adunans, neruorum uinculis commissuras eorum constrinxit, sic eis acceptricem sensuum circumfundendo carnem impassibiliora et robustiora in superficie comprehendentem.

58/98 magis – ostensus est] cfr GAL., *Plac.* 1, 8, 13 (p. 208); *UP* 5, 9 (vol. 3, p. 378); 8, 5 (vol. 3, p. 633); 8, 6 (vol. 3, p. 636-637); 9, 14 (vol. 3, p. 740-741); 11, 18 (vol. 3, p. 925); 12, 2 (vol. 4, p. 3); 16, 2 (vol. 4, p. 270-271)   72/74 quoniam – spirantia] cfr ARIST., *PA* 4, 5, 681a18-20

48 non ergo] οὐκοῦν *PG Forb.*   51 umido] hum- *B*   53 tertia] *correxi*, -cia *B*   56/57 dum administrationem – neglectum corpus] ἧς ἐπιλειπούσης πάρετον (πέρατον *PG*, τὸ σῶμα *add. q*) γίνεται καὶ νεκρῶδες τὸ μέρος *PG Forb. q*   59 intelligere] intelle- *B*   65 characteribus] car- *B*   66 umiditatis] hum- *B*   67 umido] hum- *B*   68 ad characteres] πρὸς τοὺς τύπους *PG Forb.*   characteres] car- *B*   70 pulcherrimae] *correxi* (*cfr* τοῦ καλλίστου τῶν κατὰ τὴν φύσιν ἐνεργημάτων *PG Forb.*), -me *B*   73/74 secundum marina spirantia] κατὰ τοὺς θαλασσίους πνεύμονας *PG Forb.*

9. Huic igitur solidae ossuum naturae, ueluti quibusdam co-
80 lumnis pondus ferentibus, totum corporis imponens grauitatem,
non os indiuisibile uniuersitati infudit. Si enim sic constitutionem homo haberet, immobilis et inactualis permaneret, ueluti
quaedam arbor in uno loco manens, neque crurum successione in
id quod ante est motum praecedente, neque manuum subminis-
85 tratione utili huic uitae existente. Nunc uero gressibile esse et ac-
tuale organum propter hanc intelligentiam emachinatum est,
uoluntario spiritu per neruos ueniente dans motus corpori; inde 244C
manuum administratio uaria et multum uersibilis et ad omnem
cogitationem oportuna; hinc ceruicis circumuolutiones capitis-
90 que inclinationes et erectiones et ipsa secundum maxillas agilitas,
palpebrarum quoque distinctio simul cum nutu facta, reliquorum
item artuum motiones, neruis quibusdam retractis seu laxatis, ueluti ex machina quadam operantur. Ipsa uero per haec digna uirtus
proprium quendam imperatiuum possidet motum qui prompto
95 spiritu iuxta quandam naturae administrationem, in his quae per
singula sunt operatur. Radix autem omnium principiumque eorum motuum qui per n⟨eru⟩os sunt ipse neruosus ΥΜΗΝ, hoc est
membranula quae cerebrum continet, ostensus est.

10. Non iam igitur duximus oportere sciscitari si circa quandam
100 uitalium particularum tale quippiam sit, ostensa in eo motiua B112ʳ244D
operatione. Quia uero maximum quiddam ad uitam cerebrum
perficit, euidenter quod ex contrario accidit declarat: si enim
quoddam uulnus aut scissuram ΥΜΗΝ qui est circa ipsum patiatur,
continuo mors passionem sequitur, neque aduersus paruitatem
105 uulneris natura praeualente, ueluti fundamento quodam sub-
tracto totum aedificium cum parte concutitur. Si igitur eo patiente totius animalis corruptio manifesta est, hoc proprie fortassis uitae causam habere confessum.

87/96 uoluntario – operatur] uide Gvill. S. Theod., *Nat. corp.* 54-55 (p. 125, 665-677) quasi uerbatim   96/98 radix – ostensus est] uide Gvill. S. Theod., *Nat. corp.* 54 (p. 122, 662-664)   102/105 euidenter quod – praeualente] uide Gvill. S. Theod., *Nat. corp.* 54 (p. 122, 660-662)

79 solidae] *correxi* (*cfr* ταύτῃ τοίνυν τῇ στερρᾷ τῶν ὀστέων φύσει *PG Forb.*), -de *B*   86 intelligentiam] intelle- *B*   93 digna] διεξιοῦσα *PG Forb.*, ἐξ ἴσου *q* (ἀξιοῦσα *E. legisse uel intellexisse uidetur*)   94/95 prompto spiritu] προαιρετικῷ πνεύματι *PG Forb.* (*quod supra [l. 87] E. per* uoluntarius spiritus *interpretatus est*)   97 per neruos] *correxi* (*cfr* κατὰ τὰ νεῦρα *PG Forb.*), per nos *B*   107 proprie] *correxi cum Capp.* (*cfr* κυρίως *PG Forb.*), -iae *B*

11. Si autem et in desinentibus uiuere, insita naturae extincta caliditate, quod mortuum est gelidum efficitur, per hoc etiam in calido uitalem causam intelleximus: si enim eo deficiente mors secuta est, omni necessitate praesentia ipsius animal consistere confitendum est. Talis autem uirtutis ueluti quendam fontem cor esse cognouimus, ex quo fistulares pori multipliciter diuisi, alius ab alio nascentes, uniuerso corpori calidum igneumque spiritum effundunt.

12. Quoniam uero omnino etiam oportebat cibum quendam calido ex natura conuenire – non enim recipit ignis a se ipso manere, nisi ex conuenienti cibo nutritus – propterea sanguinis riuuli, ueluti ex fonte quodam ex epare surgentes, cum calido spiritu ubique per corpus transeunt, ne separatum, altera ex altera passio facta, naturam corrumperet. Erudiat inordinatos erga aequalitatem, ex natura discentes quia superfluitas corruptrix passio est.

13. Sed quia solus Deus non indigens est, humana autem paupertas ea quae extrinsecus sunt ad suam constitutionem appetit, propterea his tribus uirtutibus quibus diximus totum corpus administrari, influentem extrinsecus introducit materiam, differentibus uiis quod conuenit eis administrans.

14. Nam fonti sanguinis, qui est epar, quod ex cibo praebetur suggerit: quod enim ex eo semper introducitur in fontes eparis ex epare praeparat manare, quemadmodum in monte nix ex proprio humore fontes qui circa radices montis sunt auget, suum umidum ex profundo in uenas quae deorsum sunt comprimens.

15. Spiritum uero qui in corde est ex uicino introducit per propria uiscera, quae quidem uocantur pulmones. Est autem pulmo aeris receptaculum, ex imposita arteria quae extrinsecus spiritum respirationibus attractum in os administrat; in cuius (pulmonis

---

109/123 si autem – passio est] uide GVILL. S. THEOD., *Nat. corp.* 56 (p. 122-123, 678-689)   109/114 si autem – cognouimus] cfr PLAT., *Tim.* 70ab; GAL., *UP* 6, 7 (vol. 3, p. 436)   117/122 quoniam – corrumperet] cfr GAL., *UP* 6, 10 (vol. 3, p. 444); 16, 13-14 (vol. 4, p. 338-342)   135/146 est autem – infundens] cfr GAL., *UP* 6, 7 (vol. 3, p. 433); 6, 10 (vol. 3, p. 448); 6, 15 (vol. 3, p. 481)   135 pulmo] uide etiam IOH. SCOT., *Periphys.* 5 (p. 121, 3900-3913) (= col. 947AB).

110 quod mortuum est] τὸ (σῶμα add. q) νεκρωθέν PG Forb. q   113 fontem] *scripsi* (*cfr* πηγήν *PG Forb.*), fortem B   120 calido] τῷ θέρμῳ PG Forb., *non praeb.* q   130 introducitur] *correxi cum Capp.* (*cfr l. 134; cfr* ἐπεισαγόμενον *PG Forb.*), -dicitur B   132/133 umidum] hum- B   134/135 spiritum uero – per propria uiscera] τὸ δὲ ἐγκάρδιον πνεῦμα διὰ τοῦ γείτονος ἐπεισάγεται σπλάγχνου PG Forb.   137/138 pulmonis scilicet] *glossa uidetur*

scilicet) medio cor inuolutum, ad imitationem operationis mobilis semper ignis, indesinenter etiam ipsum mouetur, quemadmodum in aerariis officinis fabrum folles faciunt, attrahit ad se ipsum, ex uicino spiritu per uiscerum distentionem suas implens concauitates suumque igneum exsufflans, in habitis arteriis inspirat, et hoc faciens non desinit hunc quidem aerem perfecto extrinsecus per distentionem in suas concauitates attrahens, illum uero a se ipso per concasum – hoc est per contractionem – arteriis infundens.

16. Mihi uidetur etiam spontaneae huius spirationis causam in nobis fieri. Nam saepe animus quidem in aliis sollicitus est, uel etiam per omnia in omnibus soluto in somno corpore silet, flatus uero aeris non desinit, in nullo ad hoc uoluntate cooperante. Arbitror enim, quoniam pulmone cor comprehenditur eique pars eius retro naturaliter adheret, suis distentionibus et contractionibus uiscera commouens, aeris demersionem et expirationem pulmoni emachinatum fuisse. Compactus enim quidam est et omnes in se concauitates iuxta fundamentum arteriae apertas habet, contractus quidem et concidens, receptum in concauis spiritum necessario elidit, ipseque spiritus foras prosilit, recedens autem atque reductus per distentionem ad id quod mouetur aerem per pondus attrahit.

17. Et haec est spontaneae huius spirationis causa, ipsa impossibilitas igneum quiescere. Nam quia proprium caloris est ipsa quae in motu est operatio, huius autem caloris principia in corde intelleximus, assiduitas in hac parte motus incessabilem aeris tractum et exspirationem per pulmones operatur; ac per hoc, superaddito contra naturam igneo, calidi anelitus in febribus ardentius fiunt, ueluti corde festinante impositam in se flagrantiam recentiori spiritu extinguere.

18. Sed quia egena quaedam est natura et eorum quae ad suam constitutionem sunt per omnia indiget, non aeris solummodo speciem appetit et spiritus calorem suscitantis, qui extrinsecus ad animalis conseruationem semper introducitur, sed etiam escam quae superapparentem corporis molem adicit necessariam habet.

---

140 fabrum] *scripsi* (*cfr* οἷόν τι ποιοῦσιν ἐν τοῖς χαλκείοις αἱ φύσαι *PG Forb.*), fabrini *B*   145 hoc est per contractionem] *non praeb. PG Forb.*   147 spontaneae] -ee *B*   153 et] *suppl. s.l. B*   158 ad id quod mouetur] πρὸς τὸ κενούμενον *PG Forb.*, πρὸς τὸ κινούμενον *q Forb.*[u.l.]   160 spontaneae] -ee *B*   166/167 recentiori] *correxi, recensioris B*   168 est natura] ἐστὶν ἡμῶν ἡ φύσις *PG Forb.*

Et propterea frumento et potu replet quod deest, tractiuam quandam illius quod deficit uirtutem et repulsiuam illius quod superfluum est corpori ingerens, neque ad hoc ignis qui in corde est paruam naturae praestat cooperationem.

19. Nam quia potissima uitalium particularum iuxta redditam rationem cor est, quod calido singulas partes uiuificat, undique ipsum efficax esse actuosa uirtute formator noster fecit, ut nulla pars eius otiosa et stolida ad uniuersitatis administrationem linqueretur. Propterea retro quidem pulmonem subingrediens et per assiduum motum ad se ipsum uiscera contrahens, amplificat ad pondus aeris poros reserans iterumque spirare quod assumitur praeparat, in his uero quae coram ipsum sunt capacitati uentris calidum infundens, ipsum quoque ad suas operationes moueri facit: non in spiritus attractum resuscitans, sed in receptionem cibi conuenientis. Nam proxime sibi inuicem naturaliter subsistunt introitus spiritus et cibi, adherent autem per longum alterum ad alterum, aequalique mensura sursum uersus finem conperficiunt, ita ut etiam ad se inuicem conterminentur, et in ore uias in unum consumment; unde in uno quidem cibi, in altero uero spiritus fit introitus.

20. Sed in profundum non semper adherens pororum simsugia permanet. Nam cor medium utriusque collationi insertum, uni quidem ad respirationem, alteri uero ad escam uirtutes ingerit. Naturaliter autem igneum quidem succendentem materiam quaerere consueuit, hoc autem circa receptaculum cibi necessario contingit: quanto magis enim ardor ex uicina caliditate efficitur, tanto magis quae calorem subnutriunt trahuntur. Huiusmodi autem motum concupiscentiam nominamus.

21. Si uero sufficientem materiem id quod cibum continet comprehendat, neque sic operatio ignis quiescit; sed ueluti in conflatorio conformationem quandam materiae intus facit, soluens constituta et ueluti ex quodam cacabo perfundens ad consequen-

---

173/175 tractiuam – ingerens] cfr GAL., *Nat. Fac.* 3, 8 (p. 177); *UP* 4, 7 (vol. 3, p. 275)
187/192 nam proxime – introitus] cfr PLAT., *Tim.* 78b   201/211 si uero – homo] cfr PLAT., *Tim.* 72e-73a; ARIST., *PA* 3, 14, 675b22-26; GAL., *UP* 4, 2 (vol. 3, p. 267-269); 4, 17 (vol. 3, p. 325)

175 ingerens] *correxi*, iggerens B   178 calido] τῷ θερμῷ πνεύματι PG Forb.
183 assumitur] *correxi*, assummitur B   190 in ore] ἑνὶ στώματι PG Forb. (ἐν στώματι E. *legisse uel intellexisse uidetur*)   193 simsugia] τῆς συζυγίας PG Forb., τῇ συζυγίᾳ q Forb.[u.l.]

tes uias participat, deinde quod crassius est ex sincero segregans, subtile quidem per riuulos quosdam in eparis portas ducit, feculentum uero cibi subponderatum in latiores poros interiorum repellit, ac multiformibus eorum anfractibus retorquens morose in uisceribus detinet, ne per rectum porum facile animal degerens continuo iterum concupiscentiam moueat, ac tali sollicitudine nequaquam quiescat secundum irrationabilium naturam homo.

22. Quoniam uero maxime epari caloris operatione opus erat ad umidorum in sanguinem conuersionem, distat autem illud a corde secundum positionem (non enim possibile erat, ut arbitror, principium quoddam radixque uitalis dum sit uirtutis ab altero principio coartari), ne quid administrationi calidae essentiae quae segregatum est noceret, porus neruosus – qui ab his qui talia sapiunt arteria nominatur – igneum spiritum ex corde accipiens, fert eum ad epar ubi, iuxta introitum humorum consumatus umiditatemque per caliditatem refocillans, quiddam in umido reponit, cognatione ignis igneo colore, sanguinis speciem rubrificans.

23. Inde occasionem accipientes gemini quidam riuuli, uterque fistulariter proprium suum comprehendentes, spiritum uidelicet et sanguinem (ut facilis esset humoris meatus, cum motu caloris proficiscens), per cauatum corpus multipliciter diuisum scatent in innumerabilia riuulorum principia diffusionesque per omnem partem discissi. Miscendo autem ad se inuicem uitalium uirtutum duo principia, illud uidelicet quod calidum ubique in corpus et illud quod umidum immittit, ueluti quoddam publicum uectigal necessarium ex his quae sunt in principaliori uitalis administrationis munera ferunt.

24. Est autem ipsum principium, quod secundum membranas cerebrumque consideratur, ex quo omnis quidem articuli motus omnisque cohibentium congrauatio, omnis item spontaneus spiritus per singulas particulas infusus, efficacem mobilemque ter-

---

212/214 quoniam uero – positionem] cfr GAL., *UP* 4, 3 (vol. 3, p. 269); 4, 14 (vol. 3, p. 311) 217/231 porus – ferunt] cfr GAL., *UP* 16, 10 (vol. 4, p. 266) 217/218 porus – accipiens] uide etiam IOH. SCOT., *Periphys.* 2 (p. 76, 1778-1779) (= col. 581C) 221 cognatione – rubrificans] cfr PLAT., *Tim.* 80e; GAL., *UP* 4, 4 (vol. 3, p. 272) 232/258 est autem – custodiretur] cfr GAL., *UP* 6, 2 (vol. 3, p. 416); 8, 9 (vol. 3, p. 659); *Sem.* 1, 8 (vol. 4, p. 541)

205 participat] μεταχεῖ *PG Forb.* (μετέχει *E. legisse uel intellexisse uidetur*) 206 subtile] -lem $B^{a.c.}$ 213 umidorum] hum- *B* 219 ubi] uni *Capp.* 219/220 umiditatemque] hum- *B* 220 umido] hum- *B* 225 diuisum] *correxi*, deu- *B* 229 umidum] hum- *B* publicum] puplicum *B* 232 membranas] μήνιγγας *PG Forb.*

renam nostram statuam ueluti ex machina quadam ostendunt. Nam calidi purgatissimum umidique subtilissimum, ab utraque uirtute per quandam mixturam concretionemque adunata, nutriunt et componunt ex uaporibus cerebrum. Ex quo iterum in purius extenuata ab illo reflatio, membranam quae continet cerebrum sublinit, quae desursum in profundum fistulariter perueniens, per quae colla quae deinde sunt se ipsam insitamque sibi medullam deducens, spinae basi conterminatur – ueluti quidam auriga ipsa indit per singula motionis et stationis appetitum atque uirtutem.

25. Propter hoc uidetur mihi etiam tutiori custodia dignam esse, in capite quidem duplis ossuum amictibus in gyro inuoluta, per colla uero spinarum ordinibus multiformibusque secundum figuram perplexionibus, per quae in omni impassibilitate custoditur per comprehendentem se custodiam munimen habens.

26. Similiter autem si quis etiam de corde considerarit quia, ueluti quaedam domus munita, per robustissima ossa circumstantiis quae in gyro sunt uallata et circumpacta est; retro quidem enim est spina, aequalibus latitudinibus hinc inde munita; in utraque uero obliquitate laterum positio comprehendens, medium impassibile perficit; in his uero quae ante sunt, pectus et ualuae singugia praemittitur, et undique ei munimen ab his quae extrinsecus perturbant custodiretur.

27. Possibile est autem per agriculturam uidere, imbre ex nubibus uel ex fluminibus irrigatione umidum subiectum faciente. Hortus autem quidam sermoni supponatur, innumerabiles quidem arborum differentias uariasque ex terra nascentium species in se ipso nutriens, quorum etiam figura et qualitas, coloris item proprietas, in multa differentia per singula inspicitur. Tantis igitur per unum locum humore nutritis, ueluti singula subirrigans una quaedam uirtus est secundum naturam; ipsa uero nutritorum specialitas humorem in qualitates differentes transmittit. Idem enim

---

246/250 propter – habens] cfr Plat., *Tim.* 75c   259/296 possibile – producit] cfr Gal., *Nat. Fac.* 1, 6 (p. 11)

---

237 umidique] hum- B   239/240 in purius] *correxi* (*cfr* ἐπὶ τὸ καθαρώτατον *PG Forb.*, ἐπὶ τὸ καθαρώτερον *Forb.*$^{u.l.}$), impurius B   240 membranam] ὑμένα *PG Forb.*   243 conterminatur] πάσαις ὀστέων τε καὶ ἁρμονιῶν συμβολαῖς καὶ μυῶν ἀρχαῖς *add.* *PG Forb.*   254 aequalibus latitudinibus hinc inde munita] ταῖς ὠμοπλάταις ἑκατέρωθεν (ἀμφοτέρωθεν *q Forb.*$^{u.l.}$) ἠσφαλισμένη *PG Forb. q*   256 singugia] συζυγία *PG Forb.*   260 umidum] hum- B   265 ueluti singula subirrigans] ἡ μὲν ὑπονοτίζουσα τὰ καθ᾽ ἕκαστον *PG Forb.*

DE IMAGINE, XXX

amaricatur quidem in absintho, in corrumpentem fluctum in conio transmutatur, et alius in alio fit, in croco, in balsamo, in papauere: in uno enim calificatur, in altero friget, in tertio mediam qualitatem infundit, in lauro et schino et in talibus bene spirans est; in ficulnea et [ΟΓΧΝΗ est species piri quam uolemam Latini uocant: hinc Virgilius *grauibus uolemis*] ochna dulcis efficitur, et per uineam botrus uinumque factus est, et mali succus, et rosae rubedo, et clarum lilii, et ceruleum ΙΟΥ, et purpureum yachintinae tincturae, et omnia quaecumque per terram uidenda sunt, ex uno eodemque humore pullulantia in tantas differentias secundum figuram et speciem et qualitates discernuntur. Tale aliquot miraculum etiam per animatum nostrum aruum a natura fit, magis autem a domino nature. Ossa, ilia, arteriae, nerui, coniunctiones, carnes, cutis, adipes, capilli, adenes, ungues, oculi, aures, et omnia huiusmodi et innumerabilia alia, cum his differentibus proprietatibus a se inuicem discreta, ex una specie escae conuenienter eorum naturae nutriuntur, ita in unoquoque subiectorum, cuicumque ingesta fuerit secundum illud mouetur in escam, conuenientem propriamque et connaturalem proprietati partis factam. Nam si in oculo fiat ac spectiuae particulae contemperatur, in quae differentiis tunicarum quae circa oculum sunt proprie in unumquodque partitur; si autem partibus quae per auditum sunt influxerit, auditoriae miscetur naturae; et quod in labium uenit, labium factum est; et in osse figitur, et in medulla mollificatur, roboratur in neruo, in superficie extenditur, in unguem ingreditur, in capillorum generationem conuenientes uapores subtiles facit. Si quidem per poros perplexos prodeat, crispos tortuososque capillos effundit, si uero per rectas poros uaporum capillos facientium fuerit processio, rectos planosque producit.

---

273 grauibus uolemis] cfr VERG., *Georg.* 2, 88; SERV., *Aen.* 3, 233: "... unde et pyra quaedam uolema dicuntur, eo quod uolam impleant" 292/296 in capillorum – producit] cfr PLAT., *Tim.* 76b-c; ARIST., *PA* 2, 14, 658a -15, 658b; GAL., *UP* 11, 14 (vol. 3, p. 901)

268/269 in conio] ἐν τῷ κωνείῳ *PG Forb.* 271 infundit] ἔχει *PG* (ἐγχεῖ *E. legisse uel intellexisse uidetur*) schino] ἐν σχοίνῳ *PG*, ἐν σχίνῳ *Forb.* 272/273 ΟΓΧΝΗ est species – uolemis] *glossa E. uidetur* 273 ochna] ὄχνη *PG Forb.*, ὄγχνη *Forb.*ᵘ·ˡ· 279 tertio] terc- *B* 280 ossa – nerui] ὀστέα καὶ χόνδροι, φλέβες, ἀρτηρίαι, νεῦρα *PG Forb.* (φλέβες *om. E. ut uid.*) 281 adenes] ἀδένες *PG Forb.* oculi aures] ὀφθαλμοί, μυκτῆρες, ὦτα *PG Forb.* (μυκτῆρες *om. E. ut uid.*) 287 spectiuae] ὁρατικῷ *PG Forb.*

28. Sed multum ab his quae proposita sunt nobis sermo uagatus est, in operibus quae in profundis naturae sunt, et quodammodo quae in nobis constituta sunt et quae extrinsecus efficiunt quae per singula quae ad uiuendum sunt conantes subscribere, etiam cum his alia quaedam secundum primam diuisionem intelleximus.

29. Nam propositum erat seminalem constitutionis nostrae causam ostendere neque incorporalem esse animam neque corpus exanime, sed ab animatis et uiuentibus animatum ad primam constitutionem innasci. Accipiens uero humana natura ueluti quendam cibum propriis escis eam (dico causam) nutrit; utramque uero partem (materiam uidelicet et uitam) nutrit, et conuenienter in utraque parte incrementum manifestum habet. Continuo quidem per hanc artificalem et disciplinalem formationem coniunctam ei animae ostendit uirtutem, obscurius quidem per primam manifestationem, deinde uero cum organi perfectione elucentem.

30. Sicut in lapidum sculpturis est uidendum. Proponitur enim artifici animalis cuiusdam in lapide speciem ostendere; ad hoc autem qui ponitur, primum quidem lapidem ex connaturali materia excidit, deinde, ipsius superflua amputans, prius duxit quodammodo per primam figuram imitationem ipsius quod est secundum propositum, ita ut etiam inexpertum animal per uisibilia in speculatione artis consideretur; iterum operans, plus similitudini eius quod in studio est appropinquat; deinde, perfectam diligentemque speciem materiae ingerens, artem adduxit ad perfectionem: et est leo, uel homo, uel quodcumque consequens fuerit ab artifice factum paulo ante lapis informis. Non materia in speciem submutata, sed specie in materia superartificata: tale aliquid etiam in anima cogitans, ab eo quod consequens est non aberrabit. Nam omnia machinante natura et ex eiusdem generis materia acci-

---

306/318 utramque – propositum] uide Gvill. S. Theod., *Nat. corp.* 57 (p. 123, 690-698)

297 multum] *correxi*, -am *B*   298/301 et quodammodo – quaedam] καὶ ὑπογράφειν ἐπιχειρῶν ὅπως ἡμῖν καὶ ἐξ ὁποίων συνέστηκε τὰ καθ᾽ ἕκαστον, τά τε πρὸς τὸ ζῆν καὶ τὰ πρὸς τὸ εὖ ζῆν καὶ εἴ τι μετὰ τούτων ἕτερον *PG Forb.*   304 exanime] *correxi (cfr* μήτε ἄψυχον σῶμα *PG Forb.*), -mae *B*, ex anima *Capp.*   uiuentibus] σωμάτων *add. PG Forb.*   animatum] ζῶν (ζῶον *q*) καὶ ἔμψυχον *PG Forb. q*   constitutionem] ζῶον *PG Forb.*, ζωὴν *q Forb.*ᵘ·ˡ·, *om. Forb.*ᵘ·ˡ·   306 escis] δυνάμεσι *PG Forb.*, τροφαῖς *q*   dico causam] *non praeb. PG Forb.*   307 materiam uidelicet et uitam] *non praeb. PG Forb.*   326 et] *suppl. s.l. B*

DE IMAGINE, XXX

piente, in se ipsa ex homine partem ad creandum quam statuam dicimus. Ipsa paulo post sicut in operatione lapidis speciem consecuta est, obscuriorem quidem primo, ⟨euidentiorem uero et perfectiorem post operis consummationem. Sic ergo in sculptura organi animae species secundum subiecti analogiam praemonstratur, imperfecta in imperfecto, in perfecto perfecta futura. Quae ex principio perfecta esset, si in suo principio corrupta natura per malitiam non fuisset. Propterea nascimur ut pecudes, nec continuo nec nisi cum magnis et diuturnis laboribus relucere potest in nobis factoris imago, sed longa quadam uia per materiales et pecuales animae proprietates ad perfectionem suam homo ducitur.⟩

⟨...⟩

33. ⟨...⟩ ut sollicitudinem consequerentur suggerit, dicens *spoliari* oportere *ueterem hominem, et indui renouatum ad imaginem creantis.*

34. Vt redeamus iterum in diuinam gratiam illam, in qua creauit ab initio hominem dicens Deus: *"Faciamus hominem ad imaginem et similitudinem nostram"*! Cui gloria et potentia Patri et Filio et Sancto Spiritui in saecula. Amen.

340/342 Col. 3, 9-10   344/345 Gen. 1, 26

329/338 euidentiorem – ducitur] uide Gvill. S. Theod., *Nat. corp.* 57-58 (p. 123, 699-708) uerbatim

329 obscuriorem quidem primo] obscurioremque de primo *Capp.*, per quoque add. B *Capp. sed fortasse* perfectioremque *legendum* (*cfr* τελειότερον δὲ *PG Forb.*)   329/338 euidentiorem – ducitur] restitui ex Guill. S. Theod. (*uide app. parall.*), *non praeb.* B *Capp.*   332 imperfecto in] *hic des.* q   339 *§31-32 et partim §33 desunt iuxta ed. Forb.*   345/346 Patri et Filio et Sancto Spiritui] *non praeb.* PG Forb.

INDICES AD EDITIONEM CARMINVM
IOHANNIS SCOTTI ERIVGENAE
(pag. 3-66 huius uoluminis)
PERTINENTES

Index locorvm S. Scriptvrae

Index fontivm

Index metricvs

Index nominvm

INDEX LOCORVM SACRAE SCRIPTVRAE

		Op.	*lin.*	*pag.*
Genesis				
1, 2	cfr	Carm. 5	9/10	16
1, 27	cfr	Carm. 5	13	16
2, 2	cfr	Carm. 9	3	28
2, 10	cfr	Carm. 9	82	31
22, 9-13	cfr	Carm. 5	25/26	16
Exodus				
3, 22	cfr	Carm. 6	10	18
4, 1-10	cfr	Carm. 2	15/18	7
7, 8-13	cfr	Carm. 2	15/18	7
12, 7		Carm. 5	27/28	17
12, 12-13		Carm. 3	27	12
12, 26		Carm. 3	29	12
14, 26-28	cfr	Carm. 2	37/41	8
Numeri				
21, 7-9		Carm. 2	49	9
IV Regum				
18, 4	cfr	Carm. 2	49	9
Esther				
1, 6	cfr	Carm. 25	86	54
Psalmi				
19, 10	cfr	Carm. 17	7	40
35, 10	cfr	Carm. 8	28	24
71, 11	cfr	Carm. 10	4	32
106, 14	cfr	Carm. 6	23	18
Prouerbia				
9, 1	cfr	Carm. 25	74	53
31, 10	cfr	Carm. 4	25	15
Canticum Canticorum				
2, 2	cfr	Carm. 20	23	45
Ieremias				
42, 4 (LXX)	cfr	Carm. 25	93	54
Ezechiel				
40-48	cfr	App. 12	7	62

		Op.	*lin.*	*pag.*
40, 19	cfr	Carm. 25	87	54
Daniel				
9, 20-26	cfr	App. 12	8	62
Ionas				
2, 1-11	cfr	Carm. 9	5/6	28
Matthaeus				
1, 1	cfr	Carm. 8	39	25
7, 12		Carm. 1	78	6
7, 24	cfr	Carm. 20	16/17	44
12, 29		Carm. 1	40	4
25, 19	cfr	Carm. 1	82	6
26, 34	cfr	App. 6	3	57
26, 57	cfr	Carm. 9	44/45	29
26, 65	cfr	Carm. 9	45	29
26, 74-75	cfr	App. 6	3	57
Marcus				
3, 27	cfr	Carm. 1	40	4
14, 30	cfr	App. 6	3	57
14, 36		Carm. 9	79	31
14, 68	cfr	App. 6	3	57
14, 72	cfr	App. 6	3	57
16, 10	cfr	Carm. 2	56	9
Lucas				
1, 8-20		App. 15	5	64
1, 26	cfr	Carm. 25	14	51
1, 38	cfr	Carm. 8	61/62	26
2, 4	cfr	Carm. 25	52/53	53
6, 31	cfr	Carm. 1	78	6
10, 42	cfr	Carm. 23	12	49
22, 34	cfr	App. 6	3	57
22, 60-61	cfr	App. 6	3	57
24, 34		Carm. 9	29	29
Iohannes				
1, 1-3	cfr	Carm. 8	25/26	24
1, 5	cfr	Carm. 9	12	28
1, 14	cfr	Carm. 8	47	25
	cfr	Carm. 9	19	28
1, 18	cfr	Carm. 7	3/4	20
6, 37-40	cfr	Carm. 8	74/76	26
6, 55	cfr	Carm. 25	57	53
7, 42	cfr	Carm. 25	52/53	53
8, 12	cfr	Carm. 8	69	26
13, 38	cfr	App. 6	3	57

		Op.	*lin.*	*pag.*
18, 27	cfr	App. 6	3	57
19, 37	cfr	Carm. 1	23	3
19, 41	cfr	Carm. 1	38	4
20, 15		Carm. 2	53	9
20, 18	cfr	Carm. 2	56	9

Actus Apostolorum
| 17, 34 | | Carm. 10 | 12 | 32 |
| | cfr | Carm. 21 | 1/2 | 46 |

Ad Romanos
| 5, 12 | | Carm. 9 | 57 | 30 |
| 8, 15 | | Carm. 9 | 79 | 31 |

I ad Corinthios
1, 24		Carm. 2	57	9
2, 8		Carm. 9	49	30
15, 20	cfr	Carm. 3	59	13
15, 21		Carm. 3	57	13
15, 23	cfr	Carm. 3	59	13
15, 52-53	cfr	Carm. 25	41	52

II ad Corinthios
| 12, 2 | cfr | Carm. 21 | 16 | 46 |

Ad Galatas
| 4, 6 | | Carm. 9 | 79 | 31 |

Ad Philippenses
| 2, 7 | | Carm. 9 | 50 | 30 |

II ad Timotheum
| 4, 11 | cfr | App. 15 | 2 | 64 |

Ad Hebraeos
| 1 Cor. 1, 24 | cfr | App. 2 | 11 | 55 |

I Petri
| 5, 13 | cfr | App. 14 | 1 | 63 |

Apocalypsis
| 1, 16 | cfr | Carm. 12a | 10 | 34 |

INDEX FONTIVM

		Op.	*lin.*	*pag.*
Alcimvs Ecdicivs Avitvs				
Carmina				
1, 167	cfr	Carm. 3	63	13
4, 655	cfr	Carm. 2	42	8
5, 241	cfr	Carm. 3	27	12
6, 406	cfr	Carm. 22	10	48
Alcvinvs				
Carmina				
1, 1	cfr	Carm. 2	57	9
	cfr	App. 2	11	55
1, 640	cfr	Carm. 2	25	8
1, 1244	cfr	Carm. 1	79	6
1, 1508		Carm. 25	74	53
		Carm. 25	87	54
9, 159	cfr	Carm. 9	41	29
62, 117	cfr	Carm. 9	41	29
Aldhelmvs				
Aenigmata				
55, 1	cfr	App. 12	5	62
60, 10	cfr	App. 2	2	55
Carmina ecclesiastica				
4, 2, 26		Carm. 20	15/16	44
De laude uirginitatis				
praef. 4	cfr	App. 10	14	60
65		App. 12	11	62
154		App. 10	11	60
309		Carm. 8	38	24
403		Carm. 8	38	24
1044		App. 10	11	60
2232		App. 12	11	62
2896		App. 12	11	62
Anonymvs Bobbiensis				
79, 5, 1		Carm. 21	9	46
89, 5, 1		Carm. 20	1	44
89, 5, 4		Carm. 20	21	45

CARMINA 173

		Op.	lin.	pag.
Anthologia Latina				
678, 7	cfr	Carm. 6	18	18
678, 9		Carm. 7	21	21
ARATOR SVBDIACONVS				
Historia apostolica				
Act. 1, 287	cfr	Carm. 9	15	28
AVGVSTINVS				
De ciuitate Dei				
13, 12	cfr	Carm. 9	15	28
AVSONIVS				
Carmina				
21, 2, 36		App. 9a	2	59
21, 2, 36		App. 9b	2	59
21, 2, 36		App. 9c	3	59
BEDA VENERABILIS				
De die iudicii				
109	cfr	Carm. 20	7	44
Vita Cuthberti metrica				
1, 8		Carm. 21	11	46
11, 16	cfr	App. 10	1	60
47, 11	cfr	Carm. 10	5	32
CHALCIDIVS				
Translatio Platonis Timaei				
27c-28b	cfr	Carm. 3	7/8	11
CANDIDVS FVLDENSIS				
De uita Aeigili				
17, 93	cfr	Carm. 2	13	7
18, 4	cfr	Carm. 1	41	4
CORIPPVS				
In laudem Iustini Augusti minoris				
1, 341	cfr	Carm. 9	27	29
2, 59	cfr	Carm. 25	66	53
3, 176	cfr	Carm. 10	19	32
Iohannidos libri VIII				
1, 144	cfr	Carm. 4	43	15
2, 90	cfr	Carm. 9	41	29
4, 592	cfr	Carm. 8	27	24

	Op.	lin.	pag.
6, 518	cfr Carm. 9	41	29

Ecbasis cuiusdam captiui per tropologiam

cit. 603	Carm. 3	71	13

Ermoldvs Nigellvs

Carmen elegiacum in honorem Ludowici

2, 586	cfr App. 2	14	55
4, 174	cfr App. 2	14	55

Florvs Lvgdvnensis

Carmina

3, 116	cfr Carm. 9	82	31

Gregorivs Magnvs

Homiliae in Ezechielem Prophetam

2, 6 (col. 1007B)	Carm. 25	87	54
2, 6 (col. 1067D)	Carm. 25	87	54

Hericvs Avtissiodorensis

Vita metrica sancti Germani, episcopi Autissiodorensis

inuoc. 44	Carm. 8	5	22
inuoc. 69-70	Carm. 8	2/3	22
inuoc. 72	Carm. 8	6	22
6, 338	Carm. 25	9	51

Hieronymvs Stridonensis

Aduersus Rufinum

2, 25	cfr Carm. 20	16	44

Hildvinvs

Passio metrica sancti Dionysii

1, 579-580	Carm. 25	57/70	53

Passio sancti Dionysii

cap. 5	App. 8	5/8	58

Hrabanvs Mavrvs

Carmina

2, 25	cfr App. 2	17	56
83, 1	cfr App. 2	17	56

Hymnus Nynie

2, 1	Carm. 8	28	24

CARMINA 175

	Op.	lin.	pag.

IOHANNES SCOTVS ERIVGENA

Expositiones in hierarchiam coelestem

| 7, 83-84 | cfr Carm. 8 | 9 | 22 |

Glosse in Martianum Capellam

10, 3	cfr. Carm. 3	14	11
285, 14	cfr Carm. 8	19	23
428, 23	cfr Carm. 8	9	22
486, 3	cfr Carm. 8	21	23

Maximi confessoris Ambigua ad Iohannem iuxta Iohannis Scoti Eriugenae latinam interpretationem

| prooem. | cfr Carm. 22 | 15/16 | 48 |

Periphyseon

1, 14 (col. 459D)	cfr Carm. 8	29	24
1, 14 (col. 463A)	cfr Carm. 8	14	23
1, 20 (col. 461B-D)	cfr Carm. 24	20	50
2, 2 (col. 526C)	cfr Carm. 8	34	24
2, 23 (col. 542A-542B)	cfr Carm. 7	12	20
2, 28 (col. 535C), *schol.*	cfr Carm. 24	6	50
2, 47 (col. 541B-541C)	cfr Carm. 8	35	24
3, 9 (col. 642A)	cfr Carm. 5	3	16
3, 15 (col. 665Aff.)	cfr Carm. 5	3	16
3, 32 (col. 688B)	cfr Carm. 8	28	24
3, 33 (col. 718B)	cfr Carm. 3	19	12
4, 1 (col. 741C)	cfr Carm. 8	28	24
4, 20 (col. 741C)	cfr App. 2	9	55
5, 34 (col. 952B-C)	cfr Carm. 25	43/44	52
5, 35 (col. 954C)	cfr Carm. 8	35	24
5, 7 (col. 875C)	cfr Carm. 9	29	29
5, 8 (col. 994B)	cfr Carm. 9	30/31	29

Versio operum sancti Dionysii Areopagitae

| col. 1032D | cfr Carm. 21 | 14 | 46 |
| col. 1052D | cfr Carm. 21 | 5/6 | 46 |

Ilias latina

| 184 | cfr Carm. 9 | 41 | 29 |
| 233 | cfr Carm. 9 | 41 | 29 |

ISIDORVS HISPALENSIS

Expositio in Exodum

| 12-21 (col. 292-297) | cfr Carm. 2 | 33 | 8 |

Expositio in Genesin

| 23 (col. 251ff.) | cfr Carm. 5 | 25/32 | 16/17 |

IVVENCVS

Euangeliorum libri quattuor

| 1, 424 | cfr Carm. 2 | 23 | 8 |

	Op.		lin.	pag.
1, 455	cfr	Carm. 1	51	5
3, 314	cfr	Carm. 8	78	26

LVCRETIVS

De rerum natura

2, 314	cfr	Carm. 9	13	28
4, 221		Carm. 8	1	22
4, 221		Carm. 9	51	30
5, 96	cfr	Carm. 3	5	11

MACROBIVS

Commentarii in Ciceronis somnium Scipionis

1, 6, 11-13	cfr	Carm. 8	19	23

MARTIANVS CAPELLA

De nuptiis Philologiae et Mercurii

1, 66	cfr	Carm. 8	23/24	23
2, 116, 1	cfr	Carm. 25	63	53
7, 37	cfr	Carm. 3	19	12
7, 738	cfr	Carm. 8	19	23
8, 810	cfr	Carm. 7	1/2	20
9, 951	cfr	Carm. 3	19	12

OVIDIVS

Amores

3, 11, 29	cfr	Carm. 8	19	23

Epistulae ex Ponto

4, 4, 5		Carm. 8	15	23

Epistulae heroidum

6, 115	cfr	Carm. 8	19	23
12, 81	cfr	App. 2	19	56

Fasti

3, 269	cfr	Carm. 8	19	23
6, 321	cfr	Carm. 8	19	23

Metamorphoses

6, 72	cfr	Carm. 10	14	32
8, 11		Carm. 3	13	11
10, 479		Carm. 3	13	11
12, 38	cfr	Carm. 2	41	8
12, 264		Carm. 3	13	11

Tristia

1, 10, 33	cfr	Carm. 4	49	15
4, 2, 57		Carm. 8	15	23
4, 10, 124	cfr	Carm. 20	15/16	44

	Op.		lin.	pag.

PAVLINVS NOLANVS

Carmina

22, 61	cfr	App. 10	3	60
22, 83	cfr	Carm. 8	43	25
32, 163	cfr	Carm. 9	55	30

PAVLVS PETRICORDIAE

De uita sancti Martini

3, 202	cfr	Carm. 25	66	53

PROSPER AQVITANVS

Liber epigrammatum

41, 3	cfr	Carm. 8	42	25
42, 3	cfr	Carm. 9	60	30
58, 1	cfr	Carm. 5	21	16

SEDVLIVS

Carmen paschale

1, 30	cfr	Carm. 9	59	30
5, 230	cfr	Carm. 1	39	4
5, 357		App. 11	2	61

SEDVLIVS SCOTTVS

Carmina

1, 4, 1	cfr	Carm. 9	15	28
1, 1, 24	cfr	Carm. 25	1	51
2, 7, 153	cfr	App. 2	1-2	55

SERVIVS

Commentarius in Vergilii Aeneida

10, 636	cfr	Carm. 5	30	17

STATIVS

Thebais

5, 324	cfr	Carm. 6	19	18
9, 777	cfr	App. 10	7	60

THEODVLFVS AVRELIANENSIS

Carmina

1, 40		App. 10	14	60
39, 3	cfr	Carm. 2	61	9
41, 1, 23		Carm. 7	7	20
69, 1	cfr	Carm. 8	69	26

		Op.	*lin.*	*pag.*
Venantius Fortunatus				
Vita Martini				
2, 15, 15	cfr	Carm. 1	7	3
2, 16, 70	cfr	App. 2	10	55
3, 6, 17	cfr	Carm. 1	25	4
4, 240	cfr	Carm. 21	15	46
6, 5, 34	cfr	App. 2	10	55
10, 6, 5	cfr	Carm. 22	10	48
10, 6, 81	cfr	Carm. 22	10	48
Vergilius				
Aeneis				
1, 36		Carm. 9	53	30
1, 229		Carm. 8	48	25
1, 439		Carm. 8	47	25
1, 544-5		App. 10	5	60
2, 15		Carm. 4	7	14
2, 174		Carm. 8	47	25
2, 200		Carm. 1	61	5
2, 483		Carm. 3	71	13
2, 515	cfr	Carm. 25	94	54
3, 242	cfr	Carm. 8	70	26
3, 249		Carm. 1	67	5
3, 438	cfr	Carm. 4	37	15
3, 550	cfr	App. 2	1	55
4, 128		Carm. 8	47	25
4, 145	cfr	Carm. 25	94	54
4, 350		Carm. 1	59	5
5, 478	cfr	Carm. 8	36	24
6, 475	cfr	App. 6	1	57
7, 64		Carm. 8	47	25
8, 252		Carm. 8	47	25
8, 285	cfr	Carm. 25	94	54
10, 635	cfr	Carm. 23	2	49
11, 316		Carm. 9	63	30
11, 899		Carm. 9	33	29
12, 497		Carm. 9	33	29
Eclogae				
1, 51	cfr	App. 4	2	56
8, 74	cfr	Carm. 25	94	54
Georgica				
2, 490		App. 2	3	55
4, 179		Carm. 25	90	54
4, 471		Carm. 7	5	20

INDEX METRICVS*

Acrostichi uersus
    KAROLVS REX 22, 1–10

Breues in arsi
    Christiferā 2, 14
    mannā 5, 30
    petrā 5, 29

Errores prosodici
    abbă *pro* abbā 9, 79
    Ariopāgites *pro* Ariopăgites 21, 2; 22, 16
    Āthenis *pro* Ăthenis 10, 12
    călĭgo *pro* cālīgo 8, 4
    dēdicat *pro* dĕdicat 3, 52; dĕdicans 435
    dēorsum *pro* dĕorsum 25, 94
    diābolici *pro* diăbolici App. 1, 3
    Ĕoo *pro* Ēoo 1, 33
    făros *pro* phăros 25, 95
    ferĕbatur *pro* ferēbatur 3, 17
    fuerāt *pro* fuerăt 5, 25
    īdŏnea *pro* ĭdōnea 24, 16
    implētā *pro* implĕtā 5, 33
    indĕ ΓΝΟΦΟΣ 8, 6
    lurĭculas (= loriculas) *pro* lurīculas 25, 90
    mactāt ipse 3, 53
    mōlestum *pro* mŏlestum 1, 77; 20, 9; mōlestos 6, 38
    orthōdoxus *pro* orthŏdoxus 2, 67; 9, 78; 17, 2
    parălelos *pro* parallelos 25, 1
    plācens *pro* plăcens 3, 54
    plācita *pro* plăcita 4, 40
    pōtitur *pro* pŏtitur 2, 41; 6, 32
    polygŏnos *pro* polygōnos 25, 88
    sĕdulus *pro* sēdulus App. 15, 2
    suprā *pro* suprā 4, 52
    symfŏnat *pro* symfŏnat 25, 33
    tetragōnum *pro* tetragōnum 25, 6
    theōlogos *pro* theŏlogos 10, 11
    theōremata *pro* theōremata 22, 14; 25, 17
    typicūs Isaach 5, 26

---

* Whole poems in Greek and verses entirely in Greek are excluded, as are most Greek words and names except those in common Latin usage.

Hiatus 1, 65; 5, 13; 5, 18; 5, 22; 5, 43; 24, 15; App. 5, 1; App. 12, 4; App. 16, 7

Productio finalis ante -que *encliticam*
    indomitaque diu 6, 14
    notaque propago 4, 5

Synaloephe 3, 45; 4, 1; 5, 33; 5, 39; 9, 19; App. 2, 8; App. 2, 9; App. 10, 13; App. 11, 16; App. 12, 13

Voces in tmesis
    theo ... logia 24, 19

-us *finalis pro* u' *more antiquo*
    aedibus *pro* aedibu' 3, 70
    mentibus *pro* mentibu' 3, 62
    graculus *pro* graculu' 10, 1

INDEX NOMINVM*

ΑΓΑΡ (i.e. Hagar?) *gl. deest* Fr. 1, 11
Adam 25, 61
ΑΔΗΝ ('Hades') 7, 13; 9, 4
Aebraicis *sc.* auribus 3, 1
Aegoceros ('Capricorn') 25, 11
Aegyptus 2, 34; 3, 31; 5, 27
Agarenus ('Saracen') 10, 1
ΑΙΔΕΝ ('Eden'), *gl.* locus deliciarum, Fr. 1, 6
ΑΜΜΟΝΙΑ *sc.* litora ('Egypt') 3, 39
Arcadicis *sc.* uersibus 1, 10
ΑΡΗΣ ('Mars, planet') 8, 20
Ariopagites *sc.* Dionysius 21, 2; 22, 16
ΑΡΧΩΝ (*gen.*, 'order of angels') 21, 21
Athenae (i.e. the city) 10, 12; 21, 1
Attica *sc.* tela 20, 2
Attidas ('people of Attica') 21, 10
Ausonia 3, 2
Auernus App. 13, 7
Ausoniis *sc.* usibus 20, 8
Bacchus ('wine') 19, 1; (i.e. the god) App. 3, 2; App. 4, 1 (*bis*)
Bethleem 25, 52
Caesar *sc.* Karolus App. 1, 1
Caesareos *sc.* uultus 22, 2
Caiphas 9, 45
Cancer ('sign of zodiac') 25, 11; 25, 14
Cecropides ('the Athenians') 20, 12; 21, 14
Ceryb ('order of angels') 2, 7
Cherubim 21, 17
ΧΟΡΩΝ (*gen pl.*, 'order of angels') 21, 21
Christicolae ('Christians') 4, 28; 22, 7
Christifera *sc.* crux 2, 14; cfr Xristiferum
Xristiferum *sc.* patrum 22, 10
Christigenus 4, 46
ΧΡΙΣΤΟΣ 5, 49; 8, 85; 11, 2; 11, 3; 13, 2; 14, 3; 17, 7
Christus 1, 7; 1, 17; 1, 31; 1, 64; 1, 79; 2, 33; 3, 45; 3, 59; 3, 63; 3, 68; 4, 15; 4, 34; 4, 38; 5, 7; 5, 39; 5, 39; 5, 49; 7, 7; 7, 25; 8, 41; 8, 68; 8, 69; 9, 23; 9, 71; 10, 3; 14, 7; 21, 11; 25, 2; 25, 21; 25, 53; App. 2, 16; App. 6, 4; App. 10, 15; App. 12, 8; App. 12, 9; App. 12, 11; App. 12, 3; App. 13, 1
Crios ('Ram, sign of zodiac') 25, 10; 25, 12

---

* Latin words in this index are lemmatized by nominative of nouns and adjectives; the exception is names in adjectival form followed by *sc.* and the noun with which they are construed. Greek, other foreign and hybrid words are entered according to the forms given in the text.

INDEX NOMINVM

Cypris (i.e. Venus) 4, 14
Danihel App. 12, 8
Dauid 8, 39; 25, 52; 25, 73; App. 10, 11
Dauiticus *sc.* heres 5, 46
Dionysius (i.e. 'the Ariopagite') 10, 12; 21, 1; 22, 15; ('martyr') App. 8, 2
Dominatus ('order of angels') 21, 19
ΕΛΛΗΝ 15, 1 (*bis*); cfr Hellinas
Εοο (*gen.*, 'East') 1, 33
Erebus ('hell') 1, 42; 2, 20; 3, 48; 7, 11; 9, 77; App. 6, 4
ΗΡΜΙΝΔΡΟΥΔΑ 15*, 1; cfr Yrmindrudis
Erythreas *sc.* undas 3, 33
ΕΡΥΤΡΕΑΣ *sc.* undas 2, 23
Flegetontis 9, 7; cfr Pyrflegetontis
Franci 4, 27; App. 1, 1; cfr ΦΡΑΓΓΩΝ
Francia 22, 3; App. 10, 1; cfr ΦΡΑΓΓΙΑ
Francigenae 20, 3
Furiae 6, 3
Gallia 10, 13
Gotia App. 10, 2
Graecus 15, 4 (*bis*); 20, 1; 22, 11; App. 17, *inscr.*
Graiugena *sc.* Maximus ('the Confessor') 24, 2
ΓΡΑΙΥΓΕΝΑ App. 2, 1
Gregorius (i.e. Gregory of Nyssa) 22, 13
Hebrea *sc.* gens App. 13, 5
Hellinas 1, 1; cfr ΕΛΛΗΝ
Herodes 9, 44
Hieremias App. 12, 6
Hieronimus 20, 16
Hiezechihel App. 12, 7
Hincmarus 12b, 5; App. 9a, 1; cfr ΙΝΚΜΑΡΟΣ, Igcmarus, Incmarus
Hluduwicus 1, 65; Hludouuic App. 10, 5
Homerus 1, 1
Ierothea (*acc.*) 21, 6
Iesus App. 13, 3
Igcmarus App. 9b, 1; cfr Hincmarus
Iliacas *sc.* flammas 1, 5
Incmarus App. 9c, 1; cfr Hincmarus
ΙΝΚΜΑΡΟΣ 12b, 2; cfr Hincmarus
Iohannes (i.e. Eriugena) 2, 70; 15, 3; 20, 2
ΙΩΑΝΝΗΣ 7 *inscr.*; 8 *inscr.*; 11 *inscr.*; 15, 1; 17 *inscr.*
ΙΩΗΑΝΝΙΣ ΣΚΩΘΘΙ 9 *inscr.*
Iohannes (i.e. 'the Evangelist') App. 12, 12; App. 16, 1
Isaach 5, 26
Isaias App. 12, 5
ΙΣΙΔΑΜ (i.e. Isis) 3, 26
Israhelites 3, 29
Italicam *sc.* plebem App. 14, 4
Iudaeus *sc.* graculus 10, 1
Iudaicum *sc.* pectus 9, 64
Iudith (i.e. the empress) App. 10, 7
ΚΑΡΟΛΟΣ 2, 68; 5, 49; 7 *inscr.*; 8 *inscr.*; 11 *inscr.*; 11, 3; 17 *inscr.*; 15*, 1; 17, 1; 17, 8; 17, 13

CARMINA

Karolus (i.e. Charles the Bald) 1, 47; 1, 57; 1, 62; 2, 61; 3, 68; 4, 26; 6, 35; 7, 22; 10, 8;
   10, 15; 20, 2; 25, 78; 25, 84; App. 1, 1; App. 10, 2; App. 10, 9; App. 11, 9; App. 16, 8;
   Karle App. 8, 1
Karlomannus (i.e. son of Charles the Bald) App. 5, 3
Librae ('sign of zodiac') 25, 10; 25, 15
Liuddo 15, 4
ΛΙΥΔΔΩ 15, 2
Lucas App. 12, 11; App. 15, 1
Magdaline 2, 51
Marcus App. 12, 10; App. 14, 1
Maria *sc.* dei genitrix 25, 82
Maro (Vergil) 1, 2
Mars ('war') 9, 33
Mattheus App. 12, 9; App. 13, 2
Maximus (i.e. 'the Confessor') 22, 11; 22, 20; 24, 2
Moysa 1, 13; cfr Musa
ΜΟΥΣΕΑ (*acc.*, Moses) 8, 7
Moyses 2, 15; 2, 33; 3, 25; 3, 33; App. 15, 7
Musa 6, 39; cfr Moysa
Neptunia *sc.* arua 3, 37
Neptunus ('the sea') 2, 3; 3, 11
ΝΕΡΕΑ (i.e. Nereia) 3, 11
Oceanus 4, 50
Palladios *sc.* digitos 4, 12
Pallas (i.e. Athena) 4, 7; 8, 19
Parcae 6, 3
Paulus (i.e. the apostle) 10, 12; 21, 11; 21, 15; App. 15, 2
Pelasga *sc.* lingua App. 2, 2
Petrus (i.e. the apostle) App. 14, 1
Pharao 2, 17; 2, 37; 3, 35
Pharaonicus *sc.* hostis 3, 43
ΦΟΕΒΕ ('the moon') 8, 20
Phoebus ('the sun') 21, 3
ΦΟΕΤΟΝ (i.e. Phaethon) 8, 21
ΦΡΑΓΓΙΑ 17, 14; cfr Francia
Potentes ('order of angels') 21, 19
Pyrflegetonis 6, 18; cfr Flegetontis
ΡΟΜΑΙΟΥ *sc.* ΔΗΜΟΥ 15, 1
Romani 15, 3
Romuleas *sc.* ΤΕΧΝΑΣ 20, 5
Sabaoth *sc.* rex App. 2, 13
Salomon 4, 23
Salomonica *sc.* iura App. 10, 12
Scotti 19, 1
ΣΚΩΘΟΙ 9 *inscr.*
Selena ('the moon') 21, 3
Seraphym ('order of angels') 21, 17
Seraphin 8, 9
Seraphyn 2, 7
Sina (i.e. Sinai) *gl.* prae montis Fr. 1, 12
ΣΤΙΛΒΩΝ (i.e. 'Mercury, planet') 8, 20; 12b, 1; 17, 11

Styx 1, 32; 2, 6; 6, 4
Syrtes 4, 49
Tartareus 2, 6; 3, 50; 7, 6; 9, 52
Tethis ('the sea') 3, 44
ΤΕΘΙΣ 8, 22
Throni ('order of angels') 21, 18
Titania *sc.* lampas 25, 2
ΤΡΙΑΔΙΣ *gl.* Trinitas Fr. 1, 1
Troas ('Trojans') 1, 1
Tullia *sc.* castra 23, 2
Virtutes ('order of angels') 21, 19
Vulfadus (i.e. abbot of St. Médard at Soissons) App. 5, 5
Yrmindrudis (i.e. wife of Charles the Bald) 4, 1; cfr ΗΡΜΙΝΔΡΟΥΔΑ

INDICES AD EDITIONEM SERMONIS DE IMAGINE
IOHANNIS SCOTTI ERIVGENAE
(pag. 69-165 huius uoluminis)
PERTINENTES

Index locorvm S. Scriptvrae

Index fontivm et locorvm parallelorvm

INDEX LOCORVM SACRAE SCRIPTVRAE

		Cap.	*lin.*	*pag.*
Genesis				
1, 1	cfr	I	27/28	72
1, 26		III	13/15	76
		VI	25/26	79
		VI	32	80
		VI	43/44	80
		XI	25/26	92
		XVII	2/3	110
		XVII	7/8	110
		XVII	54	112
		XXX	344/345	165
1, 27		XVII	55/56	112
		XVII	68/69	113
		XVII	71/72	113
		XVII	79/80	113
		XVII	81	113
		XVII	96/97	114
		XVII	99/100	114
		XVII	161/162	116
		XVII	176	117
2, 1		I	64/65	73
2, 4		I	5	71
2, 7	cfr	XXVIII	16/17	147
2, 9		XXI	38	128
2, 16		XX	24/25	125
2, 17	cfr	XXI	42/43	128
3, 6		XXI	55/57	129
9, 3		XVI	27/28	109
40, 1	cfr	XIV	145/146	104
41, 1-36	cfr	XIV	151/172	105
Exodus				
33, 17		XXI	16/17	127
Numeri				
16, 5		XXI	15/16	127
Deuteronomium				
4, 23		XXIX	94	153
IV Regum				
5, 10-14	cfr	XXVII	43/44	145

INDEX LOCORVM SACRAE SCRIPTVRAE

		Cap.	lin.	pag.
Psalmi				
7, 10		XII	102	96
8, 6		XVIII	44/45	119
36, 4		XX	39/40	126
48, 13		XVIII	74/76	120
48, 21		XVIII	74/76	120
93, 9		VI	22/23	79
94, 4	cfr	XXVI	25/26	143
103, 29-30		XXV	193/195	142
103, 31		XXV	196	142
103, 35		XXV	196/197	142
143, 4		XXI	65	129
Prouerbia				
3, 18		XX	40/41	126
9, 5		XX	11	125
17, 6a	cfr	Praef.	2	69
Ecclesiastes				
1, 8	cfr	X	8/9	89
Isaias				
12, 3	cfr	XX	14/15	125
25, 6	cfr	XX	14/15	125
Ieremias				
36, 23-31	cfr	XIX	83	123
Daniel				
2, 19-46	cfr	XIV	151/172	105
7, 10	cfr	XVIII	38/39	119
13, 42		XVII	148	116
		XXIX	10/11	151
Amos				
8, 11		XX	18/19	125
Matthaeus				
1, 11	cfr	XIX	83	123
4, 4		XIX	93/94	124
6, 25		XXVIII	22/23	147
7, 23		XXI	18	127
22, 30		XVIII	28/30	119
	cfr	XIX	94/95	124
22, 37	cfr	VIII	79/80	85
Marcus				
5, 22-43		XXV	95/97	139
12, 16	cfr	XVII	138/139	115

		Cap.	lin.	pag.
12, 30	cfr	VIII	79/80	85
13, 1		XXV	29/30	137

Lucas

		Cap.	lin.	pag.
1, 2		XVII	156	116
4, 23		XXV	168/169	141
4, 38-39	cfr	XXV	81/83	138
7, 11-17	cfr	XXV	100/129	139/140
7, 13-15		XXV	125/127	140
10, 27	cfr	VIII	79/80	85
16, 19-31	cfr	XXVII	25/28	144
17, 12	cfr	XXVII	44/45	145
20, 35-36		XVIII	28/30	119
20, 36	cfr	XIX	94/95	124
23, 27-29	cfr	XXV	32/42	137

Iohannes

		Cap.	lin.	pag.
1, 1		V	22/23	78
4, 46-54	cfr	XXV	86	138
4, 49		XXV	86	138
7, 37		XX	13	125
10, 5	cfr	XXX	13/14	154
11, 1-44	cfr	XXV	132/158	140
13, 35		V	29/30	78

Ad Romanos

		Cap.	lin.	pag.
11, 34		XI	15	92
14, 17		XIX	92/93	124

I ad Corinthios

		Cap.	lin.	pag.
2, 14-15		VIII	93/95	85
2, 15		XXI	13	127
2, 16	cfr	V	23/24	78
3, 1-2	cfr	XXV	75/76	138
3, 2-3		VIII	91/92	85
15, 12		XXV	184/185	142
15, 51-52		XXII	55/57	131

II ad Corinthios

		Cap.	lin.	pag.
12, 4	cfr	XVIII	21/22	118
13, 3	cfr	V	23/24	78

Ad Galatas

		Cap.	lin.	pag.
3, 28		XVII	73/74	113
	cfr	XVII	98	114

Ad Ephesios

		Cap.	lin.	pag.
4, 23	cfr	VIII	75/76	85
5, 18	cfr	VIII	75/76	85

	Cap.	*lin.*	*pag.*
Ad Colossenses			
2, 8	XXV	191	142
3, 1	XIX	64/65	123
3, 9-10	XXX	340/342	165
I ad Thessalonicenses			
4, 16	XXV	159/160	141
4, 17	XXII	70/71	132
5, 23	VIII	75/76	85
I ad Timotheum			
6, 10	XXI	28/29	127
II ad Timotheum			
2, 19	XXI	15/16	127
Ad Hebraeos			
2, 7	XVIII	44/45	119
5, 14	XXI	10/12	127
11, 3	XXIII	10/12	133
	XXIII	15/16	133
I Iohannis			
4, 7-8	V	27/28	78

INDEX FONTIVM ET LOCORVM PARALLELORVM

		Cap.	*lin.*	*pag.*
Alexander Aphrodisiensis				
De anima cum mantissa				
p. 94, 7-11	cfr	XII	8/15	93
p. 96, 5-6	cfr	XII	27/30	94
Aristoteles				
De partibus animalium				
2, 14, 658a – 15, 658b	cfr	XXX	292/296	163
3, 14, 675b22-26	cfr	XXX	201/211	160
4, 5, 681a18-20	cfr	XXX	72/74	156
Physica				
8, 2, 252b26-27	cfr	XVII	11/12	111
Basilivs Caesariensis				
Homiliae de creatione hominis				
1, 3 (p. 170-172)	cfr	III	3/27	75
1, 4 (p. 172-176)	cfr	VI	27/44	79
1, 6 (p. 178-180)	cfr	XVII	27/31	111
2, 14 (p. 266-268)	cfr	XVII	8/23	110
2, 15 (p. 268-270)	cfr	VIII	5/10	82
Homiliae in Hexaemeron				
1, 3 (p. 12-14)	cfr	XXIII/XXIV	4/42	132
2, 2 (p. 42-44)	cfr	XXIII/XXIV	4/42	132
9, 2 (p. 273-274)	cfr	VIII	5/10	82
9, 6 (p. 294)	cfr	VI	27/44	79
Chalcidivs				
Platonis Timaeus a Chalcidio translatus commentarioque instructus				
2, 197 (p. 218)	cfr	XXVIII	41/43	148
2, 213 (p. 228)	cfr	XII	15/22	93
2, 220 (p. 232-234)	cfr	XII	8/15	93
2, 224 (p. 238-239)	cfr	XII	8/15	93
2, 224 (p. 239)	cfr	XII	27/30	94
2, 231 (p. 245)	cfr	XII	15/22	93

		Cap.	lin.	pag.
EMPEDOCLES				
Fragmenta				
fr. B117 DK (p. 358-359)	cfr	XXVIII	41/43	148
CLAVDIVS GALENVS				
De naturalibus facultatibus				
1, 6 (p. 11)	cfr	XXX	259/296	162
3, 8 (p. 177)	cfr	XXX	173/175	160
De Hippocratis et Platonis placitis				
1, 8, 13 (p. 208)	cfr	XXX	58/98	156
2, 4, 17 (p. 230)	cfr	XII	15/22	93
6, 3, 4 (p. 520)	cfr	XII	30/32	94
De semine				
1, 8 (vol. 4, p. 541)	cfr	XXX	232/258	161
De usu partium				
4, 1 (vol. 3, p. 266-267)	cfr	XXX	27/31	155
4, 2 (vol. 3, p. 267-269)	cfr	XXX	201/211	160
4, 3 (vol. 3, p. 269)	cfr	XXX	212/214	161
4, 4 (vol. 3, p. 272)	cfr	XXX	221	161
4, 7 (vol. 3, p. 275)	cfr	XXX	173/175	160
4, 14 (vol. 3, p. 311)	cfr	XXX	212/214	161
4, 17 (vol. 3, p. 325)	cfr	XXX	201/211	160
5, 9 (vol. 3, p. 378)	cfr	XXX	58/98	156
6, 2 (vol. 3, p. 412)	cfr	XXX	27/31	155
6, 2 (vol. 3, p. 416)	cfr	XXX	232/258	161
6, 7 (vol. 3, p. 433)	cfr	XXX	135/146	158
6, 7 (vol. 3, p. 436)	cfr	XII	27/30	94
	cfr	XXX	109/114	158
6, 7 (vol. 3, p. 435-436)	cfr	XXX	15/27	154
6, 10 (vol. 3, p. 444)	cfr	XXX	117/122	158
6, 10 (vol. 3, p. 448)	cfr	XXX	135/146	158
6, 15 (vol. 3, p. 481)	cfr	XXX	135/146	158
8, 4 (vol. 3, p. 625)	cfr	XII	30/32	94
8, 5 (vol. 3, p. 633)	cfr	XXX	58/98	156
8, 6 (vol. 3, p. 636-637)	cfr	XXX	58/98	156
8, 9 (vol. 3, p. 659)	cfr	XXX	232/258	161
9, 8 (vol. 3, p. 714)	cfr	XXX	32/38	155
9, 14 (vol. 3, p. 740-741)	cfr	XXX	58/98	156
11, 14 (vol. 3, p. 901)	cfr	XXX	292/296	163
11, 18 (vol. 3, p. 925)	cfr	XXX	58/98	156
12, 2 (vol. 4, p. 3)	cfr	XXX	58/98	156
14, 1 (vol. 4, p. 142-143)	cfr	XXX	15/27	154
16, 2 (vol. 4, p. 270-271)	cfr	XXX	58/98	156
16, 10 (vol. 4, p. 266)	cfr	XXX	217/231	161
16, 13-14 (vol. 4, p. 338-342)	cfr	XXX	117/122	158

DE IMAGINE

		Cap.	lin.	pag.
GREGORIVS NAZIANZENVS				
Orationes				
2, 17 (p. 112)	cfr	XIII	5/21	97
37, 15 (p. 302)	cfr	XXVIII	8/14	147
38, 11 (p. 124)	cfr	XVII	8/23	110
GREGORIVS NYSSENVS				
De anima et resurrectione				
p. 26, 12-16	cfr	XVII	126/144	115
p. 26-27	cfr	XVI	5/53	108
p. 36, 9-17	cfr	XIX	84/85	124
p. 40, 11 – p. 42, 4		VIII	33/105	83
p. 42-43	cfr	XIX	35/67	122
p. 53, 13-15	cfr	XXVII	4/93	143
p. 55, 1-5	cfr	XXVII	4/93	143
p. 56, 10-11	cfr	XXVII	4/93	143
p. 80, 8 – p. 81, 2	cfr	XXIX	4/119	150
p. 84, 14 – p. 85, 9	cfr	XXVIII	8/14	147
	cfr	XXVIII	99/102	150
p. 85, 9 – p. 87, 1	cfr	XXVIII	41/43	148
p. 94, 21 – p. 95, 28	cfr	XXVIII	14/25	147
p. 104, 7 – p. 105, 2	cfr	XXV	64/185	138
De vita Moysis				
2, 319 (p. 143, 19)	cfr	XIX	84/85	124
2, 40 (p. 44, 11-19)		XXVIII	36/39	148
Oratio catechetica				
p. 16, 16 – p. 18, 7	cfr	XVII	102/118	114
p. 19, 15 – p. 20, 5	cfr	XVII	119/125	115
p. 24, 1-6	cfr	XVII	129/137	115
p. 29, 13 – p. 30, 9	cfr	XXI	60/63	129
p. 55, 4-21	cfr	XVII	129/137	115
p. 55, 21 – p. 56, 2	cfr	XXII	11/16	130
p. 56, 6 – p. 57, 3	cfr	XXI	3/68	126
GVILLELMVS A SANCTO THEODORICO				
De natura corporis et animae (*CC CM*, 88)				
52-54 (p. 121-122, 630-658)		XXX	15/40	154
54 (p. 122, 660-662)		XXX	102/105	157
54 (p. 122, 662-664)		XXX	96/98	157
54-55 (p. 125, 665-677)		XXX	87/96	157
56 (p. 122-123, 678-689)		XXX	109/123	158
57 (p. 123, 690-698)		XXX	306/318	164
57-58 (p. 123, 699-708)		XXX	329/338	165
61 (p. 124-125, 738-751)		XVI	5/53	108
62 (p. 125, 752-759)		X	26/33	90
62 (p. 125, 759-764)		XI	3/8	91
63 (p. 125, 765-767)		XI	21/23	92

	Cap.	lin.	pag.
63 (p. 125, 767-769)	XI	8/11	91
63 (p. 125, 772-776)	XII	4/7	93
64 (p. 125-126, 778-784)	XII	96/103	96
64-65 (p. 126, 784-795)	XVI	42/51	110
65-66 (p. 126, 796-808)	XII	110/123	97
66 (p. 126, 810)	IX	11	86
67-68 (p. 126-127, 814-828)	IX	11/31	86
68-69 (p. 127, 828-838)	IX	39/54	87
70-71 (p. 127-128, 845-862)	IX	59/79	88
72 (p. 128, 869-876)	VI	5/13	79
72-73 (p. 128-129, 877-886)	XI	26/39	92
73 (p. 129, 887-890)	VIII	5/9	82
73 (p. 129, 892-895)	XV	15/19	107
74 (p. 129, 896-899)	XV	7/10	107
74 (p. 129, 901-908)	XIX	13/21	121
75 (p. 129-130, 914-918)	XIX	21/25	121
76-77 (p. 130, 919-932)	XIX	40/54	122
77 (p. 130, 932-933)	XIX	25/26	122
77 (p. 130, 935-939)	II	34/38	75
77-78 (p. 130, 939-950)	IV	5/12	76
78 (p. 131, 951-952)	VII	4/5	80
81-82 (p. 132, 990-995)	VII	5/11	80
82 (p. 132, 995-999)	VII	19/22	81
82 (p. 132, 1002-1003)	VII	23/25	81
82-83 (p. 132-133, 1003-1021)	VII	30/50	81
85 (p. 133, 1029-1042)	IV	14/26	77
86 (p. 133, 1043-1054)	XVII	114/125	114

IOHANNES SCOTVS ERIVGENA

Commentarius in Euangelium Iohannis

1, 23 (p. 49-50) (col. 298BC)	V	22/23	78
3, 6 (p. 89, 15-20) (col. 320D-321A)	XVII	8/26	110

De praedestinatione

4, 5 (p. 44, 24 – p. 46, 8) (col. 373AB)	XVII	113/125	114
18, 7 (p. 196, 10 – p. 198, 5) (col. 434AC)	XXII	4/22	129
18, 8 (p. 198, 15-18) (col. 434D)	XVIII	60/64	120
19, 1 (p. 204, 4-7) (col. 436D)	XXVI	15/20	143

Epistula (= Epistulae uariae III)

14 (p. 159, 3-4)	XVII	159	116

Expositiones in hierarchiam caelestem

6, 1 (p. 87-88, 35-42)	XXII	13/15	130

Glossae in Martianum Capellam

152, 3 (p. 82, 10)	XVII	159	116
208, 11 (p. 105, 23-28)	XII	30/56	94

Glossae in Martianum Capellam (ex ms. Ox.)

p. 102-103	XII	30/56	94

	Cap.	lin.	pag.
p. 122	XXVIII	40/48	148
Homilia super 'In principio erat uerbum' (*CC CM*, 166)			
4, 1 (p. 8, 35)	I	78	74
6 (p. 11-13)	V	22/23	78
19 (p. 35, 12-15)	XVII	84/87	113
19 (p. 35, 21-22)	XVII	185/191	117
Periphyseon			
1 (p. 10, 198) (col. 447A)	XIII	39	99
1 (p. 41, 1188-1190) (col. 470A)	XVII	126/138	115
1 (p. 50, 1488-1516) (col. 477B)	I	30/41	72
1 (p. 52, 1562-1564) (col. 479A)	XXIV	4/37	134
1 (p. 53, 1583-1586) (col. 479B)	XXIV	4/37	134
1 (p. 54, 1635-1639) (col. 480C)	XII	30/56	94
1 (p. 73, 2243-2245) (col. 494D)	VIII	5	82
1 (p. 76, 2345-2349) (col. 497A)	XXIV	4/37	134
1 (p. 81-82, 1562-1564) (col. 501C)	XXII	26/34	130
1 (p. 83-84, 2570-2603) (col. 502B-503A)	XXIV	4/37	134
2 (p. 11, 193-199) (col. 531AB)	XVII	7/137	110
2 (p. 19, 393-396) (col. 538A)	XVII	7/137	110
2 (p. 21-22, 434-437) (col. 539D)	XVIII	65/78	120
2 (p. 59, 1353-1354) (col. 569A)	XV	4/35	107
2 (p. 60, 1375-1383) (col. 569CD)	X	3/62	89
2 (p. 75, 1745-1752) (col. 580D)	VIII	50/55	84
2 (p. 76, 1778-1779) (col. 581C)	XIV	40/49	101
	XXX	217/218	161
2 (p. 76, 1787-1795) (col. 582A)	XXVIII/XXIX	6/119	147
2 (p. 81, 1894-1899) (col. 584D-585A)	XI	3/39	91
2 (p. 81, 1900-1902) (col. 585A)	XVII	7/137	110
2 (p. 81, 1914-1920) (col. 585B)	XI	33/39	92
2 (p. 82, 1941-1944) (col. 586A)	XI	3/39	91
2 (p. 94, 2224-2231) (col. 594B)	XXI	13/18	127
2 (p. 100, 2399-2402) (col. 598BC)	XVII	126/138	115
2 (p. 100, 2404-2405) (col. 598C)	XIII	39	99
2 (p. 111, 2720-2723) (col. 605D)	XXIV	4/37	134
3 (p. 135, 3925-3929) (col. 714A)	I	5/41	71
3 (p. 149, 197-199, nota ⟨34⟩) (col. 723C)	XVIII	47/54	119
3 (p. 160, 4666-4671) (col. 730C)	XII	30/56	94
3 (p. 162, 4732-4735) (col. 732A)	X	3/62	89
3 (p. 166, 4876-4881) (col. 735AB)	XXIX	35/50	151
3 (p. 167, 4910-4924) (col. 735D-736A)	VIII	36/49	83
3 (p. 167, 4925-4930) (col. 736AB)	XV	20/24	107
3 (p. 169, 4964-4967) (col. 737A)	XVI	5/7	108
3 (p. 169, 4967-4970) (col. 737A)	XVI	22/25	109

	Cap.	lin.	pag.
3 (p. 172, 235-239, nota ⟨38⟩ = p. 682, 8878-8886 / 8986-8993) (col. 739C)	XVI	30/34	109
4 (p. 19, 498-502) (col. 754A)	XV	4/35	107
4 (p. 21, 551-553) (col. 755B)	VIII	50/55	84
4 (p. 25-26, nota ⟨8⟩ = p. 242, 1199-1219) (col. 758C)	III	5/15	76
4 (p. 32, 840-842) (col. 763A)	XVIII	5/78	118
4 (p. 45, 1211-1214) (col. 771C)	XI	36/39	92
4 (p. 60, 1660-1662) (col. 782B)	II	3/38	74
4 (p. 65, 1839-1840) (col. 786B)	VI	31/44	80
4 (p. 67, 1903-1904) (col. 788A)	XV	4/35	107
	XVI	5/53	108
4 (p. 68-69, 1918-1954) (col. 788B-789A)	XI	3/39	91
4 (p. 69-70, 1955-1997) (col. 789a-790B)	XIII	5/48	97
4 (p. 70, 1998-2003) (col. 790B)	XIII	59/63	99
4 (p. 71, 2016) (col. 790C)	XIII	39	99
4 (p. 72, 2057-2069) (col. 791C-792A)	XIV	4/15	100
4 (p. 72-73, 2073-2106) (col. 792AD)	XV	4/35	107
4 (p. 73-74, 2108-2125) (col. 792D-793A)	XVI	38/53	109
4 (p. 74-79, 2141-2332) (col. 793C-797C)	XVII	7/191	110
4 (p. 78, 2296) (col. 797A)	XVII	159	116
4 (p. 80-81, 2333-2384) (col. 797D-799A)	XVIII	30/78	119
4 (p. 83, 2460-2466) (col. 800C)	XXVIII/XXIX	6/119	147
4 (p. 84-85, 2472-2500) (col. 801AC)	XXVII	31/58	144
4 (p. 86, 2548-2550) (col. 802C)	XXVII	53/56	145
4 (p. 100, 2969-2975) (col. 812A)	XVIII	59/65	120
4 (p. 100-101, 2982-2989) (col. 812B)	XVIII	65/72	120
4 (p. 110-111, 3291-3339) (col. 819A-820A)	XX	5/51	124
4 (p. 111-114, 3340-3417) (col. 820A-821D)	XXI	3/68	126
4 (p. 118, 3531-3538) (col. 824C)	XXI	5/6	126
4 (p. 118, 3542-3545) (col. 824D)	VIII	50/51	84
	XV	4/35	107
	XVII	66/82	113
4 (p. 123-124, 3736-3742) (col. 828C)	XXI	20/22	127
4 (p. 125, 3800-3801) (col. 830A)	XXI	5/6	126
4 (p. 131, 3973-3980) (col. 833D)	XVII	76/77	113
5 (uersio II iuxta codd. *HM*, p. 19, 514-536) (col. 872BC)	XXVII	29/49	144
5 (uersio II iuxta codd. *HM*, p. 23, 641-648) (col. 875A)	XIX	4/9	121

DE IMAGINE

	Cap.	lin.	pag.
5 (uersio II iuxta codd. *HM*, p. 23, 648-656) (col. 875AB)	XIX	13/21	121
5 (p. 36, 1085-1089) (col. 884C)	XXVIII/ XXIX	6/119	147
5 (p. 81-82, 2579-2620) (col. 917A-918A)	XIX	54/57	122
5 (p. 81-82, 2580-2620) (col. 917A-918A)	XXII	4/43	129
5 (p. 88-89, 2821-2852) (col. 922D-923C)	XVII	161/191	116
5 (p. 121, 3900-3913) (col. 947AB)	XXX	30	155
	XXX	135	158
5 (p. 128, 4148-4150) (col. 952B)	XVII	105/111	114
5 (p. 149, 4837-4838) (col. 966D)	XVII	115/125	114
5 (p. 150, 4862-4864) (col. 967B)	XVIII	5/78	118
5 (p. 164, 5340-5343) (col. 977C)	X	10/34	89
5 (p. 167, 5439-5441) (col. 979D)	XVIII	5/78	118

MARTINVS LAVDVNENSIS

Verba graeca Prisciani

p. 135	cfr	XVII	159	116

METHODIVS OLYMPIVS

De resurrectione

1, 14 (p. 237, 1)	cfr	XXVI	15/20	143
2, 10 (p. 349, 10)	cfr	XVII	11/12	111
2, 24 (p. 240-241)	cfr	XVII	138/140	115
2, 29 (p. 386, 4-15)	cfr	XXVI	3/5	142

ORIGENES

De principiis

2, 9, 2 (vol. 253, p. 354)	cfr	XVII	126/154	115
4, 3, 8-10 (vol. 268, p. 368-380)	cfr	XXVIII	8/14	147
4, 4, 7 (vol. 268, p. 416-418)	cfr	XXIII/ XXIV	4/42	132
4, 4, 8 (vol. 268, p. 422)	cfr	XVII	126/154	115

OVIDIVS

Metamorphoses

| 1, 76-88 | cfr | VIII | 5/10 | 82 |

PHILO ALEXANDRINVS

De opificio mundi

| 72-75 | cfr | VI | 27/44 | 79 |

198 INDEX FONTIVM ET LOCORVM PARALLELORVM

			Cap.	*lin.*	*pag.*
Plato					
Phaedrus					
246c		cfr	XXVIII	99/102	150
246d		cfr	II	23/24	75
Res publica					
8, 560b		cfr	XII	16	93
10, 617e		cfr	XVII	123/124	115
Timaeus					
29d-30a		cfr	XVII	102/109	114
30a-31a		cfr	XVII	11/12	111
45a-b		cfr	XII	7	93
70a		cfr	XII	7	93
		cfr	XII	16	93
70ab		cfr	XXX	109/114	158
70c-d		cfr	XXX	27/31	155
72e-73a		cfr	XXX	201/211	160
75c		cfr	XXX	246/250	162
76b-c		cfr	XXX	292/296	163
78b		cfr	XXX	187/192	160
80e		cfr	XXX	221	161
Porphyrivs					
Ad Gaurum					
9, 1 (p. 45, 5-10)		cfr	XXVIII	14/25	147
Priscianvs					
Institutiones grammaticae					
6, 72 (vol. II, p. 256)			XVII	159	116
Servivs grammaticvs					
In Vergilii Aeneida commentarius					
3, 233		cfr	XXX	273	163
Vergilivs					
Georgica					
2, 88		cfr	XXX	273	163

CONSPECTVS MATERIAE

Preface – Andrew Hicks .... V-VI

Iohannis Scotti Eriugenae
Carmina
Michael Herren with the assistance of Andrew Dunning

Introduction	IX-LXXIX
I. Biographical	IX-XXII
A. Life	IX-XIII
B. Literary milieu	XIII-XV
C. Writings	XV-XXII
II. Literary	XXII-LVIII
A. The poems: editions and scholarship	XXII-XXVII
B. The manuscripts and the transmission of the text	XXVII-XXXVIII
1. The main collection of John's poetic work (nos. 1-19)	XXVIII-XXXIII
2. The dedicatory poems (nos. 20-22)	XXXIII-XXXIV
3. *Aulae sidereae* (no. 25)	XXXIV
4. The poems of the appendix (App. 1-17)	XXXIV-XXXVIII
C. The corpus of John's poems and problems of authenticity	XXXVIII-LVIII
1. Overview	XXXVIII-XLII
2. Problems of authenticity in Ω	XLII-XLV
3. Poems of the appendix	XLV-LVIII
4. Spurious poems	LVIII
III. John as a poet	LVIII-LXXIV
A. John' poetic reading and citation	LVIII-LXIII
B. The diction of John's poetry	LXIII-LXIX
1. Greek	LXIII-LXVIII
2. Latin	LXVIII-LXIX
C. Prosody	LXIX-LXXI
D. Poetic techniques	LXXI-LXXII

E. Structure	LXXIII
F. Conclusion	LXXIV
IV. Editorial principles	LXXIV-LXXVI
Addendum	LXXVII-LXXVIII
Acknowledgements	LXXVIII-LXXIX

MANUSCRIPT REPRODUCTIONS (PLATES I-V)	
BIBLIOGRAPHY	LXXXI-XC
Primary Sources	LXXXI-LXXXV
A. Editions of the Poems of John Scottus Eriugena	LXXXI
B. Editions of works cited	LXXXI-LXXXV
Secondary literature	LXXXV-XC

Iohannis Scotti Eriugenae
De imagine

INTRODUZIONE	
a cura di Chiara Ombretta TOMMASI ...	XCIII-CXLV
I. La tradizione manoscritta	XCIX-CVII
II. Il *De imagine* nelle opere di Eriugena ...	CVIII-CXX
A. Le citazioni del *De imagine* nel *Periphyseon*	CVIII-CXV
B. Presenza del *De imagine* in altre opere eriugeniane	CXV-CXX
III. L'esemplare greco	CXXI-CXXV
IV. La circolazione del *De imagine*	CXXVI-
A. Il *De imagine* a Bamberg	CXXVI-CXXVIII
B. Il *De imagine* nel catalogo di Cluny .	CXXVIII-CXXXIII
V. Il *De imagine* in Guglielmo di Saint-Thierry	CXXXIV-CXXXVIII
VI. La destinazione dell'opera	CXXXVIII-CXLIII
Conclusioni e ringraziamenti	CXLIV-CXLV

BIBLIOGRAFIA	CXLVII-CLVII
Edizioni	CXLVII-CL
A. *De imagine*	CXLVII
B. Altre opere di Eriugena	CXLVII-CXLVIII
C. Altri testi	CXLVIII-CL
Studi	CL-CLVII

Iohannis Scotti Eriugenae
Carmina
edidit Michael HERREN
adiuuante Andrew DUNNING

CONSPECTVS SIGLORVM	2
EDITIO TEXTVS	3-66

Iohannis Scotti Eriugenae
De imagine
cura et studio
Giovanni MANDOLINO

CONSPECTVS SIGLORVM	68
EDITIO TEXTVS	69-165

Indices ad editionem Iohannis Scotti Eriugenae *Carminum* pertinentes

Index locorum S. Scripturae	169-171
Index fontium	172-178
Index metricus	179-180
Index nominum	181-184

Indices ad editionem Iohannis Scotti Eriugenae *De imagine* pertinentes

Index locorum S. Scripturae	187-190
Index fontium et locorum parallelorum	191-198
CONSPECTVS MATERIAE	199-201

CORPVS CHRISTIANORVM
CONTINVATIO MEDIAEVALIS

ONOMASTICON

Abbo Floriacensis 300
Adalboldus Traiectensis 171
Adelmannus Leodiensis 171
Ademarus Cabannensis 129, 245, 245A
Adso Dervensis 45, 198
Aelredus Rievallensis 1, 2A, 2B, 2C, 2D, 3, 3A
Agnellus Ravennas 199
Agobardus Lugdunensis 52
Alcuinus Eboracensis 249
Alexander Essebiensis 188, 188A
Alexander Neckam 221, 227
Ambrosius Autpertus 27, 27A, 27B
Andreas a S. Victore 53, 53A, 53B, 53E, 53F, 53G
Anonymus Bonnensis 171
Anonymus Einsiedlensis 171
Anonymus Erfurtensis 171
Anonymus in Matthaeum 159
Anselmus Laudunensis 267
Apuleius (pseudo) 143
Arnoldus Gheyloven Roterdamus 212
Arnoldus Leodiensis 160
Ars Laureshamensis 40A
Ascelinus Carnotensis 171
Asclepius 143

Balduinus de Forda 99
Bartholomaeus Exoniensis 157
Beatus Liebanensis 58
Benedictus Anianensis 168, 168A
Beringerius Turonensis 84, 84A, 171
Berno Augiensis 297
Bernoldus Constantiensis 171
Bovo Corbeiensis 171
Burchardus abbas Bellevallis 62

Caesarius Heisterbacensis 171
Carmen Campidoctoris 71
Christanus Campililiensis 19A, 19B
Christianus Stabulensis 224
Chronica Adefonsi imperatoris 71
Chronica Adephonsi III 65
Chronica Albeldensis 65
Chronica Byzantia Arabica 65

Chronica Hispana 65, 71, 71A, 71B, 73
Chronica Latina Regum Castellae 73
Chronica Muzarabica 65
Chronica Naierensis 71A
Claudius Taurinensis 263
Collectaneum exemplorum et uisionum Clarevallense 208
Collectio canonum in V libris 6
Collectio exemplorum Cisterciensis 243
Commentaria in Ruth 81
Conradus Eberbacensis 138
Conradus de Mure 210
Constitutiones canonicorum regularium ordinis Arroasiensis 20
Consuetudines canonicorum regularium Springiersbacenses-Rodenses 48
Constitutiones quae uocantur Ordinis Praemonstratensis 216

Dionysius Cartusiensis 121, 121A
Donatus ortigraphus 40D

Eterius Oxomensis 59
Excerpta isagogarum et categoriarum 120
Excidii Aconis gestorum collectio 202
Explanationes fidei aevi Carolini 254
Expositiones Pauli epistularum ad Romanos, Galathas et Ephesios 151
Expositiones Psalmorum duae sicut in codice Rothomagensi 24 asseruantur 256
Extractiones de Talmud 291

Florus Lugdunensis 193, 193A, 193B, 220B, 260
Folchinus de Borfonibus 201
Frechulfus Lexoviensis 169, 169A
Frowinus abbas Montis Angelorum 134

Galbertus notarius Brugensis 131
Galterus a S. Victore 30
Garnerius de Rupeforti 232
Gerardus Cameracensis 270
Gerardus Magnus 172, 192, 235, 235A
Gerardus Moresenus seu Csanadensis 49
Gerlacus Peters 155

Germanus Parisiensis episcopus 187
Gesta abbatum Trudonensium 257, 257A
Gillebertus 171A
Giraldus Floriacensis 171A
Gislebertus Trudonensis 257A
Glosa super Graecismum Eberhardi Bethuniensis 225
Glosae in regula Sancti Benedicti abbatis ad usum Smaragdi abbatis Sancti Michaelis 282
Glossa ordinaria in Canticum Canticorum 170.22
Glossae aeui Carolini in libros I-II Martiani Capellae De nuptiis Philologiae et Mercurii 237
Glossae biblicae 189A, 189B
Gozechinus 62
Grammatici Hibernici Carolini aevi 40, 40A, 40B, 40C, 40D, 40E
Magister Gregorius 171
Guibertus Gemblacensis 66, 66A
Guibertus Tornacensis 242
Guillelmus Alvernus 230, 230A, 230B, 230C
Guillelmus de Conchis 152, 158, 203
Guillelmus Durantus 140, 140A, 140B
Guillelmus de Luxi 219
Guillelmus Petrus de Calciata 73
Guillelmus a S. Theodorico 86, 87, 88, 89, 89A, 89B
Guitbertus abbas Novigenti 127, 127A, 171

Haymo Autissiodorensis 135C, 135E
Heiricus Autissiodorensis 116, 116A, 116B
Henricus a S. Victore 30
Herbertus Turritanus 277
Herimannus abbas 236
Hermannus de Runa 64
Hermannus Werdinensis 204
Hermes Latinus 142, 143, 143A, 144, 144C
Heymericus de Campo 292A
Hieronymus de Moravia 250
Hieronymus de Praga 222
Hildebertus Cenomanensis 209
Hildegardis Bingensis 43, 43A, 90, 91, 91A, 91B, 92, 226, 226A
Historia Compostellana 70
Historia Roderici vel Gesta Roderici Campidocti 71
Historia Silensis 71B
Historia translationis S. Isidori 73
Homiletica Vadstenensia 229

Homiliarium Veronense 186
Hugo Pictaviensis 42
Hugo de Miromari 234
Hugo de Sancto Victore 176, 176A, 177, 178, 269, 276
Humbertus de Romanis 218, 279

Iacobus de Vitriaco 171, 252, 255, 279
Iohannes Beleth 41, 41A
Iohannes de Caulibus 153
Iohannes de Forda 17, 18
Iohannes Duns Scotus 287
Iohannes Hus 205, 211, 222, 238, 239, 239A, 253, 261, 271, 274
Iohannes Rusbrochius 101, 102, 103, 104, 105, 106, 107, 107A, 108, 109, 110, 172, 207
Iohannes Saresberiensis 98, 118
Iohannes Scottus Eriugena 31, 50, 161, 162, 163, 164, 165, 166, 167
Iohannes Soreth 259
Iohannes Wirziburgensis 139
Iosephus Scottus 284

Lanfrancus 171
Liber de gratia Noui Testamenti 195 + suppl.
Liber de uerbo 40E
Liber ordinis S. Victoris Parisiensis 61
Liber prefigurationum Christi et Ecclesie 195 + suppl.
Liber Quare 60
Liber sacramentorum excarsus 47
Liber sacramentorum Romane ecclesiae ordine exscarpsus 47
Liudprandus Cremonensis 156
Logica antiquioris mediae aetatis 120
Lucas Tudensis 74, 74A

Magister Cunestabulus 272
Margareta Porete 69
Martianus Capella 237
Metamorphosis Golie 171A
Metrum de vita et miraculis et obitu S. Martini 171A
Monumenta Arroasiensia 175
Monumenta Vizeliacensia 42 + suppl.
Muretach 40

Nicolaus de Aquaevilla 283
Nicolaus Maniacoria 262

Opera de computo s. XII 272

Oratio S. Brandani 47
Oswaldus de Corda 179
Otfridus Wizemburgensis 200

Pascasius Radbertus 16, 56, 56A, 56B, 56C, 85, 94, 96, 97
Paulinus Aquileiensis 95
Petrus Abaelardus 11, 12, 13, 14, 15, 190, 206, 206A
Petrus de Alliaco 258
Petrus Blesensis 128, 171, 194
Petrus Cantor 196, 196A, 196B
Petrus Cellensis 54
Petrus Comestor 191
Petrus Damiani 57
Petrus Iohannis Oliui 233, 275
Petrus Marsilii 273
Petrus Pictaviensis 51
Petrus Pictor 25
Petrus Pisanus
Petrus de S. Audemaro 25
Petrus Venerabilis 10, 58, 83
Polythecon 93
Prefatio de Almaria 71
Psalterium abbreviatum Vercellense 47
Psalterium Suthantoniense 240

Rabanus Maurus 44, 100, 174, 174A
Radulfus Ardens 241
Radulfus phisicus 171A
Radulphus Cadomensis 231
Raimundus Lullus 32, 33, 34, 35, 36, 37, 38, 39, 75, 76, 77, 78, 79, 80, 111, 112, 113, 114, 115, 180A, 180B, 180C, 181, 182, 183, 184, 185, 213, 214, 215, 246, 247, 248, 264, 265, 266
Rainherus Paderbornensis 272
Ratherius Veronensis 46, 46A
Reference Bible – Das Bibelwerk 173
Reimbaldus Leodiensis 4
Remigius Autissiodorensis 136, 171
Reynardus Vulpes 171A
Robertus Grosseteste 130, 268
Rodericus Ximenius de Rada 72, 72A, 72B, 72C

Rodulfus Trudonensis 257, 257A
Rogerus Herefordensis 272
Rudolfus de Liebegg 55
Rupertus Tuitiensis 7, 9, 21, 22, 23, 24, 26, 28, 29

Saewulf 139
Salimbene de Adam 125, 125A
Scripta medii aeui de uita Isidori Hispalensis episcopi 281
Scriptores Ordinis Grandimontensis 8
Sedulius Scottus 40B, 40C, 67 + suppl., 117
Sermones anonymi codd. S. Vict. Paris. exarati 30
Sermones in dormitionem Mariae 154
Servatus Lupus abbas Ferrariensis 289B
Sicardus Cremonensis 228
Sigo abbas 171
Smaragdus 68
Speculum virginum 5
Stephanus de Borbone 124, 124A, 124B

Testimonia orationis christianae antiquioris 47
Teterius Nivernensis 171
Thadeus 202
Theodericus 139
Thiofridus Epternacensis 133
Thomas de Chobham 82, 82A, 82B
Thomas Gallus 223, 223A
Thomas Migerius 77

Vincentius Belvacensis 137
Vitae S. Katharinae 119, 119A
Vita S. Arnulfi ep. Suessionensis 285
Vita S. Hildegardis 126

Walterus Tervanensis 217
Wilhelmus Iordani 207
Willelmus Meldunensis 244
Willelmus Tyrensis 63, 63A

December 2019